# Traxel, Trexel, Trexler, Trissler, Trostle, Troxel

## A Resource Book

HERITAGE BOOKS, INC.

# HERITAGE BOOKS

*AN IMPRINT OF HERITAGE BOOKS, INC.*

## Books, CDs, and more—Worldwide

For our listing of thousands of titles see our website
at
www.HeritageBooks.com

Published 2009 by
HERITAGE BOOKS, INC.
Publishing Division
100 Railroad Ave. #104
Westminster, Maryland 21157

Other books by the author:

*Hawley, Halley, Holley and Families of Similar Surnames Found in the Early Records of Maryland and Virginia Whose Descendants Migrated to Alaska, Arkansas, California, Connecticut, Ohio, Florida, Georgia, Iowa, Kansas, Kentucky, Missouri, Nebraska, New York, North Carolina, Ohio, South Carolina, Texas, Washington and West Virginia: A Resource Book*

*Hawley, Halley, Holley and Families of Similar Surnames Found in the Early Records of England, Maryland and Virginia: A Resource Book*

International Standard Book Numbers
Paperbound: 978-0-7884-1453-4
Clothbound: 978-0-7884-8258-8

# TRAXEL ❧ TREXEL
# TREXLER ❧ TRISSLER
# TROSTLE ❧ TROXEL

*and*
*Similar Surnames Beginning with the Letters*

**T** *and* **D**

*Found in the Early Records of Georgia, Indiana,*
*Kansas, Kentucky, Louisiana, Maryland, New Jersey,*
*New York, North Carolina, South Carolina, Ohio,*
*Pennsylvania, Virginia, West Virginia and Wisconsin*

## A Resource Book

*Laura Hawley*

HERITAGE BOOKS
2009

To

my father

John Edward Hawley
September 10, 1889 - November 5, 1961

my mother

Daisy Adelaide Trexler Hawley Childress
June 15, 1915 -

my daughter

Susan Marie Dovel
December 10, 1970 - February 25, 1999


my husband

Thomas Charles Jarvis
November 21, 1936 - September 5, 1996

# TABLE OF CONTENTS

A.      Introduction  xi

B.      Abbreviations  xvi

C.      Family Units 1

D.      Cemetery Records 79

      Kentucky 79
      Maryland 79
      Ohio 84
      Pennsylvania 84
      Virginia 91

E.      Census Records 93

      Kentucky 93
      Maryland 94
      New Jersey 99
      North Carolina 99
      South Carolina 100
      Pennsylvania 100
      Virginia 108

F.      Church Records 115

      France 115
      Germany 116
      Maryland 116
      Pennsylvania 135
      Virginia 179
      West Virginia 180

G.      City Directory Notes 181

      Maryland 181
      Pennsylvania 182
      Virginia 182

H.  Court and Legal Records 184

Chancery/Civil Records 184

Kentucky 184
Louisiana 184
Maryland 185
Pennsylvania 188

Probate, Wills, Estate Documents 191

Kentucky 191
Maryland 191
New Jersey 206
North Carolina 206
Ohio 208
Pennsylvania 208
Virginia 253

I.  Immigration Records 256

Georgia 256
Louisiana 256
Maryland 257
Ohio 260
Pennsylvania 260

J.  Land Records 269

Maryland 269
Pennsylvania 281
Virginia 297

K.  Tax and Voting 296

Maryland 296
Ohio 296
Pennsylvania 297
Virginia 311

# TABLE OF CONTENTS

L.   Marriage Records 312

     Kentucky 312
     Maryland 312
     North Carolina 314
     Ohio 317
     Pennsylvania 317
     Virginia 321

M.   Military Records 323

     Revolutionary War Service 323

          Maryland 323
          Pennsylvania 324

     War of 1812 Service 327

          Indiana 327
          Louisiana 327
          Maryland 327
          North Carolina 330
          Ohio 330
          Pennsylvania 331
          Virginia 335

     Militia Service 337

          New Jersey 337
          Pennsylvania 337

N.   Newspaper Abstracts and References 339

     Kentucky 339
     Maryland 339
     North Carolina 341
     Ohio 342
     Pennsylvania 342
     Wisconsin 344

# TABLE OF CONTENTS

O.   Additional Data 345

        Louisiana 345
        Maryland 347
        North Carolina 349
        Ohio 349
        Pennsylvania 350
        Virginia 356

P.   Sources 358

Q.   Full Name Index 363

R.   General Index 431

## A.                    INTRODUCTION

The research that led to this resource book began with my desire to learn more about my Trexler ancestors. The resulting pronunciation of the T and D at the beginning of the German surname creates an interchangeable sound. This requires checking the records under surnames beginning with both the letter T and D

While searching for my Trexler family I was able to identify 173 families with identical or similar surnames. Initially my primary research surnames were Traxel, Trexel, Trexler, Trissler, Trostle and Troxel. However, my research demonstrates that evolution of the subject surnames resulted in multiple spelling distortions over the years. Often a single document contained several variations of a surname spelling, and this occurred frequently in the records of the time.

As Americans we descend from individuals who came to this country for many reasons, dreams and aspirations. Suddenly thrust into a new and challenging environment our immigrant ancestors were logically more concerned with establishing a life than preserving the spelling their surnames had taken in the native country. It is logical that some immigrants would have made his or her mark, or signed his or her name, on what ever surname spelling the person handling the documentation provided. Eventually a particular surname was adopted by each individual, and this resulted in many early surname distortions being accepted and in contemporary use. Because family members broke away from the family unit, and migrated over various time periods within America, they frequently took with them the surname spelling they accepted as correct. Today our telephone directories and census records are filled with many of these surname variations. Although all nationalities experienced surname changes, I have personally found what I have come to refer to as the *surname distortion factor* most evident with German surnames.

Surname spelling distortions create an obstacle for researchers attempting to obtain information on an individual or family in many of the early records in this country. Frequently a family historian must determine, as I did, under which surnames to

## INTRODUCTION

search for their ancestors. This difficulty is most evident with a surname that is infrequently found. This is the case with the six primary subject surnames of this research.

These spelling distortions possibly resulted because of the native language differences between those speaking the surname and those recording the records; was possibly affected by regional influences; or the various dialects spoken; or perhaps an attempt on behalf of some records clerks to anglicize names.

I have found many of the multiple surname spellings largely ignored in previously published family histories. Many earlier family historians gathered up all those individuals they considered to be in their line and gave them their personal research surname. Some disregarded the surname distortions, found in the actual source records, and often failed to even comment on these variations. Because of this I have referenced previously published research, and have included additional surname research findings in a resource data section.

My extensive attempts to reach the authors or individuals referred to as having source records was often difficult or impossible. Many of the early historians are deceased and the reported source records referenced have vanished with time. In many instances published, as well as non-published, family histories referenced in historical societies were found to be out of print and not on file with the depositories referenced in the work. I have made every effort to locate and receive the permission of earlier researchers to cite their findings. In all instances I have shown sources of information and the earlier researchers' findings have been proved, or supplemented, in the resource data records, sections D thorough O.

I have focused, when possible, on 18th century records because this is the time period in which I found the greatest variation in the subject surname spellings. The records demonstrate that beginning in the early 19th century a pattern most often had developed with more consistent use of one

# INTRODUCTION

surname by a given individual or family.

I did not begin my research with the intention of collecting the amount of data that I ultimately acquired. However, because I found myself time and time again returning to information I had initially discounted for more extensive research, it became prudent to record every possible spelling variation for a given surname when it was located. It had become apparent that I would need to examine many surname spellings in the various source records to construct accurate research on a given individual or family.

My research was initially conducted in Pennsylvania, Maryland and Virginia records. But it soon became apparent that individuals with the subject surname spellings were found in the records of Georgia, Indiana, Kansas, Kentucky, Louisiana, Maryland, New Jersey, New York, North Carolina, South Carolina, Ohio, Pennsylvania, Virginia, West Virginia and Wisconsin. Therefore, I broadened my research area accordingly.

My purpose in publishing this resource book is to help individuals working on these and similar surnames to identify target individuals easily regardless of the surname changes that resulted as the family evolved. Because of this I have not included extensive family histories. I have documented 173 individual family units, and have furnished the actual source records from which they were documented. A researcher interested in a particular individual or family unit will be able to quickly eliminate a great deal of background research, and he or she can concentrate on the particular geographic area in which the individual is found and the variations in surname spellings under which they are found.

I have intentionally not grouped the core 173 Family Units of my research in any type of order, but have denoted them by individual unit research numbers. This is shown as (Rsh.#) before each Family Unit, and before individuals who belongs with that unit, throughout the text. The numbers have no weight but merely reflect the numerical order in which each unit was identified as I

# INTRODUCTION

conducted my research. When conclusive evidence was not found to tie a particular individual to a family unit, but a match is possible, I have recorded that individual with a question mark (?) before the given name. This will indicate to a researcher that more research is needed for definitive proof.

When proof of the parents of a Family Unit male head is proved in the supplemental resource records, sections D through O, I have cited the parents through the use of a corresponding unit research number in the Family Units section A. More importantly, after every initial surname is recorded, I have recorded every variation of the surname spellings that I found in my research for the particular individual/unit.

Because the primary focus of my study is extraction of information on individuals found under several surname spellings, I have not concentrated on female lines when the surname changed at the time of marriage. The unfortunate result is that many female lines, in this research, end with marriage. The clarification of the male surname line will result in more efficient research clues, and hopefully this will aid in tracing female lines.

The resource data records, sections D through O, include cemetery, census, church, city directory, chancery, probate, wills, distributions, immigration, deeds, land, tax records, marriage records, Revolutionary War, War of 1812, Militia Records, newspaper references, and miscellaneous records which did not fit into one of the previously defined groups. They include both published and non-published sources with all variations of the subject surnames. They are grouped under each heading by geographic locality, followed by the name of the record, and then by the name of the individual in the record. Individual unit research numbers are recorded when it is clear, from the records documented by my research, that the individual belongs with that unit.

I visited courthouses and historical depositories in an attempt to find documents which have not been previously

# INTRODUCTION

published. I have also included many individuals with whom the subject families were interacting in everyday life to furnish researchers additional clues. Some sections of the resource data records are more complete than others as they reflect the path of my personal research.

I am most grateful to the many research facilities that allowed me access to their records. I would also like to thank my cousin, Donn Gregory Trexler, who lives in Richmond, Virginia, for his help and encouragement in compiling this research. Donn is an avid and excellent family historian and because of his efforts the Trexler family history in Richmond has been documented and preserved.

Laura Hawley
August 28, 2000

# Abbreviations

\# - number
ac. - acre, acres
adm. - administer
adms. - administrators
admx. - female administrator
agm. - agreement
av. - avenue
B & S - deed of bargain and sale
b. - born
bapt. - baptism
bu. - buried
d. - died
dau. - daughter
daus. - daughters
dec. - deceased
disc. - discharged
enl. - enlisted
exr. - executor
exrs. - executors
exrx. - female executor
grandau. - granddaughters
husb. - husband
imm. - immigrated
inv. - inventory
luth. - lutheran
m. - married
mo. - month
mortg. - mortgage
occu. - occupation
orig. - originally
pg. - page
pgs. - pages
vol. - volunteer
vol. - volume
w/o - widow of
w. - wife

**Rsh.1** George, Troxell, Trexel, Draxer, Draxser, Draxelxel, b. 1735
m. Elizabeth_____, lived in Frederick Co., Md., Washington Co.,
Md., Will, Washington, Co., Md., known children:
> Magdalena b. 1762
> Peter b.1765
> Abraham b. 1769
> Catherine b.1774
> Johann Daniel, b. February 11, 1776, sponsor to bapt.
> > Johann Daniel Bender
> Phillip Olinger b. 1783, bapt. at Reformed Church of
> > Hagerstown, Washington Co., Md.

**Rsh.2** John Drexel (?son of Rsh.5), Stone Cutter, m. Susanna___
Will, April 20, 1849, Cumru Twp., Berks Co., Pa., known
children:
> Reuben m._____, children, Mary m. Samuel D.
> > Missimer, Thomas Drexel, Henry Drexel, William
> > Drexel, Reuben Drexel, Emma Louisa m. Samuel
> > Seidel, Lillie m. David Regar
> Jacob wounded in Civil War and d. shortly
> > thereafter, never m.
> John m._____, d. May 1849, Adam K. Drexel,
> > son and Charles Drexel, a son
> Henry m._____
> George W.
> Samuel
> Catharine m. Bernard Driefuss, children:
> > Fannie m. Raphael Austran; Rosa m. Paul B.
> > Waldman; Katie m. Greisemer; Harry Dreyful;
> > Emanuel Dreyful; Lillie m. Louis Heilbron;
> Susanna d. January 15, 1894, m. Henry Wagner, child Rosa
> > Steinauer
> Rosianna m. Cornelius K. Rothenberger, one
> > daughter
> Charles, was b. after his fathers death,
> > unbaptized d. one week old

**Rsh.3** John Peter Trexler,Drechsler (son of Rsh.116) b. February

26, 1680 in Dettingen, on the Mainz River, in Hessen-Darmstadt, Germany, m.Catherine Breing and left Germany, arriving in England May 3, 1709. They sailed from England May 6, 1709 on St. Catherine's for New York State. In 1710 and 1712 he lived in the Mohawk Valley of the State of New York. As early as September 20, 1720 he was one of petitioners of Oley Twp., Berks Co., Pa., a short time later settled near Breinigsville and on November 18, 1729 obtained a deed for this land from Casper Wister. Tract known as Macguney Twp., County of Bucks, Pa., this tract was called Gonser farm in 1909 when History of Berks was written. He was naturalized Maxatapany Twp., Philadelphia Co., now Berks Co., Pa., d. c. 1758, History and Genealogy of the Trexler Family, his Will, dated December 17, 1744, probate October 21,1758, Philadelphia, Pa., names the following 6 children.

> Jeremiah Trexler (Rsh.115) m. Maria Catherine
> > Shumacher
> Peter (Rsh.85) m. Catherine Winck
> John Joseph (Rsh.114), named as youngest son in
> > father's Will
> Anna
> Catherine m. John George Schumacher on November 9,
> > 1732
> Margaret m. John Albright

**Rsh.4** Goodhart Dressler, Dressel, Troxler, Tosler, Truxel, Dresser, Trexsel, (? Rsh.134) m. Anna Catherina Klemmian on July 24, 1756, in Matetcha, Trappe, Montgomery, Co., Pa.; lived in ?Monocacy, ?Fort Frederick, ?Frederick Co., Md., ?Washington Co., Md., known children:

> Frederick b. October 22, 1758, sponsor to bapt. Frederick
> > Marstella
> Maria Dorothea b. April 8, 1759
> Johann Nicholas b. May 24, 1760, sponsor to bapt.
> > Joannes and Anna Marie Schilling
> Rosina b. June 8, 1761
> Johan Jacob b. March 31, 1762, ?m. Margaret
> Margaret b. May 29, 1768
> Abraham b. 1772
> Elizabeth b. November 1781, bapt.February 3, 1782

note: similar surname individuals c 1743 in Montgomery Co., Pa., records are David Dressler m. Barbara; Sophia Dressler m. Matthews Otto, she d. then he m. Johanna M. Dressler; also George Hantsch m. Regina Dressler in Bethlemem Pa.

**Rsh.5** Anthony Trexel, Drexel, Dreskzell, Trecksler, Trecksal, Trecksall, Troxel, Trixel, Tixel, Troxell, Tresler, Dreckel, Dreckler, Truel, Traxler, Trexsel, ?Immigrant, a Mason by Trade, m. Catherine Kuhn, daughter of John George Kuhn and Catherine Riffel, (the widow Kuhn remarried Joseph Ermann after husbands death) on February 13, 1776, at Goshenhoppen, (Bally) Berks Co., Pa.,in St. Paul's Catholic Church; found in the Salford Store Ledger, Montgomery Co., Pa., June 6, 1767, where his occupation is shown as a Mason at Henry Landis; lived in Adams Co., York, Pa., where 7 children are shown in 1790 census, then Frederick Co., Taneytown, Md., Election Dist. 5, then leased lot N.E. Richmond St., Baltimore, Md. 1806, where family is found in the St. John's German Catholic Church Records. Anthony served in the Revolutionary War, York Co., Pa., (Catherine Kuhn Trexel's sister Mary m. Peter Klunk), known children:

> ?Joseph (?Rsh.61)
> Jacobus James (Rsh.18) b. July 27, 1777, sponsor to bapt. James Kuhn and Theresa Kuhn (mother's brother and his wife), Goshenhoppen, Bally, Pa.; m. Elizabeth Riffle
> Peter, b. 1777
> ?Anthony, b. July 4, 1779, York, Pa., m. Nancy Reiley, February 16, 1801; ?she d., he m. Mary Ellen Stroh
> ?John b. 1780 (?Rsh.2, ?Rsh.104, ?Rsh105)
> ?Ignatius (Rsh.76) b. 1787 m. Anna Murray, d. Richmond, Va.
> Samuel Anthony (Rsh.9) b. 1799 m. Margaret Ann Buckman, sponsor to bapt. (Rsh.29) Anthony Hitzelberger and Mary Topper (Madalean Tapper was married to a Kuhn)
> ?Appolonia (Rsh.29) m. Anthony Hitzelberger
> ?Catharina m. Herman C. Martin (Hermanus Mertengel) February, 1808

?Theresa m. John Hoffman, 1816 St. Johns German
Catholic, Baltimore
?Maria m. John Gliffendorpfler (?Kapler/Capler), May 1,
1806, St. Johns German Catholic, Baltimore, Md.
?Judith
?Jonathan P. (Rsh.20) b. 1794, m. Deborah Starr in
Baltimore, Md.
?Jacob (Rsh.132)
?Sophia (Rsh.10) m. George Zimmerman

note: Both DGM and Troxell Trails lists Rsh.5 as
being a child of Rsh.43. After careful research, I do
not believe this is true. To date there is not
conclusive evidence in favor of the earlier
researchers beliefs. I believe Rsh.5 to be my
ancestor therefore I am still searching for additional
evidence. LH

**Rsh.6** Anthony Drexler, Trexler, Trexel, Prexley, Throxel, Truxel,
Troxel, Dresler,(?son of Rsh.5) b.July 4, 1779, York Co., Pa., m.
Nancy Reiley, February 16, 1801, Adams Co., Pa., Cumberland
Dist., Conewago Catholic, ?then Mary Ellen Stroh and moved to
Dakota, Wisconsin. Wisconsin newspaper Obituary, in the
possession of Mrs. Betty Trexel Kuhnert of Bristol, TN., said he was
m. twice and gave his birthdate and birthplace as above. He served
in the War of 1812, known children:
Sarah
Anthony III
Richard
Joseph

**Rsh.7** Michael Drechsler, Drecksler, Drexler, Trexler, Trecksler,
Techsler, m. Elisabeth Kraus, Cumberland Co., Pa., Shippensburg,
Pa., Michael Drecksler is first found in the Shippensburg Church
Records on September 9, 1778. They were members of the
Reformed Lutheran Church whose records were in German, known
children:
Johannes b. April 7, 1779, sponsors to bapt. Johannes
Engle and Elenora his wife
Jacob b. August 8, 1786, sponsors to bapt. Christian
Weisser and wife Susannah

Elizabeth b. August 8, 1786, sponsors to bapt. Christian
    Weisser and wife Susannah nee Kunckel
Susanna b. October 10, 1788, sponsors to bapt. Christian
    Weiger and wife Susannah
Magdalena b. December 10, 1790, sponsors to bapt.
    Peter Kramer and Magdalena
Anna Margaretha b. May 1, 1793, sponsors to bapt. Adam
    Blum and Anna Margaretha
Catherine b. June 5, 1803, sponsors to bapt. Johannes
    Bauer and Catharina
Susanna b. September 4, 1804, sponsor to bapt.
    Susanna Weiser
Sara Anna b. June 11, 1807, sponsor to bapt. Susanna
    Weiser
Elizabeth b. September 12, 1811, sponsors bapt. parents
Margaretha b. January 30, 1814, sponsors bapt. parents
Anna Maria b. March 30, 1816, sponsors bapt. parents
Anna Catharina b. November 6, 1818, sponsors to bapt.
    parents
Christina b. March 9, 1821, sponsors to bapt. parents


**Rsh.8** Abraham Troxel (?son of Rsh.45) b. 1788, m. Sarah Ann
Boucher, on April 22, 1813, at St. Peters Catholic Church,
Baltimore, Md., served in the War of 1812, he volunteered at
Adams Co., Pa., discharged Baltimore, Md. He lived in Baltimore,
Md., where he was on July 29, 1871 as found in War of 1812
documentation, NA.

**Rsh.9** Samuel Anthony Trexler, Driseler, Truxler, Dreckseler,
Troxel, Truxel, Drescler (son of Rsh.5) bapt. May 12, 1799, m.
Margaret Ann Bookman (Buckman), daughter of George
Buchman and Barbara nee Fisher, on May 29, 1819, lived in
Baltimore.Md. where they are found in Catholic Church records,
known children:
        Anna Barbara, bapt. April 1820, sponsors Joannes
            Schbces and Conflany Edwart, she m. Lemuel
            Debow
        Anthony b. February 17, 1822
        Marianna (Mary Ann) b. November 20, 1824, bapt.
            December 8, 1824, sponsors Joannes Gross and

Margaretha Lee, she m. Jacob Piery,
Catherine Maria, bapt. on November 8, 1825, sponsors
Barbara Bushmiller (Grandmother) she m. William
Braden

**Rsh.10** Sophia Trexler, Dreckseler, (?dau. of Rsh. 5) m. George
Zimmerman in Baltimore, Md., where they are found in the Catholic
Church records.    He lived, possibly in Frederick, Md., then
Baltimore, Md., faith Catholic, known children:
Anna Margareta bapt. on October 23 1819, sponsor bapt.
Mary Geffentio
Elizabeth, bapt. on October 22,1819, sponsors Joannes
Hoffman, Theresia Hoffman
Anna Margaretha, bapt. on April 1820, sponsors Mary
Geffentio and Francis S. Geffentio

**Rsh.11**   John George Michael Trister, Triesler, Drissler, Trissler,
Trisler, Troxel, Trexler, Trixler, Dressel, Traxel, Dressler, Troecksel,
Tosseler, (son of Rsh.145), Immigrant, (twin w/ Rsh.39) b.December
25, 1721, Wolfersheim, Germany m. Anna Maria Margaret Weill
(?Barbara) on October 17. 1742, the marriage is found in the John
Casper Stover Register and names her as Margareth Wellin; In
1745, they lived in Bucks Co., Pa., then in Warwick, Lancaster, Pa.,
then in Lehigh Co., Pa., where they were members of the Egypt
Reformed Church, then lived in Monacacy Settlement north of
Frederick, Md., then they returned to Guyoneld (Gwyette) Twp., Pa.,
he d. September 1772, his Will is found in Philadelphia, Pa., <u>DGM</u>,
<u>LDS</u>, known children:
Anna Catrina bapt. Frederick Co., Md. October 17, 1743,
sponsor to bapt. Jacob Wedel and
Maria
John Nicholas b. September 17, 1753 (Rsh.47) m. Anna
Margaretha Becker (Baker), lived in Easton Pa.
Margaret b.1755
Magdalena Christina Margaretha b. April 6, 1758, d.
September 10, 1840,   m. Peter Fleck, lived in
Huntington Co., Pa.
Christina b. 1757
Elizabeth b. October 11, 1760, bapt. in Frederick, Md.
Evangelical Luth., lived in Easton, Pa., named in
fathers 1772 Will, Church record in 1782 shows her

as single

George b. January 12, 1760, sponsor to bapt. on February 3, 1760, George Schmitt and Margareta Eichebergerin

Henry b. 1763, mentioned in father's Will, found in 1790 Montgomery Co., Pa., Census, as head of household with 2 males over 16 and one female.

George Michael (Rsh.17) m. Susanna Becker (Baker), lived in Lancaster, Pa., then Easton, Pa.

Christian b. c. 1767, listed in father's 1772 Will

Ann b. 1770-1772

George Jacob bapt. on December 26, 1760, at age 6 wks old, sponsor to bapt. Jacob Kohler, Magdalena Drachselln, Eva Schneider; he had Rev. Service with the Militia of Philadelphia, he is shown in 1790 Montgomery Co., Pa., Census with 3 children, on Tax lists for Gwynedd Twp., Pa., 1785-93, 1800 Census Hilltown Twp., Pa.

Catherine Elizabeth b.April 8, 1759 bapt. April 8, 1759, sponsor to bapt. Johann Schneider, George Koehler, Catherine Elizabeth Kern, Barbara Neuhardt, lived in Easton, Pa., single in 1778

Peter b. c. 1757, named in father's 1772 Will

Anna Mary b. 1751, mentioned in father's 1772 Will, m. but no m. name given

John (Rsh.19) b. about 1749, m. Elizabeth Groff, lived in Montgomery Co., Pa., then in Huntington Co., Pa.

Juliana Barbara b. c. 1747 m. Henrich Schneider lived in Easton Pa., 6 children, active in Evangelical Reformed Church in Easton, Pa.

**Rsh.12** John Frederick Triesch, m. Anna Elizabeth, lived in Lancaster Pa., where they are found in the Trinity Lutheran Church Records, known children:

Henrich Wilehlm bapt. September 7, 1751, sponsor _____ Schell and wife

**Rsh.13** George Frederick Troxell, Traxel, Draxel, Dressel, Dreschel, Traxall, Drezel (son of Rsh.22) bapt. July 28, 1741, at Egypt Reformed Church, Leehigh Co., Pa., m. Appolonia Lay (Loy), they lived at Monocacy, Frederick Co., Md., he d. October 1795,

<u>DGM,LDS,</u>known children:

> Elizabeth b. March 11, 1769 m. Nicholas Zimmerman June 6, 1793
>
> Anna Maria b. November 20, 1764, sponsors to bapt. Johannes Traxel and Sybilla Bayin, bapt. March 20, 1765
>
> Michael b. November 4, 1766, bapt. April 1, 1767
>
> Jacob Michael b. April 1, 1767, never m., d. May 9, 1831
>
> John Frederick (Rsh.65) b.December 23, 1773 m. Elizabeth Young on May 7, 1801
>
> Johannes (Rsh.60) b. December 22, 1772 m. Elizabeth Dotterer dau. of Conrad who was brother to Sophia Rsh.43
>
> Mary b. November 5, 1764 never m., d. March 15, 1844
>
> Catherina Magdalena b. April 4, 1776 never m., d. December 7, 1823
>
> Margaret b. February 7, 1779 never m., d. October 6,1857
>
> George (?Frederick) Peter b. Sept. 28, 1781 never m., d. March 31, 1832

**Rsh.14** George Trisler, Driszler, Drissler, Dressler (son of Rsh.47) b. December 5, 1775, a Millwright by Trade, m. Rosina (Rosanna) Margaret Sheib (Sheip) on September 25, 1797 and they lived in Easton Pa., Northampton Co., Pa., then Frederick Co., Md., where they were active in the Evangelical Lutheran Church, in the City of Frederick, Md. She d. May 25, 1861. He was Executor to father's Will in Easton Pa., in 1821, <u>Troxell Trails,</u> known children:

> Carl b. July 10, 1798, bapt. 1798
>
> John b. April 10, 1801
>
> George b. August 8, 1803
>
> Henrietta b. February 1,1805, sponsor to bapt. Margaret Dressler, m. James Weaver on July 3, 1821 in Maryland
>
> Maria b. March 30, 1806
>
> Julianna Margaret b. May 6, 1808, bapt. May 29, 1808, sponsor bapt. John Schnobily and wife Catharina
>
> David b. ?August 17, 1808
>
> Jeremiah b. February 16, 1811
>
> Thomas N. b. April 28, 1813
>
> George b. September 8, 1816, sponsor bapt. parents
>
> Rosanna b. February 4, 1817

**Rsh.15**  Christian Traxal, Cocksel, Crocksel, Troxel, Droxell, Traxall,Trachsel, Sr.,(son of Rsh.22) bapt. April 16, 1739, he was a twin to sister Juliana Margaretha, DGM, m.Catherine Doerr in 1761, they are found in Glade Reformed and Evan. Reformed Church records in Frederick, Md., then leased land September 15, 1765 in Conegocheague Manor, Washington Co., Md. found there as late as 1783,LDS, Troxell Trails says descendants are found in Wayne Co., Ky. in 1810.

> known children:
>
> Christian b. 1768, Frederick, Md.
>
> Johannes bapt. March 5, 1775, Loudoun Co., Va., sponsor bapt. Johannes and Margaretta Mencher
>
> David b. 1765, Egypt, Bucks, Pa.
>
> Christopher b. before 1765
>
> Peter b. 1777, Loudoun Co., Va., m. Sally Seratte on December 7, 1802, d. before 1850
>
> Jacob b. 1772, Loudoun Co., Va., m. Susan Troxel in 1844
>
> Daniel bapt. on October 25, 1772, sponsor bapt. Jacob Braungul and Sophia Troxel
>
> Daniel b. 1778, Loudoun Co., Va., m. Harrett M. McQuit
>
> Catherine b. 1780, Loudoun Co., Va., m. Jesse Burton on March 14, 1805 in Pulaski, Kentucky

**Rsh.16**  Joseph David Trissler, Treissler, Driesler, Tresler, Dressler, Trestler, Treistler, Immigrant, son of Joseph David Trissler of Canstatt, Wurtenberg, where he was b. December 21, 1698, his Certificate of Lawful Birth is in the possession of the LHS, a Glaser by Trade, m. 1st Anna Catharina Schott then m. Maria Susannah Drusina (Drusing) Rautenbush on March 27, 1739, they were active in Trinity Lutheran Church, Lancaster Co., Pa.,
known children:

> Martin Frederick b. February 28,1742
>
> Maria Elizabeth b. October 2, 1743 bapt. York, Pa., Trinity Lutheran, sponsor to bapt. Jacob Spanseiler, Catherine Beyerlin
>
> Johann Jacob (Rsh.30) b. August 25, 1744, sponsor bapt. Jacob Jayser, Jacob Spanseiler, Cath. Beyerlin
>
> Margaretha Barbara b. August 11,1748, sponsor to bapt. Benjamin Spiecker and Barbara Margaretha his wife

Catharine Barbara b. December 16,1750 d. January 16, 1752

note:    ?Rsh.16 is possible brother to Rsh.109 Christopher Trencken

**Rsh.17** George Michael Trissoler, Trisler, Traseler, Troxler (son of Rsh.11) b. November 16, 1765 m. Susannah Becker (Baker) November 1, 1792, in Lancaster Co., Pa., his Rev. War Service is shown in the Northampton Co., Pa. Militia, they lived in Frederick Co., Md., then Easton, Pa. They were members of the German Reformed Church in Easton, Pa., he d. August 16, 1808, Easton, Northampton, Pa., <u>LDS,</u> <u>Troxell Trails,</u>
known children:
> Maria Catharine b. June 3,1792, m. Jacob Dengler, 5 children
> Elizabeth b. October 26, 1793, m. John Warmkessel
> Susanna b. August 13, 1796
> Michael Samuel b. June 1798 m. Margaret Siebers, children Theodore Michael b. December 3, 1831; Matilda Ann b. August 8, 1834; Louisa b. 1836; Samuel; Henry b. January 27, 1839
> Julia b. February 23, 1800
> Sarah b. June 3, 1804
> Edward b. June 12, 1806 m. Elizabeth, children James Jacob b. October 25, 1827; John b.1831; Susan b. 1837; Michael b. 1840; Aureth b. 1842; Benjamin b. 1844; Louisa b. 1845; Elizabeth b. 1849
> John b. November 22, 1794

**Rsh.18** Jacobus James Tresler, Treskler, Dressel (son of Rsh.5) b. July 27, 1777, m. Elisabeth Rifle (Riffle), who was b. April 10, 1780 d. ?March 3, 1850, ?then m. Susan, they lived in Adams Co., Pa., and are found in the Conewago Catholic records there, then ?Hanover,Pa., ?Cambia Co., Pa., Allegheny Twp., ?then Washington Co., Md. in 1802, he d.?May 24, 1833,
known children:
> Catherine b. August 17,1800, sponsors bapt. Anthony Tresler and Catherine Coon (Kuhn) (Rsh.5) Grandparents
> ?Catherine b. February 3, 1805

?Sarah b. June 10, 1807
?Mariana b. July 3, 1807
?David b. October 1808
?Abraham b. January 10, 1810
?William b. December 17, 1811
?Henry b. July 19, 1815
?Samuel b. 1818


**Rsh.19**  John Troxel (eldest son of Rsh.11), b. c. 1749, he was a Tanner by Trade, m. Elisabeth Groff, daughter of John Groff of Philadelphia, Pa., they lived in Huntington Co., Pa., and his Rev. Service was with the Philadelphia Co., Pa. Militia, <u>Troxell Trails</u>, known children:

> Jacob b. 1775
> John (Rsh.49) b. between 1775 and 1780, lived in Cambia
> Co., Pa.
> Henry (Rsh.59) b. August 14, 1788 m. Catherine Keltner,
> moved West

> note:  Census Records show 2 sons and 2
> daughters

**Rsh.20**  Jonathan (Jonas) P. Trexler, Trusler, Tresler, Fixler (?son of Rsh.5, ?Rsh.48) b. c. 1794, m. Deborah Starr, on October 27, 1820 in Baltimore, Md., she d. September 1837 in Baltimore, Md., they are found in the Chancery Court Records for Baltimore, Md., he d. May 15, 1849 and is buried in Dorchester Co., Md., known children:

> Samuel P. Trexler b. 1821
> Isaac S.Trexler b. October 6, 1824 m. Elizabeth found in
> 1870 Dorchester, Md. Census, dau.Elizabeth
> Nevade (Nevada) b. November 26, 1866 at
> Lakesville
> Peter Albert b. November 12, 1828 m. Martha Ellen Ball on
> March 8, 1851

**Rsh.21**  Johann Andreas (Andrew) Dressler, Tressler, Dresler, Traxel, Sr.,(son of Rsh.134) Immigrant, b. November 30, 1714, in the Jagsthausen District of Heilbronn, Wurtemberg, he was a Blacksmith and Farmer by Trade, he m. Anna Barbara Bernhardt, who was the daughter of Batholomaus Bernhardt at the District Liebenzell Duchy of Wurtemberg on September 10, 1737, he came to this Country on the Ship Edinburgh August 13, 1750 from Sachsenhausen, Wertheim, landing at Philadelphia, Pa., they settled first in the Goshenhoppen, Pa., area near present day Pennsburg in Mont.,Co., then in Berks Co., Pa., in Greenwich Twp., his Rev. Service is in the Pennsylvania Militia, known children:

Maria Barbara b. September 7, 1738

Maria Magdelena b. April 19, 1741

Anna Maria B. April 19, 1741

George David b. April 11, 1744

John Andreas, Jr. (Rsh.54) B. May 28., 1747

**Rsh.22** Peter Trachsel, Drachsel, Troxel, Toeschler, Troksell, Dreschler, Deshler, Troxell, Immigrant, b. Lenk, Canton Berne, Switzerland on November 6,1691 (son of Rsh.143), and taken by his parents to Rhineland Palatinate in the Homburg-Starr area in Germany near the French border prior to immigration to this Country on the Ship Samuel. He m. Anna Julianath Catherinath Trauthager who was b. in 1703 and the daughter of Johannes, Hans Trauthager, Trauthager, Fraudhuger, Freydinger, Freydig, and Barbara Jaggi (Jacky), of Katzenthal Alsace France; they lived in Leehigh Valley Pa., then Frederick Co., Md., he d. January 25, 1766 in Frederick Co., Md., <u>DGM</u>, <u>LDS</u>,
known children:

Peter, (Rsh.58) b. December 28, 1723, Katzenthal Alsace France, m. Anna Maria_____ then Hannah Zirckle a widow

Johann Daniel (Rsh.43) b. December 8, 1726, Katzenthal Alsace France, m. Sophia Dotterer, whose family was from Kinzheim Alsace

David (Rsh.52) b.July 27, 1734 in Egypt, Whitehall Twp., Lehigh Pa., m. Anna Elizabeth

John (Rsh.147) bapt. October 26, 1736 in Egypt, Whitehall Twp., Lehigh Co., Pa., m. Maria Margaretha

Christian, a twin, (Rsh.15) b. c. April 16, 1739, Egypt Whitehall Twp., Lehigh Pa., bapt. April 16, 1739, m. Catherine Doerr in 1761

Juliana Margaretha, a twin, bapt. April 16, 1739, sponsor bapt. George Kern, Lorentz Gut, Michael Hoffman, Anna Barbara Neuhart, Apolonia Troeschler (?sister to Rsh.22), Maria Margaretha Neuhart

George Frederick (Rsh.13) bapt. July 28, 1741 m. Appollonia Lay, Frederick Co., Md.

Mary Margaret b. October 25, 1744, bapt. December 26, 1744, Egypt, she m. Johannes Abraham Watring, Vautrin, Voiturin, Wotring, son of Abraham Vautrin and his wife Anne Margaret nee Mertz, and moved c. 1786 to Aurora, W.Va.

**Rsh.23** Jacob Tracksel, Troxel, Draxel (son of Rsh.58) b. c. 1758, m. Anna Margaretha Eberhart, daughter of Joseph, on August 10, 1783, his father deeded him land in Leehigh Co., Pa., in 1783, they also lived in Northampton Co., Pa., where they were active in Jordan Reformed Church, DGM, LDS, known children:

Susanna b. January 11, 1786 m. Conrad Kerschner

Daniel b. March 26, 1788, Census Records show 4 children

John Jacob, b. January 30, 1789, bapt. February 8, 1789

Anna Barbara, b. June 28, 1790, bapt. July 11, 1790

Eva bapt. May 13, 1793

Johannes Jacob b. January 8, 1796 (or January 30, 1789) m. Elizabeth, children Edwin b. June 13, 1831; Joshia b. 1833; Sally Ann b. 1835; Henry b. 1836; Walter b. 1838; Aaron b. 1839; Levi b. 1840; Samuel b. 1851

Henrich b. June or July 6, 1798 m. Kate (Catherine), children Henrich Tighman b. November 24, 1832, Amandus b. 1833; Elemina b. 1836; Sarah Ann b. 1838; Leanda b. 1845; William b.1851; Levi b. 1852; Susanna b.1847

**Rsh.24** Adam Troxel, Dressler, Deshler, Trucksill, Trxter, Drocksel, Troxeler, (son of Rsh.43) b. March 15, 1758 in Leehigh Co., Pa., m. Christine Miller, they lived in York and Adams Co., in Germany Twp., Pa., and were active in the St.John's Evangelical Lutheran Church, they later lived in Taneytown, Md. in Frederick Co., Md., which is slightly south of St. Johns Evangelical Lutheran Church, Adams Co., Pa., his Will is found in Frederick Co., Md., dated February 28, 1820 and probate is dated April 18, 1820, DGM, LDS, known children:

Sophia b. May 10,1790 bapt. July 27, 1790, sponsor bapt.

Sophia Troxelin (Rsh.43) the Grandmother, she m. John Wivell

Jacob b. April 11, 1793 in Maryland, sponsors bapt. parents at St.Johns Lutheran, Germany Twp., Pa., he m. Elizabeth, lived in Carroll Co., Md., known children Hetty b. 1839; Jacob b.1842

John b. Maryland, December 26, 1795, sponsors bapt. Jac. Smith and Elis m. Lydia lived in Carroll Co., Md., known child James b. 1832

Elizabeth b. February 17, 1800, sponsor bapt. Jac (Jacob) Smith (Smidt) and Elis, she is listed in father's 1820 Will

John b. January 1, 1803

Susanna b. after 1805 to 1810, she is listed in father's Will

Catherine b. after 1805, she is listed in father's Will

**Rsh.25** George Trisler, Trissler (?son of Rsh.75) was baptized January 29, 1769 at Monocracy Lutheran Church, Frederick, Md., and Schraff's History says his parents brought him to Frederick, Md. from Lancaster Pa.; he was a Merchant and had a store in Frederick Town where he imported German and Irish linens, he was also a Writer and a Poet, he m. Catherine Breitenbach in March of 1794 in Baltimore, Md., he ?m. 2nd Rosanna b. November 19, 1799, she d. October 19, 1826; He lived in Frederick, Md. and he d. September 16, 1845 in Frederick Town, Md.,
known children:

William

George m. Susan D. Kurtz October 11, 1827

Margaret

Henritta Weaver

**Rsh.26** George David Trissler, Dressler, Drisler, Sr., Immigrant, b. March 2, 1723, Canstadt, in Dukedom, Wurtemberg, he was a Saddler by Trade, and he m. Anna Maria Crohn, in 1750 in Lancaster Co., Pa., she was b. September 12, 1730 in Staudernheim in the Palatinate, he d. July 21, 1809, she d. July 11, 1812,
known children:

Maria Margaret Catherine b. February 20, 1752, d. 1753

George David (Rsh.27) b. January 25, 1754 m. Elizabeth Robinson March 1, 1776

Susanna Maria bapt. June 3, 1756 m. Johannes Jacob

Groeff (Graeff) April 15, 1776, 13 children
Catharina, b. November 27, 1758 d. November 22, 1760
Johannes (Rsh.44) b. March 17, 1761 m. Anna Marie
    Reichart then Rebecca Graff
Philip, bapt. August 29, 1763 d. within 28 hours
Christian b. August 20, 1764, d. November 12, 1857,
    single
Elizabeth    b. March 12, 1767 m. Michael Steiner,
    Carpenter, August 28, 1791
Anna Magdalena, twin, b. September 30, 1772 m. George
    Thomas
Catharine m. ,twin, b. September 30, 1772 m.Johannes
    DeMuth, a Carpenter's Helper on October 17, 1793,
    in Lancaster, Pa., Moravin Litz
George (Rsh.135) m. Catherine Oehler (Ehler)
Elizabeth b. 1783 d. 1789
Susanna b. July 1775, d. July 1775
Catherine b. 1785 d. 1787

**Rsh.27** George David Trissler, Drachzel, Trisler, Tressler, Tristler, Drisler, Dissler, Dresler, Driessler, Jr. (son of Rsh.26) b. January 25, 1754, he was Tavern Keeper and Ferryman at Wrights Ferry, Pa., on the Susquehanna River, m. Elisabeth Robinson on March 1, 1776, daughter of James and Elizabeth Robinson, she was b. 1749, New Castle Co., State of Delaware, he was a Captain in Rev. War Service, they lived in Lancaster Co., Pa., he m. 2nd Susanna____ and they lived in York Co., Pa., where he d. September 30, 1796 in Hallam Twp., estate papers show he owned land in Washington Co., Pa., Church Records say there were 7 children, four sons and three daughters, known children:
    Magdalena Drachzel bapt. November 9, 1777
    Maria bapt. January 23, 1780, m. Conrad Doll October 17,
        1801
    Elizabeth b. November 2, 1783 d. December 17, 1789
    Catharine b. February 6, 1785 d. February 6, 1787
    Jacob b. February 6, 1788 d. August 16, 1796 ?m.
        Catherine Doll
    Anna Margaret bapt. October 11, 1789
    George David
    John (Rsh.28)

**Rsh.28** John Trissler (son of Rsh.27) b. ?February 21, 1773, he was a Riflemaker, he m. Catherine Huber (Hoover) in 1802, she was a Catholic, they lived in Lancaster Co., Pa., he served in the Rev. War and the War of 1812, he d. January 30, 1840, Church Records show 3 sons and 6 daughters, known children:

> Maria b. January 25, 1805
> John b. May 14, 1807 d. April 3, 1811
> George b. January or June 11, 1811 (Moravian Register)
> Catharine b. August 8, 1812
> Sophia b. February 11, 1814
> Christina b. March 6, 1818
> David b. August 18, 1820

**Rsh.29** Apollonia Trexel, Trexell, Troxel, Drexel, Drexler, Drechseler (?dau. of Rsh.5) m. Anthony Hitselberger, a Mason by Trade, on February 26, 1801, Zion Lutheran Church, Baltimore, Md., he was b. in Lancaster Pa., and he was a Catholic, their children were raised in the Catholic Faith, known children:

> Jacob, b. 1802, a Stone Mason, m. Hannah Haas
> William
> Joseph b. March 12, 1807, a Carpenter, m. Elizabeth Smith
> Stephen Franklin b. February 28, 1813
> George Washington b. February 28, 1813
> Mary Roseanna Trexell (reportedly an old family name) b. July 2, 1815 m. Frederick Horze (widower) April 14, 1831. She d. of T.B.
> Maria Theressa b. October 22, 1817 m. Christopher C. Fifer, May 14, 1844, no children. She d. of T.B.

**Rsh.30** Johann Jacob Trissoler, Driesler, Trisler, Trissler (son of Rsh.16) b.August 25, 1744, m. Mary Maria_____, In August 1776, they lived in Georgetown Hundred, Montgomery Co., Md., this area became District of Columbia in 1800, 8 white inhabitants shown in 1783 census, ?later they were possibly in Frederick Co., Md., He is shown in the Rev. War Records for Montgomery County, Md., he d. October 20,1821, known children:

> Elizabeth b. 1769
> John George b. 1772
> John b. 1774
> Jacob Jr., b. 1775

?Adam

**Rsh.31** Christian Troxel (son of Rsh.39) b. near Egypt Pa., about 1754 m., Anna Margaret_____, they patented land in Luzerne Co., Pa., on January 4, 1793, they are found in Jordan Reformed Church Records, Leehigh Co., Pa., DGM, known children:
> ?David
> Catherine Elisabeth b. August 11, 1776
> Maria Barbara Troxel b. August 15, 1781 bapt. October
>    7,1781

**Rsh.32** Abraham Troxel m. Maria Barbara Rhorer, daughter of Christian and Francis Rhorer. They lived in Washington Co., Md. where one of her bothers Samuel Rhorer is shown in the records as residing in Huntington, Pa., The Rhorer Family was from Bolligen, Canton Berne, Switzerland, National Genealogical Magazine 1919. Washington Co., Md. Court Records say they left the State of Maryland, Washington Co., years ago in March 18, 1813 document to reside elsewhere.

**Rsh.33** Johann George Troxller, Troxclaire, Trosclair, Troscler, Truxcler, Immigrant, b.1698, in Alsatian (Alsace) of Lichtenberg in Germany, he was a Mason by Trade, and a Catholic, m. Madeline Husserman, first she probably d. c. 1735 then he m. Mary Agnes Loy c. 1738. They arrived in New Orleans c. 1719-1721. They settled 35 miles above New Orleans on the Mississippi River in a German Village named Hoften, Louisiana. This family intermarried with French Arcadian descendants.
> known children by Magdelaine Hausserman:
> Jean Nicholas b. 1734 m. April 28, 1750, Catherine
>    Materne, children, Nicholas George, Catherine,
>    Jacques
> Anne Marie m. April 15, 1750, Francois Savigon
> known children by Marie Agnes Loy:
> Marie Agnes bapt. 1739 m. Mathieu Savant 1752
> Anne Margaurite bapt. September 4, 1741
> Jean Jacques bapt. December 4, 1742 m. Jeanne Dorvin
>    then Elizabeth LeRous April 1770, children: Felicite,
>    Emelite, Raphael Godfrey, Jean Jaques, Adelaide,
>    Celeste, Marie
> Christian Christophe bapt. November 15, 1744 m. Rose

Haydel, children: Pierre, Christophe
Charlotte bapt. November 1745
Jean Baptiste d. January 1748
Catherine
Marguerite m. Bartholomew Lambert 1764 then Antonio
Purel 1796

**Rsh.34** John Jacob Troxel, Troxell, Trexler, Droxel, Troscel, Trocksell, Sr. (son of Rsh.42) b. September 17, 1747 m. Elisabeth Martin, August 28, 1770 at Germantown Market Square Presbyterian Church, Germantown, Pa. She was a daughter of John Martin of Upper Dublin Twp., Montgomery Co., Pa., and a sister to Matthias Martin. Elizabeth d. May 25, 1825, they lived in Bucks Co., Pa., Philadelphia, Pa., Frederick, Md., Emmitsburg, Md. They were members of Thurmont Lutheran Church. He built Troxell Mills in Frederick, Co., Md., where he d. April 21, 1830, Troxell Trails, known children:

John b. December 23, 1773
Magdalena m. a Hinch
Peter (Rsh.102) b. May 7, 1777 d. May 26, 1816 m.
Mary Magdalena, she d. May 23, 1850
Maria Barbara b. March 30, 1779, sponsor to her bapt.
Mathias Martin and Anna Barbara Troxell, she m.
William Greenmeyer he d., then she m. a Hinkle
John b. August 7, 1781 d. December 7, 1853 m. Sophia
Wilhide, children: Jephania b. 1842, Ann Elisa b.
1843, John F. b. 1845, Oscar J. b. 1847
?Ann m. Joseph Ridenour, m. Washington Co., Md.
January 18, 1794, not named in father's Will
Mary m. Callinger (Curlinger,Collingen)
Jacob b. January 31, 1787 d. June 7, 1833, father gave
him by Will 50 acres of mountain land, in 1831 he
placed part of this in trust for John an invalid
Margaret m. John Marks, had children mentioned but not
named in father's Will
Catherine m. a Mince
Elizabeth b. February 27, 1792 m. Adam (Thomas)
Showers (Shover) July 15, 1796, Baltimore Co.,
Md.

**Rsh.35** Peter Dreschler, Trexler, Troxell, Desler (?son of Rsh.5) m.

?Margaret Schley, ?December 21, 1766, they lived in Allegheny Twp., Cambria Co., Pa., found there in 1802 Tax list, he d. before July 2, 1844, Cambria Co., Orphans Ct. Records, known children:
?Joseph m. Mary, child Margaret b. 1806

> note: a Joseph Trexler administered estate of Margaret Trexler in 1844, see Cambria Co., Pa., Probate Records and Catholic Baptisms for Loretto, Pa.

**Rsh.36** George Jacob Trachsel, Drachsel (son of Rsh.42) b.1765, m. Maria (Mary) Groschang, April 24, 1787, at Monocacy Church, Frederick Co., Md., he d. 1807 in Frederick Co., Md., known children:
Elizabeth b. 1792

**Rsh.37** Adam Trexler (son of Rsh.122) b. 1784, m. Polly Mesimer, lived in Rowan Co., N.C. where he d. May 24, 1849. He is buried in St. Matthews Cemetery, Rowan Co., N.C., <u>History and Genealogy of the Trexler Family</u>, known children:
Sophia m. Henry Peeler
John m. Margaret Holshouser and Harriet James
Margaret M. Solomon Nussman
Eva Ann m. Simeon Kluttz
Caleb C. m. Elizabeth L. Lyerly
Katherine m. David D. Peeler
George
Adam m. Margaret Lyerly

**Rsh.38** Joseph Drexler, Trexee, Troxell, Trexler (?son of Rsh.5) m. ?Elisabetha Will, April 24, 1807, lived in Tyrone Twp., Adams Co., Pa., active in Conewago Catholic Church, witnesses to wedding Joseph Storm and Susan O'Bold., ?lived in Cambria Co, Allegheny Twp., Pa., where 1802-1815 Tax Lists a Joseph Drexler, or ?d. June 8, 1812, Adams, Pa., Conewago Records, known children:
Maria Drexler bapt. March 13, 1808, sponsor bapt. Joseph and Christina O'Bold
Johannes Drexler bapt. February 25, 1810
Peter b. April 15, 1808
?Ann Magdalen
?Mary

?Joseph b. February 15, 1816
?Jacob
?John
?David

note: Joseph Zindorff m. Elizabeth (?Will) Drexel, Catholic Conewago Records, she was b. 1784 d. November 13, 1859, Catholic Conewago. The records are not clear if this Elizabeth's maiden name was Will or Drexel, she was possibly the widow of a Joseph Drexler who died in 1812, her known children: Joseph, John, Pius, Andrew, George, Elizabeth

**Rsh.39** John (Han) Nickel (Nicholas) Traxel, Trachsel, Troxel, Draxel,Traxall (son of Rsh.145), Immigrant, b. December 25, 1721, Twin, in Wolfersheim, Germany, m. Catharina_____, lived in Whitehall Twp., members Egypt Reformed Church, Leehigh Co., Pa., she was bapt. on February 8, 1761, he d. April 27, 1797, in Leehigh Co., Pa., Egypt Church Records say they had 9 children, <u>DGM,LDS</u>, his estate papers say he had 9 children,
known children:

     Christian b. about 1754 (Rsh.31) m. Margaret_____
     Adam b. about 1758 (Rsh.48) m. Anna Marie Hecker and
          then Eva Catharine (Geiger) Kern
     Maria Barbara b. March 1, 1766 bapt. March 9, sponsor
          Peter Kern and Catherine, not named in father's Will
          possibly d. young
     Eva bapt. June 19, 1768 m. John Stoiffiet, and had five
          children, She d. April 22, 1840.
     Peter b. about 1760 (Rsh.62) m. Sibilla Veronica Hecker
     Mary Magdalena m. John Horn, named in father's Will
     ?Peter (Rsh.108) m. Magdalena_____
     ?Stephen

**Rsh.40** Peter Troxell, Traxel, Draxel, Troxall, Jr.,III, (son of Rsh.58) b. March 28, 1751 near Egypt, Pa., m. Helena Catharine Schoener, daughter of Henry Schroener of Allen Twp., Pa., he is believed to have remained his entire life near Egypt, Pa., Active members of Jordan Reformed Church., his Rev. War Service was in the Pennsylvania Militia, he d. April 11, 1816, <u>DGM,LDS</u>,
known children:

     Maria Susanna, b. February 10, 1783 m. George Adam

Kemmerer, 5 children

John (Rsh.152) b. August 9, 1784 m. Elisabeth Hittel (?Hottel), 10 children

Daniel (Rsh.15) b. January 1, 1786 m. Elizabeth Siegfried, 6 children

Peter (Rsh.154) b.January 20, 1788 m. Elizabeth Mickley, 7 children

Abraham b. October 18, 1789 d. in childhood

Magdalana, b. September 9, 1791 m. Peter Schaadt and moved west

Jacob (Rsh.156) b. June 25, 1794 m. Elizabeth Bieler, Bleiler, 11 children

Solomon (Rsh.157) b. August 26, 1796 m. Salome Leisenring, 7 children

Elizabeth b. June 12, 1799, d. in childhood

**Rsh.41** Henry Trisslar, d. in Botetourt Co., Va., probate January 1820, Probate Records, known children:

William
Jacob
Henry
Peter
Sally
George
Moses
Nancy
Michael
Barbara wife of Wm. Persinger
Mary wife of Adam Quickie
Catherine wife of George Mallow
Elizabeth wife of Jacob Pence

**Rsh.42** John Peter Troxel, Trostal, Deutsel, Deshler, Trechseler, Tracksel, Trenchsell, Deschler, Troxell, Traxel, (son of Rsh.145), Immigrant, b. April 3, 1719 in Wolfersheim, Germany, m. Anna Barbara Saeger, she d., then m. Catharine Maria Magdalena (Modolona) Schreiber in 1754, lived in Philadelphia, Pa., then Montgomery Co., Pa., then Bucks Co., Pa., then Leehigh Co., Pa., then York Co., Pa., and moved in 1776 to Frederick, Md., then Ft. Frederick, Washington Co., Md., he d. in Frederick, Md. January 25, 1779, and is buried Tom's Creek, Md., DGM, LDS,

known children:
by Anna Barbara Saeger were:

John (Rsh.34) b. September 17, 1747 m. Elizabeth Martin

Anna Barbara b. September 2, 1748 m. April 24, 1770 in Philadelphia, Germantown Market Square, Presbyterian Church to Mathias Martin brother of Elizabeth Martin Troxell (Rsh.34) one daughter m. Lewis Motter

by Catharine Maria Magdalena (Modolona) Schreiber, who was the daughter of John Jacob and Anna Madalena, nee Roth, Schreiber were:

Mary Magdalena (Modolona) b. May 17,1761 m. Christia Kuhn lived in Frederick Md. She d. December 5, 1825

Jacob (Rsh.36), b. 1765 m. Magdalena Cushion (Groschang), d. 1807 Frederick Md.

Elizabeth b. February 6, 1767 m. Peter Krise (Crise) lived in Frederick, Md.,she d. February 18, 1809

Peter b. October 23, 1768 d. 1856 m. ?Amanda, buried in Frederick, Md.

Maria b. February 15, 1771 d. August 4, 1794

George (?Rsh.98) b. February 27, 1773 m. Elizabeth Crabbs on August 2, 1805 lived in Frederick, Md., he d. January 21, 1853, in Frederick, Md.

Catharina b. April 19, 1775

Solomon b. April 21, 1777 bapt. St. Matthews Lutheran York Co., Pa. He was confirmed in Christ Lutheran, York Pa.

George Frederick b. February 27,1779, bapt. June 27, 1779 in Frederick Co., Md., m. Catherine Wilson, March 27, 1802 then Susannah Wilson, children: Joseph b. February 14, 1803 m. Amy Haff, children, Ann Elizabeth b. 1830, James Wilson b. April 1, 1831, Francis Katherine, Susan Rebecca b. 1838; Frederick (Rsh.160) b. March 29, 1811 m. Sarah J. Rowe, lived in Emmitsburg, Md. child Charles b. June 1850; Catherine b. 1810 m. a Jones; Thomas m. Naomi Hause, d. July 2, 1850 Emmitsburg, Md.

Jacob b. March 30, 1781

Sarah b. August 23, 1788

**Rsh.43** John S. Daniel Trachsel, Troxel, Drachsel, Troxler, Truxall, Troksell, Troxell, Trackseler, Traxell, Trucsill, Trucksaal, Trexell, Tresler, Tressler, Drechler, Troxeler, Trucksil, Immigrant, (son of Rsh.22) b.1726 m. Sophia Dotterer, b. March 5, 1726, who was daughter of Michael Dotterer and Anna Maria nee Fisher. They lived in Leehigh Co., Pa., then in Germany Twp., York Co., Pa. They worshipped at Jordan Reformed Church, Whitehall, Pa., and then Christ Church at Littlestown, Conewago Twp., Pa., where it is believed they moved in the 1760's, he d. 1814, buried at Christ Reformed Church, DGM,LDS, probate records not located, known children:

> Jacob Samuel John (Rsh.101) b. 1754 or ?May 3, 1761
> > m. Elisabeth
>
> Daniel b. March 8,1750
>
> Adam (Rsh.24) b. March 15, 1758 m. Christine Miller
>
> John David, (Rsh.45) b. May 3, 1761, as a widower, m.
> > Elisabeth Mohler, widow, in Philadelphia, Pa.
>
> Elizabeth b. April 8, 1763 d. December 1, 1837
>
> ?John ?David, (Rsh.91) b. January 26, 1755, d. February
> > 2, 1840

> note: Troxell Trails pg.14, lists a David b. January 26, 1755 d. February 2, 1840, buried in Evergreen Cemetery, Gettysburg, Pa. There is confusion between this individual my Rsh.91 and my Rsh.45. Richard Troxell, Troxell Trails, and Jack Salmon, DGM list a John as having been b. May 3, 1761. In 1783 York, Pa., Tax List a David (?John) is shown as having 3 children. Because David, a widower, Rsh.45 m. Elizabeth Mohler, a widow in 1781 (see marriage records), some of these children must have been from a previous marriage. However, there is another son "John" or "David",my Rsh.91, b. c. 1755 who had children. The Rev. Wm. B. Dutters in the History of Dotterer Family, lists a son, of my Rsh.43, as "unclassified" and unnamed who had children David T. b. January 3, 1836 m. Anna W. and had daughters Jennie and Fannie, and C.W.T. b. 1847 and had CWT, Jr., b. 1867. Also, LDS lists a son Anthony b. about 1752 m. Catherine Ehrman (Rsh.5) whom I cannot tie to Rsh.43.

**Rsh.44** Johannas Trissler, Dressler, (son of Rsh.26) b.March 17,

1761, d. July 28, 1844, by Trade a Saddler, m. Anna Maria Reichart, daughter of Adam Reigart, Lancaster Town, Pa., then m. Rebecca Graff on May 23, 1818, Moravian Church Records say 3 sons and 5 daughters, known children:

> John Adam (Rsh.46) b. August 9, 1787 m. Juliana Reed
> Catharine b. July 24, 1791 m. Jacob Eichholtz, portrait painter, 9 children
> Johannas b. January 3, 1798 d. March 5, 1802
> Elizabeth b. December 29, 1800
> Susanna b. June 9, 1803
> Rebecca b. July 25, 1806

**Rsh.45** John David Drechler, Drechsler, Troxel, Trachsel, Traxel, Trexil, Troxil, Trucksill, Trexel, Trucksaal, Troxler, Trostell, (son of Rsh.43) b. May 3, 1761, at Bethlehem, Northampton Pa., YCHS, a Weaver by Trade, DGM, as a widower he m. Elisabeth Mohler (Molow), b. 1763, d. September 1, 1828, New Lancaster, Fairfield, Ohio, who was a widow, in Philadelphia on June 26, 1781, lived in Northampton Co., Pa., then Frederick Co., Md., then York Pa,, then Adams Co., Pa., Germany Twp., d. October 2, 1855, at age 94. Reportedly they were among first settlers of Gettysburg, Pa., where he is buried, Troxell Trails, LDS
known children:

> John J. (Rsh.81) b. 1781, d. February 3, 1855, Gettysburg, Pa., m. Catherine Ackerman
> Salome b. April 13, 1784 m. Peter Sheads, 13 children
> Ann Margaret b. August 28, 1789 bapt. at St. Johns, Germany Twp., Pa., sponsor bapt. Elis Bischoffin, single
> David b. January 30, 1790 d. June 14, 1844, buried in Gettysburg,Pa.
> Michael (Rsh.163) b. April 11, 1793, m. Margaret Merkle (?Markel) May 21,1816, at Zion Lutheran Church, Baltimore, Md.
> Anna Marie b. May 11, 1794 d. August 9, 1871
> Hannah m. a Carpenter
> Sarah
> Abraham (?Rsh.8) b. c. 1788 1st child b. in Gettysburg,Pa., moved to Baltimore, Md.
> Anna Marie b. May 11, 1794 d. Aug. 9, 1871
> Jacob b. Maryland exact date not known.  Moved to

Fairfield Co., Ohio found there in 1830 Census. His mother d. there.

**Rsh.46**  John Adam Trissler (son of Rsh.44) b. August 9, 1787, by Trade a Carpenter, he m. Juliana Reed on September 24, 1811, and they lived in Lancaster Town, Pa., where he d. May 5, 1825, known children:

>  Richard (Reichart) Dehuff Trissler b. April 7, 1813, d. July 12, 1813
>  Johann Abraham Trissler, b. November 28, 1818, bapt. March 21, 1820, Pa. Vital Records and Moravian Church Burial Book
>  Margaret R. m. Levi Weaver
>  Maria Susanna b. June 2, 1814

**Rsh.47**  John Nicholas Traxel, Trisler, Draxel, Troxel, Troxell, Trixsell (son of Rsh.11), b. 1753, by Trade a Baker, m. Anna-Margaretha Becker, daughter of George Ernst and Magdalena Helena Becker in 1772 at Northampton Co., Pa., lived in Easton Twp., Pa., had Rev. War Service in the Pennsylvania Militia, Troxell Trails, LDS, known children:

>  George T. (Rsh.14) b March 6, 1775, d. June 5, 1861 m. Rosina (Rosanna) Seib (Seip)
>  John Nicholas (Rsh.50) b. April 11, 1778 m. Elisabeth Bishop
>  Michael b. September 6, 1781 m. Catherine Bishop, lived in Easton, Pa., children:  Peter b. September 1, 1804, Margaret b. October 31, 1806, Thomas Nicholas b. December 5, 1810, Elizabeth b. December 24, 1812, Mary Ann b. May 17, 1816, Abraham b. November 20, 1808
>  Jacob  b. March 15, 1784 m. Maria Gehry, children Samuel b. May 4, 1807, Juliana b. July 17, 1808, Aaron b. November 16, 1810, Sarah Ann b. January 12, 1813, Christina b. December 25, 1814, Anna Maria b. April 13, 1816, Nicholas b. August 13, 1819, Jacob b. August 19, 1821, Nathaniel b. 1823, Keziah b. March 5, 1831.
>  Henrich b. March 17, 1786 m. ?Sara, possibly d. before 1800 Census
>  Abraham b. August 8, 1788 d. February 26, 1827,

Peter b. August 23, 1790

Elisabeth b. November 17, 1792 bapt. November 30, 1792 m. Valentine Deily (Deitz), five children

Wilhelm b. February 23, 1795, d. May 23, 1802

Joseph b. October 6, 1797 m. Susan Moser, lived in Easton, Pa., children, William Henry b. 1820, Alexander b. October 8, 1822, Abraham b. 1824, Maria Sabina b. September 4, 1829, Benjamin b. 1831, Louisa b. June 22, 1835, Margaret b. August 16, 1837, Joseph b. 1840.

Daniel b. December 4, 1799 m. _____, lived in Easton, Pa. Census shows no children in 1840.

**Rsh.48** Adam Troxell,Trachsel,Deshler,Teschler,Deschler, (son of Rsh.39) b.about 1758, he m. Anna Maria Catherine Hecker, she d. February 8, 1812, then he m. Eva Catherine (Geiger) Kern, a widow, they lived in Northampton Co., Pa., they were members of the Egypt Reformed Church, Leehigh Co., Pa., reportedly he lived his entire life in Pa., Troxell Trails, known children:

Magdalena b. September 28, 1778, sponsor bapt. Peter Deshler and wife Magdalena (Rsh.108)

John Nichollas (Rsh.80) b. October 29, 1780 bapt. November 26, He m. Maria Heller, 4 sons 6 daughters

Maria Susanna b. May 7, 1781, sponsor to bapt. Johannes Baer and w. Susanna

Peter b. December 30, 1781 m. Catherine Christina Knoc, members of Egypt Reformed Church, children: Hanna b. 1807; Carl b. 1809; Robert b. 1811; Edward b. 1813; Drusilla b. 1819

Catharina b. July 29, 1783 sponsor bapt. Peter Shreiber and Catherine Kern

Christian (Rsh.70) b. May 1, 1784 m. Barbara Cru

Hanna b. October 5, 1786 m. Rev. John Gobrect, she d. March 17, 1819

Elisabeth b. April 25, 1789

Jonas (?Rsh.20) b. March 26, 1793 m. Sarah Geiger, and removed to Maryland, he and his wife sponsored a baptism at Egypt Reformed Church in 1814. known child, Isabella bapt. April 16, 1815 with Stephen, her Uncle, as sponsor.

Stephan b. December 29, 1798

**Rsh.49** John Trexel, Troxel, (son of Rsh.19) b. c. 1775, Philadelphia Co., Pa., lived in Montgomery Co., Pa., m. Mary_____, and lived with parents Huntingdon Co., Pa., then moved to Cambia Co., Pa., known children:

> John
> Adam m. 1824 Cambia Co., Pa.
> George b. 1813
> Perry b. 1824
> Sarah
> Samuel b. 1820

**Rsh.50** John Nicholas Traxel (son of Rsh.47) b. April 11, 1778, m. Elizabeth Bishop on August 11, 1799, they lived in Easton, Pa., he d. August 5, 1825, Troxell Trails, LDS, see Northampton Co., Pa., probate, known children:

> Sarah b. January 22, 1800 m. John Miller
> Susanna b. July 13, 1801
> William b. December 6, 1802, m, Sarah Overfield
> Lawrence (Lorentz) b. November 28, 1804, m. Hannah
> Henry Sperring b. March 1807
> Christina b. September 5, 1813
> Susanna Wilheimina b. May 5, 1816
> Johan Moritz b. October 11, 1818
> Christina
> Juliana
> John K.

**Rsh.51** John (Martin?) Stephen Tranckel, Trenckel, Troester, Troster (son of Rsh.109) m. Eva Catharine Hambrechtin on March 27, 1739. They lived in Lancaster Pa., then Breinigsville Pa., then Berks, then E. Lebanon Pa., Londonberry Twp., Shamokin, Pa., and Frederick Co., Md., known children:

> ?Jacob
> John Adam bapt. July 8, 1739, sponsor bapt. John Adam Hambrech and his wife Elizabeth
> Barbara Elizabeth Magdalena bapt. January 13, 1740 sponsor bapt. Jacob Spanseiler and wife
> Catharina bapt. March 27, 1741 sponsor Jacob Spannseiler and wife Catharina Beyerlin

John Martin b. March 2, 1743 sponsor bapt. Ulrich Spiers
   and wife
Stephen b. March 13, 1743, sponsor bapt. March 27
   Christopher Dranckel and wife
?Abraham
?Barbara
John Michael b. November 18, 1746, bapt. December 21,
   1746, sponsor bapt. Michael Axer and wife
Anna Catharine b. January 2, 1749 m. George Dietrich,
   sponsor bapt. Johan Jacob Diemer and Anna
   Catherine, his wife, at Trinity Lutheran Lancaster Pa.
Anna Maria Agensa bapt. February 12, 1751 sponsor
   Johan George Honig and wife Maria Agnesa
   note: Lancaster, Pa. and Frederick, Md. Church
   Records show Catherine sponsoring children of
   Daniel Kramer (Cramer,Creamer) and Catherine
   Kurrin (Currin) 1758-1770

**Rsh.52** David Troxel, Draxel, (son of Rsh.22) b.July 27, 1734 and
bapt.in Egypt Reformed Church, Leehigh Co., Pa., moved to
Maryland m. Anna Elizabeth_____, lived in Frederick Co.,
Md.(Conococheaque), then Washington Co., Md., Troxell Trails says
moved to Loudoun Co., Va. ?1774, there in 1782 Tax List DGM,
known children:
   George Jacob. b. 1758, Frederick Co., Md.
   Frederick b. March 27, 1762,
       sponsors to bapt. Johann Nichol and Appollonia
       Guntz
   Jacob b. 1786, Washington Co., Md.
   ?John b. 1760
   ?Mary b. 1766
   ?Peter b. 1764
   ?David b. 1770
   ?Catherine b. 1772
   ?Abraham b. 1768

**Rsh.53**   John Conrad Dreschler, Trincker, Trickler, Trackler,
Dreckler, Truncker, Tranckler, Drunckler, Drenckler, Trunckhler,
Drinckler, Trenckler, Tronckler, Trunckler, Immigrant, he came to

this country on the Ship Rawley, landed in Philadelphia, Pa., October 23, 1752 m. Catherine Magdalena Christein_____, they lived in Williams Twp., Northampton, Pa., known children:
John Jacob b. 1755, (Rsh.56) m. Rosina Catherina

**Rsh.54** Johann Andreas (Andrew) Tressler, Drissler, Dressler, Dresler, Truschel, Deuschel, Douschel, Drussel, Tresler, Treslar, Jr., (son of Rsh.21), by Trade a Farmer and Blacksmith, b. May 28, 1747 in Jagsthausen, Germany m. Mary (Maria) Margaret Ley (Loy), daughter of Mathias Ley and sister of Michael Ley, they lived in Berks Co., Pa., then York Co., Pa., then Frederick Co., Md., he had Rev. War Service in the 2nd Battalion of Berks Co., Pa., Militia., known children:
Anna Catharina bapt. March 6, 1768 in York Pa., by Jacob Lischy
John Jacob b.December 25, 1770/73 d. April 3, 1852 in Schulykill Co., Pa., m. Susannah Hamman, daughter of Frederick and Mary Hamman
Maria Magdalena b. May 4, 1771, bapt. June 21, 1772, Lutheran Church Frederick Co., Md., sponsors bapt. Henrich and Rosina Voelckner
Johann Andreas Tressler,Dressler 2nd m. Catherine Hamman (Hammon), daughter of Frederick and Mary Hammon, they lived in Albany Twp., Berks Co., Pa., members New Jerusalem Church, known children: Mary Magdalena b. July 15, 1786 m. Jacob Arnold, 6 children, Farm Loysville
Catherine Shearer b. 1788 m. Philip Smith, 4 children, she d. January 14, 1888
Jonathan b. August 23, 1792, d. April 3, 1869, m. first Rebecca Halm. Second marriage Elizabeth Phillips. 8 children. Jonathan migrated to Williams Co., Ohio
David b. May 23, 1794, d. December 16, 1852, m. Mary Catherine Bernheisel, 12 children, owned a farm in New Bloonfield, Pa.
Esther b. May 8, 1795 m. George Scheibley
Mary Rebecca b. December 4, 1796 m. George Titzel, buried Union Cemetery at Marksville, Perry Co., Pa.
Salome Sarah Doser b. May 23, 1798 m. John Kistler,

Carlisle, Pa., she d. September 9, 1841

Joseph b. August 23, 1799, d. May 28, 1890, 1st m. Sarah Koser, 10 children, 2nd Cathrine Shearer, 7 children. Joseph moved to W. Jefferson, Williams Co., Ohio

Jeremiah d. at 4 years of age

John b. July 22, 1803, d. May 4, 1859, m. Elizabeth Loy, 13 children

Elizabeth b. January 8, 1806, m. Samuel Waggoner (Wagner), 11 children

Mary (Polly) b. July 22, 1810 m. George Hohenshilt

**Rsh.55**  George Michael Dressler m. Eva Barbara Kast, in Berks Co., Pa., Rockland Twp., known children:
Dorothea bapt. 1755
Daniel b. 1762

**Rsh.56**  John Jacob Drecksler, Drescher, Drenckler, Deischer, Diescher, Trinkler, Trinckler, Drissler, Drinckler, Trenckler, Tronckler, Trunckler, (son of Rsh.53) b.1755 (?m. 1st Susannah Edelman), m. Rosina Catherina_____, lived in Williams Twp., Northampton Co., Pa., known children:
Susanna Catharine b. 1774, ?daughter of Susannah Edelman Ist wife
Julia

**Rsh.57**  Lorentz Troxell, Troxel (son of Rsh.58) b. 1767 in Whitehall Twp., Northumberland Co., Pa., he m. Christina Reichard on December 3, 1793, lived in Weisenburg Twp., Bucks & Leehigh Co., Pa., d. September 20, 1826, DGM,
known children:
John (Rsh.158) by Trade a Carpenter, b. January 9, 1795 m. Salome Mickley
Salome b. January 11, 1796
Jonathan b. February 6, 1797 christened February 24, 1797, m. Elizabeth, very active in Egypt Reformed Church, known children, Edward b. August 23, 1818, Milton b. June 17, 1819, Amandus b. August 25, 1821, Sophia b. October 9, 1823, Edmund b. May 22, 1829, Abraham b. December 21, 1833.
Catharine b. February 17, 1799

Maria Magdalena b. August 24, 1812, daughter m. Abraham
Diehl
?possibly another son

**Rsh.58** Peter Troxell, Troksell, Draxel, (son of Rsh.22) b. December
28, 1723 in Wolfersheim, Germany, by Trade a Tavern Owner, he
was naturalized March 9, 1741, Philadelphia, Pa., m. Anna Maria
Margarethain_____ on May 19, 1747, in Bucks Co., Pa., lived in
Whitehall Twp., Leehigh Co., Pa., she d., then m. Hanna Zirckel on
May 11, 1799, he was in French and Indian War, and Revolutionary
War under Capt. Henry Reitz, Northampton, Co., Pa., He ran a
tavern in 1761 and he d. February 28, 1811 and is buried at Jordan
Reformed Church, Leehigh Co., Pa., the Egypt Church Records say
he had 7 sons and 7 daughters, <u>DGM</u>
known children:
>      Peter (Rsh.40) b. March 28, 1751 m. Helena Catharine
>           Schoener
>      Daniel (Rsh.148) m. Maria Veronica_____
>      John (Rsh.149) b. about 1755 m. Catharine_____
>      Jacob Troxell (Rsh.23) m. Anna Margaret Eberhard
>      Margaret b. 1759, m. Gottfried Roth
>      Barbara b. December 13, 1762 m. Peter Gross
>      Maria Susannah b. March 9, 1765
>      Lorentz (Rsh.57) b. 1767 m. Christina Reichard in
>           Weisenburg, Twp., Leehigh Co., Pa.
>      Eva Catherine b. August 12, 1769 m. Peter Guth
>      Christian b. December 6, 1771 m. ?Barbara
>      Magdalena b. April 30, 1774
>      ?Nicholas
>      ?Adam
>      ?William found in Frederick, Md. land Records at Tom's
>           Creek May 14, 1788
>      ?Frederick, b. March 28, 1779

**Rsh.59**    Henry Troxel, (son of Rsh.19) b. August 14, 1788, in
Huntington Co., Pa., d. January 14, 1844 at Pyrmont, Indiana m.
Catherine Keltner, daughter of Michael, lived in Carroll Co., Indiana,
<u>Troxell Trails</u>, known children:
>      Margaret b. November 29, 1810
>      Susanna b. February 21, 1813
>      Elias b. October 10, 1815

Elizabeth b. March 3, 1819
Sarah b. July 15, 1821
Jacob b. August 14, 1823
Henry b. May 9, 1825
Andrew b. March 1, 1829
David b. March 1, 1829
Catherine b. October 23, 1832
Nancy b. December 21, 1836

**Rsh.60** John Troxell (son of Rsh.13) b. December 22, 1772, m. Margaret Elisabeth Dotterer, she d. 1854, she was the daughter of Conrad Dotterer who was brother to Sophia Dotterer (Rsh.43), they lived at Creagerstown, in Frederick Co., Md., and were members of the Apples Lutheran Church, he d. September 17, 1857 at Frederick, Md.,<u>DGM</u>,
known children:

Peter b. June 23, 1801, apparently d. before age 10 as per census

David b. September 27, 1805 m. Juliann Feiser (Fizer), children I. Lewis Joseph, John F., b.September 10, 1831, d. October 15, 1892, m. Susan Rebecca Hesser; Emanuel b. March 26, 1836 d. April 15, 1876 m. Mary J. Colliflower; William W or H b. c. 1841 m. Mary E. Stattlemayer; Margaret Saville b. c. 1843 m. Edward Boller; Jacob Lewis b. May 24, 1847 d. February 4, 1918 m. Mary Ann Barton, daughter of Henry Barton; Samuel J. b c. 1850 d. 1927 m. Sophia Elizabeth Colliflower - known children Joseph C. b. 1870 d. March 3, 1871; Robert L. b. 1871 d. 1951 m. Gertrude A.; Ada b. c. 1874; Maurice L. b. 1875 d. 1946; Frank A. b. April 8, 1877 d. July 12, 1953; Frank A. b. April 8, 1877 d. July 12, 1953 m. Elsie E.; Flora b. c. 1879)

Frederick b. November 13, 1807, a Shoemaker, m.Sophia Barbara Firor, and he d. February 27, 1891, known children, William D. b. c. 1839 m. Sarah Pusey; Susan M. b. July 7, 1841 d. January 24, 1917 m. George M. Harbaugh, Martin D. b. c. 1844 d. August 25, 1901 m. Jeanetta C. Boller; Mary Elizabeth b. July 4, 1846 d. April 10, 1924, never m.

Matilda b. May 16, 1809 (Polly) Anna Maria b. April 20,1810
aka Mary Ann, m. Jacob Biggs, 5 children
Abraham b. January 12, 1816 m. Isabella Agnes Welty, on
April 8, 1865, daughter of John J. Wealty, lived in
Emmitsburg, Md.,where they are both buried,
known children William H. b. 1866 m. Mary Topper;
Elizabeth b. 1868 m. John Shorb; Frederick D. b.
1871 m. Elsie S. Ott

**Rsh.61** Joseph Drechsler, Drexler, Trexler (?son of Rsh.5,
?Rsh.124), m. Elisabeth Kafeld (Kafelt), at Christ Reformed Church,
Lutheran Reformed Church, on September 1, 1805 at York, Pa.,
known children:
Daniel bapt. 1803 m. ?Susanna Shepp
Catherine bapt. October 5, 1806
Jeremiah bapt. September 3, 1809 m. Charlotte Wehrly,
son Jacob bapt. January 1, 1831 Christ Reformed
Lutheran Church, York Co., Pa.

**Rsh.62** Peter Traxel, Drachel, Draxel, Drachsel, Drexel, Trascel (son
of Rsh.39) b.about 1760, m. Sybilla Veronica Hecker, s. d. March 8,
1844, in Leehigh Co., Pa., active in Egypt Reformed Church,
Leehigh Co., Pa., also found in Tohickon Reformed Records. He d.
1816, Troxell Trails,
known children:
Johannes b. October 4, 1788, sponsor Johann Nickel
Traxel and wife Catherine
Magdalena b. September 8, 1790 m. Jacob Jones
Peter b. September 25, 1792
Catharina b. March 6, 1795, sponsors bapt. Niclaus Balliet
and Sarah Kock
Susanna b. December 27, 1796 m. John Schoenberger,
sponsor bapt. Nicklaus Drachsel and Maria Stoffiet
Salomon b. November 28, 1799 m. Barbara Schmidt on
December 17,1824, he d. January 12, 1836, 3 sons
and 1 daughter, daughter Leweine b. October 11,
1825 m. John Volweiler, she d. 1866
Joel b. November 27, 1802, sponsor bapt. Peter Traxel,
single
Elias b. January, 20, 1804, sponsor bapt. Peter Wutring

and wife Elizabeth, he m. Ruth_____ , 4 children, he d. 1824

**Rsh.63**  Henry Tressler, b. 1791, by Trade a Farmer, m. Margaret Jordan near Emmitsburgh, Md., on March 24, 1820. He was b. near Abbottstown, Pa., and he was drafted in 1812 War at Emmitsburgh, Frederick Co., Md. , He d. August 23, 1844 at Brookfield, Stark Co., Ohio, August 23, 1844. Moved to Ohio from Emmitsburgh, Md. in 1834.

**Rsh.64**  Dr. Peter Trissler, Trisler, Trister, Trislie, Trislit, by Trade a Medical Doctor, found at Jessamine Creek, Kentucky where he was living on Main Fork, Fayette Co., Ky. on June 5, 1798. ?Possible brother to Rsh.82., he m. Catherine_____.
known children:
>Jacob
>Joseph
>Peter

**Rsh.65**  John Frederick Tresslar, Troxel (son of Rsh.13) b. December 23, 1773, d. September 17, 1857, m. Elizabeth Young on May 7, 1801, in Frederick Co., Md. at Apples Lutheran Church, <u>DGM</u>, known child:
>Matilda b. May 17, 1809, sponsor bapt. Catherine Young

**Rsh.66**  Jacob Dressler, Dresler m. Salome Susannah_____, lived in Dauphin Co., Pa.,
known children:
>Hannah, bapt. August 9, 1805, sponsor bapt. Jacob Leitner and wife Hanna
>David, bapt. April 23, 1810 sponsor bapt. Abraham Erdman and wife Elizabeth
>Janathan, b. May 21, 1801, bapt. June 21,1801, sponsor Simon Scherman and wife Marg. Elizabeth
>Rebecca, b. February 13, 1804, bapt. March 13, 1805 sponsor Jacob Hannan and Cadarina Erdmann

**Rsh.67**  Abraham Troxel (?son of Rsh.32), m. Margaret Lymann, m. January 1822, Canton, Ohio,, he served in the Pa. Militia in Capt. John Jenkins Co., War of 1812. He d. in Goff, Newsha, Kansas in August 1847. Witness for year 1847 widow's pension were Peter

Troxel who had known Margaret for 57 years and Clarasy Troxel had known Margaret for 51 years. ?Brother and sister-in law.

**Rsh.68** Daniel Troxell m. Catherine Jacoby, on October 9, 1815, at Trexlertown, Leehigh Co., Pa., Solome Wiedes gave test. of wedding for War of 1812 pension application.

**Rsh.69** Jacob Troxel (?son of Rsh.101),b. 1794 m. Elizabeth Green, in 1838, in 1871 his residence was Piney Creek, Carroll Co., Md., in War of 1812 he was a Pvt. in Capt. S. Ogles Co., Maryland. Militia, he was discharged under Col. Heath, in Baltimore Md. in July 1813

**Rsh.70** Christian Troxell (son of Rsh.48) b. May 1, 1784, bapt. on May 30, in Egypt Reformed Church, Leehigh Co., Pa., m. Barbara Cru on January 15, 1806 (she may have been the widow of a Horn) m. by Minister Rev. Gobrecht, at Allentown, Leehigh Co., Pa., He enrolled in War of 1812 at Allentown, Lehigh Co., Pa., under Capt. Dinkeys Co., Pa. Militia, and was discharged at Philadelphia, Pa., church records say 9 children,
known children:
> Christian b. 1802
> Juliana b. March 12, 1807
> Samuel b. July 22, 1808
> Wilhelm b. May 2, 1810
> Margaretha b. August 9, 1812

**Rsh.71** Jacob Troxell b. 1796 in Union Co., Pa., m. Sarah Grimm, in 1819 at Swimeford, Pa., service conducted by Rev. Freize, he Volunteered at Union Co., Pa., for his War of 1812 Service. They moved to Illinois in 1842, he d. August 1852 in Pleasant Valley, Ill., Sarah had d. by 1879.

**Rsh.72** William C. Troxell m. Mary Brubaker, he enlisted for War 1812 in Greenfield, Ohio, he d. May 23, 1856 in Greenfield, Ohio

**Rsh.73** Barney Troxler, Dropler, Trousdale, Immigrant, ?b.1743, he was naturalized September 22, 1764 m. Elizabeth_____, lived in Orange Co., N.C. on Great Allmance River, in 1790 found in Orange Co., St. Asphas Dist., Hillsboro Twp., N.C., Will, written 1814,
known children:
> Philipena m.David Coble

Mary m.Lauwich (Ludwick)Albright April 1, 1784
Jacob appointed overseer of roads, May 1794 Orange
      Co., N.C.
Elizabeth m.Peter Huffman, ?son of John Huffman
Catharine m. James McCamey on December 26, 1806
David Troxler m. Betsey Graves on May 5, 1822
Powell C. m. Mary Whilesil (Whitesill) on March 8, 1810
Barnabus, Barney, Jr. b. 1795 m. Polly Pnletck, lived in
      Summerfield, Guilford Co., N.C. after War of 1812
      service.
George m. Barbara Peeler on October 2, 1811

**Rsh.74** Peter Tresler, Tressler, Teisher, Trisler, m. Fanny_____,
Will, written 1789 Washington Co., Md.,and proved October 16,
1808, known children:
    John
    Susanna
    Mary Gersh
    Elizabeth Grove, had dau. Elizabeth
    Dorathena
    Jacob was deceased in 1789, he had dau. Susanna,
    Mary Ratzell had children.

**Rsh.75** Michael (?George) Trisler, Trissler, Dressler, Drizler,
Troecksel, Trosler, Trosher (?son of Rsh.16 by 1st marriage of
Father) b. 1741, by Trade a Joiner (Carpenter), he m. Mary Margaret
_____,she was b. in 1742 and d. April 5, 1828, her Will settlement
December 1833 in Frederick Co., Md., reportedly they came to
Emmitsburg, Frederick Co., Md. from Lancaster, Pa. His burial
October 23, 1805, known children:
    Mary had daughter Mary Casper
    Magdalena Margaretha b. April 6, 1758, bapt. April 23,
        1758, sponsor bapt. Johannes Schard and wife, d.
        August 10, 1758
    Elizabeth b. October 11, 1760, bapt. November 23, 1760,
        sponsors to bapt. Valentine Schreiner and wife
        Elizabeth, ?possibly her daughter m. Jacob Houch
        March 26, 1811
    George (?Rsh.25),b. January 12, 1760, bapt. February 3,
        1769, sponsor George Schmitt and Margaretha
        Eichelbergerin, known children: William

Trisler,(buried 1842), George Trisler, Margaret
Trisler, Henritta Weaver
Valentine (Rsh.110) b. 1762 m. Mary Ream

note: ? a possible sister to Rsh.75, a Barbara m. John
Weller, as per Monocracy Lutheran Church Records,
Frederick, Md.

**Rsh.76** Ignatius Trexler, Dreckseler, Trucksall, Trexlear, Reseler,
Dresler, Preseler, Truxall, Tresslear, (?son of Rsh.5) b.c. 1787, by
Trade a Cooper, m. Anna (Nancy) Murray on November 8, 1812 at
St. Johns German Catholic Church in Baltimore, Md., they moved
to Richmond, Va. in 1817. At the rank of Corporal, he served in the
Battles of North Point and Ft. McHenry in Baltimore, Md., War of
1812. Buried, without appropriate marker, at Shockoe Hill
Cemetery, Richmond, Va.,
known children:
  John Joseph b. October, 1813, a Cooper by Trade, lived
   in Franklin Co., Va., never m., buried at Mt.Calvery
   Cemetery, Richmond, Va.
  William (Rsh.140) b. August 11, 1815, d. February 8,
   1855, a Cooper by Trade, m. Nancy Ann Ellis,
   daughter of Jeremiah and Virginia Ellis, 5 children
  Appolonia Julia (Abby Gail) b. May 2, 1817, bapt. at St.
   Johns German Catholic Church, Baltimore, Md.,
   sponsors to her bapt. were Rsh.29, m. William Miller
   July 6, 1839. She d. May 9, 1850 in Richmond, Va.
  Mary Ann b. July 7, 1821, m. Christian S. Allbrecht
   February 16, 1842, children Joseph Allbrecht, Eutaw
   Allbrecht, Christian Allbrecht
  Rosetta b. October 8, 1825, m. Gottlieb Allbrecht
   (Allbright), June 22, 1843, children: Mary Louise,
   Nonnie m. Wm. Kuhn, Margaret m. Christian
   Schneider, Virginia m. Robert Shilling

**Rsh.77** John (?Jacob) Tressler, Tresler, (?son of Rsh.78) ,m.
Barbara_____, lived in Washington Co., Md. where a Distribution
Account dated November 17, 1798, is found listing admr. as
Barbara with 1/2 to widow and equal portions to:
  Frederick
  Jacob

George
Adam
Elizabeth Sunday
Mary
George Tresler, Sr.

**Rsh.78** David Dressler, m. Phillipina_____, granted land in Lancaster, Pa., on August 20, 1740, his Will, dated April 13, 1752 names son-in-law John Thomas. She is still alive July 3, 1758 with land adjacent to Dehuff family,
known children:

         _____m. John Thomas

         note: ?possible brother to Rsh.16

**Rsh.79** George D. Jacob Dressler, Tressler, Trisler, Tresler, Dresler, Sr., (?son of Rsh.27), Weaver by Trade, m. Catherine Doll, daughter of John and Mariah Doll, (her brother Conrad m. Marie Trisler of Lancaster on September 8, 1801), Will, York Co., Pa., 1799, probate June 25, 1805 (with sureties John G. Odenman, Christian Wirst) Paradise Twp., York Co., Pa.,
known children:
         Frederick
         Anna Mary
         ?John
         note: 1783 Census Paradise Twp., York Co., Pa., shows 7 inhabitants

**Rsh.80** John Nicholas Trosell, (son of Rsh.48) b. October 29, 1780, a Farmer, m. Maria Heller, lived in Whitehall Twp., Pa., members of Egypt Church, Leehigh Co., Pa., d. August 6, 1829, <u>Troxell Trails</u>,
known children:
         Maria b. February 11, 1805
         Elizabeth b. August 24, 1806
         Adam b. February 17, 1808
         Sarah b. October 25, 1809
         Charles b. September 6, 1811
         Catharine b. March 26, 1813
         Lydia b. February 27, 1815
         Susanna b. May 2, 1817
         Joseph b. November 20, 1820

Nicholas b. September 28, 1822

**Rsh.81** John J. Troxel, Jr. (son of Rsh.45), b.1781 in Maryland, m. Catherine Ackerman, of Lancaster Borough, Pa., lived in Gettysburg, Pa., <u>DGM</u>, then Frederick Co., Md., where he d. December 7, 1853. He is buried at Elias Lutheran Church, Frederick Co., Md., known children:

> John b. September 2, 1807
> David b. Sept. 4, 1809
> Jacob (Rsh. 161) b. November 19, 1812 m. Susan Ziegler, he was a Coach Painter

**Rsh.82** Michael Trisler, Treshler, Tressler, Trehsler, Tresler, b. c. 1750, at Wittenberg, Germany (?brother to Rsh.64) m. Catherine_ ____, lived in Hagerstown, Washington Co., Md., then Baltimore, Md, then Jessamine Co., Kentucky, known children:

> Joseph
> Peter
> Johann Jacob b. November 24, 1786, bapt. May 20, 1787, Zion Lutheran, Baltimore, Md., sponsors Hemrich and Catherine Brutel
> John b. December 31, 1789, Hagerstown, Washington Co., Md.
> ?Catherine d. July 1795, 8 years 11 months old

**Rsh.83** Adam Deshler,Teschler m. Apel (Appolonia)_____, Whitehall Twp., Pa., where he d.1781, Egypt Reformed Church Records, Leehigh Co., Pa., say they had 3 sons, 3 daughters, known children:

> Peter b. March 18, 1743
> Adam the younger had daughter as per Egypt Church Records: Maria Barbara Teschler daughter of Adam Treschler the younger bapt. July 28, 1771

**Rsh.84** (Philip) John Trexler,Truxall, Sr. (son of Rsh.115) b.1729,m. Maria Elizabeth_____, then Susanna Bauer Hassler, widow, and daughter of Casper Bauer, they lived in Northampton, Leehigh Co., Pa. His Will, dated January 26, 1795, probated March 10, 1795,<u>History and Genealogy of the Trexler Family</u>, (in 1796 she is named Susanna Leer and she was exr. of husbands estate along with John Kromer), known children:

Isarel m. Hanna Ott, lived until death Hanover Twp., Pa.,
children, Emanuel Uriah m. Caroline Hoover,
Joanthan m. Clarissa M., Israel, Jr.m. Catherine,
John Jacob m. Harietta Miller, Reuben A., Abraham
R.b. 1831 m. Sarah C. Walp, Charles H.m. Elizabeth
Mosser, Polly Maria m. James Bush, Salome
m.Solomon Wantellbush (Wandel).
Emanuel b. 1760 (Rsh.106) m. Catherine Cameron of
Lancaster, Pa., in Washington Co., Maryland
Maria Elizabeth m. Jarrett (Joseph?), 1 child John Jarrett
See Pennsylvania probate record of Lawrence
Trexler
Phillipina m. John Albright then John Nyce, 1 child
Margaret b. December 4, 1771 m. John Kroner, 9 children
Ferdinand (Rsh.125) m. Catherine Swartz
Peter (?Rsh.74,?Rsh.90) said to have moved West
Jeremiah (Rsh.88) m. Elizabeth Reiss and was for many
years a Justice of the Peace at Trexlertown

**Rsh.85** John Peter Trexler, Drexler, Traxler, Trisler, Trescler, Sr.,
(son of Rsh.3) known as Macungie Peter, b. February 11, 1721, d.
August 25, 1798) m. Catherine Winck, daughter of Casper and
Gertrude (nee Kemp) Winck, at Berks Co., Pa., Macungie Twp.,
Leehigh Co., Northampton Co., lived in Easton, Pa., found at lower
Merion Twp., in 1779. Both are buried near Breinigsville, Pa. He
was deeded the family homestead in 1748. He sat in the Colonial
Courts at Easton, Pa., History and Genealogy of the Trexler Family,
known children:
?David b. 1744
John Peter (Rsh.87) b. August 15, 1748, m. Catherine
Grim
John (?Joseph) (Rsh.124) b. October 12, 1750, moved to
York Co., Pa., about 1784, on same page in 1783
tax record for York in Paradise Twp., as George
Tressler Rsh.79
Rachael m. Philip Fogel
Maria Christine b. November 3, 1753 m. Peter Haas, 10
children
Elizabeth m. Peter Christman
Jonathan (Rsh.89) b. May 1, 1762, m. Elizabeth Horlacher
Gertrude b. June 8, 1764, m. Henrich Grim

**Rsh.86** John Peter Trexler, Drechseler, Trescler, Trayxler, Trexlere, Traxler, Drexler, Drechssler, (son of Rsh.115) b. February 27,1727 m. Mary Catherine (Catharina) Allbright, lived in Berks Co., Pa. He d. November 7, 1784, his estate papers say he is of Lower Merion Twp., Montgomery Co., Pa. He is buried at St. Pauls Cemetery at Ardmore, Pa., she d. Ardmore, Pa., 1800, <u>History and Genealogy of the Trexler Family</u>,

> known children:
>
> ? Jeremiah
>
> Johannes George (Henrich?) bapt. April 29, 1759 at 14 weeks of age, sponsors George Hoffman and Catherina Schumacher,single, ?became a butcher, ?d1824.
>
> Joseph b. 1751, a Farmer, administration of his estate granted in 1811 to widow, Philadelphia, Pa., he d. intestate, widow, Elizabeth nee Horn, they lived in Northern Liberties. She remarried John Yocum, adm. granted to pay the heirs of Peter Trexler deceased on December 15, 1814, adm. states Lawrence Trexler, Catherine Bloom and Christina Hyde have moved away to parts unknown and are supposed to be dead.
>
> (?Susannah) Catherine b. 1756 m. Bloom
>
> Elizabeth b. 1758 m. John Horn at St. James Episcopal, Montgomery Co., Pa.
>
> Rachael b. 1760 m. Isaac Wood,
>
> ? Christopher confirmation 1761 at Ziegel Church
>
> Johhann Henrich, bapt. May 24, 1761, 9 weeks old, sponsors John Henry Wetzell and Catharina Drechselern
>
> Lawrence d. 1825, Montgomery Co., Pa., adm. account November 21, 825, Joseph Jarrett, adm., account does not name heirs.
>
> Christina Ann b. 1763 m. John Hidy (Hyde), lived in Highland Co., Va., buried Crabbottom, Va. west of Staunton, Va.
>
> Susanna Catharina b. January 14, 1768, sponsor to bapt. Joseph Allbright
>
> Maria b. July 15,1774
>
> Peter, d. 1825
>
> David m. September 10, 1799 to Anna Catharina Fisher,

dau. of Henry and Sarah Fisher, had sons John Trexler, Joseph Trexler, Sarah Reakirk, Hannah Fisher, grandsons, David Trexler, son of Joseph and David Fisher son of daughter Hannah Fisher, appoint Joseph Jarrett of Up. Merion Twp., exr., Sarah was christened June 6, 1802 at St. Michael's Lutheran Church Germantown, Pa.; Ann christened March 21, 1812 at St. Peter's Lutheran Church, Philadelphia, Pa.

**Rsh.87** John Peter Trexler, Trechseler, Trexsler, Drescher, Trscher, Trescler, Traxler, Treixer, (son of Rsh.85) known as Mertztown Peter, b. August 15,1748 m. Catherine Grimm, daughter of Henry Grim youngest son of Gettie Grim, he was a Capt.in the Rev. War.and represented his home area in the Pennsylvania General Assembly. He d. March 13, 1828, Berks Co., Pa., they both are buried in Mertztown, Pa., History and Genealogy of the Trexler Family, known children:

> Maria b. July 13,1774 m. John Polk (Folk) and had 7 children

> John Peter b. February 2, 1777, d. March 6, 1828 m. Rachael Fogel and had children Caroline m. Horlacher, Sarah m. Seiberling, Maria m. Fogel, and Jonas

> Jacob b. September 7,1779 m. Lydia Egner, lived in Longswamp, Will, Berks Co., Pa., 1829 and had children Reuben m. Sarah Ann Mattern, David m. Esther, John Peter m. Maria Margaretha Heller, Jacob m. Mary A. Schmoyer, Susanna m. James Breinig and Catherine m. Jacob Breinig,Jr. and Levina (Leweina) m. Stephen Smoyer (Sawyer)

> Ruben b. November 22,1781, d. 1846 m. Anna Leaher (Lesher) dau. of Jacob who lived in Longswamp, Ruben was an Ironmaster. They resided in Mertztown, they had children Col. William (1816-1905) m. Mary Ann Singmaster and Amelia Scholl, Horatio m. Sarah Ann Hunter and Mary Louisa Bell, lived in Reading, Pa., Dr. Lesher m. Elmina Schindel of Ft. Wayne, Mrs. Judith Reno, Lucinder m. General James Rittenhouse, Caroline wife of William Schall

Benjamin b. February 3, 1784 d. 1855, m. Maria Dresher - March 10, 1805 and Catherine Bolich,lived in Catawissa Valley, then Albany, Berks Co., Pa. children: 9 sons and two daughters, Daniel m. Anna Dietrich, Benjamin m. Susanna Leininger, Amos m. Elizabeth Dietrich, Anna, Jonas m. Ubbia Smith, Aaron m. Eliza Kercher, Jarius m. Polly Maria Komp, Nathan m. Lydia Bauscher, Peter m. Margaret Marr and Catherine. Benjamin is buried New Jerusalem Cemetery at Stony Run, Pa.

Catherine b. January 26, 1787 m. Jonathan Haas June 17, 1804, they lived in Longswamp Twp., had 14 children

Jonas b. June 26, 1789, lived in Longswamp Twp., m. Sarah Hottenstein then Maria Diefenderper, had children Jonas m. Mary Elizabeth Good, Willoughby m. Amelia Filbert, Abyle (Abiel) H. m. Angeline C. Breinig, David H., John Peter m. May Himmel, Sarah m. Ludwig, Angeline m. Ahlum and Elizabeth m. Harry Miller.

Anna b. October 1,1791 m. Philip Dresher and John P. Albright, and had 2 children

Judith b. April 9,1793 d. 1885, m. Rev. Isaac Roeller, she d. leaving no children

Nathan b. August 5,1795, m. Phoebe Hirst and they lived in Longswamp Twp., he d. February 1785. They had children Edwin Hirst m. Eliza Schwartz, Mary m. George Schall, Amelia (Emeline) m. Jonathan Bieber Grim and Sarah m. Joseph Esterly, Charles August b. May 19, 1843

Daniel b. November 1,1799 d. July 2, 1829, lived in Union Twp., Huntington Co., Pa., unmarried

Mattias, named in father's Will.

note: History of Berks Co., Pa., does not name Mattias as a child but names Benjamin whom the Will does not name. Perhaps they are the same?

**Rsh.88** Jeremiah Trexler (son of Rsh.84) b.March 24, 1751, m. Elizabeth Reiss, he d. February 25, 1827 in Trexlertown, Pa., as per

known children:

    John b. April 18, 1773, d. 1828, m. Hannah Schneider, 9 children, one son Joseph m. Elizabeth Haines

    Catherine b. September 5,1775

    Margaret b. February 26,1780 m. Andrew Shiffert

    Charles b. December 3,1782 m._____children: Amanda m. Sarah, Manasses m. Irene, Charles, Mary m. Philip Potts, Francis m. John J. Bohler, John Tilghman, Mary Ann, Rebecca

    Jeremiah b. April 17,1785, was a Tailor near Cedar Creek, Allentown, Pa., m. Catherine Griesmer, children: Monroe m. Sarah Ann_____, then Eleminia Kuhns, Mary C. m. George F. Roth, both buried in Allentown, Pa., Caroline m. Reuben Henninger, James m. _____, Levina m._____, Floriann m. Peter Ritz, Francis m. Matilda _____, John m. ____ Ellemina m. _____. Jeremiah

    James b. July 7,1789 m. Jeanette Dunkel

    James bapt. June 11,1790 m. Elizabeth Leibengood, children: James Allen m. Margaret Sattler, then Ellen Jane Trumbauer, Franklin m. Charity_____, William H.H. b. April 11, 1838 m. Emma E. Knerr, Anna Eliza m. Jacob Henry Schall

    Lucas b. March 21, 1795 m. Elizabeth Haines, children Sabilla m. Jepe Roseberry; Lavinia m. Bachman; Elizabeth m. Newcomb; Mary See; Benjamin Seibert; Caroline m. Fred Hahn; Emma S. m. Samuel Snyder; Jeremiah

    note: This family is found in History of Berk's Pa., and in the land records of Berk's Co., Pa., see Land Records for Pennsylvania.

**Rsh.89** Jonathan Trexler (son of Rsh.85, Macungie Peter) b.May 1, 1762, d. May 11, 1845 or May 9, 1846, m. Elizabeth Horlacher, Harlacker, both are buried near Breingsville, Pa., in old family cemetery, History and Genealogy of the Trexler Family, descendants found in Berks History, pg.1606, known children:

    Sophia b. March 4,1793, never m.

Anna b. November 10,1794 m. General Benjamin Floyd (Fogel)

David b. November 27,1796 d. August 20,1823

Christine Diana b. January 7,1799 m. Joseph Schmoyer (Joshus Schmeier), January 3, 1818

Catherine b. October 22,1801 m. Joseph Miller

Jonathan b. November 25,1803 m. Judith Lichtenwalner

Lydia b. September 1,1807 m. John Metzger

Solomon b. May 21,1810 d. August 31,1814

**Rsh.90** Peter Tresler, Traxler, Trussler (?son of Rsh.84), m. Barbara _____, lived in Rockingham Co., Va., where he d. in 1785. Henry Tresler administered Will and Estate, known children:

Charles

John

**Rsh.91** ?John David Troxell, Drachsel (?Son of Rsh.43) b. January 26, 1755, m. ?Elizabeth_____, d.in Adams Co., Pa., probate March 7, 1840, known children:

?Magdalena Drachsel of David and Elizabeth b. October 4, 1777 bapt. November 9, 1777, sponsor bapt. Sophia Drachselin (?Rsh.43), Magdalena m. Stephen Wible

Polly m. Wible, her children Stephen, John, Joseph

Elizabeth m. Wolf

Catherine m. Essick

Mary m. Spangler

David

Susannah m. Keephaver

**Rsh.92** John Trissler, Sr., lived in City of Lancaster, Pa., a Butcher by Trade, m. Catharine_____, Will, probate November 1843, witness Wm. Frink, John Lnummer, known children:

Michael

John

**Rsh.93** Henry Dresslar m. Elizabeth_____, at Bath Co., Va.,on March 19, 1818, moved to Johnson Co., Indiana, he enlisted at Fincastle, Va., for the War of 1812, and was discharged in Norfolk, Va.

**Rsh.94** James Trusler b. 1794 m. Anna Martin, lived in Brookville, Ind., Fayette Co., Indiana, served in the Indiana Militia, during the War of 1812

**Rsh.95** Townsend Trisoler, Trusler, hired Edmund M. Cobbs as substitute for his War of 1812 service at Lynchburg, Va. Edmund Cobbs served in the Va. Militia, for 6 months at Ft. Barber near Norfolk, Va. as a substitute for Townsend Trisoler

**Rsh.96** George W. Trexler, m. Mary_____, History and Genealogy of the Trexler Family known children:

Isaac S. b. July 11, 1818, d. April 23, 1895 m. Emeline V. Himebach, both buried where the family lived for several generations in Newtown Pa., children:

1. George W. b. June 15, 1841 d. June 18, 1919 m. Joanna C., children Charles H. m. Carrie Leins; Isaac S. m. Laura C.; William L. m. Zada E. Johnson
2. Charles H. b. November 6, 1843 d. 1940 m. Elizabeth M., children Joseph S. m. Ida M.; William A.
3. Mary F. b. September 25, 1845 m. Isiah M. VanHorn 5 children
4. William A. b. March 11, 1847 d. December 4, 1904
5. Charity E. b. December 5, 1849 m. D. Jolly Balerston, 7 children
6. Sarah E. b. July 22, 1852 d. March 9, 1876
7. Joseph L. b. September 20, 1854 m. Flora B., children Emma m. George Watts; Catherine
8. James P. b. November 4, 1856 d. February 18, 1925, m. Mary Ellen Saxton, children, George W. b. February 8, 1883; Clara H. b. December 13, 1885 m. Thomas B. Argust; Smith S. b. February 26, 1895 m. Elizabeth Knerr; Rebo O. b. July 6, 1896 m. Raymond F. Clayton; Maude b. 1904 m. Raymond Dansbury
9. Anna M. b. December 29, 1858 m. B. Frank Carter, 10 children

**Rsh.97** Elias Troxell, m. Ruth_____, and lived in Frederick Co., Md., where he d.c. 1821, Executor of estate George M. Echelleeger, known heir as taken from Will: Peter Troxell, brother. Bondsman were George Toxell and George Flock

> note: final account distribution April 1821 pays Samuel Aman, Peter Troxell for Mary Troxell, Joseph Baugher for Isaac Baugher, David Risk, Michael Sporrseller, Peter Troxell, Robert L. Aman, Samuel Johnson, Henry G. Waters assignee of William Henry Sleely, Jannis A. Shorb, Patrick Owings administer of Patrick Lowe in full.

**Rsh.98** George Troxler, Troxell, Troscel, Trosel,(?son of Rsh.42) b.1794 m. Elizabeth_____, lived in Frederick Co., Md., where he d. July 20, 1832, his probate 1833. She d. July 28, 1850 in Frederick, Md. probate. Her Will, witnessed by John Troxell, names known children:

> Mary Ann Smith
> Johanna m. Gleason (Grayson) then White (Winter)
> Barbara m. Joseph Welty
> Jermima  m. Jacob Motter
> Joshua
> William George (or George W.)
> Joseph Peter

**Rsh.99** George Drachsel m. Margaret____, they lived in Lancaster Pa., where they were active in the Trinity Lutheran Church, ?possibly moved to Frederick, Md.,
known children:

> Maria Magdalena b. 1761, sponsor to bapt. Jacob Heinrich Wolf and Christina Schmidtin
> John Peter b. February 5, 1764, sponsor to bapt. John Peter Funkhauser and wife Eva
> Johann George b. 1766, sponsors to bapt. John Urich Ehlsperger and Barbara his wife

> note:  see church records Frederick, Md. 1787, ?possible sponsorship of child of Adam Hoffman and Maria Christina

**Rsh.100** John Tisher, Troxell, Teisher, d. 1828 to 1835 m. Mary_

____, and lived in Washington Co., Md., where probate papers show known children:

>____m. John Siebert
>____m. Jacob Hart
>____m. David Shower
>Mary
>John
>Jacob

**Rsh.101** John Jacob Samuel (Jack) Troxell, Tresset, Treset, Trucksil, Tressent (son of Rsh.43), m. Catherine Elis (Elisabeth)__ lived in York, Adams Co., Pa., at Littlestown, DGM, then in Emmitsburg,(Pipe Creek-Kreiders Church area) Frederick Co., Md., his probate April 7, 1845 at Emmitsburg, Frederick Co., Md., known children:

>John (?Jacob) (?Rsh.69) b. March 30, 1786 ?m.Elizabeth Green in 1838
>Sophia Elisabeth b. January 17, 1787 sponsor to bapt. Sophia Troxelin (Rsh.43) the Grandmother, d. Aug. 23, 1825 or April 30, 1853 - (two records were found) m. Michael Wise, widowed then m. John D. Nickum
>Mary A. (Magdalena) bapt. January 31, 1790, sponsor to bapt. George Ad. Ohler and Catherine Ohler,(?Rsh.135) at St.Johns Evan. Lutheran, Germany Twp., Adams Co., Pa., she m. John A.Davis
>Catharine m.James W. Baugher (Bayer)
>Samuel, owned tannery, not m., probate January 14, 1851
>William
>Amanda

**Rsh.102** Peter Troxel (son of Rsh.34) b. May 7,1777 d. May 26, 1816 m. Mary Magdalena_____, they lived in Emmitsburg area, Frederick Co., Md., where she d. May 23, 1850, as per estate, children were under 21 in 1830, known children:

>George
>Charlotte
>Elizabeth
>John

Harriett (Henrietta)

**Rsh.103** Jacob Drissler m. Elizabeth_____, lived Elizabeth Twp., Lancaster Co., Pa., where probate of his Will is in July 1828, witnesses to Will, Sebastian Root, Peter Dinger, known children:
      Elizabeth
      Daniel
      Catherine
      Mary m. Emanuel Gojlin
      Jacob
      Henry, had son in 1828
      David, had son in 1828

**Rsh.104** Johannes Drexler (?son of Rsh.5), m. Maria Ilsabetha Craddock, in Baltimore, Md., on May 1, 1833, at St. Johns German Catholic Church, she d. December 18, 1833, age 21.

**Rsh.105** Lewis Trisler, Trissler, Trisseler, b. 1747, a Blacksmith by Trade, (?known as Lodowick) m. Catherine_____, she was b.1749, he is found on Tax list in Alexandria, Va., as early as 1787 with no persons listed, known children:
      Peter m. Priscilla. Priscilla d. 1848.

**Rsh.106** Emanuel Trexler, Traxler, Trexell (son of Rsh.84) b.1760, in Northampton Co., Pa., m. Catherine Cameron, of Lancaster, Pa., in May of 1822, History and Genealogy of the Trexler Family, they lived in Washington Co., Md., Chillicothe, Ohio, Jackson Co., Ohio, where land patents were received by Emanuel and son Samuel, known children:
      Samuel b. June 19, 1786 bapt. at Reformed Church of
            Hagerstown, Washington Co., Md.on April 31, 1787
            m. Harriet Mercer May 1828
      Susanna m. April 25,1809 John Jacobs
      Mary (Polly) b. May 11, 1819, Jackson, Ohio m. William
            Spriggs
      Hannah m. December 1,1814 Nottingham Mercer
      Rachel m. March 5,1815 Nathan Stewart
      Catherine b.1803 m. Moses Faught
      Elizabeth m. Collins Bennett
      Jonathan b.November 4,1791 m. Rachel Martin, d.
            January 29, 1880, children, John m. Mary Nancy

Jane Dixon and Polly A. Dobbins; Mary m. Thomas
Foster; Johnson m. Sarah Jane Ward and Mary A.;
Jackson m. Louiza Mercer and Deborah; Jonathan
m. Drusilla Foster; David m. Sarah Jane Brown;
Rachel m. Toland, William W. m. Sarah M.,
Catherine E., m. James B. Johnson; Vinton b. July
31, 1833 m. Nancy Ann
John m. May 4,1825, Nancy Price
David m.April 23,1826 Sarah Crabtree, Will, Book C.
Montgomery Co., Ohio
?Abraham, see probate records

**Rsh.107** Peter Truschel, Drushal, Draxsel, Drushall, m. Mary_____
lived at Gunpowder Falls and Lick Glad, Maryland, purchased tract
of land named Addition to Michaels, in Baltimore, Co., Md. in 1791
which he sold to Melcher Warren of York Co., State of Pa. Land
transactions between 1790 and 1793 Baltimore Co., Md. referring
to Addition to Michaels tract.

**Rsh.108** Peter Deschler, Doeschler, Deshler,(?son of Rsh.39) m.
Magdalena_____ children bapt. at Egypt Reformed Church,Leehigh
Co., Pa., known children:
Johann Peter b. April 5,1767, sponsor bapt. Martin Mickle
and Barbara Doeschler (?Rsh.42 wife of Mathias
Martin)
David b. April 8, 1773, sponsor bapt. Jacob Mueckle and
wife Susanna, m. Catherine, son John b. July 19,
1806
Catherina b. April 19, 1775, Peter Burkhalder and wife
Catherine
Jacob b. March 30, 1781, sponsor bapt. Jacob Shreiber and
wife Eliza
Sarah b. August 23, 1788, sponsor bapt. Adam Deshler
and w. Maria Catherine

**Rsh.109** John Christopher Trencken, Traenckel, Trescher,
Drechselern, Trostler, Immigrant, b. 1690, m. Anna Maria
(Margaretha) Spengler on November 17, 1741 (?brother to Rsh.16),
he is found in Trinity Lutheran Church Records in Lancaster, Pa.,
where he d. in October 1752 in his 62nd year of a long and illness
of dropsy,

known children:
John Stephen (Rsh.51)

**Rsh.110** Valentine Trisler, Tiriszler, Trissler (son of Rsh.75),b. 1762, m. Mary Ream on October 9, 1783, she was b. in 1760 and d. October 15, 1826, <u>MGS</u>. Valentine Trisler in 1778 took communion in Evangelical Reformed Church, Frederick, Md., and is found in the 1790, 1800 and 1810 Md.Census records for Harford Co., Md., at Harve de Grace. 1790 Census shows 1 male 16+ (Valentine), 1 male 16-, 3 females,(one of whom must be wife). Evan. Reformed Church, Frederick, Md., confirmation (communion) of Valentine in 1778, he d. December 20, 1813, <u>MGS</u>. In 1815 one Margaret Trisler of Frederick Co., Md. gives land to Mary Trisler widow of Valentine Trisler deceased.

**Rsh.111** Jacob Traxel m. Elizabeth_____, found in Tohickon Reformed Church Records, Leehigh Co., Pa., known children:
Jacob b. December 8, 1781
Elizabeth b. July 30, 1787
Catherine b. September 18, 1789
Magdalena b. February 27, 1792
Margaret b. February 24, 1794
Sarah b. July 3, 1798

**Rsh.112** Abraham Draxel, Trachsel, Trexel, Drachsel, Druxel, Traxell, Troxel, Traxel, Tracksell, Amish Preacher, Immigrant 1749, b.c. 1711,m.Anna_____, they lived in Lebanon Twp., Lancaster, Pa., reference in <u>1989 Mennonite Family History</u>, Will of Abraham written June 17, 1781 and proved November 16, 1784, Lancaster Pa., names wife Anna, and known children:
Abraham
Christian
John b. 1743 d. c. 1775, (letters adm. granted Jacobena Traxerll and Joseph Torney, in Lancaster Co., Derry Twp.,) m. Jacobina King, daughter of Jacob King in Derry Twp., Dauphin Co., Pa., son Jacob b. 1766 d. 1794 in Londonderry Twp., Dauphin Co., Pa., m. Elisabeth, they had son John b. Londonderry Twp., Dauphin Co. Pa., 1794, he m. Hanna Stora (Jury), he d. 1822, Upper Paxton Twp., Dauphin, Pa., Jacobina King Trachsell remarried after John's

death to Daniel Hershberger.    They lived in Lebanon Co., Pa., then in Dauphin Co., Pa.
Feromica

**Rsh.113**    Abraham Troxel, Traxel, Traxelsin, Troxell, Trochsel, Trexell, Trochsall, Truxell, Trochsal m. Catherine_____, they are found in Hagerstown, Washington Co., Md., His Will, written March, 1786 proved October, 1786 names known children:
>David
>Catherine Swilar
>Magdelena
>Anna
>Susannah
>Sarah Salome

**Rsh.114**    John (?Joseph) Trexler, (son of Rsh.3) History and Genealogy of the Trexler Family, he is named as the youngest son in his father's Will, written in 1744, known children:
>Lawrence (Rsh.122)
>Peter (Rsh.123) d. June 23, 1837

>note:  correspondence with other researchers reveals that these two sons moved to North Carolina.  To date I do not have a clear line on this family

**Rsh.115** Jeremiah Trexler, Traxler, Drechssler, Drechseler, Trosler, Traxell, (son of Rsh.3) b.1708 m. Maria Catherine Schumacher in 1726, at Berks Co., Pa. In 1732 he had a Public House (Tavern) in Trexlertown, Pa.  He moved to Easton, Pa., where he was Tax Collector in 1768. He moved back to Macgunie Twp., Berks Co., Pa., where he d. intestate in 1783,(probate at Northampton shows Joseph Trosler adm. estate of Jeremiah) History and Genealogy of the Trexler Family, known children:
>John Peter (Rsh.86) b. December 1727 m. Maria Catherine Albright
>Margaret
>John (Rsh.84) m. Maria Elizabeth_____, then Susanna
>>Bauer Hassler
>?Benjamin

**Rsh.116** Nicholas Drechsler (son of Rsh.118) b. November 12,1657, m. Elizabeth Zimmerman, she was b. May 5,1679 in Sternbach, Germany, he d. May 12,1690, History and Genealogy of the Trexler Family, known children:
> George
> Jacob
> John Peter (Rsh.3) b. February 26, 1680 d. 1758 m. Catherine Breinig

**Rsh.117** Valentine Drechsler (son of Rsh.118) b. 1656 History and Genealogy of the Trexler Family, says 12 children, however, none are named.

**Rsh.118** Conrad Drechsler b. May 1624 m. Catherine_____ she was b.in Hirelanbach, Germany, History and Genealogy of the Trexler Family, he d. March 7, 1694, known children:
> Valentine (Rsh.117) b. 1656
> Nicholas (Rsh.116) b. November 12, 1657 d. May 12,1690 m. Elizabeth Zimmerman, she was b. Sternbach Germany

**Rsh.119** Jacob Trexler, Immigrant, came to America in 1820 from Switzerland and settled in Lancaster, Pa., m. Martha_____, History and Genealogy of the Trexler Family,
known children:
> Anthony m. Louisa Marshall, children Elizabeth m. B.M. Root, 6 children; Emma m. A.L. Urban; Marshall m. _, children 2 daughters; Harriet m. John L. Allen
> Joseph
> Elizabeth
> Rosanna m. ___Centner

**Rsh.120** Abraham Drostel,Trostle, Sr., m. Susanna Benz, daughter of Whylich Bentz and wife Anna Maria, at York Pa., they lived in Heidelberg Twp., Berks Co., Pa., then York Co., Pa., his Will, dated September 4, 1813 and probate September 18, 1819, in York Co., Pa., with executors Joseph and Abraham Trostel,
known children:
> (?John) Jacob b. May 23,1774 m. Elizabeth (?Catherine) his Will, March 27, 1843, in Hamilton Twp., Adams Co., Pa., names brothers John and Peter, land in

Paradise Twp., exr. Peter Trostle of John Trostle, sons Samuel, John, Daniel, Jonas and Moves, daughter Elizabeth m. Samuel Weist, dau. Polly m. Mathias Trimmer, Dau. Susannah m. Henry Sontag, dau. Rebecca and dau. Catherine m. John Cooksey

Anna Mary b.February 18,1776

John m. ?Elizabeth, ?Catherine

John George, his Will, June 8, 1863, Cumberland Twp., Pa., dau. Elizabeth m. Joseph Maleny, son Michael, son John, son Henry, dau. Mary m. Bernhardt Goeslner, dau. Susan M. John W. Weigle, dau. Lindia m. Wm. Newman, son Daniel Trostle, dau. Anna M. George Breischer, son William, son Jacob and dau. Lydia

Abraham b. 1779 confirmed Whitsunday 1793 York Pa. Christ Evan. Lutheran Church, lived in Paradise Twp., York Pa. 1830, then Huntington Twp., m. ?Catherine, his Will, October 1, 1853 son Isaac B.Trostle, Andrew, dau. Sarah m. George Stock (Stoke), dau. Elizabeth m. John Beam, son Jacob M. Trostle, son Abraham Trostle, Jr., son Isaac R. Trostle, son Abraham Trostle

Henry, his Will, on March 15, 1853 names wife Jane, son Emanuel, dau.Catherine, youngest child Jullianne not of age

William b. 1778. confirmed Whitsunday 1793 York Pa., Christ Evan. Luth.Peter b. February 26,1788, bapt. March 30,1788

Elizabeth b. March 31,1782 m. Frederic Reimer (Rehmer)

Catharine b. December 12, 1789, m. Jacob Herbst, March 23, 1818, at Christ Evan. Luth Church, York Pa.

Susanna (?Peggy) m. Jacob Stover, 1812 Christ Evan. Lutheran Church York ,Pa.

Daniel

**Rsh.121** Philip Tristeler, Tristler, Trissler m. Maria_____, found in Tonickon Reformed Church Records, Leehigh Co., Pa., known children:

Sarah b. September 24, 1792

John b. June 18, 1795

Hannah b. June 18, 1797
David b. 1801
Margaret b. September 13, 1804

**Rsh.122** Lawrence (Lorentz) Trexler, Trexeller,(son of Rsh.114) b. 1758 m._____, lived in Rowan Co., N.C., d. Sept. 13, 1827, <u>History and Genealogy of the Trexler Family</u>, death date from Mrs. Gearldine Miller, of Rockwell, N.C., known children:

    Adam (Rsh.37), b.1784 m. Polly Mesimer
    John m. Katie Cauble, children, Sarah Elizabeth m. Michael Davis; Alexander m. America Brown; George; David m. Sally Ellen; Mary m. Christopher Lyerly; Eliza m. John Shuman
    Jacob b. March 6, 1784 m. Mary Peeler, children, Moses Peter m. Eva Kluttz; Jacob m. Clementine Fraley; John Peter m. Sarah Clementine Peeler; Alexander; Margaret m. Moses Lyerly; Louisa m. Moses Lingley; Eva m. Moses Kluttz; Sarah m. Daniel Peeler
    Henry b.October, 1792 m. Elizabeth Earnhart, children, Adam m. Elizabeth Bisher; Sophia m. John Bescherer, Jacob m. Julie Fritz Butner; Lawrence; Milas; Moses; Commilla m. George Miller; Mary C.m. William A. Cauble; Lizzie
    Catherine m. Peter Baringer, 1 child
    Elizabeth m. Samuel Peeler
    Polly m. George Miller

**Rsh.123** Peter Trexler, Trexeller, (son of Rsh.114) m._____ d.June 23,1837, North Carolina, possible children:
    ?Jacob
    ?Henry
    ?Levi

**Rsh.124** John (?Joseph) Trexler (son of Rsh.85), b. October 12,1750, m. _____moved to York Co., Pa., about 1784, m.____, some of children's births found in Christ Reformed Lutheran, York, Pa., d. June 22,1829, buried near Breinigsville, Pa., on Gonser Farm in old family cemetery <u>History and Genealogy of the Trexler Family, History of Berks Co., Pa.,</u>
known children:

Solomon m Cathrine, children: Lydia m. Charles Borger
of Breinigsville;Jonas; Reuben; Daniel christined
November 2, 1803, York Pa., Daniel lived in York
Co., Pa., in 1869
?Rachael
?Leah
?Susannah

note: Rsh.61 is also active in Christ Church, York, Pa.

**Rsh.125**  Ferdinand Trexler (son of Rsh.84) b. June 15,1769, Berks
Co., Pa., m. Catherine Swartz, History and Genealogy of the Trexler
Family, known children:
Benjamin m. Rachael Wetzel, child Benjamin F.Wetzel of
Allentown, Pa., Freiedenshole
Catherine b. October 25,1796
John, b. October 6,1799

**Rsh.126**  Francis Peter Drexler, Trexler, Drescler, Tessier, Drecksler,
Immigrant, was apprenticed to Joseph Smith, on October 26, 1772,
for 3 years, at York Pa., m. _____, known children:
Joseph Peter m. Mary Ferry, at St. Joseph Catholic
Church, Philadelphia, a child Francis b. May 26,
1797 and Francis Peter b. Jan. 7, 1800
Mary
Margaret

**Rsh.127**  Martin Treichler, Dreichler, (son of Rsh.128) b.1764 m.
Barbara Fitz, lived in York, Pa., known children:
Baltzer b. c 1794 m. Sally Johnson, May 17, 1819, New
Hanover, Montgomery Co., Pa.
John b. c. 1796
Jacob b. c. 1798

**Rsh.128**  John Treighler, Treichler, Treickler, Trenhler, Trenchler,
Dreichler, Trenghler, Teigler, Traichler, Dreickler, Traighler, Trickler,
(son of Rsh.139) b. 1743, he m. Elizabeth Leupsin she d. 1780, then
m. in 1781 m. Dorothy Neiswanger, her Will, dated August 12, 1801,
and probate July 2, 1810, named exr. Peter Gut, York Co., Pa. They
lived in York Twp., Pa., and his Will, written June 15, 1799, and
probate July 27, 1799, York, Pa., shows exr. Jacob S. Trinchler and

Andrew Ferree, family legend says that three Treichler Brothers came from Germany about 1730, one John (Rsh.128) settled in York Co., Pa., one settled in Berks Co., Pa., (Rsh.__?_) one settled near Pittsburgh Pa., Rsh.__?_ known children:

John b. 1761, never m.
Barbara b.1762, m. Peter Gut (Good), no children
Martin (Rsh.127) b. 1764 m. Barbara Fitz, 3 children
Anna b. 1768 m. Abraham Schoock, their children never m.
Henry b. 1768 d. 1788, never m.
Maria (Mary) b. 1770 m. John Miller in 1796, 4 children
Magdalena (Molly) b, 1773 d. 1869, never m.
Daniel b. 1774, m. Catherine Schroll, in 1810 York Co., Pa., they moved to Buffalo near the Niagara River in 1833, children Elizabeth b. 1811, Daniel b. 1813, John b. 1815, Henry b. 1820, Jacob b. 1823, Samuel b. 1826, Benjamin b. 1829, he d. in 1860.
Elizabeth b. 1779, m. Joseph Strickler
Susanna Sophia m. Jacob Bixler
Eve m. Mathias Stewart
Catharine b. 1782, m. Henry Grove (Gould, Groul), 2 children
Salome b. 1784 m. John Strickler, 3 children

**Rsh.129**  Charles Troxell,(son of Rsh.152), b. July 7, 1807, at Northampton Co., Pa., m. Susanna Frack, sister of the founder of Frackville, Schuylkill Co., Pa., lived in South Whitehall, Leehigh Co., Pa., before moving west, d. Tiffin, Seneca Co., Ohio, <u>DGM</u>, known children:

Joshia b. c. 1830
Alfred W. b. c. 1833 m. Emeline (Amelia) Newhard, children Alavesta b. c. 1849 m. Edwin Hunter; Clara m. Francis Kromer; Elemina m. Nathan Howerter; Willard J.C. b. c. 1867 m. Jennie Geranflo, children Marguerite and Bertram; Frank J.; Harvey J.; Lillie M.
Benjamin b. c. 1835
Alleminah b. c. 1857
Rebecca b. c. 1840 m. Benjamin Troxell

Maria b. c. 1845 m. James Kuder
Sarah b. prob. after 1850 m. Edward Frey
Walter b. prob. after 1850 d. young

**Rsh.130** James Trexler b. 1809, m. Cinetta Dankel, he d. September 7, 1886, they are both buried at Hamburg, Pa., History and Genealogy of the Trexler Family, known children:
> Jeremiah S. b. 1832, d. September 24, 1901, buried Kutztown, Pa.
> William Alexander b. February 14, 1836 m. Kennie, children Fannie; Jeanette; Nellie; Molly
> Nelson H. m. Nellie_____, then Cordelia Fisher, children Annie C. m. George W. Bear; Elizabeth E. m. A.P. Wertley; James G. m. Amelia A. Rumble; Franklin J. b. July 1, 1879 m. Laura M. Hollenbach; Ella m. J.A. Hatzfield

Lavinia

**Rsh.131** Jacob Dresser m. Margaretha Danner, on April 27, 1790, she was the daughter of Abraham Danner. They lived in Rockland Twp., Berks Co., Pa.

**Rsh.132** Jacob Dressel, Driskle (?son of Rsh.5) m. Anna Maria Chrisimer, on March 31, 1799, at Conewago Catholic Sacred Heart of Jesus Church, at Edge Grove, Pa. Witnesses to wedding Martin Black, Elizabeth Chamber, known children:
> Ann b. March 14, 1802
> Theresia b. January 2, 1804

> note: notation in original Conewago Catholic records says "is not Driskle the same as Drexel?"

**Rsh.133** John Troxell (son of Rsh.152) b. March 22, 1827 m. Mary (Mollie) A. Newhard, lived in North Whitehall Twp., Lehigh Co., Pa., DGM, known children:
> Phanus J.J. b. March 4, 1852 m. Augusta E.E. Resh, daughter of Ephraim and Caroline (Mills) Resh, known children Jennie M.; Wilson J.H.; Mable; Mantana R.; Claude E.
> Josiah b. August 31, 1853 d. July 4, 1854
> Martha J. b. May 30, 1855, m. William Reinert

Joseph Peter b. November 10, 1856 m. Catherine Biery, known children Gertrude; Minnie; Edna; Frederick

Allen Mathias b. June 16, 1859 m. Jane Lynn daughter of John, Sr., known children Preston M.; Laura; Hattie

Sarah b. c. 1861 m. Charles Radeline

Jacob b. March 30, 1862 d. 1862

James b. April 5, 1863 d. 1863

Mantana A. b. August 22, 1867 d. 1868

Savannah E. b. March 30, 1869 d. 1872

Catherine b. July 17, 1873 d. 1873

Daisy R. b. January 14, 1876 d. 1877

**Rsh.134**    Johann   Jacob   Dressler,   Journeyman   Smith   of Massenbach, Jagsthausen Dist. Heilbronn, Wurtemberg Germany, b.c 1650 m. Rosina Dorothea Schmied (Smith), April 28, 1705, she d. March 6, 1707 then he m. Eva Magdalena Rathgeber in 1707, she was b. c. 1687 known children:

Maria Elizabeth b. February 3, 1708

Eva Magdalena b. February 3, 1708 m. 1732

Johann Peter b. July 4, 1710, had son David

Johann Philipp b. February 26, 1712, deceased March 22, 1735

Maria Christina b. July 16, 1713

Johann Andreas (Rsh.21) b. November 13, 1714 m. Anna Barbara Bernhardt

Anna Katherina b. January 16, 1717 m. 1747

George Michael b.January 19, 1719, <u>YCHS</u> file says he landed at Philadelphia September 17, 1771

Maria Elizabeth b. August 3, 1720 m. 1749

Maria Dorothea b. October 31, 1722 d. November 1,1722

Anna Maria b. September 10, 1724 d. June 2, 1725

Maria Magdalena b. August 3, 1726

Anna Maria b. December 26, 1728

**Rsh.135** George (?Adam) Trissler, Coppersmith, (son of Rsh.26), m. Catherine Oehler (Ehler,Erler) in 1801 she was b. May 2, 1779 and was the daughter of Daniel and Margaret Oehler (Ehler) nee VonderSmith, George and Catherine Trissler lived in Lancaster, Pa., ?Adams Co., Pa., and later in Erie Co., Pa., where she d. August 9, 1826,
known children:

Elizabeth b. December 29, 1801, m. Peter Gander
        Eberman
George Conrad b. August 28, 1803 m. Sarah Dietrich, 2
        sons, 2 daughters
Anna Maria b. June 4, 1805 m. Josiah Brecht
Catharina b. March 8, 1807, m. Daniel Weidler, a Saddler
Henritta b. November 20, 1801
Daniel Heinrich b. February 19, 1811
John b. January 31, 1813
William B. May 4, 1815

note: Catherine Oehler (Ehler) Trissler's death records says
6 daughters and four sons, see Moravian records

**Rsh.136** George Trostel, Troxel, Troscle m. Rosina_____, lived in
Brecknock, Berks Co., Pa., where his probate is found on
September 28, 1804, widow renounced probate Cumru Twp., Berks
Co., Pa., April 28, 1814, known children:
        William d. 1841, children Sarah m. Benjamin Strink,
                Samuel, John, Elizabeth m. Solomon Boyer, Aaron,
                Eli, Leva, Mary and William. note: a Reuben Troxell
                was paid for a note in William's estate settlement.
        Abraham b. April 6, 1783, sponsor bapt. John Laub and
                wife Elizabeth, he m. Anna Maria_____
        John
        Margaret

**Rsh.137** Henry (Henrich) Trostel m. Catherine_____. They lived
in Becknock, Berks Co., Pa., where he d. December 15, 1824,
intestate, known children:
        John
        Henry
        Catharine
        Peggy (Susannah)
        Barbara b. February 6, 1786, sponsor bapt. Johannes
                Trostel and Barbara Schweicker

                note: probate shows there were minor children in
                1824 and estate guardians appointed were John
                Weiss and Israel B. Mussellman.

**Rsh.138** William Trexler, Txler, (son of Rsh.140), was b. on May 8, 1855, in Richmond, Va. He was by Trade a Builder. He m. Mary Margarett Poh (Poe) daughter of Jacob and Eva Poh who were both b. in Germany. He built the old Henrico Courthouse and much of his work is seen today in the Fan District of Richmond. He d. June 3, 1931, known children:

> William, III, m. Addie Webb, and had Marie T. m. Heath, George Nelson Trexler, Robert G. Trexler, stepchildren: William E. Trexler, Mrs. Charles Burnner, Mrs. Leo Kudig

> Charles Augustus b. April 6, 1876 in Richmond, m. Susie B.Davis, children Sara B. Trexler and Charles William Trexler.

> Rosa Alice b. September 5, 1882 d. July 12, 1918

> Eva b. June 15, 1884, d. February 2, 1920

> Jacob Eddie b. March 8, 1878 d. May 30, 1895

> Minnie m. M. Wardell then Bernard Morgan she d. October 8, 1928.

**Rsh.139** John Teighler, Dreishles, Dreichler, Dreighler, Treichler, Trexler (?son of Rsh.3) m. Barbara_____, d. February 6, 1756, probate April 2, 1757 in York Co., Hellam Twp., Pa., known children:

> John (Rsh.128) b.1743 m. Elizabeth Leupsin then Dorothy Neiswanger

> Mary b. 1744 - chose John Strickler of Hellam Twp., as guardian when father d.

> Kathrina

> Elizabeth b. c. 1751, named by mother as youngest daughter, John Strickler of Hellam Twp., Pa., her guardian

**Rsh.140** William Trexler, (son of Rsh.76), b. August 11, 1815, bapt. at St. John's German Catholic Church, Baltimore, Md., by Trade a Cooper, m. Nancy Ann Ellis on May 29, 1843, (she was the widow of James Hughes), d. February 8, 1855, in Richmond, Va., Funeral Mass said at St. Peters Catholic Church, Richmond, Va., buried at Shockhoe Hill Cemetery, Richmond, Va., in an unmarked grave, known children:

> John Ignatius (Rsh.142) b. September 2, 1844 d. April 26, 1905 m. Mary A. Elizabeth Simpson, 6 children

Rosetta b. March 17, 1847 d. May 13, 1857
Isabella b. October 15, 1849 d. October 12, 1851
Joseph b. September 23, 1852 d. May 21, 1857
William (Rsh.138) b. May 8, 1855 d. June 3, 1931 m. Mary Margaret Poh (Poe), 6 children

note: after her husbands death in 1855 Nancy Ann Ellis (Hughes) Trexler m. Albert Liggon, a Policeman with the City of Richmond, Va., known children:

> Reuben Henry b. February 3, 1858 m. Sarah_____ children, Edgar and Nellie
>
> Alonzo Columbus b. April 5, 1864, m. Willie Ann Wright, children, Ivy E., Annie Alease, Lottie Dell, Alonzo, Jr., Willie Pleasant, Ruby May, Irvine Edgar

**Rsh.141** Michael Dreicher, Tretcher, Teisher, Deicher, Teitcher m. Barbara Seichrest, daughter of Hans Ulchrist Seichrest. They lived in York Co., Pa., known children:

> Susannah b.1772-1779

**Rsh.142** John Ignatius Trexler, Txler, (son of Rsh.140), b. September 2, 1844, in Richmond, Va., m. Mary A. Elizabeth Simpson, daughter of James M. and Sarah Simpson of Buckingham Co., Va., on September 6, 1865. He served in both the Confederate States Army and Navy. It is believed that his employment at Tredegar Iron Works, which made armaments for the Confederacy, had influence on his dual military service. He d. on April 26, 1905 and is buried in an unmarked grave in Riverview Cemetery, Richmond, Va., known children:

1.  Isabella Trexler b. April 29, 1866, m. Charles Dance, m.second Powhatan J. Dance who was nicknamed "Pop" and had no children, known children by Charles Dance:
    Mrs. J.A. Carter
    Mrs. Albert Haas
    Mrs. William Wright
    Mrs. H.D. Pettis
    Ella Dance m. Cole
    Loretta R. Dance
    Annie Phippen Dance
    Lawson H. Dance

2.    John Joseph Trexler b. April 2, 1876, a Commercial
      Painter, m. the widow Lena Madeline Bennett Totty,
      known children:
      Joseph Edward Trexler, Sr., m. Helen Leary, children
            Joseph Edward Trexler, Jr., Francia L. Trexler,
            and Madelyn Trexler
      Frank James Trexler, noted Richmond, Va. Baseball
            Player, m. Ruth S. Bowles, children Donald Lee
            Trexler, Frank James Trexler, Jr.
      Violet Trexler m. Dewey W. Blanton
      Mary Trexler m. Lee Tyler
      Eunice Trexler m. Robert Winfrey Shepherd
            note: Lena Madeline Bennett m. first a Totty and
            had Estelle Totty and Hazel Totty

3.    James Washington Trexler, b. February 22, 1878, Shop
      Foreman at Richmond, Fredericksburg, and Potomac
      Railroad, m. Lottie May Perkins.  Lottie was the daughter
      of Egbert A. Perkins and his wife Emma K. Seay Perkins,
      the widow of a Mr. Bessnard.  Egbert Perkins was the son
      of Joseph E. Perkins and Pauline T., nee Lloyd, Perkins,
      and Emma K. Seay was the daughter of W. and E.R.
      Seay, known children:
      John Joseph Trexler m. Margaret (Mary) Virginia Talley,
            children Herbert Julius, John Joseph, Jr., Robert
            Earl, George Herndon, Margaret, Joyce Ann,
            Lottie May, Mable Lorraine
      Grace Bell Trexler m. Carlyle Noel, children, William
            Carlisle, James Leslie, Charles Jefferson, Marian
            Coleman, Alvin Douglas, Grace Laverne and
            Delores Ann
      Mable Lorraine Trexler m. Percy Linwood Butler, children
            Edith May, and James Linwood
      James Herman Trexler m. Helen Gertrude Fines, children
            Charlotte Ann and Rose Edith
      Ruth Virginia Pastora Trexler d. young and unmarried.
      Walter Ignatius (Edward) Trexler m. Nettie M. Blair,
            children, Walter Warren, Nancy Lorraine
      Edward Coleman Trexler m. Mary Ida Hicks, children,
            Edward Coleman, Jr., Mary Diane, Peter Lynn,
            Jeremiah

Gladys May Trexler m. Earl Kessler Auld, d. childless

Daisy Adelaide Trexler b. June 15, 1915 m.John Edward Hawley and had the following children, Laura Mae, (author of this publication) and Betty Sue. Daisy Adelaide Trexler m. 2nd Horace Beverly Childress, Sr. and had no children.

Herbert Leslie Trexler, d. as a baby

4. Charles Herndon Trexler, Sr., b. March 20, 1881, a Machinist, m. Etta May Johns daughter of Dr. and Mrs. John Alexander Johns, nee Elizabeth F. Roach, children: Lucille Herndon Trexler m. John Schluter and then John Basala

   Minor Davidson Trexler m. John Letcher Stone

   Marian May Trexler m. Newell Hamilton Houchens

   Evelyn Edward Trexler m. Silas Westly Craps

   Carlton Urban Trexler m. Grace

   Charles Herndon Trexler, Jr., nickname "Doc" m. Pearl Estelle Gerhardt, child, Donn Gregory Trexler

5. Nancy McCarthy Trexler, b. May 8, 1885, m. Arthur T. Ford, d. January 1930 in Richmond, Va., children:

   Georgie Ford m. a Trainum then James H. Burns

   Mrs. H. B. Tucker

   Doris Ford

   Margaret Ford

   Harden Gartney Ford

   Ashley F. Ford

   Mowray A. Ford

   Clyde J. Ford

6. Bertha McCarthy Trexler b. June 1, 1888, m. Clyde H. Childress, d. May 20, 1964, no children.

**Rsh.143** Jacob Trachsel, Tracksel (son of Rsh.144) bapt.on March 5, 1652 at the Reformed Church, Lenk, Semmental, Berne Canton, Switzerland, m. January 18, 1684 Margaretha Brengel, b. 1662, daughter of Steffen and Elizabeth Bratten Brengel, Bringel, Bringold, residents of St. Stephan in Semmental, Switzerland. Reportedly their children were all b. in Lenk, Berne Canton Switzerland. As far as is presently known those that came to this country settled in the Egypt

area of Lehigh Co., Pa., he d. December 24, 1721 in Wolfersheim, Pfatz, Germany, LDS, DGM
known children:
1. Elizabeth bapt. November 2, 1684
2. Jacob b. May 1, 1687, d. October 9, 1687
3. Johannes (Rsh.145) bapt. October 4, 1689 m. Anna Maria (Mary), she d. then Anna Magdalene Roth Schreiber the widow of John Jacob Schreiber.
4. Peter (Rsh.22) b. November 6, 1691 m. Julianeth Catherinath Fraudhueger daughter of Johannes Hans Fraudhueger and Barbara Jaggi (Jacky).
5. Christen, b. February 2, 1694
6. Bendikt (Rsh.146) bapt. January 1, 1697 m. Katherine

**Rsh.144** Hans Trachsel, son of Hans Jacob Trachsel and Anna Berchten, b. October 23, 1631 in Lenk, Bern, Switzerland, m. Elizabeth Gungsel, daughter of Heinrich Gunset and Christina Bertschen, on April 7, 1751, in Lenke, Canton Berne, Switzerland DGM, LDS,
known children:
Jakob (Rsh.143) bapt. March 5, 1652 m. Margaretha Brengel
Elisbeth bapt. October 2, 1653, in Lenk, Bern Switzerland, M. Jakob Thomann on March 13, 1685, Lenk, Bern, Switzerland
Anna bapt. November 29, 1655, Lenk, Bern, Switzerland
Hans, bapt. February 7, 1658, Lenk, Bern, Switzerland, m. Catharine Eydam on June 22, 1688, Lenk, Bern, Switzerland
Heinrich bapt. June 10, 1660, Lenk, Bern, Switzerland, m. Maria Dumang, October 22, 1697, Lenk, Bern, Switzerland, he d. August 5, 1738, Lenk, Bern, Switzerland
Gwer, bapt. December 28, 1662, Lenk, Bern, Switzerland
Peter, bapt. March 25, 1666, Lenk, Bern, Switzerland
Christen, bapt. November 29, 1667, Lenk, Bern, Switzerland, m. Barbara Schuler, June 16, 1693, Lenk, Bern, Switzerland
Casper, bapt. October 28, 1670, Lenk, Bern, Switzerland, m. Magdalena Buhler March 1, 1714, d. January 26, 1726, Lenk, Bern, Switzerland

Benedikt, bapt. January 14, 1672, Lenk, Bern, Switzerland

Urich, b. June 13, 1675, Lenk, Bern, Switzerland, m. Anna Walten, he d. January 9, 1750, Lenk, Bern, Switzerland

**Rsh.145** Johannes Trachsel, Troxel, Troxell, Immigrant, from Lenk, Canton Berne, Switzerland (son of Rsh.143) bapt. on October 4, 1689 m. Anna Maria (Mary)_____ then Anna Magdalena Schreiber (nee Roth) in 1750 widow of John Jacob Schreiber. Came to America in Ship Samuel, landed Philadelphia Pa., August 30, 1737. His children all b. Wolfersheim, Germany. 1st went to Egypt, Pa., then Bucks Co., which became Northampton in 1752 and Leehigh in 1812. Active members Reformed Church, Egypt, Pa., <u>DGM,</u> <u>LDS,</u> known children:

John Peter (Rsh.42) b. April 3, 1719  m. Anna Barbara Saeger then Catherine Maria Magdalena Schreiber

John George Michael (Rsh.11) b. December 25, 1721 m. Anna Margaretha Weill.

Johanne Nicholas (Rsh.39) b.December 25, 1721 twin m. Catherine_____.

Johann Jacob b. February 16, 1723, Katzenthal Alsace France

Cathrina b. March 20, 1728 d. December 2, 1777, buried Egypt Union Church, Leehigh Co., Pa.

**Rsh.146** Bendikt Trachsel, Trossell, (son of Rsh.143), b. 1687, m. Anna Maria Catherine_____, <u>DGM,</u> <u>LDS,</u> known children:

Maria Angelike (Catherine)

Jerick

Maria Crete Rossell

?Jeremiah

note: daughter, Maria Angelika was b. in Wolfersheim, Germany; bapt. April 4, 1728 at Walsheim (Blies), sponsors bapt. Bartel, son of Jacob Hunsecker of Wolfersheim; Anna, daughter of Christian Brengel of Wolfersheim; and Anna Maria daughter of Stephan Ruben (Rieben) of Wolfersheim. Records for this area should be checked for other births.

**Rsh.147** John Troxel, Troxwell, Troxall (son of Rsh.22) b. October 26, 1736, a Miller by Trade, m. Maria Margaretha_____, and moved to Frederick Co., Md. in 1758 then on to Hardy Co., W.Va. He d.in Scott Co., Ky. in 1795, where he lived on North Elkhorn Creek, Troxell Trails, LDS, known children:

> Elizabeth m. John Hornecker, Baltimore, Md.
> ?Jacob
> Frederick, a minor in 1795, possibly b. W.Va.
> Mary Ann, b. about 1755-60, probably Lehigh Co., Pa., m.
> > a Mitchell or Haun, then as a widow m. Jacob Schroyer in 1786, Frederick Co., Md.
> John lived in Pulaski Co., Ky., children Nicholas, Susanna
> ? daughter m. Col. James Grant
> _____dau., m. Col. James Grant

**Rsh.148** Daniel Troxell, Traxel, Droxel,Draxel, Troxel,Trascel, (son of Rsh.58) b.about 1753 Bucks Co., Pa., near Egypt where he was active in Jordan Reformed Church, m. Maria Veronica Blank, (Marcia Fronica) in 1774 and was deeded land by father in 1790. He d. 1814 at S.Whitehall Twp., Leehigh Co., Pa., DGM, LDS known children:

> Peter (Rsh.151) b. September 1, 1775 d. August 3, 1841,
> > m. Madalena Seigfried on April 1, 1799. Jordan Reformed,Lehigh Co., 12 children
> Elizabeth bapt. April 27, 1777 m. John Blank, d.
> > September 15, 1831, 8 children
> Catherine b. November 14, 1779 m. John Biery, July 17,
> > 1798, 12 children

**Rsh.149** John Troxell, Troxall, (son of Rsh.58), a Farmer by Trade, lived in Egypt, Leehigh Co., m. Catherine Diehl ,LDS, DGM, known children:

> Daniel b. October 20, 1787
> Salome bapt. May 2, 1795 at Egypt Reformed Church,
> > Leehigh, sponsors Peter Draxel, Sr. and wife Anna Maria
> Catharine b. January 15, 1801, bapt. at Egypt Reformed
> > Church

**Rsh.150** Frederick Treister m. Margaretha_____, lived in Bethel

Twp., Berks Co., Pa., March 2 1761, probate of Frederick show bonds by brother Martin Treister and Gottfried Rohrer of Tulpecron Twp., Pa., Inn Keeper,
known children:

> Maria Dorother, b. 1747, guardian Peter Kitzer, George Wolf, William Keiser
> John Jacob, d. prior to 1763
> John d. prior to 1763
> George Frederick b. 1759
> Peter b. 1760

**Rsh.151** Peter Troxel, Troxell, (son of Rsh.148), b. September 1, 1775 m. Magdalena Siegfried, daughter of John Sigefried, Faurier, and Gertraut Sigefried of Maxtawany Twp., Berks Co., Whitehall Leehigh Co., Pa., members Jordan Reformed Church. His Berks Co., Pa., probate May 28, 1821, witness Henry Grim and Reuben Grim, <u>DGM</u>, known children:

> Isaac A. b.January 2, 1800, d. Trumbull Ohio 1872 m.
>> Esther Unger, children , William, d. young; George, d. young; Susan Caroline m. Daniel Reinhard, 2 children; Elizabeth Ann m. Edward Keck, 2 children Alfred John m. Nancy Heaton and then Kate A. Smoyer - children Esther M., George Franklin, Mary, Nancy and by second wife Emery J., Harry Augustus, Frankie Kate, Susie Belle and Algy John; Willoughby Isaac Peter b. September 17, 1835, m. Catherine Moyer, and Mary Murburger Osbborne, children Daniel Oberlin, Isaac Willoughby, Esther Ellen, Byron F. all by first wife; Peter Francis b. c. 1837 m. Cleopatra Hunter, known child Bertha; Hiram Robert b. September 28, 1839 m. Achsah Gilkerson, two known children M. Eva and Archie H.; Almira Ellen "Ella Kitty" b. December 12, 1843 m. Elisha D. Van Wye and then Joseph W. Van Wye; Mathias Ephram; Kate b. c. 1842; Mary Magdalena, d. young.
>
> John b. August 10, 1802, m. Anna Maria Steckel, children William Henry b. August 28, 1830, Emalina b. October 6, 1832, Anna Maria b. September 10, 1834
>
> Abraham d. July 9, 1850, Roaring Creek Twp., in

Columbia Co., Pa., m. Sarar_____

Magdalena (Polly) b. October 5, 1804, m. Joseph Guth

Jeremiah, b. c. 1806 m. Eliza Troxell b. c. 1814, dau. of
    Peter and Elizabeth (Mickley) Troxell.

Lydia b. 12 April 1808 m. Adam Troxell

Hannah b. c. 1811 m. Thomas Worman, Leehigh Co., Pa.,
    4 children

Peter b. May 31, 1812 m. Leah Fenstermacher, children,
    Thianna b. 1839 m. Jesse Bernt, Elizabeth b. c.
    1841, Elmira b. c. 1843, Horatio b. c. 1846, Adamisa
    b. 1849, Hiram b. 1852

James b. March 13, 1816 m. Maria Troxell dau. of John
    and Elizabeth Hittel Troxell, children Phaon b. July
    12, 1842 m. Amanda Biery, known children Francis
    b. 1868 and Anna B. 1870; James F. B. September
    3, 1845 m. Elemina Koch, children Edwin J. b.
    January 30, 1867 m. Amanda Lorish, known
    children James R. and Frank; Annie M. b. August
    1869 m. Danie A. or Uriah Seidel, 3 children; Ellen
    J. m. David DeLong, 4 children; William G. b. July
    31, 1872 m. Annie Miller; Sarah Troxell m. Jonas
    Kuhns; Charles T. b. January 3, 1877 m. Perma
    Wertman,; Harvey J. b. January 28, 1878 m. Lizzie
    Ruch; Mary m. Edgar Wenner; Albert J. b. October
    9, 1849; Salinda b. May 1, 1852 m. Lewis D.
    Hunsicker

Phillippine Phoebe b. April 2, 1818, m. Henry Joh, moved
    to Indiana

Ursula m. 1st Elias Guth, 2nd Schlough, 3rd Rev. Yingst

Juliana b. November 26, 1820


**Rsh.152**  John Troxell (son of Rsh.40) b. August 9, 1784, m.
Elizabeth Hittel, <u>DGM</u>, known children:

Charles (Rsh.129) b. July 7, 1807 m. Susanna Frack

Stephen (Rsh.164) b. August 2, 1809 m. Esther Mickley

Lucianna b.October 14, 1811 m. Peter Ruch

Tilghman H. b. November 13, 1813 m. Anna Susanna
    Troxell, daughter of Nicholas and Marie (Heller)
    Troxel, children Priscilla E., m. Elias Hoffman, 5
    children; Isreal J.N., b. July 22, 1843 m. Sarah
    Meyer daughter of Simon and Coletta (Steckel)

Meyer, only known child Tilghman C.P. b. August 1, 1874 m. Ella George

Elias b. February 25, 1816 m. Lucinda Guth, known children: Serena (Sarah Ann) b. c. 1840 m. Samuel Mohr; Adeline b. c. 1841 m. Willoughby Kuhns; Louisa R. b. 1843 d. 1847; Claretta b. c. 1848 m. James Eberhard; Maria b. c. 1853 m. Hiram Seislore

William b. May 13,1818 d. August 2, 1838

Maria b.October 28,1820 m. James Troxell, known children Phaen, James, Albert

Margaret b. April 23,1823 m. Edward Guth, 2 known children

Elizabeth b. March 19, 1824 m. Peter Mohr, 4 known children

John (Rsh 133) b. March 22, 1827 m. Mary (Mollie) A. Newhard

**Rsh.153**   Daniel Troxell (son of Rsh.40) b. January 1,1786, d. August 6, 1826 m. Elizabeth Siegfried, daughter of Henry Siegfried of Maxtawany Twp., Berks Co., Pa.  She is named in her fathers October 25, 1821, Berks Co., Pa., probate record, DGM, known children:

Helena Catherine b. May 24, 1815

Daniel b. February 2, 1819 m. Elizabeth Ann Butz, children Thomas D.F. b. 1850 d. prior to 1914; Nathan P. b. 1852 d. prior to 1914; Savannah M.E. b. 1856 m. Dr. F.J.A. Minnich moved to St. Louis, one daughter; daughter may have d. young; Norman L.C. b. May 11, 1866 m. Clara K. Strause, dau. of Emanuel S. and Angelina L. (Lainbach) Strause; one son Byron E.D. b. April 29, 1888

Simon b. 1827 m. Elizabeth, moved to Missouri, known children George b. c. 1855; Agnes b. c. 1857; Allen Richard b. c. 1858

Mary m. Joshua Grim

Elizabeth

Charles b. April 6,1821 d. May 14, 1900 m. Sarah, children Sarah Amelia b. February 7, 1843 d. m. Walter P. Rhoads, son of Daniel; Mary A. b. c. 1845

m. John Stofflet, son of Jonas and Margaret (Saeger) Stofflet; Charles D.C. b.c. 1846 m. Rosanna; Simon C. b. c. 1852; Charity b. c. 1855; Isabella b. June 8, 1857 m. Milton Steckel, son of Ephraim Steckel; Margaret b. c. 1860; Eliza b. c. 1863, note: either Margaret or Eliza m. Charles Miller

**Rsh.154**   Peter Troxell (son of Rsh.40) b. January 20, 1788 m. Elizabeth Mickley, <u>DGM</u>, known children:

Reuben b. March 11, 1811 m. Caroline Amelia Haines (note: Reuben owned property that was in 1914 owned by Col. H.C. Trexler which later became part of the Trexler Game Reservation) children Lillian M. m. E.R. Hurd children Beatrice and James; Ida Louise m. Harry B. Loose, 2 known children; Joseph I.P. m. Lillian Christman, one known child Ruben

Elizabeth b. September 7, 1813 m. Jeremiah Troxell son of Rsh.133

Aaron b. January 23, 1815 m. Angeline Jarrett, daughter of John Jarrett, known children, Elmira b. c. 1838; Ella E. b. c. 1840; m. Alfred Saeger; Emma b. c. 1842; a son d. young; Florence b. c. 1854; note one daughter m. Francis K. Smith and another Thomas E. Saeger

Gideon

David b. August 19, 1819 m. Maria Ann (Mary) Schaadt then Esther (Hettie) Schaadt, children Alexander P. b. 1845 m. Mary Frey known children Bertha and Alexander P.; Oscar L. b. c. 1847; Eli D. b. August 18, 1848 m. Emma Koch, known child 1; Alfred J. b. March 28, 1850 known child Ida; Sarah b. c. 1851 m. Henry Yundt; Franklin b. c. 1853; Elmira b. c. 1854 m. Elias Guth; Louisa b. c. 1855 m. Rev. Frank Guth; Alice b. c. 1858 m. Vincent Koehler, and by 2nd wife Esther, Reston b. c. 1861; Anna b. c. 1864; Francisca b. c. 1866

Ephraim   b. February 1, 1823 m. Caroline A. Fogel, daughter of Solomon and Anna (Stahler) Fogel of Fogelsville, Pa., Ephraim and his family moved to

Wilkes-Barre, Pa., children: Clementine Rose b. c. 1846; Edgar R. b. April 3, 1850 m. Maria B. Nugent, children, Helen Ella; Thomas Nugent; Edgar R.; Margaret; George; Elsie and Gilbert

Francis P. b. c.1834 m. Fannie Balliet dau. of Stephen Balliet, Francis was a doctor and he d. San Diego, California, known children Marian b. c. 1867; Frederick b. c. 1870

**Rsh.155** John Trachsell m. Catherine_____. They lived in Cogolleio Twp., Lancaster Co., Pa., where 1773 probate excludes some of his children by a previous wife. One excluded was Catherine who had children but was deceased in 1773. Second wife Anna Maria _____was left estate. Exr. of his Will, John Ober friend, known children:

Catherine m._____

**Rsh.156** Jacob Troxell (son of Rsh. 40) b. June 25, 1794 m. Elizabeth Blieler, lived in Salisburg Twp., Northampton Co., Pa., area became Leehigh Co., Pa., DGM, LDS, known children:

Reuben
Elizabeth m. Nicholas Lacy
Maria m. Reuben Schaffer of South Whitehall
Elemina b. c. 1828
Reuben Daniel b. 1830
Helena b. c. 1832
Catherine b. c. 1834
Franklin b. c. 1835, m. Mary b. 1846, 2 children
Ephriam b. c. 1837, m. Susan, b. c. 1840, 8 children
Peter Ludwig b. c. 1839
Maria b. c. 1841
child
child

**Rsh.157** Solomon Troxel (son of Rsh.40) b. August 26, 1796, d. October 16, 1860. He was baptized at Jordan Reformed Church and he m. Salome Leisenring and settled in Northampton Co., Pa., DGM, known children:

Gideon b. 1826 d. 1846
Alexander b. 1827 d. 1900
Catherine b. 1831

Reuben b. 1833
Tilghman H. b. 1835 c. 1863
Eliza Ann b. 1838
David b. 1839 d. 1881

**Rsh.158** John Troxell (son of Rsh.57) b. January 9, 1796, d. February 24, 1867, a Carpenter by Trade, m. Salome Mickley, daughter of Peter and Salome (nee Biery) Mickey, DGM, known children:

> Levina b. August 9, 1818 m. Capt. Thomas Ruch
>
> Thomas b. December 22, 1820 m. Mary then Rebecca
>
> Mary Ann b. 1821 m. probably to her sister Levina's widower Capt. Thomas Ruch
>
> Owen b. November 8, 1822 m. Algelina Moyer (Meier), known children John A. b. c. 1851; Ellen J. b. c. 1852 m. Albert Peters; Lewis J. b. c. 1856; Sarah b. c. 1858 m. Jonas Buck; Joseph b. c. 1861 unmarried; Mary b. c. 1864 m. Clinton Moyer
>
> William b. February 13, 1825 d. March 21, 1835
>
> Emilia b. March 7, 1826
>
> Leanda, a twin, b. March, 7, 1830 m. Henry West
>
> Eleanor, a twin, b. March 7, 1830
>
> Rufus b. October 11, 1832
>
> Elevest m. Edwin Snyder
>
> Edwin b. c. 1836 m. Elemina, children, Charles b. c. 1858; Synobe b. c. 1859; Ellen b. c. 1860; William b. c. 1863; George b. c. 1869/70
>
> Sarah b. c. 1842 m. West or Wert

**Rsh.159** Johann David Trexler b. October 11, 1783, Wurtemberg, Germany, d. July 12, 1863, Mertztown, Pa., History and Genealogy of the Trexler Family, known child:

> John b. October 27, 1814 d. July 21, 1900 m. Maria Geist. children: David b. December 13, 1837 d. December 13, 1860; Jonas m. Killy Amanda Fenstermacher; John m. Catherine Pauli; Caroline m. Elijah Miller; Henry G. m. Sally E. Sterner; Alvin G. m. Anna Caroline Frederick; Elmira m. Simeon Abraham Heffner; Emeline m. George H. Wetzel

**Rsh.160** John Trexler m. Elizabeth Morgan on February 2, 1813, lived in Rowan Co., N.C.,active in St. John's Lutheran Church in Salisbury, <u>History and Genealogy of the Trexler Family</u>,<u>History of Rowan Co., N.C.</u>, known child:

> David Trexler b. November 26, 1827 d. January 18, 1890 m. Christina C.Riblin, children, Levi b. August 6, 1855 d. August 13, 1940 m. Agnes Jane Eagle Riblin, their children Theodore; William Grant; Bertha Caroline; Esther m. Morgan; Luther Lee m. Mary Addie File.

**Rsh.161** Jacob Troxell, (son of Rsh. 81), b. November 19, 1812 m. Susan Ziegler. He was a Coach Painter by Trade, they lived in Gettysburg, Pa., <u>DGM</u>,
known children:

> David b. January 3, 1836  m. Annie M._____.
> Anna b. c. 1839 m. Robert M. Elliott
> Samuel Ackerman b. c. 1842
> Charles William b. 1847 d. October 5, 1896 m. Margaret
> Henry b. c. 1856
> Eddy buried at Gettysburg
> infant, "Our Babe" buried at Gettysburg

**Rsh.162** William Trexler b. July 6, 1815, d. December 10, 1886 m. Elmira White, both are buried in Buck Creek Cemetery? no location noted <u>History and Genealogy of the Trexler Family</u>,
known children:

> Harry L. b. June 18, 1837
> Martha J. b. September 2, 1839 m. Abraham Bittner
> Sarah C. b. July 14, 1843 m. James Confer and William Williams
> Fleming P. b. July 13, 1846, m. Clara Birchard and Josephine Stoudt, children 1st wife Percy Thomas m. Jane Eby Garner, 2nd wife Lynn m. Mary Boyer; Lloyd m. Cora Snyder; Sintha m. Steven Deise
> Annie E. b. September 4, 1848 m. Charles Johnson
> John S. b. May 28, 1850, d. March 2, 1918

**Rsh.163** Michael Troxell, Trexel, Troxel (?son of Rsh.45), m. Margaret Merkle, who was b. 1794, at Zion Lutheran Church, Baltimore, Md. on May 21, 1816, moved to Jackson Co., Alabama then Carroll County, Indiana and finally to Pillsboro, Hendricks Co.,

Indiana, <u>DGM</u>,
known children:

> Jacob b. 1828
>
> John George b. December 3, 1830 Jackson Co.,
> Alabama m. Mary E. Gosnell

**Rsh.164** Stephen Troxell, (son of Rsh. 152), b. August 2, 1809, Northampton Co., Pa., m. Esther Mickley, Lehigh Co., Pa., d. Chinton Co., Indiana in 1865. This Family moved to Clinton Co., Indiana in 1860's, <u>DGM</u>, known children:

> Sabina b. January 31, 1836
>
> Adam John Peter b. September 25, 1837, a Blacksmith and Farmer, children Iva V.; Emma M.; Alice A.: Nevin; and Henry Stephen
>
> Clinton Tilghman Martin b. March 18, 1840 m. Eliza Maria Heilman then Magdalene (Hellick) Burkhalter, children by first wife Milton H.; Anna Maria; Minnie Catherine; Uriash Stephen; Callie/Carrier Esther; Lillian Irene; Mantania (Tena May); Edison Welcome
>
> Allen J. b. October 5, 1842 m. Louisa C. Semmel (Samuel) children Clara C.;Mary E.; Eva; Ellen V.; Emerson; Orpha M.; Daisy Bell; Cora A.; Pearl J.; Evy D.
>
> Jane Amanda b. March 21, 1844 m. Christian Miller, 8 children
>
> Walter N.,b. December 18, 1847 m. Mary A. Calloway, one child Emmet C.
>
> Elemina Louise b. April 29, 1849 m. William Rothenberger then William Kent
>
> Annie Maria b. July 4, 1854 m. Dr. J.E.Shaw, one son
>
> Daniel Joseph b. May 3, 185?, m. Sarah Elizabeth Kreisher, children Myrtle B.; Estella, Cecil Daniel; Gearlding
>
> Mathias Silas b. December 8, 1857 m. Mary A._____.
>
> Isaac Benjamin b. 1862

**Rsh.165** Peter Drecksler m. ?Maria Weiser, lived in Cumberland Co., Shippensburg, Pa., first found in the church records 1798. Members Memorial Lutheran Church, communicants as late as May 30, 1819, known children:

> Susanna b. January 19, 1798, sponsor to bapt. February

25, 1798 Christian Drexler and Sarah
Johannes b. July 4, 1804, sponsor to bapt. parents
Samuel b. April 22, 1807, sponsor to bapt. Jacob Weiser
Sara Anna, b. January 5, 1810, sponsor to bapt. parents
Helena b. December 21, 1815, sponsor to bapt. parents
Peter b. February 7, 1819, sponsor to bapt. parents

**Rsh.166** Conrad Drechsler, Dreittsler m.Fronica,(Freny, Franny, Froehry, Frohery), _____,lived in Cumberland Co., Shippensburg, Pa., members Memorial Lutheran Church, first found in records on July 11, 1797, and communicants as late as April 23, 1815, known children:
> Anna Maria b. July 11, 1797, sponsor bapt. Peter Kremer (Cramer) and Maria
> Susanna b. July 17, 1798
> Sally b. September 16, 1802 sponsor bapt. Michael Dreksler and Elisabeth, (Rsh.7)
> Johannes b. July 19, 1804, sponsor bapt. Henrich Pilgrim and Dorothea
> Rosanna b. April 6, 1813, sponsor bapt. Jacob Cremer (Cramer) and Anna Maria

**Rsh.167** George Dreschler m. Catharine_____, lived in Cumberland Co., Shippensburg, Pa., members Memorial Lutheran Church, first found in the records February 20, 1795, known children:
> Elizabeth b. February 20, 1795, bapt. May 24, 1795, sponsor bapt. Frederich Kelppinger and Barbara

**Rsh.168** Daniel Drechler m. Elizabeth_____, lived in Cumberland Co., Shippensburg, Pa., members Memorial Lutheran Church, known children:
> George b. November 2, 1814, sponsor to bapt. George Kremer (Cramer) and Maria
> Maria b. December 24, 1820, sponsor Jacob Kremer (Cramer) and Maria

**Rsh.169** John Drecksler m. Schinne, Ginny, Christina, _____, lived in Cumberland Co., Pa., found in Memorial Lutheran Church Records, known children:
> Alena b. October 20, 1800, sponsor Conrad Drcksler and

Fronica
Sara Anna b. February 4, 1819, sponsor Michael Drechsler and Elisabeth (Rsh.7)

**Rsh.170** Jacob Traxler m. Elisabeth_____, lived in Cumberland Co., Pa., found in Memorial Lutheran Church Records, known children:
Catharine b. March 27, 1826 sponsor parents
John b. September 22, 1828 sponsor parents

**Rsh.171** Franz Joseph Drexel m. Magdalin Wilhelm, they were from Dornbirn in Vorarlberg, Tirol, near Lake Constanz, known children:
Francis Martin Drexel b. April 1, 1792, by Trade a Portrait Painter, and Banker, immigrated to America leaving Amsterdam May 18, 1817. In 1821 he m. Katherine Hookey at St. Mary's Catholic Church, Philadelphia, Three sons and three daughters, known children: Francis Anthony (Rsh.172) b. January 20, 1824, Anthony J., and Joseph W.

**Rsh.172** Francis Anthony Drexel, (son of Rsh.171), b. January 20, 1824 m. Hannah Langstroth, who was born January 14, 1826 the daughter of Piscator Langstroth and Eliza Lehman Langstroth. Hannah Langstroth was a Baptist Quaker, known children:
Elizabeth
Katherine Drexel, founder of the Sisters of the Blessed Sacrament, a Catholic Order, currently in line for sainthood

note: Mrs. Hannah Langstroth Drexel died shortly after Katherine Drexel's birth and her husband m. Emma Bouvier, daughter of Michael Bouvier of Philadelphia and Louise C. Vernou Bouvier on April 10, 1860. They had a child Louise who was born October 2, 1863.

**Rsh.173** Jacob Troxel, Troxell m. Elizabeth, lived in Hilltown Twp., Bucks Co.,Pa., d. March 12, 1806,
known children:
Jacob Troxell
Elizabeth Troxell m. Kerns
Mary Troxell

Margaret Troxell m. Van Havernees
John Troxell
Sarah Troxel

# D.     CEMETERY RECORDS

## KENTUCKY CEMETERIES

Kentucky Pioneers and Their Descendants, Kentucky Society
Daughters of Colonial Wars, 1941-1950 Rogers Printing Co.,
Frankfort Kentucky
Unmarked Graves, 1900's
>> pg.116, Troxel, Esculine, Troxell, Lidia, Troxel, Martha,
>> Troxel, William L.
>> pg.268, Trisler, Fannie, Joseph, Mrs. Joseph
>> pg.140, Dresel, Mrs. Clarence, Fred, George, Harry,
>> Marg, J.

## MARYLAND CEMETERIES

Baltimore, Md., The Redemptorist Cemeteries (Catholic), Most
Holy Redeemer Cemetery, 4430 Belair Road, Baltimore, Md.
21206

Lot No. 1/2 39 J 41 Section F:
>> Drexler, Anna M., d. 7/10/1926 bu. 7/15/1926, 65 years
>> old, b. 1861
>> Drexler, Charles, d. 2/8/1943, bu. 2/12/1943, 88 yrs. old,
>> b. 1854
>> Drexler, Joseph, b. 4/23/1902, orig. bur. #453 Row, age
>> 12 mo., original death date unknown
>> Drexler, Mary K., d. 6/27/1921, bu. 6/30/1921, box 1896,
>> age 25 yrs.
>> Drexler, Frederick (Ferdianand) d. 10/7/1918, bu. 1890,
>> age 27 yrs. 9 mo.

Lot No. 110, Section F.
>> Dreschler, Catherine F., bu. 9/25/1899, age 2 years 6 mo.
>> Dreschler, Frank bu. 10/2/1899, no age
>> Dreschler, Fred, d. 11/2/1925, bu. 11/5/1925, 62 yrs. old,
>> b. 1863
>> Dreschler, Theresa, bu. 4/8/1913, age 51 years, b. 1862
>> Dreschler, Thomas, bu. 10/2/1899, no age

Lot No. 8, Section H
>> Drexler, Charles C., bu. 9/22/1903, age 19 yrs. 7 mo.

Drexler, Ferdinand, bu. 6/15/1897, age 73 years, b. 1824
Drexler, John A., bu. 7/21/1892, age 1 yrs. 4 mo.
Drexler, John M., bu. 2/6/1900, age 47 yrs., b. 1853
Drexler, Margaret, bu. 3/3/1888, age 1 yr. 10 mo.
Drexler, Margaret, bu. 1/7/1894, age 1 month
Dexler, Mary, bu. 2/26/1895, age 66 yrs., b. 1829
Drexler, Mary E., bu. 12/27/1895, no age

Lot No., 63, Section O

Trexler, Charlotte, bu. 9/21/1910, age 12 days old

Lot No. 348, Section Q

Dexel, Barbara, d. 5/28/1971, bu. 6/1/1971, b. 8/15/1881,
parents Dexel, Michael and Catherine
Dexel, Caroline M., bu. 10/6/1908, no age, orig. bu. on
#1140 Row, original Death date unknown
Dexel, Catherine, d. 11/23/1926, bu. 11/26/1926, age 81
years 7 months. b. 1845
Dexel, Cunigunda, bu. 10/6/1908, no age orig. bu. on #7
02 Row, original death date unknown
Dexel, Philip, bu. 9/11/1908, age 34 years
Stiller, Albert, bu. 9/12/1910, removed from St. Alphonsus
Cemetery, no age given
Drexel, Catherine, bu. 9/12/1910, no age, was originally
bu. in St. Alphonsus Cemetery, no longer in
existence
Drexel, Michael and wife, bu. 9/12/1910, no ages,
originally bu. in St. Alphonsus Cemetery

note: Lot owner was Dexel, Catherine, who is bu.
in this lot

Lot No. Rear 1/2 212, Section V.

Drexler, Crescentia, d. 2/20/1934, bu. 2/23/1934, age 26
yrs. 8 mo.
Drexler, Frank P., d. 5/19/1984, bu. 5/25/1984 b.
5/18/1901

Lot No. 254, Section X.

Deixler, Mary, d. 2/24/1918, bu. 2/27/1918, age 23 years
Deixler, John, d. 3/12/1918, bu. 3/15/1918, age 32 years

Lot No. 326, Section X

Drexler, Anna, d. 10/18/1918, bu. 10/21/1918, age 26
years

Lot No. 155, Section CC

Dreschler, George J., d. 2/2/1942, bu. 2/5/1942, age 35 years, 8 months

Drexler, Margaret, d. 4/7/1938, bu. 4/11/1938, age 34 ye ars

Drechsler, Mary C., d. 4/23/1965, bu. 4/26/1965, b. 1882, age 83 years

Lot No. 138, Section LL

Drexler, George, d. 11/25/1926, bu. 11/29/1926, age 37 years

Lot No. 925, Section LL

Infant of Drexler, Frank and Mary, d. 6/5/1945, bu. 6/6/1945, infant

Drexler, Mary C., d. 12/12/1966, bu. 12/16/1966, b. 4/8/1914, age 52

Duschl, Caroline, d. 3/13/1942, bu. 3/16/1942, age 60 years, 11 mons.

Duschl, John, d. 4/9/1930, bu. 4/12/1930, age 20 yrs. 10 mo.

Duschl, Mathias, d. 8/18/1956, bu. 8/22/1956, age 75 years

Lot 79, Section Little Flower

Drescher, John C., d. 7/24/1951, bu. 7/27/1951, age 56 years

Drescher, Mary, d. 2/6/1947, bu. 2/10/1947, age 55 years

Lot No. Front 1/2 31, Section Sacred Heart

Dresler, Anna M., d. 12/10/1970, bu. 12/14/1970, b. 12/11/1897

Dreslerk, Max P., d. 9/5/1961, bu. 9/9/1961, b. 1890, age 71 years

Lot No. 117, Section St. Henry

Trexler, Margaret A., d. 11/16/1992, bu. 11/18/1992, b. 9/17/1907


Carroll Co., Cemeteries, Vol.2, East-Central, compiled by Carroll Co., Genealogical Society, Westminster, Md. 1990. F187.C25C35 Pub. by Carroll Co., Genealogical Society, C/O Carroll Co., Public Library, 50 E. Main St. Westminster, Md. 21157

pg.176, Drechsler, Anna Barbara b. 4/24/1924 d. 3/19/1984 age 59 (10 25), bu. Trinity Luth (12 09) husb. John Henry, lot 26 pg.176, Drechsler, John Henry b. 4/9/1820 d. 12/24/1882 (63 8 15) mo., Trinity Lutheran, lot 26

> pg.176, Drechsler, Wayne Herman b. 2/14/1960 d. 4/30/1988 (28 2 16), Deer Park, SRA, U.S. Air Force

## Dorchester Co., Md., Tombstone Records,1678-1964, by Nellie M. Marshall

Rsh.20 pg.67, James White property, Chesapeake Bay side Middle Hooper Island, Hooper Island Dist. Trexler, Elizabeth, wife of Trexler, Isaac S., b. 10/6/1834, d. 9/16/1869.

Rsh.20 pg.68, S. Hubert Applegarth Home Place, Honga Hooper Island District, Trexler, Jonathan P., d. 5/15/1849, age 55 years.(b. 1794)

## Frederick Co., Md.,Tombstone, Inc., Elias Evangelical Lutheran Church, Emmitsburg, The Maryland and Delaware Genealogist, Vol.VI #1, January 1965

Rsh.34 Troxel, Elizabeth, (b.1751) wife of Troxel, John, mother of 10, d. 5/25/1825. Age 74, 10 mo. 13 days.

Rsh.34 Troxel, John, b. 9/17/1747, d. 4/21/1830, age 82 years, 7 months, 4 days.

Rsh.102 Troxel, Peter, b.1777, d. 5/26/1816, age 39 years, 19 days

Rsh.34 Troxel, Magdalene, consort of Troxel, Peter, d. 5/23/1850, age 68

> Troxel, Joseph Peter, b. 5/19/1822, d. April 14, 1862

Rsh.98 Troxel, Elizabeth wife of George d. 7/28/1850, age 69 years, 10 months, 6 days.

Rsh.98 Troxel, George, b.1794, d. 7/20/1832, age 38 years, 10 months, 23 days.

> Troxel, George Washington, d. 1/3/1815, Age 1 year, 4 months 11 days.

Rsh.101 Troxel, Sophia Elizabeth, b.1787, wife of John Nickum, d. 8/23/1825 in her 38th year

> Weaver, Lewis, b. June 18, 1804, d. August 26, 1805, 1 year, 2 mo, 3 days

> Houch, Mary, consort of Houch, George d. 7/26/1828, Age 72 years.

> Weaver, Elizabeth, wife of Weaver, John d. 8/4/1739, age 62 years, 3 months 9 days.

Rsh.101 Troxel, Catherine d. 3/30/1845, age 51 years, 6 months, 16 days.

Rsh.101 Troxel, Samuel Troxel b. 6/2/1823, d. 1/9/1851

Rsh.34 Troxel, Jacob (b1787) d. 6/7/1833, age 46 years, 8 months, 7 days

Rsh.101 Nickum, Elizabeth, wife of Nickum, John, b.1812, d. 4/30/1852, age 40 years, 18 days,
Note: stone made by Meade of Gettysburg, she was daughter of Jacob.
Troxel, Catharine Ann, b. 1835, d. 1897

Rsh.34 John Troxel, of John,(Rsh.45) b.1781, d. 12/7/1853, age 72 years, 4 months 4 days.
Troxel, Peter Van Buren, d. 1/11/1837, age 13 months.


Names in Stone, Frederick Co., Md. Vol.I & II, Jacob Mehrline Holdcraft, Ann Arbor, Michigan, 1966.

Rsh.42 Troxel, Peter, b. 4/3/1719, d. 1/25/1799, Toms Creek Lutheran Church, East side Four Points Bridge Rd.
Troxel, Maria Magdelena, b. 1/6/1806, d. 1821

Rsh.36 Troxel, Jacob, b. 1765, d. 1807
Troxel, Peter, b. 5/26/1816, bu. Emmitsburg Lutheran, Emmitsburg, Md.
Troxel, Magdelena, d. 5/1850, age 68

Rsh.42 Troxel, Peter, son of Peter, b. 10/1768, d. 1856

Rsh.34 Troxel, John, b. 9/17/1747, d. 4/1830
Troxel, Frederick, b. 1807 d. 1891, bu. Thurmont Apples Church, Northern outskirts of town
Troxel, Elizabeth, b. 1774 d. 1856
Troxell, Catherine, b. 1776 d. 1823

Rsh.25 Trisler, George, b. 1768, d. 1845 age 77, bu. Frederick Reformed Lutheran

Rsh.25 Trisler, Rosanna, b. 11/19/1799 d. 10/12/1826

Rsh.75 Trisler, Mary, w/o Michael d. 4/4/1828, age 87 (b. 1741)
note: plaque on site shows her name as Margaret.

Rsh.75 Trisler, William H., bu. 1842 - no age


MHS - Deaths

Rsh.25 Trissler, George, d. 9/16/1845 in Frederick Co., b. 1768

Rsh.75 Trisler, Michael, d. 10/22/1805

Rsh.75 Trisler, Mary Margaret, d. 4/5/1828, age 87, wife of

Michael, Frederick Co.
Rsh.25 Rosanna Trisler, d. October 19, 1826, wife of George
Trisler, Frederick Co.

## OHIO CEMETERIES

Cemetery Records, Ohio Jackson Township, DAR Library,
Washington, D.C.
    Trissell Cemetery
    Trissell, David, b.1761, husband of Anna, d. 8/30/1836,
        age 75 years 3 months
    Trissel, David, b.1792, husband of Mary, d. 3/11/1854,
        age 62 years 14 days.

Cemetery Records, Ohio Miami Township DAR Library,
Washington, D.C., Vol.IV, Mont. Co., Cemetery Records, compiled
by Lindsay M. Brian
    Found on the Troxel Farm
?Rsh.32 Troxel, Abraham, b.1771, d. 1/13/1845, age 74 years, 10
        mo. 2 days
    Troxel, Barbary, d. June 20 - no year given
    Troxel, Samuel, b.1791, d. 6/23/1826, age 35 years 1
        month 9 days.
    Shower, David, d. 10/1826

## PENNSYLVANIA CEMETERIES

Cemetery Inscriptions, Adams Co., Pa., DAR publication DAR
Library, Washington, D.C.
Rsh.81 Troxell, John, d. 2/3/1855, age 74 (b. 1781)
Rsh.81 Troxell, Catherine d. 7/9/1870, 84 years old (b. 1786)
?Rsh.45 Troxel, John, Sr., 1st Settler of Gettysburg, b. Bethel
        Pa., 5/3/1761 d. Gettysburg 10/2/1855, age 94

Adams Co., Pa., Notes, York County Pa., HSYC
Evergreen Cemetery, Gettysburg, Pa.,
?Rsh.45 Troxell, John, Sr., 1st Settler of Gettysburg, b.
        Bethlehem, Pa., 5/3/1761, d. 1855 in Gettysburg,
        10 children, 71 grandchildren, 120 great grand

children, 20 great great grandchildren, Tombstone
date 1855
?Rsh.45   Troxel, David, son of John


Pa. German Tombstone Records, Vol.2, pub. by Lt. Col. Oscar H.
Slorh, R.D. 4, Box 925, Harrisburg, Pa., 17112 F160.G3587, 1980,
Vol.1
pg.43, Drexler, Regina nee Kienert, b. 7/6/1776, d. 4/27/1856, 79
       yr, 9 mo. 21 da., Herford Twp., Berks Co., Huffs
       Church

Rsh.136 Trostle, Abraham, d. 2/12/1861, 78 years
Rsh.136 Trostle, Anna Marie, w. of Abraham, d. 12/1/1862 - 78
       yrs,2 mo., 24 days
       Trostle, Catherine, b. 11/27/1822, d. 1/15/1895
       Trostle, Abraham, b. 11/27/1822, d. 11/12/1886
       Trostle, Melle, nee Redge, wife of Adam, b. 4/2/1803 d.
       8/20/1853
       Trostle, Maria, dau. of Abraham & Maria d. 1/1837, 19
       years, 3 mo
       Trostle, George, b. 4/6/1812, d. 5/16/1898

Jim Wirth, Trexler Historian:
1st Lutheran Cemetery in Chambersburg, Pa., bu., Tressler,
Rachel, 1808-1840, daughter of Tressler, Frederick and Elizabeth

Franklin Co., Pa., Shippensburg in the Civil War, Author William
H. Burkhart, et al, publ. by SHS, The News-Chronicle Company,
Shippensburg, Pa., 1964
Otterbein Evangelical United Brethren Church Cemetery,
pg.287, #21. Traxler, Jacob R., b. 9/23/1822, d. 3/22/1874;
       Traxler, William A., d. 1/26/1902, age 55 years and 2 days


Franklin Co., Pa., SHS
       Carrick Cemetery, Metal Twp., Traxler, Charles Walker,
       Sr., Fannettsburg, retired farmer, b. 1/2/1888 in Shade
       Valley, Huntingdon Co.,the son of Traxler, Doris and Mary
       Jane,(nee Wiser) d. 7/12/1982

**Tombstone Inscriptions from Graveyards in Lancaster Co., Pa., copied by William Frederick Worner, the Librarian of the Lancaster County Historical Society, Lancaster Pa., 1935 - book at Historical Society. Lancaster, Pa.**

Vol.6, pg.92, Trexler, Anthony, Methodist Church yard, Soudersberg, Pa., Trexler, Anthony, d. 8/17/1854 in the 40th year of his age (b.1814)

Vol.8, pg.237, Trexler, J.F., (J.F. Trexler, Deputy Coroner)

Trissler, Elizabeth, Shreiner's Cemetery, b. 12/29/1800, d. 6/17/1883. Aged 82 years, 5 months and 18 days

Vol.11, pg.55, Traxler, Elizabeth, Lancaster Cemetery, Section 1, (stone worn) ?5/2/1822, ?8/28/1851

Vol.11, pg.246, Trissler, David, Lancaster Cemetery, Section 9, Company A (stone sunk)

Vol.11, pg.246, Trissler, John, Lancaster Cemetery, Section 9, in 84th year, b. 11/9/1815, 12/30/1898

Vol.11, pg.246, Trissler, Lillie D., Lancaster Cemetery, Section 9, wife of Trissler, Joseph R., 2/20/1851, 3/20/1886

Vol.11, pg.246, Trissler, Louisa Miller, Lancaster Cemetery, Section 9, 29th Year, 5/25/1887

Vol.11, pg.247, Trissler, Rachael W., Lancaster Cemetery, Section 9, wife of Trissler, John, 4/1/1819, 8/30/1885

Vol.11, pg.273, Trissler, Louisa, Lancaster Cemetery, Section 10, wife of John A. Trissler 8/23/1839, 10/14/1888

Rsh.29 Vol.19, pg.330, St. Mary's Roman Catholic Church, Lancaster, Pa., Hiltenberger, _____mason of this church, d. 8/25/1794, on pg.346 there is a note that this reference is as recorded in American Catholic Historical Society, Vol.24, (1914) 1788-1804, pp. 274, 344-351

**Lancaster Moravian Church Records, Part 1, Marriages and Burials 1743-1875, LHS Photocopy of Typescript in the possession on the congregation 1985 Burial Book of the Moravian Church, Lancaster, Pa., 1744 - 1821, LHS**
**Burials:**

Rsh.26 bu. 7/31/1753, Dressler, Maria Catharine, daughter of George David and Anna Maria b. Cron age 1 yr. and 5 mo

bu. 10/29/1752, Trissler, Margaretha Catherine, 11 mo., daughter of J. Michael Lauburger

Rsh.26 bu. 11/22/1760, Dressler, Catharine, dau. George David and Anna Maria b. Cron, age 2 years less 5 days

Rsh.26 bu. 8/25/1763, Drissler, Philip, (28 hrs) 2 days, son of George David and Anna Maria b. Cron

Rsh.26 bu. 7/11/1775, Trisler,Susanna, dau. George David and Anna Maria b. Cron b. July 6, 1775

Rsh.26 bu. 8/23/1778, Graff, Mattheus, son of Graff, Jacob and Maria b. Trissler b. 2/16/1777

Rsh.26 bu. 2/23/1782, Graff, Matthews, son of Graff, Jacob and Maria b. Trissler, b. 10/21/1781

Rsh.26 bu. 7/8/1783, Graff, Andreas, son of Graff, Jacob and Maria b. Trissler b. 7/1/1783

Rsh.27 bu. 2/6/1787, Trissler, Cathaine, dau. of George and Anna Maria Cron b. 12/4/1785

Rsh.27 bu. 12/17/1789 Trissler, Eliza, dau. George and Anna Maria b. Cron b. 11/2/1783

Rsh.26 bu. 2/4/1795 Demuth, Sophia Elizabeth Demuth b. 7/7/1794 dau. of Johannes Demuth, Riflemaker, and Cathaina b. Trissler

Rsh.27 bu. 1/25/1792, Trissler, Elizabeth. She was b. 9/1749 in New Castle Co., Del. Her parents were Robinson, James and Elizabeth. She m. in 1776 to the widower George David Trissler, Jr. a Saddler

Rsh.26 bu. 2/4/1795 DeMuth, Sophia Elizabeth, b. 7/7/1794 daughter of DeMuth, Joannes, Riflemaker, resident and Trisslery, Catharine.

Rsh.27 bu. 8/16/1796, Trissler, Jacob, b. 2/6/1788 in Lancaster son of Trissler, George David, and the late Elizabeth nee Robinson. He was with his father, at present the Tavern Keeper and Ferryman on the other side of the Susquehanna, at the so called Wrights Ferry where the lad died.

Rsh.27 bu. 9/30/1796, Trissler, George David, b. 1/25/1754, a Saddler, from Lancaster. Learned the trade of Saddler with his father. He married Elizabeth b. Robinson in 1776. They had 4 sons and 3 daughters of whom 3 sons and a daughter survive. He married a second time.

Rsh.44 bu. 3/5/1802, Trissler, Johannes, b. Lancaster 1/3/1798

son of Trissler, Johannes, a Saddler, and wife Anna Marie
b. Reichart

Rsh.44 bu. 2/16/1808, Trissler, Anna Maria, b. Reichart 7/6/1767
m. Trissler, Johannes. This union was blest with 3 sons
and 5 daughters of whom 1 son is deceased

Rsh.27 bu. 7/21/1809, Trissler, George David, Sr., b. at Canstadt
in the Dukedom Wurtemberg on 3/2/1723. In 1750 he m.
in Lancaster to Anna Maria nee Cron of Lancaster. This
union was blest with 11 children and as far as known, 2
sons Johannes and Christian and 4 daughters survive.
He lived to see 48 grandchildren and 10 great
grandchildren

Rsh.26 bu. 2/3/1810, Steiner, Michael, b. 9/10/1764, m. in 1791 to
Elizabeth b. Trissler. 7 children 2 sons 5 daughters all
survive. Trissler, Elizabeth, d. 5/20/1811

Rsh.28 bu. 4/3/1811, Trissler, John, b. 5/14/1807, son of Trissler,
John and Catherina nee Huber. He was baptized by a
Catholic priest, as his mother is a Catholic. The father is
a Riflemaker.

Rsh.28 bu. 6/17/1811, Trissler, George, b. 6/11/1811, son of
Trissler, John and Catharina b. Huber

Rsh.26 bu. 1/25/1812, Thomas, Catharines, single. b. 10/22/1793
dau. of Thomas, George and Anna Magdalena b. Trissler

Rsh.26 bu. 4/13/1812, Steiner, Rebecca, single, b. 8/20/1795,
dau. of Steiner, Michael and w. Elizabeth b. Trisslery

Rsh.26 bu. 7/11/1812, Trissler, Anna Maria, widow, b. Chron,
9/12/1730 at Staudernheim, in the Palatinate. She
entered the married state in 1750 with Trissler, George
David, and was blessed with 11 children, 2 sons and 3
daughters survive. 49 grandchildren, 16 great
grandchildren.

Rsh.27 bu. 7/11/1812, Trissler, Anna Maria, b. Chron 9/12/1730
in Stauderheim, Palatinate m. 1750 to George David
Trissler, surviving 1. Johannes, 2. Christian, 3. Elizabeth
Steiner, 4. Susanna Maria Graeff, 5. Anna Magdalena
Thomas

Rsh.46 bu. 7/12/1813 Trissler, Richard Dehuff, son of Trissler,
Adam and Juliana Reed, b. Reichard. He was b. 4/7/1813

Rsh.26 bu. 9/8/1815, Graeff, Johann Jacob, b. 12/17/1753, m.
4/15/1776 to Trissler, Susanna Maria, 13 children of whom
10 survive

Rsh.26 bu. 1/1/1816, Thomas, George, b. 9/19/1776 m. 6/26/1791 to Trissler, Anna Magdalena 6 children 5 survive

Rsh.26 bu. no year given, 3/8, Demuth, Johannes, age 50, 2 months 16 days m. widow, Trissler, Catharine in 1790

Rsh.46 bu. 3/21/1820, Trissler, Johann Abrahamr, b. 11/28/1818, son of Trissler, Adam, resident Carpenter and Juliana

Rsh.46 bu. 8/14/1822, Trissler, Julianna, age 33 years 5 months 29 days b. 2/16/1789 m. Trissler, John Adam, 5 children 2 sons and 3 daughters, both sons dead

Rsh.46 bu. 5/5/1825, Trissler, John Adam, age 37 9 months less 4 days

Rsh135 bu. 8/9/1826, Trissler, Catharine, b. Ehler daughter of Ehler, Daniel and Margaretha Ehler b. Vonder Smith, Catherine b. 5/2/1779 m. Trissler, George, in 1801, 6 daughters 4 sons

Rsh135 bu. 9/15/1838, Trissler, George Conrad, b. 3/19/1803 son of Trissler, George and Catharina on 3/19/1829 m. Dielrich, Sarah, had 2 sons and a daughter

Rsh.28 bu. 1/30/1840, Trissler, John, son of Trissler, George David and wife Elizabeth b. Robinson. He was b. 2/21/1773, in 1802 he married Hoover, Catherine, and they had 5 sons and 6 daughters

Rsh.44 bu. 7/28/1844, Trissler, John, widower, of Trissler, David and Anna Mar. b. 3/17/1761 m. twice. Second time Rebecca Graff, had issue, 83 years 4 months 11 days

Rsh.26 bu. 11/20/1857, Trissler, Christian, single, son of Trissler, George David and Anna Maria b. 8/20/1764, had little good of this life

Rsh.44 bu. 2/19/1867, Eichhotz, Catharine Trissler, 2nd wife of Jacob Eichholtz, Portrait Painter. She was b. 7/24/1791 to Trissler, John and Mary nee Reigart. 9 Children


Lancaster Co., Pa., Cemetery Surname Index, compiled by Bob and Mary Closson, printed by Closson Press, 1935 Sampson Drive, Appolo, Pa., 15613, F157.L2C54, 1988

pg.24, Drescher, Landisville Menn, Mastersonville
pg.24, Draucher, Quarrysville
pg.24, Dracher, Quarrysville
pg.107, Treichler, Hans Graft Graveyard, Mt. Tunnel

Trexler, Landisville Menn
Trichler, Mt. Tunnel
Trissler, Landisville Menn, St. James Episcopal, Millersville
    Menn
Troxel, Old Weaverland

Leehigh Co., Pa., Eyerman "Graveyards of Old Northampton",
Easton German Reformed Church Yard, Vol.1, page 33:
Rsh.11 "Henrich Schneider, b. March 17, 1735 married Juliana
    Troxel, 15 1/2 years, 2 sons, 4 daughters, d. 3/17/1778,
    age 43 years." Her brothers Nicholas and Michael and
    sisters Catharine and Elizabeth went to Easton Pa., with
    her.

City of Philadelphia, Index to Registration of Deaths, 1803-1860,
Transcription of index prepared by WPA project 11791, original
records are deposited with the Genealogical Society of Pa., 1300
Locust Street, Philadelphia, Pa., kF158.25.I43, 1934   numbers 7/8
for D and 31 for T
pg.331  Trexler, Mary Ann, interred in Williamsburg, St. Mary's
R.C. J. Chambers, Sexton, date of death, 10/28/1845, age 29
    Trexlen, Jacob, death 9/15/1835 cause diarrhoea, age 50,
Doctor I. Kline b.1785
    Trexler, male child of Mrs. Trexler, bu. Mutual Kensington,
9/11/1841, still b., Doctor J.P. Bethell
    Trexler, no first name, Mrs. bu. Odd Fellows, d. 5/5/1859
of old age, age 79, Dr. R.G. Mansfieldl b.1780
    Trexler, no first name, Mrs. bu. Mutual Kensington, d.
9/11/1841 from rupture of uterus, age 20, doctor J.P. Bethell,
b.1821
    Trexler, Catherine, bu. St. Marys, d. 10/10/1845 of fever,
age 39, Dr. W.R. Clapp b.1806
    Trexler, Charles, bu. Union Kensingtron, d. 1/28/1857, of
scarlet fever, age 2, Dr S. Updegrove, b. 1835
    ?Rsh.85  Trexler,David, bu. German Lutheran, d. 10/1812,
no cause given, age 68 (b.1744)
    Trexler, George, bu. St. Johns Epis., d. 12/26/1820, age
14, b. 1806
    Trexler, Jacob, bu. St. Johns Epis., d. 11/27/1820, age 15,
b. 1805
    Trexler, Mary Ann, bu. Odd Fellows, d. 1/30/1856, of small

pox, age 21, Dr. S. Updegrove, b 1835

Trexler, Rachel, bu. St. Johns Episcopal, d. 2/7/1822, age 3 weeks

Trexler, Rebecca, bu. Laurel Hill, d. 3/23/1848, of Pulmonary Comsumption, age 25, Dr. W. Williamson, b. 1823

Trexler, Sarah, d. 12/16/1834, of mania a potu, age 29, corner, b. 1805

Trexlet, no name, bu Mutual Family, d. 7/12/1845 of apoplexy, age 60, Dr. A.H. Grimshaw, b. 1785

Trextler, no name, child of Mrs. Trextler, buried Old Kensington, d. 4/6/1857, of pheumonia, age 7 Dr. S. Updegrove

Traxler, Francis, bu. in Blockley, d. 5/21/1841 of Rubeola, age 5 years 6 weeks, Dr. R. Foster

Troxell, no name, son of Troxell, Abraham, bu. New Reformed German, d. 1/23/1819, still b.

Troxel, Andrew, bu. Mutual of Kensington, d. October 10, 1839, of puerperal, age 6, Dr. J.K. Knorr

Drexell, Mary R., bu. Woodland, d. 8/7/1855, Maramu s, age 13, Dr. J.L. Ludlow

Drexler, H., bu. German Baptist, d. 12/20/1858, of encephalitis, age 2, Dr. G. Maeheinger

Rsh.86 Drexler, Joseph, bu. German Lutheran, d. 9/1811, age 60, b. 1751

pg.352

Disler, George, bu. Alms House, d. 2/24/1849, chronic diarrhea, age 8 days, Dr. B.F. Wendel


## VIRGINIA CEMETERIES

Alexander, Va., Trisler file at National Genealogical Society, Arlington, Va., Rsh.105

A former cemetery on the outskirts of Alexandria, Va. known as Triangle Market area, because it occupied a triangle formerly bounded by Duke St. and Telegraph Rd., was located 1/4 miles N.W. of the Masonic Memorial. The inscriptions on the following stones were recorded before being destroyed:

Catherine Trisler, consort of Lewis Trisler died 10/12/1830 Age 81 years. Lewis Trisler d. 12/15/1814, age 67 years.

Ann (Ana or Ada?) daughter of Peter and Priscilla Trisler

d. 8/3/1822, age 3 years, 10 months, 26 days.

3 infants, children of Peter and Priscilla Trisler, no date.
Amanda Trisler daughter of Peter and Priscilla Trisler d.
10/12/1836, age 5 years, 1 month 26 days.

Priscilla Trisler, wife of Peter Trisler d. 3/12/1848 age 54
years.

Footstone next to Priscilla, no marking, except for initials
P.T. on back.


Shockoe Hill Cemetery, Richmond, Va., Alice Bohmer Rudd,
F234.R5R8, Vol.1 & 2
Vol.1

Rsh.76 Trexler, Anthony, pg.8, 6/8/1824, 8 mo. old

Rsh.76 Trexler, Ignatius, pg.5, 8/6/1827, 40 years old, note: War
of 1812 Veteran, Grave unmarked.

Rsh.76 Trexler, Virginia, pg.6, 8/1/1828, 8 months old
Vol.2

Rsh140 Trexler, Isabella, pg.4, 10/13/1851, 2 years old

Rsh140 Trexler, William, pg.22, 2/10/1855, (less than year old)

Rsh140 Troxler, Rosetta, pg.34, 5/14/1857, 10 year, 2 mo.

Rsh140 Trexler, Joseph D., pg.34, 5/22/1857, 5 year, 6 mo.

Rsh140 Trexler, Katy, pg.l55, 9/5/___, 1 mo. 8 days, b.d. Rich.
Railburg, John Edward, 2/10/1868, 1 year 2 mo)

Rsh142 Trexler, Adelaide, pg.93, 9/30/1870, 7 mo. 4 days

Rsh138 Trexler, Rose Alice, pg.l36, II/27/1881, 23 mo. b. William
Trexler's house

Rsh138 Trexler, William H., pg.133, 1/12/1881, 6 years, 8 mo. 25
days

Rsh138 Trexler, Minnie A., pg.153, 10/5/1887, 1 yr.4 mo.4 days
old

Rsh.76 Truxler, Joseph, pg.155, 8/15/1888, 18 days old, b.d.
Richmond

Rsh.76 Trexler, Ada Lee, pg.l60, 6/ 1/1890, 3 mo. 23 days b.d.
Richmond

Rsh.76 Trexler, Nancy, pg.95, w/o of Ignatius Trexler formerly
Nancy Anna Murray, bu.5/12/1871, 75 years old, b.
Baltimore, Md., d, Richmond,Va.

**E.** **CENSUS RECORDS**
**KENTUCKY CENSUS**
<u>1810 Census, NA, Kentucky</u>

Tressel, Wm., Lewis Co., pg.101
Rsh.64, Trisler, Catharine, Jessamine Co., pg.48
Trisler, Jacob, Jesamine Co., pg.48
Trisler, Joseph, Jesamine Co., pg.48
Trisler, Peter, Jesamine Co., pg.48
Troseaxe, Isaac, Adair Co., pg.14
Trosell, Frederick, Grayson Co., pg.243
Troxel, Christopher, Wayne Co., pg.365
Troxel, Daniel, Wayne Co., pg.365
Troxel, Peter, Wayne Co., pg.365
Troxell, Jacob, Wayne Co., pg.362
Troxell, Peter, Wayne Co., pg.362
Troxely, John, Gattalin Co., pg.193
Trussel, Sally, Logan Co., pg.167
Trussel, Jilson, Bourbon Co., pg.111
Trussel, Nahum, Bourbon Co., pg.111

## MARYLAND CENSUS

<u>1776 Census, Mdhr, Index 46</u>

Rsh.1 Elizabeth Hundred, Hagerstown, 1814, Frederick Co., Md.,Box 2, Folder 7, pgs.8,12,19,44, Abraham Draxel, age 7, b. 1769, Daniel Draxel, age 6 months, Elizabeth Draxel, age 26, b. 1750, George Drascel, age 41, b. 1735, Peter Draxelxel, age 11, b. 1765, Magdalena Draxeixel, age 14, b. 1762, Catharine Draxser, age 2, b. 1774.

<u>Census of 1776, Recorded August 22, 1776, Mdhr, Index 46</u>

Rsh.30 Georgetown Hundred, Frederick Co., Md., Box 2, Folder 8, pg.16, George Trissoler, age 4, b. 1772, Jacob Trissoler, age 32, b. 1744, Jacob Trissoler, Jr. age 1, b. 1775, John Trissoler age 2, b. 1774, Mary Trissoler age 23, b. 1753, Elizabeth Trissoler, age 7, b.1769, the last two are on pg.18 with females all of whom are listed separately as a group.

<u>Mdhr, Oaths of Fidelity, Maryland, it was required that every man</u>

in Maryland over the age of 18 in the year 1777, take an Oath of Fidelity, Mdhr.

Anne Arundel County - James Tootell, Richard Tootell Baltimore County - John Delcher

Frederick County - John Theser, Benjamin Thrasher, John Trasher, Thomas Trasher, Michael Tripler, John Troxall

Queen Anne County - Charles Tressies

Montgomery County - (Rsh.30) Jacob Trissler, John Trundel, Josias Trundel, Thomas Trundel

Washington County - Goodhart Tresal, George Troseel, Abraham Troxal, Abraham Troxel, George Troxel, Louson Troller

## 1790 Census

Maryland, Mdhr, Census Tabulations, numbers at end of line indicate males 16+, males 16-, females, slaves

Tresel, Peter, pg.32, Baltimore Co., 1, 2, 4
Troxill, George I., pg.115, Washington Co., 1, 2, 2
Tresler, Michael, pg.117, Washington Co.,1, 3, 4
Trestler, Goodhart, pg.120, Washington Co., 0, 1, 3, 4
Troxall, David, pg.64, Frederick Co., 1, 0, 6
Troxall, Frederick, pg.64, Frederick Co., 0, 2, 3, 5
Troxall, Jacob, pg.63, Frederick Co., 0, 1, 3, 4
Troxall, Jacob of Peter, pg.65, Frederick Co., 1, 2, 1
Troxall, John, pg.65, Frederick Co., 0, 1, 3, 5
Troxall, John, Jr., pg.65, Frederick Co., 3, 3, 6, 3
Troxall, Peter, pg.65, Frederick Co., 3, 2, 1
Tressair, John, Queen Annes Co., 0, 2, 2, 2
Trissler, Valentine, pg.79, Harford, Co., 1, 1, 3
Trisler, Michael, Frederick, Co., pg.68, 0, 2, 1

## 1800 MARYLAND CENSUS, NA

Index

Rsh.75  Trisler, Michael, Frederick Co., (NA 2  850  14)

Rsh.110 Trissler, Valentine, Harford Co., Md.,pg.97, Harve de Grace

Rsh.15  Troxal, David, Washington Co., Conococheague Dist. (NA659 8)

## 1800 Census Tabulations

?Rsh.101  Tresler, Jacob, Frederick Co., pg.175, Taney Town Elec. Dist.#5, males under 10=2, 10-16=2, 16-25=0, 26-45=1, 45+=0, females under 10=3, 10-16=1, 16-25=0, 26-45=1

Rsh.5  Trexel, Tixel, Anthony, Frederick Co., pg. 180, (NA12001 21101-00), Taney Town Elec. Dist # 5 males under 10 =1, 10-16 = 2, 16-25 = 0, 26-45 = 0, 45+ = 1, females under 10 = 2, 10-16 = 1, 16-20 = 1, 26-45 = 0, over 45 = 1

Rsh.42  Troxel, George, Frederick Co., Emmitsburg Elect. Dist. 4, males under 10=0, 10-16=0, 16-26=2, 26-45=0, over 45=0, females 1 over 45, 1 slave

Rsh.34  Troxel, Jacob, Frederick Co., Emmitsburg Elect. Dist #4, males under 10=2, 10-16=1, 16-26=1, 26-45=1, over 45=0, females under 10=2, 26-45=1, 1 slave

Troxel, Jacob, Emmitsburg, males 16-26=2, 26-45=1, females 16-26=2, 26-45=1

Troxel, Jacob, Emmitsburg, males under 10=3, 10-16=2, 26-45=1, females under 10=2, 26-45=1, over 45=1, 2 slaves

Troxel, John, Emmitsburg, males 10-16=1, 16-26=2, over 45=1, females under 10=2, 16-26=1, over 45=1, 2 slaves

Troxel, Peter, Jr., Emmitsburg, males 16-26=1

Rsh.24  Troxel, Adam, males under 10 = l, 0 males 10-16, males 45+ = 1

Troxill,(Troxall) Peter, Washington Co., Fort Frederick, (NA 651-1), white males 10-16=1, 16-25=0, 26-45=2, 45+1, Females

10-16=1, 16-25=0, 26-45=1, 45=0

## 1800 Census, Mdhr Microfilm M2056-2
Census Tabulations

Rsh.110  Valentine Trisler, pg.97, Town of Harve de Grace, 0 males under 10, 0 males 10-16, 0 males 16-26, 1 male 26-45, 0 males 45+, 0 females under 10, 1 female 10-16, 1 female 16-26, 0 females 26-45, 1 female 45+, 0 free, 0 slaves

## 1810 MARYLAND CENSUS,Mdhr Index

Toxen, Christopher, Baltimore, pg.604, Pipe Creek

Tresler, David, Washington Co., pg.419, Jerusalem twp.

Tressler, J., Frederick Co., pg.411, no twp.

Rsh.110  Trisler, Valentine, Harford Co., pg.65, Harve De Grace

Trissler, G., Frederick Co., pg.424, no twp.

Trissler, M., Frederick Co., pg.424, no twp.

Truller, William , Baltimore Co., pg.666, Gunpowder

## 1810 Census Tabulations

Tresler, Jacob, Washington Co., pg.433, Jerusalem Township, 1 male under 10, 2 males 16-26, 1 male 16-45
Tresler, Jacob, Jerusalem, Upper Antietam Hundred, 2 males under 10, 1 male 16-26, 1 male 26-45, 1 female 26-45
Tressler, Jacob, Washington Co., pg.433, Jerusalem Township, which today is Funkstown, Md., 1 male under 10, 2 males 16-26, 1 male 16-45
Trisler, (Tristee,Tresler), Philip, Balt., pg.361, Baltimore, l male under 10, 1 male 10-16, no males 16-26, l male 26-45, l male 45+, females 3 under 10, l 10-16, l 16-26, l 26-45, l, 45+
Troxal, F., Frederick, pg.257, no twp., 1 male under 10, 1

male 16-26, 2 females under 10, 2 females 10-16, 1 female 16-26
Troxal, F., Frederick Co., pg.259, no twp., 1 male 26-45, 1 female under 10, 1 female 16-26

Troxal (Troseal), G., Frederick Co., pg.257, no twp., 1 male 16-26, 3 females under 10, 1 female 16-26, 2 slaves

Troxal, J., Frederick Co., pg.251, no twp., 1 male 16-26, 1 male 26-45, 1 male over 45, 2 females 16-26, 1 female 45+, 2 slaves

Troxal, M., Frederick Co., pg.256, no twp., 2 males under 10, 3 males 10-16, 1 male 16-26, 4 females under 10, ? females 10-16, 1 female 16-45

Troxal (Troseal), P., Frederick Co., pg.243, no twp., 1 male under 10, 1 male 26-45, 2 females under 10, 1 female 26-45

Rsh.5 A. Troxelll, Frederick, pg.293, no twp., 1 male under 10, 0 males 10-16, I male 16-26, 0 males 26- 45, 1 male 45+, 3 females under 10,0 females 10-16, 1 female 16-26, 1 female 26-45, 1 female 45+, 0 other free, 0 slaves, (Microfilm Mdhr M2060-6, pg.293,519)

Troxell, Daniel, Washington Co., Marsh Hundred,number 465, 1 male 10-16, 1 male 26-45, 1 female 26-45

Troxell, David, Washington Co., Marsh Hundred, Conochch. Dist., 09, 1 male 10-16, 1 male 26-45

Troxel, Peter, Washington Co., Fort Frederick, Hagerstown, pg.549,  3 males under 10, 1 male 10-16, 1 male 16-26, 1 male 26-45, 4 females under 10, 1 female 26-45

Troxet, Peter, Washington, 514, (Fort Frederick is to the west of Hagerstown, Md.), 1 male under 10, 3 males 10-16, 1 male 16-26, 1 male 26-45

### 1820 MARYLAND CENSUS, NA Index
Dressler, Henry, Frederick Co., pg.150, no twp.
Dressler, Jacob, Frederick Co., pg.150, no twp.
Trenkle, Jacob, Frederick Co., pg.142, no twp.
Teighter, Joseph, Washington Co., pg.73, 1st Elect. Dist.
Trickell, Fred, Washington Co., pg.112, 3rd Elect. Dist.
Troxal, Christian, Frederick Co., pg.179, no twp.
Troxel, David, Washington Co., pg.151, no twp.
Troxell, Elias, Frederick Co., pg.145, no twp.
Troxell, Frederick, Frederick Co., pg.146, no twp.
Troxell, Frederick, Frederick Co., pg.165, no twp.
Troxell, George, Frederick Co., pg.143, no twp.

Troxell, Jacob, Frederick, Co., pg.141, no twp.
Troxell, Jacob, Frederick Co., pg.162, no twp.
Troxell, Jacob of John, Frederick Co., pg.147, no twp.
Troxell, John, Frederick Co., pg.141, no twp.
Troxell, John, Frederick Co., pg.158, no twp.
Troxell, Mary, Frederick, Co., pg.145, no twp.
Troxell, Mary Magdalene, Frederick Co., pg.147, no twp.


### 1830 MARYLAND CENSUS, Mdhr,Index
Rsh.20  Trexler, Jonas P., Baltimore Co., pg.412, 11th Ward
Rsh.9  Trexler, Samuel, Baltimore Co., pg.210, 4th Ward
Trizzeler, Stephen, Baltimore Co., pg.201, 6th Coll


### 1840 MARYLAND CENSUS, Mdhr, Index
Tressler, Goodhart, Alle. Co., pg.087, Littlec.
Tressler, Joseph, Washington Co., pg.101, Hagerstown
Trexler, Benjamin, Washington Co., pg.98, Hagerstown
Trisler, George, Frederick Co., pg.109, Frederick
Trusler, Baltimore Co., pg.188, Baltimore


### 1850 MARYLAND CENSUS, Mdhr, Index
Tressel, Thomas,  Baltimore, pg.269, 20th Ward
Tressler, Goodhard, Alleghney Co., pg.87,  Little C.
Tressler, Joseph, Washington Co., pg.101, Hagerstown
Trexler, Catherine,  Baltimore, pg.385, 8th Ward
Trexler, Nancy, Frederick Co., pg.145, 10th Add.
Trexler, Mary, Baltimore pg.217, 19th Ward
Trisler, George, Frederick, pg.109, Frederick
Tabulations
Tressel, John,  Baltimore, pg.215, 2nd Ward, a Baker, b. Germany, 34 yrs. old

Tresler, Christian, Baltimore, pg.333,  3rd Ward, Boot and Shoe Maker, b. Germany 33 yrs. old

### 1870 MARYLAND CENSUS, Mdhr, Index, Partial Tabulation
Rsh.20 Dist. 5, Dorchester Co., Md., Household # 202 - Isaac


98

Trexler age 47 (b.c.1823)

## NEW JERSEY CENSUS

1830 CENSUS, NA
Elizabeth Traxler, HunterDon Co., New Jersey, Kingwood Township

## NORTH CAROLINA CENSUS

1790 Census Index - North Carolina, NA
Rsh.73 Troxler, Barney, pg.95, Orange Co., St.Asaphs Dist, Hillsboro
Troxler, Jacob, pg.96, Orange Co., St.Asaphs Dist., Hillsboro

1800 Census Index - North Carolina, NA
Rsh.123   John Trexeller, Rowan Co., pg.291, Roll 33
Rsh.122   Lawrence Trexeller, Rowan Co., pg.304
Rsh.123   Peter Trexeller, Rowan Co., pg.304
Peter Trexeller, Rowan Co., pg.310
John Trexler, Rowan Co., pg.278

Census Index - 1810 North Carolina, NA
Rsh.37 Adam Trexler, Rowan Co., pg.067, no twp.
Rsh.122   Jacob Trexler, Rowan Co., pg.078, no twp.
John Trexler, Rowan Co., pg.089, no twp.
Rsh.123   Peter Trexler, Rowan Co., pg.076, no twp.
Peter Trexler, Rowan Co., pg.040, no twp.

1820 Census Index - North Carolina, NA
Rsh.37 John Trexler, Rowan Co., pg.274, no twp.
John Trexler, Rowan Co., pg.280, Salisbury Twp.

note: In 1766 Salem was established by the Moravians it later became Winston-Salem. Salisbury is located south of Winston-Salem and north of Charlotte.

# SOUTH CAROLINA CENSUS

1800 Census Index, comp. Brent H. Holcomb, Baltimore
Genealogical. Pub. 1980
John Drexler, Charleston pg.122


# PENNSYLVANIA CENSUS

The following time line of county formation has been furnished to aid in tracing individual family units through the census records for Pennsylvania:

Adams, seated in Gettysburg, was formed in 1800 from York Co.

Allegheny seated Pittsburgh formed 1787 from Westmoreland, Washington

Beaver seated Beaver formed 1800 from Allegheny, Washington

Berks seated Reading formed 1752 from Bucks, Lancaster, Philadelphia

Bucks, seated in Doylestown, is an original county with census reports from 1790-1880

Cambria seated Ebensburg (Loretto area) formed 1804 from Somerset, Bedford, Huntington

Chester seated West Chester, original County formed 1682

Cumberland seated Carlisle formed 1750 from Lancaster

Delaware, seated Media, formed 1789 from Chester

Franklin seated Chambersburg formed 1784 from Cumberland

Huntington, seated in Huntington, was formed in 1787 from Bedford Co.

Lancaster, seated in Lancaster, was formed in 1729 from Chester

Lehigh seated Allentown formed from Northampton

Luzerene, seated in Wilkes-Barre, was formed in 1786 from Northumberland

Lycoming, seated in Williamsport, was formed in 1795 from Northumberland

Montgomery seated Norristown formed 1784 from Philadelphia

Northampton seated Easton formed 1752 from Bucks

Philadelphia, seated in Philadelphia, was formed in 1682, original county

Washington seated Washington formed 1781 from Westmoreland

Westmoreland, seated in Greensburg, was fromed in 1773 from Bedford

York Co, seated in York, was formed in 1749 from Lancaster


note:    In addition to a formal Census Index and recorded Census Tabulations, additional data is presented in this section to serve as a census, because it indicates that an individual was in a certain area during a given time period.

A New Index to Lancaster County, Pennsylvania, before Federal Census, Vol.1, Index to 1780 Tax Records, Gary T. Hawbaker and Clyde L. Gross, Hershey Pa., 1981,call F157.L2H39 Vol.1
Rsh.27, David Trissler, year 1770, Lancaster, Sadler (shown as Drisler, in 1772)
Rsh.27, David Trissler, Lancaster Borough, 81, Oath Taken
Rsh.79, George Trissler, Lancaster Borough, 81 Oath Taken

New Index to Lancaster before the Federal Census, Vol.5, Index to 1770 Tax Records, Gary T. Hawbaker and Clyde L. Groff

Rsh.27, David Trissler, year 1770, Lancaster Borough, Sadler; shown as Drisler in year 1772

Michael Traxall, 1770, Paxton, Assessment of Non-Assoc.

Abraham Traxel, 1769, Lebanon, Farm

Christian Traxel, 1759, Leacock, Freemen for Themselves

John Traxel, 1769, Londonderry, 1775

## 1790 Pennsylvania Census Index

?Rsh.43, Troxell, Daniel, pg.290, York Co., Mixed Twp.

Rsh.79, Tresler, George, pg.277, York Co., Paradise Twp.

Trackseler, Daniel, Leehigh Co.,Whitehall Twp.

?Rsh.9  Traxeler, Jacob, Leehigh Co., Whitehall Twp.

Traxler, Peter, Leehigh Co.,Whitehall Twp.

Rsh.24, Traxel, Adam, Leehigh Co., Whitehall Twp.

Trexeler, Jaramiah pg.176, Northampton Co.

Rsh.88, Trexeler, Jermiah, pg.163 Montgomery Co.

Rsh.85, Trexeler, Peter, pg.176, Northampton Co.

Rsh.87, Trexeler, Peter,Jr. pg.176, Northampton Co.

Rsh.5, Trexell, Anthony, pg.290, York Co.

Trexler, David, pg.204, Philadelphia Co.

Trexler, Joseph, pg.164 Montgomery Co.

Trexler, Lawrantz pg.166 Montgomery Co.

Troxel, Jacob, Montgomery Co.

?Rsh.43 Trexell, Daniel, York Co.

Special Publication #18, April 1982, 1800 Census, Adams County, Pa., compiled by Wm. C. Lightner, pub. by South Central Pennsylvania Genealogical Society,Inc.,P.O.Box 1824, York, Pa., 17405

Tabulations

pg.478,  Cumberland Co., Trexel, Jacob, 1M 45, 1F 10, 1F 26

?Rsh.6, pg.473 Cumberland Co., Trexel, Anthony, 1M 26, 1F 26

pg.497, Straban Co., Troshell, George, 1M 10, 2M 26, 1F 10, 1F 45

pg.476, Cumberland Co., Truxel, David, 1M 10, 1F 10, 1F 16, 3F 26, 1F 45

?Rsh.170, pg.478 Cumberland Co, Truxel, John, 3M 10, 1M 16, 1M 45+, 2F 10, 1F 16, 1F 45

1800 Census Index, Pennsylvania Census, Vol. 2, Ronald Vern Jackson, Ed., Accelerated Indexing Systems 1972, copyright, 1972, RVJ, AIS, Inc. 3346 So. Orchard Drive, Bountiful, Utah 84010, and NA Index

Deshler, Adam, Northampton Co., pg.535
Deshler, widow, Northampton Co., pg.598
Deshler, Charles, Esq, Northampton Co., pg.598
Deshler, David, Northampton Co., pg.639
Deshler, David, Northampton Co., pg.519
Deshler, Peter, Jr., Northampton Co., pg.520
Deshler, Peter, Sr., Northampton Co., pg.520
Dissler, David, Lancaster Co., pg.194
Dissler, Jacob, Lancaster Co., pg.194
Disler, John, Berks Co., pg.642
Draxell, Adam, Northampton Co., pg.639
Draxell, Daniel, Northampton Co., pg.639
Draxell, Jacob, Northampton Co., pg.639
Draxell, John, Northampton Co., pg.639
Draxell, Lawrence, Northampton Co., pg.639
Draxell, Peter, Northampton Co., pg.639
Draxell, Peter, Northampton Co., pg.639
Draxell, Peter, son of David, Northampton Co., pg.639
Draxell, Peter, Jr., Northampton Co., pg.639
Dresh, Andreas, Northampton Co., pg.611
Dresh, Dewalt, Northampton Co., pg.611
Dresher, Abraham, Montgomery Co., pg.851
Dresher, George, Montgomery Co., pg.873
Dresher, Samuel, Berks Co., pg.692
Dressler, Andrew, Northampton Co., pg.631
Dressler, David, Berks Co., pg.605
Rsh.79, Dresler, George, York Co., pg.1336
Dressler, Jacob, Berks Co., pg.692
Dressler, Jacob, Berks Co., pg.665
Dressler, Peter, Berks Co., pg.605
?Rsh.124, Drexler, John, York Co., pg.1358
Drish, Adam, Lancaster Co., pg.64
Drischol, Charles, Lancaster Co., pg.194
Drissel, John, Bucks Co., pg.244
Drissel, Olery, Bucks Co., pg.244
Driskle, Charles, Adams Co., pg.520
Driskle, James, Adams Co., pg.504

Driskle, Charles, Adams Co., pg.504
Druch, George, York Co., pg.1318
Drucher, Martin, York Co., pg.1339
Traseler, Michael, Huntington Co., pg.143
Trastle, John, Berks Co., pg.567
Trastle, Jacob, York Co., pg.1336
?Rsh.137, Trastle, Henry, Berks Co., pg.567
?Rsh.136, Trastle, George, Berks Co., pg.567
Draxal, Abraham, Daulphin Co., Pa., pg.214
Traxal, Abraham, Jr., Daulphin Co., Pa., pg.214
Traxel, Abraham, Northumberland Co., pg.728
Traxel, Henry, Berks Co., pg.550
Traxel, John, Berks Co., pg.589
Traxel, John, Daulphin Co., Pa., pg.214
Trefsler, Godhart, Somerset Co., pg.534 - 21001-2100100
Treisler, Jacob, Northampton Co., pg.02
Tresecl, Jacob, Adams Co., pg.478
Tresler, Daniel, Berks Co., pg.624
?Rsh.45 Tresler, David, Montgomery Co., pg.849
Tresler, Philip, Bucks Co., pg.239
Tresley, Jacob, Philadelphia Co., pg.499
Tresley, George, Philadelphia Co., pg.499
?Rsh.166,Trexler, Cooney, 142:04, Cumberland Co., STL, pg.278
Trexler, David, 117:07, Montgomery Co., Whitparrie
Trexler, Jeremiah, 67:07, Montgomery Co., Moreland
Trexler, Jeremiah,, Northampton Co., pg.584
Trexler, Jeremiah, 062A:03 Northampton Co., MC Twp., pg.584
Trexler, John, 062A:03 Northampton Co.,MC Twp., pg.584
Trexler, Jonathan, 062A:03 Northampton Co., MC Twp.
Trexler, Joseph, 7l:07, Montgomery Co., Norriton Twp. pg.757
Trexler, Peter, 142:04, Cumberland Co., Shippensburg Twp.
Trexler, Peter, Montgomery Co., pg.893
Rsh.165, Trexler, Peter, Cumberland Co., pg.279
Trexler, Peter, Berks Co., pg.621
Trexler, Peter, Northampton Co. pg.58
Rsh.7, Trexler, Michael, Cumberland Co., Hopewell Twp. pg.273
Trexler, Philip, Cumberland Co., Hopewell Twp., pg.274
Trexley, David, Philadelphia Co., pg.93
Trexter, Jonathan, Northampton Co., pg.584
Trexter, Jonathan, Northampton Co., pg.584
Trish, Christian, Bedford Co.,pg.436

Trisler, Jacob, Northampton Co., pg.666
Trisler, David, Lancaster Co., pg.40
Trisler, Philip, Bucks Co., pg.98
Trissel, John, Bucks Co., pg.285
Trissel, Joseph, Bucks Co., pg.285
Rsh.28, Trissler, John, Lancaster Co., pg.33
Trixler, Peter, Northampton Co., pg.667
Trixler, David, Montgomery Co., pg.835
Rsh.120, Trostle, Abraham, York Co., pg.1337
Trostle, John , York Co., pg.1341
Troxel, Christian, Berks Co., pg.690
Troxell, George, Northampton Co.,pg.538
Troxel, Jacob, Bucks Co., pg.238
Rsh.19, Troxel, John, Huntington Co., pg.150
Troxell, John, Northampton Co., pg.538
Troxell, Michael, Northampton Co., pg.538
Troxell, Nicholas, Northampton Co., pg.538
Troshell, George, Adams Co., pg.497
Trushel, Jacob, Lancaster Co., pg.270
Trushe, Lewis, Philadelphia, Pa., pg.126
?Rsh.27 Truxel, David, Adams Co., Cumberland Twp., pg.476
Rsh.170 Truxel, John, Adams Co., Cumberland Twp., pg.478
Truxel, Jacob, Bedford Co., pg.383
Tuxler, Jeremiah, Montgomery Co., pg.749

Tabulations, NA
Rsh.6 Trexel, Anthony, pg.8, reel 1, Adams Co, CB Township,
Anthony Trexel,  Adams, pg.473-7, Cumberland Dist. 1 male 16-
45 1 female 16-45

Trexel, Jacob, 10:01  Adams Co. Cumberland Dist., Ad pg.478,
10, Cumberland Dist, 1 male 26-44.

Index to the Pennsylvania Census of 1810, compiled by the Ohio
Family Historials, published 1966 by MicroPhoto Division, Bell and
Howell Co., Cleveland, Ohio 44112
Dishler, Thomas, Berks Co., Bern Twp., pg.670
Disler, Goopey, Berks Co., Bern Twp., pg.671
Dissler, Jacob, York Co., Windsor Twp., pg.1084
Dissler, John, Berks Co., Reading Twp., pg.593
Dissler, John, Berks Co., Reading Twp., pg.595

Traxel, George, Northampton Co., Easton Boro., pg.71
Traxel, Jacob, Northampton Co., Easton Boro., pg.109
Traxel, Michael, Northampton Co., Easton Boro., pg.70
Traxel, Nicholas, Northampton Co., Easton Boro., pg.71
Traxel, Nicholas, Northampton Co., Easton Boro., pg.109
Traxeler, Peter, Northampton Co., Shamokin Twp., pg.271
Treasler, Adam, Bedford Co., Woodberry Twp., pg.520
Treasler, Daniel, Centre Co., Potter Twp.
Treichel, Chas, Phila City, No. Mulberry Wd. pg.367
Treichler, Abm, Montgomery Co., Upper Providence, pg.1221
Treisler, Conrad, York Co., Hanover Twp., pg.129
Tresher, Conrad, Berks Co., Longswamp Twp., pg.789
Tresher, John, Berks Co., Longswamp Twp., pg.789
Tresher, Lorentz, Berks Co., Longswamp Twp., pg.789
Tresher, Phillip, Berks Co., Longswamp Twp., pg.789
Tresher, Samuel, Berks Co., Longswamp Twp., pg.789
Tresler, Andrew, Cumberland Co., Toboine Twp., pg.104
Tresler, Jacob, Phila Co., Lower Dublin Twp., pg.45
Tresler, John, Northampton Co., Macungie Twp., pg.22
Tresler, Philip, Bucks Co., Haycock Twp., pg.995
Tresler, Philip, Bucks Co., Hilltown Twp., pg.980
Treslor, Anderson, Mifflin Co., Greenwood Twp., pg.973
Tressel, Christian, Washington Co., Strabane Twp., pg.539-14
Tressel, John, Bucks Co., Tinicum Twp., pg.984
Tressler, Jacob, Berks Co., Rockland Twp., pg.851
Tressler, Jacob, Berks Co., Upper Mahantongo Twp., pg.824
Tressler, Samuel, Somerset Co., Brothers Valley Twp., pg.404
Tressler, Jacob, Berks Co., Rockland Twp., pg.851
Tressler, Jacob, Berks Co., Union Twp., pg.824
Trester, Daniel, Berks Co., Bern Twp., pg.660
?Rsh.11 Trexel, Henry, Montgomery Co., U.Hanover Twp., pg.235
Trexel, John, Adams Co., Gettysburg Twp., pg.86
Trexel, John Jr., Adams Co., Gettysburg Twp., pg.86
Trexler, Charles, Northampton Co., Macungie Twp., pg.22
Trexler, David, Montgomery Co., Plymouth Twp., pg.205
Trexler, George, Philadelphia Co., N. Liberties Twp., pg.181
Trexler, Jacob, Philadelphia Co., Upper Delaware Ward, pg.166
Trexler, Jeremiah, Montgomery Co., Abingdon Twp., pg.60
Trexler, Jeremiah, Northampton Co.,Macungie Twp., pg.22
Trexler, John, Northampton Co., Macungie Twp., pg.22
Trexler, John, Montgomery Co., Upper Dublin Twp., pg.228

Trexler, John, Esq., York Co.,Codorus Twp., pg.1132
Trexler, Joseph, York Co., York Twp., pg.1021
Trexler, Peter, Northampton Co., Macungie Twp., pg.22
Trexler, Rachel, Montgomery Co., pg.229 Upper Dublin
Trexler, Samuel, Somerset Co., Brothers Valley Twp., pg.404
Trichler, Jacob, Bucks Co., Springfield Twp., pg.922
Trishler, Barbara, York Co., Hellam Twp., pg.1031
Trisler, Philip, Bucks Co., Bedminister Twp., pg.990
Trissel, Joseph, Bucks Co., Tinicum Twp., pg.984
Trissler, no lst name, Lancaster Co., Lancaster Boro, pg.595
Trissler, George, Lancaster Co., Lancaster Boro. pg.596
Trissler, John, Lancaster Co., Lancaster Boro. pg.597
Trostel, Abraham, York Co., Paradise Twp., pg.1004
Trostel, Henry, York Co., Paradise Twp., pg.1000
Trostel, Jacob, York Co., Paradise Twp., pg.1009
Trostel, John, York Co., Paradise Twp., pg.1007
Trostel, William, York Co., Paradise Twp., pg.1004
Trostle, Abraham, York Co., Paradise Twp., pg.1017
Trostle, Jacob, Lancaster Co., Caernarvon Twp., pg.455
Troxall, Jeremiah Sr., Northampton Co., Macungie Twp., pg.22
Troxall, John, Northampton Co., Macungie, Twp., pg.22
Troxall, Jonathan, Northampton Co., Macungie, Twp., pg.22
Troxel, Abraham, Westmoreland Co., Mt.Pleasant Twp., pg.827
?Rsh.27 Troxel, David, Adams Co., Cumberland Twp., pg.112
Troxel, Jacob, Cambria Co., Allegheny Twp., pg.15
Troxel, Jacob, Westmoreland Co., Unity Twp., pg.805
Troxel, John, Berks Co., Cumru Twp., pg.696
Rsh.19, Troxel, John, Westmo. Co., E.Huntington Twp., pg.828
Troxell, George, Northumberland Co., Lewisbury Twp., pg.328
Troxell, John, Northumberland Co., Beaver Twp., pg.280
Rsh.17, Troxler, G.,Huntington Co., Tyrone Twp., pg.217
Rsh.17, Troxler, M., Huntington Co., Dublin Twp., pg.210
Troxsell, Christian, Northampton Co., Whitehall Twp., pg.42
Troxsell, Christian, Northampton Co., Whitehall Twp., pg.43
?Rsh.11 Troxtell, H., Huntington Co., Alleghany Twp., pg.220A
?Rsh.11 Troxtell, J., Huntington Co., Alleghany Twp., pg.157
?Rsh.11 Troxtell, J., Huntington Co., Alleghany Twp., pg.220A
Trussel, Henry, Washington Co., Amwell Twp., pg.642
Trussell, David, Fayette Co., Luzerne Twp., pg.964
Truster, Martin, Northumberland Co., Berlin Twp., pg.329
Truxale, Adam, Westmoreland Co., Hempfield Twp., pg.851

Truxale, Jacob, Westmoreland Co., Hempfield Twp., pg.851
Truxall, Abraham, Northum.Co., Chillisquaque Twp., pg.362
Truxel, Christian, Mercer Co., Springfield Twp., pg.935
Truxel, Daniel, Westmoreland Co., Greensburgh Boro., pg.830
Truxile, Joseph, Adams Co., Tyrone Twp., pg.2

Tabulations, NA
Trexler, John, Esq., pg.209, York Co., Codorus Twp., 1 male 45+
Trexler, Joseph, pg.153, 1021, York Borough, 1 male under 10, 1
    male 26-45, 1 female under 10, 1 female 26-45
Trexler, Solomon, pg.209, York Co., Codorus Twp., pg.208/1132,
    1 male under 10, 1 male 26-45, 2 females under 10, 1
    female 26-45
Trisler, George, pg.596, Lancaster Borough, Pa., 1 male under
    10, 1 male 10-16, 1 male 16-26, 1 male 26-45, 4 females
    under 10, 1 female 16-26, 1 female 26+
Rsh.120 Trostle, Abraham, pg.151, Borough of York, #1011, 1
    male 45+, 2 females 26-45, others I
Trostle, George, Adams Co., pg.93, Strabon Twp., 1 male 10-16,
    3 males 26-45, 1 female 10-16, 1 female 26-45
Trostle, Peter, Adams Co., pg.70, Manallen Twp., 1 male 10-16,
    1 male 16-26, 1 male 45+, female under 10, 2 females
    16-26, 3 females 45+, I other, 1 slave.
Troxel, David, Adams Co., pg.2, Cumberland Town, 1 dist.
    pg.112, 1 male 16-26, 1 female 16-26

## 1820 PENNSYLVANIA CENSUS, NA, Index
Tessier, Anthony, Philadelphia City, South Ward pg.153
Tessler, Jesse, York Co., E. Manche, pg.67
Trexler, George, Philadelphia, Kensengl, pg.141
Trexler, Jacob, Philadelphia, Upper De, pg.200
Trexler, John, Philadelphia City, 5th Ward, pg.026

## VIRGINIA CENSUS

### 1787 Census Index, NA
note in index: Also see surname spelling Snoxall
#'s are: Whi.21+, Whi. 16+, Bla.16+, Bla.16-, Horses
Andrew Tresler, 0, 0, 0, 3, 6, Shenandoah Co.
Jacob Tresler
George J. Troxall, 0,0,0,0,0, Loudoun Co.

Adam Troxell, 0,0,0,3,0, Augusta Co.
John Troxell, 0, 0,0, 3, 6, Hardy Co.
John Snoxall, 0,0,1,1,2, Stafford Co.
Edward Snoxall, 1,0,0,3,5, Stafford Co.
Ann Snoxable, 0,0,0,1,3, Stafford Co.
Sarsfield Snoxable, 0,0,0,1,3, Stafford Co.

## 1790 Census, NA, Virginia

Tresler, Andrew, T498, Roll 3 , pg.64, Shenandoah Co, 11 white
souls, no blacks, census taker, Alex Hite

## 1810 Census, NA, Virginia

Tesler, George, Shenandoah Co., pg.29
Trisler, George, Frederick Co., pg.328
Trisler, Kitty, Frederick Co., pg.329
Trisler, Mary, Frederick Co., pg.328
Tresler, Philip, Shenandoah Co., pg.31
Tressah, Robert, Rockbridge Co., pg.395
Troxtell, David, Washington Co., pg.205
Troxale, Daniel, Rockbridge Co., pg.403
Tressel, David, Rockbridge Co., pg.132
Troxtell, Deniel, Washington Co., pg.205
Trossler, Henry, Boutetourt Co., pg.645
Troshcver, George, Berkley Co., pg.571
Tresler, Philip, Shenandoah Co., Roll 71, pg.31 00201-04

## 1820 Census, NA, Virginia

Tresler, Ignatius, HnCo 193 Richmond,Tresler, Ignatius
Henrico Co.,pg.193, City of Richmond  Roll 131, page 192
A
Trester, Mary  Fred 046 no twp.
Tresler, George, Frederick #138, 045,  no. twp.
Tressler, Elizabeth, Botetoute Co. #130, 074 no twp.
Henry Tressler and William Tressler
Trissle, Abraham, Rockbridge Co., pg.169, no twp.
Trissle, David, Rockbridge, Co., pg.168, no. twp.
Trissle, Jacob, Rockbridge, Co., pg.168, no twp.
Trissle, Joseph, Rockbridge, Co., pg.168, no twp.
Troxall, Abraham, Augusta, Co., pg.007 mixed twp.
Troxall,David, Augusta Co., pg.007, mixed twp.

Troxall, Peter, Augusta Co., pg.84, mixed twp.
Troxall, Peter, Augusta Co., pg.07, mixed twp.
Truxell, Jacob, Frederick Co., pg.4, no twp.
Truxell, John, Frederick Co., pg.15, no twp.

## 1830 Census, NA, Virginia

Rsh.76, Trixler, Nancy , Richmond, Henrico, Roll 195, pg.400,
Monroe Ward, 1 male, age. 10-15, 1 male, age 15-20, 1 female
under 5, 2 females age 5 to 10, 1 female of 20 and under 30
Trexler, Ann, Frederick Co., pg.153, Roll #190 Winchester
Trexler, George, Frederick Co., pg.153, Roll #190, Winchester
Tresslett, Nathaniel, Fauquier Co, pg.484
Teshler, Abraham, Rockbridge Co., pg.269
Tristler, Mary, Frederick Co., Winchester
Trisler, Jacob, Ohio Co., pg.282, Wheeling

## 1840 Census, NA, Virginia

Tresler, Susan,  Fairfax, Roll 558, Fairfax Co., Va., #156,
Trishler, Jacob, Jr., Mono., pg.80, E. Monog
Trishler, George, Ohio, pg.66, Wheeling
Trissell, Joseph, Rockbridge, pg.101, no twp.
Trisler, Joel, Ohio, pg.74, Wheeling
Troxall, Abraham, Augusta, pg.42, no twp.
Troxall, Peter, Augusta, pg.42, no twp.
Troxel, Daniel, Jr., Wash, pg.251, no twp.
Troxel, Daniel, Sr., Wash., pg.251, no twp.
Trussel, F., Ohio, pg.78, Wheeling
Trussel, John, Clair, pg.10, no twp.
Trussel, Nimrod, Clair, pg.010, no twp.
Trussel, Thomas, Loudoun, pg.152, Jonah HO
Truxell, Daniel, Ohio, pg.60, Wheeling
Truxell, John, Ohio, pg.59, Wheeling

## 1850 Census, NA, Virginia

Tresler, Joseph, Richmond, pg.191, Lunenburg Co.
Trisler, Casper, Ohio, pg.160, 44th Dist
Trisler, David, Mono, pg.284, 36th Dist
Trisler, George, Ohio, pg.139, 44th
Trisler, James, Ohio, pg.131, 44th
Trisler, Joel, Ohio, pg.126, 44th
Trisler, John, Preston, pg.349, 45th

Trisler, Lewis, Fairfax, pg.113, no twp.
Trisler, Peter, Fairfax, pg.114, no twp.
Trisler, Samuel, Mono, pg.288, 36th
Trisler, Susan, Alexan., pg.316, Alex.
Trisler, William, Ohio, pg.,209, 44th
Trissell, Jacob, Rockbridge, pg.312, 57th
Troxell, Abraham, Augusta, pg.281, 2nd
Troxell, Andrew, Rockbridge, pg.422, 51st
Troxell, David, Augusta, pg.285, 2nd
Troxell, Jeremiah, Augusta, pg.280, 2nd
Troxell, Phillip, Brax(u), pg.221, Dist.
Troxell, Rachael, Augusta, pg.281, 2nd
Troxell, Sarah J., Augusta, pg.280, 2nd
Troxwell, William, Morg, pg.87, Bath 42n
Trussel, John, Jeff, pg.422, Harpers Ferry
Rsh.79, Albright, Christian age 38, male, born Europe, value real
estate 150, Albright, Mary Ann, pg.29, female, born Va., Joseph,
8, male, born Va., Eutau, 7,male, born Va., Christian, 3 male, born
VA.
Rsh.79 Albright, Geo.(Gottleib),40, male, born Germany,
profession Carpenter, value real estate 800, Rosetta, 24, female,
born Va., Virginia, 4, female, born Va., Mary, 2, female, born Va.
Rsh.140, Trexeler, William, Henrico Co., Roll 951, pg.291,
Richmond, occupation Cooper, real estate worth 1500, born 1815
in Maryland, 35 years old, living in Henrico Co., Nancy Trexler,
wife, age 31, born 1819 in Virginia, Ignatius Trexler b. 1845, age
5, male born Va., Rosetta Trexler, age 3, female, born Va.,
Isabella Trexler, age 1, female, born Va., Nancy Trexler, age 60,
born 1790, female, born in Maryland.

## 1860, Census, NA, Virginia

Trexler, Nancy, Henrico Co., Va., #650, 3rd Ward,Richm.,
Ennum. in household of, William Gibhardt, age. 33, male,
silvermaker, birthplace Prussia, Married within year to Mildred
Gibhardt, age 32, female, birthplace Prussia, Albert Gibhardt, 3/12
male born Virginia, Nancy Trexler age 34, Born 1826, birthplace
Maryland.

Rsh.79, Trexler, John, Franklin Co., Va. #321, Boons Mill P.O.
Age 42, born 1818, occupation Cooper, born Virginia. (note:

birthplace Virginia is in error as his birth is shown in Maryland Church Records). Counted with household of Jaeah Neff, age 60, and wife Susan Neff, age 55, children Mary Neff, female, age 25, Susan Neff, female age 23, Magnadline Neff, male age 21, Isaac Neff, age 17 male, William Neff, age 13, male and Daniel Hunt, age 23, male, a Carpenter.

Tresler, Peter, Fairfax Co., Va., born 1789 in Fairfax Va., Farmer, 4000 value real estate, 2500 value personal property, pg.814, S.O.& A.R. Rd.

Trusler, Hezekiah, Nelson Co., pg.757, Rockfish P.O.

Trusler, John, Augusta Co., pg.572, Staunton P.O.

Trusler, John, Nelson Co., pg.760, Rockfish P.O.

Trusler, Joseph, Nelson Co., pg.757, Rockfish P.O.

Trusler, Julia. Nelson Co., pg.758, Rockfish P.O.

Trusler, Mary, Augusta Co., pg.1089, BurkesMill P.O.

Trusler, Richard, Rockbridge Co., pg.258,Lexington P.O.

Trusler, William, Augusta Co., pg.683, Staunton P.O.

Triall, Elizabeth, Fluvanna Co., pg.748, Central

Triall, Stephen, Fluvanna Co., pg.747, Scottsville

Troxall, Jeremiah, Augusta Co., pg.691, Stanton

Tressell, Charles, Clark Co., pg.629, Castlemans Ferry

Trussell, Archibald, Loudoun Co., pg.575, Paris P.O.

Trussell, Moses B., Clark Co., pg.627, Castlemans Ferry

Trussell, Samuel, Frederick Co., pg.699, Stephensburg P.O.

Trussell, Thomas, Loudoun Co., pg.575, Paris P.O.

Trussell, Thomas W., Frederick Co., pg.518, Winchester P.O.

Troxall, David, Augusta Co., pg.672, Staunton P.O.

Troxall, Jane, Augusta Co., pg.691, Stanton P.O.

Troxall, William H., Augusta Co., pg.691, Staunton

Troxall, Abraham, Augusta Co., pg.690, Staunton

Troxell, William, Washington Co., pg.529, Liberty Hall P.O.

Troxey, H., Meckbg., pg.201, Clarksville P.O.

Troxwell, George W., Washington Co., pg.525, Liberty Hall P.O.

Troxwell, Greenbury, Washington Co., pg.526, Liberty Hall P.O.

Rsh140, Liggon, Albert, Henrico Co., pg.546, 3rd Ward, Richmond, Va. July 29, 1860, 607 family contacted, age 45 male, profession, City Police, value real estate owned 2,500, born Virginia, Nancy Liggon, age 38, female, Reuben H. Liggon, age 1yr, male, (Rsh.142) Ignatius Txler, age 16, male, school within year, (Rsh.138) William Txler, age 5, male, Robert Blackburn, age 40, male, City Police.

## 1870 Census, NA, Virginia

Tresler, Jesse Wise, age 14, m, w, (born) Va., Jacksonville Twp., Floyd Co., Va.

Tresler, Susan, age 50, f, w, Va., 4th Ward, Alexandria, Va.

Trisler, Lewis, age 43, m, w, Va., 3rd Ward Alexandria,Va., Rsh. 105

Treser, Ann, age 34, f, w, Va., St. George Parish, Accomack
M593, 1673

## 1880 Census NA, Virginia

Trusler, Jessee W., w, m, age 23, Va.. living Floyd Co., Jacksonville Dist., Nancy Trusler, wife, age 22 Va., John M. Trusler, son age 1 Va., James W. Trusler, son Age. 2 born Va., Horlilly M. Trusler Dau. 3 1/2 born Va..

## Virginia 1890, Special Census of Veterans, Ronald Vern Jackson, Accelerated Indexing Systems International

Charles T. Trexler, Elizabeth City, Va., 148, National Home for Disabled Veterans.

George W. Trexler, Elizabeth City, Va. 078, National Home for Disabled Veterans

## 1900 Census, NA, Virginia - Soundex T624

Traxler, Frederick, Vol. 3, Ed. 99, Sheet 5, Line 95 White, Jan 17, Age 24, Switzerland birthplace, Alexandria Co., Va., Enn. Ft. Meyer Troop H. 3rd Calvery, Private.

Troxler, G.W., Vol. 26, Ed. 30, Sheet 12, line 84, white, Nr Henrico Co., Fairfield Dist. 21st Street (living alone)

Tresler, Isaac N., white, June 1851, age 48 years, birthplace Pennsylvania, living Henrico Co., Fairfield Dist., Annie E. Tresler, wife 3/1856 , age 44, born Maryland, Rosa Mary, dau. 8/81, age 18, born Pennsylvania, Clara C., dau. 6/1884, age 15, born Pennsylvania, Trosler, Myrtle, born July 1895, age 5, born in Va., enumerated with Southward, Zawood, grandfather.

Tresler, Oscar T., born Oct. 1876, age 23, born in New Jersey, living in Henrico Co., Fairfield Dist., at 1216 State Street, wife, Lilian Tresler, born Oct. 1873, age 26, born in Md.

Troxler, Samuel D., born Feb. 1873, age 27, born in N.C., living in Henrico Bookland Dist., Northside, 4th Avenue. Boarder with Elizabeth M. Williams.

Rsh.138, Trexler, William, occupation carpenter, born May 1863,
age 37, born in Va., living Richmond at 508 Delsom
Street, wife, Mary born July 1851, age 48, born in
Va.,dau. Rosa, born Sept. 1882, age 17, Va., dau.Eva,
born June 1884, Age 15, Va., dau. Minnie, born Aug.
1890, age 9, Va.., son Willie born Feb. 1894, age 6,
Va.,ED 67, sheet 10, Line 47, National Archives Roll 1738.

## 1910 Census, NA, Virginia

Troxler, Eva,, granddaughter, 6 years old, Andrew, grandson, 13
years old, Myrtle, granddaughter, 17 years old, Katie,
granddaughter, 7 years old, Enumerated with grandfather,
Southworth, Zazhary

Truxler, Forest, B.O. age 32, both parents born Va., Richmond
City, enumerated with Mary Layne

Tresler, Oscar B. born 1877, age 33, father born in Maryland,
Mother born in Va., wife, Lillian age 37, born New Jersey,
dau., Margaret E. age 7 born Va., dau. Ellie, age 7 born
Va., son Henry, age 4, born Va., dau. Nora I. age 2 born
Va.

Trexler, Walter H., born 1874, age 36 father born N.C. mother
born Va., living in Washington, Abingdon, 098 0122 0094
wife, Manewa age 26 born N.C., son, Bernard age 4 born
N.C., dau. Ruth, 2 years old, born N.C., son, Walter R.J.,
no age recorded, born Va.

**F.**  **CHURCH RECORDS**

## EUROPE
## FRANCE

Private Researcher and Contributor to Morman Records - Carolyn Reinbold, 998 Bloomington Drive South, St. George, Ut 84770 Copyright 1987

Rsh.22, Trachsel, Troxell, Peter, b. 11/6/1691, Lenk, Bern Switzerland, d. 4/16/1766, Frederick Co., Md., bu. Jordan Reformed Church, Frederick Co., Md.

> Wife: Anna Juliana Catharina Trauthager, Fraudhueger, Freydinger, Freidig, Freydig, Fraudhueger, b. 1703, Katzenthal Alsace France, d. 1795, father, Johannes Hans Trauthager, mother Barbara Jaggi Jacky

> children:

1. Rsh.58, Troxell, II, Peter, b. 12/28/1723, Katzenthal Alsace France, d. 2/28/1811, Lehigh Co., Pa., m. 5/19/1747, one wife. authors note: the records indicate he m. a second time.
2. Trachsel, Johann Jacob, b. 2/16/1723, Katzenthal Alsace France
3. Rsh.43, Trachsel, Johann Daniel, b. 12/8/1726 Katzenthal Alsace France d. 1814 m. Sophia Dotterer.
4. Traxhsel, Maria Barbara, b. 9/17/1728, Katzenthal Alsace France
5. Rsh.52, Trachsel, David, b. 7/27/1734, Egypt, Whitehall Twp., Lehigh, Pa.
6. Rsh.147, Trachsel, Johannes, b. 10/26/1736, Egypt Whitehall Twp., Lehigh Pa., d. 10/1795, w. Maria Margaretha
7. Rsh.15, Trachsel, Christian, (twin) c. 4/16/1739 Egypt Whitehall Twp., Lehigh Pa.
8. Trachsel, Juliana Margaretha, c. 4/16/1739, Egypt, Whitehall Twp.
9. Rsh.13, Trachsel, George Frederick, c. 7/28/1741 Egypt Whitehall, d. 1796 m. Appollonia Lay (Loy)
10. Troxell, Mary Margaret, b. 10/25/1744, Egypt Whitehall Twp., m. Abraham Wotring

note: some of these births can be found in Pennsylvania Archives, 6th Series, Vol. 6, pgs.5,6,8,133

# GERMANY

YCHS File 1879

Rsh.21, Dressler, Sr., Johann Andreas, Tressler, George David, Rsh.54 Dressler, Jr., Johann Andreas, Rsh.134 Dressler, Johann Jacob, are each found in the Parish Register at Jagsthausen, District of Heilbronn, Wurtemberg.

# USA
# MARYLAND

## Anglican

Cecil Co., Md., St. Stephen's Parish, Cecil Co., Md., MHS
Preslar, Andreas and Wells, Ant Je Ann, children: Presler, Andrew b. 2/4/1732, Presler, Christian c. 6/6/1725, Presler, John Volintine c. 1/9/1726, Presler, Sarah c. 5/24/1728, Presler, Thomas, c. Aug. 27, 1730
>   author's note: Presler is included here because one variation of the subject surnames beginning with the letter P. is found in several records. Most notably this variation has taken the form of Prexley.

Cecil Co., Md. Early Anglican Church Records of Cecil Co., by Henry C. Peden, Jr., Family Line Publications, 1990
pg.32, St. Stephen's Parish (North Sassafras Parish) Andrew Prosler son of Andrew and Ann, grandson of John Vollintine Prosler b. 2/4/1732/3

St. Andrews Parish St. Mary's Co., Md. 1728-1886 - Vol. 1, MHS Leonardtown
Ticklen, Jeremiah, St. Mary's Co., Md.

## Catholic

The northern part of Maryland is on the border of Pennsylvania and includes an area that was disputed for several years by both Pennsylvania and Maryland, and ultimately settled by the Mason Dixon Survey Line. Those individuals researching families in this area should be aware that the area was initially served by the Jesuits from Southern Maryland and was later served by the Mission at Conewago, Pennsylvania. The site of the Conewago Mission was located in 1995 in Adams Co., Pa. This Mission, which also served all of Western Maryland, attracted many settlers from the Catholic Mission at Bally, Gosenhoppen, Washington Co., Pa.

Baltimore, Md. Early Catholic Church Records in Baltimore, Md. 1782-1800, by Mary and Stanley G. Piet,
Rsh.9, pg.18, Buckman, Joseph b. 7/17/1797, bapt. 7/23, son of George and Barbara Buckman, Rsh.9 Buckman, Margaret, b. 1/23/1800, bapt. 1/26/1800, dau. of George and Barbara Buckman (m.Samuel Anthony Trexler Rsh.9)
Rsh.9, pg.128, marriage of Buckman, George to Barbara Fisher, 3/28/1796

Baltimore, Md, St. Peters Catholic, City of Baltimore, Md. Mdhr, M 1511, Vol. 5-8, 1775 - 1806
Rsh.29, Vol.5, pg.77, Hitzelberger, 3/7/1813 was bapt. Stephen Franklin b.2/28 of Anthony and Appolonia Hitzelberger, sponsor Joseph Hitzelberger and Mary Keisendaffer. Enoch Fenwick, Rector of St. Peters
Rsh.29, Vol.5, pg.77, Hitzelberger, George Washington, bapt. twin brother of Stephen Franklin of Anthony and Appolonia, sponsor Samuel Schrode and Theresa (Teresaell) Drehcell (Drexel, Drexell) Enoch Fenwick, Rector of St. Peters
Rsh.29, Vol.5, pg.220, Hitzelberger, Mary Rosanna b. 7/2, bapt. 7/9/1815, dau. of Hitzelberger, Anthony and Appolonia, sponsors Samuel Drexell and Mary Ann Bowen, Enoch Fenwick, Rector of St. Peters
Rsh.29, Vol.5, pg.384, Hitzelberger, bapt. 11/16/1817 Maria Teresa b. 10/22 of Anthony and Appolonia, sponsor John and Teresa Hoffman, Enoc Fenwich, Rector, St. Peters
Rsh.29, Vol.6, pg.189, Lewis, (Corban) Anthony, b. 6/17/1821, bapt. 7/8/1821, lawful son of John Lewis and Appoloni Hitzelberge, sponsor Anthony Hitzelberger, James Whitfield, Rector
Rsh.9, pg.229, Trexler, Anthony, bapt. 4/8/1822, b. of Samuel Trexler and Margaret on 2/17 last sponsor Joseph and Mary

Bookman, James Whitfield Pastor of the Cathedral

Baltimore, Md., Mdhr, M1525 - B.C. Sacred Heart baptisms,
began pg.90, 6/1/1820 author's note: these records were read
to pg.155, the beginning of year 1832.
Rsh.29, pg.93, Hitzelberger, 9/21/1820 bapt. Emilia Catharine, b.
7/11 dau. (legitment) Petri Hitzelberger and Margaretha Norbeck,
sponsors Felix Weifs and Barbara
Rsh.29, pg.94, Hitzelberger, 2/4/1821, Stephanus Vincent, b.
1/22/1821 to Nicolas and Emilia Couk (or Cook) , sponsors Petri
Hitzelberger and Rebecca Carroll.
Rsh.9, pg.109, 12/8/1824, Driseler, Marianna, b. 11/20/ dau.
Samuel Driseler and Margaret Buckman, sponsors Joannes Gross
and Margaretha Lee
Rsh.9, pg.89, 3/29/1820, Drecksler, Anna Barbara, dau, Samuel
Drecksler and Margareta Buckman, sponsor Joannes Hckbos and
Conflany Edwart bapt. 4/16/1820
Rsh.9, pg.109, Dresher (Drocksel,Drexel), 7/31/1824, bapt.
Marianna (?) b.12/4/?1823 dau. to Herbemanl and Sarah,
sponsor Elizabeth Hohler.

Baltimore, Md., St. James Catholic Church Records, Baltimore,
Md.,1804-1811 M. 1584, Microfilm Mdhr
Rsh.9, pg.89, Dreckseler, Anna Barbara Dreckseler, b.3/11/1820
to Samuel Dreckseler and Margaret Buckman.

Baltimore, Md., St. Johns German Catholic Church, City of
Baltimore, Md, Mdhr, M. 1584
Parish: author's note: these have been read to page 156, year
1832/1833.
Rsh.29, year 1804, Hemelt, September legit thoro, Appolonia,
parentibus Petro and Maria Hemelt, patrimerant, Peter, et
Hitzelberger, Appolonia bapt. 36th juiben
?Rsh.5, XIX, 4/1808, Gliffendorfer, Joannes, Dreckseler, Anmarie
1806
?Rsh.5, pg.126, Klunk, 2/6/1828, Catharina Maria baptized dau.
Peter Klunk, et Elizabeth Kintz, sponsor Maurietias Schumacher,
Catherine Robinson.

Baltimore, Md., Mdhr M1584, page 8,9. St. Johns German
Catholic Church Parish Records

118

Rsh.10, ?Rsh.5 Baptisms, 10/23/1819, Zimmerman, Anna Margrreta, Father George Zimmerman, Mother Sophia Dreckseler (Trexler), Sponsor Mary Gei_en_er and _____ ____
Rsh.20, 10/27/1820, Trexler, Jonathan, and Deborah Starr, #310 no minister listed.

Baltimore, City, St. Johns German Catholic, Mdhr M1584, Cemeterio Record
?Rsh.5, pg.XIII, Cemeterio/Burial Record, St. Joavanis Appostalistic of Germany in Baltimore: Dreckseler, Catharina, 10/28/1807
Marriage Record author's note: these records have been read to year 1828
?Rsh.5, pg.XIX , 5/1/1806, Gliffendorfer, Joannes, (author's note: later in the records this name is shown as Kapler) m. to Maria Dreckseler
?Rsh.5., pg.XXI, 2/21/1808, Mertengel, Hermangel C., (author's note: later this name is shown as Martin) m.to Catharina Dreckseler
Rsh.76, pg.XXIV, 3/20/1810, Werner, Joannes m. to A. Elizabeth Bergmann, Witnesses, Jeffes Joseph Bergmann and Ignatius Drecksler
Rsh.76, pg.XXVIII, 11/8/1812, Drecksler, Ignatius m. Moury, Anna, Sebastian George Poe, Johannes Robeson
Rsh.76, 11/12/1812, Poe, Georgeous m. King, Margaretha, witnesses (Rsh.5) Peter Klonk and Ignatius Drecksler (?Pilhertc)
?Rsh.5, pg.XXXIII, _____, 1816, Hoffman, Joannes m. Drecksler, Theresia Drecksler, witnesses names not clear very light
Rsh.9, pg.XXXVI, 5/30/1819, Dreckseler, Samuel m. Buckman, Margaret (Ann), witnesses Joseph Buckman and David Weekler, Minister Mertz

Baptisms
?Rsh.5, pg.14, Gluffen, Kapler, Carpler, Capler, Croper, 5/22/1808, Maria Magdalena dau. of Joannes, and mother Maria Drecksler
?Rsh.5, pg.20, 10/23/1808, Martin, Antoniua, dau. Hermann and mother Catherine Drecksler, sponsor Maria Gliffimorert (?Kapler), bapt. 9/1807
?Rsh.5, pg.33, Gliffendorpfler (?Kapler), 8/29/1811, b. Elisabet

dau. (author's note: someone has written in d.August 30, 1849) of Joannes, and mother Maria Drecksler, sponsor to bapt. 10/8/1811 Judith Drecksler

Rsh.76, pg.46, Dreckseler, Joannes Joseph, 10/1813, son of Ignatius and mother Anna Murry, sponsors Joannes Gross and Barbara Gross, bapt. 10/4/1813

Rsh.76, pg.56, Drecksler, William, 8/11/1815, son of Ignatius and Anna Maurry, sponsors Joannes Murry and Emertinia Mourry, bapt. Sunday, 8/29/1815

Rsh.76, pg.69, Dreckseler, Appolonia Julia, 5/7/1817, dau. Ignatius and Nancy Mourry, sponsor Anthony Hitzelberger and Appolonia Dreckseler, Rsh.29, bapt. 5/25/1817/1819

Rsh.9, pg.74, Gruber, William, 11/4/1819, son Joannes Gruber and Susannae Gilman, sponsor Joannes Dreskler and Margaretha Buckmann

Baltimore, Md. St. John's German Catholic Church, (M1525), M1584 Microfilm, MDHr, Parish Records, 2/9/1804 to 6/11/1841 Marriages; index of Bapt. on pg.LXXXV (85); index of Marriages on pg.LXXXVII (87), MDHR M-1584-2,
author's note:  these records were read to pg.139, date 1828. They are also recorded in an additional record book (see above) in a different handwriting.

Rsh.29, pg.7, Hitzelberger, 4/16/1806, Jacobus Antonius Frthisglor son of John Hitzelberger and Mary Gonig, sponsors William Antonius Hitzelberger and Appolonia Hitzelberger, bapt. 9/23/1806

Rsh.29, pg.10, Hitzelberger, 3/12/1807, Josephus son of Antonia Hitzelberger and Appolonia Drecksler, sponsors Josephius Hitzelberger and Catherine Walters.*

?Rsh.5, pg.14, Gluden (?Kapler), 5/22/1808, Maria Madgellena dau. of Joannes Kapler and Maria Drecksler, mother, bapt. 7/2/1808, Rev. John Nicholas Mertz

?Rsh.5, pg.19, Kingbert, 5/23/1809, Anna Maria dau. of Jacob Kingbert and Hariot Kazen, sponsors Peter Klouk and Frau Klonk, bapt. 6/23/1809

?Rsh.5, pg.21, Klonk, 10/17/l809, Josephus, son of Peter Klonk and Elizabeth King, sponsors Joseph Klonk and Margaretha King, bapt. 10/29/1809

?Rsh.5, pg.33, Gliffendorffler, 8/9/1811, Elizabet dau. (author's note: someone has written in d. 8/30/1843 of Joannes

Gliffendorffler and Maria Dreckseler, sponsor Judith Dreckseler, bapt. 10/7/1811

Rsh.76, pg.46, Dreckseler, 10/1813, Joannes Joseph, son of Ignatius Dreckseler and Anna Murry, sponsors Joannes Gross, and Barbara Gross, bapt. 10/4/1813

Rsh.76, pg.56, Drecksler, 8/11/1815, William, son of Ignatius Drecksler and Anna Maurry, sponsors Joannes Murry and Emertinia Mourry, bapt. Sunday, 8/29/1815

Rsh.76, pg.69, Drecksler, 5/7/1819, Appolinia Julia dau. of Ignatius Drecksler and Anna Maurry, Nancy, sponsors Anthony Hitzelberger and Appolonia Drecksler, bapt. 5/25/1819

Rsh.10, pg.73, Zimmerman, Elizabeth, 10/22/1819, dau. George Zimmerman and Sophia Dreckseler, sponsors Joannes Hoffman, Theresia Hoffman

> pg.73, note: there is a Hagerstown, Md. baptism recorded on this page, indicating that the Priest was visiting Hagerstown during this period.

Rsh.9, pg.74, William Hitz, son Jreamns Gruber and Susan nee Gillmor, sponsor Samuel Dreckseler and Margaretha Buckman

Rsh.9, pg.89, Drecksler, 3/29/1820, Anna Barbara, dau. Samuel Drecksler and Margaretha Buckman, sponsor Joannes Hckbos (Schbces) and Edwart Conflany, bapt. 4/16/1820

Rsh.10, pg.89, Anna Margaretha, 4/1820, dau. George Zimmerman and Sophia Drecksler, sponsor Mary Geffentio, Gesseno and Francis S. Geffentio

Rsh.9, pg.___,Marianna, b. 5/20, bapt.12/8/1824, Samuels Drescler and Margaretha Buckman, sponsors Joannes Gross and Margaretha Lee

pg.109, Susanna, bapt. subject to conditions, 12/4/1824, b. 7/31/1824, parents Gerhardt Drocksel and Sabra Dresler, sponsors _____ and Elizabeth Mohler

Rsh.9, pg.116, Catharine, bapt. 11/8/1825, dau. Samuels Drecksler and Margaret Buckman, sponsor Barbara Bushmiller

?Rsh.5, Catharina Maria, 2/6/1828, dau. Peter Klunk and Elizabeth Kintz, sponsors Mrurilus Schumacher and Catherine Robinson

> * a Nicholas Walter was schoolmaster in Adams Co., Pa., for Dreckseler,Trexler, Klunk children as he was paid from their stepgrandfather Joseph Ehrman's estate.

Baltimore, Md. St. Peter's Roman Catholic Church, Baltimore, Md. Mdhr MF 1517

Rsh.8, pg.310 Troxell, Abraham m. Sarah Amboucher, 4/22/1813

Cecil Co., Md.,Bohemia Catholic Parish Collection, Mdhr,MSA SC 3572
Baptisms, Births 1787-1842, 1790-1882, no Trexlers or similar research surnames found

Frederick Co., Md.,Emmitsburg, Md.,Mt. St. Mary's Catholic Parish, Emmitsburg, Md. Mdhr, MSA SC2575, 1815-1871, no Trexler, etc found.

Frederick Co., Md.,Emmitsburg, Md., Mt. St. Mary's Catholic Parish Registers, Emmitsburg, Md.
Mdhr, M1999 1815-1850 - 800582, Restricted Roll, searched baptisms, marriages and deaths to 1830, no Trexler, etc. found

Harford Co., Md.,St. Ignatius Catholic Church  Mdhr, MSA S C 2686
M2849 - 1817 - 1854, M2850 - 1874-1909, no Trexler, etc. found

St. Mary's Co., Md. The Jesuit Missions of St. Mary's Co., Maryland by Edwin Warfield Beitzell, LC 77-75320
pg.105, Troxsell, John, 1786, date he belonged to Church, St. Francis Xavier Church, Newtown 1766

### Lutheran

In searching Maryland Church Records the following Pennsylvania Lutheran and Reformed Churches are close to the border. The dates their records begin is noted. Moving from east to west.
1. Bethlehem, Steltz, York Co., (Union) 1794
2. St. David's, West Manheim Township, York Co., (Union) 1751.
3. St. Matthews Lutheran, Hanover, York Co., 1743
4. Christ Reformed, Near Littlestown, Adams Co., 1747
5. St. Johns Lutheran, near Littletown, Adams Co., 1763
6. Salem Reformed (Beshore's) near Waynesboro, Franklin Co., 1785

Baltimore, Md., Zion Lutheran Church, Baltimore, Md.
Rsh.82, pg.4, Tresler, Johan Jacob b. ll/24/1786, bapt. 5/20/1787, parents, Tresler, Michael and Catherine, sponsors, Hemrich and Catherine Brutel

pg.338 number 28, Tressler, Trehsler, Catherine, 7/1795, 8 years, 11 months (?burial)

Baltimore, Md., First German Reformed Church, Balt. Md., Mormon Film, No. 13700, Year 1786-1849
Vol.1
pg.15, year 1801, Trehsler, Jr., Christian
pg.98, year 1813, bapt., Resseler, Anna Catharne b. 11/25/1812, bapt.1/27/1813, Christian and w. Christian Resseler.
Vol.2
Rsh.8, pg.202, Trachsel, 11/5/1826, Abraham Trachsel
pg.205, Troxel, 5/25/1828, Abr. Troxal
pg.206, Troxel, 4/19/1829, Sarah Troxal

Carroll Co., Md., St. Benjamin, Pipe Creek, Kreiders, Westminster,Md., Baptism Records 1763-1836 -Mdhr 1159, # 5, Oldest Record of Lutheran Congregation of St. Benjamin or Kriders Church near Westminister Md.,in Region called Pipes Creek in former days, Evangelical Lutheran Krauters Church.
note: If a guess was made by author this is indicated by a ? These names were translated from German
Rsh.101, pg.13, John Tressent?, parents Sam and w. Elis, b. 3/30/1786, baptized 4/13/1786, sponsor Casp. Bayer and w. Cathrine

Dorchester Co., Md.,Church Creek Charge Records, DCPL
Rsh.20, Elizabeth Nevade dau. of Isaac S. and Elizabeth Trexler, b. 11/26/1866 at Lakesville

Vol.1 Maryland German Church Records, Records of Christ Reformed Church, also known as the German Reformed Church (a congregation of the United Church of Christ) Middletown, Frederick, Co., Md. 1770-1840 - translated and edited by Frederick S. Weiser, Noodle-Doosey Press, Manchester, Md., 1986 F190G3W38
pg.8, Thaler, Johannes, son of Schim (Jim) and Margaretha Thaler (umlat over a) b. 1776, bapt. 1776, sponsors Caster and Susanna Beckebach

Vol.2 Maryland German Church Records, Records of Zion Lutheran Church, Middletown, Frederick Co., Md. 1781-1826,

translated by Charles T. Zhan, edited by Frederick S. Weiser, Noodle-Doosey Press, Manchester, Md.
no Trexlers, etc. found

<u>Vol.3 Maryland German Church Records, Baptismal records of the Monocacy Lutheran Congregation, and its successor, the Evangelical Lutheran Church of Frederick, Frederick Co., Md. 1742-1779 Translated and edited by Frederick S. Weiser, Noodle Doosey Press, Manchester, Md.</u>
pg.41, Weller, Joann Georg, son of Johannes and Barbara Weller, b. 6/6/1776, bapt. 9/25/1776, sponsor mother, Barbara Dressler, (Drissler,Treisler)
pg.41 Schmid, 11/25/1763 Henrich Schmid and Eliesbeth, a little son Michael, sponsors Michael Drissler and Margaretha, bapt. 12/4/1763 (?Rsh.75)
Rsh.54, pg.65 Dressler, Maria Magdalena, dau. of Andreas and Maria Dressler, b. 5/4/1771, bapt. 6/21/1772, sponsors Henrich and Rosina Voelckner
Rsh.11, pg.5 Dressel, 7/20/1743, Gotthart Dressell, a dau. Anna Catrina, sponsors Jacob Wedel and w. Maria, bapt. 10/17/1743
Rsh.13, pg.47 Drezel 11/20/1764, Fredrich Dressel and Appalonia, a little dau. Anna Maria, sponsors Johannes Traxel and Sybilla Bayin, bapt. 3/20/1765
pg.67, Drealer (Driealer) , Johann Georg, son of Jacob and Maria Driealer, b. 1/20/1772, bapt. 7/22/1772, sponsors Johannes and Rebecca Gost
?Rsh.75/25,pg.57, Dresele, date not given, Johann Georg parents Michael Dresele and Margaretha, bapt. 1/29/1769, sponsors Valentine Schwartz and Susannah
pg.66, Dewald, son of Dewald and Eva Hickel b. 10/1/1771, bapt. 6/28/1772, sponsors Stephan and Catharina Trenckel Rsh.51
?Rsh.75, pg.60 Triesler (Dressler) Georg Michael, son of Johannes and Barbara Weller, b. 6/19/no year, bapt. 7/7/1771, sponsors Georg Michael and Anna Margareth Treisler ?Rsh.75
pg.70, Susanna, dau. of Valentin and Susanna Breitenbach, b. 4/10/1773, bapt. 5/2/1773, sponsors Caspar and Susanna Tritsch

<u>Vol.4 Maryland German Church Records, Baptismal Records of the Evangelical Lutheran Church of Frederick, Frederick Co., Md. 1780-1811, translated and edited by Frederick S. Weiser, Historical Society of Carroll Co., Westminister, Md.</u>

pg.4, Debeler, Juliana, dau. of Adam and Philippina Debeler, b. 10/28/1780, bapt. 12/7/1780, sponsors Christian and Juliana Ostertag

pg.11, Schnautigel, Margareth, dau. of Jacob and Maria Barbara Schnautigel b. 3/17/180, bp. 3/30/1783, sponsor Margreth Drieslern

pg.15, Currens, Amos son of Robert and Rachael Currens, b. 8/10/1763 bapt. 10/5/1783 sponsors Georg and Sophia Deschner

pg.33, Hoffman, Maria Catherina dau. of Adam and Maria Christina Hoffman, b. 4/8/1787, bapt. 7/15/1787, sponsors Georg and Sophia Margreth Daeschner

pg.56, Hoffman, Johann Georg son of Adam and Maria Christina Hoffman, b. 12/5/1790, bapt. 5/1/1791, sponsors Johann Georg and Sophia Daeschner

Vol.7 Maryland German Church Records, Saint Mary's Church, Silver Run, Carroll Co., Lutheran records 1784-1863; reformed records 1812-1866, extracts from a ledger of both congregations, 1820-1823, translated and edited by Frederick S. Weiser, Noodle Doosey Press, Manchester, Md.

pg.22, Booss, Solomon Susanna, dau. of Daniel and Elizabeth Booss, b. 9/6/1834, bapt. 11/9/1834, sponsors John and Rachael Troxel, Susanna Fiesser

pg.61, bapt., 9/1818, Elisa, dau. of not given, b. not given, sponsor Adam Traxel

Carroll Co., Lutheran Silver Run, Saint Mary's Lutheran, Baptisms, 1784-, Md. Hist. Soc., Nat. Gen.Soc., No Trexlers, etc., until 1840

Carroll Co., Lutheran Zion Church, originally Balt. Co., c. 1760, Mdhr 1159, #6, Bapt. 1760-1836
Translated to English, no Trexlers, etc. through 1804

Frederick, Md., All Saints Parish, now Montgomery, All of Frederick, part of Carroll, Washington , Allegheny, and Garrett Counties, Maryland, Baltimore Co., Md. Vital Record, Mdhr, No. 281, Pg.39

Rsh.110, Trisler, Valentine m. Mary Ream, October 9, 1783, Minister Nickolas Pomp, minister at the Reformed Church

Frederick Co., Nd, Graceham (Graceheim), Moravian Church c

1747, Mdhr M2117 #6, 1759-1871
Troxel, David (l:85) son of John Troxel
Rsh.60, Troxel, David, son of John Troxell m. 8/31/1830 to Juliana
Feiser.
Rsh.65, Troxel, John (2:230) b. 12/23/1773 d. 9/17/1857 m.
Elizabeth Young (2:228)


Frederick Co., Md, Moravian Families of Graceham, Maryland, the
families belonging to the Moravian Community and Congregation
at Graceham in Maryland and some of their neighbors 1759-1871,
translated and edited from the parish register by Henry James
Young 1942, pub. 1988, Family Line Publications F187.F8Y68
1988
pg.16  Drachsel, Mary Ellen (1:217) illegitimate daughter of Elias
Drachsel and Sarah Seiffert, b. 6/15/1812 and bapt. 4/24/1815.
Maria Schenkel was this child's foster mother
Rsh.60, pg.95  Troxel, Abraham  m. Isabella, issue William Henry
2:129, 1/12/1866, bapt. 11/4/1866
Troxel, Charlotte m. George Wolf
Rsh.60, Troxel, David, 1:85 son of John Troxel m. 8/31/1830
Juliana Feiser 2:241 she was b. 11/9/1809, she d. 8/5/1865, and
was b. at Apples Church 8/6.
Elias Troxel m. Sarah, issue Mary Ann or Mary Ellen m. William
Little
Rsh.60, Emanuel Troxel 2:250 d. 4/15/1876 in Washington Co.,
bu. 4/16/1786  Apples Church
Rsh.60, John Troxel m. Elizabeth Dodero, issue Maria 1/86 m.
Jacob Biggs
Rsh.65, John Troxel 2:230 b. 12/23/1773, d. 9/17/1857, b.
9/18/1857 at Apples Church, he m. Elizabeth Young 2:228 who
was b. 6/8/1774, d. 12/4/1856 b. 12/6/1856 Apples Church
Rsh.60, John Troxel m. Susanna Rebecca Hesser, issue Abraham
Alexander 2:58 b. 11/16/1860, bapt. 9/12/1862, George William
2:121 b. 11/23/1854, bapt. 5/27/1855
Rsh.60, Lewis Troxell m. Mary Ann Barton, issue Julia Sabina
2:136 b. 3/17/1880, bapt. 7/17/1880
Rsh.60, Margaret Savilla Troxel m. Edward Boiler
Rsh.60, Samuel J. Troxel m. Sophia Elizabeth Colliflower, dau. of
Joseph and Harriet Elizabeth (Shuff) Colliflower, issue Clarence
Joseph, b. 7/6/1870, bapt. 9/22/1870, Robert Lee b. 1871, Addie
Bruce b.1873, Morris Luther b. 1875, Alva Franklin b. 1877,

Florence Ellen b. 1870, Zeppa Grace b. 1880
Sarah Troxel m. Tobias Newcomer

Frederick Co., Md. Baptismal Records of the Apples Church,
Originals at College of the Evang. and Reformed Church,
Lancaster, Pa., FCHS Md. 1773-1848 (Church is near Thurmont,
Md.)
Rsh.34, Troxel, Johannes and Elisabeth, dau. Maria Barbara, b.
3/30/1779, bapt. 6/27/1779, sponsor Mathais Martin and w.
Rsh.34, Troxel, Johannes and Elisabeth, son Johannes, b.
8/7/1781, bapt. 9/5/1781, no sponsors named
Droxel, Johannes, Elisabeth, son Johannes b. 6/17 bapt.
9/3/1801, sponsors Johannes Martin and Ana Maria
Rsh.60, Draxel, Johannes and Elisabeth, son David b. 9/27 bapt.
11/16/1805, sponsors Conrad Dothero and Catharine
Rsh.60, Droxel, Johannes, Elisabeth, son Frederick b.11/13/1807,
bapt. 4/7/1808, sponsor Fridrich Draxel and Elisabetha
Rsh.60, Troxell, Johannes, Elisabeth, Anna Maria, b. 4/20/1810,
bapt. 6/3/1810, Anna Maria Dottero
Rsh.60, Troxel, Johannes, Elisabetha, son Abraham, b. 1/12/1816,
bapt. 3/25/1816
Rsh.13, Troxel, Frederick and Apollonia, son Johannes, b.
12/22/1773, bapt. 4/20/1774, sponsors, Johannes Troxel and
Maria Margaretha
Rsh.13, Troxel, Frederich, Appolonia, dau. Catherina Magdalena,
b.4/4/1776, bapt. 6/30/1776, sponsor Magdalena Jung (Young)
single
Rsh.13, Troxel, Frederich, Appolonia, dau. Margaretha b.
2/7/1779, sponsor Johannes Troxell and Margaretha
?Rsh.58, Troxel, Peter and Magdalena son Fridrich, b. 3/28/1779,
bapt. 6/27/1779, sponsor Fridich Troxel and w.
Peter Drauss and Juli, son George Peter, b. 7/21/1780, bapt.
10/12/1780, sponsor Fridrich Troxell
Jung (Young) Johannes, Magdalena, son Johann Jacob, b.
6/7/1787, bapt. 8/19, sponsors Fridrich Troxel, Abolonia

Frederick Co., Md., Evangelical Reformed Church, Frederick,
Mdhr 2116-5
pg.197, Index of Marriages:
Rsh.15, Traxel, Christian and Catherine Doerr, 5/31/1761, 1-267

Frederick Co., Md., Record of Marriages and Burials in the
Monocacy Church in Evangelical Lutheran in City of Frederick by
Frederick Sheely Weiser 1743-1811 FCHS
Rsh.36, pg.52, Trachsel, 4/24/1787, Jacob Trachsel and Maria
Groschang, near Krugerstown, proclaimed witness, Johan and
Peter Trachsel, Matthis Martin, Matthis Schrupp, Abraham and
Johann Groschang.

Frederick Md. Records of Marriages and Buriels, Moncracy,
Evangelical Lutheran, 1743-1811, National Genealogical, Society.
Washington, D.C. 1972, Frederick Md. Evangelical Lutheran,
Marriages
?Rsh.75, 3/13/1811, Jacob Houch and Elisabeth Trisler, by
license at Mr. Trishers, 10/19/1803, John Leyth and Marsha
Trechern at the "Trepp" Mr. Treschners house
10/20/1803, Wm. Lamar and Drusilla Trescher at the "Treb" Mr.
Treschers house
?Rsh.75, 1805, Mr. Trissler, Sr., bu. 10/23/1805 d. of
consumption age 64 or 65, b. c. 1741, (?son of Rsh.16 by first
marriage)

Frederick Co., Monocacy Church, Settlement, north of Frederick,
Evangelical Lutheran,in City of Frederick, c 1738, Mdhr - M723 A
#9, Translated from German -
Rsh.11, Dressel, Gotthart, dau. b. Anna Catrina, 7/20/1743,
sponsors Jacob Wedel and w. Maria
pg.223, Toxler, Peter and Marcia, son Stephan b. 8/6/1758
(66)
Rsh.4, Troxler, George and Catharina, dau. Maria Dorothea b.
4/8/1759 (71)
Rsh.11, Trixsler, Michael and Margaret, dau. Elizabeth b.
10/11/1760, bapt. 11/23/1760 (76)
Henrich Schmid and Elizabeth had son Michael b. 11/25/1763,
bapt. 12/4/1763, sponsors Michael Drissler and Margareth Rsh.11
Weller, b. George Michael son of Johannes and Barbara Weller,
b. 6/19 bapt. 7/7/1771, sponsors George Michael and Anna
Margreth Triesler. Rsh.11
Rsh.4, pg.49, Doseler (Tosler), George and Catherine, dau.
Rosina b. 6/8/1761, bapt. 9/16/1761, (77)
Rsh.11 Dosler, George and Catherine, dau. Margaret b. 1/1768,
bapt. 5/29/1768 (94)

Rsh.54, Dressler, Andreas and Maria, dau. Maria Magdelena, b. 5/4/1771, bapt. 6/21/1772, sponsors Heinrich and Rosina Voelckner

Dossler, Peter and Margaret, son Peter b. 10/15/1771, bapt. 11/19/1771 (109)

Driealer, Jacob and Maria, son Johann George b. 1/20/1772, bapt. 7/22/1772, sponsors Johannes and Rebecca Gost

?Rsh.99 Dessler, George and Margaret, son Peter, b. 10/10/1777, bapt. 11/16/1777 (145)

Dossler, Peter and Margaret, dau., Elizabeth b. 2/27/1781, bapt. 5/3/1781 (164)

Rsh.4, Trexsel, Gotthard and Catherine, dau. Elizabeth b. November, bapt. 2/3/1782 (167)

Rsh.14, Driszler, George and Rosina, dau. Henrietta, b. 2/1/1805, bapt. 4/14/1805 (242)

Rsh.4 , Dosler, George and Catherine, dau. Catherine, b. 10/4/1805

Evangelical Reformed Church, Frederick, Mdhr 2116-5
Rsh.75, Valentine Wolff (w. Susannah), dau. Margaretha b. 3/6/1763, bapt. 3/13/1763, sponsor Michael Triseler and w.

Rsh.75, Michael Trisler and Margaretha, dau. Elizabeth b. 10/11/1760, bapt. 11/23/1760, sponsors Valentine Sohreiner and w.

Christian Teubelbis, and Maria Magdalena, dau. Margaretha b. 7/18/1778, bapt. 8/30/1778, sponsors Margaretha Trister (Rsh.75)

Rsh.75, Dreszler, A. Marg, year 1767, communion at Picket Mountain, Lower Church

Rsh.75, Drizler 130, George, year 1787, communion

Rsh.75, Driszler, Elizabeth, year 1799

Rsh.75, Taescler, Elizabeth, pg.133, confirmations, year 1767,

Lower Church
Rsh.110,Triszler, Valentine, year 1778

Index of Marriages pg.197
?Rsh. 35, Desler, Peter and Margaret Schley, 12/21/1766, 1-270

Rsh.15, Traxel, Christian and Catherine Doerr, 5/31/1761, 1-267

Frederick Co., Md.,Maryland Church, Monocracy Lutheran and Evangelical Lutheran, Fred S. Weiser, 1987, Cannageschick

(Conococheaque) Frederick Co., Md., MHS
Rsh.52, pg.32, Draxel, 3/27/1762, son Freiderich b. to David
Draxel and w. Anna Elisabetha, bapt. 6/16/1762, sponsors Johann
Nicol Guntz and Appollonia

Frederick Co., Md., Evangelical. Reformed, Frederick Md., NGS
1988,
Rsh.11, Fridrich Huter on 8/29/1779 m. Maria Anna Schreinern by
license, witness, Valentine Schriener and w. Elisabeth, Michael
Driesler and w. Margaret, (?Rsh.75) Jacob Muller, Thomas Preuss

Frederick Co., Md., Index to Evangelical Lutheran Church
Records, MHS
Drachsel, Elizabeth pg.475, Jacob, pg.304, Johann pg.475
Drachset, David & Elizabeth pg.567
Drazel, Anna Maria pg.540, b. 1764, Zion Luth. Frederick, Md.
Drazel, Frederick and Appolonia pg.540, pg.541
Drazel, Johannes pg.54
Dressler, Andreas pg.572
Dressler, Maria pg.572
Driesler, Jacob and Maria pg.576
Dreisler, Johann George pg.576
Dreisler, Margaretha pg.417, pg.709

Frederick Co., Md. Monocracy Congregation, Lutheran Births and
Baptisms, until 1756, and listed by Miss Miller in 1910 - book was
found at FCHS but no one at FCHS knew just who Miss Miller
was, but here is her list.
?Rsh.11, 7/20/1743, Drossell, (Trossel), Barthart (Bernard) a dau.
Anna Cathrina, witness Jacob Wedel and w. Maria, bapt.
10/17/1743

Frederick Co., Md., Moncracy, Evangelical Lutheran, Records of
Marriages and Burials, 1743-1811, NGS, Washington D.C. 1972
Rsh.36, 10/9/1787, Groschang, Johannes and Anna Maria
Geigorn, proclaimed marriage, witness Jacob Drachsel,
Leonhardt Geiger, Owen McDonald

Frederick Co., Md.,Records of Evangelical Reformed, 1747-1800,
Family Line 1980
pg.46, Tresel, Gotthard, Catharina, dau. Elisabetha b. 11/1781,

bapt. 2/3/1782, sponsor Henrich Hildebrand and Elisabetha
Rsh.13, pg.118, Death Records, 10/10/1795 - Draxel, George
Frederick, 55 years old 0 months 0 days

Frederick Co., Md., Monocacy Church, Settlement, north of
Frederick, Evangelical Lutheran, in City of Frederick, c 1738,
Mdhr, M723 A #9, Translated from German
Rsh.13, Draxal, Frederick and Appollonia, son Michael b.
4/1/1767, bapt. 4/20/1769 (91)
Rsh.13, Drezel, Anna Maria bapt. 3/20/1765, dau. b. to Frederick
and Appolona Drezel, sponsors Johannes Traxel and Sybilla
Bayin

Frederick Co., Md. Monocracy Lutheran and Evangelical
Lutheran, Fred S. Weiser, 1987, Cannageschick
(Conococheaque) FHS/MHS
Rsh.15, pg.32, 6/3/1762, Walder (?Walter), Jacob and Catharina,
son Christian bapt. 5/8/1763, sponsors Christian Draxel and w.
Catharina
?Rsh.75, pg.41, 11/25/1763, Schmid, Henrich and Elisabeth, son
Michael, sponsors, bapt. 12/4/1763, Michael Drissler and
Margaretha
Rsh.13, pg.48, Traxel, Michael, b. 11/4/1766, bapt. 12/25/1766,
sponsors Drederich and Appalonia Draxel
Rsh.13, pg.47, Drezel, Fredrich, 11/20/1764, Fredrich Drezel and
Appalonia, dau. Anna Maria, sponsors bapt. 3/20/1765 Johannes
Traxel ?Rsh.147 and Sybilla Bayin
pg.60, Weller, George Michael, son of Johannes and Barbara
?Rsh.11, Weller, b. 6/19/1771, bapt. 7/7/1771, sponsors George
Michael and Anna Margareth Triesler

Frederick Co., Md., Rocky Hill Lutheran Church, Woodsboro,
Frederick Co. Md., 1767-1853. Trans by Mrs. Jacob Kintz 1930
FHS
Rsh.13, 1769, Dreschel, Elisabeth b. 3/11/1769, bapt. 4/4/1769,
sponsor parents Fredrich Dreschel and Appolomia his w.

Frederick Co., Md., Records of Evangelical Reformed, 1747-1800,
Family Line 1980
Rsh.13, pg.20, Draxel, Fredrich and Applonia son Michael b.
4/1/1767, bapt. 4/20/1767, at the Glade, sponsor Jacob Herrman

and Margaretha Draxel

Frederick Co., Monocacy Church, Settlement, north of Frederick, Evangelical Lutheran, in City of Frederick, c 1738, Mdhr, M723 A #9, Translated from German
Rsh.14, Driszler, George and Rosina, dau., Henrietta, b. 2/1/1805, bapt. 4/14/1805 (242)

Frederick Co., Md., First German Reformed Church, Mormon Film, 13,935, Frederick Co., Md.
Rsh.14, pg.401, Drissler, Henrietta b. to George and Rosina, 2/1/1805, christened 4/14/1805, witness Margaret Dressler
Rsh.14, pg.419, Drissler, Julianna Margaret b. to George Drissler and w. Rosina, 5/6/1808, christened 5/29, witness John Schnobily and w. Cathina
Rsh.14, pg.467, Trisler, George b. 9/8/1816 to George Trisler and w. Rosina, witness George Trisler and w.

Frederick Co., Walkersville, Glade Reformed, UCC, Mdhr M2116-7, 1763-1822
Translated from German
Rsh.15, Troxel, 10/25/1772, bapt. Daniel, son of Christian and Catharine (Katharina) Troxel, sponsors  Jacob Braungul and Sophia Troxel
Rsh.15, Troxel, 3/5/1775, bapt. Johannes, son of Christian and Katharina Troxel, sponsors Johannes and Margaretta Mencher

Washington Co., Maryland, Church Records of the 18th Century, 1768-1800, Hagerstown, Clearspring, Williamsport, Leitersburg, Funkstown, Clearfoss, Family Line Pub. Westminister, Md. 1988
Rsh.106, pg.86, Trexler, Samuel, Reformed Church of Hagerstown, Samuel of Emanuel Trexler and mother Catharina, both married people, b. 6/19/1786, bapt. 4/31/1787, sponsor himself

Washington Co., Reformed Church, Salem (Zion) near Hagerstown, Mdhr M859, note: first part German/typed English, second part, bapt.records, 1787-1823
Teisher, Jacob bu. in Salem Baptist Cemetery, no date

Washington Co., Maryland, Church Records of the 18th Century, 1768-1800, Hagerstown, Clearspring, Williamsport, Leitersburg, Funkstown, Clearfoss, Family Line Pub., Westminster, Md. 1988 pg.21, Evangelical Lutheran at Elisabethtown (Hagerstown), Elis of Benjamin Reitnauer and w. A. Maria, b. 6/10/1798, bapt. 6/14/1799, sponsor Juliana Trisher

Rsh.113, pg.35, Schwertzol, Salem Reformed, Abraham of Mathaus Schwertzol and Catharine Barbara, married people, b. 3/9/1774, bapt. 7/19, witness Abraham Traxel and his housewife Catharina

Rsh.113, pg.34, Roth, Salem Reformed, Catharina of Johannes Roth and Juliana, m., b. 1772, bapt. 3/28/1773, witness Catharina Traxel

Rsh.113, pg.32, Willige, Salem Reformed, Abraham of Johannes Wilige and Elisabeth, m. people, b. 2/2/1771, bapt. 7/20, witness Abraham Troxel

Rsh.113, pg.69, Wingert, Reformed Church of Hagerstown, Anna Catharina of Peter Wingert and mother Elisabeth, both m., b. 4/4/1772, bapt. 6/8/1772, sponsors Meister Jonathan Hoeger and Catharine Traxelsin

Rsh.113, pg.71, Schneider, Reformed Church of Hagerstown, Jonathan of Jacob Schneider and mother Catharina both m. people, b. 1/3/1773, bapt. 2/14/1772, sponsor Jonathan Thager and Catharina Traxel

Rsh.113, pg.77, Traxel, Reformed Church, Johannes of Johannes Traxel and mother Elisabetha, both m. people, b. 4/13/1776, bapt. 7/16/1776, sponsor Catharina Traxelsin

pg.40, Mueller, Salem Reformed, David of Daniel Mueller and Juliana, m. people, b. 12/15/1780, bapt. 2/25/1781, witness David Traxel

pg.73, Bitinger, Reformed Church of Hagerstown, Susanna Maria of Philip Bitinger and mother Juliana Philabner, b. 7/14/1773, bapt. 8/28/1773, sponsor Gotthart Dresel and Maria Dresel

Rsh.1, pg.77, Truxel, Reformed Church of Hagerstown, Johann Daniel of George Truxel and mother Elisabetha both m. people, b. 2/11/1776, bapt. 6/25/1776, sponsor Johan Daniel Bender

Washington Co., Md., MHS. Norris Harris Church Registers Index
Drassel, Elizabeth, dau. of Peter Drassel and w. Margaretha, b. 2/14/1811, bapt. 6/9/1811, Evangelical Lutheran Congregation, Hagerstown, Md., Washington Co., #38, pg.78

Draxal, Sarah, b. 9/1/1813, bapt. 10/31/1813, dau. of Jacob and Susarina, Evangelical Lutheran and Reformed Church, Provinz, Md., Washington Co., Md., #13, pg.42

Draxel, Marianna, b. 7/3/1807, bapt. 11/1/1807, dau. of Jacob and Elizabeth Drexel, Evangelical Lutheran & Reformed, Provinz, Md., Washington Co., Md., #13, pg.42

Draxel, Polly, communicant Whitsuntich 1804, Evangelical Lutheran & Reformed, Hagerstown, Wash.Co., Md., #8, pg.162,

Dressler, Barb, m. 3/1799, Jacob Knodel Dressler, Evangelical Lutheran, Hagerstown, Wash Co., Md., #8, pg.116, she was the mother of Jacob Dressler b. 5/19/1810, bapt. 8/5/1810, Evangelical Lutheran Church, Hagerstown, Wash. Co., Md., #8 pg.74, Barb Drestler and Jacob Dressler were communicants for Whitsuntide, 1808, pg.174 Drexel, David, b. 10/1/1808, bapt. 5/8/1808, son of Jacob and Elizabeth Drexel, Evangelical Lutheran & Reformed Church, Provinz, Md. Wash. Co., Md., #13, pg.34

Drexel, Elizabeth, Communicant for 1802 day before W/S Evangelical Lutheran Church, Hagerstown, Washington Co., Md.,#8, pg.153

Drexel, Jacob, w. Elizabeth, dau. Marianna b. 7/3, David b. 10/1/1808, Evangelical Lutheran and Reformed Church, Provinz, Md., Washington Co., Md., #13, pgs.31,34

Drexel, Maud Comm. 1802, day before W/S Evangelical Lutheran and Reformed Church, Hagerstown, Washington Co., Md., #8, pg.153

Droscel, David, w. Maria, wit. at bapt. of David Drexst 5/8/809, Evangelical Lutheran and Reformed Church, Provinz, Md. Washington Co., Md., #13, pg.34

Traxell, Margaret, dau. of Peter and Margaretha, b. 2/2/1815, bapt. 9/1816, sponsor Henry Lohrey, Evangelical Lutheran and Reformed Church, Hagerstown, Washington, Co., Md., #8, pg.99

Traxel, Mary, dau. of Peter and Margaretha. b. 2/1/1814, bapt. 9/18/1816, sponsor father, Evangelical Lutheran and Reformed Church, Hagerstown, Washington Co., Md., #8, pg.99


Washington County, Maryland, Church Records of the 18th Century, 1768-1800, Hagerstown, Clearspring, Williamsport, Leitersburg, Funkstown, Clearfoss, Family Line Pub. Westminister, Md., 1988

?Brother to Rsh.113, pg.67. Reformed Church of Hagerstown,

Elisabetha of George Troxel and mother Margaretha, both m. people, b. 7/10/1771, bapt. 8/25/1771, sponsor Melchor Boltzhuber and his housewife Elisabetha

## PENNSYLVANIA

### Pennsylvania Catholic

Adams Co., Pa., John Timon Reily, Historical Notes, Genealogy Conewago Valley, 1988 -Reily - F159C648R44, John T. Reily, Genealogy of the Conewago Valley, Abstractions from John Timon Reily's books relating to the Conewago Valley, Copyright 1988, by John Timon Reily Historical Society, researched and published by Volunteers of The John Timon Reily Historical Society, Hanover, Pa., 17331, under the direction of Francis W. Miller, Chairman, Publishing Committee, Adams Co., Pa., John Timon Reiley, Conewago Valley
Rsh.9 Record 4505, Dreskzell, Samuel (Trexell) Vol.6, pg.36, key relative, Dreskzell, Anthony (Trexell),Father, Mother was Catharine, baptized 1799/05/12, sponsors Anthony Hithlberger (Rsh.29) (Hitselberger) and Mary Topper
Record 807, Drexel, ??? (Elder) Vol.4, pg.66, Related to the O'Bolds on Mother's side, was a frenchman who spoke English, Spanish and German. Dealt with many immigrants.
Record 1868, Drexell, Miss Vol.4, pg.179, Zindorff, Pius (son) she was godmother of Adam Oaster, b. 1816, the Zindorff family scattered in Ohio and Virginia
Record 7761, Lottie Tressler, np/173, her father is Edmund Sanders
Record 4900, Drexler, Anthony, Vol.6, pg.66, marriage date 1801/02/16, key relative, Riley, Nancy, w.
Record 2991, Drexler, Joseph, Vol.6, pg.87, death date 1812/06/?, bu. 1812/06/08
Record 4911, Drexler, Joseph, Vol.6, pg.67, marriage date 1807/04/24 key relative, Will, Elizabeth, w., witnesses, Joseph Storm and Susan O'Bold
Record 4641, Drexler, Mary, Vol.6, pg.46, key relative, Drexler, Joseph father, mother was Elizabeth, baptized 1808/03/13, sponsors, Joseph and Christina O'Bold

Record 3081, Driscal, Jacob, Vol.6, pg.92, death date 1815/08/?, bu. 1815/08/07

Record 6574, Driscoll, James, Vol.7, pg.60, he was a teamster for the Jesuits carried letters to Baltimore to Bishop Carroll from Fathers Pellentz and Gallitzin

Record 4408, Driskell, Charles Vol.6, pg.29, key relative, Driskell, Charles, father, mother was Anna, baptized 1798/09/07, sponsors, Jacob Driskell and Betsy Staub

Record 4372, Driskell, John, Vol.6, pg.26, key relative Driskell, Henry, father, mother was Margaret, baptized 1797/06/06, sponsors James Driskell and Mary Anna Will

Record 4279, Driskell, William, Vol.6, pg.19, key relative Driskell, Charles father, mother was Nancy, baptized 1796/09/25, sponsors, James and Margaret Driskelll

Record 4809, Driskle, Anna (Driskell), Vol.6, pg.60, key relative Driskle, Jacob (Driskell) father, mother was Mary Chrisimer, baptized 1801/03/19, sponsors, Henry and Catharine Becker

Rsh.18, Record 4579, Treskler, Catharine, Vol.6, pg.41, key relative Treskler, Jacob, father, mother was Elizabeth Rifle (Riffle), baptized 1800/08/17, sponsors, Rsh.5, Anthony Tresler and Catharine Kuhn

Record 7177, Mary Trexell, Vol.8, pg.142, sister is Elizabeth Trexell, brothers are John Trexell, Charles Trexell. note: there is a Charles and a John Driskell in these records, possibly the same people.

Record 1703, Trexell, Miss, Vol.4, pg.201, Key relative Zindorff, Miss Trexell, husb. Zindorff

Record 1420, Trostle, Jacob Mrs., Vol.5, pg.212, death date 1897/10/09, key relative Hoover, Lizzie, Mrs., dau.

Record 7178, Joseph Zindorff, w. Mrs. Trexell, they had Joseph, John, Pius, Andrew, George who went west and Elizabeth

Record 1702, Zindorff, m. Miss Trexell, she was godmother of Adam Oaster in 1830's.

Record 6306, Elizabeth Zindorf, b. 1784, d. 1859/11/13, husb. Joseph Zindorf, Sr., bu. at Conewago

Record 4952, Pius Zindorf son of Joseph Zindorf, mother was Elisabeth Drexler, baptized 1822/02/24, sponsors John Oaster and Catharine Schisler

Record 4920, Joseph Zindorff m. 1817/11/16 to Elisabeth Will, witness Joseph Krichten and Catharine Will

Adams County Church Records of the 18th Century, Family Line Publications, F157.A2,A33 - 1990
Conewago Chapel Roman Catholic Records
Rsh.18, pg.203, Catherine Tresler of James and Elisabeth Rifle Tresler b. 8/17/1800, bapt. 9/22/1800, sponsors, Anthony Tresler and Catharine Coon: I-36

Berks Co., Pa., Records of the Catholic Historical Society of Philadelphia, published by Society 1891, Pennsylvania General Findings in the Allemangel Area of Berks and Lehigh (Northampton) Cos. and adjacent areas. Catholic Goshenhoppen Registers Complied by Warren J. Ziegler, Box 503, Milford, NJ 08848 - Reprint August 1985.
Rsh.5, pg.l3, Drexel, Anthony 2/13/1776, m. at Goshenhoppen, Berks Co., Bally to Catherine Ermann, (author's note: actually this is Catherine Kuhn her stepfather was Ermann) 2/385. Son, (Rsh.18) James b. to Anthony & Catherine 2/341 b. 7/27/1777, bapt. 7/30/1777, in the Chapel, sponsors James Kuhn and Teresa Kuhn
Rsh.5, pg.39, Jacob Kuhn on 3/3/1768 m. Madalen Tapper, Bally 2/380 note: this Jacob Kuhn is a brother of Catherine Kuhn (mother remarried Joseph Ehrmann) m.Anthony Drexel (Dreckseler) (Rsh.5)
Rsh.5, pg.53, Catherine Riffel on 11/27/1744 m. John George Kuhn, Allen (Berks Co.)
note: when Balley is cited it is the Church or the Chapel and the Priest's home. In cold weather it could mean the parishioners home nearby.
Rsh.5, pg.39, Anna Marie Kuhn, b. 5/18/1783, bapt. 5/23/1783, dau. of John and Teresa (nee Fricker) Kuhn, Bally, sponsors Anthony Butz and Marie Butz, 2/366

Berks Co., Pa., The Goshenhoppen Registers, 1741-1819, reprinted from Records of the American Catholic Historical Society of Philadelphia Co., Pa., Groshenhoppen (Bally) Washington Twp., Berks Co., Berks Co., Pa., Pa. Genealogical Publishing Co. Inc., Bentley, Baltimore,1984 - Registers of Baptisms, Marriages, and Deaths of the Catholic Mission at Goshenhoppen (Bally), Washington Township, Berks County, Pennsylvania
Rsh.5, pg.64, Drexel, James of Anthony and Catherine b.

7/27/1777, bapt. 7/30 in the Chapel, sponsors James Kuhn and Theresa Kuhn. note: this was St. Paul's Chapel, Bally, Washington Twp., Pa., still standing in 1995 and known as the Church of the Most Blessed Sacrament
Rsh.5, pg.8, bapt. Martin Lochler, son of George Ernest and M. Magdalen Lechler, bapt. 7/24/1744 at parents house Oley, sponsors Martin Reisel and Catharine Riffel
Rsh.5, pg.9, bapt. Schmidt, Catherine, of Phillip and Eva Mary Schmidt, sponsors George and Catherine Kuhn, no date noted.
Rsh.5, pg.15, marriage, 11/27/1744, in John Kuhn's house, John George Kuhn to Catharine Riffel, witnesses the bridegrooms parents and brothers and others
Rsh.5, pg.3, Kuhn, Anna Barbara, of Henry and Margaret Kuhn bapt. 3/28/1742 in John Kuhn's house (Cedar Creek),sponsors John and Anna Barbara his wife
Rsh.5, pg.7, Margaret Kuhn of Henry and Margaret Kuhn, bapt. 4/22/1744, in John Kuhn's house, sponsor John Eckenroth and Margaret Wise his wife
Rsh.5, pg.10, George James Kuhn of George and Catherrine Kuhn, bapt. 3/31/1745, sponsors Jacob Riffel and Ollita Meyers
Rsh.171, pg.13, Anthony Hucki (Hookey) of Nicholas and Catharine (Kleyss) Hucki born 9/29/1751, bapt.10/17 following in Edward Carty's house, sponsors Anthmy Gursser (umlat over u) and Elizabeth (Kleyss) his wife. Ancestor of Drexel family of Philadelphia

Cambia Co., Pa., Western Pennsylvania - Catholic Baptisms in Western Pennsylvania, 1799-1828, Father Peter Helbron's Greensburg Register, Baltimore Genealogical Publishing 1985
pg.43, Baptism of Gery (Gary) Margaret of Michael and Mary Gery, Bapt. October 7, 1805, sponsors Peter and Margaret Dreschler

Cambia Co., Pa., SOUVENIER OF LORETTO CENETENARY 1799-1899 Compiled by Ferdinand Kittell
pg.34, Loretto was founded by people from Conewago area in Pennsylvania, these individuals were led there by Capt. M.McGuire, an Irishman, in 1788. In August of 1799, Father Gallitzin came to McGuire's settlement and built the first church between Lancaster, Pa., and St. Louis. Father Gallitzin had previously been at Baltimore, Md. then at Conewago where he

was a missionary priest who rode horseback throughout the countryside. He visited, from Conewago, Taneytown, Pipe Creek, Hagerstown, and Cumberland in Maryland, Chambersburg, Path, Shade Valley, Huntingdon and the Allegheny mountains in Pennsylvania. On March 23, 1804 Cambria County was formally organized.

pg.69. "Father Kittell found the records of Father Gallitzin, from 1800 to a few days before his death in 1840, written on loose sheets and kept in a box. He arranged the sheets in chronological order, and had them bound...he took these with him to Rome in the spring of 1896 and during three months of the summer season which he spent in the ancient monastery of Galloro, on the Alban hills, six miles from the Eternal City, he made up his "Index of Parish Records, Loret, Pa., 1800-1896...This index comprises an alphabetical list of 1301 marriages, 6949 baptisms...arranged in family groups under the names of the parents...the number of families represented in this Index is 2143."

Matrimonial and Baptismal Records of Rev. D.A. Gallitzin
note: "Father Gallitzin in making entries of baptisms, was not accustomed to express the maiden surname of the mother. Hence such surnames, when not found in the Matrimonial Register, have been in some instances supplied from other sources, but in too many cases they are unfortunately wanting...But it is certain that he performed many baptisms and marriages which he failed to record, for the reason that, administering these sacraments while traveling among his scattered flock, he would frequently, as he himself stated, lose the memoranda which he intended, on returning home, to copy into the Registers."

Benden, Robert and Mary Caroline Trexler, m. 8/21/1838, child Mary Elizabeth, record for year 1839

Byrne, Barnabas and Mark Driskel, m. 10/11/1825. children, Mary Magdalen, Sarah Jane, Juliana, Anastasia, Silas Augustine, Michael, Charles Thomas, Agnes Elizabeth, Margaret Catherine. Record 1826-1838.

Byrne, Augustine and Mary Ann Driskel, m. 5/6/1828, children, Michael, Alice, Thomas, Mary, Margaret, Sarah Ann, Jane Matilda. Record 1829-39.

Cronyn, Philip and Sarah Troxell. children John. Record 1828

Driskel, Charles and Ann, children Mary, Michael. Record 1805-

07

Driskel, James and Mary Ann Barnicle, m. 5/16/1822. children, Mary Ellen, Charles, Michael John, Elias. Record 1823-35
Driskel, Michael and Matilda Kaylor, m. 4/12/1836. children Catherine, John. Record 1837-38
Lilly, Samuel and Catherine Troxell, m. 2/3/1825. children , Thomas, Joseph, William, Isidore. Record 1826-39
Rsh.38, Trexler, Joseph and Elizabeth. children, Peter, Ann Magdalen, Mary Joseph, Jacob, John, David. Record 1808-22. note: it is not certain that this dau.'s name was Mary Joseph or if this entry was a dau. and a son.
?Rsh.35, Trexler, Peter and Ann Margare Donoughe, m. 5/21/1833. children Mary Elizabeth and Ann Margaret. Record 1834-35.
Rsh.38, Trexler, Joseph, Jr. and Susan Krise, m. 6/26/1838. children John Andrew, Jacob. Record 1838-40. note: it is not certain that these children are not three instead of 2.
Troxell, Jacob and Susan, children, Catherine, Sarah, Abraham, William, Henry, Samuel. Record 1805-18.
Troxell, Joseph and Mary, children, Margaret. Record 1806.
Troxell, John and Susan, children, Mary. Record 1826.
Troxell, William and Jane Wharton m. 4/16/1839.

Register of Deaths in St. Michael's Parish, Loretto, Pa., from 11/17/1793 to 10/10/1899. - "...these are from many sources, but chiefly from the headstones in St. Michael's cemetery..."

Byrne, Augustine b. 1807, d. 5/18/1867, Mrs. Augustine (Mary Ann Driskel) b. 1805, d. 1/17/1890
Callahan, Andrew d. 1/17/1874, Mrs. Andrew Callahan (Ann Magdalena Trexler) d. 12/4/1878
Driskel, Michael L., b. 11/2/1842, d. 8/18/1888.
Lilly, Mrs. Samuel (Catharine Troxell) b. 10/20/1805 d. 11/29/1865.
Tomlinson, Mrs. Francis (Mary Matilda Driskei) b. 11/28/1850 d. 8/4/1886
Rsh.35 Trexler, Peter, b. 4/15/1808 d. 11/25/1885
Trexler, Joseph, b. 2/15/1816, d. 1/10/1892
Trexler, Mrs. James b. 11/15/1822, d.1888
Troxell, Jacob, b. 1779, d. 5/14/1833
Troxell, Mrs. Jacob (Susan) b. 4/10/1780, d. 3/3/1850
Troxell, Sarah, b. 6/10/1807 d. 10/25/1850

Troxell, Abraham, b. 1/10/1810, d. 7/24/1852
Troxell, William, b. 12/17/1811, d. 10/2/1847
Troxell, Henry, b. 7/19/1815, d. 11/17/1883
Troxell, Mrs. Henry (Hannah McElmee) b. 1827 d. 4/11/1886
Troxell, John J. (Mary J. Gallagher) b. 1/26/1832 d. 1/18/1887

Paschal Communions. Paschal Confessions. Confirmation
"...Father Gallitzin had written down the names of those who
fulfilled the precept of Paschal Communion in 1810, and of
Paschal Confession in 1811 and 1813, as also the names of
those who where confirmed by Bishop Egan in 1811..."
Paschall Confessions - 1811: Driskel, Ann, Trexler, Peter, Trexler,
Elizabeth, Troxell, Jacob, Troxell, Susan, Troxell, Margaret
Confirmation - "names of those who were confirmed in the old log
church, Loretto, by Rt. Rev. Michael Egan, first Bishop of
Philadelphia, in September or October, 1811:" Driskel, James
1795, Driskel, William 1797, Driskel, Charles 1799, Driskel, Ann
1802, Driskel, Mary Ann, November 2, 1805, Driskel, Michael
8/18/1807, Trexler, Peter no date, Trexler, Mrs. Peter, no date

"From a list of subscribers for monument of Father Gallitzen -
probably made up in 1847" Michael Driskel $2.00

"From subscription list of new brick church at Loretto - 1847:
Michael Driskel $60.00

"Loretto, June 1850 - Memorandum of men who worked at the
digging of foundation, and of inspectors who came to examine
the foundation and work." - "David Trexler saw and examined the
foundation."

Cambria County, Pennsylvania - Catholic Trails West, The
Founding Catholic Families Pa., Gateway Press, Baltimore 1989,
Vol.2, Edmund Adams and Barbara Brady O'Keefe
note: this area was initially Allegheny Twp.
pg.650, Vol.2, St. Michael, Loretto, Trexler Family member
confirmed 1811
pg.647, Jacob Troxel, signed petition, 4/24/1807, Conewago
pg.651, War of 1812, Jacob Troxel, Jacob and John Will from St.
Michaels at Loretto, Prince Gattilzin assisted in drilling the troops,
1st Battalion 142 Regt. Pa. Mil. Supp. attack against Niagria Falls.

Rsh.38, pg.708, Joseph Troxell (Trexler), 1802-15 Tax List, m. Elizabeth, 1811 Pascal Confession, children Peter b. 4/15/1808, Ann Magdalen, Mary, Joseph b. 2/15/1816, Jacob, John, David, 1808-1822

Rsh.35, pg.708, continued, Peter Troxell (Trexler), 1802-15 Tax list, 1811 Pascal Confession, confirmation, m. Margaret, d. before 7/2/1844, Cambria Co. Orphans Court Records, 1811 Pascal Confession, confirmation

?Rsh.18, Jacob (James) Troxell (Trexler) b. 1779, d. 5/24/1833, 1807 Gallitzin Petition, 1808-15 Tax List, 1810 Allegheny Twp., Cambria Co. Census, 1812 War of, 1811,1813 Pascal Confession, m. Susan, b. 4/10/1780, d. 3/3/1850, 1811 Pascal Confession, children Catherine b. 3/3/1805, Sarah b. 6/10/1807, Abraham b. 1/10/1810, William b. 12/17/1811, Henry b. 7/19/1815, Samuel b. 1818

?Rsh.38, pg.708, continued, Joseph, (?son of Peter and Margaret) m. Mary, child Margaret b. 1806, note a Joseph Trexler was administer for Margaret Trexler, 1844, Cambria Co., Orphans Court Records


Lancaster Co., Pa., Catholic, Marriages, Baptisms, Burials at St. Mary's Church, Lancaster, Pa., 1787 to 1804. Barbara Brady O'Keefe, Miami, Fla.19832, call F159.L2 033 1983
note: The American Catholic Historical Society Journal is held in most Diocesan Headquarters. the Lancaster Historical Society holds all volumes to current.
pg.4, John Triskell m. Maria Oekin, 6/3/1803, in the presence of John Luch, Alexander Oekin and Maria Luck


Lancaster, Pa., Marriages, Baptisms, burials at St. Mary's Church, Lancaster, Pa., 1787 to 1804/ Barbara Brady O'Keefe, Miami, Fla, 19832, call F159.L2 033 1983
Triskil, Margaret, bapt. 10/6/1792, dau. of John Triskil and his w. Mary, sponsors John Lick and Anna Rohner 5-7 1/2?


Lancaster, Pa., Journal of the American Catholic Historical Society, 1758-1781
Baptismal Records St. Mary's Church, Lancaster, Pa., pg.352, A.D. 1789, List of those m. with the assistance and benediction of John Charles Helbron, as parish priest and qualified witness. June 3, 1789, John Triskell and Maria Oekin, in

the presence of John Luck, Alexander Oekin and Maria Luck

Lancaster, Pa., Records of Catholic Historical Society of Philadelphia, Vol.XXV, published by the Society 1914, American Catholic Historical Society
Baptismal Records St. Mary's Church, Lancaster
pg.262, A.D. 1796, b. 12/27 and bapt. 12/29, Mary and Margaret, twin daughters of James and Catharine Murray (?Rsh.76), sponsors, Margaret and James Reedy and Margaret McConally, Louis Barth Priest
pg.39, year 1787, John, lawful son of John Luck and Mary Margaret Agatha(?) sponsors John Driskel (Driscoll?) and Eva Lochler. He was b. 8/29.
pg.39, 10/18/1787, Anthony, lawful son of Caspar Trippel and his w. Catharine Anthony. sponsors, Anthony Keine and his w. Dame Catharine Algeyer. He was b. on 10/10
pg.45, bapt. on 10/6/1792, Margaret Triskil, dau. of John Triskil and his w. Mary, sponsors, John Lick and Anna Rohnen 5-7 1/2(?)

Philadelphia, Pa., Pennsylvania Catholic Trails West; founding Catholic families of Pennsylvania,, by Edmund Adams and Barbara Brady O'Keefe.Balt. Genea.Publ. 1988, Vol.1 & 2, E184.C3 A15 1988
Vol.1, St. Joseph Church, Philadelphia
Rsh.126, Peter Tessier (Texler) m. Mary Ferry, child Frances b. 5/26/1797 and child Francis Peter b. 1/7/1800

Philadelphia, Pa., Journal of the American Catholic Historical Society, 1758-1781, St. Josephs Catholic Church, Philadelphia, Pa.
Vol.1, William Fitzgerald, son of William Fitzgerald and Margaret Triskel (Driscoll) b. 10/9/1774, bapt. 5/28, sponsors John Cobole and Joanna Swinney
Daniel Smith of Daniel and Mary Smith b. 8/1/1772, bapt. 8/14, sponsors Samuel Ridney and Anna Triskel.
author's note: Catholic Conewago records contains a notation "is not Triskel the same as Drexel?"

Philadelphia, Pa., Katharine Drexel, a biography, by Sister Consuela Maria Duffy, S.B.S. Mother Katharine Drexel Guild,

**Sisters of the Blessed Sacrament, Cornwells Heights, Pa., 19020
1977**
Rsh.171, In 1821 Francis Martin Drexel and Katharine Hookey
were married by Bishop Conwell in St. Mary's Church in
Philadelphia, Pa. The Hookey family had been prominent in St.
Augustine's church almost from the time the church was built.
Three sons and three daughters blessed this marriage one of
them Francis Anthony Drexel was b. 1/20/1824 and m. Hannah
Langstroth a Baptist Quaker (brethren/dunkard). Francis A.
Drexel was founder of Drexel and Company the highly successful
investment firm in Philadelphia, Pa. Their dau. Katherine will be
cannoized in the year 2000. She established the Order of the
Blessed Sacrament which ministered to and educated African
Americans and Native Americans. With the help of her sister
Louise she established a school for African Americans in
Powhatan, Va. which is outside of Richmond, Va. The Blessed
Sacrament Order is located at the Mother House in Bensalem,
Pennsylvania.

**Philadelphia, Pa., Father Farmer's Marriage Registers, 1758-1786,
St. Josephs Church, Philadelphia, Pa., Barbara Brady O'Keffe,
March 1983 2120 S.W 127 Avenue, Miami, Florida 33175**
pg.22, Joseph Harakaum m. Mary Magdalen Trostler, widow,
9/5/1758 in the Philadelphia chapel.(?widow Rsh.109)


## Lutheran

**Adams County Church Records of the 18th Century, Family Line
Publications, F157.A2,A33 - 1990**
**Germany Township, St. John's Evangelical Lutheran Church,
pg.183**
Rsh.24, Elis. Troxel of Ad. and Christina, b. 2/17/1800, bapt.
4/14/1800, sponsor, Jacob Smidt and Elis.
Rsh.24, Joh. Troxel of Ad. and Christina, b. 12/26/1795, bapt.
3/12/1796, sponsor, Jac. Smith and Elis.
Rsh.24, Jacob Troxel of Adam and Christina, b.4/11/1793, bapt.
6/1/1793, sponsor, parents
Rsh.24, Abraham Miller of Georg. and Magdl., b. 12/15/1788,
bapt. 4/10/1789, sponsor, Ad. Troxel and Christina
Rsh.45, An.Mar.Traxel of Dav. and Elis., b. 8/18/1789, bapt.

10/11/1789, sponsor, Elis. Bischoffin, single
Rsh.101, Magdl. Traxel of Jac. and Elis., b. 12/18/1789, bapt.
1/31/1790, sponsor, George Ad. Ohler and Cathr.
Rsh.24, Sophia Troxel of Ad. and Christina, b. 5/10/1790, bapt.
6/27/1790, sponsor, Sophia Troxelin, the grandmother (Rsh.43)
Rsh.43, Sarah Porter of Reinhardt and Barb., b. 1/16/1787, bapt.
3/11/1787, sponsor, Sophia Traxelin
Rsh.101, Elis. Troxel of Jac. and Elis, b. 1/17/1787, bapt.
4/9/1787, sponsor, Sophia Troxelin, the grandmother
Rsh.101, Jacob Kragel (Kraglo) of Georg and Barb., b. 4/2/1785,
bapt. 5/29/1785, sponsor, Jac. Traxel and Elis (Rsh.101)
Rsh.101, Elis. Traxel (Troxel) of John and Elis., b. 1/22/1786,
bapt. 4/30/1786, sponsor, Elis. Traxelin
Elisabeth Baschman (Buschman?) of Jacob and Catharine, b.
4/4/1782, bapt. 8/21/1782, sponsor, Jacob Traehxel (Traxel) and
Elizabeth (?Rsh.91).
Rsh.45, Elis. Bauer of Joh. and Marg., b. 2/22/1783 (?2/22/1883),
bapt. 11/1/1783, sponsor, Dav. Trachsel and Elis.
Sophia Rommel of Ludwig and Ana Maria, b. 8/1/1777, bapt.
9/14/1777, sponsor, Sophia Drachselin, w. of Daniel Drachsel
(Rsh.43)
?Rsh.91, Magdalena Drachsel of David and Elisabetha, b.
10/4/1777, bapt. 11/9/1777, sponsor, Sophia Drachselin (Rsh.43)

Littlestown, Pa., Christ Church , No date, pg.86
Membership - Daniel Troxel, David Troxel, Elizabeth Troxler
Rsh.43, pg.85, List of Communicants 4/21/1776, held by Rev.
Charles Lewis Boehme, Sophia Troxeler

Berks Co., Pa., Pennsylvania Vital Records (Church Records),
F148, 1983, Vol.1,2,3
Vol.3, Tohickon Reformed Records
Rsh.111, pgs.403,159, Jacob Traxel and his w. Elizabeth have the
following children and have entered them here as an evidence of
their baptism, Jacob. b. 12/8/1781, Elizabeth b. 7/30/1787,
Catherine b. 9/18/1789, Magdalena b. 2/27/1792, Margaret b.
2/24/1794
Rsh.121, pgs.409,165, Philip Tristler w. Maria, Sarah b. 9/24/1792,
John b. 6/18/1795, Hannah b. 6/18/1797
Rsh.111, pgs.410/166, Jacob Troxel, w. Elizabeth dau. Sarah b.
7/31/98

Rsh.121, pgs.421,177, Philip Tristeler, w. Maria, dau. Margaret b. 9/13/1804

pgs.428,184, David son of John and Elizabeth Steinbach, bapt. 1/7/1810, witness Jacob Baker and Polly Tristler

pgs.445, 201, Maria Tressler b. 9/4/1820, parents John and Margaret Tressler, Witness Henry Zep and Sarah Tressler

Rsh.111, pgs. 519,275, Burials by Rev. Jacob Senn, 3/2/1806, Jacob Troxel

pgs.527,283, 1820 buriels, 11/18/1820, John Tressler, 25 years 6 months

pgs.534,291, 11/11/1834, bu. widow Tressler, 71 years old

pgs.573,327, Calechumens in Flaland, 11/1813, Anna Treichler, age 17, father John

Rsh.121, pgs.575,329, Calechumens at Tohickon, 5/28/1819, Hannah Tressler, age 20, father Phillip

Rsh.121, pg.330, David Trissler, age 18, father Phillip

Vol.3, Goshenhoppen

pg.98, Goshenhoppen, year 1793, Jacob Geri m. Elizabeth Dreisler

pg.110, list of communicants, Fall 1808, Sally Troxel, Catherine Huber, Christine Huber, Elisabeth Rother

?Rsh.47 10/24/1813 communicants, Henrich Traxel, Sara his w.

Rsh.47, pg.111, 4/9/1814, Easter Day, Lords Supper, Henrich Traxel, Sara his w.

Rsh.47, pg.112, 9/25/1814, communicant, Elizabeth Traxel

pg.120 year 1770, 12/28, b. Johannes, son of George Draxel, witness Johannes Koebler (Keebler) and w.

pg.201 and 208, name of Calechumens year 1814, Elis. Traxel age 16

pg.209 year 1816, Calechumens, Sophia Traxel, age 16 years

Berks and Leehigh Counties, Pennsylvania Archives, 2nd Series, Vol.9

pg.443, Rev. Johannes Helfrich Personal and Pastorial Records

Rsh.87, Jonathan Haas and Catharina Trexler, m. 6/17/1804, Longswamp, Berks Co.

Rsh.87, Benjamin Trexler m. Maria Drescher, 3/10/1805, Longswamp Berks.

Rsh.148/151, Peter Traxal m. Magdalend Sigfried 4/1/1799, at ministers home.

John Walbert m. Catharina Dresher 2/8/1801, Longswamp Berks

Co.

Frederick Braum m. Elizabeth Dexel, 5/1/1803, Longswamp Berks Co.

Nicholas Hartman m. Susanna Drescher 3/2/1807, Ministers home.

Rsh.62, Soloman Trexel a son is b. to Peter and Sybilla Trexel, 11/28/1799, he m. Barbara Schmidt 12/17/1824 and d. 1/12/1836, 3 sons, one dau. His dau. Leweine b. 10/11/1825 m. Johannes Vollweiler and d. 1846.

Rsh.57, Lorentz Troxel m. Christine Reichard, 12/3/1793, Weisenbert, Leehigh Co., Pa.


Berks Co., Pa., Ministerial Acts (Baptisms and Confirmations of Daniel Schumacher, Lutheran Pastor, 1754-1774, newly translated by Frederick S. Weiser, 1967, Lutheran Theological Seminary, Gettysburg, Pa.

Rsh.11, pg.64, Drachsell, 12/26/1760, Jurg Jacob 6 weeks old Egypt, son of Michael Drachsell and Margaretha, sponsors Jurg Kohler, Jacob Kohler, Magdalena Drachselln, Eva Schneider

Rsh.86, pg.50, Drechseler, 4/29/1759, Johann Jurg, 14 weeks old bapt. Schmaltzgass, son of Peter Drechseler and Catharina, sponsors Jurg Hoffman, Catharina Schumachern, single

Rsh.86, pg.68, 5/24/1761, Johann Henrich, 9 weeks old in the Schmaltzgass, son of Peter Drechseler and Catharina, sponsors Johann Henrich Wetzell, single, and Catharina Drechselern, single

Rsh.86, pg.137, 6/12/1768, bapt. Susanna Catharina b. 1/14 in Macugie at home, dau. of Peter Drechseler and Maria

Rsh.86, Drechseler,Catharina sponsors child of Joseph Allbrecht and Susanna Catharina

pg.191, Dreschseler, year 1769, confirmed in the Ziegel or St. John's Church, Sunday Quasimodo Maria Drechselern, Barbara Treschern

pg.185, Treber confirmed in Windsor Twp., year 1765, Catharine Trebern

pg.132, Trescher, year 1767, the 29th bapt. Christina, 8 days old Weissenburg, parents Christopher Trescher and Margaretha, sponsors Peter Biber and Christina. note: this is found in between October and December notes

pg.80, year 1761, confirmed in Weisenburg Church, Christopher Trescher

pg.189, year 1768 Easter, in Ziegel Church, Conrad Frescher,

Maria Margarfetha Treschern
pg.191, year 1769, in the Ziegel or St. John's Church, Sunday
Quasimodo Maria Drechselern, Barbara Treschern

Berks Co., Pa., Source and Documents of the Pennsylvania
Germans: XIII, Records of Pastoral Acs at Christ Lutheran Church,
Stouchsburg, Berks County, Pennsylvania, Part 1, Baptisms,
1743-1819, translated and edited by Frederick S. Weiser,
Birdsboro, Pennsylvania, The Pennsylvania German Society, 1989
pg.100, Dresser, Margreth, dau. of Daniel and Eva Dressler b.
1/1/1799, bapt. 1/20/1799, sponsors Joh. Nocol. Cllllemens, w.
pg.109, Drostel, Rachel, dau. of Georg and Susanna Drostel, b.
1/26/1795, bp. not given, sponsors parents, Maria, dau. of Georg
and Susanna Drostel, b. 9/27/1796, bapt. not given sponsors
parents, Susanna, dau.of George and Susanna Drostel b.
9/17/1798, bapt. not given., sponsors, parents, Sarah, dau. of
Georg and Susanna Drostel b. 11/31/1801, bapt. not given
sponsors, parents

Berks Co., Pa., Albany Twp., Jerusalem Lutheran Church, Pa.,
1959 Number 23, CS 42.N43, publication of the National
Genealogical Society located at rear of LHG RR Library of
Congress
Rsh.54, pg.20, Esther, b. 5/8/1795, bapt. 7/19/1795, dau. of
Andreas Dressler and Cathar., sponsor Fridrich Luden, Cathar

Berks Co., Pa., Horns Church (St. John's Reformed), known as
Hains Church, Heidelberg Twp., Berks Co., Pa.
Rsh.120, pg.442, 5/23/1774, John Drostel son of Abraham and
Susannah, sponsors Christian Benz and w. Anna Mary
Rsh 120, pg.444, 2/18/1776, Anna Mary Drostel, dau of Abraham
and w., sponsors George Ruth and w. Anna Mary
Rsh.120, pg.445, 1/19/1778 , John Leonhard son of Jacob and
w., sponsors Abraham Drostel and w. Susanna
Rsh.120, pg.452, 3/31/1782, Elizabeth Drostel dau. of Abraham
and w., sponsors Peter Dechert and w. Elizabeth

Berks Co., Breinigsville, Pa., today Berks and eastern Lebanon,
Sources and Documents of the Pennsylvania Germans VII,
Tulpehocken Church Records, 1730-1800, Christ Church (Little
Tulpehocken) and Altalaha Church, Rehrersburg, translated by

148

Frederick S. Weiser, Breinigsville, Pa., the Pennsylvania German
Society, 1982
pg.56, Drebler, announced for communion 3/21/1761, Mechior
Drebler and Friderich Taxis
?Rsh.51, pg.23, Troster, umlat over o, Joh. Martin Troster,
3/20/1743 son Joh. Martin bapt. 3/17/1743, sponsors Ulrich Spies
and his w.
Rsh.51, 11/18/1746 a son Joh. Michael Troster bapt. 12/21/1746,
sponsors Joh. Michael Axer and his finance
pg.40, child of Michael Schneider, Maria Catharina b. 1/3/1768,
bapt. 2/7/1768, sponsors Martin Troster and his w. (Rsh.51)
Rsh.51, pg.72, Martin Troster son Johan Wilhem, month not
shown but between February and October on the 21st year 1758,
bapt. shortly thereafter in home, sponsors Wilhelm Stein and
Margaretha Gebhardin
Rsh.51, pg.73, Martin Troster, son Johannes b. and bapt.
1/3/1760, Oculi Sunday, sponsors Johannes Gebhartt and Anna
Maria Brackin
Rsh.51, pg.77, Martin Troster, dau. Catharine b. 1/1/1764,
Sexagesima, sponsors Daniel Kramer and Catharina Kurrin
Rsh.51, pg.83, Martin Troster and w. sponsor on 3/1/1767, Judica
Sunday, Maria Catharine dau. of Johannes Rettmann
Rsh.51, pg.85, Martin Troster son Johann Martin, 8/6/1768, 17th
Sunday after Trinity, Martin Troster and w.
Rsh.51, pg.88, Martin Troster in Schamicki (Shamokin), dau.
Maria Cathrina, b. 5/22/1770, bapt. 4/25/1771, sponsors
Bartblomaus Ziebach and w.

Cumberland Co., Pa., Memorial Lutheran Church, Shippensburg,
Pa.,
1775-1845, Translated Records, SHS
Rsh.7, pg.8, section 12, baptisms, child Johannes, b. 12/7/1779,
parents Michael Drecksler, sponsors Johannes Engel and Elenora
pg.11, section 16, child Johannes, b. 1/2/1785, bapt. 5/15/1785,
parents Jacob Witmer and Anna Maria, sponsors Michael Drexler
and Elisabeth
Rsh.7, pg.11, section 17, child Jacob, b. 8/8/1786, bapt. not given
1786, parents Michael Trexler and Elisabetha, sponsors Christian
Weisser and Susanna
pg.13, section 19, child James b. 3/19/1787, parents William
Armstrong and Elisabeth, sponsors Michael Drechsler and

Elisabeth

pg.13, section 20, child Anna Catharine b. 5/5/1787, bapt. 5/27/1787, parents Christian Weisser, Lutheran deacon, Susanna nee Kuckelin, sponsors Michael Drechsler and Elisabeth, nee Krausin

Rsh.7, pg.15, section 22, child Susanna b. 10/10/1788, bapt.12/2/1788, parents Michael Trexler and Elisabeth, sponsors Christian Weiser and Susanna

Rsh.7, pg.16, section 23, child Magdalena, b. 12/10/1790, parents Michael Trexsler and Elisabeth, sponsors Peter Kramer and Magdalena

Rsh.7, pg.18, section 25, child Anna Margaretha, b. 3/1/1793, bapt. 5/12/1793, parents Michael Trecksler and Elisabeth, sponsors Adam Blum and Margaretha

pg.20, child Johannes, b. 2/23/1794, bapt. 4/27/1794, parents Peter Kramer and Maria sponsors Peter Trexler and Veronicka Vogt

Rsh.166, pg.24, section 30, child Anna Maria, b. 7/11/1797, bapt. 8/27/1797, parents Conrad Drechsler and Phronica, sponsors Peter Kremer and Maria

Rsh.165, pg.25, section 31, child Susanna, b. 1/17/1798, bapt. 2/25/1798, parents Peter Drechsler, Maria, sponsors Christian Drexler and Sara

Rsh.169, pg.27, child Alena, b. 10/20/1800, parents Joh Drecksler and Schinne/Ginny?, sponsors Conrad Drcksler and Fronica

pg.30, Communicants 5/10/1799, Conrad Drecksler and w., Fronica Drecksler

pg.31, Communicants 5/21/1800, Fronica Dreckslern and Conrad Drecksler, Reichert Treisch and w., Peter Kramer

pg.54, with permission of both church councils this bill is signed Shippensburg, May 12, 1788, Michel Treckler

Rsh.166, pg.64, Communicants 8/27/1797, Conrads Drechsler, Maria Weiser, m. to Drechsler, Phronica Drechsler

pg.65, Communicants 7/29/1798 Peter Drechsler, Maria Drechsler

pg.77, child Joh Martin, 2/13/1800, parents Martin Kladdi, Catha, sponsors Conrad Dreittsler and Fronica

Rsh.166, pg.79, child Sally, b. 9/16/1802, parents Conrad Dreksler, Freny, sponsors Michael Dreksler and Elizabeth

Rsh.7, pg.80, child Catharina, b. 6/5/1803, parents Michael Drecksler and Elizabeth, sponsors Johannes Bauer and Catharina

Rsh.166, pg.82, child Johannes, b. 7/19/1804, parents Conrad

Drechsler and Franny, sponsors Henrich Pilgrim and Dorothea
Rsh.7, pg.83, child Susanna, b. 9/4/1804, parents Michael
Drechsler and Elizabeth, sponsor Susanna Weiser
Rsh.165, pg.83, child Johannes, b. 7/4/1804, parents Peter
Drechsler and Maria, sponsors parents
pg.84, child Robert, b. 4/13/1805, parents Robert M'Conche and
Elizabeth, sponsors Michael Drechsler
Rsh.165, pg.86, child Samuel b. 4/22/1807, parents Peter
Drechsler and Maria, sponsors Jacob Weiser
pg.86, child Johannes, b. 10/22/1806, parents Johannes
McConachy and Susanna sponsors Peter Drechsler and Maria
Rsh.7, pg.86, child Sara Anna b. 6/11/1807, parents Michael
Drechsler and Elizabeth, sponsors Susanna Weiser
pg.89, child Maria, b. May 9, 1809, bapt. 6/25/1809, parents
Johannes Miller and Catharine, sponsors Peter Drechsler and
Maria
Rsh.165, pg.92, child Sara Anna, b. 1/5/1810, bapt. 5/12/1810,
parents Peter Drechsler and Maria, sponsors parents
Rsh.7, pg.97, child Elisabeth, b. 9/12/1811, bapt. 8/14/1812,
parents Michael Drechsler and Elisabeth, sponsors parents
Rsh.166, pg.100, child Rosanna, b. 4/6/1813, bapt. 9/26/1813,
parents Conrad Drechsler and Roehny, sponsors Jacob Kremer
and Anna Maria
Rsh.7, pg.103, child Margaretha b. 1/30/1814, bapt. 9/11/1814,
parents Michael Drechsler and Elisabeth, sponsors parents
Rsh.168, pg.104, child George, b. 11/2/1814, bapt. 5/7/1815,
parents Daniel Drechsler and Elisabeth, sponsors George Kremer
and Maria
Rsh.165, pg.108, child Helena b. 12/21/1815, bapt. 5/5/1816,
parents Peter Drechsler and Maria, sponsors parents
Rsh.7, pg.109, child Anna Maria b. 3/30/1816, bapt. 8/25/1816,
parents Michael Drechsler and Elisabeth, sponsors parents
Rsh.165, pg.118, child Peter, b. 2/7/1819, bapt. 5/30/1819,
parents Peter Drechsler and Maria, sponsors parents
Rsh.7, pg.118, child Anna Catharina b. 11/6/1818, bapt.
5/30/1819, parents Michael Drechsler and Elisabeth, sponsors
parents
Rsh.169, pg.119, child Sara Anna, b. 2/4/1819, bapt. 8/22/1819,
parents Johannes Drechsler and Christina, sponsors Michael
Drechsler and Elisabeth
Rsh.168, pg.124, child Maria b. 8/24/1810, bapt. 12/24/1820,

parents Daniel Drechsler and Elisabeth, sponsors Jacob Kremer and Maria

pg.124, child Johannes b. 8/16/1820, bapt. 3/4/1821, parents Jacob Aue and Susanna sponsors Peter Drechsler and Mary

Rsh.7, pg.125, child Christina b. 3/9/1821, bapt. 7/8/1821, parents Michael Drechsler and Elisabeth, sponsors parents

Rsh.170, pg.142, child Catharine, b. 3/27/1826, parents Jacob Traxler and Elisabeth, sponsors parents

Rsh.170, pg.142, child John, b. 9/22/1828, bapt. 7/26/1829, parents Jacob Traxler and Elisabeth, sponsors parents

pg.172, child George Cremer, b. 10/31/1843, bapt. 1/25/1844, parents Jacob Trexler and Mrs. Trexler sponsors parents

pg.183, 9/22/1801 Communicants, Anna Treisch, Conrad Drecksler, w. Fronica

pg.188, May 22, 1813, Communicants, Conrad Drechsler, w., pg. 189, Jacob Dreisch, w., Anna Maria Dreisch, Elizabeth Dreschsler, Maria Drechsler

Rsh.166, pg.190, 4/23/1815, Communicants Elizabeth Drechsler, Froehnry Drechsler, Elisabeth Drechsler, Maria Drechsler

pg.193, Communicants 4/6/1817, Elizabeth Drechsler, Elizabeth Dreisch

pg.194, Communicants May 30, 1819, Peter Drechsler and w., Maria, Maria Drechsler, Elisabeth Drechsler, Michael Drechsler, Elizabeth Drexler, Eleonore Drexler

pg.228, Union between Evangelical Lutheran and Evangelical Reformed Congregations made 9/9/1778, signature - Michael Trechsler

Cumberland Co., Pa., Records of the Reformed Church, Shippensburg, Pa., Cumberland Co., Pa., F. 159.S56L54, 1982, trans. from German by Wm. C. Lightner + Tombstone Inscriptions, Shippensburg, Pa., pub. South Central Pa., Genealogical Soc., Inc., P.O. Box 1824, York, Pa., 17405, copyright 1982

Rsh.7, pg.1, signers to church agreement 9/9/1788, Michael Trexler

Rsh.7, pg.3, 4/7/1779, b. Johannes, parents Michael Drexler, sponsor Johannes Engel and Elenora, his w.

Rsh.7, pg.4, bapt. 1/15/1785, Johannes of Jacob Witmer and Anna Maria, sponsor Michael Drexler and Elizabeth

Rsh.7, pg.5, dau. Elizabeth, parents Michael Trexler and

Elizabeth, 8/8/1786, sponsor Christian Weisser and w. Susannah
Rsh.7, pg.5, Jacob b. to Michael Trexler and Elizabeth 8/8/1786,
sponsor Christian Weisser and w Susannah
Rsh.7, pg.6, Anna Maria, dau. deacon Weisser and Susanna nee
Kunckel, bapt. 6/17/1787, Michael Drechsler and Elizabeth nee
Kraus
Rsh.7, pg.8, dau. Susanna b. 10/10/1788, bapt. December,
Michael Trexler and Elizabeth, sponsor  Christian Weiger and w.
Susanna
Rsh.7, pg.10, Anna Margaretha, Michael Trexler and Elizabeth, b.
3/1/1793, bapt. May., sponsor Adam Blum and Anna Margaretha
pg.11, Peter Treisch b. to Jacob and Catharina, 12/2/1793, bapt.
1794, sponsor Peter Treisch and Elizabeth
pg.11, Johannes b. to Peter Kramer and Maria, bapt. 4/27/1794,
sponsors Peter Trexler and Amanda
Rsh.167, pg.12, Elisabeth b. to George Drechsler and Catharina,
2/20/1795, bapt. 5/24/1795, sponsor Frederich Kelppinger and
Barbara
pg.12, Susanna b. to Jacob Helm and Rosena, bapt. 8/17/1794,
sponsor Peter Treisch and Elizabeth
pg.13, Johannes b. to Jacob Treisch and Catharina, 12/6/1795
bapt. 4/10/1796, sponsor Peter Kremer and Anna Maria
Rsh.166, pg.14, Anna Maria b. to Conrad Drechsler and Phronica,
7/11/1797, bapt. 8/27/1797, sponsor Peter Kramer and Maria
Rsh.165, pg.15, Susanna b. to Peter Drechsler and Maria,
1/19/1798, bapt. 2/25/1798, sponsor Christian Drechsler and
Christina
pg.16, Susanna b. to David Treisch and Maria, 8/13/1798,
sponsors parents
Rsh.169, pg.18, Alena b. to John Drecksler and w. 10/2/1800,
sponsors Conrad Drecksler and Fronica
pg.28, m. 8/27/1787, Jacob Frey (umlat over y) and Susanna
Treysch (umlat over Y)
Rsh.166, pg.31, Communicants 5/10/1799, Conrad Drecksler and
w., Fronica Drecksler, Jacob Treish and w.
pg.32, Communicants 5/21/1800, Reichert Treisch and w., Jacob
Treisch, Conrad Drecksler

Dauphin Co., Pa., Zion Lutheran Church, Harrisburg, 1795-1827,
translated and edited by Frederick S. Weiser, Birdsboro, Pa., The
Pennsylvania German Society 1989, The Pennsylvania German

Society, Box 397, Birdsboro, Pa., 19508
F 159.H3W45 1987
pg.77, Doscher, Betzi m. 4/16/1807 John Quick
pg.80, Troesner, Betzi m. 12/10/1810 Andres Schulter

Dauphin Co., Pa., Records of the Klinger Church, compiled by
Mary Ellen Bowman, RR 5, Columbia City, Indiana 46715, August.
15, 1975, pub. 1978 by The Bookmark, P.O. Box 74, Knightstown,
In 46148 F159.E68R4
Rsh.66, pg.22, Dresler, Hannah, Jacob, Susanna, 8/9/1805, dau.
Hanna to Jacob and w. Dusanna (Dresler) sponsors Jacob
Leitner and w. Hanna
pg.29, Dressler, David, son bapt. 4/23/1810, Jacob Dressler and
w. Susanna, sponsors Abraham Erdman and w. Elizabeth
pg.16, Dressler, Jacob and w. Salome, son Janathan b.
5/21/1801, bapt. 6/21/1801, sponsors Simon Scherman and w.
Marg. Elizabeth
 pg.20, Dressler, Jacob and w Susanna dau. Rebecca, b.
2/13/1804, bapt. 3/13/1805 sponsors Jacob Hannan and Cadarina
Erdmann

Lancaster Co., Pa., Pennsylvania Archives 6th Series, Vol.6,
Microfilm, LC
pg.196, Baptismal and Marriage Records, Rev. John
Waldschmidt, Lancaster Co., Pa., 1752-1786
Rsh.136, Trostel, Abraham son of George and w. Rosina b.
4/26/1783, bapt. 6/15/1783, sponsors Johanne's Laub and w.
Elizabeth
Rsh.137, Trostel, Barbara dau. Heinrich and w. Catharina b.
2/6/1786, bapt. 5/7/1786, sponsors Johannes Trostel and Barbara
Schweicker

Lancaster, Pa., Sources and Documents of the Pennsylvania
Germans; VIII, Records of Pastoral Acts at Lancaster, Co., Pa.,
Emanuel Lutheran Church, known in the eighteenth century as
the Warwick Congregation, near Brickerville, Elizabeth Township,
Lancaster Co., Pa., 1743-1799, translated by Frederick S. Weiser,
Breingsville, Pa., The Pennsylvania German Society, 1983
pg.74, Deigler, b. 6/22/1765, Jacob sponsors Joannes Deigler
and w. bapt. 8/4/1765
pg.11, Dreisch, Adam b. 8/13/1776 to Christoph Gold and Maria,

bapt. S9/15/1776, sponsors Adam  Dreisch and Marlena
pg.134, George b. 11/1/1784 of Nicholaus and  Elisabeth Klein
and bapt. 5/8/1785 sponsors Adam Dreisch and w.
pg.142, b. 7/20/1787 son/dau of Michael and Catherine Klein,
sponsor Adam Dreisch and Magdalena
pg.161, Michael b. of George and Barbara Stober, 4/13/1793
bapt. 5/20/1793 sponsors Jacob Stober and Peggy Dreischin
Rsh.11, pg.98, Dessel - list of married persons in the Warwick
Congregation - Gotthart Dressel and Anna Maria Weilin,
10/16/1742 (1743)
Rsh.75, pg.59, Troecksel, Georg, dau. Magdalena Margaretha
b.4/6/1758, bapt. 4/23/1758, sponsors Johannes Schard and his
w., d. 8/10/1758
Rsh.75, pg.59, Georg Troecksel, a son Georg b. 1/12/1760, bapt.
2/3/1760, sponsors Georg Schmitt and Margreta Eichelbergerin,
both single, d. 8/5/1760

Lancaster Co., Pa., Sources and Documents of the Pennsylvania
Germans: V Records of Pastoral Acts at the Lutheran and
Reformed Congregations of the Muddy Creek  Church, East
Cacalico Township , Lancaster County  Pennsylvania, 1730-1790,
translated by William J. Hinke and Frederick S. Weiser,
Breinigsville, Pennsylvania; The Pennsylvania German Society
1981
pg.78, Dreigeler (Deigler), Johannes Eberhart a son Joh. Jacob.
b. 5/21/1755, bapt. 7/20/1755, sponsors Johannes Teicheler and
his w.
pg.79, Johannes Deigeler a dau. Mariua Catharina b. 10/30/1756
and bapt. 12/5/1756, sponsors Frederich Stohr, umlat over o, and
w. Dorothea
Rsh.11, pg.115, Dressel, List of persons married by John Casper
Stover, Gotthart Dressel and Anna Maria Weilin, Warwick
10/16/1743

Lancaster, Pa., Lutheran Reformed Church, Lancaster, Pa., 1773-
1848, FCHS.  Note with book says "church is near Thurmont,
Md."
Rsh.65, Fredrich Troxell and Elisabetha, child Matilda b.
5/16/1809, bapt. 7/1/1809, sponsor Catharina Yung (Young)
Jacob Weller and Anna, dau. Elisabeth, b. 6/3/1785, bapt.
6/22/1785, sponsor, Elisabet Troxel (Rsh. 65) Weller

Lancaster, Pa., 1st Reformed Church Lancaster Pa., LHS
Rsh.16, Martin Frederick Trissler, son of Joseph David and Maria
Drusina, b. 2/28/1742
Christian Groh m. Anna Marie Trieser, 2/20/1759
Rsh.79, Conrad Doll m. Marie Trisler, of Lancaster, 9/8/1801
Rsh.17, George Rissler m. Susanna Becker of Lancaster,
11/1/1792

Lancaster Moravian Church Records, Part 1, Marriages and
Burials 1743-1875, Photocopy of Typescript in the possession on
the congregation 1985, copy found at LHS
Marriages
Rsh.26, pg.99, 6/26/1791, George Thomas single b. 9/19/1766 a
Carpenter's Helper son of George Phillip Thomas and w. Julianen
Barbara Steinerin and Anna Magdalena Trisslerin b. 11/10/1769 a
dau. of George David Trissler and Annen Marien Crohnin
Rsh.26, pg.100, 8/28/1791 Michael Steiner, single, a carpenter
from Harrisburg, Dauphin Co., Pa., b. 9/20/1764, son of Jacob
Steiner and w. Margartha Thomas of Frederickstown, Md. and
Elizabeth Trisslerin b. 3/12/1767 dau. of George David Trissler
and Anna Maria Crohnin
Rsh.26, pg.103, 10/24/1793 Johannes Demuth, single, b.
12/20/1771 son of Christopher Demuth, Tobacconist, and w.
Elizabeth Hartaffel and Catherine Trissler in b. 9/30/1772 dau. of
Geroge David Trissler and Anne Maria Chrohniny
Rsh.44, pg.134, 9/24/1811, Johann Adam Trissler b. 8/9/1787,
son of Johannes and Maria Reichart Trissler and Julianna Reed b.
2/16/1789 dau. of Robert and Mary Reedy
Rsh.26, pg.146, 9/5/1813 Joseph Eberman, single, Clockmaker,
son of John Eberman and Elizabeth Frank and Maria Thomas
dau. of George Thomas and Anna Magdalena Trissler
Rsh.44, pg.164, 5/23/1818, Johannes Trissler, widower, and
Rebecca Graff, single dau. of Andreas and Catharine Graff
Rsh.135, pg.208, 5/26/1822 Peter Gander Eberman m. Elizabeth
Trissler, single, dau. of George Trissler and w. Catharina b. Ehler
(Ohler)
Rsh.26, pg.214, 7/6/1823 Henry Huest m. Sophia Theresa
Kreiter, widow, dau. of late John Demuth and w. Catharina b.
Trissler
Rsh.26, pg.227, 9/19/1824 Rudolph Stoner, m. to Henriette
Witmer, he is son of Michael Stoner and w. Elizabeth b. Trissler,

both lately deceased

Rsh.135, pg.263, 9/13/1827  Daniel Weidler, single, a Saddler and Catharina Trissler, single, dau. of George Trissler, Coppersmith, and his w. Catharine Ehlerk (Oehlery)

Rsh.46, pg.332, Levi Weaver to Margaret R. Trissler dau. of Adam and Juliana Trissler

Rsh.135, pg.360, Josiah Brecht to Margaret Trissler dau. of George and Catharine Trissler, both of Erie Co., Pa.

Buriels

Rsh.26, 7/31/1753  Maria Catharine Dressler, dau. of George David and Anna Maria b. Cron age 1 yr. and 5 mos

10/29/1752 Margaretha Catherine Trissler, 11 mos., dau. of J. Michael Lauburger

11/22/1760  Catharine Dressler dau. George David and Anna Maria b. Cron, age 2 years less 5 days

8/25/1763  Philip Drissler,(28 hrs) 2 days, son of George David and Anna Maria b. Cron

?Rsh.27, 7/11/1775  Susanna Trisler dau. George David and Anna Maria b. Cron b. 7/6/1775

8/23/1778  Mattheus Graff son of Jacob Graff and Maria b. Trissler b. 2/16/1777

February 23, 1782  Matthews Graff son of Jacob Graff and Maria b. Trissler, b. 10/21/1781

7/8/1783  Andreas Graff son of Jacob Graff and Maria b. Trissler b. 7/1/1783

Rsh.27, 2/6/1787  Cathaine Trissler dau. of George and Anna Maria Cron b. 12/4/1785

Rsh.27, 12/17/1789  Eliza Trissler dau. George and Anna Maria b. Cron b. 11/2/1783

2/4/1795  Sophia Elizabeth Demuth b. 7/7/1794 dau. of Johannes Demuth, Riflemaker, and Cathaina b. Trissler

Rsh.27, 1/25/1792  Elizabeth Trissler.  She was b. 9/1749 in New Castle Co., Del.  Her parents were James and Elizabeth Robinson.  She m. in 1776 to the widower George David Trissler, Jr. a Saddler

Rsh.26, 2/4/1795 Sophia Elizabeth DeMuth b. 7/7/1794 dau. of Joannes DeMuth, Riflemaker, resident and Catharine Trissler

Rsh.27, 8/16/1796  Jacob Trissler b. 2/6/1788 in Lancaster son of George David Trissler and the late Elizabeth b. Robinson.  He was with his father, at present the Tavern Keeper and Ferryman on the other side of the Susquehanna at the so called Wrights

Ferry where the lad d.

Rsh.27, 9/30/1796 Geroge David Trisssler b. 1/25/1754, a Saddler, from Lancaster. Learned the trade of saddler with his father. He m. Elizabeth b. Robinson in 1776. They had 4 sons and 3 daughters of whom 3 sons and a daughter survive. He m. a second time.

Rsh.44, 3/5/1802 Johannes Trissler b. Lancaster 1/3/1798 son of Johannes Trissler, a Saddler, and w. Anna Marie b. Reichart

Rsh.44, 2/16/1808 Anna Maria Trissler b. Reichart 7/6/1767 m. Johannes Trissler. This union was blest with 3 sons and 5 daughters of whom 1 son is deceased

Rsh.27, 7/21/1809 George David Trissler, Sr., b. at Canstadt in the Dukedom Wurtemberg on 3/2/1723. In 1750 he m. in Lancaster to Anna Maria b. Cron of Lancaster. This union was blest with 11 children and as far as known, 2 sons Johannes and Christian and 4 daughters survive. He lived to see 48 grandchildren and 10 great grandchildren

2/3/1810 Michael Steiner b. 9/10/1764, m. in 1791 to Elizabeth b. Trissler. 7 children 2 sons 5 daughters all survive. Elizabeth Trissler d. 5/20/1811

Rsh.28, 4/13/1811, John Trissler, b. 5/14/1807, son of John Trissler and Catherina Huber. He was baptized by a Catholic Priest, as his mother is a Catholic. The father is a Riflemaker.

Rsh.28, 6/17/1811 George Trissler b. 6/11/1811 son of John Trissler and Catharina b. Huber

1/25/1812 Catharine Thomas, single. b. 10/22/1793 dau. of George Thomas and Anna Magdalena b. Trissler

4/13/1812 Rebecca Steiner, single, b. 8/20/1795, dau. of Michael Steiner and w. Elizabeth b. Trissler

Rsh.26, 7/11/1812, Anna Maria Trissler, widow, b. Chron, 9/12/1730 at Staudernheim, in the Palatinate. She entered the married state in 1750 with George David Trissler and was blessed with 11 children, 2 sons and 3 daughters survive, 49 grandchildren, 16 great grandchildren

Rsh.27, 7/11/1812 Anna Maria Trissler b. Chron 9/12/1730 in Stauderheim, Palatinate m. 1750 to George David Trissler, surviving 1. Johannes, 2. Christian, 3. Elizabeth Steiner, 4. Susanna Maria Graeff, 5. Anna Magdalena Thomas

Rsh.46, 7/12/1813 Richard Dehuff Trissler son of Adam and Juliana Reed Trissler b. Reichard. He was b. 4/7/1813

9/8/1815 Johann Jacob Graeff b. 12/17/1753 m. 4/15/1776 to

Susanna Maria Trissler 13 children, of whom 10 survive, 1/1/1816. George Thomas b. 9/19/1776 m. 6/26/1791 to Anna Magdalena Trissler, 6 children 5 survive
(no year given) March 8 Johannes Demuth age 50, 2 months 16 days m. widow Catharine Trissler 1790
Rsh.46, 3/21/1820 Johann Abraham Trissler, b. 11/28/1818, son of Adam Trissler, resident Carpenter and Juliana
Rsh.46, 8/14/1822 Julianna Trissler age 33 years 5 months 29 days b. February 16, 1789 m. John Adam Trissler, 5 children 2 sons and 3 daughters, both sons dead
5/5/1825 John Adam Trissler age 37 9 months less 4 days
Rsh.135, 8/9/1826 Catharine Trissler b. Ehler dau. of Daniel and Margaretha Ehler b. Vonder Smith, Catherine b. 5/2/1779 m. George Trissler in 1801 6 daughters 4 sons
Rsh.135, 9/15/1838 George Conrad Trissler b. 3/19/1803 son of George and Catharina Trissler on 3/19/1829 m. Sarah Dielrich had 2 sons and a daughter
Rsh.28, 1/30/1840 John Trissler son of George David Trissler and w. Elizabeth b. Robinson. He was b. 2/21/1773 in 1802 he m. Catherine Hoover and they had 5 sons and 6 daughters
Rsh.44, 7/28/1844 John Trissler, widower, of David and Anna Mar. Trissler b. March 17, 1761 m. twice. Second time Rebecca Graff, had issue, 83 years 4 months 11 days
11/20/1857 Christian Trissler, single, son of George David and Anna Maria Trissler b. 8/20/1764, had little good of this life
2/19/1867 Catharine Trissler Eichhotz, 2nd w. of Jacob Eichholtz, Portrait Painter. She was b. 7/24/1791 to John Trissler and Mary Reigart. 9 Children

Lancaster Co., Pa., Trinity Lutheran Church records, Lancaster, Pa., Debra D. Smith and Frederick S. Weiser, Apollo Pa., Closson Press 1988, Apollo, Pa., Vol.1, F 157.L2T75 1730-1767
Rsh.99, pg.20, Johann Peter Drachsel, b. 2/5/1764, parents George and Margaret Drachsel, bapt. 5/7/1764, sponsors John Peter Funkhauser and w. Eva.
Rsh.16, pg.342, David Driesler, Maria Susanna Drieslerin, prepare for communion 1750.
Rsh.16, pg.30, Maria Elizabeth Driessler bapt. 10/2/1743, parents Joseph David Driessler and w. Maria Drusina, bapt. by Kraft, York Register
Rsh.99, pg.175, Maria Magdalena Trachsel b. 9/15/1761, bapt.

10/18/1761, parents George and Margaret Trachsel, sponsors
Jacob Heinrich Wolf and Christina Schmidtin, singles

Rsh.16, pg.46, m. 3/27/1739, Joseph David Triessler and Maria
Drusiana Rautenbuschin.

Rsh.12, pg.96, b. 9/7/1751, Henrich Wilhelm Triesch, bapt.
9/22/1751, parents Fred. and Anna Elizabeth Triesch, sponsors
Self and w.

Rsh.16, pg.63, Margaretha Barbara Triesler b. 8/11/1748, parents
Joseph David, Maria Susanna, sponsors Benjamin Spiecker and
Margaretha his w.

Rsh.51, pg.46, m. John Stephen Tranckel and Eva Catharina
Hambrechtin, 3/27/1739

Rsh.16, pg.419, Joseph David Triessler and w., son Johan Jacob
b. 8/25/1744, bapt. 9/2/1744, sponsors Jacob Jayser, Jacob
Spanseiler, Cath. Beyerlin

Rsh.16, pg.285, Catharina Barbara, beloved little dau. of Joseph
David and Maria Susanna Trissler, b. 12/16/1750, d. 1/16/1751,
bu. on the 17th of same month, age 1 year 1 month.

Rsh.99, pg.222, Johann George Drachsel, b. 6/26/1766, bapt.
11/9/1766, parents George and Margaret Drachsel, sponsors
John Urich Ehlsperger and Barbara his w.

pg.376, those announced for Communion Easter 1751 - John
Frederick Draesch, w. Anne Elizabeth, Catherine Elizabeth
Draeschin

pg.377, Anna Maria Draescherin

Rsh.16, pg.89, Catharina Barbara Driesler b. 12/16/1750, bapt.
12/21/1750, parents Joseph David and Maria Susanna, sponsors
Benjamin Spieker and Barbara Marg. his w.

Rsh.16, pg.290, Joseph David Driessler, Glaser, d. 8/4/1754, bu.
the following day. Age 55 yrs. 7 mos. -b. 1699

Rsh.51, pg.21, 7/21/1739, John Adam of John Stephen Tranckel,
bapt. 7/8/1739, sponsors John Adam Hambrecht and his w.
Elizabeth Barbara

Rsh.51, pg.36, Stephen Tranckel, 1/12/1740, Elizabeth Magdalena
Tranckel bapt. 1/13/1740, sponsors Jacob Spanseiler and w.

Rsh.51, Stephen Tranckel, 3/23/1741, dau. Catarina bapt.
3/27/1741, sponsors Jacob Spannseiler and w. Catharina Beyerlin

Rsh.51, Stephen Tranckel, 3/13/1743 b. Maria Eva, bapt.
3/27/1743, sponsors Christopher Dranckel and w.

pg.77, b. 10/1/1749, Anna Maria Hoffilch a twin to Johannes, bapt. 10/8, parents Conrad and Anna Ottilia, sponsors David Triesler and Anna Maria, his w., Rsh.16

pg.275 , 10/6/1766, m. by Pastor Gerock, John Weller of Lancaster County and Barbara Treister, Spinster,

pg.330, 7/27/1748, Intention to Commune, Eva Catharina Schreinerin, see Rsh.11, Hans George Koehler, Christoph Trenckel Rsh.109, Anna Maria Trencksin, Maria Susanna Trislerin

pg.22, Johann Adam Durslter (umlat over u) b. 9/14/1766, bapt. 10/19/1766, parents Adam and Regina Durslter, sponsors Adam Brenner and Anna Maria, w.

pg.142, Barbara Driesch, b. 12/7/1757, bapt. 12/18/1757, parents Freidrich and Cath. Eliza. Driesch, sponsors Loranz Marquetant, Barbara, w.

pg.161, Friedrich Joseph Driesch, bapt. 3/19/1760, bapt. 3/21/1760, parents Fredrich and Cath. Driesch, parents sponsors

pg.186, Fred.Sehner, b. 11/14/1762, bapt. 12/19/1762, parents Gottlieb and Mar. Barbara, sponsors Fredrich Driesch and w.

pg.190, Christian Driesch, b. 4/12/1763, bapt. 4/10/1763, parents Fridr. and Catharina Driesch, sponsors Christian Liebpe and Catharina, w.

pg.296, child of Fried Driesch, 1 1/2 years d. 4/2/1757, bu. the next day.

pg.303, Maria Barbara, child of Friedrich Driesch, age 1 year, 6 months, d. 5/27/1759, bu. the following day.

pg.378, Holy Communion, 3 weeks after Easter, 4/1765, Johann Fred. Driesch, Catharina Elizabeth Drieschin

Rsh.16, pg.342, David Driesler, Maria Susanna Drieslerin, communion 1750

Rsh.109, pg.4, Christopher Dranckel (umlat over a), 5/29/1743, had church pews made 9/21/1743, donated 1 lbs, for funeral cloths.

pg.268 Adam Durstler (umlat over u), from Neidenstein m. Anna Regina Doschin, single on 7/2/1765

Rsh.51, pg.397, Holy Communion 1752, Sunday of Trinity, Christopher Trinckel, Rsh.___ Stephen Trinckel

Rsh.51, pg.392, 1752 Communion, Cath. Trinckeln

Rsh.51, pg.67, Anna Catharine Trenkel, b. 1/2/1749, bapt. 1/6/1749, parents Stephen and Eva Catharina, sponsors, Johan Jacob Diemer and Anna Catharina, his w.

Rsh.51, pg.324, 10/10/1747, Communion Catharina Trenksln, Stephen Trenkel

Rsh.51, pg.333, 11/27/1748 - Communion, Matthaeus Buger, servant of Stephan Trenkel

Rsh.51, pg.334, 11/1747, announced intention to commune, but did not come, Stephen Trenkel and Eva Catherina Trenkeln.

pg.350, 2/18/1750, Eva Barbara Geiger, communion

pg.338, Zinzendorfus from Moravians, Anna Christine Schmiditn, age 66, Joseph Spanseilers mother-in-law

Rsh.51, pg.345, 5/27/1749, Eva Catherine Trencken, Stephen Trenckel

pg.54, b. Maria Elizabeth Loeser, bapt. 9/16/1750, father, the Schoolmaster, Johann Jacob Loeser, sponsors Christop. Trenckel and Anna Maria, w., Rsh.109

pg.86, Elizabeth Zinzendorffisch - Moravin

Rsh.51, pg.91, b. Anna Maria Agensa Trenckel, 2/12/1751, parents Stephen and Eva Catharina Trenckel, sponsors, Johann George Honig and Maria Agnesa, his w.

Rsh.51, pg.282, Anna Cath. Trenckel dau. of Stephen and Eva Trenckel, b. January 2, 1751, d. 1/9/1751

Rsh.109, pg.397, Chris. Trenckel, w. Anna Maria, Stephen Trinckel, Communion

Rsh.51, pg.398, Stephen Trinckel and w. Catherine, Johannes Honig, Communion 1752

Rsh.109, pg.338, 3/13/1749 - Christopher Trenkel, Anna Maria Trenckeln

Rsh.109, pg.287, Christopher Trenckel, d. 10/1752, in his 62 year, long illness with dropsy, bu. 10/2/1752


Lancaster, Pa., Pennsylvania Vital Records (Church Records), F148, 1983, Vol.1,2,3

Vol.1, Trinity Lutheran

pg.17, Henry Wilhelm Triesch, son of Fried, mother Anna Elizabeth, b. 9/7/1751, bapt. 9/22/1751

Rsh.99, pg.62, Johann Peter Drachsel, son of George and Margaret, b. 2/5/1764, bapt. 5/20/1764

Rsh.99, pg.72, Johann George Drachsel, father George, mother Margaret b. 6/27/1766, bapt. 11/9/1766


Lancaster Pa., Pennsylvania (Lutheran) German Church Records from the Pennsylvania German Society Proceedings and Addresses, Vol.I,II,III, Baltimore Geo., Pub.

Trinity Lutheran,

Rsh.16, pg.234, 2/28/1742, a son is b. to Joseph David Trissler and Maria Drusina Trisler, named Martin Frederick
Ist Reformed Church,
Christian Groh m. Anna Marie Trieser, 2/20/1759
Rsh.79, Conrad Doll m. Marie Trisler, of Lancaster, 9/8/1801
Rsh.17, George Rissler m. Susanna Becker of Lancaster, 11/1/1792

Lancaster, Pa., Pennsylvania German Church Records, Balt. Genealogical 1983, 3 Volumes.
Donna R. Irish, F160 G.3174., 1982
Trinity Lutheran, Lancaster, Pa.
Rsh.16, Margaretha Barbara Driesler dau. b. to Joseph David and Maria Susanna Triesler, 8/11/1748.
?Rsh.99, Johann George Drachsel son b. to George and Margaret, 6/26/1766, bapt. November
Rsh.16, Catharina Barbara Driesler, dau. Joseph David and Maria Susanna b. 12/16 bapt. 12/21/1750

Leehigh Co., Pa., Great Swamp Reformed Church, Lower Milford Town.LeeHigh Co.
History taken from Goshenhoppen Reformed charge, DAR
Rsh.23, Jacob Tracksel son of Peter and Margareteth is m. to Eberhart dau. of Joseph, 8/10/1784

Leehigh Co., Pa., Schwartzwald Reformed 1781-1811, DAR
Jacob Dressler m. Margaretha Danner, 4/27/1790, Rockland

Leehigh Co., Pa., Pennsylvania (Lutheran) German Church Records from the Pennsylvania German Society Proceedings and Addresses, Vol.I,II,III, Baltimore Geo., Pub.
Jordan Reformed Church, South Whitehall Town,
Rsh.40, Peter Traxal, Jr. and w. Elizabeth Mickly, son Ruben b. 3/11/1811, sponsors, Peter Traxel Sr. and Helena.
Rsh.58, Maria Koch dau. of Henry and Hanna Zirckel Kock, Hanna Zirckel Knock is now the w. of Peter Draxal, child b. 12/2/1799

Leehigh Co., Pa., Pennsylvania Archives, 2nd Series, Vol.9, LeeHigh Co., Great Swamp Reformed Church, Lower Milford Town, Microfilm LC, History taken from Goshenhoppen Reformed

charge,
Rsh.58, Jacob Tracksel son of Peter and Margareteth is m. to
Eberhart dau. of Joseph, 8/10/1784


Lehigh Co., Pa., Pennsylvania Archives, Series 6, Vol.6, records
Egypt Reformed Church, Lehigh County Pa., Microfilm LC
Rsh.22/52, pg.5, year 1734, David Traxel, son of Peter Traxel b.
7/27/1734 bapt. 9/23/1734 by Rev. Boehm, sp. Nicholaus Kern
and w. Maria Margaretha
Rsh.147, pg.5, year 1736, Johannes Traxel, son of the
respectable Peter Traxel church censor of the reformed
congregation here and w. Juliana Catharina Traxel bapt.
10/26/1736 by Rev. Goetsch, sp. Nicholas Kern, Johannes
Egender, Margaretha Egender
Rsh.22, pg.5, 4/16/1739, Christian Traxel baptized son of Peter
Traxel and w. Juliana Catharina, sponsors Christian Bregel, Peter
Traxel, Salome Gut
Rsh.22, pg.5, 4/16/1739, Juliana Margaretha Traxel baptized, dau.
above mentioned Peter Traxel and his w., twins, sponsors
Johannes Bertsch, Catharine Elizabeth Kern, Maria Margaretha
Neuhart.
Rsh.22/13, pg.6, Georg Frederick Traxel, son Peter Traxel,
deacon of the reformed congregation here and w. Juliana
Catharina Traxel, bapt. 7/28/1741, sp. Georg Kern, Frederich
Neuhart, Salome Gut, Lortentz Guts w., Susanna Ruch, Georg
Ruch's w., bapt. by Rev. Mr. Boehm
Rsh.22, pg.8, year 1744, Margaretha dau. Peter Traxel and w.
Juliana Catharine b. 10/25/1741, bapt. 12/26/1741, sp. Georg
Kern, Lorentz Gut, Michael Hoffman, Anna Barbara Neuhart,
Apolonia Toeschler, Maria Margaretha Neuhart
pg.8, 1744, Johann Peter Trachsel, Peter Trachsel's son, Apolonia
Toeschler, Cornela Kern dau. of Nicholas Kern
pg.133, confirmations list of the children permitted by me to come
for the first time to the table of our Lord, year 1753, Rsh.22,
Rsh.15, Christian, Peter Traxel's son, Johann Nickel Fuchs,
servant with Peter Traxel, Juliana Margaretha, Peter Traxel's dau.
pg.135, notes number 12, John Traxel arrived at Philadelphia on
8/20/1737. He secured land in Whitehall Township, but d. a few
years later
Rsh.22, pg.134, number 4, Peter Traxel emigrated from
Switzerland and landed at Philadelphia with two sons, (Rsh.58)

Peter and (Rsh.43) Daniel, 8/17/1733. He settled at Egypt but later removed a few miles westward and built a stone house in 1744 which still stands. He purchased a large tract of land some of which is still owned by descendants.

Rsh.58, pg.135, number 20, Peter Traxel, son of Peter Traxel was b. 1/1724 and d. 2/28/1811. His w. Anna Maria was b. 3/6/1727 and d. 7/10/1795. He m. 5/19/1747 and had seven sons and seven daughters.

Rsh.43, pg.138, number 31, Daniel Traxel was the second son of Peter Traxel, the emigrant and arrived with his father at the age of nine years. He m. Sophia Dotterer and later removed to Adams County, Pa.

Rsh.145/39, pg.139, number 38 John Nicolaus Traxel had nine children among whom were Adam, Peter, Magdalena, w. of John Jorn and Eva w. of John Stoffiet, John Nicholaus d. in 1797

Rsh.145/11, pg.12 year 1759 - Catharina Elisabetha Traxel dau. Joh Michael Traxel and w. Margaretha b., bapt. 4/8/1759, sponsors Johannes Schneider, Georg Koehler, Catharine Elisabetha Kern, Barbara Neuhart

Rsh.145/39, pg.13, year 1766, bapt. Maria Barbara Trachsel, dau. Nikel Trachsel and w. Catharina b. 3/1, bapt. 3/9, sponsor Peter Kern and Catharina Balliet

Rsh.108, pg.14, year 1767, Johann Peter Doeschler, son Peter Doeschler and w. Magdalena b. 4/5/1767 bapt. 4/20/1767 sponsor Martin Mickle and Barbara Doeschler

Rsh.39, pg.15, Eva Trachsel, dau. Nickel Trachsel and w. Catharina bapt. 6/19/1768, sponsor Paul Balliet and w. Nickel Mark and w.

year 1771, Maria Barbara Teschler dau. Adam Teschler the younger bapt. 7/28/1771

Rsh.108, year 1773, pg.18, David Deschler son Peter Deschler and w. Magdalena b. 4/8 bapt. 5/23/1773, sponsors Jacob Mueckle and w. Susanna

Rsh.108, pg.22, Catharina Deschler dau. Peter Deschler and w. Magdalena b. 4/19/1775 bapt. 5/28/1775, sponsors Peter Burckhalder and w. Eva Catharina

Rsh.48/80, pg.27, Nicolaus Trachsel, son Adam Trachsel and w. Anna Maria b. 10/29/1789 bapt. 11/26/1780 sponsors Joh. Nicolaus Trachsel and Barbara w. of Michael Neuhart. Rsh.48, pg.28, Peter Trachsel, son Adam Trachsel and w. Anna Maria, b. 12/30/1781, bapt. 1/27/1782, sponsor Henrich Stoeckel and Maria Barbara Trachsel

Rsh.48, pg.34, 1786, Hanna Traxel dau. Adam Traxel and w. Anna Maria, b. 10/51786 bapt. 11/4/1786 sponsors Michael Neuhart Sr., Catharina w. of Nicolaus Traxel

Rsh.62, year 1788, pg.37, Johannes Traxel, son Peter Traxel and w. Sibilla Veronica b. 10/4/1788, bapt. 10/19/1788, sponsors Johann Nickel Traxel and w. Catharina

Rsh.62, pg.44, Peter Troxell bapt. 11/4/1792, sponsors Jost Wilhelm Hecker and w. Regina

Rsh.62, pg.48, year 1795, Catharina Traxel dau. Peter Traxel and w. Sybilla b. 3/6/1795, bapt. 4/6/1795, sponsors Nicolaus Balliet and Sarah Koch

Rsh.62, pg.50, 12/27/1796, Susanna Drachel dau. of Peter Drachsel and w. Sibilla, bapt. 1/29/1797, sponsors Nicklaus Drachsel and Maria Stoffiet.

Rsh.62, year 1799, pg.54, Solomon Draxel, son Peter Drexel and w. Sybilla, b. 11/28/1799, bapt. 12/26/1799, sponsors Nicolaus Wotring, Maria Koch

Rsh.62, pg.59, b. 11/27/1802, Joel Traxel son of Peter Traxel and w. Sybilla Veronica, bapt. 1/1/1803, sponsor Peter Traxel, single

Rsh.62, pg.61, b. 1/20/1804, Elias Traxel son of Peter Traxel and w. Sybilla Vernoica, bapt. 2/6/1804, sponsors Peter Wutring and w. Elisabeth

## Leehigh Co., Pa., Jordan Reformed Church, South Whitehall Town, DAR

Rsh.40, Peter Traxal, Jr. and w. Elizabeth Mickly, son Ruben b. 3/11/1811, sponsors, Peter Traxel Sr. and Helena.

Maria Koch dau. of Henry and Hanna Zirckel Kock, Hanna Zirckel Knock is now the w. of Peter Draxal (Rsh.58), child b. December 2, 1799

## Leehigh Co., Pa., Pennsylvania Vital Record Vol.3, Tohickon Reformed Records, DAR

Rsh.48, pgs.35,261, Anna Maria Hecker m. Adam Troxell of Whitehall Twp., Leehigh Co., She d. 2/8/1812, children Nicholas, Peter, Christian, Hanna and Jonas. Hanna m. John Gobrect

Rsh.62, pgs.36,262, Sibylla Veronica Hecker m. Peter Troxell, she d. 3/8/1844, children: John, Magdalena m. Jacob Jones, Peter, Susanna, Catherine and Solomon

Leehigh Co., Pa., PA. Archives, Series 6, Vol.6, LeHigh Co. Pa., Records of Egypt Reformed Church, Microfilm, LC

Rsh.83, pg.7, b. 3/18/1743, Peter Teschler son of Adam Teschler and w. Apel Teschler.

Rsh.11, pg.12, bapt. 4/8/1759, Catharina Elizabetha Traxel, dau. of John Michael Traxel and w. Margaretha Traxel, sponsors Johann Schneider, George Koehler, Catharina Elizabetha Kern, Barbara Neuhardt

Rsh.39, pg.12 , 2/8/1761, bapt. Traxel, w. of Han Nickel Traxel

Rsh.39, pg.13, b. 3/1/1766, Maria Barbara Trachsel dau. of Nickel Trachsel and w. Catharine, bapt. 3/9/1766, sponsors Peter Kern and Catharina

Rsh.108, pg.14 , b. 4/3/1766, bapt. 4/20/1766, Johann Peter Doeschler, son of Peter Doeschler and w. Magdalena, sponsors Marg. Mickle (Rsh.108) and Barbara Doeschler (Rsh.108)

Rsh.39, pg.15, Eva Trachsel bapt. 6/19/1768, Eva Trachsel, dau. of Nickel Trachsel and w. Catharina, sponsors Paul Balet and w., Nickel Mark and w.

Rsh.39, pg.16, bapt. 7/28/1771, Maria Barbara Teschler, daughter Adam Teschler, the younger.

pg.18, David Deschler, baptized the son of Adam Deschler and w. Catharina, 10/17/1773, b. 9/17/1773, sponsors David Deschler and w. Susanna, David Kern and Susanna Baillet.

Rsh.108, pg.22, b. 4/19/1775, Catharina Deschler, dau. Peter Deschler and w. Magdalena, bapt. 5/28/1775, sponsors, Peter Burckhalder and w. Eva Catharina

Rsh.48, pg.25, b. 9/28/1778, Magdalena Deschler dau. of Adam Deshler and w. Maria Catharine, bapt. 10/4/1778, sponsors Peter Deshler and w. Magdalena Rsh.108

Rsh.48, pg.27, b. 10/29/1780, Nicolaus Trachsel, son of Adam Trachsel and w. Anna Maria. bapt. 11/26/1780, sponsors John Niclaus Trachsel and Barbara w. of Michael Neuhard

Rsh.108, pg.28, b. 3/30/1781, Jacob Deshler son of Peter Deshler and w. Magdalena, bapt. 5/6/1781, sponsors Jacob Shreiber and w. Elizabeth

Rsh.48, b. 5/7/1781, Maria Susanna Deshler dau. of Adam Deshler and w. Maria Catharina, bapt.6/3/1781, sponsors Johannes Baer and w. Susanna

Rsh.48, b. 12/30/1781, Peter Trachsel son of Adam Trachsel and w. Anna Maria, bapt. 1/27/1782, sponsors Henrich Stoeckel and Maria Barbara Trachsel Rsh.39

Rsh 48, pg.30, b. 7/29/1783, Catharina Deshler dau. of Adam Desher and w. Maria Catharine. bapt. 9/20/1783, sponsors Peter Shreiber and Catharina Kern.

Rsh.48, pg.31, b. 5/1/1784, Christian Trachsel son of Adam Tachsel and w. Anna Maria, bapt. 5/20/1784, sponsors Christian Drachsel and Sibilla Veronica Hecker.

Rsh.48, pg.34, b. 10/5/1786, Hanna Traxel dau. Adam Traxel and w. Anna Maria, bapt. 11/4/1786, sponsors Michael Neuhard, Sr. and Catharina w. of Nicolaus Traxel

Rsh.108, pg.37, b. 8/23/1788, Sara Deshler dau. of Peter Deshler and w. Magdalena, bapt. 9/21/1788, sponsors Adam Deshler and w. Maria Catharina

b. 8/31/1788, Elizabeth Deshler dau. of George Deshler and Susanna A. Mueckli, bapt. 9/21/1788, sponsors Jacob Mueckl and w. Susanna. Rsh.62, pg.37, b. 10/4/1788, Johannes Traxel son of Peter Traxel and w. Sibilla Veronica, bapt. 10/19/1788, sponsors Johann Nickel Traxel and w. Catharina

Rsh.48, pg.38, b. 4/25/1789, Elisabeth Deshler dau. Adam Deshler and w. Maria Catharine, bapt. 5/10/1789, sponsors Peter Burghalder and w. Eva Catharina

Rsh.48, pg.45, b. 3/26/1793, Jonas Traxel son of Adam Traxel and w. Anna Maria, bapt. 4/13/1793, sponsors Jonas Hecker and Maria Stofflet

Rsh.62, pg.48, b. 3/6/1795, Catharina Traxel dau. Peter Traxel and w. Sybilla, bapt. 4/6/1795, sponsors Niclaus Balliet and Sarah Kocky

Rsh.149, b. 5/2/1795, Salome Draxel dau. of John Draxel and w. Catharina, bapt. 5/24/1795, sponsors Peter Draxel, Sr. and w. Anna Maria

Rsh.62, pg.50, b. 12/27/1796, Susanna Drachel dau. of Peter Drachsel and w. Sibilla, bapt. 1/29/1797, sponsors Nicklaus Drachsel and Maria Stoffiet.

Rsh.48, pg.52, b. 12/29/1798, Stephan Trachsel son of Adam Trachsel and w. Maria, bapt. 1/28/1799, sponsors, Stephan Balliet and w. Magdalena

b. 9/7/1798, David Deshler son of David Deshler and w. Catharine, bapt. 9/18/1798, sponsors Christian Deyli and w. Maria Catharina. pg.57, b. 4/4/1801, Maria Deshler dau. of David Deshler and w. Catharina, bapt. 5/17/1801, sponsors Nicolaus Kern and w. Catharina. Rsh.62, pg.59, b. 11/27/1802, Joel Traxel son of Peter Traxel and

w. Sybilla Veronica, bapt. 1/1/1803, sponsor Peter Traxel, single Rsh.62, pg.61, b. 1/20/1804 , Elias Traxel son of Peter Traxel and w. Sybilla Vernoica, bapt. 2/6/1804, sponsors Peter Wutring and w. Elisabeth

Rsh.48, pg.63, b. 2/11/1805, Maria Traxel dau. Johann Nicolaus Traxel and w. Maria, bapt. 3/17/1805, sponsors Adam Traxel and w. Maria rsh.48

pg.66, b. 7/19/1806, John Deschler son of David Deschler and w. Catharina, bapt. 8/10/1806, sponsors Peter Schreiber and w. Susanna. Rsh.48, b. 8/24/1806, Elisabeth, dau., J. Nocolaus Traxel and w. Maria, bapt. 9/21/1806, sponsors David Heller and w. Elizabeth

Rsh.48, pg.67, b. 1/16/1807, Hanna Traxel dau. of Peter Traxel and w. Catharina, bapt. 2/15/1807, sponsors Adam Traxel and w. Maria (Rsh.48)

Rsh.48, b. 3/12/1807, Juliana Traxel, dau. of Christian Traxel and w. Barbara (Rsh.70), bapt. 4/4/1807, Adam Traxel and w. Maria Rsh.48

Rsh.48, pg.69, b. 2/17/1808, Adam Traxel son of Nicolaus Traxel and w. Maria, bapt. 3/11/1808, sponsors Christian Traxel and w. Barbara (?Cru)

Rsh.48, pg.70, b. 7/22/1808, Samuel Traxel, son of Christian Traxel and w. Barbara,(Rsh.70) bapt. 8/21/1808, sponsors Johann Nocolaus Traxel and w. Maria Rsh.48

1809 - Debora Deshler, father David, mother Catharina Carl Traxel father Peter mother Christina, Sara Traxel father Nicolaus mother Maria. 1810 - Wilhelm Traxel, father Christian, mother Barbara. 1811, Robert Traxel, father Peter, mother Christina, Carl Traxel, father Nicolaus, mother Maria 1812 - Margretha Traxel, father Christian, mother Barbara 1813 - Catharine Traxel, father Nicolaus, mother Maria, Edward Traxel, father Peter, mother Christina. 1815 - Isabella Traxel, father Jonas Traxel, mother Sara. 1817 - Anna Susanna Traxel, father Nicolaus, mother Maria. 1818 - Edward Traxel, father Jonathan, mother Elisabeth, Levina Traxel, father John, mother Salome. 1819 - Drusilla Traxel, father Peter, mother Christina, Milton Traxel, father Jonathan, mother Elisabeth, Joseph Traxzel, father John Nicolaus, mother Maria. 1821 - Thomas Traxel, father John, mother Salome, Amandus Traxel, father Jonathan, mother Elisa. 1822 - Nocolaus Traxel, father John Nicolaus, mother Maria, Owen

Traxel, father John, mother Salome
1823 - Sophia Traxel, father Jonathan, mother Elisabeth
1824 - Paul Traxel, father Christian, mother Magdalena
1825 - William Traxel, father John Traxel, mother Salome

Montgomery Co., Pa., 1765-1832, from the Library of Dr. and Mrs.
Glenn P. Schwah, "Schuylkill Roots" Researchers
pg.5, Baptisms by Rev. John Henry Helffrich, 1773-1810,
Catharine Barbara, b. 9/14/1773, bapt. 11/14/1773, Peter Mohn &
Catherine, sponsors David Dressler & Barbara
pg.26, baptisms as above, Jacob b. 11/24/1799, bapt. 3/16/1800,
parents Jacob Lang and Anna Barbara, sponsors Jacob Dressler
and Margaret ?Rsh.4
Rsh.85, pg.18, baptisms as above, Peter b. 8/3/1781 bapt.
9/16/1781, parents Peter Christman and Elizabeth, sponsors
Michael Cristman and Rachel Drexler Rsh.86
?Rsh.4, pg.3, baptisms as above, Jacob Tressler and Margaret
sponsors bapt. of Leah Angstadt dau. of Jacob and Mary Ann
Angstadt, bapt. 6/21/1818
Rsh.85, pg.60, Cemetery, Christ or Maxatwny (Delongs), Gertraut
Grim nee Trexler w. of Henrich Grim b. 6/8/1764 d. 3/4/1845,
(80.8.26)

Montgomery Co., Pa., Pennsylvania (Lutheran) German Church
Records from the Pennsylvania German Society Proceedings and
Addresses, Vol.I,II,III, Baltimore Geo., Pub.,Vol.III
Goshenhoppen Reformed Charge, Montgomery Co., Pa., 1731-
1833, Index of Church Records (Records not in book, just index)-
Elis Traxal 208, Elizabeth Traxel 112, Henrich Traxel 110, 111,
Sara Traxal 111, Sarah Traxal 110, Sophia 209, Sally 110, George
Draxal 120, Johannas Draxal 120, Elizabeth Dreisler 98.
Upper Hanover Town,
Jacobb Geri m. to Elizabeth Dreisler 1793

Mont. Co., Pa., The Trappe Records, Augustus Church Records,
Trappe New Providence, Mont Co., Pa., Evan. Lutheran, German
Travelling Ministry.
Maria Elizabeth Drautel (umlat over a) is b. to Michael and
Elizabeth Drautel, 10/6/1742, sponsor Crassman (umlat over
a)and w. Anna Marie.
Rsh.4, Dresser, Johan Nicolas, son to George and Catharina

3/24/1760, bapt. 8/24/1760, sponsors Johannes Schill and w. Anna Marie

Rsh.4, Dressler, Frederick, son of Jurg and Catharina, bapt. 10/22/1758, sponsor Frederick Marstella

Rsh.4, Johan Jacob Dressler son of Jurg and Cathrina b. March baptized 5/16/1762, sponsors parents.

Rsh.4, Jurg Dressler m. Catharina Klemmian 7/24/1756 in the church. They live in Matetcha.

Montgomery Co., Pa., Pennsylvania Archives, Series 2, Vol.8, German Reformed Church, Pa., 1748-1802 -LC

pg.112, Moravian Bethlehem 1742-1800, Sophia Dressler and Matthews Otto, 9/7/1753

Rsh.26, pg.145, Moravian Litz, Catherine Trisler and Johannes Demuth, 10/24/1793

Rsh.26, Elizabeth Trisler and Michael Steiner, 8/28/1791

Rsh.86, pg.177, St. James Episcopal, Marriage Record, Perkiomen, Mont. Co., Pa., Elizabeth Traxler and John Horn 1/16/1794, Susanna Traxler and Philip Krickbaum, 11/24/1791

Montgomery Co., Pa., Pennsylvania German Church Records from the Pennsylvania German Society Proceedings and Addresses, Vol.I, II, III, Baltimore Geo., Pub.
Vol.Lutheran Church at Trappe, Montgomery.Co., Pa.

Rsh.4, pg.446, Marriage, 7/4/1756, Jurg (George) Dressler and Catharina Klemmin, in the Church, they live in Matelcha

Rsh.4, pg.411, Dressler, Johannes, parents George and Catherina b. 5/24/1760, bapt. 8/24/1760, sponsor Johannes Schilling and w. Anna Maria

Rsh.4, pg.412, Anna Catharina Dressler (Mrs.) and Jung Dresser sponsored bapt. 8/24/1760 of Maria Catharina Schilling, dau. of Johannes and Anna Maria Schilling.

Rsh.4, pg.406, son is b. to Jurg (George) and Catharina Dressler, 10/22/1758, named Frederick Dressler, sponsor at bapt. Fried Marstella

Rsh.4, pg.415, b. 3/31/1762, bapt. 5/16/1762, sponsors parents, a son is b. to Jurg (George) and Cath. named Johan Jacob Dressler

Rsh.4, 5/1760 a son is b. to George and Catharina named, Johannes Dressler

Montgomery Co., Pa., Falkner Swamp Lutheran, New Hanover Town,DAR
Rsh.127, Balsar Treichler m. Sally Johnson, 5/17/1819

Montgomery Co., Pa., Pennsylvania (Lutheran) German Church Records from the Pennsylvania German Society Proceedings and Addresses, Vol.I,II,III, Baltimore Geo., Pub.
Whitpan Reformed
John Harris M. Rachael Trexler, July 23, 1814

Northampton Co., Pa., Pennsylvania German Church Records, Births Marriages, Buriels, Vol.1,2,3
Baltimore Genealogical, 1983
Northampton County, pg.57, Williams Twp.,Congregation,
Rsh.53, Conard Trackler and w. Catharina sponsors bapt. Johann Conrad Holms son of Johann George and Anna Barbara Holmes bapt. 6/26/1758
Rsh.53, pg.117, Conrad Trackler and w. Catharine communicants 7/1/1770
Rsh.53, pg.68, Conrad Drinckler and w. sponsor bapt. 10/23/1780 of Michael Schleienson of Johann Michael Schleier and w. Anna.
Rsh.53, pg.116, Conrad Drinckler and w. Catharine communicants 10/9/1768
Rsh.53, pg.129, Conrad Drinckler, communicant 1st Sunday after Whitsuntide 1778
Rsh.53, pg.128, communicant 1/29/1777, John Conrad Drinckler, Jacob Drinckler
Rsh.56,pg.130, communicant 10/24/1779, John Jacob Drecksler
Rsh.56/53, pg.114, Holy Good Friday 1787, Jacob Drenckler, Catharina, Conrad Drenckler
Rsh.56, pg.119, confirmed 10/4/1770, John J. Drenckler, 15 years b. 1755
Rsh.56, pg.70, Rosina Catharina w. of Jacob Drenckler was baptized Easter Day 4/16/1786
Susanna Catharina Drenckler bapt. Age 12
Rsh.56, pg.126, communicant, 10/28/1775, Conrad Trinckler, w. Catharina, son Jacob, Michael Schleier, son Michael and dau. Anna, Maria Catherine Schumacher, Maria Elis Edelman, Anthony Dech
Rsh.56, pg.129, connumicants lst Sunday after Whitsuntide 1778 , Conrad Drinckler

172

pg.116, communicants 5/22/1768, Margaret Dech.

Rsh.56, pg.129, communicants lst Sunday after Whitsuntide 1778, Conrad Drinckler

Rsh.56, pg.132, confessional 10/28/1780, Conrad Drinckler, Jacob Drinckler

pg.57, Johann Conrad Dankel and w. Catharine, on 5/7/1758, sponsor bapt. of Johann Conrad son of Michael and Elizabeth Hechelman

Rsh.56, pg.117, communicants 6/1769, Conrad Trunckler and w. Catharina

communicants 7/1/1770, Conrad Tranckler and w. Catharine

Rsh.56, pg.138, communicants 1784, Johann Jacob Trinckler and w. Catharine

Rsh.56, pg.121, communicants 6/6/1772, Conrad Trinckler, w. Catharina and son Jacob

Rsh.56, pg.124, communicants 12/18/1773, John Jacob Trenckler, Cath. Diescher, Christ.Deischer

Rsh.56, communicants 4/9/1774, Conrad Trinckler, w. Catharina, son Jacob

Rsh.56, pg.120, communicants Conrad Trinckler, w. Catharina, son Jacob

Rsh.56, pg.64, Jacob Trinckler and Susannah Edelmann, sponsor on 7/29/1773, Johann Jacob son of Johannes, and w. Phoebe, Schrantz

Rsh.56, pg.137, 1784, communicant Joh Jacob Trinckler

Rsh.56, pg.131, confirmed 5/28/1780, Conrad Tronckler, Jacob Tronckler

Rsh.56, pg.74, Conrad Trunckler, Magdalena Catharine Christein 5/15//1788, sponsor bapt. of Magdalane dau., b. in Springfield, of Heinrich Schmidt

Rsh.56, pg.120, communicant 4/9/1773, Conrad Trinckler, w. Catharina, son Johann Jacob

pg.56, John Jacob Deischer, dau. Julia


Northampton Co., Pa., Pennsylvania Vital Records (Church Records), Library of Congress, F148, 1983, Vol.1,2,3

Rsh.53, Vol.2, pg.64, Williams Township Congregation, 1773, 7/29 bapt. Scrantz, Johann Jacob, parents Johann and Phoebe, sponsors Jacob Trinckler and Susanna Edelman

Rsh.53, pg.68, year 1780, Johann Michael Schleier, son of Michael and w. Anna, bapt. 11/26/1780, sponsor Conrad Drinckler and w.

Rsh.53, pg.57, year 1758, Johann Conrad Hohms, son of Johann George and w. Anna Barbara bapt. 6/26/1758, sponsors Conrad Tranckler (unlaut over A) and w. Catharina

Rsh.56, pg.70, Rosina Catharina w. of Jacob Drenckler was bapt. 4/16/1786, on Easter Day 1786

Rsh.56, Susanna Catharina Drenckler was bapt. in the 12th year of age.

Rsh.53, pg.117, Williams Communicants, 6/1769, Conrad Trunckler w. Catherine

Rsh.53, pg.114, Williams, Holy Good Friday, 1787, Conrad Drenckler, Jacob Drenckler, Catharina Drenckler and Frederick Gross

Rsh.56, pg.119, 10/4/1770, confirmed John J. Drenckler, 15 years old.

Rsh.53, pg.116, communicants 10/9/1768, Conrad Drinckler w. Catharina

Rsh.53, pg.120, communicants 4/9/1773, Conrad Trinckler, w. Catharine, son Johann Jacob

John. Jacob Deischer, dau. Julia

Rsh.53, pg.121, communicants 6/6/1772, Conrad Trinckler w. Catharine son Jacob, Peter Gross

Rsh.53, pg.124, communicants 12/18/1773, Conrad Trinckler, w. Catharina, son Joh Jacob Trenckler, christ. Deischer, Phillip Gross, John George Gross

Rsh.53, pg.126, communicants 10/28/1775, Conrad Trinckler w. Catharina, son Jacob

Rsh.53, pg.128, communicants 1/29/1777, John Conrad Drinckler, Jacob Drinckler

Rsh.53, pg.129, communicants 1st Sunday after Whitsuntide 1778, Conrad Drinckler

Rsh.53, pg.132, confessional 10/28/1780, Conrad Drinckler, Jacob Drinckler

Rsh.53, pg.136, communicants, Jacob Drinckler, Johann Jacob Gross,

Rsh.53, pg.138, DomXXII, Trinit 1784, Trinit. 10/24/1779, Joh Jacob Drecksler

Philadelphia, Pa., Pennsylvania Vital Records (Church Records), F148, 1983, Vol.1,2,3
pg.719, Zion Evangelical Lutheran, SE Corner 4th & Cherry,

Margaretha Lauxin m. 10/27/1793, witness, John Jac Laux father, Franz Wolff, Conrad Rohrman, George Draecher, Fried Plensing, John Henry Rohrman

Rsh.127, pg.360, New Hanover Lutheran, Balser Treichler m. Sally Johnson, 5/17/1819

pg.408, Bethlehem, Pa., Old Moravin Cemetery,John Matthew Otto, 1714-1786, physician, native of Meinungen, Saxony, he m. Johanna M. Dressler, she d. 1776.

pg.422, George Hantsch 1690-1754 b. Ottendorf, Saxony, came to Bethlehem in 1743, with w. Regina, whose maiden name was Dressler. He served as Lay Evangelist in Eastern, Pa.


Philadelphia, Pa., Pennsylvania (Lutheran) German Church Records from the Pennsylvania German Society Proceedings and Addresses, Vol.I, II, III, Baltimore Geo., Pub.
Swatara Reformed Church
Anna Magdalena Draxlerin m. 12/19/1749, at Jonestown, to Hans Jurg Romer (umlat over o) witness Jacob Barthel, Jacob Unbehind, Petter Poot, Michael Kuntz
First Reformed Church
Anna Marie b. to John George Drescher and Anna Marie Swalb, 12/20/1754
Joseph Traxal m. Maria Winkhaus, 12/18/1814
Plainsfield Reformed Church
John Trexel, w. Anna Heimer, son Levi b. 2/1/1823, sponsors George P. Dreisbach and w. Margaret Binder


Philadelphia, Pa., Germantown Pa., Reformed Church, New Market Sq., Germantown, Pa., MCHS
Rsh.42, Martin Matthias m. Barbara Traxal, Whitpan, 4/24/1770, Matthias Martin was a brother of Elizabeth Martin Trexel Rsh.34


Philadelphia, Pa., Vol.9, Marriage Record 1745-1800, St. Michaels and Zion Lutheran Church
Rsh.45, pg.373, 6/26/1781, David Drechsler, widower, m. Elizabeth Molow, widow
pg.370, 10/22/1779, Michael Trissler, (Baker) m. Catharine Radinger
pg.322, 2/10/1763, Elias Ludwig Treichel m. Maria Elizabeth Pfeiffer

Somerset Co., Pa., Church Records of Berlin, Somerset Co., Pa., 1788-1856, Translated from German by E.C. Saylor, Closson Press, 1935 Sampson Drive, Appollo, Pa., 15613-9238, CR 1989
pg.3, George Frederick Tressler b. 6/17/1777, parents George and Christina Tressler
pg.20, John Tressler b. 9/16/1785, parents George and Christina Tresslersh
pg.15, John George Trushel, b. 2/8/1782, parents George Trushel
pg.114, John Tressler b. 3/13/1819, parents Samuel Tressler and Maria

York Co., Pa., Pa., Archives, 2nd Series, Vol.9, Microfilm, LC
York Co, 1st Trinity Reformed Church
Rsh.61, Joseph Drechsler m. to Elizabeth Kafeld, 9/1/1805

York Co., Pa., HSYC.
Rsh.16, m. 3/27/1739, Maria Drusiana Rautenbush to Joseph David Triessler resident of Lancaster, John Casper Stoever, Register of Baptisms and Marriages
Elizabeth Drushel m. Martin Fleischman, 5/11/1790, St. Matthews Lutheran Church, Hanover Twp., Pa., York Co., Pa. (1/2,1/2a,1/2b,y3,y4)
Rsh.115/86, Johann Peter Drechssler b. 12/1727, christened 8/19/1730, Father Jeremias Drechseler, John Casper Stoever Record of Baptisms and Marriages, KII, Kila, sponsor Johann George Schuymacher
Rsh.6, Anthony Dresler m. Nancy Reiley, m. 2/16/1801, Conewago Chapel, Edge Grove Pa., Conewago Catholic Chapel, Sacred Heart of Jesus
Rsh.61, Joseph Drechsler m. 9/1/1805, Elizabeth Kafelt, 1st Reformed Church and Trinity 1st Reformed Church, York Pa., (JJ3,JJ3a,Jjb,JJ)
Rsh.54, Anna Catharina Drussel, christened 3/6/1768, father Andreas, mother Margaretha, sponsors Christopher Ragy and Susanna Kuntzin. Lischy's Private Reg. KK6, KK6A
Rsh.120, Peter Trostle, b. 2/27/1788, christened 3/30/1788, parents Abraham and Susannah, Wolfs-St.Pauls, Lutheran and Reformed, W.Manchester Twp., York Co., Pa.
Philipina Trusler d. 10/6/1844, 53 years old, 9 months and 5 days, Schewsburg Twp., Christ (Solomons) Lutheran, York Co., Pa.

York Co., Pa., Mormon Record
Christening 9/19/1856, St. Jacobs (Stone) Lutheran and Reformed
Church, Brodbecks, York, Pa., Rosina Drexell, father John Drexel
mother Sussanna,

York Co., Pa., Christ Evangelical Lutheran, Part VI F 157.Y6C4,
Vol.6, Confirmations 1770-1799, Burials 1801-1856, Bapt. 1882-
192 F157Y6C4, Vol.I, part 1. Bapt. 1733-1794
Baptisms
pg.86, Gertrude Duenckel, of John Daniel and Anna Margaret
Dunenckel, b. 10/26/1758, bapt. 11/8/1758, sponsors
grandparents, John William and Gertrude Ruhl
pg.8, John Henry Dreher, b. 1/28/1758, bapt. 5/7/1758, parents
David and Anna Marg. Dreher, sponsors Henry and Maria
Catherine Peters
pg.244, Anna Maria, b. 4/2/1794, bapt. 6/27/1784, parents William
Dreher and Catharine, sponsors Peter Wiederencht and w.
 pg.254, Jacob b. 11/21/1786, bapt. 12/31/1786, parents William
Dreher and Catharine, sponsor Jacob Shafer and w.
pg.263, Michael b. 10/18/1789, parents William Dreher and
Catharine, sponsors Christopher Heibele and w. Sophia Catharine
pg.263, Rebakah, b. 9/8/1789, bapt. 11/24/1789, parents Jacob
Dreher and Veronica, sponsor mother
Confirmations,
Rsh. 87, WhitSunday 1794, Soloman Trechseler, Age 16, b. 1778
Rsh. 42, WhitSunday 1793 - George Trostal, Age 17, b. 1779
Rsh.120, Abraham Trostel, age 17, b. 1779
Rsh.120, Wilheim Trostel, age 16, b. 1778
Marriages, F157Y6C4V4, Part IV, 1735-1848
pg.29, 9/10/1812, Jacob Dreher and Catherine Gackle
Rsh.120, pg.31, 1812, Jacob Stover and Susan Trostel
Rsh.120, pg.41, 3/23/1818, Jacob Herbst and Catharine Trostle
pg.42, 10/15/1818, Daniel Dreher and Elisabeth Miller
Rsh.61, pg.42,  Daniel Drexler and Susanna Shepp
Rsh.61, 6/22/1828, Jermiah Drexler and Charlotte Wehrly
10/27/1840, Joseph Haelkerun and Catharine Dreher
10/24/1841, John Dreher and Catharine Small

York County Church Records of the 18th Century, Marilene
Strawser Bates and F. Edward Wright, Family Line, Westminster,
Md. 1991. York County, Pennsylvania

Vol.l

Rsh.54, Andreas Douschel witness to bapt. of Anna Maria Maison, 9/30/1786

York Co., Pa., Ziegler's (St. Pauls) Lutheran Church

pg.117, George Descher, dau. Maria Catharine b. 2/14/1783, dau. of George and Rosina. Witness Maria Catherine Hassler, York Co.

St. Matthews Lutheran Church

pg.206, Soloman Deutsel b. son of Cathaine and Johannes Deutsel b. 4/21/1777

York Co., Pa., St. Matthews Lutheran Church

pg.227, Elizabeth Drushel m. Martin Fleischman

Vol.2

Christ Evangelical Lutheran Church, City of York, Pa.

pg.265, Elizabeth Trostel dau. of George and Catherine Trostel, b. 5/7/1798

pg.298, Rosina Deschner sponsored bapt. of Funffrockc child 4/5/1789, bapt. by Paster Goerine 1788-1789 in the vicinity of York.

Vol.3

York Pa., Wolf (St. Pauls) Reformed Church

Rsh.45, pg.137, David Trachsel and w. sponsor bapt. of Susanna Conrad, 11/16/1780 dau. George Conrad and Maria Conrad

Rsh.120, pgs.141,142, Cathrina Trostel b. 12/12/1789, dau. of Abraham and Susanna Trostel, Susanna and Abraham Trostel sponsor dau. of Peter and Catharine Heilman bapt.4/12/1791, Peter Drostel b. 2/26/1788 son of Abraham and Susanna Drostel

Rsh.120, pgs.145,146, Jacob and Elizabeth Trostel sponsor Jacob son of Peter Bott, bapt. 3/4/1799

York Pa., Jacob Lischy's Private Pastorial Record

Rsh.54, pg.272, Anna Christina bapt. 9/6/1765 dau. of Andreas Truschel and Margaretha

Rsh.54, pg.276, Anna Catharina, dau. of Andreas and Margaretha bapt. 3/6/1768

Rsh.42, Solomon Trechseler, confirmed 1794 age 17, Christ Lutheran Church, York, Pa., Weiser, JJ1-JJLE, Becker JJ1F, Young JJ1-JJ1-9

Abstracts from the Journal of Bishop Christian Newcomer for Years 1795-1830

Abraham Draksel d. 1824/25, Westmoreland Co., Pa., lived with

family in Lancaster Pa., in 1797, then moved to West October 2, 1804, later some of family moved to Mont. Co., Ohio, on tax list for Mont 1810/16 Troxel
Mariana Dresell b. 7/3/1807 bapt. 11/1/1807, father Jacob, mother Elizabeth, St. Paul Lutheran and Reformed Church, Clearspring, Washington Co., Md.
St. Paul, ibid. Sarah Draxel b. 9/1/1813 bapt. 10/31/1813, sponsor parents, Jacob Draxel father, mother Susanna
Conewago Chapel, Sacred Heart of Jesus, Mary Driskle (Dresser) m. 10/24/1802, Edgegrove to Samuel Brady, child. Capt. Thomas Brady.

## VIRGINIA

The Report, #38, A Journal of German American History, pub. by Soc. of History of The Germans in Md. 1975, Baltimore, Md. For those individuals researching Virginia German Records, this issue contains location of the Virginia German Church Records.
"It is also probable that German families of southwestern Frederick County, Md. used the ministrations of the New Jerusalem Lutheran and St. James Reformed Churches at Lovettsville, Loudoun Co., Va., New Jerusalem Church, Lovettsville, Loudoun Co., same Minister who served Frederick Md. served Loudoun Co., Va.

1.New Jerusalem Lutheran, 1784-1845 at Lutheran Theological Seminary, Gettysburg and at Nat. Gen. Soc., and Utah Gen. Soc.
2.St. James Reformed. 1786-1857, have been Xeroxed. Transcript?

Also, two pioneer clergymen:
1.John Casper Stoever, Lutheran, Frederick Co., Md. and adjacent Va., 1730 through 1740's, Baptisms and marriages pub. by F.J.F. Schantz, in 1896 and record is at Hist. Society of Pennsylvania.
2.Jacob Lischy, reformed, baptisms, 1744-1769, published by the Pennsylvania German Society. He ministered in Carroll and Baltimore Counties, Md."

## WEST VIRGINIA

In West Virginia, on the border of Maryland:
1.St. Peter's Lutheran and Christ Reformed, Shepherdstown, W.V.
Christ Reformed published, 1791-1818, by Gladys Hartzell, "On this Rock" Transcript at DAR

# G.  CITY DIRECTORY NOTES

Compiled by: Donn Gregory Trexler, P.O. Box 323, Midlothian, Va. 23113

## MARYLAND

1796 Baltimore City Directory
(Baltimore Town & Fells Point)
?Rsh.5, James Murray, Painter and Glazier, Old Town, Low Street
Christian Delcher, Old Town, 45, French Ft.
Valentine Delcher, Miller, Old Town, French ft., precincts

1804 Baltimore City Directory
Rsh.29, Antoni Hitzelberger, Brick Layer, North Eutaw St.
Rsh.5   Jacob Kuhns, Storekeeper, Hookstown Road

1807 Baltimore City Directory
Rsh.5   Jacob Kohn, (Kuhn) Storekeeper, Hookstown Rd

1806 Baltimore City Directory
Rsh.5   John Kohn, Storekeeper, Hookstown Rd., pg.74

1810 Baltimore City Directory

Rsh.29, Anthony Hitzelberger, Stonemason, No. Calvert St.
Rsh.5, Peter Klunk, Carpenter, New Lane, W.P., pg.110

1814/1815 Baltimore City Directory
Rsh.76, Ignatius Trexler, Grocer, Hookstown Road, W.P.
Rsh.5, Peter Klunk, Carpenter, New Lane W.P. pg.98

1816 Baltimore City Directory
Rsh.76, Treaxler and Baker, Coopers, 100 N. Howard Street
Rsh.5, Klunk, Peter, Carpenter, New Lane W.P. pg.98

1817 Baltimore City Directory
Rsh.76 Ignatius Truxler, Cooper, 117 N. Howard

1819 Baltimore City Directory
Rsh.29 Anthony Hitzelberger, Booths Alley

J. Trexler, Plasterer, Carperter's Alley, west of Howard St.
Rsh.9   Samuel Trexler, Stonemason, Harford Avenue, South side
Rsh.29  Anthony Hitzelberger, Stonemason, Lerews Al.N.of
Madison

1855 Baltimore City Directory
Isabella Troxall, 107 Mulberry


## PENNSYLVANIA

Year 1780, History of Lancaster, Pennsylvania, Everets and Peck,
1883, Author Ellis Franklin
pg.370, Lancaster, Pa., Directory, Those who trade as Saddlers:
David Trissler, George Trissler

1806 Philadelphia City Directory
John Traxler, Shoemaker, 460 North 3rd

1807 Philadelphia City Directory
John Traxler, Shoemaker, 260 St. John

1810 Philadelphia City Directory
John Trexler, Shoemaker, alley
Joseph Trexler, Gentlemen, 386 N. 3rd., wife Maria

1811 Philadelphia City Directory
John Trexler, Shoemaker, Rachael
Jacob Trexler, Hairdresser, 143 N. Front
Joseph Trexler, Gentlemen, 386 N. Third

1813 Philadelphia City Directory
Jacob Trexler, Hairdresser, 143 N. Front St.
John Trexler, Shoemaker, Rachel
Trexler, widow of Joseph, 386 N. 3rd.

1837 Philadelphia City Directory
Mary Trexler, widow, Nurse, 2 Jone's Alley

1840 Philadelphia City Directory

Mary Trexler, widow, Nurse, 2 Jone's Alley

1843 Philadelphia City Directory
Isaac S. Trexler, Cordwainer, 2 Jone's Alley


# VIRGINIA

1850 Franklin County, Va., Franklin County, Virginia, 1786-1986: a
Bicentennial History/John S. Salmon and Emily J. Salmon,
Franklin County Board of Supervisors, 1993, All rights reserved,
Rocky Mount, Va.
Blacksmiths listed in 1850, Stephen Trisler
Rsh.76, Coopers listed in 1860, John Trexler

1869 Richmond, Va., City Directory
Rsh.142  John Trexler, Machinist bds 208 W. Broad

1873 Richmond, Va., City Directory
Rsh.142  John Trexler, Engineer, h. 2412 E. Broad

1874 Richmond, Va., City Directory
Rsh.142  John Trexler, Laborer h. 206 W. Broad

1875 Richmond, Va., City Directory
Charles Trexler, Moulder, bds 507 E. Marshall
Ignatius Trexler, Machinist, bds 208 W. Broad
Rsh.142 John Trexler, Machinist, Tredegar Co.
Rsh.138 William Trexler, Carpenter, h. 206 W. Broad

1875 - 1904 Richmond, Va. City Directories
Rsh.142 John Trexler, Machinist

H.            COURT AND LEGAL RECORDS
              CHANCERY/CIVIL RECORDS
              KENTUCKY

Kentucky County Court Records, Grant, Harrison, Pendleton,
Pease Abstracts Publications, compiler Janet K. Pease, Pub.
Grant Co. Hist. Soc, Williamstown, Ky 1985
pg.246, Pendelton Co., Order Book A., pg.14, Petition of Henry
Troxell and Thomas Shell, 9/1799, Letters of Adm.pg.262,
Pendleton Co., Order Book A., pg.107, Henry Troxell, 12/2/1801,
adm. estate of Peter Horn, deceased.
pg.271, Pendleton Co., Order Book A., 2/1803, Henry Troxell
adm. of John Horn

Kentucky Court and other Records, Vol.II, compiler, Mrs. Wm.
Breckenridge Ardery, Genealogical Publishing Co., Baltimore,
1972
pg.181, Jessamine (Oldham) Vital Statistics, Mary Trisler, Age 70,
widow, born Maryland daughter of ____Barr, d. 11/6/1852
pg.15, Bourbon Co., Estate Record, Elizabeth Hand, to Edward
Fugate, to son John, son Robert, son Henry, to Ann Trussel and
Milly White furniture.

**LOUISIANA**

The German Coast, Abstracts of the Civil Records of St. Charles
and St. John the Baptist Parishes 1804-1812, by Glenn R.
Conrad, Center for Lousiana Studies, University of Southwestern
Louisiana, Lafayette, Louisiana, Copyright 1081, University of
Southwestern Louisiana, Lafayette, La. F377.S124C65
Rsh.33  pg.165. No. 13, date 4/28/1809, Inventory of the
Community Property of the Late Jacques Troxler and his wife,
Elisabeth Leroux, one son Jacques Troxler, Jr. deceased with
three children Firmin 12, Marceline 10 and Emeline 8 represented
by their grandfather and tutor Jean Desnoyes. Other heirs born
to Jacques Troxler's second marriage to Elisabeth LeRoux were
nine children one dead but who had four children. These four
children represented by their uncle and turtor, Alphonse Haydel.
Other children were Marie, wife of Alphonse Haydel, Christophe,
Cleste, wife of Jacques Haydel, Adellaide, wife of Nicholas
Haydel, Emelie, wife of George Haydel, Maximillien, Godefroy,

and Andre. The four children represented by Alphonse Haydel their uncle and tutor, were Joseph, Carmelite, Nathalie, and Moyse (?) Haydle who were heirs through their mother Felicite Troxler, left farm 12 arpets wide located about 37.5 miles above New Orleans, 40 arpets deep with 40 arpets of cultivable land fenced.

## MARYLAND

Baltimore, Md., MdHR Index 59, Chancery Court-Index to Litigants, Ships,Streets, & Tracts 1668-1807;1817-1851. Records between 1807 and 1817 are not indexed, Tracts for 1790-1799 are in Index 61.
#82, pg.74, date 9/27/1810, The Reverend John Tesier (Tisser), lease, lot at Euthaw and Franklin, Balt. City, $31. Annual Rent, leased then sold his interest.
#3619, Balt. Co., 10/20/1847, C221, Thomas F. Troxell, Lot on Charles St. Mdhr 200-3593, 2/15/14/3

Baltimore, Md., Mdhr, Index 117, Chancery Papers #55, Baltimore City Superior Court, date 01/30/1852, C132, Mdhr 40,200-4455 - 1/3 2/15/14/57
Rsh.9 Barbara Bushmiller, Lemuel and Barbara Debow, Mary Ann and Jacob Pierey, Catherine and William Braden, Henry and Joseph Boughman, Anthony Trexler vs George William Boughaman, Petition to sell Lot on Britton St., George Baughman d. intestate 2/1833, leaving widow Barbara who later married Bushmiller since dead. Children of George Baughman and Barbara were Joseph, Margaret and George. Margaret married (Rsh.9) Anthony Trexler and died leaving 4 children. 1. Barbara who m. Lemuel Debow, 2. Mary Ann who m. Jacob Piery, 3. Catherine who m. William Braden and 4. Anthony Trexler, George died leaving George William Boughman and Henry Boughman. George W. Boughman is a lunatic without any means of support and resides at the Mt. Hope Lunatic Asylum in City. Henry D. Boughman and Eleanor his wife and Samuel Martin, trustee for George W., obtained judgment for $22.50 against Anthony Trexler on 1/28/1854, trustees sale.

Baltimore, Md., Mdhr, Index 117, Computer, Baltimore City/County Chancery Papers, # 3269, number 3932,

Rsh.20 Baltimore Co., Md. Chancery Record date 10/18/1845, C 252, Mdhr 40,200-3269-1/4, 2/15/13/78, Samuel P. Trexler and Isaac Trexler vs. Peter Trexler, Jonathan P. Trexler, Catherine Starr and John Teas, Estate of Deborah Trexler, Lot on Church St., suit involves land on south side of Vulcan Alley, now new Church St. in City of Baltimore, Jonathan P. Trexler was indebted to his mother-in-law Catherine Starr for $594.60 and he mortgaged this property on June 1, 1833 at Sharpe St. and Vulcan Alley for this amount. He placed this land, at the request of his mother-in-law, in trust for his wife Deborah Trexler. Deborah Trexler was the wife of Jonathan P. Trexler and mother of Samuel P. Trexler, Isaac Trexler, each over 21, and Peter Trexler an infant under the age of 21 on January 20, 1846. Deborah Trexler d. in September of 1837. Jonathan P. Trexler, left town and these three children lived with their grandmother Catherine Starr for years, after the death of their mother. Joseph Starr of the City of Baltimore was appointed guardian for Peter Trexler, infant, on 11/18/1846. When property was initially placed in trust for Deborah Trexler it was held by John Teas and trust stipulated that children of Deborah Trexler were to have property if anything happened to their mother. Jonathan P. Trexler has no interest in property, two supenos for him have been returned and numerous ads in newspapers have received no response. Children are petitioning Court to sell property. Other spellings are Truscler, Tresler. Other references pertaining to this property and included above are Liber, N.G. #20, folio 576, N.G. # 20 folio 574

Baltimore, Md., Mdhr, Index 117, Computer, Baltimore Chancery Papers
Rsh.8 # 1383, Baltimore Co., date 05/29/1833, C 419, Abram Troxal vs. Catherine Erek, petition to release mortgage on Mulberry & Eutaw St., Mdhr 40,200,1373, 2/15/12/41
Rsh.8 #117, 979, date 11/07/1829 C463, Mdhr 40,200-970 1/5/2/15/12, Abraham Troxel, lease on lots on Fayette and Pine Sts.
Rsh.8 #2914, Mdhr 40,200-2892-1/2, 2/15/13/53 year 1843, mtg. foreclosure Lot on Ross St., C269, Abraham Troxel

Frederick Co., Md.,Index 59, Chancery Court 1668-1807, 1817-1851, 1807-1817 not indexed, Mdhr

Rsh.34 Frederick Co., Md., Book 69, pg.466, year 1807, John Troxall and George Bower vs. William, James and Henry Shields and others regarding lots in Town of Emmitsburg, Frederick Co., bought of Shields on 3/29/1795.

Frederick Co., Md., MdHR Index 59, Chancery Court-Index to Litigants, Ships, Streets, & Tracts 1668-1807;1817-1851. Records between 1807 and 1817 are not indexed, Tracts for 1790-1799 are in Index 61.
Rsh.13 Chancery 5083, location 1/37/2/16, John Troxall vs. Mary, Jacob, Elizabeth, Frederick, John, Catherine, Margaret and George Troxall heirs of Frederick Troxal of Frederick Co., Md. year 1801. Frederick Troxell on 5th day of July 1795 made his last Will, 5 years after his death money to be divided among his children, Mary, Jacob, Elizabeth, Frederick, John, Catherine, Margaret and George. Exr., son-in-law Nicholas Zimmerman and Son Jacob. Proved 11/1/1796 by witnesses, David Stoner and Matthew Young.

Frederick Co., Md., Mdhr,Chancery Papers 1650, location 1/36/2/28
Rsh.34 date 2/15/1811, Jacob Eversole vs. Jacob Greenamyer, John Troxall of Frederick, Md. John Troxall, adm. of Wm. Greenamyer deceased as of date 2/1806, suit mentions Jacob Greenmyer who resides in Adams Co., Pa., and John's name is spelled John Troscel and he is said to reside in Frederick Co., Md. receipt signed by Wm. Greenamyer before his death on 4/18/1800 shows he resided in Emmitsburg.

Washington Co., Md., Mdhr Index 59, Chancery Court-Index to Litigants, Ships,Streets, & Tracts 1668-1807;1817-1851. Records between 1807 and 1817 are not indexed, Tracts for 1790-1799 are in Index 61.
Rsh.32 Chancery 17, 898-4118, location 1/37/1/10, Washington Co., Md., date 3/18/1813 (1814), David Rhorer, Daniel, Benjamin, Barbara vs. Christian, Samuel Rhorer, Jacob Troxel and Maria his wife, suit involves Christian Rhorer's estate. Wife named Francis, Christian had 7 children as named Daniel, Barbara wife of Daniel Bragonier, Christian, Samuel, Jacob and Maria who married Abraham Troxell and Ann Miller.
author's note: This is lengthy file, however, it is clear that it is

Abraham Troxell and not Jacob Troxel who is married to Maria
Rhorer, file states that Abraham, whose name was entered in the
suit as Jacob in error, and Maria Barbara Rhorer Troxel left the
state of Maryland years ago for the purpose of residing
elsewhere. Samuel Rhorer is said to reside in Huntington,
Commonwealth of Pennsylvania.

Washington Co., Md., Mdhr, Index 59, Chancery Court 1668-1807,
1817-1851, 1807-1817 not indexed
Book 24, pg.580, year 1792, David Jones, Gentlemen of
Washington Co., Farmer, his Will, witnesses John Kershner,
Abraham Troxell, David Kesher. Wife Margaret Jones, 11
children, John, David, Peter, Margaret, Elizabeth, William,
Jonathan, Thomas, Catherine, Susanna, Ann, Will written
12/22/1779, son Peter Jones had moved to Hampshire Co., Va.
when Will was proved in 1792.
Book 38, pg.469, Michael Trisler, witness along with Joseph
Wood and George Dixon to Will of Arthur Carlton, Authur's wife
Eleanor, on 12/1/1770, of Frederick Co., Fredericktown. Will
proved 9/21/1771.
Book 149, pg.783, Frederick Troxel is Justice of the Peace for
Frederick Co., 11/21/1829
Book 153, pg.26, Baltimore Co., year 1834, Abraham Troxel,
pd.43.77.
Book 153, pg.18, Frederick Troxell witness in Frederick Co., Md.
date 3/31/1825 to indenture between John Harris and John Black.
Book 173, pgs.957, 1001, 1833, Abram Troxel, in July of 1848,
Abram Troxel assigned 7/18/1833, a lot on Pierce St. bounded by
Goosberry Alley, Liber TR number 29, pg.485, to Beale Randall
for annual rent of $38 in Baltimore Co., recorded Liber TKN #229,
pg.485.


## PENNSYLVANIA

Northampton Co., Pa., Prothonotary, NCA
Traxsell, George, Jr., plf., cont. 11/26/1827, George
Troxell,Traxsel, Jr., vs. Mr. Robert Butz, 7/29/1828, default on
promissory note, amicable action in case, 27/54.
Trexler, Peter, exr. dft., 3/1760, Peter Trexler, Jr. dft, 12/1769, sum
in case.

Peter Trexler, w. plt, cont. 9/1770, ejectment, Timothy Peaceable, lessee of Peter Trexler, et ux vs Lawrence Kuhnle, 3/1773, trespass and ejectment, Adam Epler vs. Peter Traxler, Jr., summons served, 3/1760, Melchor Smith vs. Peter Trexler, exr. sum case ended, 6/21, 9/453. Traxler, Jr., Mrs. Peter, husband, plf., 9/1770 term, Ejectment, cont. Mrs. Trexler, cont. Mrs. Traxler, lessee of Peter Traxler, et ux., vs. Lawrence Kicknle, trespass and ejectment; Peter Tresler, Jr. vs. Jacob Wetzell, summons for Jacob Wetzell, 9/1770, final; 8/1823, 11/8, 10/82.

Traxel, Hannickle, Alt, dft., year 1768, ejectment, lessee of Lawrence Breder, Breader, et al vs. Hannickle Traxel, et al, trespass and ejectment, enters into the common rule, 12/1769, 9/382, 10/5.Troxell, Michael E., plf., vs. Amanda Troxell, Michael Troxell's sister is Mrs. Ellen Smith and his mother Elizabeth is 58 years old of Buskill Twp., his father is Edward Troxell, Shoemaker, 8/1864, divorce.

?Rsh.53 Trexler, John, plf., 9/1765 to 9/3/1768, ejectment, Timothy Peacable, lessee of John Trexler, vs. Thomas Troublesom, Jacob Swartz, Tenant, 4/1766, John Trexler vs. Jacob Swartz, John Trexler vs. Jacob Swartz, 3/1767, John Trexler vs. Leonary Moyer 3/1770, referred by consent of Parker to David Deshler, Peter Rhode and John Crisman or any two of them who are to audit and make report 6/1770, 9/94, 9/144, 9/368.

Traxler, John, dft., 12/1757, sum in case; Ludwig Betting vs. John Traxler, 9/21/1757 to 12/1757, sum in case, narrative filed, 5/124, 5/169, 5/82.

Trexler, John, plf.,6/16/1761, lessee of John Trexler vs. Christopher Badtitle, Mr. Johnson appears for Jacob Swartz, enters into common rule, 6/16/1761, 6/205, 6/229.

Rsh.115 Trexler, Jeremiah, vs. Jacob Swartz, 4/1762, amicable action on the case on motion by confer of parties all matters in variance between are referred to George Brering, Esq., (?Rsh.85) Philip Fogel and John Ronig or any two of them who are to hear.

Trexler, Jeremiah, plt, 4/1792 to 4/1798, amicable action in case, 15/347, 18/119.

Trexler, Jeremiah, vs. Joseph Albrecht and Susannah Albrecht, adm. of Joseph Abrecht deceased, sum case settled before court, 4/1798, 18/119.

Traxsell, Nicholas, dft, 8/1798, sum in case, Henry Miller vs. Nicholas Traxele, 18/165.

Traxsell, Peter, Jr., dft. 4/1798, sum in dower, 1/7/1799 to 8/1799 to 11/15/1799, Christina Ritter, late Christina Gobel who was the w. of Adam Gobel, 56 vs. Peter Traxsele, Junior, sum + dower, summons served, 8/1798, 18/120.

Traxel, Mary, al, dft, 4/12/1807, Peter Troxel, Jr., Jacob Shryver, Juliana Shuyver, partition, Peter Traxel, al, dft, 4/25/1807, partition, Jacob Shuyler, (Shryver, Schrieder) 7/29/1807, Peter Traxel, Jr. charge his w., Mary Traxel, late Mary Shryver, 4/25/1807, informed petition be made 7/29/1807, 20/218.

Troxsell, Troxell, Daniel, al, dft, cont, 11/7/1809, ejectment, Troxsell, Daniel; John Wagener vs. Caspar Shenebruch, John Shenebruch, John Rhoades and Daniel Troxsell, sums in ejectment 11/1809 to 7/27/1811, 21/146.

# PROBATE RECORDS, WILLS, ESTATE DOCUMENTS

## KENTUCKY

Marylanders to Kentucky, 1775-1825, Henry C. Peden, Jr., Family Line Pub. 1991
 pg.147, Wm. Trimbul, 8/9/1830, names in his Will, sister-in-law, Rachel Troxell

## MARYLAND

Baltimore, Md., Survey of Probate Records, Baltimore Co., Md., Mdhr
1. Estate Dockets, Adm. Docket, WK 1094-95-1/2/3
2. Orphans Court Proceedings Index 1,2,3
3. Wills Index 114
4. Inventory Index Wk1096, 1,2,3

1. Baltimore Co., Estate Docket Adm. Docket Index 1772-1851 Mdhr 12,054, location 2/33/6/10 1789
#1 pg.55, 2/10/1789, John Delcher, dec., Mary Delcher exr., sureties: Conrod Riely, Christian Delcher
#3, pg.71, 1804 John Delcher, 4/18/1804, John Delcher, Will, Kitty Delcher exr; sureties, Samuel Crawford, Edward Brown
?Rsh.5, 1805 James Murray
7/16/1808, Henry Drescher, Will, John March A.W.A.; sureties Nicholas Popplim, Peter Forney
#4, pg.69, 1808 Christian Delcher, 9/28/1808, Christian Delcher, Intestate, James Beers adm; sureties, John McCaffer, Thomas Bradley, Henry Anderson
# 6, pg.74, 1815 Valentine Delcher, #6, pg.75, Valentine Delcher, 5/31/1815, Intestate, adm, Daniel Brand; sureties John Gross, Lewis Gross Adm. acts. index, Microfilm CR 10599, 1st. Act. 4/7/1818, buyers at sale are John Delcher, Mrs. Ann Delcher, George Delcher; Accounts of Sale Index, Baltimore 1780-1851, 1-2, 12,058-1, location 2/32/14/41,Microfilm CR 9513 P-1, Baltimore Co., 1818, #6, 1816-1818. Book 2, pg.273, paid to heirs of Valentine Delcher $587.41 each to John Delcher, George Delcher, Wm. Rutler who married Ann Delcher, Sarah Delcher and George Delcher guardian of Harriet Delcher for her portion, 4/7/1818,

Daniel Brand, Adm.
#6 pg.83, 1817 George Delcher
#7 pg.69, 1822 Jermiah Delcher
#7, pg.69, Jerimah Delcher, Intestate, James Clark, admr;
sureties George Rodenmayer, Ignatius Herder

2. Baltimore Co., Orphans Court Proceedings Index, Mdhr
#1 1777-1817
1795 Michael Thrash, Book 3, pg.133, Michael Thrash an orphan
13 years old, 10/14/1795 is bound to Daniel Evans to learn the
trade of Tanner and Currier
#2 1818-1833
1818 Harriett Delcher, Book 10, pg.178
1822 Jeremiah Delcher, Book 11, pg.329,331
1822 Harriet Delcher Book 11, pg.331
1826 Jemima Delcher Book 13, pg.278
#3 1834-1848
Rsh.20, 1847 Peter Trexler, Book 23, pg.41

3. Baltimore Co., Md. Wills Index
        1789 John Delcher, Book 4, pgs. 327 to 329, John
Delcher of Baltimore Town 1/8/1789, son Christian 20' of the lot I
live on with the house and other improvements, this 20' is next to
William Pooles house, son Valentine 16' of same lot with house
and improvements on that portion, dau. Catherine Riley, dau.
Christina Bumberger, son John Delcher to have a house and lot,
son George Delcher a house and lot where Wm. Nailor now lives,
wife to have remainder of estate during her natural life and after
her demise to be divided among my children above named.
Loving w. and son in law William Bumberger joint Exrx. and Exrs,
of this my last Will...witness Wm. Asquith, John Delp, James
Semons, proved 2/10/1789
        1804 John Delcher Book 7, pg.276, John Delchier, w.
Kittey house and lot for her life then to son John Delcher if he has
heirs, if he has no heirs to niece Catherine Bumbarger dau. of
sister Christina Bumbarger if niece Catherine dies then to niece
Nancy Bumbarger. Balt. Co., witnesses, James Baker, signed,
Samuel Granford, mark, Edward Brown signed, proved April 18,
1804
        1806 Henry Dresher, Book 8, pg.340,December 15, 1801,
William Henry Dresher and Mrs. Roelofes, man and w. (translated

from the Dutch), made March 16, 1806, appeared before one Antonie Lodwwyh Heysteck, notary at Amsterdam, administered by the Court of Holland, William Henry Dresher and Mrs. Roeloles, man and w., residing in this City on the Princegraft above the Devehoolf, both in healthy and perfect state, do make this their Last Will and Testament...first dying appoints the other universal heir, minor children, not named, witness messrs Johann George Poppleim and Johann Nicholas Popplin both of Amsterdam, living at the corner of Heegraft and Huiden St.

    1817 George Delcher Book 10, pg.337, George Delcher, Balt. Co., April 16, 1817, Brother John Delcher $1., Sister Ann Rutler $l., Sister Sarah $1, Sister Harriott $1, dear and loving w. Jemmina to have all...witness Joshiua Turner, John Valiant, Lambert Thomas, proved July 30, 1817

    1825 Harriet Delcher Book 12, pg.173

4. Baltimore Co., Md. Inventories Index WK 1096
        1763 Martin Thrash, Book 10, pg.45
        1769 Thomas Trussel Book 9, pg.44
        1804 John Delcher Book 23, pg.176
        1812 Henry Dresher Book 27, pg.282
        1815 Valentine Delcher Book 29, pg.445
        1817 George Delcher Book 30, pg.592
        1820 George Delcher Book 32, pg.123
        1822 Jermima Delcher Book 33, pg.323
        1826 James Datzell Book 35, pg.585
        1826 Harriet Delcher Book 36, pg.99

Baltimore Co., Md., Estate Docket Adm. Docket Index 1772-1851 Mdhr 12,054, location 2/33/6/10
    Rsh.76 1816, John E. Murray, 8/3/1816, Book 6, pg.189, Intestate, Immavanchaanau Murray, Admx; sureties Ignatius Trexler, Samuel Robinson, inv. total $625.56, found in Book 30, pg.23,231, 8/14/1816, location 2/29/9/31, includes 6 windsor chairs, 53 vols. of books, 12 3/4 yards of carpet, 2 maps, family bible, lots of queensware and stoneware, etc. large inv. Inv. is found on WK 1096.2 microfilm, and was taken by Benjamin Grammer and Wm. C. Byrd, Test Jacob Kettering.

Baltimore Md., Orphans Court Proceedings 1816, Vol.9, pg.320, June Term 1816, Mdhr

Rsh.76 On application of Immaranchannau Murry admx.
of John E. Murray dec., it is ordered that said admx. give notice
required by law for creditors to eschiliete their claims against the
estate of the dec. and that the same be published once a week
for 6 weeks in the American and the Federal Gazette in the City of
Baltimore, Md.

<u>Baltimore, Md., Mdhr, Year 1809 Acts 67/236/256</u>
Benjamin Debruler

<u>Baltimore, Md., Mdhr, This record located in Adm CR 10674,</u>
<u>1810-1814</u>
Rsh.58/7/1814, John Ehrman, Will, Catherine Exrx, sureties,
Andrew Shorb and John Crouse, Exrx. has moved to the back
country and has been summons to February 1814 Court.

<u>Baltimore Co., Md., Wills, Mdhr</u>
Rsh.5, John Ehrman of the City of Baltimore , Book 9, pg.28,
beloved w. Catharina for her full use...Anthony Steele of the City
of Philadelphia, my nephew, to receive after wife's demise.
Nephew to pay John Black of the City of Baltimore 10 lbs and 10
lbs to Mary Mitchell my granddau....two lots of ground in old town
on High Street.  Signed Joannes Ehrman, 8/14/1810.  Witness
Theophilus F. Dougherty, John Crouse, Erasmus Uhller
        Year 1812, Accounts Index, Wk1094, Henry Dresher,
Book 18, pg.529, Wk 1016-1017-I, Accounts of Sales, Book 18,
pg.529, expenses paid for dec. and his w. to be buried, money
paid for translating Will, balance due heirs of the two dec. estate
who reside in Holland
        Year 1818, Wk 1018-1019, 22/348, George Delcher, all
money retained by Thomas Curlett in right of his w. who is the
only child of the dec.
        Year 1823, WK 1017-1018, Book 23, Jeremiah Delcher,
pg.41, $852.23 due the estate, June 5, 1823, Wk 1019-1020,
Book 24, pg.289, Jeriam Delcher, cash paid $416.72 George
Rodenmayer, present guardian for Harriet Delchers for whom dec.
was guardian.
        Year 1827, 1019-1020, Book 25, pg.100,312, due est.
$246.24, Harriet Delcher, wearing apparel devised to Sarah
Delcher, balances paid to Clemey Hughes guardian of Legatee
William Ruther, Nephew

<u>Baltimore, Co, Md., Mdhr, Test Proceedings, Index 2</u>
        Baltimore Co., 1767, pg.130, Frederick and John Troxall, exrs.of Peter Troxall, late of Frederick Co., Md.
        Baltimore Co., Vol.43, pgs.206, 258, 324, 5/4/1769, inv. for Thomas Truxsells.

<u>Baltimore, Md., Death Certificates, City of Baltimore, Mdhr, Microfilm</u>
        CR 48,050
        Permit #17658, Certificate of Death, Date of Death 5/20/1877, Name: Samuel R.B. Trexler, age one year, white, b. Baltimore, place of death, 34 North Bond, cause: Whooping Cough, ill five weeks, buried Green Mt. Cemetery, 5/21/1877
        CR48,046
        Permit #03306, Dates 5/1875 to 10/1875, Certificate of Death 2831-6210, John Drexel, 6 months old

<u>Charles Co., Md., Mdhr,Test Proceedings, Index 2, Charles Co., Vol.32, pg.50</u>
        Rhodam Truxill of Charles Co., Md., female, 2/18/1746

<u>Frederick Co., Md. Register of Wills Microfilm, Mdhr</u>
CR 8502  Will Index
CR 49,160-2, 1783-1803, GM 3,i, Frederick Co., Md.
        Rsh.13  pg.141, Frederick Troxell, dau. Catherine, dau. Margaret, sons Jacob, adm., Frederick, John, George, daus. Mary, Elizabeth, m. Nicholas Zimmerman, adm., signed 7/5/1795, entered into Probate 11/1/1796.
        Rsh.42, pg.271, Peter Troxol, 12/15/1798, w. Modolona, sons Frederick, 270 ac. plat, George, 200 ac. plat, John, Peter, house in Emmitsburgh, Jacob, daus. Barbara Martin, Modolona Coon, Elizabeth Crise; exr. Jacob Troxell son and Peter Crise, entered into Probate 2/7/1799
CR49,162-2, 1816-1822 HS 2,1, Frederick Co., Md.
        Rsh.24, pg.353, Adam Troxall, Will, w. Christine, son John, daus. Elizabeth, Susanna and Catherine, Catherine to have weavers loom without gears, son Jacob, oldest son, dau. Sophia m. John Wivell, Jacob Troxall exr., signed and sealed 2/28/1820, entered into Probate 4/18/1820.

CR 49,163-1, HS, Frederick Co., Md.

Rsh.97 pg.270, Elias Troxell of Frederick County, Md. weak of body...to my lawful children...in case either of them shall die before he or she reaches lawful age estate shall be divided among surviving...beloved w. Ruth, brother Peter Troxell, friend G.M. Echellbergr, exr. Signed Elias Troxell, witness George Black, George Troxell, Robert L. Annan, final account December 23, 1829 G.M.E. 6/33

pg.270, Elizabeth Troxell, exr. Peter Troxell et al.,4/20/1824 probate

Rsh.97 pg.272, to Orphans Court, Frederick Co., Md., I Ruth Troxell do hereby renounce bequest made by my late husb. Elias Troxell dec. and will take my legal share of his estate. Witness G.U. Eichelberger, date 6/9/1824

CR 49,164, 1828-1834, GME 1,i, Frederick Co., Md.

Rsh.13 GME 1, pg.366, George Troxell of Frederick, sisters Mary Troxel and Margaret Troxel sole heirs, friend Daniel (Davie) Hoover, sole exr., probate 5/14/1832

Rsh.34 GME 1, pg.129, John Troxell of Emmitsburg,Md., Mary Troxell, late w. and w/o son Peter Troxell, dec., Mary and Peter Troxell's children George, Charlotte, Elizabeth, John and Henrietta, sons Jacob, John, daus. Magdalina Hinch (or Finch) Elizabeth m. Adam Thomas, exr., Barbara Hinkle m. William Grenamyer, Mary Collingen, Margaret Marks m. John Marks, Catherine Mince. Jacob Troxell exr. along with Adam Thomas, probate 2/11/1829, witness Jacob Dannay, Jacob Harrier, John Zimmerman

Rsh.75 GME, pg.517, Margaret Trisler of Emmitsburg, Md., son George Trisler, his children William Trisler, George Trisler, Margaret Trisler and Henrietta Weaver, grandau. Elizabeth Houch m. Jacob Houch, $1,000 paid to Mary Wigle, exr. George Baltgell, witnesses Richard Potts, James Coates, N.A. Randall, probate 10/17/1833 to 12/17/1833

GME 1, pg.121, George Trisler, exr. Susan Trisler, Will, 11/1843, no children named or mentioned, left everything to Susan probate 10/21/1845

GME, I, pg.129, John Troxell, Sr., exr. Adam Shover, probate 4/26/1836

CR 49,166-1 GME, Frederick, Md.

Rsh.13 GME 3, pg.30, Mary Troxell of Frederick Co., Md., exr. friend Daniel Hoover, give and bequeath all estate to sister Margaret Troxell to her heirs and assigns. Witness William B. Pellengen, John Head, Warner T. Gremed. She made mark, probate 4/1/1844

Rsh.98 pg.84, Elizabeth Troxell, County of Frederick, Md., devise and bequeath as follows, my interest and estate in farm and mountain land owned by me and my son Joseph P. Troxell to said Joseph P. Troxell, he is to pay $1200 to be distributed to my dau. Barbara Welty, w. of Joseph Welty dec., dau. Mary Ann Smith, to George Grayson, son of dec. dau. Joann Winter, dau. Jeremia Motter, w. of Joseph Motter, son George W. Troxell, son Joshua Troxell, Witness John Troxell, Samuel Maxel, Deitrichson Leek, probate 9/3/1850, final 3/1873.

Rsh.101 pg.85, Catherine Troxell, Town of Emmitsburg, Md., being sick, two sons Samuel and William. Real estate Shields Addition, one story frame house, one story stone house, two story brick house. Land bounded by Jacob Winder and Robert Brooks and Gunblat, dau. Elizabeth, w/o Michael Wise, dau. Mary Ann m. John A. Davis, dau. Catharine m. James W. Baugher, dau. Amanda under 18. Witness Samuel Baumgaden, Nathaniel Ron, Joseph Murtiz, probate 4/7/1845

CR 49,166-2 TS 1, Frederick Co., Md.

Rsh.101 pg.110, Samuel Troxell, of Frederick Co., Md., exr. brother William Troxel, brother William to have all I have in Tannery, brother William and four sisters, Elizabeth m. John Nichum, Mary Ann m. John Davis, Catherine m. James Baugher, Amanda Troxel. Bequest to German Reformed Church, Witness George U. Aughenlaugh, Joshua Rowe, Isaac R. Jiarsone, probate 1/14/1851

CR 8-2-1, Frederick Co., Md.

Rsh.60 GH1, pg.252, John Troxell of Frederick Co., dec. exr. David Troxell, son Abraham to have home and 139 acres where I now dwell, son David Troxell, son Frederick Troxell, dau. Polly m. Jacob Biggs, signed John Troxell, witness John Zimmerman of V, George Zimmerman of V, Elijah F.T. Zimmerman, Charles Broadrauf, John A.J. Zimmerman, probate 10/10/1857, written 11/1842

Rsh.60 pg.253, Margaret Troxell of Frederick Co., exr.

David Troxell, give to Julian Troxell, w. of David Troxell and her dau. Margaret S. Troxell all my furniture and clothing, give to Margaret Troxell, dau. of David and Juliaan $90, give to my brother John $300, give and bequeath to the following names sons of David Troxal $20 each, namely, Emanuel Troxel, William W.Troxel, I. Lewis Troxal and Joseph Troxal, remainder divided between the forenamed dau. and sons of David Troxell, witness Nicholas Snider, Michael Crouse, Builes Bemnett, George S. Crouse, probate 10/26/1857, written 9/1855.
A 1 pg.170 Martin Thrisher, no exr., not probated

CR 11-1 HL 1, Frederick Co., Md.
    Frederick Troxell, exr. William D. of Frederick Co., estate to be equally divided between my following named children: son William Daniel, son Martin D., dau. Susanna w. of George M. Harbvaugh, dau. Mary Elizabeth, witness Mrs. David Fisher, Mrs. John Troxell, signed Frederick Troxell, probate 4/19/1891

Frederick Co., Md., Mdhr, Index 83, Orphans Ct. 1777-1808
    Rsh. 13 Frederick Traxall dec., Mary, Frederick, John, George, Catharine and Margaret Troxall summonsed to effect distribution of estate. MDHR 12292, Book GM3, pg.96.

Frederick Co., Md., Mdhr, Index 83, Orphans Ct. Minutes MDHR 12293, Book RB1, pp 90,pgs.263,264
    Rsh.36 Jacob Troxell, year 1806, Frederick Co., Orphans Ct., dec. His admx. directed to sell property per inv. except negroes and to advertise for creditors claims, pg.90
    Rsh.36 Jacob Troxel, year 1807, dec. former co-exer. of Peter Troxell. His widow and admx. Mary Troxel and Peter Crisel, acting exr. of Peter Troxel dec., ordered to pay L83/7/6 1/2 and L149/4/9 resp. to Peter Troxel admr. of Magdelena Troxel, w/o Peter, both dec. pg.263,264

Frederick Co., Md., Mdhr, Orphans Ct., Distributions, Index 83
    John Troxell, Frederick Orphans Ct. Minutes (distributions) year 1778-1784, adm. of Paul Marshall, Mdhr 12290, Book GM 1, pg.87.
    Bernard Tresner, years 1778-1784, adm. of Jacob Tresner, Mdhr, 12290, Book GM1., pg.117
    John Tressler, year 1805, Frederick Orphans Ct. Minutes,

with Leonard Yaste approved as securities for Richard Tomplin guardian to 5 children of Christian Mosseter (q.v.) heirs of Michael Runner, Mdhr 12293, Book RB 1 pg.54.

<u>Frederick Co., Md., Mdhr Index 124, Wills</u>
Rsh.22 Book 1, pg.213, 4/1766, Peter Troxel, children Peter, Daniel, David, John, Christian, Frederick, Julinah Troxell of Margaretha Troxell, grandau. Julinah Catherinath to receive share of estate.

<u>Frederick Co., Md., FCHS</u>
Baltimore Reformed Church, Baltimore, date 9/12/1786 Jacob Schreier m. Mary Mitshall, witnesses Elizabeth Drachsel, dau. of John Drachsel, and John Hornecker. author's note: a John Troxells Will, Scott County, Kentucky in the late 1700's, names a John Hornecker as son-in-law.

<u>Frederick Co., Md., Mdhr, Adm. Records 1815-1816</u>
Rsh.24 Adam Troxel exr. of Jacob Troxel, Rsh.101, bonds Henry Plaek, Jacob Bumgartner, inv. 5/8/1820, Book H54, pg.204, additional inv. HS5202, lst Act. 10/5/1821, Nhs5/11 no final account
Abraham Troxel, adm. David Troxel, final account 6/12/1877, Book JRR3, pg.418.

<u>Frederick Co., Md., Mdhr, Adm.</u>
Rsh.97 Elias Troxel, exr. George M. Echelleeger, 4/20/1824, bondsmen George Flock, George Troxell, Final Act. 12/23/1829, Book GME 6 pg.33, First Act. 4/20/1821
Rsh.97 Elias Troxell, his final account by George M. Echelberger, exr. of Elias Troxel. Paid Samuel Aman in Full of his 1 dividend...on his age, paid Peter Troxell for Mary Troxell in full for her 2, paid Joseph Baugher for Isaac Baugher, paid David Risk in full, paid Michael Sporrseller in full, paid Peter Troxel in full at .24 on the dollar on his age, paid Robert L. Aman at 2 on his age, paid Samuel Johnson in full at 2 on his age, paid Henry G. Waters assignee of William Henry Sleely in full of his 2, paid Jannis A. Shorb in full his paid, paid Patrick Owings adm. of Patrick Lowe in full of his 1st dividend.

<u>Frederick Co., Md. Wills, Mdhr</u>

Rsh.13 Book GM 3, pg.141, 7/1795 proved 11/1796, Frederick Troxel, dau. Mary, sons Jacob, Frederick, John, dau. Catherine, dau. Margaret. Son John left Loom with all gears and appurtences. Children to stay on "Plantation" for five years then real and personal property to be disposed of. Son in law Nicholas Zimmerman.

Rsh.22 Peter Troxell, Book A. No.1, pg.213, Peter Troxell, written 4/1766, probate 5/6/1766, sons Frederick and John Troxell, adms.,w. Julianath Catherinath to have her 1/3, eight children, Peter, Daniel, David, John, Christian, George Frederick, Julinah Troxell of Margaretha. Granddau. Julianna Catharina to receive share of Estate, Will was translated from the Dutch Language; Witnesses Philip Klingenmith, Adam Reydenour, Peter Shaffer

Rsh.34 John Troxell, Book GME 1, pg.129, John Troxell year 1830, Emmmitsburg, Mary Troxel, widow, of son Peter Troxel, dec., son Jacob, children of Mary and Peter are George, Charlotte, Elizabeth, John and Henrietta, all are under 21. daus. of John, Magdelina Hinch, Elizabeth Shower, Barbara Hinkle, whose husb. is Wm. Greenmyer/Grimamger, Mary Cattinger, Margaret Marks, whose husb. is John Marks, Catherine Mince.

Rsh.42 Peter Troxell, Book GM No.3, pg.271, Peter Troxell, 2/7/1799, Will, written 12/15/1798, beloved w. Modolona, to have back room on stone part of the house to live there, sons Frederick, George, John, Jacob, Peter, daus. Barbara Martin, Modolna Coon, Elizabeth Crise, House in Emmitsburg is bequeathed, adms., Jacob Troxel and Peter Crise, witness Wm. Emmit, Frediand Lay.

Rsh.47 Margaret Trisler, Book GME 1, pg.517, 12/1833, son George, Rsh.14, grandau. Elizabeth Houch w. of Jacob Houch, grandchildren William, George, Margaret Tipler and Henrietta Weaver who are the children of son George Trisler.

Rsh.98 Elizabeth Troxell, Book TS 1, pg.84, year 1850, son Joseph P. Troxell, dau. Barbara who is w. of John Welty, dec. dau. Mary Ann Smith, George Grayson son of dec. dau. Joanna Winter, dau. Jeremiah Motter, w. of Jacob Motter, son George W. Troxell, Son Joshua Troxel.

Rsh.101 Catherine Troxell, Book GME 3, pg.83, Emmitsburg year 1846, sons Samuel and William, land "Shields Addition" 4 daus., Elizabeth Wise, w/o Michael, Mary Ann m. John A. Davis, Catherine m. James W. Baugher, Amanda under 18.

Rsh.101 Samuel Troxell, Book TS 1, pg.110, 1/1851, brother William with whom he owns a Tannery jointly, sisters Elizabeth m. John Nickum, Mary Ann m. John Davis, Catherine m. Baugher and Amanda Troxell.

George Trisler, Book GME 3, pg.121, 11/1843, w. Susan no children named or mentioned. Left everything to Susan.

Frederick Troxell, Last Will and Testament, Book JKW No.1, 5/8/1893, Wm. D. Troxell exr., Wm. D. Troxell a son, Susannah Harbaugh a dau., Martin D. Troxell a son, Mary E. Troxel a dau.

Frederick Co., Md. Adm. Records Mdhr

Rsh.34 John Troxel, Sr., Book GME No.9, 3/25/1833, Jacob Troxel exr. of John Troxel, Sr. of Frederick Co., Md. Distribution as per Will to Magalena Hinch, Elizabeth Shower, Barbara Hinkle, late Greenmeyer, Mary Callings of Stewartshim, Pa., Catharine Mince portion to be placed on interest for her benefit, Margaret Mark her children as directed by Will.

Rsh.60 Margaret Troxell, APK1, pg.390, David Troxel, exr.,11/9/1857, personal property bequeathed to Juliana Troxel and Margaret S. Troxell, legacy conveyed by Will, to Mary A. Biggs, Frederick Troxell, Abraham Troxell, David Troxell, Samuel J. Troxell, Jacob S. Troxell, Emanuel Troxell, William W. Troxell

Rsh.60 John Troxell, Book APK1, pg.250, 1st and final account of David Troxell, exr. of John Troxall 10/26/1857. A.J. and John Zimmerman paid for proving Will. The following heirs paid: David Troxel a son, Frederick Troxel a son, Mary Biggs a dau., Abraham Troxell, a son.

Rsh.98 Peter Troxel, Book GME 13, pg.38 Joseph Welty adr. of Peter Troxel of J., late of Frederick, dec. 12/19/1836, large estate, many payments, no heirs named none evident.

Rsh.98 Elizabeth Troxell, exrs. Joshua and Joseph P. Troxell, 10/18/1850, bonds John Troxell and Jesse Landes, final 3/25/1873, Book SGC 3, pg.505.

Frederick Troxell, exr. William L. Troxell, final 5/8/1893, Book IRW 1, pg.49

Rsh.9 George Troxeler, final account by Fred Crabbs, Book GME,pg.128, 8/12/1833, paid Mary Ann Smith a dau., Johanna Gleason a dau., Barbara Troscel a dau., Jermima Troscel a dau., Joshua Trosela a son, William George Troscel a son, Joseph Peter Trosel a son. Received from Jacob Trosel, Tanner, on act, Frederick Troxel, on act., George Loy, amount of his note, Faurier A. Shorb on account and Peter Trosel.

Rsh.98  Peter Troxell of J, GME 13, pgs.395, 595, 10/29/1839, Joseph Welty of Peter Troxel of J., late of Frederick Co., 12/19/1836, balance $2,364.07, 3/4 allowed to Joseph Welty by Orphans Court.

Rsh.98  Elizabeth Troxel, Joshua Troxell, exr., of Frederick Co., Md., 3/25/1873, Book SGC, pg.505, paid to Barbara Welty w. of Joseph Welty a dau., heirs of Mary Ann Smith, George Grayson a son of Joanna White dec. who was a dau. of testix, Jermiam Motter, w. of Jocob Motter a dau. of the textrix, Joshua Troxel a son of the testix.

Rsh.101  Catherine Troxel, Samuel Troxel exr. 4/8/1845, final 5/29/1847, Book TS2, pg.25,

Rsh.101  Samuel Troxell, exr. William Troxel, Book TS5, pg.614, 2/17/1857,bonds Henry Winder and John D. Nickham

Rsh.101  Catherine Troxell, Book TS 2, pg.17, 5/26/1847, Samuel Troxell adm. of Catherine Troxell, paid to Samuel Troxell, son, paid to William Troxell son, paid to Elizabeth M., late Elizabeth Wise a dau., paid to Mary A. Davis a dau., paid to Catherine Bayer a dau., paid to Amanda Troxel a dau.

Rsh.101  Jacob Troxell, Book TS5, pg.595, Joshua Mottey, Isaac Motley, Lewis M. Motley, exrs. of Lewis Motley dec. who was adm. of Jacob Troxell late of Frederick Co., Md. settled by Joshua Motley. Distribution of estate: Catherine Troxel widow, Elizabeth Wise dau., Mary A. Davis dau., Catharine Troxell dau., Samuel Troxell son, William Troxel son, Amanda Troxel dau..

Rsh.101  Samuel Troxel, Book TS5, pg.614, 7/23/1852, William Troxell adm. of Samuel Troxell dec. Paid to John D. Nickum, the husb. of a sister of the dec., paid to John D. Davis the husb. of a sister, paid to J.W. Baugher the husb. of Catherine a sister, paid to Amanda Troxel a sister of dec., paid to William Troxel a brother of the dec.

Rsh.102  Peter Troxell, Jacob Troxell, adm. of Peter Troxell of John, 1820, dec., Book H.S.4, pg.159, 1/31/1820 late of Frederick Co. Deceased owned 25 shares of Westminister and Emmitsburg T.P. Paid to Mary Troxell w/o dec. 1/3 of shares, paid to children, George, Charlotte, Elizabeth, John and Harriett Troxell each 1/5 of remaining shares.

Frederick Co., Md.,  Orphans Distributions, Mdhr, 1778-1784
Mdhr 12, 290-2, Loc.1/50/7/46, pg.102

author's note:  there is no index, I have read entire book.
    Rsh.79  Conrad Doll and Catherine Terech, exr. of
Anthony Terech, balance due on paying final acct. 44.56 1/2.  No
date or heirs.  This entry is not dated but the Book begins in
August 1778 and ends with pg.122.  Estimated date: 1784
    pg.117, Jacob Tresner,Bernard Tresner, his adm.,
balance due on paying 1st act. 9-2-4.

Frederick Co., Md., Mdhr, Wills,
    Michael Trisler, 12/1/1770, Will of Arthur Carlton of
Frederick Co., son Thomas Carlton, w. Eleanor, dau. Alice m. to
Casper Shaaff they have son Arthur Shaaff, Arthur Carltons
Children Alice Shaff, Eleanor Murdock, Mary Charlton Grosh,
Usher Charlton, Anne Pheby, Penn Charlton and Jane Charlton,
witnesses Michael Trisler and Jos. Wood, George Dickson.
Proved 9/21/1771

Harford Co., Md., Mdhr, Index to Estate Docket Cr 10962
author's note:  this record has been read to June 1816
    6/19/1781 Jonathan Tossett, Francis Trossett adm., Book
JJB No.1, pg.195, inv. Book G.B., pg.80

Harford Co., Md., Mdhr, Wills Index, Mdhr AJ#C 1803-1812,
83,274, loc 1/5/3/18
    Elizabeth Totell made mark, left everything to grandau,
Priscilla Dallam.  Richard Totell son one dollar if demanded, dau.
Helen Paca one dollar if demanded, friend Richard Boothley
Dallas exr., witness Philip Henderson, Thomas Archer, Frances
Ann Henderson, proved 3/22/1803

Washington Co., Md., Distributions 1778-1805, County Agency
Index.  Mdhr 9152, Loc. 1/63/3/25
    Rsh.77  John Tresler, pg.93, 11/17/1798, John Tresler, his
adm. Barbara Tresler, 1/2 to widow, equal portions to Frederick
Tresler, Jacob Tresler, George Tresler, Adam Tresler, Elizabeth
Sunday, Mary Tresler, George Tresler, Sr.
    Rsh.79  Henry Doil, No date but in 1780 time period,
pg.18, Henry Doil, his admr Mary Doil, 1/3 to widow, remainder to
children, Adam, Catherine Stein her two children, Elizabeth Doll,
George Doll, Conrad Doil, Henry Doil, Mary Doil each.

Washington Co., Md. Probate Indexes, Hall of Records, Annapolis, Md.

Rsh.77   John Tresler, balances, Index 3, Drawer 30, year 1798, Washington Co., Md., Balance Book 1778-1805, pg.93

Washington Co., Md. Wills Liber A/215,

Rsh.74   Peter Teisher, 10/31/1789, proved 10/16/1808, w. Fanny, son John to adm. and have estate after death of mother, dau. Susanna, dau. Mary Gersh, dau.Elizabeth Grove, who has a dau. Elizabeth, dau. Dorathena, grandchild Susanna Trisler dau. of son Jacob Tresler dec., children of dau. Mary Ratzell dec., names them but writing is not clear.

Washington Co., Md., Mdhr, Wills, Hagerstown

Rsh.1   George Troxell, Book A, pg.77, 2/6/1783 proved 3/15/1783, w. Elizabeth, son Peter, son Abraham, dau. Magdelen, dau. Catherine, son Daniel and the one my w. is now big with to share equally.

John Tisher, adm. Mary Tisher, Bond C8 and other accounts no evidence of a Will, date 2/19/1820

Washington Co., Md., Distributions 1778-1805, County Agency Index.  Mdhr 9152, Loc. 1/63/3/25

Rsh.113   David Troxell, pg.64, 1/15/1791, his admr. John Hager, Abraham Troxell, to widow not named, David Troxell 2 shares, Catherine Swilar, 1 share, Magdelena Troxell 1 share, Anna Troxell 1 share, Sarah Salome, 1 share, Susannah 1 share.

Washington Co., Md., Distributions, Coagser m150, Cr9438-1,Cr9438-1,Cr9438-1, Microfilm, one reel.

Rsh.100   John Tisher, pg.183, 1828-1835, 1/3 widow Mary $832.37, heirs, John Siebert and w. $277.46; Jacob Hart and w. $277.46, David Shower and w. $277.46, Mary Teisher $277.46, John Teisher $277.46, Jacob Teisher $277.46.  author's note: When Mary d. her estate was paid to these heirs.

Washington Co., Md., Distributions 1778-1805, County Agency Index.,Mdhr 9152, Loc. 1/63/3/25

Rsh.1   George Troxell, pg.33, Will, 6/10/1785, exrs. John Cellar and Jacob Rorse, dist. agreeable to test. Will, widow 30.11.1, Peter Troxel 49.11.1, Abraham Troxell 45.18.7, Daniel

Troxell 22.11.1, Catherine Troxell 22.11.1, Phillip Olingor Troxell 22.11.1, ____Troxell 22.11.1.

Washington Co., Md. Distribution Accounts Mdhr 16315, 1836-1850, location 1/63/3/26
Mary Troxel, Philip Householder her adm.,2/1849, 1/4 each to Mary Troxel, Levi Troxel, Abraham Troxel, Philip Troxel

Washington Co., Md., Wills, Hagerstown
Rsh.113 Abraham Troxell, Will, Book A. pg.128, written 3/30/1786, proved 10/21/1786, w., mentioned but not named, son David, daus. Catherine, Magdelena, Anna, Susana, Salone

Washington Co., Md., Mdhr, Distributions 1778-1805, County Agency Index. Mdhr 9152, Loc. 1/63/3/25
Rsh.113 Abraham Troxel, (no index) pg.9, 4/18/1780, William Maphel dec., Wm. Band and Abraham Troxel the exrs., dist. Agreeable to test Will, 1/3 to widow, remainder equally divided upon children, Elizabeth, Margaret and the child unborn.
Rsh. 113 Abraham Troxel, exr. 8/12/1783 of Balsor Hawleybows, to be paid according to Will of Balsor Hawleybows, to widow, to each of children. These not named

Washington Co., Md., Distribution of Estate Accounts,1778-1850, by Dale Walton Morrow and Deborah Jensen Morrow F187.w3m66, copyright 1982,
Rsh.1 George Troxell, pg.9, his adm. John Cellars, Jacob Rowe 6/18/1785; widow 30.11.1; Peter, Abraham, Daniel, Catherine, Philip Orlinger each 22.11.1 T 216.5.2
Rsh.77 John Tresler, pg.9, his adm. Barbara 11/17/1798, 1/2 To widow 82.1.3 1/2, Frederick, Jacob, George, Adam, Elizabeth Sunday, Mary, George Sr. each 11.14.5 1/2; T164.2.7
Rsh.113 Abraham Troxell, pg.4, adm. of Hawleybower, Balsor, 8/12/1783, the widow 19.8.9, each child 5.11.1 T58.6.3 note: T58.6.3 minus 19.8.9 equals 38.17.8 and this divided by 7 equals 5.11.1 which suggests there were 7 children
Rsh.113 Abraham Troxell pg.9, his adm. David Troup, John Hager 1/15/1791; widow 142.4.3; David, 2 shares 80.5.3; Catherine, Magdalena, Anna, Sarah, Susanna each 40.12.7 T426.12.11: 6/22/1793: 1/3 to widow 170.9.11 1/4; David 97.8.6 1/2; Catherine Swilar, Magdalena, Anna, Susanna, Salome each

48.14.3 1/4 T511.9.10

Washington Co., Md. Estate documents
        Rsh.77  John Tressler, Book F, year 1796 supporting
documents for estate settlement,
        Ab. Troxell, Book FW, year 1786
        George Troxell, Book FW, year 1783
        John Tisher, (supporting documents for estate settlement)
year 1820
        Manry Troxell, Book F, year 1848
        Fannie S. Troxell Book F, year l860
        Emanuel Troxell, Book F, year 1876
        Dav. Troxell, Book F, year 1848
        Ann R. Troxell Book FW, year 1873

## NEW JERSEY

State of New Jersey, Index of Wills, Vol.2, 1913, NGS
Hunterdon Co., Will, Mary Traxler, year 1823

## NORTH CAROLINA

Abstracts Wills, Orange County, N.C., 1782-1800, 1800-1850, Ruth
Herndon Shields, Baltimore Geo. Publ Balt. 1972
        Rsh.73  George Troxler, Book E101 pg.118, written
10/29/1825, proved February Court, year 1826, son John under
age, dau. Adeline who is the w. of Briscoe Warren, dau. Franky
w. of Henry Rich and other unnamed unmarried daus.
        Rsh.73  David Troxler, Book E., pg.1, pg.98, Will, Adam
Whitsel, exrs. John Boon and John Troxler, witness John Boon
and David Troxler.

N.C. Wills, A Testator Index 1665-1900, by Thornton W. Mitchell,
Vol. II K-Z, Raleigh, N.C. 1987, F253.M57, 1987, V2
        Rsh.73  Barney Trexler, pg.588, Co. of Orange, 1817 WB -
D507, AR, N.C. State Archives.
        George Troxler, pg.588, 1826, WB E101, N.C. Archives,
Rsh.73, John Troxler 1849, Guilford Co.
        John C. Troxler 1895, Alamance Co.
        Powell C. Troxler 1851, Alamance Co.

Rowan County, N.C. Will Abstracts Vol.11, 1805-1850, abstracts of Books G-K, 1850, Abstracted and Compiled by Jo White Linn, indexed by Edith Montcalm Clark, copyright Jo White Linn 1971, publisher, Mrs. Stahle Linn, Jr., Box 978, Salisbury, N.C. 28144

?Rsh.123 Peter Trexler, pg.29, Lewis Kaylor, Sr., sons Lewis and Leonard, daus Mary Kaylor, Mary Chloe Stucker, Mottelina Eary, Catherine Caylor, Elizabeth Cresaly and Regener Fruck, exrs w. Margaret, son Leonard and John Eary.G254, 3/1805, probate 1815, witnesses Peter Trexler, George Krile

?Rsh.123 Peter Trexler, pg.75 James Kincaid, Sr., 9/11/1816, probate 2/1827, w. Hannah, daug. Elizabeth Kincaid, living sons and daug. exrs w. Hanna, Thomas Hatch Dent, witness Peter Trexler, William Hulin

Levi Trexler, pg.98 book I pg.5, Zacariah Rodgers, 2/3/1837, probate 2/1837, w. not named, son Samuel, Alen Rodgers, son of Randel Rodgers, exrs., none, witnesses Levi Trexler, Daniel Frick, Daniel File

Jacob Trexler, pg.128 David Fraley, 7/31/1859, probate 1849 (author's note: this is not typo) Book K, pg.100, w. Ellen, children not named, exrs., son William, sons-in-law, John Lantz, Jacob Trexler, witness Samuel Rothrock, Obediah Hampton

Henry Trexler, pg.105, Will, Peter Arey, Book I, pg.102, 7/15/1840 probate 5/1841, w. not named, son Milas, land in Iredell Co., dau. Elizabeth, exr. Samuel Rothrock, witness Henry Trexler, Martin Starns

Rowan County N.C. Will Abstracts, Vol.1, 1753-1805, Abstracts Books A-F, Abstracted and Compiled by Jo Whitelinn, Indexed by Edith Montcalm Clark,Pub. Mrs. Stahle Linn, Jr., Box 978, Salisbury, N.C. 28144

pg.29, Book G:254, 3/1805, Will of Lewis Kaylor, Sr. witnessed by Peter Trexler, George Krile

pg.75, Book H:378, 9/1816, Will of James Kincaid Sr., witnesses, Peter Trexler, Wm. Hulin

pg.98, I5, 1837, Will of Jacariah Rodgers, witnesses Levi Trexler

OHIO

<u>Gateway to the West, Vol.II, Compiled by Ruth Bowers and Anita Short, Geo. Publ Co., Inc., Balt. 1989</u>
Abraham Troxell, pg.192, 11/5/1821, Catherine Gephart age 13 chose Abraham Troxell as her Guardian. Montgomery Co., Ohio
Abraham Troxell, pg.182, 11/9/1819, Abraham Troxell appointed guardian of Elizabeth, Mary, Sarah, Jacob, and Catherine Arnold 10-3 years. Father Christian Arnold, Montgomery Co., Ohio
Abraham Troxel, pg.209, 3/11/1833, Abraham Showers age 18, Polly Ann Showers age 16 and Deliah Showers 14, children of David Showers chose Abraham Troxel as their guardian. Montgomery Co., Ohio
?Rsh.106 Samuel Troxell, pg.216, 9/13/1836, Rosanna Troxell appointed guardian of Mary Troxel age 10, Lewis Troxel age 9, Abraham Troxell age 5 the children and heirs of Samuel Troxell, Montgomery Co., Ohio
?Rsh.106 Emanuel Trexler, Samuel Trexler, pg.501, 5/19/1814, John Shewards, Will, Witness Emanuel Trexler, Samuel Trexler

<u>Montgomery Co., Ohio, Index Wills and Adm. 1803-1893 Copied by Lindsay M. Brian, Doc. A1, pg.207,</u>
Rsh.106 Samuel Troxell, 1835-1837, Samuel Troxell, Doc.J., pg.225, No Will Book
David Trissel, Doc. J. pg.186, David Trissel, Will, Book C., pg.5
Abraham Troxell, 1837-1851, Abraham Troxell, Will, Book D., pg.247

**PENNSYLVANIA**

<u>Adams Co., Pa., Abstracts, Adams Co., Pa., Wills, 1800-1826, Kevin L. Greenholt, Familine, Westminster, Md. 1988, Will Book A., Adams County C.H. Gettysburg, Pa.</u>
Rsh.5 Appolonia Ehrman of Heidelberg Twp., Adams Co., Pa., Will, Book A., pg.63 No.34, 3/1800, probate 3/5/1801. To six children of my sister Mary Klunk dec., namely Joseph, Peter, John, Mary, Teresa and Catherine to each of them five pounds to be paid to them as they shall come of age, agreeable to the Last Will and Testament of my father Joseph Ehrman, dec., bearing the date of 6/16/1798....balance to Rev. Francis X. Brosius, with full confidence in him or his assigns that part of the said property

will be disposed of agreeable to my private instructions and the remainder to be applied so the said Mr. Brosius shall deem to the honor and glory of God. Do appoint my brother Jacob Kuhn my sole exr., Witness to her mark, Samuel and Henry Lilly.

Rsh.5 Anthony Drecksel makes claim against estate of Appolonia Ehrman and received 13.9.9 of total estate of L543.10.11

Rsh.81 John Troxell, pg.25, Jacob Ackerman, Gettysburg, dau. Catherine w. of John Troxell, Jr., written 11/8/1808, probate 11/14/1808, exr. son-in-law John J. Troxell, Jr., pg.16, Jacob Ackerman, Gettysburg, sick, w. Catherine, children Catharine Troxell w. of John Troxell, Jr., Mary w. of Valentine Neaswitz, Rachael, w. of George Rowe, Sarah, Rebecca, Joshua, exors, w., son-in- law John Troxell, Jr., witness, Samuel Keplinger, John Agnew, Alexander Russell, Nov. 8, 1808, probate 11/14/1808.

Rsh.5 Jacob Kuhn, pg.11, James Pellentz, Hidelberg Twp., Roman Catholic Priest, weak. Bequest to Francis Xavier Brosius, priest, including land in Rye Twp., Cumberland Co., Pa.; exr.: Brosius, witnesses: Joseph Lilly *James Driskell, Jacob Kuhn; written 6/14/1795; probate 4/23/1800, recorded pg.16.

note: notation in the Catholic Conewago records "is not Dirskell Trexel?", Jacob Kuhn is brother to Catherine Trexel, Rsh.5.

Adams Co., Pa., Courthouse Records, Gettysburg, Pa., note probate records are microfiche and are numbered

No.3419, John Tressler, adm. 9/19/1857, exr. John B. Baumgardner, inv. file 10/6/1857, Account settled 12/27/1865

No.3051, Henry Troste, Sr., adm., 4/6/1851, exr. Wm. S. Hamilson, inv. 4/29/1853, Heirs, Chtistian Zeigler, Catherine Zeigler, Susannah Trostle, her mark, George Starr, Elizabeth Starr, Peter Trostle

Rsh.38 No.487, Joseph Trexel (Trexee), adm. 12/23/1812, Tyrone Twp., exr. Benjamin Whitley, bond $500. M. Longwele, Ralph Sasbalter, 1/23/1813. Inv. 6 plates silver, 1 wash tub, 1 tea table...

Rsh.120 No.2317, John Trostle, Will, 3/27/1843, Hamilton Twp., w. Elizabeth, brothers John and Peter Trostle, land Paradise Twp., exr. Peter Trostle of John Trostle, sons Samuel, John, Daniel, Jonas and Moves, dau. Elizabeth m. Samuel Weist, dau. Polly m. Mathias Trimmer, dau. Susannah m. Henry Sontag, dau. Rebecca, dau. Catherine m. John Cooksey

Rsh.120 No.3044, Henry Trostle, Jr., Will, 3/15/1853, exr. Michael Trostle, w. Jane, youngest child Jullianne not of age, son Emanuel, dau. Catherina

Rsh.120 No.3051, Henry Trostle, Sr., adm. 4/6/1851, heirs Christian Zeigler, Catherine Ziegler, Susannah Trostle, her mark, George Starr, Elizabeth Starr, Peter Trostle

Rsh.120 No.3084, Abraham Trostle, Sr., Will, 10/1/1853, brother Peter Trostle, Peter Trostle, Sr., exr. son, Isaac B. Trostle, member German Church, Huntington Twp., son Andrew Trostle, dau. Sarah Stock w. of George Stock, dau. Elizabeth Beam w. of John Beam, son Jacob M. Trostle, son Abraham Trostle, Jr., son Isaac R. Trostle.

Rsh.120 No.3210, Jacob Trostle, Will, 3/3/1855, of East Berlin, w. Catherine, sons exrs. John and George Trostle, dau. Elizabeth m. David Moul, sons John and George

Rsh.120 No.3727, Catherine Trostle, w/o Abraham, Will, 4/11/1861, she made mark, exr. Isaac B. Trostle, son, children, Andrew Trostle, Elizabeth Beam m. John H. Beam, Jacob B. Trostle, Abraham Trostel and Isaac B. Trostle, Grandchildren, Catherine C. Stoke, Henry Stoke, Sarah A. Stoke, Joseph Stoke, William Stoke, Abraham Stoke, ___ Stoke, George Stoke, Samuel Stoke, Jacob F. Stoke,in Orphans Court Records, Abraham Trostle; Catherine Trostle, Henry, Franklin, Catherine, Sarah, Samuel, Henry Stoke, 1854, Reel 215, pg.938.

Rsh.120 No.3928, George Trostle, Cumberland Twp., Wll 6/8/1863, exr. John Trostle, and D. A. Buehler, dau. Elizabeth m. Joseph Maleny, son Michael Trostle, son John Trostle, son Henry Trostle, dau. Mary m. Bernhardt Goeslner, dau. Susan m. John W. Weigle, dau. Lindia m. Wm. Newman, now dec., son Daniel Trostle, dau. Anna m. George Breischer, now dec., son William Trostle, son Jacob Trostle, children of dau. Lydia now dec..

Rsh.120 No.3964, Peter Trostle, Will, 9/28/1863, exr. Samuel Herbs and Daniel Stallsmitt.

Rsh.120 No.7452, Abraham Trostle, 9/12/1895 death date, Borough of York, w. Lydia, he has marriage contract with her, daus. Mary A. and Catherine, sons Henry J. Trostle and George H. Trostle, and son Hiram Trostle, dau. Sarah A. Harris, dau. Mary A. dau. Hannah L. dau. Catherine, dau. E. Shaw, Will, Book K., pg.219, sett. April 20, 1901,

No.2153, David Troxell, Will, 3/7/1840, Straban Twp., exr. Abraham Spangler, dau. Magdalena dec. she m. Stephen Wible, he dec. also, dau. Polly Wible, her children Stephen, John, Joseph, 5 children, dau. Elizabeth m. Wolff, dau. Catherine m. Essick, dau. Mary m. Spangler, son David Troxell, dau. Susannah m. Keephaver (Keefauver)

?Rsh.43  No.2411, David Troxel, Will, 6/17/1844

No.3394, John Troxell, adm. 4/24/1850, exr. David Troxel

?Rsh.45  No.3419, John Tressler, adm. 9/19/1857, exr. John H. Baumgardner, Act. Sttl. 12/27/1865.

Allegheny County Pa., Wills, Index, Vol.1 throu. 12, 1789-1869, compiled by Bob and Mary Closson copyright June 1979 F 157.A4C55

Michael Driscoll, Book 11, pg.572, year 1866

John Tragesser, Book 11, pg.159, year 1864

Armstrong County Pennsylvania Willbook Index 1805-1900, Compiled by Diana Bowman for Closson Press, copyright 1987 F157.A7B68 1987 Rsh.84  Isreal Truxall, Plumcreek Twp., year 1864, Vol.2, pg.312 estate 1582

Beaver County Pa., Index, Wills 1800-1900 Bob and Mary Closson, Closson Press, Appollo Pa., 15613 copyright 1988

John Dressler, year 1898, Book L, pg.68

Bedford County Pa., Index, Wills 1771-1900, compiled by Patricia Wainwright Collins for Closson Press,  F 157.B25 C65, 1983

John Truxel, Book 3, pgs.415,454, year 1848

Berks County, Pa., Register of Wills Office, Courthouse, Reading, Pa., Estate accounts filed alphabetically and in individual files

Rsh.2  John Drexel, Stone Cutter, Cumru Twp., Berks Co., Pa. Will, 4/20/1849, w. Susanna, children now living Reuben, Jacob, John, Henry, George, Samuel, Catherine the w. of Bernard Driefuss, Susanna, Rosianna and one yet unborn (Charles Drexel)...Reuben Drexel d. 3/29/1895, Jacob Drexel was wounded in the Civil War and brought home where he d. shortly thereafter, and John Drexel, another exr. named was declared a habitual drunkard by the Court of Common Pleas of Berks Co., on 1/11/1869...Susanna Drexel d. 1/15/1894...Petitioner Mary H. Missimer, w. of Samuel D. Missimer daughter of Reuben Drexel to discharge John Drexel as ex...John Drexel d. in May 1849 and left a Last Will and Testament dated 4/20/1849...subpoena Mrs. Rosa Waldman, Mrs. Lillie Heilbron and Adam Drexel, committee; subpoena a John Drexel and Mrs. Rosianna Rothenberger, George Drexel, Henry Drexel; sworn 11/16/1895, Adam K. Drexel, son of John Drexel, Charles Drexel, son of John Drexel who d. in 1849; 11/25/1895, Emanuel B. Dreifoos, residing at 350 Burling St., Chicago, Ill grandson of John Drexel renounced his right and requested they be granted to Cornelias K. Rothenberger; 11/1895, Fannie Austrain and Lillie Heilborn of New York, granddaus. of John Drexel renounced their rights and requested they be granted to Cornelius K. Rothenberger; 11/25/1895, Harry F. Dreifoos, grandson of John Drexel, from Essex County, New Jersey, renounced his rights and requested they be granted to Cornelius K. Rothenberger; 11/25/1895

1. Reuben Drexel dec.: Children - Mary m. Samuel D.Missimer, Thomas Drexel, Henry Drexel, William Drexel, Reuben Drexel, Emma Louisa Seidel, w. of Samuel Seidel, Lillie m. David Regar;
2. Catharine Dreyfus dec.: Children - Fannie m. Raphael Austrain, Rosa m. Paul b. Waldman, Katie m. Greisemer, Harry Dreyfus, Emanuel Dreyfus, Lillie m. Louis Heilbron
3. Henry Drexel
4. Rosa Sleinauer, w. of George Sleinauer, only child of Susan Wagner, dec.
5. George W. Drexel
6. Rosa Rothenberger, w. of Cornelius K. Rothenberger
7. John Drexel, his committee is Adam K. Drexel.

note: John Drexel d. 5/1845 leaving a posthumous child since dec.,Estate of John Drexel, late of Spring Twp., dec., decedent d. in the mo. of May 1849, testate and m., leaving to survive him a widow Susanna Drexel, who had since d. to wit: January 15, 1894 and the following issue, viz: 1. Reuben Drexel, a son, who d., testate on the 29th day of March having named as his exe. Lillie V. Regar and Emma L. Seidel. 2. Jacob Drexel, a son who d. intestate, unmarried and without issue in the year 1864. 3. John Drexel, a son, who has for his committee Adam K. Drexel. 4. Henry Drexel, a son. 5. George Drexel, a son, Samuel Drexel, a son who d. in the year 1875 intestate, unmarried and without issue. 7. Catherine Dreifoos, a dau., who d. in the year 1867 leaving to survive her a husb. Bernard Dreifoos and the following issue - Fannie Austrian,

Henry Dreifoos, Emanuel Dreifoos, Rose Waldman, Katie M. Griesemer, Lillie Heilbron. 8. Susanna Wagner, a dau., who d. in the year 1892 leaving to survive her a husb., Henry Wagner and the following issue. a. Rosa Steinauer. 9. Rosa Rothenberger, a dau. 10. A posthumous child which d. without a Christian name, about a week after its birth in June 1849

Berks County, Pa., Register of Wills Office, Courthouse, Reading, Pa., Estate accounts filed alphabetically and in individual files
    Dissler, John, Sadler, Reading, Berks Co., Pa., signed 10/8/1810, beloved w. Sophia, son John, son Jacob, son George, dau. Sarah, dau. Catharina, dau. Mary
    Dissler, Jacob, Reading, Berks Co., Pa., 1822, John Disler and George Disler brothers to Jacob Disler dec. renounced rights, Maria Disler a minor under 14 years of age 12/13/1822, Ejiah Dichert (Decher) named guardian of Maria on 3/14/1824.
    Ditzler, Anthony, Tulpehouon Twp., Berks Co., Pa., d. intestate 1781, bond, Magdalen Ditzler, widow, (she made mark), Andrew Rigel and George Haugh, both of the same place bound unto Henry Christ...petition of guardianship, Michael, Margaret and Elizabeth Ditzler under the age of 14 years 3/18/1783, petition of guardianship Reading 3/18/1786 of Nicholas Sheffer who m. one of the daus. of Anthony Ditzler dec. 4/30/1783 Magdlaena Ditzler widow, adm. for guardian appointed Balser Emrock, Thomas Kurr, 8 children total, Christina, Simon, Michael, Margaret who are under 14 years of age, Thomas the eldest son, Elizabeth, Catherine the w. of Nicholas Stoffeer, Jacob, Christina, Simon, Michael and Elizabeth 8/15/1783 Jacob Ditzler minor above 14.
    Ditzler (Tritzler), William V., Will, Tulpehocken Twp., Berks Co., Pa., (he made mark), written 5/4/1758, Probate 6/14/1782, written in German, Melchior Tilzer eldest son, son Anthony Titzler, then my children shall have equal shares to wit, Melchor Titzler, Mary Magdalena Tritzler and Anthony Titzler, witness Frederick Truster, we Melchoir Ditzler in Bethel Twp., in County of Lancaster eldest son of William Ditzler late of Tulpenocken and Godfried Rohrer (umlat over o) and Charles Key of the same place bound unto Henry Christ Register of the Probate of Wills.
    Christina Ditzler, Tulpehocken Twp., Berks Co., Pa., d. int. 1808...year 1818 Catharine dau. of Christina Ditzler, late of Tulpehocken, d. 10 years ago intestate leaving 6 children, Betsy

m. to Jacob Ditzler, Catharine, Christina m. to John Smith, Molly, Thomas and Jacob the last 2 who are yet in minority. 4/10/1818 Thomas Titzler had dau. Hester, John Shaffer appointed, a son of Thomas Titzler required guardian, Molly Ditzler was a dau. of Christina 11/6/1816. Jacob Ditzler m. to Betsy Ditzler, John Smith m. to Christina Dritzler, Molly Ditzler, John Manbock guardian for Thomas Distzler and John Shaffer for Jacob Ditzler heirs and representatives of Christina Ditzler late of Tulpehocken.

Ditzler, Elizabeth, d. intestate 1833, Upper Bern Twp., Berks Co., Pa., probate January 10, 1834, Isaac Siebert, adm.

Drenkle (Drankle), Daniel, merchant d. intestate 3/15/1830/1831, Reading Borough, Berks Co., Pa., w. Elizabeth Drenkle, witness John Miller, 5/7/1838 petition of Elizabeth Sheuman (she made mark) of Cumru Twp., Berks, Co., widow, she made mark, 1839 petition for guardian of Catharine Drenkle, guardian of Sarah Drenkle, minor, guardian for Elizabeth Drenkle minor, guardian for Henry Drenkle minor, guardian for Caroline Drinkle, 1/10/1845 petition of Elizabeth Drenkle widow and Henry Drenkle, Amos Esterly who m. Maria Drenkle, Catharine Drenkle, Joseph Jackson who m. Sarah Ann Drenkle and Caroline Drenkle is a minor with Amos Esterly guardian.

Drenkle, Maria, Alsace Twp., Berks Co., Pa., 1801, John Trenckle, late husb. of Marcia Boyer, formerly the w/o Henry Schmech, late of Alsace Twp., Jorge Babb of Alce Twp., and Samuel Woolison of Reading, all of Berks Co., Pa., 10/19/1801.

Dress (Drear,Dreas), Theobald (Dewald), Longswamp, Berks Co., Pa., 3/25/1790 Elizabeth Drehs w/o Deobalt Drehs, dec. int., Tailor, late of Longswamp. Theobald/Deobalt Carl of the same place father-in-law of the dec., John Adam Gehry and Michael Drehs both of Longswamp yeoman bound John Chust. Elizabeth Dreks (she made mark), witness Samuel Hock, Adam Kaufer, on 3/5/1800, 6 children, Catherine the w. of Peter Brown, Abraham, John, Elizabeth and Jacob the three last named are in their minority. Intestate had land adjoining John Ech, John Hummer. On 9/3/1800 mother Elizabeth Dreas had d. dau. Elizabeth Dreas, who made mark, said she was a minor above 14 years of age, John Deas minor above 14, Jacob minor under 14

Dress (Dores), Valentine, 1799, Will, written in German, translated, he made mark, Manheim Twp., Berks Co., Pa., Valentine Droef letters granted George Droes and Geor Zerbe exrs. 9/30/1799, Peter Lehr and Jacob Fisher witness Will, beloved w. Barbara, only son George Droes, 3 daus. Catherine, Ann Maria and Barbara, exrs. George Droes and George Zorbe

Dress, Conrad, Longswamp, Berks Co., Pa., written in German, translated, 6/17/1790, Will, probate, written 5/29/1790, Jacob Reiner and John Wagonner witnesses, sons John Dress and Michael Dress, exrs., 6 heirs five sons and one dau., 2 lbs. Reformed Church Longswamp, 2 lbs, Lutheran Church Maccumagy (Macgunie) son Deobald, son John, son Matssias, son George, dau. Elizabeth, son Michael

Traxel, Margaret, (made mark) 4/28/1814, Cumru Twp., Berks Co., Pa., do hereby empower my brother John Laab (Laub) to administer estate of dec. husb. Abraham Traxel. Witness Sam Leather, adm. Henry Fritz, Joseph Morris

?Rsh.127  Treichler, Jacob, d. intestate 1845, Washington Twp., Berks Co., Pa., Sarah Treichler (she made mark) w/o Washington Twp., and Samuel Treichler of Hereford Twp., and Amous Shultz of Douglas Twp., Montgomery Co., Andrew Stauffer and John Roland of Washington Twp., Co. of Berks.  Samuel Treichler chooses Samuel Treichler as his guardian, Peter Hillegas of Montgomery Co., guardian of Manasseh Treichler and John Hilleson guardian of Henry Treichler, David Knetz of Montgomery Co., guardian of John and Mary Treichler.

Treshter, George, Bethel Twp., Berks Co., Pa., 1794, 4/29/1793 appeared Peter Treshter of Bethel Township, a brother of George Treshter late a soldier in the service of the United States of America dec., Christian Zerbe of same place yeoman and John Kautum of the Borough of Reading in Berks Co., Pa.

Rsh.87  Trexler, Daniel, d. 7/2/1829, of Union Twp., Huntington, Co., Pa., in the year 1833, Longswamp Twp., Berks Co., Pa., Jonathan Haas, brother-in-law contests Reuben Trexler, brother of Daniel, claim against Last Will and Testament of Daniel Trexler, dec., found for Jonathan Haas

Rsh.87  Trexler, Jacob, Longswamp, Berks Co., Pa., 1829, letters granted to Ruben Trexler, witness George Heisler and Peter Trexler, probate 8/31/1829, Reuben Trexler and Jacob Breing, exrs. paid to heirs, David Tresler's legacy; Peter Tresler's legacy; Jacob Trexler by Jacob Breings m. to Catharina; Levina Tresler's legacy, Reuben Tresler's legacy, Susanna Brening's legacy she is m. to James Brenning.

Rsh.87  Trexler, Jonas, Longswamp. Berks Co., Pa., d.

12/1841/42?, Renunciation of Sarah Trexler, w/o Jonas, Wm. Hollenstein of Maxatwny Twp., Horatio Trexler of Longswamp Twp., David Kutz and David H. Hottenstine of Maxatawny Twp., all of Berks Co., to adm. Jonas Trexler...petition 1842 Willoughley, Sarah, Caroline and Catherine Trexler minor children in 1842. David K. Hollenstein guardian of Jonas, Peter and David H. Hollerstein guardian of David, Elizabeth and Amelia and Isaac Rodler guardine of Abile, Willouby Trescler oldest son of Jonas, Sarah w., children living Angleine w. of Milton Ahum, Sarah w. of George Ludwig, Willoby Trexer, Jonas Trexler, Abial Trexler, Peter Trexler, David Trexler and Elizabeth E. Trexler. Said Sarah and Jonas are minors above age of 14. Daniel K. Hollenstine being the guardian of Jonas and the said Abial, Peter, David and Elizabeth being minors under 14 years...the Rev. Roeller being guardian of Abial, Dan K. Hollensein of Peter and David K. Hollerstein for David and Elizabeth...Jonas Trexler d. seized in his demise as of fee and in the following real estate adjoining the land of Nathan Trexler

Rsh.87 Trexler, Peter, Longswamp Twp., Berks Co., Pa., 1828, witness to Will, Nathan Trexler and Daniel Trexler; letters test: Jacob, Ruben and Jonas Trexler, sons of Peter Trexler, w. Catherine, daus. Maria, Catharina, Anna, Judith, sons Jonas, Mattias and Daniel, sons Peter, Jacob, Reuben, Jonas. Will, dated 2/15/1825, probate, 4/19/1828, John Folk m. Maria Trexler, Peter Trexler, Jonas Trexler, Reuben Trexler, Jonathan Haas, John Albright and Jonas Trexler, Judith Trexler, Nathan Trexler and Daniel Trexler

Rsh.87 Trexler, Reuben 1846, Longswamp, written 3/26/1846, granted to Horatio Trexler and William Trexler, dear w. Anna, children to share, 1/5 to dau. Lucinda, 1/5 to dau Carolina, 1/5 to son Horatio, 1/5 to son William, 1/5 to son Lesher, sons Horatio and William exr.

?Rsh.89 Trexler, Sophia, 1850, District Township (south east corner Berks Co.,) Berks Co., Pa., renunciation of David Trexler of the estate of Sophia Trexler, dec. 2/3/1850, adm. Jesse Gerhart, Samuel Walter of Pike Twp., and John Reidenour of Wash. Twp.

Rsh.150 Triester, Frederic, Intestate, 3/2/1761, adm. bond from Margaretta Treister, w/o Frederick of Bethel Twp., Berks Co., Pa., yeoman, dec. Martin Treister, brother to the dec., and Gottfried Roher of the Tulpehocken, Innkeeper, 3/2/1761 bonded for widow, guardians who were appointed by court Peter Kirtzer and

George Wolf for the children under 14 years of age as to Maria Dorothea, Anna Margaret Triester, widow, states that Frederich Triester left five children, all minors, to wit, John Jacob, John, George Frederick and Peter under the age of 14 years and Maria Dorothea, age 15 years. 17 August 1762, Dorothea Triester, between the age of 14 and 21, petitions that William Keiser of Twp. of Tulpehocken, County of Berks to be her guardian 3/26/1763, final distribution 3/26/1763, George Frederick, age 4 years, Peter age 3 years, Maria Dorrothea, age 15 years, Jacob and John, both dec., under age.

?Rsh.146  Trostel, Bernard, Longswamp, 9/8/1776, Anna Maria Trostleinn of Longswamp, w/o Bernard Trostel of same place, yeoman, Henry Haller of Reading, innkeeper and Frederick Klein of Tonameusing Twp., in Northampton County in the Province of Pennsylvania, 9/8/1766, Anna Maria Trostlerin. author's note: see Frederick, Md. Monacracy Church records

Rsh.91  Trostel, Henry, Beckwick Twp., County of Berks, Pa., 1824, Will, d. 12/15/1824, letters granted to John and Henry Trostel, sons as exrs., w. Catharina, son Henry, youngest dau. Catherine, dau. Peggy, dau. Barbara, son John

Rsh.91  Trostel, Henry, dec., Beckwick Twp., County of Berks, Pa., 1867, John Weiss, guardian of Susanna Trostel, John Trostel and Henry Trostel, minor children of Henry Trostel late of Brackwick Twp., Berks Co., discharged his guardianship to Israel B. Mussellman 3 August 1867, Orphans Court Record.

Rsh.136  Trostel, George, Yeoman, Brecknock Twp., Berks, Co.,Pa., 1804, (s.w. corner of Berks close to Lancaster Co., poss. attended church there) dec. as of 9/28/1804, Rosina Trostel widow (she made mark) of George Trostel and William Trostle son of the dec. Abraham Marquart, Jacob Remp, both of Cumru Twp., Berks Co., Pa., yeoman, adms bound Rosina Trostel and William Trostle. Disbursements 10/29/1805 include John Trostel, Margaret Trostle, Abraham Trostle

Rsh.136  Troxel (Troscle), William, (d.latter part of summer 1841) Cumru Twp., Berks Co., Pa., died intestate. Adms. Benjamin Stump, Patrick O' Deer and Daniel Knower of Cumru Twp., Berks Co., 8/6/1841 Samuel Troscle child, Julia Troscle child, Elizabeth Troscle child of William Troscle are minors above the age of 14 years and their mother is dec. As of 8/13/1842 Benjamin Strink had m. Sarah one of the children of Wm. Troxell dec. and she is above 21 years of age. William Troxel left 9 children, Sarah w. of Benjamin Strink, Samuel, John, Elizabeth, Aaron, Eli, Levi, Mary, William who are minors. He had property adjoining land of G.U. Kohl and John Troxell...in settlement Reuben Troxel was paid for note, 5/9/1845 petition of Abraham Troxell one of the heirs and representatives of Rebecca Troxell dec. Rebecca had land said William Troxell possessed and her heirs were not fully satisfied. Abraham prays Benjamin Strink to enter an account of Adm. of estate. Abraham Troxell make mark 7/1846 Samuel Troxell and John Troxel sons of William Troxel petition for settlement. 11/9/1849 Solomon Boyer who made mark petitioned that he had m. Elizabeth a dau. of Wm. Troxell.

Berks Co., Pa., Morman Microfilm, Index to Wills
     Rsh.87  1833  Daniel Trexler witness Ruben Trexler, Pendente Light Adm., 11 D.D.
     Rsh 87  1833  Daniel Trexler, Will, Book 7, pg.161
     Rsh.87  1829  Jacob Trexler witness Rueben Trexler, Will, Book 6, pg.416
     Rsh.87  1818  Peter Trexler, witness Jacob Rueben, Jonas Trexler, Will, Book 6, pg.187
     Rsh.87  1846  Ruben Trexler witness Horatio and William Will, Book 9, pg.119

Berks Co., Pa., Abstracts of Wills, Collections of the Genealogical Society of Philadelphia, Vol.2, 1798-1825, Presented to the Genealogical Society by Alfred Smith, Philadelphia 1898
     pg.481  Drenkel (Trenkel), John, Reading Twp., 8/29/1821, probate 9/3/1822, Book D, pg.346, w. not named, son John, 6 children, John, Daniel, George, Peter, Samuel and Susanna w. of Nicholas Maderia, exrs. sons John and Daniel, witness Henry Betz, Daniel Kerper
     pg.175  (Samuel Dresher) Fegely, Christian, Longswamp Twp., 3/29/1806 probate 1/10/1807, translation from German, w. Anna Maria, children Hennrich, David, Anna Maria Maslo, Christian Relitz, George and Philops, sons Christian and Peter, w. Anna Maria and son Henrich exrs., witness Samuel Dresher and John Daniel Young.
     pg.128  (Daniel Dresler) Trautman, Michael, Tulpekocken Twp., dated 8/3/1804, probate 12/3/1804, translation from German, w. Susanna, brother Valentine, brother John with son Michael, brother Philip with children, witness Leonard Zerbe, Daniel Dresler

pg.435 (Peter Dresser) Smeck, Jacob, Maxatawmy Twp., 3/21/1820, adm. to w. Susanna the widow and John G. Renchler and Peter Dresser

Rsh.131 pg.130 (Jacob Dressler) Albrecht, Conrad, Rockland Twp., 12/31/1804, adm. to Mary Albrecht and widow and Jacob Dressler, brother-in-law

Rsh.131 pg.269 (Jacob Dressler) Henry William Lies, Rockland Twp., w. Margaret, 9 children Margaret m. Henry Heanig, Maria, Peter, Daniel, Ester, Magdaline, Catharina, William and Elizabeth Lies. W. Margaret and John Haak, adm. witness Jacob Long and Jacob Dressler

Rsh.131 pg.302 (Jacob Dressler) Danner, Abraham, Rockland Twp., dated 10/26/1811, probate 6/9/1813, Book D, pg.59, dau. Margaret w. of Jacob Dressler, dau. Magdalene w. of Adam Klein, dau. Barbara w. of Jacob Long, their children daus. Maria, Catharine, Magdalena and Margaret Long, to Maria w. of Bernhard Zigler, a dau. Elizabeth, sons-in-law Adam Klein and Jacob Dressler exrs. witness George Heist and Christopher Keller

pg.402 (Peter Dressler) Kohser, George, Greenwich Twp., 1/19/1813, probate 11/9/1814, translation from German, w. Elizabeth, son George dec., sons Jacob, John, Andreas, Christian, daus. Christiana Kraft, Elizabeth Kamp, dec., Maria Wanner, son Henry, daus. Catherine Keveler, Maria Barbara, (son) Daniel, Rosina, Regina, Salome of these George and 6 last named were of 2nd w.. The others by dec. w. John Coles and Peter Dressler, exrs. witness Jacob Grim and John Zimmer

pg.472 (Peter Dressler) Witt, John Nicholas, Maxatawny Twp., 2/15/1822, adm. to John a son and Peter Dressler friend, widow renouncing

pg.142 (Joseph Drissel) Van Read, Anna, widow, Amity Twp., 4/11/1805, probate 6/1/1805, Book 4, pg.292, to Elizabeth dau. of Joseph Drissel of Tinicum Twp., Bucks Co., Pa., to Lydia w. of David Stauffer of Nocamixon Twp., Bucks Co., Pa., she being a dau. of John Drissels, to Susanna w. of Henry Stauffer of same place also a dau. of Dressels

Rsh.136 pg.335 Traxel, Abraham, Cumru Twp., 4/28/1814, adm. to John Laab a friend, widow renouncing

Rsh.136 pg.126 Trostel, George, Brecknock Twp., 9/28/1804, adm. to Rosina the widow and William, son.

Rsh.137 pg.340 Trostel, Henry, Breckmock Twp., 9/2/1824, probate 12/15/1824, Book D, pg.444, w. Catherine, son

Henry, daus. Catherine, Peggy, Barbara, son John, exrs. sons
John and Henry, witness Conrad Spatz, Samuel Bowmen

Rsh.151  pg.6271  (Peter Troxell) Sigfried, John, Faurier,
Maxtawany Twp., 2/20/1817 probate 5/28/1821, w. Gerhaut
(Gertraut), son Daniel Siegfried, land in Weisenburg Twp.,
Leehigh Co., son John, dau. Magdalena w. of Peter Troxell, dau.
Maria w. of Jacob Albrecht, dau. Catharine w. of John Bieber,
dau. Judith w. of _____Schlauch - whose children are Cathaeine
Schlauch and Joseph Schlauch. exrs. w. Gertraut, son John,
witness Henry Grim, Reuben Grim

Rsh.153  pg.481  (Elizabeth Troxell) Siegfried, Henry,
Maxatawny Twp., 10/25/1821, probate 8/30/1822, Book D, pg.344,
son Solomon, son Joseph, son John, son David farm where
Henry Poh now lives, son Abraham, brother Jacob Siegfried, w.
Magdalena, daus. Maria Uetzger (?Rsh.153) Elizabeth Troxall,
Catharine Bieber, friend and neighbor John Siegfried and son
John exrs. witness Jonathan Grim and Daniel Levan and James
Donagan

Bucks Co., Pa., Index of Wills and Administration Records 1684 to
1850 compiled by Richard T. and Mildred C. Williams, published
by same, Danboro, Pennsylvania 18916, 1971 F157.B8W5

pg.40, Dressel, Ulrich, year 1817, Lower Milford, Will/Adm.
4365

pg.40, Drissel, Joseph, 1834, Tinicum, Will, 6666
pg.40, Drissel, Henry 1834, Tenicum, Adm., 6711
pg.40, Drissel, Abraham 1837, Tinicum, Adm., 7077
pg.40, Drissel, David, 1833, Doylestown Boro, Will, 8381
pg.166, Treichler, David, 1833, Nockamixon, Adm. 6535
pg.166, Trichler, John, 1811, Richland, Adm. 3826
pg.166, Trickler, John, 1794, Hilltown, Adm. 2509
pg.166, Trissel, John, Sr., 1814, Tinicum, Will, 4068

Bucks Co., Pa., BCH

note:  these estate papers are grouped at the court house
by file numbers, therefore the file number reference
furnished will apply to all exhibits in file, when information
has been furnished it indicates that these files were read.

Drisel, David, 1847, 08381-00, 1/1/1847 probate, of Milford

Twp., Doylestown, Will, Book 12, pg.588, beloved w. Catherine to provide for my father a comfortable life, Catherine exr., written 1/6/1842.

Drissel, Abraham, year 1837, 07077-00, d. 3/1/1837, of Ginium Twp., adm. Jacob Hendricks, Nicholas H. McCarty, guardian of Leah Drissel minor child of Abraham, 8/5/1847

Drissel,Trissel, John,Sr., 1814, 04068-00,late of Tinicum Twp., Bucks Co., Will, Book 8, pg.425, total estate left to Joseph Trissel who was exr., 10/3/1814

Trichler, John, 1811, 03826-00, 12/5/1811, late of Richland Twp., Eve Trichler, Jr. and John Trichler, adms., in estate cash paid to Joseph Trighler, could find no final account, cash was paid for guardian for minor child.

Trissler, Frederick, Cabinetmaker, proved 1868, 12265-00, written 2/7/1866, probate 3/2/1868, Will, Book 17, pg.188, Richland Twp., beloved w. Catherine Barbara to have all for her natural life or remarriage, 4 children, daus, Jacobina Rosina, Catherine, sons Jacob Frederick and Joseph to share and share alike.

Troxel, Henry, 5/17/1873, 13355-00, of Sellersville, Rockhill Twp., Elizabeth Troxel, widow, Will, Book 18, pg.407, son Peter, son-in-law Doc. Lewis T. Trumbour, Jame B. Troxel, Joseph Tice, guardian of Harvey B. Troxel

Rsh.173 Troxel, Jacob, 1806, 03429-00, 3/12/1806, to Elizabeth Troxell of Hilltown, 1/3/ estate to widow Elizabeth, 1/6 of 2/3 to Jacob Troxell, Elizabeth Troxell m. Kerns, Mary Troxell, Margaret Troxell m. Vanhavernees, John Troxell, Sarah Troxell. Bond to Elizabeth Troxel, Jacob Troxel, David, Thomas and Jacob Bodder.

Troxel,Troscell, Trosall, Jacob, Hatter, 9/14/1815, 04245-0, Doylestown, bond Susanna Trosall and Christian Clmes, adms., Bond 9/1816

Troxell, Elizabeth, 1844, 08099-00, late of Doylestown, written 1844, probate 5/14/1846, Charles DuBois, adm., John Troxell paid for note.

Trussell, John E., 1008, 83558-00

<u>Index to Bulter County Pa., Wills 1800-1900, Bob and Mary Closson, copyright  F157.B87C56 1982</u>

Druschel, George, Sr., Book O, pg.343, year 1899
Druschel, Rinehart, Book J, pg.5112, year 1889

Cambria Co., Pa., (Loretto Area), Index to Cambria Co., Pa., Wills 1804-1900, F157.C16C63 1983, compiled by Pat Wainwright Collins for Closson Press Windber, Pa., Register of Wills Office,Ebensburg, Pa.

David Trexler, 18/102, year 1892
Elizabeth Trexler, 18/105, 1888
Joseph Trexler, 18/115, 1861
Joseph Trexler, 18/117, 1892
Abraham Troxel, 18/99 1852
Abraham Troxell,18/99, 1852
Anna Troxel, 18/100, 1891
George Troxell, 18/108, 1882
Mary Jane Troxel, 18/125, 1887
Samuel E. Troxell, 18/131, 1895
William Troxell, 18/136, 1889

Earliest Estates for which no date was available
?Rsh.38, Anna Elizabeth Trezler, 18/99, file 3179
?Rsh.18, James Trexler, 18/116, file 1238
Rsh.35, Margaret Trexler, 18/125, file 358
?Rsh.18, Jacob Troxel, 18/115, file 208
John Troxel, 18/115, file 557
?Rsh.18, Susannah Troxell, 18/131, file 580
William Troxell, 18/136, file 518

Chester Co., Pa., Orphans Court Dockets, Wills, CCA
Dresser, James, Thornbury Twp., file #11300, 1848; file #20, 1849, acts. 556; Jacob Dresser file #333, along with Wm. Cheyney, Francis Hickman, witness the Will of Wm. Williamson of Thornberry, proved 2/17/1812
Tresse, Hugh, file No.3, proceeding 56.58.60, Mics. 50.55
?Rsh.20 Starr, Samuel and Moses, in 1762 minors under the age of 21, children of Isaac Starr of Goshen, deceased, admitts Wm. Starr to be guardian

Cumberland Co., Courthouse, Carslile, Pa., Register of Wills
Trostle, Catherine, of Mechanicsburg, death date 12/20/1924, exr. Emanuel R. Trostle, William T. and Harry C. Trostle, Will, Book 32, pg.268
Trostle, Rev. George, Mechanicsburg, Pa., 7/21/1918, dated, exr. Gertrude Kepford, Book 30 pg.256, Will, 144

Traxler, George R., Carlisle, 9/7/1932 death, Anna M. Traxler, adm., Will, 201 Book 37, pg.49

Trostle, Helen S., Mechanicsburg, Pa., death, 6/18/1918, adm. W. H. Aulthouse, No.143, Book 30, pg.248

Trostle, Maggie, Carslile, Pa., death 10/12/1923, exr. George A. Albright, No.158, Book 32, pg.343

Trostle, McClellan A., of No. Middleton, 4/7/1927, adm. John C. Trostle and McClellen Miller, Book J. pg.519

Trostle, Peter, Middlesex Twp., Cumberland Co., Pa., death 8/18/1877, exr. George W. Jacobs, 3/15/1860, final 12/22/1863, P.Drawer, Act. 124, Christina w/o dec. Peter Trostle

Fayette Co., Pa., Index to Wills 178301900, copyright Jan. 1980 Bob and Mary Closson, F157.F2C55

John B. Truxel, Vol.4, pg.234, year 1868

Franklin Co., Pa., Courthouse, Chambersburg, Pa., Administrative Accounts

note: this Courthouse was burned during the Civil War. See land records, Section J., for clues.

No.9669, 9669 1/2 Trostle, Daniel, domicile Chambersburg, Pa., exr. M. Trostle, J. Rhoadarmer, trustee F.M. Kimmell, letters 4/24/1862, 2/13/1873, first account of F.M. Kinimmiell 8/3/1887, final 8/9/1880

No.9801 Traxler, Jacob R., Last Will and Testament, (author's note: this Will was not read for the purpose of this publication) domicile Lurjan,Curgau Twp., Franklin Co., Pa., adm. Margaret A or J. and William A. Traxler, 1/3/1873; paid Peter Conner guardian for Margaret A. and Jacob Troxler, minors, paid Lizzie Stayman, paid Rebecca O. Troxler, paid W.A. Troxler, inv. 4/27/1874

No.8188 Troxel, Barbara S., Book F., pg.440, exr. Elias Troxell 1861, Barbara Troxel w. of Elias S. Troxel of Waynesboro of Franklin Co., dispose of lot of ground which John Phillips and George Bender assigns of Elias S. Troxell my husb. by deed dated 12/31/1858 to William McLellan in trust for me until my youngest child arrives at age 21, requests same continued, Barbara S. Troxel of Washington Co., now Maryland probate 2/13/1861 witness Alex Hamilton and William Flanagan, Barbara S. Troxell late of Maryland exrs. Peter Gook and George Stover

Fulton County Pa., Will Book Index 1850-1900, compiled by
Patricia W. Collins for Closson Press, copyright Jan. 1987,
Closson Press, 1935 Sampson Drive, Appolo, Pa., 15613 F
157.F9C65 1987
    Andrew Trostle, year 1889, Book 2, pg.316
    John Truxell, year 1879, Book 1

Indiana County Pa., Wills, Index to, 1803-1900, compiled by Bob
and Mary Closson, Closson Press 1982 F 157.I3 C56 1982
    Mary Trusal, Book 5, pg.457, year 1884
    Robert Trusal, Book 5, pg.80, year 1881
    William Trusell, Book 2, pg.267, year 1856

Lancaster Co., Pa., Will Books and Intestate Records, An Index
to, 1729-1850, Eleanore Jane Fulton, Balt. Genealogical Pub.Co.
1973 - F157.L2F88 1973 John Traxel, year 1775; Rsh.78  David
Drissler, Will, 4/13/1752; Maria Drexel year 1793; Elizabeth Dissler
1832, Book F. Vol.I, pg.152; John Dissler, 1828, Book D 1,
pg.248; Margaret Trissler, year 1822, Book A 1, pg.159; Susanna
Triussler year 1798; Abraham Drexel year 1784, Book Y 2, pg.100

Lancaster Co., Pa., Abstracts of Wills 1721-1820, The
Genealogical Society of Pennsylvania, Index to Vol.24
    Rsh.112  216/217/1040/1041  Trachsell (Trexel, Draxel),
Abraham, Will, dated 6/11/1781, probate 11/16/1784, exr. John
Snyder and John Kurtz, Lebanon Twp., Lancaster Co., Pa., w.
Anna, children Abraham, Christian, John and Feromica
    Rsh.112  pg.546  Jacob King, w.'s name not given, dated
5/20/1770, probate 1/2/1775, exr. Jacob Saylor and John Knayge,
Derry Twp., Lancaster Co., Pa., son-in-law John Tracksel
    Rsh.5  pg.269,270, Peter Ehrman, dated 4/22/1809, probate
3/3/1814  exr. Peter Huber and Peter Ehrman, Warwick Twp.,
Lancaster Co., w. Elizabeth, children Elizabeth, Barbara, Ann,
John, Peter, Christian, Michael, Andrew and Margaret who m.
Huber.  Grandchildren George Ehrman son of Andrew, and Jacob
Huber

Lancaster Co., Pa., Courthouse,Administrative Bonds, Letters of
Administration, Bond Book, and Letters of Administration
note:  These books are shelved in Section 1 and the loose estate
papers referenced in these books are held by the Lancaster

County Historical Society for the time period 1729 through 1928. Those individuals wishing further information on the items below should contact LHS. Total Books of Index 27

Dershtler, Michael, Manor Twp., Lancaster Co., Pa., Book 5, pg.301, letter of adm. Jacob Schock and John Schoff, 4/28/1802

Dissler, Catherine, Wood County, State of Ohio, Lancaster Co., Pa., Book W., Vol.1, pg.111, 6/21/1866, bondsmen Robert A. Evans, William B. Wiley, Christian Witmyer. adm. Robert A. Evans

Derstler, Adam, Manor Twp., Lancaster Co., Pa., Book C., Vol.1, pg.12, letters granted to Adam Derstler and John Mann, 1/29/1825

Dissler, John, Elizabeth Twp., Lancaster Co., Pa., Book V, Vol.1, pg.248, adm. Jacos Loos and Peter Dinger

Dissler, Elizabeth, 1832, Book F1, pg.252, we Daniel Disler and Samuel Eberly, Esq. of Elizabeth Twp., and John Stober of Cocalico Twp., in the County of Lancaster post bond for estate of Elizabeth Disler, late of Elizabeth Twp., 9/26/1832.

Drissler, Daniel, Sr., d. intestate, Book E. Vol.2, pg.88, 7/6/1880, letters of adm. granted to Jacob Dissler and Daniel D. Dissler of Clay Twp., Lancaster Co., Pa.

Droxel, Maria, Book B4, pg.584, letter of adm. to Vincent Switzgable son of Maria Droxel who d. intestate late of Lancaster Co., Pa., 4/27/1793.

Rsh.155 Trachsell, John, Cogolleio Twp., Lancaster Co., Pa., dated 10/2/1773, Will, Book D. Vol, 1, pg.248, children from former w. Catherine and dead dau. Catherine's heirs excluded from estate, w. Anna Maria left all of estate, exr. John Ober, friend, probate dated 9/25/1780.

Rsh.112 Traxell, John, Derry Twp., Lancaster Co., Pa., intestate, Book 2, pg.279, letters granted to Jacobena Traxell and Joseph Torney of Lancaster Co., Pa., 1/2/1779

Trexler, Amanda, East Cocalico Twp., Lancaster Co., Pa., Book B, Vol.3, pg.324, adm. C.S. Flickwiger of Shillington, Berks Co., Pa., witness C. S. Flickwiger, Andrew E. Shmifs, Martin T. Eberly of last two of Cocalico Twp., Pa., 11/20/1906

Trisler, David, R. Vol.pg.178, William B. Wiley, Luriel Swope and E.D. Hurst all of the City of Lancaster, 12/3/1857

Trissler, Maria F/T?, Lancaster City, Pa., Book M. Vol.2, pg.284, dated 6/30/1890, adm. Ann C. Trissler, witness Ann C. Trissler, Charles T. Stregerwalt, Charles Denues

Trissler, Louisa, of Lancaster City, Pa., m. Vol.2, pg.290,

to H.H. Trissler of Altoona, Louisa Trissler d. intestate, 7/14/1890.

Trissler, Margaret, A1, pg.159, we John Trissler, Emanuel Reigart and John Bachman, all of the City of Lancaster, estate of Margaret Trissler, late Margaret Groff (Graff), of the City of Lancaster, 4/13/1822 (?Rsh44 Margaret Rebecca?)

?Rsh.16 Trissler, Susannah, Book 5, pg.165, d. intestate, letter of adm. granted to Henry Bunner, 8/15/1798.

Trissler, Ann Catherine, Lancaster City, Pa., Book U, Vol. 2, pg.59, adm. Charles T. Steigenwalt, Charles Steigenwalt, M.T. Steigenwalt, 9/8/1899.

Trissler, Annette C., Book R2, pg.78, d. intestate, of City of Lancaster, Pa., letters granted to Ann C. Trissler, 11/29/1894.

Trostle, Henry, Jr., Adamstown Borough, Lancaster Co., Pa., H2 pg.169, intestate, letters granted to Sarah Trostel of Adamstown Borough, 3/26/1884.

Trostle, Levi, Breckmund Twp., Lancaster Co., Pa., intestate,letters of adm. granted to Elmer (Elrnru) F. Trostel of Reading, Pa., 7/23/1897.

Lancaster, Pa., Administrative Index, Courthouse, and Loose Estate Papers read at LHS
Reference in Parenthesis is found in Courthouse
author's note: in November of 1994 when my husband and I visited the Lancaster Historical Society and read the index of the Administrative Book found at the Court House, the LHS representative that handles the loose papers was not there. The people there were most helpful but inexperienced. We felt that there is a great deal more information such as final account distributions possibly to be found there. Perhaps it would be best for interested individuals to call ahead and make arrangements to read these records.

Index to Administration Bonds and Letters of Administration, Bond Book/Letters of Administration Book. Period covered 1729-1928, Total index consists of 27 books which are listed by Decedent

| Decedent | year | book | vol | pg. |
|---|---|---|---|---|
| Derstler, Adam | 1825 | C | 1 | 12 |
| Derstler, Michael | 1801 | 5 | | 301 |
| Dissler, Catharine | 1866 | W | 1 | 111 |
| Dissler, Daniel, Sr. | 1880 | E | 2 | 98 |

| | | | | |
|---|---|---|---|---|
| Dissler, Elizabeth | 1832 | F | 1 | 252 |
| Dissler, John | 1828 | D | 1 | 248 |
| Droxel, Maria | 1793 | 4 | | 584 |
| Traxell, John | 1775 | 2 | | 279 |
| Trexler, Amanda | 1906 | B | 3 | 324 |
| Trissler, Annetta | 1895 | R | 2 | 78 |
| Trissler, Ann Catharine | 1899 | U | 2 | 59 |
| Trissler, David | 1857 | R | 1 | 178 |
| Trissler, Louisa | 1890 | M | 2 | 290 |
| Trissler, Margaret | 1822 | A | 1 | 159 |
| Trissler, Maria | 1890 | M | 2 | 284 |
| Trissler, Susanna | 1798 | 5 | | 165 |
| Trostle, Henry | 1884 | H | 2 | 169 |
| Trostel, Leir | 1897 | S | 2 | 196 |

### Loose Estate Papers - Lancaster Co., Historical Society

Deichler, Henry M., dec., 1896, account of Sarah L. Deichler, City of Lancaster Pa.

Dissler, Catharine, dec., her adm. Robert A. Evans, 1866, (Book W1, pg.111), of Wood County, Ohio, heir and dau. of Ann Mary Ghling (Ihling) late of the City of Lancaster Pa.

Dissler, Elizabeth, widow, dec., of Elizabeth Twp., Lancaster Co., Pa., her adm. Daniel Dissler,1832/3(Book F1, pg.252).

Dissler, John, dec., Elizabeth Twp., Lancaster Co., Pa., (1828, Book D1, pg.248) his adm. account by Jacob Loos and Peter Dinger, 3/15/1830

Doerstler, Jacob M., dec.,Manor Twp., Lancaster Co., Pa., (1825 Book C1, pg.12) 1850, adm. account of Jacob R. Doerstler, 3/19/1846 and adm. account of Adam Doerstler, Miller, 11/9/1850

Doerstler, Michael, dec., account of Jacob I. Witmer, guardian of Jeremiah Doerster, minor child of Michael late of Manor Twp., Lancaster Co., Pa., 8/16/1865.

Doerstler, Michael, dec., account Jacob S. Witmer, guardian of Carolina Doerstler, minor child of Michael Doerstler of Manor Twp., Lancaster Co., Pa., 4/1/1867.

Doerstler, Michael, Manor Twp., Lancaster Co., Pa., (1801 Book 5, pg.301) adm. account of Jacob Shock and John Schopf, 6/13/1801, 1802.

Doerstler, Michael, dec., guardianship account 6/18/1811 of Ulrich Bott of Manor Twp., for Anna Maria and Adam Doerstler, minor children of Michael Doerstler, dec. Doerstler, Michael, dec.,guardianship account 6/9/1813 of John Schock guardian of the estate of Michael and Jacob Doerstler, two of the minor children of Michael Doerstler of Manor Twp., Lancaster Co., dec.

Doerstler, Michael, dec., 2/15/1856 adm. account of Benjamin Doerstler and Christian Hertzler of the estate of Michael Doerstler of Manor Twp., accounts started 1/11/1854

Doerstler, Michael, late of Manor Twp., Lancaster Co., Pa., minor child Sarah Doerstler, account of Jacob S. Witmer, guardian of Sarah, 2/15/1862, acts. 1855-1862

Doerstler, Michael, dec., account of Jacob I. Witmer, guardian of Mary Doerstler, minor child of Michael Doerstler 1863

Doster, Rosina, dec., 5/16/1857, City of Lancaster, Pa., Last Will and Test, adm. account of William Frederick Mayer and Sebastian Graw, exrs.

Treichler, Elizabeth, dec., Village of Maytown, Lancaster Co., Pa., exrs. of Last Will and Testament 6/16/1846, Thomas Huston and Jacob S. Engle, balances to be distributed subject to collateral inheritance. note: checked to 1880, could not find final account listing heirs.

Treichler, Elizabeth, dec. late of Village of Maytown, Lancaster Co., Pa., account of Thoes Huston and Jacob S. Engle, exrs. 4/24/1866.

Triesh, Margaret, w/o Leonart Treish, dec., Cocolico Twp., Lancaster Co., Pa., 11/17/1797, Adam Treish and Michael Treish adm., estate lb. 225,16.8 to be distributed according to law.

Trissler, John, dec., City of Lancaster, Pa., 1849, City of Lancaster, Pa., adm. account of Michael and John Trissler, exrs. of John Trissler.

Trissler, David, dec., Borough of Lancaster, Pa., adm. act. by Wm. B. Wiley, 1859

Troesher, Jacob, dec., Warwick Twp., Lancaster Co., Pa., adm. act. 3/21/1825, of Last Will and Test of Jacob Troesler by Peter Erb and Christian Reist

Trostel, Abraham, dec., Brecknock Twp., Lancaster Co., Pa., adm. act. of Wm. Trostel and Henry Trostel, 3/21/1864, exrs. of the Last Will and Testament of Abraham Trostel, Sr.. Catharine Trostel paid $1.25 per week for 84 weeks for services rendered $105, Henry Trostel paid for services rendered $5.00, William Trostel for services rendered $20.58.

Lancaster Co., Pa., Courthouse Archives, Wills at Office of Records and Archives Services, 50 North Duke Street, P. O. Box 3480, Lancaster, Pa., 17603 (717) 299-8319

?Rsh.28 Trissler, David, Book J2, pg.562, Conestoga Twp., Lancaster Co., Pa., written 11/2/1886, d. 6/9/1892 at 5:30 p.m., w. Ann shall receive portion allotted to her by common law, members Lancaster Lodge International Order of Odd Fellows...1st w. Sarah, son John dec. to have tombstones, balance to share and share alike...son William, dau. Caroline m. Joseph Stoke to have pictorial family bible, dau. Angeline m. Maris McMillan, son Benjamin I., dau. Mary m. to Maris H. Groff, dau. Adaline m. David Warfel, son David, dau. Kate m. Augustus Barth, son Charles...nephew Benjamin I. Hookey, exr. Witness Henry Graves and P.G. Hiller. Probate 7/13/1892.

Rsh.92 Trissler, John, Sr., Book T1, pg.319, City of Lancaster, Pa., Butcher, dear w. Catherine, all children to share and share alike, w. Catherine and sons Michael and John exrs., John Trisler (he made mark), witness William Frink, John Lnummer, probate 11/16/1843.

Rsh.103 Drissler, Jacob, Book P1 pg.429, Elizabeth Twp., Lancaster Co., Pa., son Daniel, dau. Catherine, dau. Elizabeth, dau. Mary w. of Emanuel Gojlin, son Jacob, son Henry, son David...37 lbs 10 shillings to my grandchildren, the children of my sons David and Henry, clock and case to Daniel after beloved w. Elizabeth dies...son Daniel Exr., July 1, 1828, Sebastian Root and Peter Dinger, Witness, Jacob Drissler, probate 1/20/1830.

?Rsh.139 Drissler, Daniel, Book E2 pg.___, 7/15/1869 d. 10/27/1882, 5 1/2 p.m., Clay Twp., Lancaster Co., Pa., dear w. Mary, 3 sons John B., Jacob B. Samuel B. and w. Mary to be exrs. Probate 11/14/1882.

Derstler, Catherine Book U1, pg.333, w/o Manor Twp., Lancaster Co., Pa., George Withers nephew $1.00, son Adam Derstler, dau. Catherine, w. of Adam Shuman, dec. dau. Elizabeth former w. of Jacob Martin, her children to share equally as they reach 21, son Adam and son-in-law Adam Shuman, exrs, Catherine Derstler (she made Mark), probate 5/29/1847.

Derstler, Adam, Book F1, pg.544, 2/17/1794, Manor Twp., County of Lancaster, no w. mentioned, eldest son Adam Derstler to have my plantation and tract purchased of John Newcomer in Manor Twp., son Michael Derstler, plantation on which I now life in Manor Twp., and 4 best team horses. The Elders of Evangical

Lutheran Congregation in the Borough of Lancaster, dau. Barbara, dau. Elizabeth, friend and neighbor John Shock and son Michael exrs. Witness Henry Shopp and Casper Shaffer. Probate 2/26/1794.

Dreichler, Elizabeth, Book T1, pg.626, 3/27/1834, Donegal Twp., Lancaster Co., Pa., single woman, brother Daniel Treichler's children to share and share alike. Friends Thomas Huston of Maytown and Jacob Engle, son of Jacob at the river, to be exrs. Elizabeth Triechler (she made mark) witness Henry Engle, John Longenecker, Henry Shock, Codicle July 8, 1837 Elizabeth Triechler of the Village of Maytown do hereby give bequeath to my brothers and sisters of the Society to which I belong all my books that are in the German Language, probate 9/15/1845, Peter Albright appeared 9/15/1845 to state John Longnecker is dec.

Trisler, Elizabeth, Book E2 pg.511, d. 6/17/1883 at 2:50 p.m., spinster, beloved niece Clara R. Shreiner, niece exr. witness F.J. Heckler, William B. Girn, probate 6/25/1883.

Trissler, Michael, Book D2, pg.450, d. 8/13/1880, Butcher, City of Lancaster, Pa., estate at death of w. Catharine F. Trissler to dau. Kate, dau. Annette, dau. Maria, 2 sons of dec. dau._____ name not clear, Charles and Henry Steigewalt. Resided when Will was written on East King. St., signed 7/16/1880, witness Wm. G. Baker, Honorable H.C. Demuth. probate 8/17/1880.

Trissler, John, Book N2, pg.140, 2/17/1892, Lancaster, Pa., d. 12/1899, son Edward H., son Joseph R., dau. Ella L. Ellenburger, w. of Frank Ellenburger, remainder to four children John A. Trissler, Edward H. Trissler, Joseph R. Trissler, and Ellas L. Ellenburger, witness Charles Demers, Edward P. Brinstow, sons E.H. Trissler and Joseph R. Trissler, exrs. probate 1/24/1899.

Trissler, Annetta, Book L2 pg.382, d. 10/22/1895, 3:00 p.m. Lancaster, Pa., 9/22/1892 sister Ann C. Tressler for her heirs and assigns, request her to provide for Ann Louisa Fick, Charles Steigenwalt. Witness Ann Louisa Fick, Charles Steigenwalt

Troesher, Jacob, X2 pg.56, 1/29/1824, Warwick Twp., County of Lancaster, Pa., w.'s sister Barbara Geist, all personal property, mother Catharina Troesher in Europe, Germany, Kingdom of Wuerdenburg in the Government of Ludwigs Bury Gersingen to be paid in gold or silver with discount to the above Katharina Troesher in Germany...100 which Philip Guist has to exr. without interest and Wm. Lutz of Warwick Twp., appoint Peter Erb,

Warwick Twp., and Christian Reist exrs. Witness Henry Muller, Schoolmaster, Jacob Stoll, 2/6/1824.

<u>Leehigh Co., Pa., LCCH</u>
note: these estate papers are grouped at the Court House by file numbers, therefore the file number furnished will apply to all exhibits in file, when information has been furnished it indicates that these files were read.

Rsh.148 Droxel, Daniel, No.73, S. Whitehall Twp., Peter Troxel and Maria F. Troxel, exrs., beloved w. Marcia Fronica, 3 children, son Peter, dau. Elizabeth Blank, dau. Catherine Biery

Treichler, Jacob, No.2787, Allentown, William H. Blumer, exr., 1857

Treichler, John, No.2815, Mary A. Treichler, adm., 1857

Trexler, Amandus, No.3815, Allentown, Sarah Trexler and Lewis L. Sheldon, adrs. 1866-1867

Trexler, Benjamin B., No.6027, S. Whitehall Twp., Olive Trexler, James Troxell and Mahon Seidel adrs., 1883-1887

Trexler, Clarissa M., No.6038, Allentown, James Stahlnecker, exr.,5/2/1883

Trexler, David, No.1353, Hanover Twp., Benjamin Ludwig and Daniel Ludwig adms., 1836-1837

Trexler, David H., No.3799, Mary Ann Trexler, adm., Coopersburg, 1866-1868

Trexler, Franklin H., No.2968, L. Mcgunie Twp., Nathan Trexler, adm. 1858

Rsh.89 Trexler, Elizabeth, No.2596, Mcgunie Twp., Jonathan Trexler and John Metzger,exrs., 1854-1855

Rsh.88, Trexler, James, No.2772, U. Milford Twp., Reuben Stahler, adr., 1856-1857

Rsh.88 Trexler, Jeremiah, No.743 and 1085, Mcgunie Twp., Jeremiah Trexler and Peter Grammes, exrs., 1827-1865, beloved w. Elizabeth, dau. Catharine Ann, dau. Margaret m. Andrew Shifflet, sons Jeremiah, Lucas, James, John, Charles, Will, 10/26/1826: Rsh.88, Trexler, Jeremiah, No.1085,743, S. Whitehall Twp., Solomon Greisemer, adm., 1831-1854

Rsh.87, Trexler, John Peter, No.820, Mcgunie Twp., Solomon Fogel, adm., 1828-1847.

Rsh.89 Trexler, Jonathan, Sr., No.1959, Mcgunie Twp., Jonathan Trexler, Benjamin Fogel, Joshua Schnuyer, Joseph Miller,

John Metzger, exrs., 1846-1850, Will, in German, no translation in file, proved 5/23/1846.

?Rsh.89 Trexler, Jonathan, No.5834, 1882-1882

Trexler, Lydia, No.4175, 1870-1873

?Rsh.87 Trexler, Ruben, No.1574, 1840

Trexler, Sarah, No.5102, 1877

?Rsh.89 Trexler, Sophia, No.3620, 1864-1865

Trichel, Joel, No.3244 1/2, 1861

Tritschler, Henry, No.4777, Allentown, Twp., John Rupp, exr., Louisa Trichler and Chas. Tritschler adms., 1874-1916

Rsh.48 Troxel, Adam, S., No.63, S. Whitehall, exrs. John N. Troxel and Jonas Troxel, 1814 to 1816

Troxel, Christiana, No.3770, Lowhill Twp., Jonathan Deihl, exr., 1866-1869

Troxel, Daniel, No.701, S. Whitehall Twp., Elizabeth Troxel and John Troxel adms., 1826-1830

Troxel, Elizabeth, No.1004, S. Whitehall Twp., John Troxel, adm.,1830-1832

Troxel, Elizabeth, No.5230, Allentown, William H. Nennermachey, adm., 1878-1881

?Rsh.23 Troxel, Jacob, No.837, S. Whitehall Twp., John Troxel and Henry Troxel, exrs., 1828

Troxel, Jacob, No.1867, Salisburg Twp., Elizabeth Troxel and Peter Troxel, exrs., 1845-1847

Troxel, John, No.4026, 1868-1869

Rsh.57 Troxel, Lorentz, No.708, 1826-1831

Troxel, Nicholas, No.917, 1829-1833

Rsh.62 Troxel, Trascel, Droxel, Draxel, Peter, Sr., No.151, Hiedelberg, S. Whitehall Twp., 1816-1834, John Troxel and Peter Troxel, adm. and exrs., widow Sibila release adm. to sons John and Peter 5/2/1816, settled Northampton 4/21/1817, Will is written in German, no translation found in file.

Troxel, Peter, No.640, 1825-1826

Troxel, Peter, No.1026, 1830-1831

Troxel, Peter, Sr., No.1625, 1841-1848

Troxel, Peter, No.4268, 1871-1872

?Rsh.39 Troxel, Traxell, Stephen, No.482, S. Whitehall Twp., bond Nicholas Troxel, Henry Francz, Solomon Sherer, Co. of Leehigh, 1822-1825

Rsh.152 Troxel, Tilghman, No.4160, 1870-1871

Troxell, Adam, No.5432, N. Whitehall Twp., Lewis I. Troxell,
Edmund A. Troxell and Lucas J. Troxell, Adm. 1879-1880
Troxell, Audora, No.7047, Whitehall Twp., Franklin J. Newhard, adm., 1888-1889
Troxell, Christiana, No.6721, Catasaugua Twp., Tilghman F. Frederick and Henly Davis, exrs. 1887-1889
Troxell, Elemina, No.5955 1/2, Coopersburg, Caveat, 12/29/1882
Troxell, Jeremiah, No.3184, 1860-1861
Troxell, Magdalena, No.3106, 1860-1861
Troxell, Mary, No.2999, 1859-1859
Troxell, Nicholus, No.2268, 1850-1851
Troxell, Solomon, No.1314, 1836-1837

<u>Montgomery Co., Pa., Wills, Collections of the Genealogical Society of Pa., Vol.270, Mont. Co., Pa. Vol.122, Pub. Philadelphia 1912.  Book at National Genealogical Society Library</u>
Rsh.34  John Martin, Book 2, pg.92, Upper Dublin, written 4/9/1798, son Matthias Martin, dau. Elizabeth Trexler to have, upon death of mother.
Rsh.43  Michael Dotterer, Book NSG, Frederick, children to have equal shares except Suffia Troxel she is to have 5 shillings, children Mary Hefners, Margaret Dotterer, Mary Rife

<u>Montgomery Co., Pa., Index of Wills and Estate Settlements, 1784-1850, compiled and published by Richard T. Mildred, C. Williams, Danboro, Pa., 18916 1972</u>
authors note:  Montgomery County was established from North part of Philadelphia County in 1784)

| 1785 | Sarah Treichler | Gwynedd | OC18854 |
| 1848 | David Trexler | Plymouth | Reg.Wills |
| 6693/OC18961 | | | |
| 1848 | David Troxel | Gwynedd | OC18959 |
| 1829 | Henry Troxel | Upper Han. | Reg.Wills |
| 16923/OC19069 | | | |
| 1829 | Sarah Troxel | Gwynedd | OC18959 |

<u>Montgomery Co., Pa., Orphans Court Records, MCCH</u>
note:  the 3 sets of numbers, at the end of the referenced information, which are separated by slashes represent

volume/page/book

Dressler, Peter, RW9991, OC4474, U.Hanover, Solomon and William Dressler, adms, estate of Peter Dressler, of Upper Hanover, deceased, 10/8/1854, inventory 12/1854 continued to 10/8/1855, 4/374/7

Treichler, Abraham, OC18854, John Fronefield, guardian, 12/20/5

Treichler, John, OC18909, Christian Wismer, guardian, 12/161/9

Treichler, Lydia, OC18854, John Fronefield, guardian, 3/14/1823, Lyndia Treshler, Abraham, Treshler, Sarah Tresher, children of Linda Treshler, late, grandfather Herman Umstead, 12/181/7, Lydia Treischer, April term 1823 a petition for a guardian for Lydia, Abrm, and Sarah Treichler, 3/10/1823 to the Justices of the Orphans Court, Herman Umstead, to the honorable the Justices of the Orphans Court of the County of Montgomery the petition of the subscriber as grandmother and next friend of Lydia Trescher, Abraham Tressher, and Sarah Treischer, children of Lydia Treischer late, until minors under the age of fourteen years respectfully petition that the grandfather Herman Umstead to be their guardian, signed Barbara Umsted, witnessed Nathan Custer

Treichler, Martha, OC18909, Christian Wismer, guardian, 12/209/6

Treichler, Sarah, OC18854, John Fronefield, guardian, 12/246/3

Treichler, Samuel, Jr., OC19385, David W. and Joseph Treichler, adms., Samuel Treichler, d. intestate, unmarried and without issue, 6/13/1865, advertisement in local paper naming possible heirs, David M. Treichler, Sarah Treichler, Mary Treichler m. to Solomon Wehr, Joseph Treichler, Elizabeth Treichler m. to Charles Heinitze, George Treichler, Susanna Treichler, Annie Treichler m. to Samuel Missimer, Edward Treichler, Ellen Treichler, John Treichler, Isabella Treichler, Samuel Treichler, Manasses Treichler, Henry Treichler, John Treichler, Mary Treichler, 12/246/5

Trichler, Catharine, OC18909, James White, guardian, grandfather Harmon Umstead, 4/1823, children of Lydia Tresler, Nathan, Barbara, Catherine Ann and John, 12/47/5

Trexler, Andrew, RW6663, OC18875, G.K. Heller, exr., of Andrew Trexlelr, Cheltenham Twp., deceased, written 5/31/1865 proved 8/5/1865, 6/1868, George Hiller, adm., appeal of Ann Trexler, to George Hiller, adm., Cheltenham Twp., of Andrew,

7/1867 in the matter of the estate of the said Andrew Trexler, wife Ann Trexler, children Sarah, Hiram, Hannah and Rachel, 12/21/1

Rsh.86 Trexler, David, RW6693, OC18961, Joseph Jarrett, exr.,9/1848, of David Trexler of Plymouth Twp., who d. 1/18/1847, two children of David, Sarah Riakirt and Joseph Trexler, Last Will and Testament of David Trexler, Plymouth Twp., deceased give and bequeath to children John Trexler, Joseph Trexler, Sarah Reakirk, Hannah Fisher to share, grandsons, David Trexler, son of Joseph and David Fisher son of dau. Hannah Fisher, appoint Joseph Jarrett of Up. Merion Twp., exr. 12/57/2

Trexler, Emma R. or P., OC2723, Edward Armstrong, Peter C. Hollis, guardians, 12/76/6

Trexler, Hannah D., OC19082, George K. Heller, guardian, 8/16/1838, Petition of Hannah and Rachel Trexler, both under 14, for guardian as they have interest in estate of John Deckhard, late of said County, 12/119/1

Trexler, James E. RW6777, OC19210, 2/8/1873, Chris Santee, James M. Trexler, Chas. I, year 1877, James E. Trexler late of Twp., Whitemarsh, exrs. Charles Santee, James M. Trexler and Charles J. Miller 12/161/6, Last Will and Testament of James E. Trexler, Whitemarsh Twp., 2/24/1873, beloved w. Frederica, dau. Helen, son James, son William.

Trexler, Jonathan D., RW16984, Andrew Trexler, adm. 12/161/5

Rsh.86 Trexler, Lawrence, RW17009,OC19252, Joseph Jarrett, adm., 8/23/1826, Lower Merion Twp., dec., cash received of John Yocum for his w. Elizabeth late Elizabeth Trexler who is the adm. of Joseph Trexler, dec. as also for Joseph Trexler who was the adm. of Peter Trexler, dec., renunciation of Elizabeth Horn of the estate of Lawrence Trexler to Joseph Jarrett, 11/21/1825, Renunciation of David Trexler to Joseph Jarriett. 12/181/4, Account OC19252, Lawrence Trexlere dec. by Administrator, notices put up and published and advertised agreeable to law in the public papers at Norristown. 8/23/1826, Register, at Orphans Court held at Norristown, 8/23/1826, account confirmed Joseph Jarrett, adm. of goods and chattels of Lawrence Trexler, 4/6/1826, late of Lower Merion Township, dec., to cash received of John Yocum for his w. Elizabeth late Elizabeth Trexler who is administrator of Joseph Trexler dec. as also for Joseph Trexler who was administrator of Peter Trexler dec., $213.63.

Accountant craves allowance for cash paid Register of Philadelphia for a copy of the estate of Joseph Trexler, dec., letters of Adm., James Webb for house expenses, Geoell Potts for six searches, Benjamin Evans for services, by commissions allowed by comment of the heirs present, cash paid register, cash paid clerk, $32.18 + by balance due the estate (it does not name estate heirs who received this money $181.45 = $213.63. RW 17009, Renunciation of David Trexler, filed 11/21/1825, I do certify that I renounce and relinquish all my right of claims of administration of the estate of Lawrence Tressler and Catherine Bloom and Christianna Hyda heirs of the Estate of Joseph Trexler dec. to Joseph Jarrett, given from under my hand this 14th day of November in the year one thousand eight hundred and twenty-five, signed David Trexler...Renunciation of Elizabeth Horn, filed 11/21/1825, I do certify that I renounce and relinquish all my right and claim of Administration of the estate of Lawrence Trexler, Catherine Bloom and Christian Hyda, heirs of the estate of Joseph Trexler, dec. to Joseph Jarret. Given under my hand this 21st day of November in the year of our Lord one thousand eight hundred and twenty five, signed Elizabeth Horn; Inv. of the goods and chattels, rights and credits which were of Laurence Trexler late of Montgomery Co., dec., to heirs amount due to the said Laurence Trexler dec. estate from the estate of Joseph Trexler dec. as per settlement filed in the Registers office at Philadelphia $137.68 11/28/1825.

Rsh.86 Trexler, Peter, RW17045, OC19323, Catharine and Joseph Trexler, adms. this file is blank and there is a notation that the papers are missing in the year 1995, RW17045, Peter Trexler, L. Merion d. without Will, personally appeared Catharine and Joseph Trexler adms., Catherine Trexler, Joseph Trexler, Israel Jones and Anthony Levering, all of Twp. of Lower Merion post bond 11/18/1784, need to make adm. on or before 11/1785, Cath. Trexler made mark, notices put up at Elisha Evans, one at John Thomas and one at Isaac H. Pritners 3 of the most public places in the neighborhood of the parties interested 8/1774, payments made to Joseph Albrith, Jonathan Robeson, John Heide, Balleis Hoffman, Susannah Trealer; prays allowance for following fees for selling Jeremiah Trexler's estate at Eastown and by his expenses going to Eastown 205/13/72 due estate, 12/221/7

Trexler, Rachel, OC19082, George K. Heller, guardian, 12/229/8

Troxel, Adelaide, OC18878, Henry Troxel, guardian,

1/1874 Henry Troxel, Rockhill Twp., act. L.T. Trumbower and
N.B. Troxel, exr. minor child of Samuel Troxel deceased was
Rebecca and Henry Troxel was her guardian, Rebecca Troxel,
Lydia Troxel and Adelaide Troxel minor children of Samuel Troxel,
deceased of U. Malboreo, George S. Shumacher guardian of
Emma Troxel minor child of Samuel deceased, Rebecca and Irvin
Troxel minor children of Samuel, Catherine Troxel w/o Samuel
Troxel deceased, Samuel left 10 children, 12/20/9

Troxel, Ann, OC18859, Peter Miller, guardian, petition for
guardian for Ann Troxcel, appoint Peter Miller, U.Hanover Twp.,
8/9/1829, Sarah Troxel w/o Henry Troxel of Upper Hanover Twp.,
deceased left 10 children, Ann under the age of 14, Sara Troxel
made mark, witness Samuel Troxel, 12/20/10

Troxel, David, 1/18/1847, RW6693, OC18959, Philip Reed,
guardian, 8/1829, minor children under age of 14 of Henry Troxel,
petition for guardian, David, Sarah, Maria, apt. Peter Miller, Esq.
and Philip Reed, Esq.,12/57/5

Troxel, David, RW16887, OC18971, Henry Troxel, adm.
7/5/1882, David Troxel, deceased of Upper Hanover Twp.,
1/19/1882, 12/57/4

Troxel, Elizabeth, RW16895, OC18994, Samuel Troxel, adm., of
estate of Elizabeth Tottel late of U.Hanover, Spinster, deceased,
5/16/1859, heirs, Henry Trottel, Marian T. Summary, Julian
McClvey, Catherine Sauvrtz, Henry Reoder, David Tottel,
Preifs, Charles Rader, Aaron H. Summers for Thomas F. Readin,
Elizabeth Krumor by her attorney in fact, Henry Rouderbush,
Elizabeth Troxel, late of U.Hanover, dec. 1/12/1849, act. of
Samuel Troxel, heirs, Henry Troxel, Maria G. Summary, Julian
McElroy, Catherine Swartz, Henry Roeder, David Troxler, Firms
Levitt, Charles Rader, Aaron H. Summer for Thomas T. Rroder,
Elizabeth Krummee by her attorney in fact Henry Rouderbush,
Rachael, ____, Illo, Anna Eisenhart, Amatuina Roederbush,
12/76/1

Troxel, Erwin, OC18878, Henry Troxel, George Mumbauer,
guardians, 12/76/4

Troxel, Emma, OC18878, Henry Troxel, George Mumbauer,
guardians, 12/76/5

Troxel, Henry, OC19069, RW16923, year 1829, Samuel Troxel,
Henry Roudebush, adms., inventory 5/1829, Henry Troxel of U.
Hanover Twp., Peter Miller signed inventory, 12/118/6, Henry
Troxel, 8/17/1829, Count appoints Peter Miller, Esquire guardian

for Maria Troxel and Phillip Reed Esquire guardian for David and Sarah Troxel, minor children of Henry Troxel late of Upper Hanover Twp., of said County dec.

Troxel, Irwin, OC18878, Henry Troxel, George Mumbauer, guardians, 12/118/8

Troxel, Lydia, OC18878, Henry Troxel, guardian, 12/181/2

Troxel, Rebecca, OC18878, Henry Troxel, George Mumbauer, guardians, 12/229/9

Troxel, Samuel, RW6860, OC19388, Catharine and John Troxel, exrs., of Samuel Troxel, late of U. Hanover Twp., act. 8/1871 of John T. Troxel and Catherine Troxel exrs. of Last Will and Testament of Samuel Troxel, Will, Samuel Troxel, U.Hanover, proved 11/14/1870, w. Catherine, 2/3 to be equally divided among my children, w. exr., witness, David Troxel, Jesse Shicht; John T. Troxel and Catherine Troxel, exrs., 12/245/9

Troxel, Sarah, OC18959, Philip Reed, guardian, 12/245/7

Troxel, Sarah, RW17078, OC19380, Samuel Troxel, adm., act. of Samuel Troxel, adm. of Sarah Troxel, late of U.Hanover Twp., widow, deceased 5/16/1859 to 6/11/1859, entered Book 5, pg.14 12/245/8

Montgomery Co., Pa., Abstracts of Wills, Vol.I, 1784-1823, Vol.II, 1824-1850, Collections of the Genealogical Society of Pa., Vol.269, 270, Philadelphia 1912

pg.286, Driechler, Mary, Will of Mary Umstad, Worcester Twp., 8/11/1808, to Mary Driechler

pg.84, Dresher, George, Will of Margaret Houpt, Upper Dublin Twp., 11/25/1794, exr. George Dresher.

pg.96, Dresher, Abraham, Will of Anna Schultz, Upper Hanover Twp., 1/22/1795, remaining, to son Abraham Dresher, balance to children of Eve Dresher, dec.

?Rsh.86  pg.254  Trexler, David, Plymouth Twp., 1846, 2/19/1848, Book 8, pg.582, Estate to be sold, to sons John and Joseph and daus. Sarah and Hannah to receive sale proceeds. exrs. Joseph Jarrett, witnesses, Reuben Spalhoffer, Samuel Bactleton

pg.376, Dressler, Christopher, witness to Will

?Rsh.86  pg.306 Trexler, Lawrence, Montgomery, 11/21/1825, Joseph Jarrett, adm.

pg.319  Troxel, Henry, Upper Hanover, 6/1/1829, adm.

Samuel Troxel, Henry Roudenbush

<u>Northampton Co., Pa., NCCH</u>
John Treichler, No.10068, 9/16/1880, Bethel Borough, Northampton, Moravian Church Rites, to Sarah Clemmer dau. of Henry, to Frederick Benner w. of Abraham R. Benner, to my sister Hannah, my sister Nancy, my sister Polly, brother Jacob's children, my sister Sarah's children, my sister Elizabeth, friend Abraham R. Brenner of Beth, exr.

Samuel Treichler, No.8604, Will, Book 8,pg.543, 1871-1872, Bethlehem Twp., beloved w. Susannah, appoint John Clymer present brother-in-law adm.

Susanna Treichler, No.8960,WB8,pg.543, 1873-1875, brother John Clymer, sister Elizabeth Rilley and to Abraham R. Brenner, and to Maria Cressman, w. of Ephram Cressman, to Nancy Beiller, w/o John Beiller, to Hannah Rudolph w. of Henry Rudolf, to Emma Greensueig, w. of Edwin Greensueig, and to Christ Reformed Church, John Clymer, exr.

Elizabeth Trexler, No.9410, 11/8/1876

Rsh.88 Jeremiah Trexler,No.,1024, 1783-1801, d. Macgunie Twp., Catharine & Peter Trexler, adms., bond 1783, act. 1801.

Rsh.115 Jeremiah Trexler, file 1024, proved 7/6/1783, Catherina, Peter adms., settled 4/1802 file 168, folder 9515, Book 7, pg.98, Whitehall Twp., Peter Traxell, exr., settlement-Joseph Trosler, adm.

Rsh.84 John Trexler, Vol.1, pg.296, written 1/6/1795, proved 3/10/1795, Mcgunie Twp., Plainfield Twp., Susanna Trexler and John Kromer exrs, dearly beloved w. Susannah, her father Casper Bawr, step-children Jacob Hesler, Eliza Hesler, which are prisoners by the indians, John Hesler, William Hesler, Anna Marie Hesler, and to my youngest son Israel, sons Peter, Jeremiah, Ferdinand, son of my dau. Maria Elizabeth deceased John Jarrett is under 21, my children Peter, Jeremiah, Emanuel, Ferdinand, Philippina, Margaret and grandchild John Jarrett, wife is named in 1796 as Susanna Leer exr., file 168,folder 9511, Plainfield Twp., John Trexler, No.1686, 1795-1802, youngest son Isreal under 21, exrs. Susannah Lehr and John Kromer.

Rsh.85 Peter Trisler, Trexler, Trescler, Sr., Book 3, Vol.2, pg.166, proved 4/10/1799, Mcgunie Twp., beloved w. Catherine, son Jonathan, 7 children to rec. after wife's death in equal shares, sons Peter, John, Jonathan, exrs., Book 7, pg.134, settled, Peter and Jonathan exrs. of Peter, 8/12/1802. No.1904, Will, Book 3, pg.166, 1799-1802, Mcgunie Twp., Husbandman, beloved w. Catherine, son Jonathan, 7 c., 3 sons Peter, John, Jonathan, exrs.

Abby Troxell, file No.1178C, death 2/4/1888

Daniel Troxell, No.5169, 1843, Easton Borough, 11/1809, renunciation of Catherine Troxell, adm. granted to Jefferson K. MCKim, Hickman

David Troxell, No.10382, 9/20/1881

Edward Troxell, No.7877, 1866

George Troxell, Sr., No.7173, 1861-1864

Henry S. Troxell, No.9331, 1876

Henry M. Troxell, No.9335, 8/9/1876

John Troxell, No.4956, 1840, John Troxsell, Catherine Troxell of Upper Mt.Bethel Twp., w/o John renounces to Wm. Hummel, Merchant, David Troxell, Painter, and George Troxell, Merchant, post bond.

J. Morris Troxell, No.8215, 1869

Juliann Troxell, No.12276, 4/5/1886

Lawrence Troxell, No.5595, 1848

Mary Ann Troxell, No.5757, Will, Book 6, pg.470, 1849, Upper Mt. Bethel Twp., year 1849, beloved husband Jeremiah S. Troxel, John R. Aten and George Troxell, Jr., witnesses.

Mary Troxell, No.7067, 1861

Michael Troxell, Orphans 126/294

Rsh.47   Nicholas Troxell,Trixsell, No.3645, 1824-1828, exrs. George Troxsell, Millwright, James Black, Coppersmith and Michael Sheip, Blacksmith, all of Easton Borough, heirs, Daniel, Joseph, Abraham, Jacob Troxel, Valentine Deitz. John Troxell's heirs, Wm. Troxsell, Lawrence Troxell, John Miller and Sarah his w., John H. Troxell, J. Bishop guardian of H. Troxell, A. White, guardian of Christina, Juliana and John K.; Michael Troxell's heirs, Peter Troxell, Thomas P. Bullman, R. Hindy, Benjamin Hinds, guardian of Elizabeth and Juliana, John Clifton, guardian of Thomas Troxell, George Troxell.

Rsh.39   Nicholas Troxell, Book 3, Vol.2, pgs.101,166, proved 5/17/1797, Whitehall Twp., Peter Troxell, exr., loving w. Catherine, sons Adam and Peter, upon marriage of w. children shall share and share alike, c. not named. Witness Peter Rhoads, John Horn, Peter Rhodes, Nicholas Traxall, Book 7, pg.99, Peter

Traxell, adm. of Nicholas Tracell, Nicholas Traxell, No.1788, 1797-1802, loving w. Catherine, son Adam, son Peter, exr., nine children not named.

Rsh.157 Solomon Troxell, No.6988, 1860-1862, Solome Troxell, w/o Solomon of Allen Twp., County of Northampton renounces to sons Alexander and Reuben, 10/29/1860

Rsh.152 Tilghman H. Troxell, No.7314, 3/6/1880

Northumberland Co., Pa., Wills and Administrations, including Wills and Administrations of Union, Mifflin and Indiana Counties all formerly a part of Northumberland County, Pa., compiled by Charles A. Fisher, Genealogical Publishing Co., Inc., Baltimore, 1974 F157.N8F57

David Drisler, pg.13, 9/13/1805, Elizabeth Disler w. David Drisler, pg.31, 9/13/1805, 10/22/1805, Drissler, Mahantango Twp., w. Elizabeth, children had some, did not name then in Will.

David Drissler, pg.15, 10/22/1809, see 9/13/1805, adm. Elizabeth Drissler, sureties, John Hafley

John Troxel, pg.42, Letters of Administration, Union County, Pa., 10/24/1815, John

Troxell, Beaver Township, letters to Henry Aurand and John Troxel, sureties for administration, Frederick Bingaman, John Moyer. see Snyder Co., Pa.

Philadelphia Pa., Courthouse, Register of Wills, Room 180, Philadelphia, Pa., 19107

?Rsh.86 Joseph Drexler, adm. year 1811, No.174, Book K, pg.442, Joseph Drexler

Daniel Dexemer, Will, probate year 1759, 2-1, Dexemer, Daniel Book L, pg.317, W201, written 1759, Daniel Dexemer, City of Philadelphia, very sick, weak in body, loving w. Catherine, whole of estate after her death to son-in-law Martin Spring, son of said w. by former husb.

John Drissle, Will, probate year 1757, No.19, Book L, pg.27, John Drissel, lower Lowershire Ford, County of Bucks, w. Margaret, sons Ulrich, Abraham, witness, George Ackerman, Thomas Blackledge, of Lower Milford.

Maria Trexler, widow, of Philadelphia, Book 37, pg.367, year 1856, I give and bequeath the sum of one hundred dollars to my dau. Elizabeth Sims her exects. adms. and assigns. All the residue and remainder of my estate, both real and personal, I give bequeath and devise to my dau. Louisa George. Revoke all former Wills by me at any time made. Son in Law William Harry George. Signed with her mark, witnesses, James M. King, John Edward Siddall, Registered 11/5/1856.

Rsh.3 Peter Trexler, Will, probate year 1758, 105, Peter Trexler, Book L, pg.180, W.105, 758, written 11/17/1744, Peter Trexler, Twp., Macongey, County of Bucks, Catherine dearly beloved w., son Peter 238 acres w/warrant to 50 ac, and John Trexler, youngest son 351 lb, lawful money of Pennsylvania, Jeremiah Trexler, eldest son 20 lbs, Anna Trexler 1st of daus. 20 lbs, Catherine Trexler 2nd of my daus. 20 lbs, Margaret Trexler 3rd of my daus., Revoke all former Wills, Peter Trexler make mark, exr. Peter Trexler, witnesses: Geittie Grimm, George Shamback, Proved 10/21/1758, recorded pg.180.

?Rsh.86 George Trexler, year 1824, d. without Will, Northern Liberties, Butcher, Book M, pg.443, 1824/85, 3/11/1824, Mrs. Trexler refuses to settle estate, court appoints, John Ulrich, Northern Liberties, Shoemaker, Conrad Polk, Cabinet Maker, John Schmeyer, Constable

Rsh.86 Joseph Trexler, A174-1811, Joseph Trexler m. Elizabeth , after his death she m. John Yocum. Adm. 9/3/1811 for Joseph Drexler, Farmer to Elizabeth Drexler the w/o Northern Liberties, widow, John Sander and Jacob Belsterling. She did not sign but made mark According to the accounting of the estate there must have been no surviving children. Total $1738.69 divided by 2 = $869.35 divided by 11 heirs (children of Joseph's father Peter Trexler, dec., = $79.03 each with $869.35 to widow. note: 1 administration granted in Bucks Co., Pa.

John Trextors, Will, probate year 1777, No.338, Book Q, pg.395, Book W, pg.338, 2/1777, John Trextors, of Bedmister Twp., Co. of Bucks, sick bed, friend Ludwick Bennes of Rockville Twp., only son George 1 year 3 mos old, and of my w. Catherine

Joseph Troxell, adm., year 1833, 121 1/2, Book O, pg.77, Joseph Troxell, Maria Troxell, widow, appeared, 5/3/1833, Joseph d. without Will, George Priest (Triest), Catherine Tinkhouse administer with her, signed Benjamis Miller appraiser, Anthony Hookey, appraiser, estate 10.50

Rsh.11 Michael Troxell, abstract of Will, 9/8/1772, 203, Book P, pg.310, Michael Troxel, Michael Guyonedd, Co. of Philadelphia, Yeoman, signed 9/8/1772, w. Ann Margaret, children, Juliana, John, Ann Mary, Nicholas, Margaret, Magdalina, Peter,

Catherine, Jacob, Henry, Michael, Christian, and Ann, nephew, John Troxel, brother Nicholas exrs: Son John Troxel, Nephew John Troxel, Witness, Martin Swenk, Melchior Wagener, proved 10/1/1772.

Somerset County Pa., Wills, An Index to, 1795 to 1900 compiled by Bob and Mary Closson, Closson press 1984 F 157.S6 C58 1984
 Arneas Tressler, file 35, year 1886
 George Tressler, file 52, year 1871
 Goodhart Tressler, file 5, year 1810
 Hiran Tressler, file 10, year 1900
 Ira Tressler, file 94, year 1893
 John Tressler, file 13, year 1867
 Joseph Tressle, file 10, year 1888
 Samuel Tressler, file 59, year 1853
 Simon Tressler, file 3, year 1816
 Christena Trexel, file 7, year 1895
 Daniel Trostle, file 3, year 1879

Snyder County, Pa., Probate and Orphans Court Records, abstracts of, (1772-1855) by Dr. Charles A. Fisher, F.I.A.G Selinsgrove, Pa., F157.S5F4 Library of Congress Binding
 David Disler, pg.5, 9/13/1805 dec. David Dissler, Elizabeth Disler w., see Will
 David Disler 29, 9/13/1805, 10/22/1805, David Disler of Mahantango, w. Elizabeth children no names given, exr. John Hafflinch
 George Treaster, pg.l, 11/25/1779, dec. George Treaster letters to Martin Treaster, sureties George Troutner and Melchoir Stock
 George Treaster, pg.35, 3/11/1823, 3/20/1823, dec. George Treaster, Milleeburg, no names given
 Martin Treaster, Jr., pg.52, 8/29/1782, 6/29/1786, Martin Treaster, Jr., Elizabeth, widow, John oldest son, Margaret, George, Catherine, Jacob Joseph
 Charles Trinkle, pg.1, 11/17/1783, dec. Mathias Trinkle, letters to Charles Trinkle, sureties, George Overmire, Jacob Harpster
 Mathias Trinkle pg.1, 5/18/1786 dec. Charles Trinkle, letters to Elizabeth Trinkle, Leonard Walker, sureties Peter Kister

(Kuster) and Frederick Druckenmiller

George Troxel, pg.1, 6/22/1790, dec. George Troxel, letters to Catherine Troxel and John Troxel, sureties Henry Aurand, Nicholas Stroh

John Troxel, pg.7, 10/24/1815, dec. George Troxel, Twp., Beaver, letters to Henry Aurand, John Troxel, sureties Frederick Brigaman, John Moyer

Washington Co., Pa., Wills, an Index to, 1781 to 1900, compiled by Bob and Mary Closson, copyright 1981 F 157.W3 C56, 1981

John Droshel, Book 10, pg.638, year 1878
Charles Trusel, Book 9, pg.260, year 1867
Luther C. Trusell, Book 14, pg.464, year 1894
Manson Trussell, Book 11, pg.501, year 1883
Margaret Trussel, Book 13, pg.80, year 1889
Sarah Trussel, Book 11, pg.689, year 1884
Sarah A. Trussell, Book 10, pg.278, year 1874

Washington Co., Pa., Estate Records 1781-1796 and Deed Records 1782-1785, in Washington County, Pa., compiled by Raymond Martin Bell, Washington and Jefferson College, 2nd ed. 1977 F157.W3B39 Washington, Pennsylvania

Rsh.27 pg.11, George Tristler, Will, on file year 1796, see York Pa., loose estate papers.

author's note: Washington Pa. was formed in 1781. Before that time the source for estate records is Westmoreland Co., Pa., (abstracts of Wills in Vol.6, Genealogical Society of Pa., 1915-17) and Mohogania County, summarized in Vol.9, No. 3, The Virginia Genealogist, few earlier records can be found at Wheeling, W.Va., Morgantown, W.Va., Bedford, Pa., and Carlisle, Pa. Both Virginia and Pennsylvania claimed the region and established Courts. Permanent settlement began about the year 1770

Westmoreland Co., Pa., Wills, an Index to, 1773-1896 complied by Bob and Mary Closson, R.D. 2, Box 373A, Apollo, Penn 15613 F 157.W5C54

pg.11, Abraham Dracksel, Vol.2, pg.127, year 1824
pg.47, John Troxel, Vol.3, pg.285, year 1850

pg.286, John Troxall, Vol.5, year 1869
pg.36, Elizabeth Troxall, Vol.9, year 1893
pg.88, William Troxell, Vol.8, year 1889
pg.361, Jacob Truxal, Vol.3, year 1836

## York Co., Pa., YCHS, Abstracts of Wills - The Geo. Soc. of Pa., York Co., Philadelphia, Pa.

Rsh.79 pg.112, George Dressler, dated 7/1799, probate 6/1805, w. Catherine, children, Frederick, Anna.

## York Co., Pa., Loose Estate Papers found at Courthouse

Rsh.79 George Dressler, of Paradise Twp., York County, w. Catharina, Will, dated 7/17/1799, son Frederick, dau. Anna Mary, Will, presented to court 6/25/1805, accounting dated 4/9/1814, also, Will, Book L., pg.239, dated 7/17/1799, probate 6/25/1805.

Rsh.79 Doll, John D., 12/27/1815, pg.13, 1/1818, exr. Thomas Jordan and George McMullen, children, Jacob, Conrad, Catherine m. Jacob Tressler, Mary m. Peter Harold, Joseph, Formica m. Henry Graeff, Lettia m. John Lebberl, Elizabeth m. ____? Marx, Magdalena w. Nicholas Henry, Christina m. Jacob Harr, Susanna m. George Hoar, Margaret m. David Wilson, and Barbara m. Peter Noll. Grandchildren, John, Elizabeth, Polly, Jacob, Joseph and Catharine (children of Conrad Doll) note: Conrad Doll m. Maria Tressler brother of Jacob.

Rsh.79 John Doll of Paradise Twp., Co. of York, weak in body, son Jacob Doll, w. Mariah, dau. Catherina m. to Jacob Tressler, dau. Mary m. Peter Harrole, dau. Elizabeth m. John Mary, dau. Magdalena m. Nicholas Henry, son John Doll, dau. Christina m. Jacob Haas, son Conrad Doll, six Children, grandchildren, John, Elizabeth, Polly, Jacob, Joseph and Catharina; son Joseph Doll his children dau. Susannah m. to George Haas, dau. Magdalena m. to Joseph Hintz, dau. Eva m. David Wilson, dau. Barbara m. to Peter Noel; son Henry Doll, his children dau. Veronica m. to Henry Greff, dau. Juliana m. to John Moul, dau. Letia m. to John Sibbest; youngest son Jacob, Executers, Jacos Ernst, friend and Nicholas Henry, son-in-law dated 12/1815, probate 1/13/1818.

Rsh.5 Matthias Riffell, Mountjoy Twp., York Co., Christina Riffel, son George Riffell, probate 10/2/1792; Bond for L800, George Riffell of MountJoy Twp., Jacob Kuhn of Heidelberg Twp., Andrew Kaltenback of Frederick Co., Md. Accounting to be made by 10/2/1793, payments to Thomas Lilly, Mathias Baker, John Shorb,

Joseph Flath, Jacob Shorb, John Stehly

Rsh.5 Joseph Ehrman of Heidleberg township of York County, sick body, dated 6/16/1798, dau. Appolonia, w. Catherine, children Joseph, Peter, John, dau. Mary m. to Peter Klunk, dau. Catherina m. to Anthony Trexel, exr. Stephen Jacob Kuhn, exrx. dau. Appolonia, filed 7/24/1798.

Rsh.5 No.34 Ehrman, Appolona, Will, 3/5/1801, she made mark, exr. Jacob Kuhn, inv. 4/14/1801, act. settled 8/13/1802, Heidleburg Twp., 6 Children of my sister Mary Klunk, 5 lbs each, Joseph, Peter, John, Mary, Joseph and Catherine; Joseph Ehrman, debtor to Anthony Dreckel, short pay of the work of a house in the year 1782, the sum of 3.14.0, year 1784, short pay to making a bake oven, and sitting up a still 0.15.0, gals of brandy 0.8.0, 0.15.0. Year 1789 made well and springhouse 0.18.0. 12/17/1801, Anthony Dreckler paid 13.8.0; paid Jacob Kuhn on this act. for Joseph Ehrman dec. the sum of 3.9.10; year 1784 short pay of rye 3.16.0, Antonio Drexel signed name.

Rsh.5 No.34 Last Will and Test Joseph Ehrman of York, Yeoman dec., Henry Cerkman appraising 0.7.6; Philip Mayer for coffin 3.0.0; Jacob Adams for clerking inv. 0.15.0; Nicholas Walter, School Master, for learning 1.2.6; funeral of dec. widow 1.2.6; Est. L.183.6.4, Orphans Court Fees 11.3

Rsh.139 Barbara Treichler (she made mark) Hallum Twp., Co. of York, widow, 1/1/1838, granddaughter Susanna Treicher under 18, son Jacob Treicher, son John Treicher, exector, son Baltzer, inv. 2/1839.

Rsh.139 Martin Treighler, late of Paradise Twp., 7/7/1801, widow, Barbara, adm. Abraham Heistandt of Condorus, Balance 338,16.8

Rsh.128 Dorothea Treighler, dated 8/12/1801, probate 7/2/1810, exr. Peter Gut, Book M, pg.244, of York Township in the County of York being old and infirm...dau. Sufania (Shophia) m. Jacob Bixler, Eve m. Mathias Stewart, Elizabeth m. Joseph Strickler, Catharine m. Henry Grove, Salome m. John Strickler; seven stepchildren, dau. Catharine, dau. Salome, stepdaughter Barbara m. Peter Gut, 1/9 to heirs of Martin Trenghler, heirs of Martin Tenghler, Anna m. Abraham Shock, Mary m. John Miller, Magdalena Trenghler, Daniel Trenghler, recorded 7/2/1810.

Rsh.128 John Treighler, Will, made mark, 6/15/1799, probate 7/27/1799, Book K, pg.90, York Twp., old and informed, dearly beloved w. Dorothy to have plantation, land called the Hill

Place and 300 lbs and 1/3 of personal estate, daus. Barbara, Maria, Elizabeth and Magdalene, sons Martin and Daniel, two youngest daus., Catherine and Salome, among 9 children to share and share alike -Barbara, Martin, Anna, Elizabeth, Maria, Magdalena, Daniel, Catharine and Salome. Trusted friends Jacob Strickler, at the Stonyrun and Andrew Ferrea, both of Hellam Twp., estate inv. 7/26/1799

Rsh.128 Dorothea Treighler, made mark, 8/12/1801, York Twp., widow, beloved dau. Susana m. Jacob Bixler, Eve m. Mathias Stewart, Elizabeth m. Joseph Strickler, Catharine m. Henry Grove, Salome m. John Strickler, and unto my 7 stepchildren, 1. Barbara m. Peter Gut, unto Martin Treghler's late heirs, Anna m. Abraham Shock, Elizabeth Tenghler, Mary Trenghler m. John Miller, Magdalena Trenghler, stepson Daniel Trenghler

Rsh.27 George David Tristler, dec. 10/21/1796, late of Hallam Twp., York Co., Pa., goods and chattels, widow, Susanna, she made mark, and John Jordon, Borough of Lancaster, Christian Stake of Manor Township, Lancaster and John Stewart of York Co. Not clear what kind of record this is but these three are posting a bond along with Susanna. She signed with a mark.

Rsh.43 Will of Michael Dotterer, Sr., Philadelphia, Pa., Montgomery Co., Pa., I Michael Dotterer, late of Philadelphia Co., and Frederick Twp., and State of Pa., and now of York County, Yeoman, being in good state of health. 10/10/1783, dau. Suffia Troxel, Exr. Conrad Dotterer, proved 9/29/1786, son Michael Dotter, Mary, Margaretha, Mary Rifle, son Conrad Dotterer as exr. Michael Dotterer, probate states late of Montgomery Co., Pa., probate dated 9/29/1786.

Rsh.43 Will, and Estate papers, of Conrad Dotterer 1808, Conewago, Pa., advanced age of Conewago Twp., County of Adams, State of Pennsylvania, sons John and George Exector, sons Conrad, John, George, oldest daus. Elizabeth and Margaret dec., son Michael, dau. Julianna Spanseller, son Frederick Spanseller, dau. Julianna m. to Frederick Spanseller.

Rsh.120 Abraham Trostel, Will, dated 9/27/1819, Abraham Trostle of the Borough and County of York, w. Susannah, children Jacob, George,John, Abraham, Henry, Elizabeth m. Frederick Rehmer, William, Daniel, Peter, Catherine and Susannah m. Jacob Stover, total on accounting $14,318.40

Rsh.120 Susannah Trostel, Will, Inv. 1826, York Borough, w/o Abraham, unto my son John Jackb, John, John George,

Abraham, Henry, William Daniel, Peter, dau. Elizabeth m. Frederic Reimer, dau. Catharine m. Jacob Herbst, dau. Susannah m. Jacob Stover, inv. 1/5/1826.

Rsh.120 Abraham Trostle, 4/2/1830, Paradise Township, paid Jacob Trostel per receipt $5.00, balance $1,363.31.

Rsh.120 Whylich Bentz, Will, Book F, pg.109, 4/18/1782, Whylich Bentz, York Town, Yeoman, being in health, beloved w. Anna Maria, son Whyrich Bentz, dau. Ursula m. Jacob Lether. grandau. Catherina b. of body of dau. of Elizabeth late the w. of Peter Dechart, dau. Barbara the w. of Laurence Marcha, dau. Catherina w. of Jacob Hiller, dau. Anna Maria w. of George Rudy, dau. Susanna w. of Abraham Trostle, son Jacob Bentz, dau, Luzey w. of Jacob Sidler. dau. Salome m. Henry King, son Whyrich, four grandchildren, heirs of my son Christian Bentz, late of Lancaster Co., dec. should have equal share. He made Mark.

Rsh.120 1/8/1787, Anna Maria Bentz, w/o Whyrich, weak in body, 8 children, Christian Benta dec., his children to have his share, Anna Maria (dec.), Susannah, Elicabeth, Salome, Ursula, Whrich Bentz, Peter Bent, son-in-law Abraham Trostle to be exr.

Rsh.120 Abraham Trostel York Borough, 9/18/1819, exrs. Jacob Trostle and Abraham Trostle, Book 0, pg.198; Susannah Trostle, York Borough, 12/28/1825, exr. William Trostle, Book P, pg.359.


York Co., Pa., Courthouse Orphans Court Records, Book A. 1749-1768, April 2, 1757

Rsh.139 John Dreichler, dec., Barbara Dreichler made mark, Jacob Strickler and Henry Strickler, Jr., County of York, Pa., 1/26/1756

Rsh.139 pg.78, Barbara Dreichler w/o John Dreichler, dec., balance 219 lbs, 14 shillings, to be dist. among widow and children according to law.

Rsh.139 pg.187, John Treighler, 8/26/1761, came John Treighler, oldest son and heir at law of John Treighler, late of this County, yeoman dec.. Had plantation and 2 tracts of land in York Co., he would like to hold and make satisfaction to the other children. Committee appointed to review.

Rsh.139 pg.191, John Treichler, 8/27/1761, came to Court Mary Treichler, age 17 years, orphan dau. of John Treichler late of York Township, dec. and chose John Strickler of Hellam

Twp., her guardian.

Rsh.139 pg.191, John Treichler, 11/1/1761, came Barbara Treichler, w/o John Treichler of York Twp., yeoman and requested guardian of youngest dau. Elizabeth age 10 years. appt. John Strickler of Hellam Twp.

Rsh.139 pg.192, John Treichler plantation valued at 390 lbs, improvements at 26 lbs, land 48 lbs. John Treichler, son to pay Barbara Treighler, relict of intestate 91 lbs. 5 shillings and 7 pence every year during her natural life in satisfaction of her dower 1/3 of estate. Pay Kathrina Trexler dau. of said intestate, pay Mary Treicher dau., pay Elizabeth Treicher dau.

York Co., Pa., Orphans Court Records, Book F. 1786 to 1793

Rsh.86 Andrew Horn of Merion, Book 1, pg.15, written 3/6/1788, names sisters Mary Trayxler,(?Rsh.39) Susannah Horn, Elizabeth Trayxler, brother George Horn.

Rsh.86 Henry Fisher, Book 4, pg.195, Upper Dublin, written 8/18/1813, dec. dau. Catharine Trexler her share is to be equally divided between her children. W. Sarah Fisher, dau. Sabina, mentions sons but does not name them.

Rsh.86 Peter Trexler, Lower Merion, 11/18/1784, Catharine Trexler adm.

Rsh.141 pg.142, came to Court Susannah Dreicher age 17 years and upwards, dau. of Michael Deicher and granddau.of Hans Ulchrist Seichrest dec., and asked that her father Michael be named guardian.

Rsh.141 Book E, pg.275, Susannah Teisher 14 years old, children of Michael Teisher, grandau. of John Ulrich Segrist, late of Manchester Twp.

William Miller, New Hanover, 10/7/1819, adm. Henry Troxel, George Miller

Henry Troxel, pg.328, Upper Hanover, 6/1/1829, Samuel Troxel, Henry Roudenbush adm.

York Co., Pa., Orphans Court Records, Book H. 1798-1803 Courthouse, York, Pa.

Rsh.126 pg.78, came Joseph Trexler, Age 19 and Upwards and Mary Trexler age 16 minor children of Peter Trexler, estate to descend to them from grand uncle Joseph Smith dec.,

Casper Glatfelter of Shrewsbury Twp. named their guardian of the estate.

Rsh.126 pg.78, on application of Peter Trexler the Court appointed Abraham Damer (Rsh.131) to be guardian of the estate of Margaret Trexler, age 6 years, for the estate of grand uncle Joseph Smith dec.


York Co., Pa., Orphans Court Records, Courthouse, York, Pa., Book P.

Rsh.120 Book Q., York County, Tuesday, 5/4/1830, account of Abraham Trostle exr. of Will of Abraham Trostle, Senior, dec., balance, 1172.25

Rsh.120 pg.97, 2/13/1827, William Trostle, exr. of Susannah Trostle, Susannah Trostle, Personal Estate, Balance $669.22


YCHS, Genealogical Notes

Rsh.126 Peter Trexler, nephew of Joseph Smith, Will Book F, pg.251


York Co., Pa., Wills, Courthouse, York, Pa.

Rsh.79 pg.112, George Dressler, dated July 1799, prob. June 1805, w. Catherine, Children Frederick, Anna

Rsh.126 Book F, pg.251, 11/27/1783, Joseph Smith of York Town, gave land to Catholic Church in Lancaster, nephew, Peter Drexler, dearly beloved w. Barbara, give to Rev. James Bellentz (Catholic Priest), give 1/2 part to children of Peter Drescler which he now hath of which he may yet lawfully have by his w. Friend Thomas Lilly, Esquire, Exr., witness Valentine Frantz, George Lewis Lefter, Christian Stayer, proved 4/22/1784.


YCHS, Wills

Rsh.79 pg.117, Jacob Tressler m. to Catherine Doll in 1818, dau. of John Doll.


York Co., Pa., Orphans Court Records, Book H. 1798 - 1803, Courthouse, York, Pa.

Rsh.127 pg.420, Martin Dreichler, Abraham Heistand,

surviving adm. of all goods and chattels of Martin Dreichler, dec., balance of 1551 lbs, 14 shillings, 6 pence 1/2 penny

Rsh.127   Book I, pg.449, Martin Dreichler, comes Baltzer Treichler, John Treichler, Jacob Treishler their guardian pg.334.

Rsh.127   pg.334, 6/3/1807 came Barbara Treichler, w/o Martin Treichler dec. and prayed Court to appoint a guardian for Baltzer Treichler, age 13 and upwards, John Treichler age 11 years, and Jacob Treicher age 9, children of dec.   Court appointed Harman Long of Lancaster County their guardian.

Rsh.127   pg.449, Abraham Heistand for Martin Treichler balance 396lbs, 19 shillings, 3 pence.


York Co., Pa., Will Index, Courthouse, York, Pa.

Rsh.79   George Dressler, Sr., Paradise Twp., 6/25/1805, John G. Odenman and Christian Wirst, Book L, pg.239

John Deshner, Windsor Twp., 7/5/1786, George Dice, Daniel Cayler, Book G, pg.114.


York Co., Pa., Orphans Court, Book E., 1782-1786, pg.291

Peter Drieber, age 18, orphan of Ludwich Dreiber, late of Manchaster, Christian Lieb, former guardian, he now wants Peter Sprenckel. author's note: this entry is not dated.


York Co., Pa., Special Publication # 20, October 1982 - Surviving Early Records of York Co., Pa., more precisely being genealogical excerpts from Will Book A 1749-1762 with surname index, Mary Barr Bryant Wilt, The South Central Pennsylvania Genealogical Society, Inc., P.O. Box 1824, York Pa., 17404, 1982 copyright

Rsh.139   John Dreichler, pg.123, 2/6/1756, Letter of adm. Barbara Dreichler

Daniel Dinkle, pg.119, written 4/6/1754, proved 12/20/1755, residence York, Pa., children Daniel, Peter, Margaretha Salome, Mary Catharina, Anna Mary, Mary Dorothea; exe w. Mary Ursula, George Sohn and George Christian Sinn, Wit. Jacob Billmeyer, Jacob Fracklin, Bartholomew Maul

John Dussiel, pg.200, 3/26/1759, letter adm. Margaret and William Dussiel

York Co., Pa., Special Publication 3, 40, July to Oct. 1989, abstracts of unrecorded Wills of York Co., Pa. 1749-1798 with Surname index, compiled and pub. by the South Central Pennsylvania Genealogical Society, Inc., P.O. Box 1824, York Pa. 17405, copyright 1989 F 157.Y6 A27 1989

Rsh.5 Klunk, Peter, Jr., brother-in-law to Rsh.5, pg.37, Peter Klunk original in English, codicil in German, dated 2/3/1777, Peter Klunk of Berwick Twp., w. Mary, property adjoining Michael Kart, Jacob Slagle; children, Martin, Elizabeth, Peter, (Jr.), Margreat, Anne and Magdelen, exrs. son Martin, son Peter, w. Mary, witnesses Thomas Lilly and Nicolaus Walter, probate 6/27/1780.

Rsh.5 Ehrman, Joseph, step-father-in-law to Rsh.5, pg.128 Ehrman, Joseph dated 6/16/1798, probate 6/24/1798, exr. Jacob Kuhn and Appolonia Ehrman, Heidleberg Twp., w. Catharine Ehrman, children Appolonia, Mary m. Peter Kurk, and Catharine m. Anthony Trexel. Grandchildren Furgerson and Mary Kurk, Joseph, Peter and John Trexel

Rsh.120 pg.547, Trostel, Abraham, dated 9/4/1813 probate 9/18/1819, exr. Joseph and Abraham Trostel, York Borough, Pa., w. Susanna, children Jacob, George, John, Abraham, Henry, Elizabeth m. Frederick Rehmer, William, Daniel, Peter, Catharine and Susanna m. Jacob Stover.

Rsh.128 pg.52, Treigler, Johannes, along with George Beard witness Will of George Adam Gosslar dated 8/20/1787, York Township, original in German

Rsh.128 pg.543, Treighler, John, dated 6/15/1799, probate 7/27/1799, exr. Jacob S. Trichler and Andrew Ferree, York County, w. Dorothea Treighler, children Barbara, Martin, Anna, Elizabeth, Maria, Magdalena, Catherine, Daniel and Salome.

Rsh.128 pg.545, Trenhler, Dorothea, dated 8/12/1801, probate 7/1/1810, exr. Peter Gut, York County, children, Susanna m. Jacob Bixler, Eve m. Mathias Stewart, Elizabeth m. Joseph Strickler, Catharine m. Henry Groul, Salome m. John Stricker, Mary m. John Miller.

Rsh.141 Teitcher, Michael w. Barbara, pg.24, Hans Urich Seegrist, original in English, 1776-77 time period, dated 8/26/1774, of Manchester Twp., Yeoman, to dau. Barbara, w. of Michael Teitcher 1/3 of estate, to Susannah my grandau. and dau. of Barbara 2/3 of estate, if grandau. dies, her 2/3 to dau. Barbara, exrs. friends Casper Lichtenberger and Baltzer Zujwalt, witness John Morris and Casper Miller probate 5/6/1776.

pg.3, Teutsch, Philip, along with John Schmitt witnessed Will of John Morningstar, original in German, dated 10/19/1756.

pg.6, Teutsch, Philip, along with Casper Lichtenberger witnessed Will of Jacob Fletcher, original in German, dated 9/24/1758.

pg.8, Teutsch, Philip, along with George Ernst Mayer witness Will of Jacob Kuntzel, original in German, dated 11/4/1759.

pg.16, Teutsch, Philip, along with George Sweyer, witness Will of Jacob Muller, original in German, dated 9/29/1759.

pg.54, Treiber, Ludwig, Will of Julius Bruckhart, original in German, dated 4/17/1793, Manchester Twp., dau. Barbara m. to Ludwig Treiber, witnesses Isaac Brenneman, Balthaser Kohler and Peter Schultz.

## VIRGINIA

Alexandria City and County, Virginia, Wills, Administration and Guardian Bonds 1800-1870, Patrick G. Wardell - Heritage Books, Inc. 1986
pg.126    Tretcher, Thomas, Will, 2/2/1811, proved 10/23/1813, w. Eleanor, only child Elizabeth.

Augusta Co., Va., Deaths, DAR Library, Washington, D.C.
Abraham Troxel, 11/1/1853, age 64, b. 1789
Mrs. Jane Troxell, 10/8/1865, age 72, b. 1793
Daniel Troxel, 8/7/1870, age 71, b. 1799
David Troxell, 8/3/1896 age 76, b. 1820
Abram Troxell, 2/17/1882, age 52, b. 1830
Mary N. Troxell, 6/26/1878, age 39, b. 1839
Andrew Troxell, 11/1/1880, age 36, b. 1844
Jeremiah Troxell, 11/26/1865, age 17, b. 1848
James M. Troxell, 2/2/1876, age 23, b. 1853
Abrams Troxel, 12/23/ 1881, age 26, b. 1855
Charles L. Troxell, 11/1/1865

author's note: Botetourt County was formed from Augusta in 1770, Monongalia County was formed from Augusta in 1776, Ohio County was formed from Augusta in 1776, Rockbridge County was formed from Augusta 1778, Rockingham County was formed from Augusta 1778, Pendleton County was formed from Augusta 1788, Bath County was formed from Augusta 1791, Illinois County was formed for Augusta 1778, Yohogania County was formed from Augusta in 1776.

Botetourt County, Va. Early Marriages, Wills and Some Rev. War Records, Anne Lowry Worrell, Baltimore Geo. Publ Co., 1985
     Rsh.41  pg.64, Henry Trisslar dec. 1/1820, division of land names heirs: William, Jacob, Henry, Peter, Sally, George, Moses, Nancy, Michael, Barbara (w. Wm. Persinger) Mary (w. of Adam Quickie) Catherine (w. of George Mallow) Elizabeth (w. Jacob Pence).

Rockingham County, Virginia, Abstracts of Executor, Administrator, and Guardian Bonds  1778-1864 - compiled by Marguerite B. Priode, Harrisonburg-Rockingham Historical Society, P.O. Box 1141, Harrisonburg, Virginia 22801
     Rsh.90  pg.2, 12/26/1785, Peter Tresler, decedent, exrs., Henry Tresler, James Frazer, 300 lbs, bondsman, Frederick Armentrout.
     Rsh.90  pg.38, 3/27/1786, parent, Peter Tressler, orphan, Charles, guardian, Anthony Branaman, 300 lbs, bondsman, Henry Tussler (Trusler).
     pg.48  pg.38, 2/20/1817, John Traxler parent, Christena Traxler, orphan, Guardian, Daniel Getts, 100 lbs. bondsman, Jacob Highz.

Rockingham County, Va., Minute Book 1778-1786, Constance A. Levinson, Louise C. Levinson F232.R7L48, 1985 Greystone Publishers, Harrisonburg, Va.
     Rsh.90  Tresler, Peter, pgs.18, 306, 307, (pg.475 in original record), 1/23/1786, the appraisement bill of the estate of Peter Tresler, dec., was returned and ordered to be recorded, pgs.312,325.
     Rsh.90  Tresler (Trussler), Barby (Barbara) pg.325, (pg.520 in original record), 7/25/1786, ordered that the Overseers of the Poor bind Chas. Tresler, orphan of Peter Tresler, to be bound to Wm. Coul till he comes to the age of twenty one to learn the trade of Blacksmith, and ordered that Edward Hatfeild, orphan of Mansfeild Hatfeild be bound to George Mallow, Jr. to learn the trade

of a Weaver according to law. Ordered that Barbary Tresler be bound according to Law.

Rsh.90 Tresler, Peter, Charles, pgs.312,325, (pg.489 in original record) 3/27/1786, Charles Tresler, an orphan of Peter Tresler, dec. came into Court and chose Anthony Branamer his guardian who entered into bond with security according to Law.

Rsh.90 Tresler, Peter, Henry, pg.306,(pg.473 in original record), 11/30/1785, the Last Will and Testament of Peter Tresler was proved by the oaths of James Fraisor, Fredk. Armintrout and Jacob Kesler, whereupon Hy. Tresler, exr. herein named having complied with the law, certificate is granted him to obtain probate in due form. Ordered that Augustine Price, Sr., Capt. Jno. Rush, Jacob Keslinger and John Hendrick or any three of them being first sworn, appraise the estate and Negroes, if any, of Peter Tresler, dec., and made return according to Law.

Trussler, Margaret, pg.18, (pg.19 in original record), 9/28/1778, Deed of Bargain and Sale from Peter Trussler and Margt. his w. to Jacob Archenbright was proved by the witnesses and ordered to be recorded.

Rockingham County, Virginia Minute Book No. 2, Part, 1, January 1791 to June 1793, Constance A. Levinson and Lousie Chambers Levinson - copyright 1990, L. and C. Levinson, 46 Monument Avenue, Harrisonburg, Va. 22801 F232.R7 R59 1990

Rsh.90 pg.94, Tresler, Peter, time period 4/22/1793, Deed B&S from Tresler to John Winebareck proved by the Oaths of the Witnesses thereto and ordered recorded.

Rsh.90 pg.21, appraisement of the estate of Peter Tresler, Phil. Armontrout decd,, was returned and ordered to be recorded.

pg.57, Trissle, David, 9/24/1792, Deed B&S, Pet.Crumbaugher and Catherin his w. she being privately examined was acknowledged to David Trissle and same ordered recorded.

# IMMIGRATION

## Georgia

The Report, A Journal of German American History, pub. by the Society for the History of Germans in Md. Baltimore, Md., No.38, 975.20B
Treslers, Catherine, b. in 1710, Hans Joseph Tresler, b. 1704, occu. Farmer, native of Palatine, into the State of Georgia.

## Louisiana

F380.A2J33 1988 The German-Acadian Coast Historical and Genealogical Society, Ancestors Searching List Compiled by Harold A. Jacob
      Troxler, Jacque circa 1742-1809 parents Johann George and Agnes Laile, Jacques and Isabel LeRoux, spouse Isabelle Leroux, 2nd, 3/28/1770, file 04, note: The name Isabelle is interchangeable with Elisabeth in these records.
      Troxler, Jn George, spouse Agnes Laite, file 046.
      Troxler, Jn (Johannes) George 1698-1759, spouse Hausseran, Magdeline (1), cote des Allemands file 074, spouse Marie

The Settlement of the German Coast of Louisiana and The Creoles of German Descent by J. Hanno Deiler, Balt. Genealogical Publishing, Baltimore, 1969 Author, Professor Emeritus of German at Tulane University of Louisiana, New Orleans, La., Published through Americana Germanica Press, Philadelphia 1909 "Right bank of the Mississippi, The German Village of Hoffen, 10 Lieues above New Orleans, 11/12/1724 Rsh.33 pgs.80,81, Census Enumerator proceeds down right side of River number 3, Johann Georg Troxler, of Lichtenberg in Alsace, Catholic, 26 years old, a Mason, his wife "Fort bon Travailluer". Two and one-half arpents cleared, on which he has been only since the beginning of the year having left the village in the rear. Exposed to inundation. Absent because of bad health. His wife is also sick. Lost his crop and his house. A neighbor, who cooked in a shed attached to Troxler's house, accidentally set fire to it: year 1731, two children, two negroes, one cow. Johann

George Troxler was progenitor of all the "Troxler" and "Trosclair" families in Louisiana.

pg.84, here ends the village of Hoffen, and the census man now leaves the river front and proceeds to the two old villages in the rear, which were mentioned before. Old German Village, three-forths of a mile from the Mississippi, number 24, Balthasar Marx of Wullenberg, Palatinate (one Wollenberg near Wimpfen), Catholic; 27 years old, Nailsmith, 1775, Jean Simon Marx, son of Balthasar and Marianne Agae Marx, married Catharine Troxler, dau. of Nik.T. and Cath. Matern (St.James Parish).

pg.118, German girls took German husbands and whole families married into one another...out of the ten children of one Jacob Troxler not fewer than eight married into the Heidel (Haydel) family. In such families the German language survived the longest, and old Creoles of German descent have told me that their grandparents still understood and were able to speak the German language, although they were not able to read and write it, as there were never any German teachers on the German coast."

author's note; these records indicate that the name Troxler changed into 19 separate and distinct names: those names include Sroscler, Stroscler, Drozeler, Troesscler, Troxlaire, Drotseler, Trocsler, Trucksler, Trouchsler, Troustre, Troseler, Trocler, Trossclair, Troscler, Trocher, Drotzeler, Droezler, Troxclair, Troslisser

## MARYLAND

Monocracy and Catoctin, Vol.II, Some Settlers of Western Maryland and Adjacent Pennsylvania, and their descendants, C.E. Schildknecht, Ed,, Familyline 1989

Rsh.32 pg.88, Troxel, the Rohrer Family which intermarried with Troxel was from Bolligen, Canton Berne, Switzerland, see National Genealogical Magazine, October 1919. Frederick Co., Md., Monocracy and Catoctin, Vol.II, Some Settlers of Western Maryland and Adjacent Pennsylvania, and their descendants, C.E. Schildknecht, Ed,, Familyline 1989

Rsh.21 pg.50, Andreas Dressler (Tressler) imm. from Sachsenhausen, Wertheim, before 1761
Maryland Naturalization Records Mdhr

?Rsh.32   Abraham Troxle, Frederick Co., Md. German, Naturalized 5/5/1768

Mdhr, Index 136, Provencial Court 1658-1778, 3 Vols. Judgment, Plaintiff Index
DD No.5, parts of 1762,1763,1764, George Tosseler (Toseller, Toxeller) naturalized No.282, German Protestant received sacrament of Lords Supper of the Church of England 4/7/1764, along with George Mim and Peter Farmer, Minister Wm. Dorvee, St. Annes Parish., Church of England, (author's note: there additional oaths found from York Co., Pa. which I have not recorded here)
BT No.3, 1757 to 1759, Peter Toseler (Toxelor), Naturalized No.886, he has occupied lands of his magistys for 7 years, Frederick Co., Md., along with Barnard Hapsler and Adam Shipsler, John Conrad Stiner (Stoner) Minister of Reformed Congregation in Frederick Town adm. Lords Supper to Peter Toxler, 4/16/1759.
All became citizens under the law allowing foreign protestants to do so. Frederick Md.
DD No.14, Abraham Troscle, Naturalized, 1768, No.661, 5/5/1768, Abraham Troxel, Jacob Holf, Leonard Weber, John Rienner, Jacob Hoseler of Frederick Co., Md. natives of Germany, Jacob Holf, Leonard Weber, John Bremer, Lutheran; Abraham Toxle member of Reformed Church, Friday 3/10, Minister Conrad Baugner received Holy Sacrament of Lords Supper.

Monocacy and Catoctin, Vol.II, C. E. Schildknecht, Editor Family Line Publication, Rear 63, East Main St. Westminster, Md. 21157, 1989, all rights reserved F187.F8M66, 1985 Vol.2 copyright 1989
pg.50, Caspar Dreschler (Tressler) imm. 1840 from Darmstadt area (York Natl.)
Rsh.22   pg.50, Peter Drachsel (Troxell) from Lenk in Simmenthal, Canton Berne, Switzerland, imm. c. 1708 to Rieschweiler, W. Pfalz and c 1733 to Lehigh Valley, Pa. (23) Dsc Peter in Frederick Co., Md.
pg.88, Christian Rohrbach was b.in Rueggisberg, Canton Berne.  Christian Rohrbach m. Elisabeth Drachsel.
Rsh.22 pg.101, Peter Trachsel (Drachsel, Troxell), s/o Jakob and Margaretha (Brengel) was b. at Lenk, Canton Berne, where bap. 1691; imm. to Wolfersheim in Homburg-Saar area and to Frederick Co., Md., soon after 1754 (Will 1766)
pg.311, John and Margaret Troxell, 4/1784 sponsor child of

Jacob and Anna Christine Krall Weller.

pg.314, Frederick Troxell owned part of Arnold's Delight.

Rsh.43 pg.478, a survey for a land warrant of 1775 shows lands of Thomas Fisher adjoining those of John and Nichholas Schreyer and (Rsh.43) Daniel Droxel (Troxell). author's note: in 1773, Thomas Fisher, Esquire was called a Merchant of York County when he bought 112 acres of the tract Hibernia. He was called Merchant when he sold in 1777, 100 acres called Addition to Brook's Discovery, near later the area which was later to be Taneytown. To this and other deeds for Thomas recorded in Frederick Courthouse his wife Eve gave her consent. Thomas Fisher from Germany Township was elected to the Revolutionary War of York County, Pa., continued pg.479, he bought a lot in Taneytown, Md. in 1762 and agreed to build a house, in 1772 he bought Michael's Luck in Frederick Co., Md. from Charles Caroll of Annapolis. Eve was still living in 1780 when she gave her consent to sale of land recorded in Frederick, sometime before 1786 Eve King Fisher died and Thomas Sr. moved to Yorktown Pa. and married again. In 1778 Thomas Jr. replaced his father on the Tax list of Germany Twp., Thomas Fisher Sr. second m. Catherine Linebacher who had been married twice before and they operated a tavern in York. The farm was near Littlestown and was divided between sons Thomas, Jr. and James. In 1786 Thomas Sr. and Catherine bought 66 acres bounded by Thomas Fisher, Jr., Henry Buecher, Daniel Truxall and heirs of Peter Hooff. Thomas Fisher died in 1793 his Will made March 1790 is in York C.H. His children George, Elizabeth and Eva Schreyer, dau. Catherine Ohle, dau. Mary Selll, son Thomas,Jr. and James, new b. son John, son John Fisher and wife Ann lived in Baltimore in 1812, where he studied medicine; pg.476, earliest records of Christ Reformed Church north of Littlestown show that a Nicholas Fischer and wife Susannah Maria (Klee) came in 1738 from Rebeller or Rehweiler near Kusel in the Pfalz, then part of the doman of Zweibruecken. Their son John Nicholas was b. May 17, 1747. His bapt. was sponsored by Nicholas Klee and wife Anna Appolonia Oyler. Pennsylvania German Pioneers says that Thomas and Jacob Fisher arrived together in September 1751 at Philadelphia from Rotterdam via Portsmouth, England. Thomas must have been at least 16 and Jacob possibly older, names of children and women on this boat are not given. George Fisher had small acreage in Mt. Joy Twp. in 1783, Jacob Fisher Jr. was a Mason and he and wife Catherine were in Germany

Twp. in 1850 and 1860 Census.

Rsh.21   pg.50, Andreas Dressler (Tressler), imm. from Sachsenhausen, Wertheim before 1761.

pg.50, Conrad Dress, imm. 1746 from Aich, Wuerttemberg, to Berks Co., Pa., 6 children.


# OHIO

Montgomery Co., Ohio, Naturalization Records 1803-1931 Indexed by Nancy Glessell, printed by Wright State University
Dreshsel, Herman, Vol.PC11, pg.209
Drechsel, John, Vol.N1, pg.421
Dresher, William, Vol.X1, pg.426B
Traxler, Frank, Vol.CC14, pg.35
Trilscher, John, Vol.PC3, pg.369

# PENNSYLVANIA

Hinkle, W.J. ed. Pennsylvania German Pioneers Norristown, Pa. 1934, Vol.1
pgs.106-110, List of passengers imported in Ship Samuel, Hugh Percy, Master from Rotterdam, Qualified 8/17/1733, Rsh.22, Peter Troksell age 42, b. 1691; ?Rsh.146, Bernard Tossell, age 38; Rsh.22, Catharina Troksell, age 30, b. 1703; ?Rsh.146, Anna Maria Trossel, age 32; Rsh.58, Peter Troksell, age 9, b. 1724; Rsh. 43, Daniel Troksell, age 7, b. 1726.

pgs.110-111, Palantines imported in the Ship Samuel, of London, Hugh Percy, Master from Rotterdam, but last from Deal, as per clearance thence. Qualified 8/17/1733, Rsh.22, Peter Drachsel; ?Rsh.146, Hans Bernhardt Trossell.

pg.168, list 44A, a list of men passengers 16+ imported in Ship Samuel, Hugh Percy, Master from Rotterdam, qualified, 8/30/1737, John Tracksel, age 47, b. 1690; John Peter Tracksel, age 19, b.1718.

pg.170, list 44B, Palantines imported Ship Samuel, Hugh Percy, Master from Rotterdam, but last from Cowes, qualified 8/30/1737, Johannes Drachsell, Johann Peter Trachsel.

pg.171, list 44C, at the Courthouse of Philadelphia, 8/30/1737, the Palantines imported in Ship Samuel, did take and subscribe the oath to the government, Johannes Drachsel, Johann

Peter Trechsell

pg.322, Hans Trachsall came to America on the Brig. Mary, John Mason, Master, from Rotterdam via Cowes, arriving at Philadelphia 8/25/1742 and took the Oath of Allegiance and Abjuration at the Court House there the same day.

pg.405, George Michael and Bernard Traxel came to America on the Ship Phonix, John Mason, Master, from Rotterdam via Cowes, arriving at Philadelphia 9/15/1749, and took the Oath of Allegiance and Abjuration at the Court House there the same day. On this Ship came "261,550 whole Freights from Zweybrech, Nassau, Wirtemberg, and Palatinate."

pgs.620, 622, 624, Johann Georg Traxel, came to America on the Ship Neptune, Capt. Waire, from Rotterdam, arriving at Philadelphia 9/30/1754 and took the Oaths of Allegiance and Abjuration at the Statehouse there the same day. "260 Freights, 400 souls, Palatinate, Dormstad, Zweybrecht, 4 Roman Catholicks," listed as on board.

pgs.107,108,110,111,112, on the Ship Samuel, Hugh Percy, Master, from Rotterdam, the following persons came to America, arriving at Philadelphia 8/17/1733, Peter Troksell and Bernard Trossell taking the Oaths of Allegiance and Abjuration at the Court House the same day, Rsh.22, Peter Troksell, age 42, Rsh.146, Bernard Trossell, age 38, Rsh.22, Catharine Troksell, age 30, Rsh.146, Anna Maria Trossel age 32., Rsh.58, Peter Troksell, age 9, Rsh.43, Daniel Troksell age 7, Rsh.146, Catharine Rossell age 10, Rsh.146, Jerick Rossell, age 4, Rsh.146, Maria Crete Rossell, age 2.

Pennsylvania German Pioneers, f146.P23, Vols.I, II, III, Pennsylvania German Society, Norristown, Pa. 1934, Note: Vol.1 references are found in F160.G3S8 1966, Pa. German Pioneers, Baltimore Genealogical Publishing Company 1966

Rsh.5, Ehrman, Joseph, Vol.I pg.458, List 165C, Court House, Philadelphia, 9/14/1751, from Rotterdam, last from Cowes in England, 230 whole freights, 8 Roman Catholicks, 10 Mennonites.Remr Calvinists, Johan Phillipp Teutsch, Georg Adam Allbrecht, Josans Ehrman, Josef Ehrmann

Taxler, Hans Atam, Vol.I, pgs.694,692, List 245C at the Court House at Philadelphia, 9/26/1764, the Foreigners whose names are underwritten, imported in the Ship Britannia, Capt. Thomas Arnot, from Rotterdam, did this day take and subscribe the usual Qualifications, Hans Atam Taxler.

Tecker, (Decker) Ludwig, Vol.I, pgs.369,370, List 116B, foreigners imported in the Ship (Two Brothers?) qualified 10/20/1747, Ludwick (X) Tecker, pg.370, List 116C, at the Court House at Philadelphia 10/20/1747, foreigners whose names are underwritten, imported in the Ship ?, Master, from Rotterdam, but last from Leith, did this day take the foregoing Oaths to the Government, Ludwig (X) Tecker.

pg.195, Teckler, Valantin, Vol.111 pg.195, Ship Betsey, year 1807, American Schooner bound to Philadelphia cargo taken on board at Tonningen, 5/8/1807, Valantin Teckler, Shoemaker, 2, Hamburg, Light Completion.

Telcher, Johanes, Vol.I, pg.430, at the Court House at Philadelphia, 8/13/1750, the Foreigners whose names are underwritten, imported in the Ship Edinburgh, Capt. James Russel, Master, from Rotterdam, but last from Portsmouth in England, did this day take and subscribe the usual Qualifications, Johanes (X) Telcher, and a separate name with no X to indicate his mark, Johannes Delcher.

Tesch, Ada, Vol.I, pg.499, List 191C at the Court House at Philadelphia, Monday the 10/23/1752, the Foreigners whose names are underwritten, imported in the Ship Rawley, Capt. John Grove from Rotterdam, but last from Plymouth, this day took the usual Qualifications to the Government, Henrich Peter Tesch, Adam (X) Tesch.

Tesch, Henrich Peter, Vol.I, pg.400 , nothing on this page for Vol.1 referenced above

Tesche, Catrina, Engel, Vol.III, pg.101, List of Passengers in the Ship Columbia from Amsterdam, undated, Engel Tesch and Catrina Tesche in group number 5, after 11/19/1799.

Rsh.21, Dresler, Johann Andreas, Vol.1, pg.399, List 130C at the Court House at Philadelphia, Wednesday the 13th 7BER (September?), 1749, the foreigners whose names, etc. imported Ship Christian, Capt. Thomas Brady, from Rotterdam, last from Cowes in England did take the Oaths to Government, 300 Persons from Wirtembert, Alsace, Zweybrecht, Andreas Vogel, Rsh.54, Johann Andreas Dresler, Hs. Jacob Schumaker, Vallentine (O) Kern, Heinrich Albrecht

Titsch, Jacob, Druschel, Andres, Vol.I, pg.468, List 172C Court House, Philadelphia, Tuesday, 9/24/1751, Ship Neptune, from Rotterdam, last from Cowes, Andres Druschel (umlat over U).

Vol.1, pg.346, Rsh.53, Johann Conradt Trunckhler (umlat

over u) Truckel, Matheus

Traxal, Bernard, Vol I pg.401

Traxel, George, Vol.I, pg.405, List 133C at the Court House at Philadelphia, Friday, 9/15/1749, foreigners, imported Ship Phoenix, John Mason Master, from Rotterdam, but last from Cowes, in England, 550 whose freights, from Zweybrech, Nassau, Wirtemberg, & Palatinate, Michael (X) Traxel, George (X) Traxel, Bernard (X) Traxel.

Rsh.11, Traxel, Johann George, Vol.I, pgs.620,622,624; pg. 620, List 221A, Ship Neptune, Capt. Waire, from Rotterdam, arrived Philadelphia, 9/30/1754, John Jerg Dechert; Joh. Peter Dachert, Godfrid Gebhard; Jerge Traxel; pg.622, List 221B Ship Neptune, Capt. Waire, from Rotterdam, qualified 9/30/1754, Johann George Decher; Johann Peter Decher; Gottfridt Gebhard; Johann George Traxel; Frederick (+) Schneider; pg.624, List 221C Philadelphia, Monday 9/30/1754, Ship Neptune, Capt. Waire from Rotterdam, last from Cowes 400 souls, Palantinate, Darmstad, Zweybrecht, 4 Roman Catholicks, Johann Georg Decher; Johann Peter Decker, Andreas (X) Bringel, Gottfriedt Gebhard; Johann Georg Traxel; Johann Henrich Schneider.

Traxel, Michael, Vol.I, pg.405

Trexler, Michael Vol.I, pg.737, List 290C, 11/19/1771 at Philadelphia, Ship Tyger, George Johnson Master from Rotterdam, last from Cowes, Peter (X)Trexler; Michael (X) Trexler; Johann Adam Dracker

Trexler, Peter, Vol.I, pg.737, see above

Rsh.16 Trissler, (Dresser) Joseph David, Vol.I, pgs.246,247,248; pg.246, List 65A list of mens names imported in the Charming Nancy, Charles Stedman, Comr, from Rotterdam, 11/9/1738, Joseph David Dresser, age 38; Rsh.109, Christophel Trenkle, age 48; Rsh.51, Stephen Trenkel, age 20:

pg.247, List 65B Palatines imported in ship Charming Nancy, Charles Stedman, Comr, from Rotterdam, but last from Cowes in England, qualified 11/9/1738, Hans Christian Gerber; Rsh.16, Joseph Davidt Trissler; Jurich Geo.(X) Troulst.

pg.248, List 65C at Court House of Philadelphia, 11/9/1738, Palantines whose names are imported in ship Charming Nancy, Charles Stedman, Comr, from Rotterdam, but last from Cowes, Hans Christinan Gerber, Hans Georg (X) Reisser, Rsh.16, Joseph Davidt Trissler.

Troester (Trostel) Abraham (Abram) Vol.I, pgs.637,639,640;

pg.637, List 223A foreigners Ship Peggy, Capt. James Abercrombie, from Rotterdam, qualified 10/17/1754, Abram Troester.

Trostel, Abraham; pg.638, List 223B, Ship Peggy Capt. James Abercrombie, from Rotterdam, qualified 10/16/1754, Georg Adam Durstlelr (umlat over u); Abraham Trostel.

Truchauser; pg.739, Truchauser, Johann George (umlat over A) Vol.I, pg.739

Trunckhler; pg.500, Rsh.53, Trunckhler, Johann Conradt, Vol.1,pg.500, List 191 C, Court House, Philadelphia, Monday 10/23/1752, Ship Rawley, from Rotterdam, last from Plymouth, this day took, J Philip (X)

pg.734, Trussler, Michael, Vol.I, pg.734, List 287C., 9/17/1771, Ship Minerva, Rotterdam, last from Crows, Michael Trussler.

pg.14, Trunckel, Michael, Vol.III, pg.14, List of passengers on board the Brig Lydia, Garner Hammond, Commander, from Amsterdam 10/29/1785, number 13, Michael Trunckel.

pg.124, Tuchter, Martin, Vol.III, pg.124, List of passengers on board the Ship Traveller, from Amsterdam, 6/22/1803, *Martin Tuchter; Note states that he did not come on board the Ship.

List of Immigrants on the Ship Minerva 1769, MCHS
Antoni Drexel

Katharine Drexel, A Biography by Sister Consuela Marie Duffy, S.B.S.,Cornwells Heights, Pa. 19020 1977
Rsh.171 The European parents of the Francis Martin Drexel family were Franz Joseph Drexel and his wife Magdalin Wilhelm. They were from Dornbrin in Voralberg, Tirol, Germany, near Lake Constanz. This was five miles from the point where the Rhine River and the Lake meet. Francis Martin Drexel was b. there on 4/1/1792 and he left Amsterdam 5/18/1817 and disembarked in Philadelphia 7/28. The Ship he came on was the John of Baltimore.

Pennsylvania Oaths of Allegiance, Genealogical Publishing Baltimore, Md. 1976 Taken from Pennsylvania Archives, Vol XV111, 2nd Series, Harrisburg, Pa. 1890
John George Traxel, foreigners who took the Oath of Allegiance imported in Ship Neptune, Capt. Ware, from Rotterdam, qualified 9/30/1754.

Michael Trexler, imported in Ship Tiger from Rotterdam, last from Cowes, George Johnson Master, qualified 11/19/1771.

Pennsylvania Archives, 2nd Series, Vol.17, LC
Joannes Dechler, pg.367, Ship Duke of Wirtenberg, Daniel Montpelier, Rotterdam, last Cowes, 10/20/1752, Hans George Heitzman, Johannes Dechler, Johann Frederick Gross
Joannes Delcher, pg.310, Ship Edinburgh, James Russell, Rotterdam last Portsmouth, 8/13/1750, Johannes Delcher, 9/15/1749, George Henry Rissler.
Johan David Deschler, pg.85, Ship Hope of London, Daniel Reed, Rotterdam, 8/28/1733.
George Deschner, pg.473, Ship Betsy, John Osman, Rotterdam, last Cowes, 9/19/1765.
Rsh.134 Johan Peter Dressler, pg.185, Ship Samuel Hugh Percy, Rotterdam, 8/27/1739.
Rsh.126 Frantz Peter Drexler; pg.502, Ship Crawford, Charles Smith, Rotterdam, last Cowes, 10/16/1772.
Hans Adam Dessler, pg.215, age 38, b. 1703, Ship St.Andrew, Charles Stedman, Rotterdam, 10/2/1741.
John Henrich Dessler, pg.232, Ship Francis and Elizabeth, George North, Rotterdam, 9/21/1742.
Rsh.16, Joseph David Trissler, pg.178, age 33, List imported in the Ship Charming Nancy, Charles Stedman, from Rotterdam, 11/9/1738, b. 1705.
Trachsel, pg.289, Michael Trachsel, Bernhard Trachsel, George Trachsel, Abraham Dreachsel, Ship Phoenix, John Mason, Rotterdam, 9/15/1749.
John George Traxel, pg.436, Ship Neptune, Capt. Ware, Rotterdam, 9/30/1754.
Peter Tresler, pg.185, age 25, original list, b. 1714.
John Peter Tressler, pg.277, Ship Elliot, James Adams, Rotterdam, 8/24/1749.
Rsh.53, John Conrad Trunckler, pg.370, Ship Rawley, John Grove, 10/23/1752, Rotterdam, last Plymouth.
Michael Trussler, David Drexler, pg.496, Ship Minerva, Thomas Arnott, Rotterdam, last Cowes, 9/17/1771.

Passenger & Immigration Lists Index, 1st Edition, Vol.3, O-Z, Edited by P. William Filby, w/Mary K. Meyer -Gale Research Co., Book Tower, Detroit, Mich. 48226, pg.2119.
Trexler, Michael, no age given, Philadelphia, Pa., year 1771

Trexler, Peter, no age given, Philadelphia, Pa., year 1771

Rupp, Israel Daniel - Leipzig: Degener & Co., 1931, Reprint, Baltimore Genealogical, 1965, Lancour 144 A Collection of Upwards of 30,000 Names
pg.285, Reference No. 7820, 11/19/1771, Ship Tyger, George Johnson Master from Rotterdam, last from Cowes, the foreigners whose names are underwritten imported in the Ship Tyger, George Johnson, master, from Rotterdam, but last from Cowes, did this day take and subscribe the foregoing oaths and qualifications, consigned to Messrs Willing and Morris, 130 individuals on list among them: Michael (x) Trexler, Peter (x) Trexler.

RE:9041 - & 9042 - Strassburger, Ralph Beaver, Pa. German Society, 1934 Reprint, Baltimore, Geo. 1964 -Pennsylvania German Pioneers, Port of Philadelphia, 1727-1802
9041, pg.737, List 290 C at Messrs. Willing and Morris Store at Philadelphia 11/19/1771, present George Bryan, Esquire, Peter Trexler, no age given, Philadelphia County Pa., Year 1734
RE:7820, Rupp, Israel Daniel; pg.475.

Passengers & Immigration Lists Index - 1982 Supplement, Yoder, Don Editor, Lehigh County National Record ,The Pennsylvania Dutchman, RE: 9931, (Penn Emmig. German, Pen.)
pg.6, David Trexler, year 1805
Rsh.3    pg.475, Peter Trexler, Maxatany Twp. acres not given, RE 7820, Rupp, Israel
note:   Quit rent was a reserved rent in the grant of land handled by proprietor, payment freed landholder from other taxes.

Pennsylvania Archives, Series 2, Vol.2, (Persons Naturalized), LC
pg.376, Johan Peter Traxel, Bucks Co., Pa., 9/5/1748
pg.386, Jeremiah Tracsler, Bucks Co., Pa., 3/29/1752
pg.411, Michael Traxall, Northampton, 3/22/1761
pg.413, Daniel Traxell, Northampton, 3/15/1761
pg.414, John Nicholas Traxell, Northampton, 3/22/1761
Rsh.16  pg.429, David Tressler, Lancaster, Pa., 8/21/1761

Historic Background and Annals of the Swiss and German Pioneer Settlers of South Eastern Pennsylvania, and of their remote ancestors, from the middle of the dark ages, down to the time of the Revolutionary War. Henry Frank Eshleman, B.E., M.E. LL.B. Baltimore Genealogical Publishing Company 169 F160.S9E8 1969

pg.188, Trachsel, Anna, Deportation of Swiss in 1711 - reference 1711 Exodus into Holland - in the Ship Neuenburger were, Als Hans Zurcher, 40 years of age, cripple, of Fruitigen, and his mother Barb German, widow, seventy years old, knitter; also Anna Trachsel of Frutigen, 34 years of age, forsaken; also Verena Kallen country servant of Frutigen, twenty nine years of age, single woman, also Christina Kallen, country servant of Frutigen, 32 years of age, the complete record is undersigned Schaffhausen, the 23 of July 1711, Johann Ludwig Runckel.

pg.48, Trasser, George, meeting in Berne, Switzerland, February and March 1538, strange baptists were present and also and some of them spoke a great deal, among them was George Trasser of Bavaria.

pg.184, Trussel, Ulrich and Katherine, 1711 Exodus into Holland, the Swiss arrived on the 3rd of August in Amsterdam, great love and coordination was shown and they were made very comfortable among them was Ulrich Trussel (umlat over U) and his daughter Katherine of Sumiswald.

pg.170, Trussel, Ull, 1711, further plans to deport mennonites, Holland the final asylum, from the Dominion Sumiswald; Ull Trussel (umlat over U), Ulli Schurch, in Muller pg.290 may be found a list of prisoners mentioned in a letter from Alsace who were in the Jail of Berne, July 27, 1710, consisting of 23 Brethren and seven sisters of the Antibaptist or Mennonite faith. The names above in the reference are among them.

pg.171, Trussel, Christina, among this prisoners are sisters, Christina Trussel they are imprisoned in Berne to be sent down the Rhine to Holland.

pg.173, Trussel, Ulrich, and Trussel, Stini, Reference 1711, Joyous Swiss Mennonite Exodus into Holland, among the prisoners incarcerated on September 29, 1710 is Ulrich Trussel (umlat over u) Peter Gerber, Hans Wissler, among the women, Stini Trussel, Anna Salzmann, Margrit Gerber, Barbara Steiner

pg.189, Trusler, Niklaus, Tuscher, Anna and Tillie, reference 1711, Goal of the Emigrants to Holland, they intended to push on to America. Swiss leave Holland's Shelter, heads of families and individuals found are Niklaus Teuscher who settled at Saperneer. Also in and about Groningen were Peter Tschaggelm, Anna and

Tillie Tuscher. In the year 1721, the information was sent from Groningen to the committees at Amsterdam, that none of the Swiss were in need of any further assistance. Some of these individuals in later years immigrated to Pennsylvania.

pg.185, Teuscher, Anna and Duchtly, 1711 Exodus into Holland, in the Ship Oberlander people from up the country, there were: Anna and Duchtly Teuscher, forty years old, single women, Weavers; and Marg. Kallen of Frutigen, seventy years of age lame and daughter twenty years old, Reformed, her husband stayed behind; and Magd. Schmied, 54 years old, Baptist of Latterbach and eight children, Jobam, Abraham, Jakob, Isaac, David, Hans Rudolf, Susanna, Salome all by the last name of Lortscher and all children of the Reformed Faith.

Note: on second page of book "an authentic history from the original sources of their suffering during several centuries before and especially during the two centuries following the protestant reformation, and of their slow migration moved by those causes during the last mentioned two hundred years westward in quest of religious freedom and their happy relief in the Susquehanna and Schuylkill Valleys in the new world; with particular reference to the German-Swiss Mennonites or Anabaptists, The Amish and other non-resistant sects". The author refers to these people as Swiss Germans and traces their migration into Pennsylvania, particularly into Lancaster

## MARYLAND

Baltimore Co., Md., Mdhr, Index 117, Land Records, General Index
Charles Deschiel (Deskiel,Schiol,Tchisl,these spellings all in this document) Book W.G. No. D., pg.556, receives part of Lot 30, year 1779, Hanover Lane and German Av. from Daniel Barent, Daniels's wife Caterana.

Rsh.107 Peter Drushal, year 1790 to Samuel Owings, Book W.G.No.F.F., Addition to Michaels, 57 ac., No. 361, mort., on land located at Gunpowder Falls, and Lick Glad. Peter Druxsel (with umlat over U) signed name in German.

Rsh. 107 Peter Drushall, year 1793 Peter Drushall to Samuel Owings release, Addition to Michaels, 57 ac., Book W.G. No. L. L. pg.338, 6/18/1793, mort. paid Samuel Owings releases to Peter Drushall.

Conrad Disher, W.G.No.Z, pg.337, year 1786, Conrad Disher to John Thompson, Lot 118.

Rsh.5, Anthony Trecksall, deed Lot on Falls and Mill St., Book W.G. No.85, pg.480, year 1806

Rsh.5 Anthony Trecksall, Book W.G. 91, pg.60, Anthony Trecksall, grantee, Elisha Tyson grantor, lease lot N.E. Richmond St.

Rsh.5 Anthony Trecksal, Book W.G.110, pg.498, year 1810 Anthony Trecksal, Grantor, Rsh.29 Anthony Hitzelberger Grantee, Asst. Lot, N.E. side Richmond St., Anthony Trecksal assignment to Anthony Hitzelberger, signed in German: Antoni Tiwxl, 7/13/1810, both men of Baltimore Co., Richmond, St. Anthony Trecksal sells to Hitzelberger for $160.

Rsh.82 Michael Trisler, Book WG No. Y, pg.137, Indenture Made, year 1784, recorded 1/17/1786, Michael Trisler of Baltimore Co., State of Md., indebted to merchants, Hans Morrison, John Michle, John McDonoagh, desires to discharge debts, conveys house and lot to Trust, land in Howards Late Addition to Baltimore Town, No.789, Sharpe and Barre Streets to a point where a well that has been dug by Michael Trisler for his brother Peter to land of Benedict Swope and Jacob Hofs. Michael Trisler's lease date 1/24/1784, recorded in Book W.G.No.T, pg.155, signed name Michael Trisler, 1/17/1786.

Rsh.82 Michael Trisler, Book W.G.No.T, pg.155, lease had yearly ground rent 6lbs current money in half Johannos at 3 libs each and Mexican Dollars at 7 shillings and 6 pense each. Michael Trisler shall erect and build a good substantial dwelling house. author's note: by the time the above indenture was made in 1784 Michael Trisler had erected a house on the lot.

?Rsh.8  Abraham Troxell, year 1827, David W.B. McClellan, bond for lease 2 lots W. Pine St., Book W.G., pg.189, pg.348.

Rsh.107  Peter Truschel, year 1791, Book W.G. H.H. pg.462, Peter Truschel, 12/27/1791, of Baltimore Co., State of Maryland sells to Melcher Waren of York Co. State of Pennsylvania, tract of land called Addition to Michaels, close by a draught of the Lick Glad into the western fork of Gunpowder, 57 ac.  Signed name in German, then came Mary Truschel wife of Peter to relinquish dower.

Baltimore Co., Md.,Mdhr, Grantors Index, Microfilm WK1289-1-1, 1289-1290-1/2, 1290-1291-1/2

Rsh.5  year 1806, Book W.G.91, pg.60. Anthony Trecksall, grantee, Elisha Tyson grantor, lease lot N.E. Richmond, St.

Rsh.107  Year 1791, Peter Truschel to Melchor Warner, Addition to Michaels, 54 ac. HH 402

Rsh.107  Year 1794, Peter Drushal to Samuel Owings, mort., Addition to Michales 57 ac. Book FF, pg.361, Baltimore, Md.,Land Records, Baltimore Co., Md.

Frederick Co., Md., Deed Indices, Courthouse, Frederick, Md. 1748-1778

Deshler, Adam, Book WR16, pg.237, 7/9/1798, to Jacob Sampson, sale

Threlxeld, Henry, Book F, pg.589, 11/23/1758, from William Tretehelt, deed

Tracksall, John, Book P, pg.92, 5/27/1772, from John Shroepe, deed

Rsh.75 Tressler, Michael, Book L, pg.119, 5/20/1770, to Henry Lazarus, sale

Rsh.5, Trexler, Anthony, Book WR19, pg.49, 9/26/1799, from Andrew Bashman, deed

Trisher, Peter, Book M. pg.329, 6/29/1769, to Philip Rodeupeeler, deed

Trisler, Goodhard, Book L, pg.531, 10/21/1768, from George French, deed

Rsh.75, Trissler, Michael, Book N,pg.119, 5/26/1770, to Henry Lazarus, sale

Trocksal, Michael, Book O, pg.174, 3/26/1771, from Michael Rosoe, deed

Trocksell, John, Book P, pg.540, 1/6/1773, from John McMahon, sale

Troxall, Abraham, Book O, pg.404, 6/1/1771, from Jonathan Hager, deed

Troxell, John, Book J, pg.978, 12/18/1764, to George Neat, deed

Troxell, John, Book L, pg.379, 7/7/1768, from George Neat, mort.

Troxell, John, Book N, pg.48, 4/2/1770, to George Neat, release

Tysher, Peter, Book M, pg.631, 10/18/1769, from Jonathan Hager, deed

Tysher, Peter, Book P, pg.607, 3/8/1773, from Thomas Polhouse, mort.

1778-1803

?Rsh.77,?Rsh.27, Tressler, Jacob, Book WR17, pg.516 to George Tressler, deed

?Rsh.77,?Rsh.79, Tressler, Jacob, Book WR17, pg.517, 12/8/1798, to John Doll, sale

?Rsh.79,?Rsh43, Trexal, Jr., Book WR8, pg.194, 9/24/1788, from John Davis, mortgage

?Rsh.79,?Rsh.43, Trexall, John, Book WR10, pg.198, 8/4/1791, from Haus Hoover, deed

?Rsh.79,?Rsh.43, Trexall, Jacob, Book WR12, pg.497,498, 7/8/1794, from William Emmitt, 2 deeds

?Rsh.79,?Rsh.43, Trexell, John, Book WR21, pg.238, 6/4/1801, to William Emmitt, release

?Rsh.79,?Rsh.43, Trexell, Jacob & others, Book WR22, pg.390, 3/24/1802, agreement

?Rsh.79,?Rsh.43, Trexler, Jacob, Jr., Book WR22, pg.373, 3/19/1802 to Peter Samm, deed

Rsh.75 Trissler, Michael, Book WR2, pg.1124, 3/22/1782, and Valentine Black, Inquisition

Rsh.75 Trissler, Michael, Book WR5, pg.44, 6/17/1784, to Valentine Black, deed

Rsh.75 Trisler, Michael & w. Margaret, Book WR7, pg.2, 9/5/1786, from John Sigfried, Shoemaker, deed

?Rsh.77,?Rsh.27, Trissler, George, Book WR17, pg.516, 12/8/1798 from Jacob Trossler, deed

Trissler, George, Book WR24, pg.671, 8/18/1803, from Peter Tossler, deed

Rsh.34 Trocksell, John, Book WR7, pg.424, 8/21/1787, from Peter Hinkle, deed

Troxal, Peter, Book WR10, pg.566, 4/4/1792, from Bernard O'Neill, deed

Troxal, Peter, Book WR10, pg.621, 5/14/1792, and John Crabs, agreement

Troxal, Peter, Book WR13, pg.244, 5/14/1792, from Christian Smith, deed

Troxal, Peter, Book WR24, pg.665, 8/1/1803, from Patrick Davidson, deed

Troxal, John, Book WR11, pg.531, 5/9/1793, from David Danner, deed

Troxall, Peter, Book WR15, pg.130, 3/20/1797, from William Emmit, deed

Troxall, John, Book WR8, pg.581, 8/17/1789, to John Trexall, deed

Troxall, Jacob Jr., Book WR9, pg.10, 1/7/1790,from Joseph Hughes, deed

Troxall, John, Book WR9, pg.272, 1/8/1790, from Sheilds Heckensmith Esq., mtg

Troxall, John, Book WR9, pg.273, 1/8/1790, from John Davis, deed

Troxall, John, Farmer, Book WR10, pg.250, 9/24/1791, and John Troxall, Miller, agm.

Troxall, John, Book WR10, pg.252, 9/24/1791, and Sam Emmit, agm.

Troxall, John, Book WR10, pg.253, 9/24/1791, to John Hough, deed

Troxall, John and Peter, Book WR10, pg.327, 10/24/1791, and John Whitman, agm.

Troxall, John & others, Book WR10, pg.404, 12/21/1791, from Carolsburg, plat

Troxall, John, Book WR13, pg.75, 3/2/1795, from William Emmitt, deed

Troxall, John, Book WR13, pg.132, 3/25/1795, from Patrick Reid, deed

Troxall, John, Book WR13, pg.512, 9/4/1795, from William Emmitt, deed

Troxall, Jacob & others, Book WR13, pg.627, 11/11/1795,

from Carrolsburg, agm.

Troxall, Jacob, Book WR15, pg.433, 6/15/1797, from Andrew Hoover, deed

Troxall, Jacob, Book WR15, pg.528, 8/11/1797, from Christian Hoover, deed

Troxsel, Jacob, Book WR8, pg.17, 5/10/1788, from Michael Heckerewith, deed

Troxsel, John, & others, Book WR8, pg.70, 5/15/1788, agm.

Troxell, John, Book WR17, pgs.64,65, 6/13/1798, from Ignatius Brammer, 2 deeds

Troxel, Peter with adm., Book WR16, pg.185, 2/2/1798, to D.H. Whitmore, agm.

Troxel, Peter,Jr., Book WR17, pg.257, 9/7/1798, to Henry Whitmore, deed

Troxel, Peter, Jr., Book WR17, pg.344, 10/8/1798, from Stephen Winchester, deed

Troxel, Peter, Jr., Book WR17, pg.531, 12/13/1798, from William Diggs, deed

Troxel, Peter, Jr., Book WR18, pg.46, 2/4/1799, to Peter Crise, deed

Troxel, Peter, Jr., Book WR19,pg.97, 11/21/1799, and John Briggs, agm.

Troxel, Peter, Jr., Book WR24, pg.552, 7/16/1803, to James Hughes, deed

Troxel, Peter, Jr., Book WR24, pg.554, 6/16/1803, to James Hughes, deed

Troxel, John, Book WR5, pg.17, 6/7/1784, from Henry Geror and others, deed

Troxel, Jacob, Book WR16, pg.498, 5/10/1798, from William Emmitt, deed

Troxell, John, Book WR2, pg.41, 5/29/1779, from John Shryer, deed

Troxell, John, Book WR6, pg.461, 6/5/1786, from William Emmit, deed

Troxell, John, Jr., Book WR7, pg.244, 4/30/1787, from John Harris, deed

Troxell, John, Book WR7, pg.639, 12/19/1787, to Frederick Beard, deed

Troxell, Jacob, Book WR19, pg.98, 11/9/1799, to Philip Mailhoff, agm.

Troxell, Jacob, Book WR19, pg.196, 12/17/1799, from

Horace Hoover, deed

Troxell, Jacob, Book WR19, pg.198, 12/17/1799, to Horace Hoover, deed

1803-1815

J. Trisler, Book TB, pg.298, 1/17/1815, from Jacob Harbaugh, Jr.

Jacob Trisler, Book WR 37, pg.57  4/1810, tract "Worlds Wonder"

Jacob Tresler, Book WR39, pg.41, 2/1811, "Worlds Wonder"

Adam Troxall, Book WR33, pg.524, 9/3/1808, from John Septer and w., agm.

Adam Troxall, Book WR41, pg.393, 2/4/1812, from William Owings, deed

Peter Troxel, Book WR26, pg.183, 11/5/1803, Peter Troxel to James Hughes

Frederick Troxel, Book WR25, pg.502, 7/13/1804, to John Creeger

Frederick Troxel, Book WR25, pg.690, 7/13/1804, to Peter Shover, deed

G. Troxel, Book WR39, pg.35, 2/4/1811, from John Whitmore deed

Jacob Peter Troxel, Book WR25, pg.435, 3/10/1804, to State of Md., bond

John Troxel and others, Book WR37, pg.42, 12/9/1809, to Francis Graff, deed

Rsh.75 Michael Trisler, Book K, pg.860, 12/8/1766

Rsh.75 Michael Trisler and w. Margaret, Book WR No.2, pg.293, 11/3/1779

Rsh.75 Michael Trisler and w. Margaret, Book WR 7, pg.2, 9/5/1786

Rsh.75 Margaret Trisler, Book WR32, pg.78, 10/14/1807

Rsh.75 Margaret Trisler, Book WR28, pg.105, 12/13/1805, from John Bruner

Rsh.75 Margaret Trisler, of Frederick Town, Book WR28, pg.107, 12/19/1805, to John Brunner, 2 lots in town

J.D. Troxler, Book 26, pg.441, 2/15/1805

?Rsh.107, P. Trussel, Book WR 35, pg.24, 5/1809

1815-1833 author's note:  this index has not been read in full, only skimmed quickly.

Joseph Tresler, Book 32, pg.428, 9/1829

Joseph Tresler, Book JS 41, pg.492, 3/4/1833, Tract, Mary's Delight, south mountain west of Frederick old alternate 40 before Boonsboro.

<u>Frederick Co., Md., Deed Books, Courthouse, Frederick, Md.</u>
author's note: these records contain data which was not cited in the indices. The letter (s) along with / indicate the deed book/page.
Henry Thelhold, Merchant, of Frederick Co., Md., F/589, 11/23/1750
Rsh.5 Anthony Traxler, WR25/617, 5/22/1804, request of John McAllister, Anthony Traxler of Frederick County, Md. for consideration of 300 lbs. paid by McAllister sells part of a tract called Exchange in Frederick Co., bounded by Henry Bushmans, containing 50 ac., signed Antonio Trexel, witness Jos.Jim Smith, Thos. Jones, 4/14/1804 came Catherine wife of Anthony Trexel and relinquished dower.
?Rsh.43,?Rsh.79  Jacob Tresler, Frederick Co., Md., WR39/41, 2/4/1810, request of Jacob Harbaugh, tract called Worlds Wonder, no wife acknowledged, 12/29/1810.
?Rsh.43,?Rsh.61,?Rsh.79,?Rsh.124  Joseph Tresler, Frederick Co., JS35, 1/3/1831, Joseph Tresler, Frederick Co., from John Tresler of Adams, Co., Pa. property called NoBaiile, paid $1500 3 tracts, John and Joseph purchased from their father Jacob Tressler as joint tenants, John Tressler, selling land to Joseph, did not sign he made mark and his wife Christina made mark and relinquished dower.
Joseph Tresler, JS/41/492, 3/4/1833, record made 2/23/1833, between John Eyler of Peter and Margaret of Frederick Co., State of Maryland and Joseph Tresler of Frederick Co., Md., Eyler sells to Joseph Tresler tract of land called Mary's Delight.
Michael Tresler, K/860, 12/8/1866, sells to Maj.Conrad G. Peter Gross, household furniture, signed Michael Tresler, no wife acknowledged dower
Rsh.5 Anthony Trexler, WR19/49, 9/26/1799, at request of Anthony Trexler the following indenture recorded, Indenture made 4/5/1799 between Andrew Bushman County of Frederick Md. and Anthony Trexler of the County of York, State of Pennsylvania for 275 lbs. Land Called Exchange abutting Henry Bushman, containing 50 ac. of Land and Appurtences, 275 lbs. received by payment 4/5/1799. Andrew Bushman's wife Polly acknowledged, witness, Jno Grinn, Jos. Jim Smith

?Rsh.74    Peter Trisher, M/329, 6/29/1769, to Philip Rodenbitter, Lane, Peter Trisher signed, then came Fronica wife of Peter Trisher and acknowledged dower, witness Thomas Prather and Wm. Luckell

Rsh.75    Michael Trisler, House Carpenter, of Frederick Town, WR5/44, indenture with Valentine Black, Merchant, of Frederick Town and Michael Trisler, House Carpenter of Frederick Town, Margaret Trisler w. acknowledged 6/17/1784.

Rsh.75    Michael Trisler, N/119, 5/21/1770, Michael Trisler, Frederick Co., Md., sold to Henry Lazarus, household goods, no wife acknowledged dower.

?Rsh.32    Abraham Trocksal, O/174, Abraham Trocksal of Frederick Co., to Michael Rowe of Frederick Co., land called Michaels Folly, no date, in records C. 1772

John Trocksal, P92/1772, 5/27/1772, between William Smoyer of Frederick Co., Md. and John Trosall of Frederick Co., Farmer, tract of land called Resurvey of William's Pleasure.

Rsh.75  Michael Trosler (Trosher), L/531/119, 11/25/1767, at Request of Philip Shreiner, sale of household goods and cow by Michael Trosler of Frederick Town, Joyner, no wife acknowledged.

Rsh.34    John Troxall, Miller, and John Troxal, Farmer of Frederick Co., 8/17/1789, 8/581, then came Margaret w. of John Troxall and acknowledged dower.

John Troxall, P/540, 1/6/1773, John Troxall request Bill of Sale for negro man recorded from John McMechon Frederick Co., Farmer and John Troxel, Frederick Co., Farmer.

?Rsh.147    John Troxall (Troxel), J/978, 12/10/1764, John Troxel of Frederick Co., Md. Farmer, sells to George Neat, tract of land called Toury, John Troxall did not sign, he made mark, then came Margaret, w. of John Troxall and acknowledged dower

?Rsh.34    John Troxel, WR7/639, 12/19/1787, at request of Frederick Beard, indenture between John Troxel of Frederick and Frederick Beard of Frederick, land in Emmitsburg, John Troxel signed, wife came and acknowledged but she was not named.

?Rsh.36  Mary Troxel widow of Jacob, WR46/349, 4/12/1814, her 3 children, John, Elias, and Mary, she made mark, children signed, when signed the notation said widow of John, to Henry Koons, Jr.

Rsh.42  Peter Troxel, WR29/41, 5/17/1805, from John Troxel and others, daughter named Krise (?Peter Crise's wife)

Rsh.42    Jacob Troxell, WR22/390, 3/24/1802, at request of

Jacob Troxell and others, Jacob Troxel, Peter Troxel, George Troxell and Frederick Troxel all of Frederick County, as per last Will and Testament of Peter Troxell late of county, tract of land called Good Wife containing 44 ac. and tract part called Caroline. All signed names.

John Troxsel, William Trocksells, WR8/70, 5/15/1788, Toms Creek, agm. regarding (access) over the northern arm of William Trocksells Mill Dam, John Troxsel and others.

?Rsh.74   Peter Tysher, P/607, 3/18/1773, mort.

## Harford Co.,Md. Land Records,Mdhr

Rsh.110  Valentine Trisler, WK807-8, Books Y and Z., 1813-1817, pg.344, Margaret Trisler (Rsh.75) of Frederick Co., Md. (Margaret's son George is Rsh.25) gives with affection to Mary Casper, daughter of Mary Trisler and Granddaughter of Margaret Trisler land in Harve de Grace, Md.

Rsh.75  Margaret Trisler, WK 806, 6/13/1809, Harford Land Book U & V pg.807 to 811, Trissler, Margaret of Frederick Co. from Jacob Bare and Barbara Ann Bare, City of Baltimore, assignment of lease., page 69, Robert Young Stokes gave lease 4/2/1782 to Benjamin Bowser, Lot 194, rec. in Book JLG No.E pgs.267,268,269, Benjamin Bowser wife Catherine, 7/23/1802 granted to John Bear, Book HD No.2, pg.292, John Bear departed this life without will. Jacob Bear has taken letters of adm. on the estate granted him by the Orphans Court.  Jacob's wife Barbara Ann sold to Margaret Trisler of Frederick Co.

Rsh.75  pg.45, Margaret Trisler, 2/14/1815, Margaret Trisler of Frederick Co., Md. with affection gives land to Mary Trisler who is a widow of Valentine Trisler, deceased of Harford Co., Md. lot # 194, on the west side of Susequanna River in Harve de Grace, fronting on Union Street at 3rd lot where Congress Street intersects Union Street, 60' front 200' depth, Land had lease to Trisler on or about 4/2/1782 with rents, witnesses Frederick Co., David Bowley, Belt Brashear.

## Montgomery Co., Md. Index 127, Land Records 1777-1845, Mdhr

Nathan Ducker, Book Q5, pg.55
Jeremiah Ducker, Book B, pg.183

## Washington Co., Md., Mdhr, Index 65, Assessment of 1783, Index to Property Owners) 1782-1783

Rsh.15 Assessment 1783, pg.2, Washington Co.,Md., Marsh Hundred, part of Ringolds Manor, Christian Droxell, 60 ac., wood, 100 Total ac., 9 horses, 10 cattle, white inhabitants total 8.

Washington Co., Md., Deed Book Indices, Courthouse, Hagerstown,Md. author's note: these records are presented in order by year of transaction.
1778, Tresel, Godhart to Harman Working, Deed, A/256
1783, Troxall, Abraham, from David Heister, Deed, C/269
1783, Troxall, Abraham to Leonard Plufer, Deed, C/352
1786, Tressler, Peter to George Scott, B&S, Book E., pg.226
1791, Troxell, Catharine from David Troxell, G/300
1793, Tristler, Michael from William Boone,et al, Deed, H/47
1797, Tristler, Michael from William Boone, et al, Deed, K/147
1797, Tristler, Michael to George Scott, Deed, K/329
1798, Troxel, Peter from Michael Beard, Deed, L/110
1803, Troxell, David, et al, to State of Md. Bond, P/137
1809, Tressler, David from Peter Bowes, Deed, T/227
1810, Tressler, David to Henry Shafer, Deed, W/372, 1810
1814, Troxell, Peter, to David Troxell, Deed, AA/9
1834, Tressler, John from Samuel Prior, Deed, PP/358
1838, Troxell, John to Jacob Snivley, Bill of Sale, TT/737
1842, Trexler, Benjamin to Christianna Heckley, B&S, YY/814
1846, Troxell, Abraham and Sarah his wife, IN1/874, June 5, 1846
1849, Troxell, et al, Thomas F. from Samuel Bentz, Bill of Sale IN4/257
1857, Troxell, Peter and w., from Francis M. Davis, Deed, In 12/613
1866, Troxell, William from R.D. Kerfoot, Bill of Sale, IN14/552
1866, Troxell, Elizabeth, from William Shillings, et al, LBN1/77
1917, Tresler, A.C. from Charles E. Hawmond, Deed 150/465
1923, Tresler, A.C., Hazel, to J.J. Carey, Deed, 166/223
1924, Tresler, Nora May and Wm. F. from John S. Flohr, Mtg., 67/550
1930, Trexler, Frederick from Jacob Brogonier, Deed, KK/583

Washington Co., Md., Deeds, Courthouse, Hagerstown, Md.
Federick Dresler, Book KK, pg.4422, with D. Frederick Dresler with D. Keckerly, agm., 12/9/1828 rented a ten plat stove and pipe to David Gagler for 9 months for $3.00 for said term. Signed Frederick Dresler and Daniel Gagler, in German,

278

acknowledged the same before Justice of Peace.

?Rsh.15 Catharine Droxelle, Sr., Book G, pg.278, at request of Catharine Droxelle, Sr., the following Bill of Sale was recorded 11/18/1790. I David Droxells of Washington County, State of Md. for 451 lbs. do grant bargain and sell, all my estate and debts due me to Catharine Droxell, Sr., Witness John Stull, Josaunowr Zergenew, signed and acknowledge by David Troxel, November 18, 1790

Goodhard Tresel, Book A, pg.256, 7/12/1778, Goodhard Tresel of Washington Co., Md. to Harmon Working, signed Goodhard Tresel, witness John Stuhull and Andrew Rentch, Then came Anna McCoy wife to the said Goodhart Torscle, confirmed Goodhart Troselle, witness John Stule and Andrew Reutch, witness

Benjamin Trexler, Book YY, pg.814, year 1842, Benjamin Trexler of Washington Co., Md. to Christinna Heckley, Bargain and Sale of household goods, signed Benjamin Trexler

Frederick Trexler (Drexler), OHW1, pg.710, recorded 12/5/1843, recorded at request of Thomas South, indenture made 10/22/1842 between Frederick Trexler and Juliana, his wife in the County of Montgomery, State of Ohio of one part and Thomas South of Washington Co. Frederick Trexler does grant, bargain and sell that tract of land located in Jerusalem Town, Washington Co., Lot #57 with all improvement to Thomas South. Witness Charles A. Swain and David C. Baker. Frederick Drexler signed in German, Juliana Drexler made mark, 10/22/1842, Montgomery County, State of Ohio.

Rsh.82 Michael Trisler, Book H, pg.47, at request of Michael Trisler, purchaser as of 11/24/1792 the following deed was recorded 1/21/1793, between William Boone, Washington Co., Md. and George Boone of Berks Co., Pa., and Michael Trisler of Washington Co., Md., land called Fellowship, part of a tract called Bells Chance in Boones Berry town number 2. Witness Thomas Crampten, William Good

Rsh.82 Michael Trisler, Book K, pg.147, 5/4/1797, reference to Michael Trisler purchase of and William Boon, then came Susanna Boone, wife of William Boon and relinquished dower

Rsh.82 Michael Trisler, Book, pg.329, 7/24/1797, Michael Trisler of Frederick Co., Md., grants to George Scott land purchased of William and George Boon, then came Catreaner Trisller wife to said Michael Trisller and relinquished right of dower.

David Trissler, Book W, pg.372, David Trissler, of Washington Co., Md. sells to Henry Shaffer of Jerusalem Town, on

12/31/1810. Witness Jacob Schrelelg, Robert Douglas, then came Cristina Trissler wife of the said David Trissler and relinquished dower

Peter Trissler, Book E, pg.226, Bill of Sale, at the request of George Scott, following was recorded 12/26/1786, on 11/27/1786 Peter Trossler, Farmer, of Washington Co., Md. hath bargained and sold to George Scott of Frederick Co., 25 ac. of wheat now growing, some sours, horses and cows. Signed Peter Trissler

Rsh.113 Abraham Trochsel, pg.317, 3/19/1783, then came Abraham Trochsel of Washington Co. and then came Catherine the wife of Abraham Trochsel, deed to Alexander Clagett.

Rsh.113 Abraham Trochsal, Trochsall, pg.352, 5/3/1783, Indenture Abraham Trochsal and Leonard Phifer sells land called Michaels Folly and resurvey called Hagers Delight, witness John Barnes, A. Keutch, signed Abraham Trochsall (Truxell) then came Catherine Trochsall, his wife.

Rsh.113 Abraham Troxall, Book C, pg.269, 1783, at request of Abraham Troxall following deed recorded, indenture between David Header the younger of Philadelphia in the State of Pennsylvania attorney of Jonathan Hager the younger and Abraham Troxell of Washington Co., State of Md. exr. will of Balser Hefflebower late of Frederick.

?Rsh.15 David Troxcele (Troxel), Book AA, pg.9, 9/20/1814, David Troxcele, Washington Co., Md. Deed and Peter Troxele, Washington Co., Md. tract of land called Michaels Fancy. Peter Troxcel made mark, Witness William Yates, Jeremiah Chaser, then came Margaret Troxel, Peter Troxel's wife and relinquished dower.

?Rsh.15 David Troxel, Book G, pg.300, from David Troxel, 1/10/1791, Bill of Sale to Catharine Droxall for 56 lbs., one horse about 12 years old, 1 mare about 7 years old, 2 milkcows, old wagon, 2 beds, household and kitchen furniture, all books, witness H. Skrayork, Zefamer Zngner

Peter Troxel, Book R., pg.211, Peter Troxel, 11/30/1805, Nicholas Leach of Bedford Co., Pa., and Peter Troxel and John Smith of Washington Co., Md. purchase for $252. Addition to Buck Range containing 126 ac., then came Elizabeth B. Leach wife of Nicholas Leach

Peter Troxel, Book W, pg.691, Request of Jonathan Meyers, 8/19/1811, indenture between Peter Troxel of Washington Co., Md. and Jonathan Meyers, Jr. of Washington Co., Peter Troxcel signed, witness William Yetes, James Prathe, then came Margaret Torxel, wife of Peter Troxel and relinquished dower.

David Troxell, Book P, pg.137, Bond 6/20/1803, David Troxell and John Hager, of Washington Co., Md. $250., witness Robert Smith and Josua Price

Rsh.113 Abraham Troxell, Book HH, pg.800, John Cushwa, 2/13/1826, and Abraham Troxell, of Washington Co., signed Abraham Troxell, witness Jacob Schultz and Benjamin Yor

Philip L. Troxell, Book I No. 6, pg.284, 9/27/1851, Philip L. Troxell, Washington Co., Md. to John D. Kline, household furnishings.

## PENNSYLVANIA

Pennsylvania Archives, Series 3, Vol.26, Warranties of Land, LC Berks Co., Pa., 1752-1890
pg.324, Jeremiah Trexler, Lot 220, March 11, 1754
Peter Traxler, Esquire, 20 ac., September 13, 1788
Peter Traxler, Jr., 44.53 ac., November 6, 1788
Peter Traxler, Jr., 89.40 ac., November 6, 1788
pg.325, Christian Troxel, 400 ac., July 1, 1793
Christian Traxell, 400 ac., December 10, 1793
Christian Traxel, 400 ac., February 18, 1794
Magdalene Troxel, 400 ac., September 5, 1794
Christian Troxel, 400 ac., September 5, 1795
Nathan Trexler, 37.90 ac., September 19, 1827
Wm. Trexler, et al (and others) 106.24 ac., November 13, 1873

Pennsylvania Archives, Series 3, Vol.24, Warranties of Land, LC Bucks Co., Pa., 1733-1889
pg.169, John Troxell, 100 ac., January 18, 1737
Peter Traxell, 300 ac., May 10, 1737
Peter Traxell, 100 ac., October 15, 1737
Jeremiah Traxell, 100 ac., October 15, 1737
pg.170, John Troxel, 250 ac., October 15, 1737
Jeremiah Traxel, 50 ac., January 4, 1743
Peter Troxel, 250 ac., January 26, 1743
Peter Traxler, 50 ac., April 7, 1743
Peter Traxler, 100 ac., April 16, 1743
Hans Peter Troxel, 50 ac., May 16, 1745
John Traxler, 25 ac., April 29, 1746

pg.171, John Traxel, 50 ac., August 10, 1748
Peter Traxler, 35 ac., November 16, 1748
Peter Traxler, 50 ac., April 11, 1749
John Traxler, 25 ac., August 15, 1749
Peter Traxler, 25 ac., August 15, 1749
Peter Traxler, 50 ac., August 15, 1749
Peter Traxler, 50 ac., August 15, 1749
Peter Troxel, 25 ac., April 5, 1750
Joshua Trexler, 50 ac., August 23, 1750
John Troxle, 100 ac., August 26, 1750
Nicholas Traxel, 125 ac., November 29, 1751
Jeremiah Traxler, 50 ac., January 9, 1752
Peter Trexler, 50 ac., April 3, 1752
Lodowick Trache, 20 ac., March 21, 1755


Franklin County, Pa., Courthouse, Chambersburg, Pa.,
Grantor/Grantee Index
author's note: this Courthouse was burned in the Civil War by the
Confederate Army because the Town failed to pay 100 lbs in gold,
many records reportedly were lost. Therefore, I have included 19th
and 20th Century records in the hope they will provide clues.
Grantor, Item 1421, Traxler, Charles A., to Traxler, John E.,
guardian, grantee, 6/8/1907
Grantor, item 1509, Traxler, Daniel Errol, to Traxler, John E.,
guardian, 6/23/1910
Grantee, item 1224, Traxler, George R., from W.A. Traxler's heirs,
12/2/1903, 131/102
Grantor, item 666, Traxler, Jacob, grantee Greenawalt, Henry,
6/27/1865, 40/184, Location Southampton
Grantor, item 747, Traxler, Jacob R., Traxler, Grantor, William
A.Traxler, grantee, 4/26/1873 54/319, location Lurgan
Grantor, item 770, Traxler, Jacob R.,adm., Peter Cramer, Grantee,
4/1/1875, deed 58/455
Grantee Traxler, Jacob R., 1872, J.L. Suesserott, et. al, 50/236
Traxler, William A., 1874, 54/319
Creamer, Peter, 1876 58/455 Location of property Lugan
Grantor, item 849, Traxler, Jacob L., Creamer, Peter, guardian
grantee 4/8/1882 release 72/34, Grantee, item 1017, Traxler, William,
from Samuel S. Sentman exrs. 5/5/1888, 12/16/1892 93/211 Rsh.60?
Grantor, item 1317/8, Traxler, William A., adm., to Kohn, J.C.,

Clippenger, Levi H. year 1903

Rsh.60? Grantor, item 1323, Traxler, W.A. heirs, to Traxler, George R., adm. 1903

Rsh.77? Grantor, item 1047/48, Tresler, Joseph and Barbara A. to Hoover, Mary A., deed 4/30/1872 96/587 Land in Washington Co., now Maryland

Grantor, item 1524, Tressler, Edgar, to Bassard, M.T., 4/4/1910, Washington Co., Md.

Grantor, item 1405, Tressler, Emanuel E., to Tressler, Joseph B. 12/27/1906

Grantor, item 1527, Tressler, Francis, Jr.'s adm.to Hixon, S.T., 1/14/1911, Washington Co., Md.

Grantor, item 1517, Tressler, Hawey L., to Flohr, Daniel E., 8/13/1910

127/128? Grantor, item 837, Tressler, John to Fitz, Henry, 12/5/1840, deed 69/412

Grantee, item 764, Tressler, John, from Abraham Stoner, 11/21/1837, deed 3/26/1883, 69/411

Grantor, item 1048/50/1356, Tressler, Joseph, to Hoover, Mary A., to Murphy, Susan, 8/17/1893, to Tressler, Edgar 3/14/1905 96/589, Land Washington Co., now Maryland

Grantor, item 1406, Tressler, Joseph B., to Sample, Annie M., 12/27/1906

Grantor, item 1451/2, Tressler, Lewis E., and Ehner E., to Fitz, Laura, 2/25/1908

Grantor, item 1438, Tressler, Maryella, heirs, to Mauherz, Jesse R., adm. grantee, 12/31/1907

Grantor, item 537, Trexler, Benjamin deed to Denig,Lewis, grantee, 10/18/1848, Chambersburg, Pa., Land Book 21/282    Rsh.87? Rsh.125?

Grantor, item 568, Trexler, Benjamin to Reanser, John, 1/7/1854, 26/463, land in Chambersburg, Pa.

Grantor, item 593, Trostell, Daniel, 9/16/1858, land in Horse Valley, 32/16

Grantor, item 575/576, Trostle, John and Trostel, Sarah to Glasg, Jacob and w. deed of petition, 1/13/1855, 28/252, land in Guilford

Grantor, Item 787, Trostle, Daniel,adms, William Skinner, grantee, 4/1/1876 61/281

Grantor, item 599, Trostle, Daniel, land in Letterkenny, 9/1/1858, 32/226

Grantor, item 940, Trostle, Martha, Kimmell, F.M. 8/21/1888 82/144

Grantee, item 536, Trostle, John, From, Early, Thomas J., 4/5/1851 23/360, Guilford

item 546, From, John M. Knights heirs, 8/23/1852 25/81, Guilford
item 593 From, John Green's exrs., 7/24/1860, 34/145 Hamilton
Grantor, item 612, 613, Troxel, Barbara S. and Troxell, Elias S. grantee, John Royer et al, 12/27/1858, 32/523
Grantor, item 748/749, Troxel, E.S. and M.J., 3/3/1874, 55/19, location Waynesboro
Grantee, item 755, Troxel, Elias S., from Ella D. Troxell, et al 10/29/1881 67/31
Grantor, Troxel, Elias S., item 590, Besone, Henry 4/21/1857 31/135
item 596 Phillips, John, et al, Grantee, 6/15/1858, 321/151
item 605 McLellan, William Grantee, 2/18/1859 32/388
item 613, Royer, John, Grantee, 4/19/1859, 32/523
item 648, Flanagan, William F., grantee 3/30/1864 38/11
item 748, Reilly, Philip, Grantee, 5/9/1874, 55/19
Grantor Troxell, A.H., 820;
Grantor Ella D. Troxell and Troxell,A.H., grantees E.S. Troxell, 8/30/1880, Release, 10/29/1881, Book 67/31
Grantee, item 438, Troxell, John from Daniel Cook, 3/9/1816, A. of A. instrument, 11/9/1826, 14/53


Pennsylvania Archives, Series 3, Vol.24, Warranties of Land, LC Juniata, Co., Pa., 1833-1891
pg.327Adam Tressler, 50 ac., January 5, 1844

Pennsylvania Archives, Series 3, Vol.24, Warranties of Land, LC Lancaster, Co., Pa., 1733-1896
pg.548, John Traxell, 58,136, April 1768
Abraham Troxall, 30 ac., January 31, 1774

Lancaster County, Pennsylvania, Deed Abstracts and Revolutionary War Oaths of Allegiance Revised and Enlarged Edition, Deed Book a - M 1729, through ca. 1770 with adjoining Landowners and Witnesses, compiled by R. Thomas Mayhill, pub. 1973, F157.L2M35
        David Deshler, C13, pg.25, Deshler (Disher, Disher), David, David Deshler, 12/29/1738, 4/13/1751
        David Disher C122, pg.27, another reference to David Disher, 8/1751, Lebanon Twp.
        David Deshler, C414, pg.33, David Deshler of Philadelphia

and Richard Wister, are executors of Casper Wister Will, 6/15/1752

David Deshler, C443, pg.33, 11/1752, Catherine Wistar, David Deshler, Richard Johnson and Richard Wistar exrs. for Caster Wistar

David Deshler, D111, pg.40, Jacob Coyer of Warwick Twp., mort. to excrs of Casper Wistar, decd of Phila. Ib 200, Valentine Baker, George Koyer, Jacob Koyer, Hannes Dleinfilder, Hans Bender, John Wistar, George Koyer, Jacob Koyer, mort. money being estate of Catherine Wister and ch. Margaret, Rebecca, Sarah and Caster Wistar and Catherine Greenleaf to exrs. Catharine Wistar, David Deshler, Richard Johnson and Richard Wistar, 5/13/1754

Rsh.78 David Dressler, K/138 pg.119, Dressler, David and w. Phillipina, James Hamilton 8/20/1740, grant to John Gorner and on 1/14/1740/41, John Gorner grant to David Dressler, who by Will dated 4/14/1752, devised part of lots to his son in law John Thomas adjacent to John Dehuffs lot and resident part devised to his wife Phillipina who 7/3/1758 grant to Jacob Riegart who with wife Jane on 7/4/1758, grant half to Paul Gorner who 3/30/1763 grants to John Gorner

Leonard Treisser, M/488b pg.192, M488, Treisser, Leonard Godfried Zensinger, (Zenziger) doctor and w. Eva of Cocalico Twp., mort. to Samuel Funk, Joiner of Cacalic Twp., adj. Leonard Treisser, Jocob Seybert, Tobias Miller, Jacob Beck

G375, Martin Kendrick Treslar, pg.83, James Hamilton 5/20/1735 grant to Philip Trensler adj. owners John Ewing and also 5 ac. lot adjoining Cornelius Verhulst, Michael Moyer, Peter Talbach, Frederick Strobele; Trensler 5/17/1738 grant lots to Martin Kendrick Treslar,(Trestler, Tristler, Tristlear, Treasler, Tresler, Trissler, Trisler)

Rsh.16 David Trestler, B452/pg.19, David Trestler (Glazier) and w. Susanna, Lancaster Borough Mort. to Casper Wistar of Phila. I45 1/2 Money Lot., s.side King St., Lancaster Bor: adj. John Gurner, David Trestler, Mathias Young, James Hamilton 1/14/1740 grant to John Gurner 2 lots in Lancaster Borough, Gurner and wife Maria Phillippina 5/14/1745 grant to David Trestler, adj. owners, John Gurmner, Mathias Young, this deed is signed Joseph David Triestler

Rsh.16 David Tresler D516 - of, 55 Christophel Reigert (butcher) and Susannah of Lancaster b. lot w. side Queen St.Lancaster borough in tenure of David Tresler

Rsh.16 E24; David Trissler E78; lot Prince St. David Tresler

Rsh.16 G152B; Jurorer, David Tresler

Rsh.16 David Trissler G164; 3/20/1760 land Conestoga

Twp., David Trissler

Rsh.16 David Tresler H42; pg.88, David Tresler and w. Maria Drusing, enf to Frederick Ulman, Mason all of L. Co.lot Duke St., to Vine St. Lancaster Borough, no adj. owners., James Hamilton 1740 gr to David Tresler, 11/2/1743 or 1734, Jacob Spansailer

Rsh.16 David Trisler L385T; pg.151, Oath of Allegiance 6/13/1777, David Trisler,

Rsh.16 David Trisler L395B2; 6/13/1771 Oath of Allegiance, James Poe, David Trisler, David Bender, Matthias Kochler, John Baker, James Fisher, George Reitzell

David Tresler M504B; pg.193, John Ensminger applied to Henry Dehuff, one of burgesses of Lancaster borough for payment for wound received and Phillip Hart and David Treasler

Rsh.16 Joseph David Trisler, 2 free holders, examined certificate and was given monthly pay of Lancaster Borough, B450; & w Maria Drusing H42;

George Trisler, G148, 10/19/1761, Cacalico Twp., George Trisler

Rsh.16 Jost David Tresler, of Lancaster Borough I-1, Jost David Tresler of Lancaster Borough w. side Duke St. to Vine St. Adam Kintz

Michael Trisler, L380T2; 6/13/1777, Oath of Allegiance, Michael Trisler

Michael Trisler, L399 6/13/1777, Oath of Allegiance, 8/12 Michael Trisler


Pennsylvania Archives, Series 3, Vol.24, Warranties of Land, LC Luzerne Co.,Pa., 1787-1896
pg.286, Christian Troxial, 400 ac., January 4, 1793


Montgomery Co., Pa., Grantee/Grantor Index, MCCH Grantee
note: two sets of numbers with slash represent Deed Book and Page Grantee

Textor, John, grantee, 6/4/1787, Jonathan Frey, grantor, Franconia, 3/296

Treichler, Samuel, grantee, 10/30/1807, Jacob C. Nyce, et ux, Marlboro, 43/299

Treichler, Samuel Jr., et al, grantee, Joseph Treichler, et ux, Upper Hanover, 245/171

?Rsh.116, ?Rsh.3 Trexler, David, grantee, 3/26/1798, Aquila Tool, et ux grantor, Whitpain 11/115

Trexler, William, grantee, 1856 to 1868, Joseph W. Bigone, et ux, Limerick and Bridgeport, 103/201, 120/323, 120/325, 163/320

Troxell, Traxel, Henry, et ux, grantee, 8/17/1812, Abraham Levy, grantor, U. Hanover, 27/805

Troxel, Troxal, Peter, et al, grantee, 9/23/1799, Gwynedd Twp., 1/27/1776, Christian Betz, et al, Worchester Twp., and Liddy his w., Whitpain, mentions Dutch Calvin or Reformed Church, 12/366.

?Rsh.116, ?Rsh.3    Trexler, Peter, grantee, 10/19/1801, Thomas Armat, et ux, grantor, Lower Merion, 15/61.

Troxel, Samuel, grantor, 1/14/1830, Peter Miller, guardian, et al, Power of Attorney,___, 105/266, 125/352, 187/390

Grantor

Trasel, Joseph, et al, grantor, 4/7/1853, Sarah T. Fell, et al, grantee, Release, L. Merion 87/269

Traxell, John, et ux., grantor, 12/13/1785, George Sheive, grantee, Gwynedd Twp., 2/73

Traxell, Elizabeth, et al, grantor, 12/13/1785, George Sheive, grantee, Gwywedd, 2/73

Treichler, Abraham, by guardian, grantor, 8/21/1824, Theodore Diffenield, et al, Worchester, 40/278

Treichler, Abraham, by guardian, grantor, 1/16/1826, Joseph D. Corson, et al, grantee, Worchester, 41/422

Treichler, Abraham, et ux, grantor, 4/7/1856, John K. Beaver, grantee, U. Providence, 4/7/1856, 101/212

Treichler, Abraham, et ux, grantor, 9/3/1858, Sarah Gehman, grantee, U. Providence, 111/337

Treichler, Abraham, et ux, grantor, 4/3/1860, James Miller, grantee, U. Providence, 117/437

Treichler, Abraham, et ux, grantor, 4/9/1861, Abel Rambo, grantee, U. Providence, 122/383

Treichler, Abraham, et ux, grantor, 5/2/1866, Richard Pool, grantee, U. Providence, 145/31

Treichler, Barbara, by guardian, et al, grantor, 8/21/1824, Joseph Metz, et al, grantee, Worchester, 40/278

Treichler, Barbara, by guardian, et al, 1/16/1826, Joseph D. Corson, grantee, 41/422

Treichler, Catherine, by guardian, et al, grantor, 8/21/1824, Samuel Detweiler, et al, grantee, Worchester, 40/278

Treichler, Catherine, by guardian, et al, grantor, 1/16/1826, Joseph D. Corson, et al, Release, Worchester, 41/422

Treichler, David M., exr. et al, grantor, 9/10/1878, Frederick T. Jobst, grantee, U. Hanover, 245/173

Treichler, David M., adm. et al, grantor, 9/10/1878, Frederick T. Jobst, grantee, U. Hanover, 245/175

Treichler, Jacob, et ux, grantor, 4/22/1837, Christian Schwenck, grantee, U. Hanover, 53/504

Treichler, John, by guardian, et al, grantor, 8/21/1824, Christian Dittere, et al, grantee, Worchester, 40/278

Treichler, John, by guardian, et al, grantor, 1/16/1826, Joseph D. Corson, et al, grantee, Worchester, 41/422

Treichler, Joseph M., grantor, 7/29/1873, Perkiomen RR Co., grantee, Release, U.Hanover, 212/163

Treichler, Joseph M., grantor, 7/21/1875, Perkiomen RR Co., grantee, U. Hanover, 227/20

Treichler, Joseph, et ux, grantor, 9/10/1878, Samuel Treichler, Sr., et al, grantee, U. Hanover, 245/171

Treichler, Joseph M. exr., grantor, 9/10/1878, Frederick T. Jobst, grantee, U.Hanover, 245/173

Treichler, Joseph, adm. grantor, 9/10/1878, Frederick T. Jobst, grantee, U. Hanover, 245/175

Treichler, Joseph M., grantor, 8/20/1879, Susanna Schlicher, grantee, 250/138

Treichler, Mary, et al, grantor, 8/21/1824, Samuel Detweilder, et al, grantee, Worchester 40/278

Trexler, Agness, et al, grantor, 10/19/1801, Samuel Powell, grantee, L. Merion, 15/62; Peter Trexler and Agness his w., to Samuel Powell, 10/10/1802 land L. Merion, same land granted to Peter Trexler and w., 9/24/1796, Peter and Agness both made mark

Trexler, Ann, et al, grantor, 2/22/1844, Caroline Schall, grantee, Marlbourgh, 63/235

Trexler, Ann, et al, grantor, 9/6/1866, Alfred Lefferts, grantee, Cheltenham, 147/36

Trexler, Anna, et al, grantor, 1/14/1846, Charles F. Rapp, grantee, Pottsgrove/Pottstown, 67/187

Trexler, Andrew, 2/21/1853, grantor, John J. Roberts, grantee, Cheltenham, 86/38

Trexler, Andrew, estate, grantor, 9/6/1866, Alfred Lefferts, grantee, Cheltenham, 147/36

Trexler, Arener, et al, grantor, 1/3/1876, Thomas Y. Henry,

grantee, Hanover and Bucks County, 229/60

?Rsh.86 Trexler, Catherine, et al, grantor, 8/10/1802, Wm. Greacey, grantee, Whitpain, 16/49

?Rsh.86 Trexler, Catherine, et al, grantor, 11/10/1802, Jacob Ulric, grantee, Whitemarsh, 16/180

Trexler, David, et ux, grantor, 8/10/1802, Wm. Greacey, grantee, Whitpain, 16/49

Trexler, David, et ux., grantor, 11/10/1802, Jacob Ulric, grantee, Whitemarsh, 16/180

Trexler, David, estate, grantor, 4/5/1849, Jesse Sheport, grantee, Plymouth, 74/235

Trexler, David, estate, grantor, 4/5/1849, Jesse Sheport, grantee, Release, Plymouth, 74/237

Trexler, David, estate, grantor, 2/10/1852, Samuel Pluck, et ux., grantee, Release, Mtg., 7/236

Trexler, David, est. grantor, 4/4/1899, Ben James Wagner, grantee, Ployouth, 446/168

Trexler, Elizabeth, et al, grantor, 4/29/1817, Jachariah Buruo, grantee, Morriton and Whitpain, 33/461

Trexler, Elizabeth, et al, grantor, 4/4/1829, Joseph Taylor, grantee, Whitpain, 44/575

Trexler, Elmira, et al, grantor, 1/31/1851, Lucinda Rittenhouse, grantee, Pottsgrove and Pottstown, 79/64

Trexler, Frederica, et al, grantor, 8/3/1864, Philip Bushong, grantee, Whitemarsh, 134/413

Trexler, Frederica, et al, grantor, 5/21/1879, Thomas Hart, grantee, Whitemarsh, 249/157

Trexler, Frederica, grantor, 5/13/1880, Charles J. Miller, grantee, Charles J. Miller, grantee, Agreement, 20/247

Rsh.87 Trexler, Horatio, grantor, 1/31/1851, Lucinda Rittenhouse, Grantee, Pottstown,Pottsgrove, 79/64

Rsh.87 Trexler, Horatio, exr., grantor 4/14/1852, Charles F. Rapp, Pottstown, 82/664

Trexler, John, et al, grantor, 4/5/1849, Jesse Shepard, grantee, release, Plymouth, 74/237

?Rsh.124   Trexler, Joseph, et ux, grantor, 4/29/1817, Zachariah Buraus, grantee, Noriton and Whitpain, 33/461

Trexler, Joseph, et ux, grantor, 4/4/1829, Joseph Taylor, Whitpain, grantee, 44/575

Trexler, Joseph, et ux., grantor, 8/28/1835, Shadrach H. Dorson, grantee, Assignment and Legacy, 4/119

Trexler, Joseph, et al, grantor, 4/5/1849, Jesse Shepard, grantee, release, Plymouth, 74/237

Trexler, James E. et ux, grantor 5/1/1868, David Homer, grantee, release dower, 134/413

Trexler, James M. est, grantor, 5/21/1879, Thomas Hart, grantee, Whitemarsh, 249/157

Rsh.87 Trexler, Lesher, et al grantor, 1/31/1851, Lucinda Rittenhouse, grantee, fee, Pottstown, 79/64

Trexler, Peter, grantor, 10/19/1801, 15/62; by Marshall 27/80, Thomas Humphrey, L. Merion, July 2, 1810

Trexler, Sarah Ann, et al, grantor, 1/31/1851, Lucinda Rittenhouse, grantee, Pottstown, 79/64

Trexler, Wm., et al,grantor, 1/31/1851, Lucinda Rittenhouse, grantee, 79/64

Trissel, Joseph, et ux, grantor, 6/8/1865, John Kratz, grantee, Halfield Twp., 140/181

Troxel, Catherine, et al, grantor, 4/3/1854, Wm. Hoffman, grantee, U. Hanover, 90/530

Troxel, Catherine, et al, grantor, 4/17/1869, John McElroy, grantee, U. Hanover, 168/52

Troxel, Catherine, exr., grantor, 4/11/1871, George S. Mumbauer, grantee, U. Hanover, 187/393

Troxel, Catherine, grantor, 4/11/1881, George S. Mumbouer, grantee, Release, msc. 21/180, Troxel, David, et al, grantor, 12/15/1860, Samuel Wineberger, grantee, Release. U. Hanover, 121/419

Troxel, David, et al, grantor, 4/11/1871, Jonas Brey, grantee, U. Hanover, 187/397

Troxel, Elizabeth, et al, grantor, 1/4/1830, Samuel Troxel, grantee, Power of Attorney, 3/243

Troxel, Elizabeth, estate, grantor, 12/15/1860, Samuel Weinberger, grantee, Release, U. Hanover, 121/419

Troxel, Elizabeth, et al, grantor, 10/26/1880, Jeremiah K. Groff, exr., et al, grantee, Release, 20/470

Troxel, Henry, grantor, 11/13/1797, Matthias Felton, grantee, Whitpain, 8/661

Troxel, Henry, adm. et al, grantor, 2/19/1822, John Trumbower, grantee, Marlborough and Bucks, Shff C110

Troxel, Henry, adm. et al, grantor, 2/19/1822, Philip Reed, U. Hanover, Shff, C111

Troxel, Henry, adm. et al, grantor, 2/19/1822, Margaret

Reiter, grantee, U. Hanover, Shff, C115

Troxel, Henry, adm. et al, grantor, 2/19/1822, Frederick Hillegass, grantee, U. Hanover, Shff, C116

Troxel, Henry, adm. et al, grantor, 2/19/1822, George Kline, granett, U. Hanover, Shff, C126

Troxel, Henry, et al, grantor, 1/14/1830, Samuel Troxel, grantee, Power of Attorney, Msc. 3/243

Troxel, Henry, est., grantor, 4/3/1854, Wm. Hoffman, grantee, U.Hanover, 90/530

Troxel, Henry, adm. grantor, 4/26/1858, Lydia Mitler, grantee, U.Hanover, 110/233

Troxel, Henry, et al, grantor, 12/15/1860, Samuel Weinberger, Release, grantee, U.Hanover, 121/419

Troxel, Henry, est., grantor, 4/17/1869, John McElory, grantee, U.Hanover, 168/52

Troxel, Henry, et al, grantor, 10/26/1880, Jeremiah K. Groff, exr. et al, grantee, Msc. 20/470

Troxel, Henry, adm., grantor, 11/8/1876, Philip Super, grantee, U.Hanover, 234/78

Troxel, Irvin T., grantor, 3/2/1880, George S. Mumbouer, grantee, , guardian release Msc. 20/163

Troxel, John T., exr., et al, grantor, 4/11/1871, George S. Mumbauer, grantee, U.Hanover, 187/393

Troxel, Joseph S., et al, grantor, 5/14/1872, Henry K. Zeigler, exr., et al grantor, release msc 15/403

Pennsylvania Archives, Series 3, Vol.26, Warranties of Land, LC Northampton County 1752-1886

pg.189, Peter Troxel, 50 ac., April 30, 1752

Peter Troxel, 50 ac., August 26, 1752

Peter Troxel, Jr, 50 ac., October 26, 1752

pg.190, Peter Trexler, 25 ac., May 2, 1753

Peter Trexler, Jr., 50 ac., May 3, 1754

Jeremiah Traxler, Lot 220, March 11, 1754

Peter Troxel, 25 ac., October 8, 1754

John Traxel, 100 ac., September 2, 1755

Jeremiah Traxler, 16 ac., July 9, 1760

John Traxler, 2.15 ac., June 7, 1765

John Trexler, 101 ac., November 28, 1768

John Trexler and Jno. Albright, 2 tracts, December 6, 1770

John Traxler, 40 ac., May 4, 1773

Peter Traxler, 128 ac., July 27, 1773
pg.192, John Trexler, 15 ac., April 27, 1787
John Trexler, Jr., 30 ac., March 10, 1789
pg.193, Jeremiah Trexler, 10 ac., December 19, 1792

Pennsylvania Archives, Series 3, Vol.24, Warranties of Land, LC
Westmoreland Co., Pa., 1773-1892
pg.517, Adam Truxel, 28 ac., Feb. 7, 1812

York County Pennsylvania Deeds Vol.III, compiled by Joan L.
Alguire, pub. Alguire Abstracts, 765 E. 170th Pl, South Holland, Il
60473 1982 F157.y6A43
    Frederick Tissall, pg.32, Deed 11/15/1762 between Peter
Sprinkle of Manchaster Twp., and John Strickler of Halllam and
Elizabeth his w. and Ludwig Treiber of Codorus and Anna Barbara
his w. and Jacob Keller of Codorus Twp., and Esther his w., Henry
Landes of Newberry Twp., and Susannah his w. and Ludwig
Keepher of Codorus and Anna Margaret his w. and Abraham Keefer
of Codorus and Katharine his w. and George Springel of
Manchester, et al witnessed by Frederick Tissall
    Adam Tissel, pg.30, Deed between Henry Neaff of Dover
Twp., and Adam Tissel of same place, dated 11/16/1762
    Frederick Trissel, pg.104, Deed 11/20/1763 between
Frederick Tissel of Shrewsberry Twp., Millwright and Mary his wife
and Nicholas Henery

Pennsylvania Archives, Series 3, Vol.24, Warranties of Land, LC
Bucks Co., Pa., 1733-1889
pg.169 John Troxell, 100 ac., January 18, 1737
       Peter Traxell, 300 ac., May 10, 1737
       Peter Traxell, 100 ac., October 15, 1737
       Jeremiah Traxell, 100 ac., October 15, 1737
pg.170 John Troxel, 250 ac., October 15, 1737
       Jeremiah Traxel, 50 ac., January 4, 1743
       Peter Troxel, 250 ac., January 26, 1743
       Peter Traxler, 50 ac., April 7, 1743
       Peter Traxler, 100 ac., April 16, 1743
       Hans Peter Troxel, 50 ac., May 16, 1745
       John Traxler, 25 ac., April 29, 1746
pg.171 John Traxel, 50 ac., August 10, 1748
       Peter Traxler, 35 ac., November 16, 1748

Peter Traxler, 50 ac., April 11, 1749
John Traxler, 25 ac., August 15, 1749
Peter Traxler, 25 ac., August 15, 1749
Peter Traxler, 50 ac., August 15, 1749
Peter Traxler, 50 ac., August 15, 1749
Peter Troxel, 25 ac., April 5, 1750
Joshua Trexler, 50 ac., August 23, 1750
John Troxle, 100 ac., August 26, 1750
Nicholas Traxel, 125 ac., November 29, 1751
Jeremiah Traxler, 50 ac., January 9, 1752
Peter Trexler, 50 ac., April 3, 1752
Lodowick Trache, 20 ac., March 21, 1755

Luzerne Co.,Pa., 1787-1896

pg.286 Christian Troxial, 400 ac., January 4, 1793

Juniata, Co., Pa., 1833-1891
pg.327 Adam Tressler, 50 ac., January 5, 1844

Lancaster, Co., Pa., 1733-1896
pg.548 John Traxell, 58 ac., 136 ac., April 1768
Abraham Troxall, 30 ac., January 31, 1774

Westmoreland Co., Pa., 1773-1892
pg.517 Adam Truxel, 28 ac., Feb. 7, 1812


Pennsylvania Archives, Series 3, Vol.26, Warranties of Land, LC
Berks Co., Pa., 1752-1890

pg.324 Jeremiah Trexler, Lot 220, March 11, 1754
Peter Traxler, Esquire, 20 ac., September 13, 1788
Peter Traxler, Jr., 44.53 ac., November 6, 1788
Peter Traxler, Jr., 89.40 ac., November 6, 1788
pg.325 Christian Troxel, 400 ac., July 1, 1793
Christian Traxell, 400 ac., December 10, 1793
Christian Traxel, 400 ac., February 18, 1794
Magdalene Troxel, 400 ac., September 5, 1794
Christian Troxel, 400 ac., September 5, 1795

Nathan Trexler, 37.90 ac., September 19, 1827

Wm. Trexler, et al (and others) 106.24 ac., November 13, 1873

Northampton County 1752-1886

pg.189 Peter Troxel, 50 ac., April 30, 1752

Peter Troxel, 50 ac., August 26, 1752

Peter Troxel, Jr, 50 ac., October 26, 1752

pg.190 Peter Trexler, 25 ac., May 2, 1753

Peter Trexler, Jr., 50 ac., May 3, 1754

Jeremiah Traxler, Lot 220, March 11, 1754

Peter Troxel, 25 ac., October 8, 1754

John Traxel, 100 ac., September 2, 1755

Jeremiah Traxler, 16 ac., July 9, 1760

John Traxler, 2.15 ac., June 7, 1765

John Trexler, 101 ac., November 28, 1768

John Trexler and Jno. Albright, 2 tracts, December 6, 1770

John Traxler, 40 ac., May 4, 1773

Peter Traxler, 128 ac., July 27, 1773

pg.192 John Trexler, 15 ac., April 27, 1787

John Trexler, Jr., 30 ac., March 10, 1789

pg.193 Jeremiah Trexler, 10 ac., December 19, 1792


## VIRGINIA

Alexandria, Va., Alexandria Hustings Court, Compiled by James D. Munson, Heritage Books 1990, Deeds 1783-1797

Rsh.105 Lodowick Trissler, Deed Book F, pg.128, 5/15/1795, Town of Alexandria, Fairfax Co., State of Va., deeded to George Spangler, begin on Prince at east line of parcel conveyed by John and Jane Fitzgerald today to Lodowick Trissler.

Rsh.105 Lodowick Trissler, pg.129, 5/15/1795, John and Jane Fitzgerald to Lodowich Tressler, lease of land south of Prince, west of Royal.

Rsh.105 Lodowick Trisseler, Deed Book H., pg.195, 2/27/1796, Deed of Trust, beginning at Prince at east line of ground conveyed by Fitzgeralds to Lodowick Trisseler.

?Rsh.105 Lewis Trissler, Deed Book G, pg.168, 7/21/1796 From Abraham and Mary Faw, Town of Alexandria, State of Va., to Lewis Tristler, Blacksmith, lease s.w. corner of King St., Asaph to E. King to Street A.

Loudoun County, Virginia Minute Book 1780-1783, Copyright by T.L. C. Genealogy, P.O. Box 403369, Miami Beach, FL 33140-1369 F232.L8L64 1990

David Troxable, pg.114, 6/10/1782. Deed from David Troxable to John Stiffler proved by the witnesses and ordered recorded

## TAX AND VOTING RECORDS
## MARYLAND

Baltimore, Md., A Name Index to the Baltimore City Tax Records, 1798-1808, in the Baltimore City Archives, Publication of the Baltimore City Archives, Edited by Richard J. Cox, Balt. City Archives, 1981
Rsh.29    pg.97, Anthony Hitsenberger, Assessment Book 1800, pg.22; 1804-1808 pg.186

Baltimore Co., Md., The Particular Assessment List for Baltimore and Carroll Counties, Md. by George J. Horvath, Family Line Publications, Silver, Spring, Md. 1986 F187.B2H67
1804 Tax List for Precincts surrounding Baltimore Town,
    pg.9, Christian Delcher 74 lbs.
    rg.9, George Delcher 430 lbs.
    pg.10, John Delcher 50 lbs.
    pg.139, Valentine Delcher 282 lbs.

Frederick Co., Md., Mdhr, Poll Books, Frederick Co., Md.
Rsh.24        1808 Dist.5, Taneytown, Adams Troxeler

Montgomery Co., Md., Mdhr, Maryland Assessment 1783
Middle Potomac General Hundred,
Rsh.30    pg.12, Jacob Trisler, female slaves I, cattle I, number of white inhabitants total 8.

## OHIO

Early Ohio Tax Records, compiled by Ester Weygandt Powell, Baltimore Genealogical Publishing Co., 1985

Brown Co., Ohio, 1819 Tax List
    pg.189, John Tresler

Jackson Co., Ohio, 1819 Tax List
Rsh.106, pg.202, Samuel Trexler, Range 18, Township 6, Sec. 20, OU N.W., Original owner Samuel Trexler.

Jackson Co., Ohio 1825 Tax List
Rsh.106, pg.204, John Traxler, Samuel Traxler, Emanuel Traxler, Jonathan Traxler

Licking Co., Ohio 1816 Tax List
pg.228, Granville Twp. Phinehas Trussel

Madison Co., Ohio 1816 Tax Record
pg.240, Isaac Troxsell, John Troxel

Montgomery Co., Ohio 1810 Tax List
pg.270, Abrm Troxel (4) Jefferson Twp.

Montgomery Co., Ohio 1816 Tax List
pg.273, Abraham Troxel (3) Jefferson Twp.

Stark Co., Ohio 1810 Tax List
pg.369, Auditor of State of Ohio, Jacob Draxel, Orange Twp.

Stark Co., Ohio 1816 Tax List
pg.372, Present Owners, Jacob Troxell, Jacob Troxel, Peter Troxell

Stark Co., Ohio 1816 Tax List
pg.374, Original Owners Names, Peter Troxell

Tuscarawas Co., Ohio, 1816 Tax List
pg.389, George Tressel

Warren Co., Ohio 1810 Tax List,
pg.403, Joseph Troxell, Franklin; Wm. Treusdall, Turtle Creek; Samuel Troudall, Turtle Creek

Wayne Co., Ohio 1825 Tax List
pg.431, Jacob Troxall (2), James Trusdall (2)

author's note: Comment in this book says many pioneers before 1800 were from New Jersey, Pennsylvania and Virginia,

## PENNSYLVANIA

note: Paradise Township, is in York Co., on the Adams Co., Pa. line, (near Abbottstown). Early settlers were mostly Germans. Paradise was taken from Jackson Township. Catholic Colonial Conewego is in Adams Co., and south of York, Pa., and includes some of 1995's Frederick and Carroll Counties as far south as Westminister,Md. This includes the Pipe Creek area.

note: Hopewell Township, is in York Co., on the Maryland line between Harford and Baltimore Counties.

Berks Co., Pa., BCHS Reading Tax Lists
Drechsler, John, male/married, Longswamp Twp., 1764
Rsh.54    Dressler, Andreas   male/married,   Greenwich   Twp.,
    1762,1764,1766
Rsh.54  Tresler, Andreas, male/married,,Greenwich Twp., 1763
    Tresler, Michael,male/married, Rockland Twp., 1762

Berks Co., Pa., Archives 3rd Series, Vol.18 Berks Co., Pa., 1767
Rsh.54 pg.59, Greenwhich Twp., 1767, Andrew Tresler (Blacksmith) 130 ac. 3h, 3c, 4s, 7 tax
Rsh.54    pg.128,   Greenwich   Twp.,   1768,   Andrew   Treslar (Blacksmith),150 ac. 2 h., 3c, 4s, 7 tax

Lancaster Co., Pa., New Index Lancaster County, 1750 Tax, Vol.3, Haw, Baker and Groff, F157.L2H39 Vol.3
    John Treeler, Lancaster Borough,year 1750
Rsh.26 David Teesler, Lancaster Borough, year 1750
Rsh.26 David Tressler,Sr., Lancaster Borough 1751, Sadler in 1759
    Friterich Tresler, Bethel, year 1750
    Martin Tresiter, Bethel, year 1750

York Co., Pa., HSYC
    Manheim Twp., Tax List 1762 - Andrew Drushal

Philadelphia   Co.,   Gwinedth   (Gwynedd)   Township   1769, Pennsylvania Archives, 3rd Series, Vol.14, LC

    pg.21, Peter Troxel, Grist Mill, Saw Mill, 280 ac., 4 horses, 7 cattle, tax 48.12.0
        Michael Troxel, 130 ac., 4 horses, 3 cattle - 18.15.4

298

Lancaster, Co., Pa., 1771, Pennsylvania Archives, 3rd Series, Vol.17, LC

Manner Township 1771
pg.111, Adam Disler, 100 ac., 2 horses, 4 cattle, tax. 18.0

Lebanon Township 1771
Rsh.112  pg.142, Abra Troxel, 210 ac. 3 horses 4 cattle, 7.6

Londonderry Township 1771
pg.164,  John Traxall, 100 ac., 2 horses, 3 cattle, 10.0

Lancaster Borough 1771
Rsh.29  pg.7, Nicholas Hitzelberger, 1 cattle, tax 7.0
Rsh.29  widow Hitzelberger, tax 3.0

Northampton County, Pa., Pennsylvania Archives 3rd Series, Vol.19, LC

Easton Township 1772
Rsh.115        pg.7, Jeremias Traxler, 2.8.0 tax

Williams Township 1772
Rsh.53  pg.14, Conrad Trincker  Fa'r ?  2.17.4

Whitehall Township 1772
pg.15, Nich's Draxel, Fa'r?  12.13.4
Adam Deshler, Jr., Fa'r?  12.17.4
Peter Deshler, Fa'r?  5.6.8
Rsh.58  Peter Draxel, Fa'r?, 13.8.0
Single men,
Rsh.148  pg.18, Daniel Traxel,15.0

Northampton Town 1772
pg.41, David Deshler, Fa'r?, G.M.? S.M.? 9.16.0

Macungi Township 1772
Rsh.85  pg.46, Peter Traxler, Fa'r? 23.3.4
Rsh.87  John Traxler, Fa'r?, 6.16.0

Singleman
pg.47, Peter Traxler, 15.0

Weisenburg Township 1772
   pg.56  Christopher Tresher, Fa'r?, 2.0.0

Lancaster Co., Pa., 1772, Pennsylvania Archives, 3rd Series, Vol.17, LC

Manner Township 1772
   pg.172, Adam Destler, 112 ac., 2 horses, 3 cattle, 18.0

Lebanon Township 1772
Rsh.112  pg.285, Abra Traxel, 210 ac., 3 horses, 4 cattle,  9.6

Londonderry Township 1772
Rsh.112  pg.254, John Tracksell, 100 ac., 3 horses, 3 cattle, 7.0

Lancaster Co., Pa., 1773, Pennsylvania Archives, 3rd Series, Vol.17, LC

Lebanon Township 1773
Rsh.112  pg.420, Abraham Troxel, 210 ac., 3 horses, 5 cattle, 7.0

Londonderry Township 1773
Rsh.112  pg.376, John Troxel, 80 ac., 2 horses, 3 cattle, 7.0

Manner Township 1773
   pg.400, Adam Dristler, 100 ac., 2 horses, 2 cattle, 17.0
Lancaster Borough 1773
Rsh.29  Nicholas Hitzolbarger, Mason, 1 cattle, 7.0 tax

Philadelphia Co., Gwinedth Township 1774, Pennsylvania Archives, 3rd Series, Vol.14, LC

Rsh.40  pg.346, Peter Troxall, 170 ac., 4 horses, 6 cattle, 16.17.4
Rsh.149 John Troxall, 70 acre, 2 horses, 2 cattle, 1 8.16.0, Grist mill, Saw mill
   pg.348, John Troxall

Bedford Co., Pa., 1775, Pennsylvania Archives, 3rd Series, Vol.22, LC   pg.101, Philip Truax, 6.10 tax
   Samuel Truax, 13.7 tax

John Truax, 8.11 tax
Jacob Truax, 8.4 tax
Benjamin Truax. 8.10 tax

Bedford Co., Pa., 1776, Pennsylvania Archives, 3rd Series, Vol.22, LC

Bethel Township
pg.147 Jacob Truax, 6.6.1/4 land tax, 2.10 Provencial Tax
Benjamin Truax, 8.7.1/2, 8.1
Philip Truax, 1.9 1/2, 4.8
John Truax, 6.9, 2.1
Samuel Truax, 2.3, 5.9

Lancaster Co., Pa., 1779, Pennsylvania Archives, Series 3, Vol.17, LC
pg.238, Greenwich Twp. 1779
Rsh.54 Andrew Dresler, 126 ac., 2 horses, 5 cattle, 559
Rsh.27 David Dresler, 135 ac., 2 horses, 3 cattle, 573
pg.534, Adam Derstler, 112 ac. 4 horses, 5 cattle

Lebanon Twp. 1779
Rsh.112 pg.554, Abraham Traxel

City of Philadelphia 1779, Pennsylvania Archives, 3rd Series, Vol.14, Effective Supply Tax, LC
pg.500, Jacob Tressell, Middle Ward
pg.512, Michael Tresler, North Ward, Tax 3
pg.796, Michael Tresler, North Ward, Tax 15.0, State Tax 1779

Lower Merion Twp. 1779, County of Philadelphia
Rsh.86, pg.67, Peter Trexler, 1.5.0
Rsh.86, Joseph Trexler 1.10.0 (P.h'd)
Rsh.115, Gramier Trexler 1.10.0(P.h'd)(?Jeremiah)
Rsh.86, Lawrence Trexler 10.0
pg.628, Peter Trexler, 5
?Rsh.124, Joseph Trexler ph.d.d
Rsh.115 (?Jeremiah) Gramier Trexler p.hd.d
Rsh.86, Lawrence Trexler, 2

York Twp., Pa., Pennsylvania Archives 3rd Series Vol.21, York Co.,

Pa. Tax 1779, LC
Rsh.128   pg.145, John Treichler, 200 ac., 2 horses, 5 cattle, tax
100.0.0

York, Paradise Twnship, 1779
Rsh.79, pg.75, George Tressler, 70 ac., 2 horses, 3 cattle tax 20.0.0

York Co., Heidelberg Township,1779
pg.101, John Trussel, 1 cattle
Rsh.5, Anthony Truel, 1 cattle, 6.10.0
Rsh.5, pg.99, Joseph Ehrman, 2 cattle, tax 6.0.0

York Co., Germany Township, 1779
Rsh.43   pg.107, Daniel Troxel, 225 ac., 4 horses, 4 cattle 95.7.6
Rsh.45   David Troxel, 1 cattle, 7.10.0
?Rsh.101   Jacob Troxel, 100 ac., 1 horse, 3 cattle, 33.0.0

Tax List York Co. Pa., 1779 reprinted from Pa. Archives, Family Line
Pub. 1989
Rsh.79  pg.57, Paradise Twp., George Tressler, 70 ac., 2 horses, 3
cattle, tax 20.0.0

York Twp.
Rsh.126   pg.108, Peter Drexler, 4 cows, tax 5.5.0
Rsh.128   pg.111, John Treichler, 200 ac., 2 horses, 5 cattle tax
100.0.0

Philadelphia Co., Pa., Gwinedth Twp. 1779, Pennsylvania Archives,
3rd Series, Vol.14,LC
Rsh.149   pg.610, John Troxell, Tax 11

Buck's Co., Pa., 1779, Archives, 3rd Series, Vol.13, Bucks County,
LC
Richland Twp.
Rsh.128   pg.83, John Traighler, 140 ac. 2 horses, 3 cattle
Solesbury Twp.
        pg.9, Joseph Trisher, 25 ac. 1 horse, 2 cattle

A New Index to Lancaster County, Pennsylvania, before Federal
Census, Vol.1, Index to 1780 Tax Records, Gary T. Hawbaker and
Clyde L. Gross, Hershey Pa., 1981

302

Vol.1 ,Vol.5, Index to 1779 Tax Records, Lancaster Co., Pa.
Michael Traxel, year 1777, Paxton Twp., assessment
Rsh.112, Abraham Traxel, year 1769, Lebanon, farm
Christian Traxel year 1759, Lecock Twp., freeman
Rsh.112, John Traxel, year 1769, Londonderry, 75
Rsh.26, David Trissler, year 1770, Lancaster, Sadler (shown as Drisler in 1772.
Adam Treish, year 1771, Cacalico, inmate -not land owner

A New Index, Lancaster Pa., before the Federal Census, by Gary T. Hawbaker and Clyde L. Groff, Hershey, Pa., Call F157.L2H39
Rsh.26, David Trissler, Lancaster Borough, 81, Oath Taken
Rsh.27, George Trissler, Lancaster Borough, 81 Oath Taken
Jacob Dissler, Cocaliico, 79, Taxable, landed

Pennsylvania Archives, 3rd Series, Vol.17 (1779 Tax), LC
Lancaster Borough
Rsh.26  pg.60, David Trissler, Sadler, 1 cattle

Lancaster Borough, Effective Supply Tax
Rsh.29  Nicho. Hitzelberger, Mason, 1 cattle
Rsh.29  Peter Hitzelberger, Mason, 1 cattle

Pennsylvania Archives, Series 3, Vol.15, LC
Philadelphia Co., Gwynedth Township 1780
Rsh.149  pg.416, John Troxell, value 4,023, tax 130.12.0

Pennsylvania Archives, 3rd Series, Vol.21, York Co., LC
York Co., York Township 1780
Rsh.126  pg.177, Peter Drexler, 1 horse, 3 cattle, 3.10.10
Rsh.128  pg.181, John Treichler, 200 ac, 3 hor, 3 cat. 79.3.0

York Co., Heidelberg Township 1780
pg.259  John Trushel, 1 cattle, 3.0.0
Rsh.5, Anthony Trixel, 1 cattle, 16.0

York, Germany Township 1780
Rsh.43, pg.310 - Daniel Troxel, 150 a. 3h,3c, 58.0.0
Rsh.45, David Troxel, 1 cattle, 2.0.0
Rsh.101, Jacob Troxel, 50 ac., 2 h, 2 c, 20.0.0

York, Paradise Township, 1780
Rsh.79, pg.244 - George Tressler, 40 a, 3 horses, 2 cattle, tax 9.7.6

Pennsylvania Archives, Series 3, Vol.18, LC
Greenwich Twp. 1780
Rsh.54  pg.357  Andrew Dressler  126ac, 2h, 4c,  12.5.0
David Dressler  135 ac, 2h, 5c  13.5.0

Pennsylvania Archives, 3rd Series, Vol.15, LC
County of Philadelphia 1780, Effective Supply Tax, Lower Merion
Township
Rsh.86, pg.433, Laurence Trexler, Valuation, 1150, Tax 25.17.6
Rsh.86, Peter Trexler, Valuation 30,330, Tax 682.8.6
Rsh.115 Jeremiah Trexler, Valuation 400, Tax 9.0.0
pg.505, Elias L's Trichell, Northern Liberties, west part

Pennsylvania in 1780, Statewide Index Tax List Circa 1780, compiled
by John D. and E. Diane Stemmons, P.O. Box 20531, 3527 W. 4650
South, Salt Lake City, Utah 84119 f,148.S82 1978
Dreiber, Michael, York, Manchester,
Dresh, Rudolph, Berks, LS=Longswamp
Dresher, Conrad, Berk: LS
Dresher, George, Phila:SF=Springfield
Dresher, Lawrence, Berk:LS
Dresher, Phil., Berk:LS
Dresher, Samuel, Berk:LS
Dresher, Stofle, NHTN:WB=Northampton, Weisenburg Twp.
Dress, Dewalt, Nhtn, Mu,
Dress, George, Berk, BW,
Dress, Maw, Berk, BW
Rsh.54, Dressler, Andrew, Berk, GW=Greenwich
Rsh.27, Dressler, David, Berk, GW
Rsh.126  Drexler, Peter, York, York Town
Rsh.27, Drissler, George, Lncr, Lancaster Borough
Droslle, George, Berk, BN
Rsh.79, Tressler, George, York, Paradise Twp.
Trisler, Jacob, Buck, MF
Rsh.26, Trissler, David, Lncr, Lancaster Borough
Rsh.5, Trixel, Anthony, York, Heidelburg
Rsh.43, Troxel, Daniel, York, Germany
Rsh.45, Troxel, David, York, Germany

?Rsh.101 Troxel,Jacob, York, Germany
Troxell, George, Cumberlan,FM = Fermanagh
Troxell, John, Phil, GW = Gwynedth
Trexler, Joseph, Phil LM=Lower Merion
Rsh.86, Trexler, Lawrence, Phil, LM
Rsh.87, Trexler, Peter, Phil, LM
Effective Supply Tax


City of Philadelphia 1781, Pennsylvania Archives, Vol.15,LC
Mulberry Ward West
Rsh.87 pg.651, Peter Treixer, Val. 20, Tax. 4.4 part.

Berks Co., Pa., 1781, Pennsylvania Archives, Series 3, Vol.18, LC
Greenwich Twp.
Rsh.54  pg.485  Andrew Dressler  126 ac. 2h, 4c, 2.2.2

Bucks Co., Pa., 1781, Pennsylvania Archives, 3rd Series, Vol.13, LC
Richland Twp.
Rsh.128  pg.118, John Trickler, 140 Ac., 2 h, 5 c

York Co., Pa., 1781, Pennsylvania Archives, 3rd Series, Vol.21, LC
York, York Township 1781
Rsh.128  pg.342, John Dreickler, 150 ac., 4 horses, 5 cattle, 8.0.10

York Co., Pa., Hopewell Township, 1781
Rsh.126  pg.472, Peter Traxler, 1.15.0

York, Co., Pa., Paradise Township, 1781
Rsh.79, pg.356, George Tresler (Weaver) 95 ac. 2 horses,3 cattle,
1.18.6

York, Co., Pa., Germany Township 1781
Rsh.43, pg.454, Daniel S. Troxel, 200 ac. 3 horses, 4 cattle, 8.7.6
Rsh.45, David Troxel (Weaver) 1 cattle., 5.6
?Rsh.101, Jacob Troxel, 100 acre, 2 horses, 1 cattle, 3.16.0
Rsh.5, Anthony Troxel (Mason) 77 acre, 1 horse, 2 cattle, 2.2.9

Bucks Co., Pa., 1782, Pennsylvania Archives, 3rd Series, Vol.13, LC
Richland Twp.

Rsh.128   pg.293, John Trickler, 140 ac. 2 h, 5 c

Lancaster Co., Pa., 1782, Pennsylvania Archives, Series 3, Vol.17, LC
Lebanon Twp.1782
Rsh.112   pg.800, Abram Traxel, 7.16.0

Manor Twp. 1782
pg.742, Adam Derstler, 112 ac. 3 horses, 4 cattle, 20.0.0

York Co., Pa., Paradise Township, 1782
Rsh.79  pg.526, George Dressler, 90 acre, 2 h,2 c, 3.14.4
Rsh.44  John Dressler, single man, 3.0.0
Rsh.79  John Doll, 220 ac, 3 h., 4 c., 12.6.5

Lancaster Borough 1782
Rsh.29  pg.758, Nicholas Hitzelberger, Mason, 1 cattle 1.11.3. tax
Rsh.29  Peter Hitzelberger, Mason, 1 cattle 1.11.3 tax
York Co., Pa., 1782, Pennsylvania Archives, 3rd Series, Vol.21, York Co., LC
Rsh.126  pg.541, Peter Trexler, 100 ac, 2 horses, 2 cattle, 2.15.0

York Co., Pa., Germany Township, 1782
Rsh.43, pg.560, Daniel Trucksil, 200 ac., 2 horses, 3 cattle, 14.0.10
Rsh.45, David Trucksil, 1 horse, 1 cattle, 16.9
Rsh.101 Jacob Trucksil, 75 ac., 2 horse, 1 cattle, 5.2.8
Rsh.5, Anthony Traxler, 77 ac., 1 horse, 2 cattle, 3.16.8
Rsh.24, pg.561, Adam Trucksill, singleman, 3.10.0

Bucks Co., Pa., 1783, Pa. Archives, 3rd Series, Vol.13. LC
Richland Twp.
Rsh.128  pg.407, John Treichler, 2.10.0 tax

York Co., Pa., 1783, Pennsylvania Archives, 3rd Series, Vol.21,York Co., LC Paradise Twp.
Rsh.79  pg.723, George Tressler, 70 ac., inhabitants 7
Rsh.44  John Dressler, single man (rsh.124)

York Co., Pa., Germany Township, 1783
Rsh.43, pg.727, Daniel Trucksaal, 200 ac, inhab. 6
Rsh.45, David Trucksaal, 100 ac.

Rsh.5, Anthony Trecksler, 77 ac, 5 servants

York Co., Pa., Hopewell Township 1783
pg.779  Peter Drecksler, 60 ac, 5 inhabitants

Bethel Pa., 1784, Pennsylvania Archives, 3rd Series, Vol.22, LC
pg.293  Samuel Truax, 1 dwelling house, 9 whites
Jacob Truax, 1 dh, 11 whites
John Truax, 1 dh, 6 whites
Joseph Truax, 1 dh, 6 whites

Buck's Co., Pa., 1784, Pa. Archives, 3rd Series, Vol.13, LC
Richland Twp.
Rsh.128    pg.426, John Trickler, 140 ac. house 1, outhouses 3,
whites 12

Greenwich Twp., Pa., 1784, Pennsylvania Archives, Series 3, Vol.18,
LC
Rsh.54, pg.615, Andrew Dresler 100 ac., 2 horses, 2 cattle, 4 sheep
Rsh.27, David Dresler  135 ac., 2 horses, 3 cattle, 5 sheep

Buck's Co., Pa., 1785, Pennsylvania Archives, 3rd Series, Vol.13, LC
Richland Twp.
Rsh.128  pg.599, John Trickher, 140 ac. 3 horses, 5 cattle
pg.546, Joseph Tressell, 300 ac. 4 horses, 4 cattle
John Tressell, single man, Tinicum Twp.

Berks Co., Pa., 1785, Pennsylvania Archives, Series 3, Vol.18, LC
Greenwich Twp.
Rsh.54  pg.744, Andrew Dressler  18.0
Rsh.27  David Driessler  1.1.0

Heidleberg Township 1785
Rsh.24    pg.754, Adam Trxter  18.9
pg.122  Jacob Kressler, 200 ac, 1 cattle 15.4 tax

Longswamp 1785
pg.760, Lawrence Dresher  3.2.9
Conrad Dresher  3.2.9

Northampton Co., Pa., 1785, Pennsylvania Archives, 3rd Series,

Vol.19, LC
Federal Tax

## Allen Township 1785
pg.157  David Deshler, Grist Mill, 350 ac., 7 horses, 6 cattle, 3.13.6

## Easton Township 1785
Rsh.47, pg.83, Nich's Troxel, 1 cattle  4.1 tax

## Macungie Township 1785
Rsh.85  pg.107, Peter Trexler, 2501 ac., 4 horses, 10 cattle 3.7.11
Rsh.87  Peter Trexler, Jr., 176 ac., 4 horses, 6 cattle 2.4.0
John Trexler, 8 ac., 1 cattle  5.0
Jeremiah Trexler, 60 ac., 2 horses, 2 cattle  15.0
pg.108  Jonathan Trexler, 12.0 tax, single freemen

## Northampton Town 1785
pg.111  Charles Deshler, 1 horse, 1 cattle 7.6 tax
Peter Deshler, 4.1 tax

## Upper Milford Township 1785
pg.101  John Trexler, 34 ac. 3.11 tax

## Weisenburg Township 1785
pg.115, Peter Trexler, 20 ac., 4.6 tax
Peter Trexler, Jr., 21 ac, 7.0 tax

## Williams Township 1785
Rsh.56  pg 87, Jacob Trinkler, 90 ac. 2 horses, 2 cattle, 9.0 tax

## Whitehall Township 1785
Rsh.40  pg.125, Peter Draxel, Jr., 194 ac., 3 horses, 3 cattle, 1.17.10
Rsh.148 Daniel Draxel, 189 ac., 3h, 4c, 1.19.7
Peter Deshler, 128 ac., 2h, 3c, 1.18.2
Adam Deshler (Grist Mill) 250 ac., 4h, 4c, 3.16.3
Rsh.39  Nicholas Draxel, 325 ac., 2h, 4c, 3.2.11
Rsh.23  Jacob Draxel, 120 ac., 1h, 2c, 13.9


## Bucks Co., Pa., 1786, Pennsylvania Archives, 3rd Series, Vol.13, LC
## Solesbury Twp.

pg.677, Joseph Trissell, 1.14.9

Bucks Co., Pa., 1786, Pennsylvania Archives, 3rd Series, Vol.13, LC
Richland Twp.
pg.705, Jacob Trusler, 3.6 tax
John Frickler, 15.8 tax

Northampton Co., Pa., 1786, Pennsylvania Archives, 3rd Series,
Vol.19, LC
Federal Tax
Easton Twp.
Rsh.47  pg.186, Nicholas Troxel, Baker, 1 house, 1 lot, 6.6tax

Williams Township 1786
Rsh.56  pg.189, Jacob Trinkler, 90 ac., 2 horses, 2 cattle, 9.0 tax

Upper Milford Township 1786
pg.212, John Trexler, 34 acre, 3.11 tax

 Salisburg Township 1786
pg.214, David Deshler, Grist Mill, 50 ac., 3.18.10 tax

Northampton Town 1786
pg.217, Charles Deshler, Tinker, 1 cattle, 9.2
Peter Deshler 6.0

Whitehall Township 1786
Rsh.40  pg.219, Peter Draxel, Jr., 104 ac, 3 horses,3 cattle, 1.19.6
Rsh.148 Daniel Draxel, 189 ac, 3 horses, 4 cattle, 1.19.2
Peter Deshler, 160 ac., 2 horses, 3 cattle, 1.19.0
Adam Deshler, 250 ac., Grist Mill, 4 horses, 4 cattle,3.14.4
Rsh.39, Nicholas Draxel, 325 ac., 2 horses, 2 cattle, 3.0.6
Rsh.23, Jacob Draxel, 128 ac., 1 horse, 1 catt;e, 13.0
?Rsh.58, Adam Draxel, 2 horses, 2 cattle, 3.9
Rsh.58, Peter Draxel, 160 ac., 3 horses, 6 cattle, 1.9.4

Weisenburg Township 1786
pg.227, Peter Trexler, 13 ac. 1.6
Peter Trexler, Jr., 20 ac. 2.6
Samuel Tresser, 160 ac., 2 horses, 1 cattle, 18.3 tax

**Northampton Co., Macungie Township 1786**
Rsh 85, Peter Trexler, 300 ac., 4 horses, 8 cattle, 4.5.0
Rsh.87, Peter Trexler, Jr., 176 ac., 4 horses, 5 cattle, 2.10.0
John Trexler, 16 ac, 7.0
?Rsh.124, John Trexler, Jr., 175 ac., 4 horses, 2 cattle, 2.0.0
?Rsh.86, Jeremiah Trexler, 60 ac., 2 horses, 2 cattle, 15.0

**Bucks Co., Pa., 1787, Pennsylvania Archives, 3rd Series, Vol.13, LC**
pg.785, Jos. Trissel, Tax 1.16.0
John Trissel, single man
Richland Twp.
?Rsh.128, pg.814, John Traichler 15.10 tax

**Easton Pa., 1788, Pennsylvania Archives 3rd Series, Vol.19, LC**
Federal Tax
Rsh.47  pg.292, Nicholas Traxel, Baker, 4 ac., 1 cattle, 8.0

**Upper Milford Township 1788**
pg.309  John Trexler, 34 ac., 3.10

**Salisburg Township 1788**
pg.311, David Deshler, Grist Mill 75 ac. 4.4.4
pg.312, John Draxel, 87 ac. 2 horses, 4 cattle, 9.7

**Whitehall Township 1788**
Rsh.31, pg.316, Christian Draxel, 162 ac., 2 horses, 2 cattle, 1.8.8
Rsh.58, Peter Draxel, inholder, 262 ac., 2 horses, 1 cattle, 1.8.8
Rsh.40, Peter Draxel, Jr., 194 ac., 3 horses, 3 cattle, 1.16.10
Rsh.58, Peter Draxel, 160 ac., 2 horses, 2 cattle, 1.7.2
Rsh.148, Daniel Draxel, 189 ac. 3 horses, 3 cattle, 1.16.1
Rsh.23, Jacob Draxel, 128 ac. 1 horse, 1 cattle, 12.5
?Rsh.58, Adam Draxel, 162 ac., 2 horses, 2 cattle, 1.8.8
Adam Deshler  246 ac., 4 horses, 4 cattle, 3.16.0
Peter Deshler, 180 ac. 4 horses, 4 cattle  1.18.0

**Weisenburg Township 1788**
pg.324, Peter Trexler, Jr., 20 ac., 2.9

**Huntingdon Co., Pa., 1788, Pennsylvania Archives, 3rd Series, Vol.22, LC**
**Tyrone Township 1788**

pg.341, John Troxal, 112 ac., 2 horses, 1 cattle, 3.1 tax

<u>HSYC, notes</u>
Manheim Twp. 1795, Tax List, Peter Drushel

<u>Record Book of Overseers of the Poor, Borough of York,</u>
<u>Pennsylvania, 1799-1804, South Central Pennsylvania Geo. Soc.,</u>
<u>Inc. An Alphabetical Listing of the Assessed Inhabitants,</u>
?Rsh.5, Joseph Trexler, single man, taxed May 3, 1804
Adam Deshler taxed July 1799 and March 1800

note: This tax occurred every year and rather than put down the
individual tax dates I have just put a total period of taxation

## Virginia
<u>Richmond, Va. Personal Property Tax list</u>
1818 Ignatius Trexler .70 Tax

**MARRIAGE RECORDS**

## KENTUCKY

Marriages - Pulaski Co., Ky., 1798-1851, Pulaski County Historical
Society, National Genealogical Library, F457.P8K38 Jesse Burton
m. to Cathy ("J") Troxell 3/14/1805, Minister McWhorter

## MARYLAND

Baltimore Vital Records, Mdhr, pg.46, #132
George Zimmerman and Sophia Trickell m. 6/22/1816, Minister,
Joseph Shane, Methodist Episcopal

Baltimore County Marriage Licenses 1777-1798, Family Line
Publishers, Dawn Bieller Smith 1989
Rsh.34  Elizabeth Troxall to Adam Showers, 7/15/1796, marriage
was reported by Minister

Baltimore, Md., Zion Lutheran Church, Baltimore, Md., MHS
Rsh.45  pg.435, #19, Michael Trexil and Margaret Markel,
5/21/1816
pg.435, #23, William Wolf and Julia Ann Trexel, 6/4/1816

Frederick Co., Md., Marriages from the Land Records,
Courthouse, Frederick, Md.
author's note:  these inferences to marriage are listed by the date
of transaction.
12/10/1764, John Troxel (Troxall) m. Margaret
6/29/1769, Peter Trisher m. Fronica
Rsh.75  6/17/1784, Michael Trisler, House Carpenter of Frederick
Town, m. Margaret
4/12/1814, John Jacob Troxel, deceased m. Mary, children John,
Elias and Mary
1/3/1831, John Tresler (Tressler) of Adams Co., Pa., m. Christina

Frederick Co., Md., Marriages 1778 - 1810 - Margaret E. Meyers,
Family Line Publication, Silver Spring, Md. 1987
Rsh.65, 5/7/1801, Troxel Frederick to Elizabeth Young
Rsh.13, 6/6/1793, Elizabeth Troxell to Nicholas Zimmerman
Rsh.42, 8/2/1805, George Troxel to Elizabeth Cabbs
Rsh.42, 3/27/1802, Frederick Troxel to Catherine Wilson

David Trisler to Christiana Brouhmeyer, 3/26/1805, Minister Shumaker

Jacob Dresler m. Barbara Fare, 4/4/1805

Jacob Troxell to Elizabeth Brewer, 11/22/1806, Minister Rahauser

Peter Troxall to Margaret Erly, 2/28/1809, Minister Rahauser

Polly Thresher to Hugh Rose, 8/3/1809, Minister Borer

Jacob Troxall to Susanna Rhodes, 8/20/1812, Minister Rahausr

Abraham Troxell to Sarah Raugh, 8/19/1813, Minister Rahsoe

John Troxell to Elizabeth Cooper, 10/8/1814, Minister Rahauser

John Troxell to Mary Alter, 3/1/1816, Minister Rahauser

John Troxel to Livia Hathway, 5/15/1826, Minister Hurly

Elizabeth Troxell to Perry Prather, 8/3/1830, Minister Light

John Troxall to Christina Stansler, 7/18/1838

Sarah Troxall to Allen Dunn, 8/23/1837


Washington Co., Md. Marriages from Land Records, Courthouse, Hagerstown, Md.

author's note: these inferences to marriage are listed by the date of transaction.

7/12/1778, Goodhard Tresel,(Torscle,Troselle) m. Anna McCoy Rsh.113 3/19/1783, Abraham Troxell,(Trochsel,Trochsall) m. Catherine 7/24/1795, Michael Trisler,(Trisller m. Catreaner) 12/31/1810, David Trissler m. Cristina, 8/19/1811, Peter Troxel,(Torxel, Troxcele, Drassel, Traxel) m. Margaret 10/22/1842, Frederick Trexler, (Dexler) m. Juliana


MHS

Rsh.25  George Trisler m. Susan Kurtz, 10/11/1827

Rsh.75  Elizabeth Trisler m. Jacob Houck, 3/26/1811, Frederick, Md.

Rsh.25  George Trisler m. Catherine Breidenbach, 3/1794

Rsh.44  Catharine Trissler m. I Eicholtz, 6/23/1818

Rsh.14  Henrietta Trisler m. James Weaver, 7/3/1821, she is the dau. of George Trisler


Maryland Marriage Records, Mdhr

Rsh.140  John Trexler m. Mary E. Craddock, 5/1/1833, Number 1, Index 11

John Dressler m. Rosa Meyer, 2/17/1849, Number 408, Index 15

Rsh.20    Peter Albert Trexler m. Martha Ellen Ball, 3/8/1851, Baltimore, Md.

Morman I.G.I. 1992
Samuel Trusler and Mary Flanaday, 8/1/1815, Minister, George Roberts, Vol.2, pg.22
Philip Trisler and Ann Caroline Rag., 7/4/1837, Vol.2, pg.125, Minister Isaac P. Cook
Joseph J. Treakle and Anne E. Starr, 12/24/1850, Vol.2, pg.341
Henry C. Treakle and Mary J. Starr, 12/23/1853, Vol.2, pg.352

Maryland Marriages, compiler Robert Barnes, Genealogical Publishing Baltimore, Md. 1978 Rsh.13, pg.259, 6/6/1793, Nicholas Zimmerman m. Elizabeth Troxell, Frederick Co.; Rsh.20 Jos. Fixler to Deb. Starr, 10/28/1820, Baltimore, Md.

Transcription by Mrs. Warren D. (Louise L.) Miller at D.A.R. Library.
pg.129, 3/1799, Jacob Knodel m. Barb. Dressler, St. Johns Evan. Lutheran, Hagerstown,


# NORTH CAROLINA

Marriages of Orange County North Carolina 1779-1868, compiled by Brent H. Holcomb, with an Index by Robert and Catherine Barnes, Baltimore Genealogical Publishing Company, Inc. 1983
Rsh.73  Troxlar, David, pg.3,  John and Caty Albright 9/13/1810, bondsman David Troxlar
        Troxlar Francis, pg.260, Henry Fitch and Francis Troxlar, 7/31/1821, Daniel Hill bondsman
        Troxlar Sally, pg.11, Rev. Wm. Artz, and Sally Troxlar, 10/20/1829, Michael Holt, bondsman
        Troxler Adeline, pg.320, Warren, Biscoc and Adeline Troxler, 3/16/1824, Charles S. Darren, bondsman
Rsh.73          Troxler, Barnabe, pg.3, Jonas Albright and
                Susannah Strator, 10/17/1815, Barnabe Troxler,
                bondsman
Rsh.73          Troxler, Catherine, pg.191, James McCamie and
                Catharine Troxler, 12/26/1806, John Gibson

bondsman

Troxler, Eli, pg.161, David Johnston and Mary Mabane, 5/17/1828, bondsman Eli Troxler,

pg.205, May, Tobias and Catharine Friddle, 2/8/1798, bondsman Eli Troxler

Troxler, Jn., pg.155, Christian Isley and Nancy Whitsell, 8/17/1822, bondsman Jn. Troxler

Troxler, John C., pg.273, Soloman Sharp and Hessey Shatterby 9/17/1833, bondsman John C. Troxler

Rsh.73 Troxler, Mary, pg.3, Ludwick Albright and Mary Troxler, 4/1/1784; Thomas Mulhollay bondsman

Troxler, Milly pg.167, John Keck and Milly Troxler 1/14/1812, John Mason bondsman

pg.309, Troxlar, Condestan, and Nelly Clap, 4/1/1835, bondsman John Calp

Rsh.73 pg.309, Troxlar, David, and Betsey Graves, 5/5/1822, bondsman Barnet Troxler

pg.309, Troxlar, Haywood, and Catharine Geringer, 2/4/1840, bondsman, John Huffman

Rsh.73 pg.309, Powell Troxler and Mary Whitesill 3/8/1810, bondsman George Troxler

Rsh.73 pg.309, John Troxler and Elizabeth Whitsill, 1/25/1817, John Keck bondsman

pg.309, John C. Troxler and Fanny Wheeler, 1/22/1840, bondsman John Huffman


Marriages of Orange Co., N.C., 1779-1868, Compiled by Brent H. Holcomb, Baltimore Genealogical Pub. 1983

pg.161, 1828, Eli Troxler bondsman

pg.155, 1822 John Trexler, bondsman

Rsh.73, pg.3, Ludwick Albright m. Mary Troxler, 4/1/1784

Rsh.73, Ludwick Albright m. Betsy Sharp, 10/2/1787

pg.3, David Troxler, bondsman, 9/13/1810

pg.167, Milly Troxler m. John Keck, 1/14/1812

pg.205, 12/1825, Eli Troxler bondsman for Tobias/Burrow marriage

pg.273, 9/1833, John Troxler bondsman for Sharp/Shatterly marriage

Rsh.73, pg.309, David Troxlar m. Betsey Graves, 5/5/1822

pg.309, Condestan Troxlar m. Nelly Clap, 4/1835

Rsh.73, pg.309, Powell Troxler m. Mary Whilesil, 3/8/1810, George

Troxler, bondsman
  pg.320, Warren Biscoe m. Adeline Troxler, 3/16/1824

Marriages of Rowan Co., N.C., 1753-1868, Comp. Brent H. Holcomb, Baltimore Genealogical Pub. 1981
pg.3, John Trexler bondsman for 12/17/1811 marriage
  pg.401, marriage of Adam Trexler to Margaret Erwin took place 2/20/1820
  pg.401, Adam Trexler m. Artamessa Pinkson on 6/18/1823
  pg.401, George Trexler m. Barbara Peeler, 10/2/1811, John Trexler, bondsman
  pg.402, John Trexler M. Elizabeth Morgan, 2/9/1813
note:       Salisbury is in Rowan Co., N.C. and many more
            Trexlers are found in this records throughout the
            1800's.

Marriage and Death Notices from the Western Carolinian, (Salisbury, North Carolina) 1820-1852, an Indexed Abstract, compiled by Robert M. Topkins, Raleigh, North Carolina 1975, The Reprint Company, Publishers, Spartansburg, South Carolina 1983
  Trexler, Adam to Miss Elizabeth Bisherer, 6/16/1840, near Salisburg, 6/19/1840 paper
  Trexler, Alexander, to Miss America Brown, 6/13/1833, in Rowan County, 4/18/1833 paper
  Trexler, Henry to Miss (blank) Miller, 4/17/1835, Rowan County paper 4/18/1835
  Trexler, Levi to Miss Elizabedth Frick, 4/5/1835, in Rowan Coounty paper 5/16/1835
  Trexler, Moses to Miss Margaret Cauble, 8/22/1839 in Rowan County paper 8/30/1839
  Peter Trexler to Miss Elizabeth C. Miller, 4/16/1835 in Rowan County paper 5/2/1835
  Trexler, Miss Ann to Henry A. Walton, 1841
  Trexler, Miss Camilla to Thomas H. Dent, 1831
  Trexler, Miss Sally to Michael Davis, 1826
  Trexler, Miss Sophia to Henry Peeler, 1830
Rsh.122 Trexler, Lawrence aged about 70, 9/13/1827, in Rowan County 9/25/1827 paper.

## OHIO

Gateway To the West, Vol.I, compiled by Ruth Bowers and Anita Short, Genealogical Pub.Co.,Inc., Baltimore 1989
  pg.167, Bulter Co., Ohio Marriages 1803-1806, Frederick Troxel to Jane MCCarey, 10/15/1807
  pg.163, John Baird to Nancy Troxell, 3/10/1808
  pg.530, Greene Co., Ohio Marriages 1815 to 1818, Japheth Davis to Polly Troxel, 11/13/1817

Early Marriages of Montgomery Co., Ohio, DAR Library
pg.16, 8/19/1813, David Showers m.Catherine Troxell

Index to Marriage vows Montgomery Co., Ohio, DAR Library
pg.67, Sarah Troxell m. John A. Troxell, 11/24/1825
pg.64, Samuel Truexell m. Rose Ann Weaver, 6/16/1825

## PENNSYLVANIA

Bucks County, Pa., Intelligence, Marriage Notices, Vol.1, 1804-1834, Vol.2, 1835-1860 A to LAW, edited by Frances Wise Waite, Bucks County Genealogical Society, P. O. Box 1092, Doylestown, Pa. 18901
  Treichler, Susanna, Springfield Twp., to John McFarland, Merchant of Rockamixon Twp., 4/15/1833
  Tresler, Elizabeth, dau. of Philip Tresler, to John Stonebeck, both of Hilltown, 12/8/1805
  Tressler, Mary to Jonathan Jones, both of Bedminister, 4/11/1811
  Trissel, Margaret, to John Yettes, both of Haycock Twp., 12/25/1827
  Trissel, Jr., John, of Tinicum to Susannah Stover of Haycock, 5/3/1814
  Troxel, Elizabeth of Hilltown, to George Kern of New Britian, 3/3/1811
  Troxell, Jacob of Doylestown to Susannna Miller dau. of John of New Britian, 5/12/1812
  Troxel, Margaret to Benjamin Vanluvanee, both of Doylestown, 12/31/1812
  Troxell, Sarah to Peter Ulrich, both of Hilltown, but m. at Philadelphia, 3/23/1826

?5/2/1852, Dressel, Mrs. Catharine, Milford, and Col. George Hager, widower, by Rev. J.A. Sleassburger

Cumberland Co., Courthouse, Carslile, Pa., Marriage License Index (Female and Male)
Drexler, Carrie May, Searer, Jacob A., Book 19, pg.75, 6/10/1901;
Drexler, Emma E., Shearer, Clarence L., Book 21, pg.36, 5/8/1912;
Drexler, Mary C., Humes, William, Book 6, pg.42, 3/24/1891;
Drexler, Mildred E., Ruth, William H., Book 32, pg.265, 12/12/1929

Trostle, Annie M., Adams, Charles R., Book 15, pg.420, 1/19/1905:
Trostle, Alda C., Myers, John W., Book 19, pg.242, 12/13/1909:
Trostle, Anna Edua, Eruerick, Simon G., Book 20, pg.160, 2/13/1911;
Trostle, Blanche M., Hammond, Oliver, Book 13, pg.105, 5/18/1901;
Trostle, Bertha A., McRitter, Geroge B., Book 17, pg.219, 2/28/1907;
Trostle, Blanche R., Arbrgast, P.G., Book 17, pg.231, 3/16/1907; Trostle, Emma F., Rauls, Elmer H., Book 22, pg.26, 9/3/1913; Trostle, Fanny P., Bervermoster, James C., Book 20, pg.111, 12/24/1910; Trostle, Frances C., Yahn, Monroe C., Book 28, pg.226, 7/19/1923; Trostle, George W., Bowers, Helen G., Book 10, pg.111, 2/25/1897; Trostle, Gerhe M., McManus, William E., Book 16, pg.37, 5/27/1905; Trostle, Gertrude, Kepford, Daniel M., Book 16, pg.137, 9/12/1905; Trostle, Leurena M., Neff, Clyde C., Book 17, pg.316, 5/22/1907; Trostle, Mima, Lebo, Christian, Book 8, pg.440, 3/13/1895; Trostle, Mary E., Stake, Martin G.E., Book 13, pg.496, 7/7/1912
Trostle, Sallie M., Sowers, Peter A., Book 9, pg.108, 11/23/1895

Trexler, Bertha J., Miller, Wilbur, Book 18, pg.217, 6/17/1908
Trexler, Margaret Cecila, Ponesmith, Clinton E., Book 19, pg.473, 8/9/1910

Trostle, Zora Elizabeth, Mumper, Daniel C., Book 24, pg.16, 9/6/1916

Drexler, George A., Smith, Anna, Book 27, pg.118, 5/4/1921; Drexler, Miles Alvina, Isenberg, Laura May, Book 21, pg.221, 12/21/1912; Drexler, William H., Orler, Ella, Book 15, pg.46, 12/23/1903; Drexler, William, Koser, Ruth, Book 32, pg.255, 11/26/1929

Trostle, Boyd, Bruder, Elizabeth, Book 18, pg.145, 3/21/1908;Trostle, Charles W., Book 22, pg.108, Myers, Edna May, 11/26/1913; Trostle, David, Mathias, Rosie, Book 12, pg.223, 2/27/1900; Trostle, Ernest H., Bieam, Hannah A., Book 12, pg.446, 12/20/1900; Trostle, George W., Bowers, Helen G., Book 10, pg.111, 2/25/1897; Trostle, James S., Eicholtz, Lydia C., Book 3, pg.386, 5/6/1886

Traxler, John E., Hall, Eurma T., Book 14, pg.305, 4/9/1903; Traxler, William D., Thumma, Clara M., Book 15, pg.272, 9/19/1904

Trostle, John C., Bigler, Jemre G., Book 14, pg.430, 9/12/1903

Trostle, Lewis E., Smee, Blanche M., Book 22, pg.182, 2/4/1914

Trostle, Lester W., Blosser, Sylva E., Book 30, pg.54, 3/20/1926

Trostle, Roy John, Bear, Edith Irene, Book 19, pg.486, 8/25/1910

Troxell, Thomas, Dabw, Minnie T., Book 13, pg.166, 8/22/1901; Trostle, W.A., Schwartz, A.A., Book 2, pg.272, 12/20/1886

Trexler, William L., Mmuim, Clara J., Book 15, pg.401, 12/31/1904

Dauphin, Pa., St. Johns Lutheran, Burysburg, DAR Library
Ignatius Dresel m. 1864

Genealogies of Pennsylvania Families, from the Pa. Geo. Mag. Vol.III, Indexed by Robert and Catherine Barnes, Baltimore Genealogical Pub. 1982 pg.27, Vincent Stauffer, Warwick Twp., Lancaster Pa., Germany Twp., York Co., has child John Vincent, b. 3/12/1741 who was a Blacksmith and m. Veronica Troxel on

6/15/1762 dau. of John Draschel of LeeHigh Co., Pa. Archives 6th

Series, Vol.6, pg.256.

## Rev. Johanner Heinrich Helfrich Records, DAR Library
pg.450, 1/11/1801, John Walbert et Catharina Dresher, Longswamp Berks, Schwm

10/27/1801; Fred. Gaumer, et Salome Dach, Milford Lehigh (Dach with umlat)

pg.451, 5/1/1803, Longswamp Berks, Fred. Braun et Elizabeth Drexel, Lehigh

Rsh.87, pg.452, 6/10/1804, Longswamp Berks, Jonathan Haas et Catharina Trexsler

Rsh.87, 3/10/1805, Longswamp, Benjamin Trexsler, et Mariga Drescher

pg.454, 3/2/1807, Christian Miller et Susannah Drescher Domi

pg.451, 12/11/1803, Longswamp Berks, Samuel Drescher m. Catharina Kaysser

Rsh.57, pg.446, 12/3/1793, Lorentz Troxel m. Christina Reichard, Weisenburg, Leehigh Co., Pa.

Rsh.151 pg.449, 4/2/1799, Domi, Peter Traxel m. Magdlna Seigfried

## The Lancaster Journal Newspaper, LHS
Rsh.135 pg.550, 2/4/1801, m. Mr. George Trissler to Miss Kitty Erler; Rsh.27, pg.554, m. 10/17/1801 on Tuesday evening last, Mr. Conrad Doll to Miss Mary Trissler, all of Lancaster; pg.349, Pa. Evening Post 1775, 4/13/ Thursday m. Robert Roberts to Miss Katy Deshler, dau. of Mr. David Deshler, Merchant of Philadelphia

## Montgomery Co., Pa., Grantor Index, Deeds, MCCH
note: date furnished is that of deed not marriage. Peter Trexler m. Agness_____, 10/19/1801, L. Merion Twp., Book 15, pg.62, land was granted to Peter Trexler and Agness his wife on 9/24/1796.

## Northanpton Co., Pa., Prothonotary, NCA
note: date is that of document found in above Court record not that of marriage. Peter Troxel, Traxel, Jr., m. Mary Shryver,Shuyver, 4/12/1807, Book 20, pg.218

## Philadelphia, Pa., Pennsylvania Archives, Series 2, Vol.2, Vol.9,

Marriage Record 1745-1800, St. Michaels and Zion Lutheran
Church, LC
    pg.293, Philip Trissler, 6/12/1787
    pg.322, 2/10/1763, Elias Ludwig Treichel m. Maria Elizabeth
Pfeiffer
    pg.370, 10/22/1779, Michael Trissler, (Baker) m. Catharine
Radinger, (L)
Rsh.45, pg.373, 6/26/1781, David Drechsler, widower, m.
Elizabeth Molow, widow.

Philadelphia, Pa., American Catholic Historical Society,
pg.137,170, Father Farmer's Marriage Register 1758-1786,
Preserved at St. Joseph's Church, Philadelphia,
    9/25/1758, Chapel in Philadelphia, Joseph Harakaum m.
Mary Magdalen Trostler, widow.

York Co., Pa., Marriages found in the Land Records, Courthouse,
Lancaster, Pa.
author's note:  date is date of transaction not marriage
    11/20/1763, Frederick Trissel, Millright, of Shrewsbury Twp.,
m. Mary

York Co., Pa., Marriage Index, from Newspapers, DAR
Publication, Vol.II, 1783-1850, DAR
Rsh.61      Jeremiah Trexler m. Charlott Wearly, both of York,
           6/22/1828, Rev. Schumuker; Gazette, 6/24/1828;
           German Gazette, 6/27/1828; York Recorder,
           6/24/1828


**VIRGINIA**

Botetourt County, Va. Early Marriages, Wills and Some Rev. War
Records, Anne Lowry Worrell, Baltimore Genealogical Pub. Co.,
1985
    pg.47, Tressler, William m. Margaret Brummer, dau. John
Bummer, 5/26/1820
    pg.47, Tressler, John m. Mary Fudge, dau. Christian Fudge,
11/8/1810
DAR
    Conrad Bronamer m. Barbara Trexler, 2/4/1795, wit: Henry

Trexler, Barbara, age 21, Botetourt Co., Va.

Frederick Co., Va. Marriages, Courthouse, Winchester, Va.
George Trisler and Ann Bulger, 12/25/1792, Minister Alex Balmain
George Trisler and Rosannah Hottel, 1/2/1800, Minister Christian Streit
Susan Trisler m. Landon Cochran 1/7/1815, Minister James Walls
Catherine Trisler m. James McBride, 10/8/1798, Minister Alex Balmain

Richmond Marriage Bonds, 1797-1853, Genealogical Pub. Co., Baltimore,Md.,F234.R5R3, Ann Walker Reddy
Rsh.76, Orphan of Ignatius Trexler, Mary Ann Trexler m. to Christian S. Albrecht, 2/16/1842, pg.76,
Rsh.140, 5/1/1843, William Trexler m. to Nancy Ann, w/o James Hughes
Rsh.76, Orphan of Ignatius Trexler, Rosetta Trexler m. Gottlieb Allbrecht, 6/22/1843, pg.80

Rockingham Co., Va. Marriages, John Vogt and T. Wm. Kethley, Jr., Iberian Publ, Athens, Ga.
George Tressler m. Molly Boroughliker, 1794, of Daniel Buricker, German, brother David Buricker
Charles Tressler m. Molly Borongliker, 1794, bondsman David Buricker, German, dau. of Daniel Buricker

Shenandoah Co., Va. Marriages, DAR Library
John Trixler to Elizabeth Finder, 9/4/1799, she a widow
Margaret Tresler m. Christian Snider, 10/5/1798, brother Jacob Tresler
Mary Tresler m. Martin Feagle, 4/6/1799, brother Andrew Tresler
Mary Tresler m. John Wilkins, 12/21/1822, brother George Hottle
John Trisler, son of George, m. Jedidah Smoot dau. of Leonard, 6/29/1821

## REVOLUTIONARY WAR SERVICE
## MARYLAND

Frederick Co., Md., Pennsylvania Germans in the Settlement of
Maryland, Lancaster Pa., 1914 Daniel Wunderlich, Neade, Md.,
Lancaster Pa., 1914, Genealogical Publ. Balt. 1975
　　　　pg.174, Fort Frederick, Md. Privates Goodhert Tressel,
Abraham Troxal, Jr., Jacob Royer, Adam Coon (Kuhn), John
Robinson, in Rev. War Company as Privates on 7/27/1778
guarding prisoners in Capt. John Kershners Co.
　　　　pg.180, Rsh.42, at meeting to protest taxes, Maryland
Gazette gives account of meeting held in Frederick Co., Md.
8/28/1770, near Troxell's Mill on Tom's Creek. Present were
Charles Robinson, Frederick Troxell both citizens of Tom's Creek,
Md.
　　　　pg.222, The Flying Camp, Jno Troxel, Private, Thomas
Robison, Private, Abram Troxel
　　　　　(The German Regiment, 2 companies in Frederick Co., Md.,
　　　　　2 companies in Baltimore Co., Md.)

Mdhr, Index 47, Oaths of Fidelity
Anne Arundel Co., Md., James Tootell, Richard Tootell
Frederick Co., Md., John Theser, Benjamin Thrasher, John
Trasher, Thomas Trasher, Michael Tripler, John Troxall
Montgomery Co., Md., Jacob Trissler, John Trundel, Josiah
Trundel, Thomas Trundel.
Rsh.30 Jacob Trissler

Mdhr 1778, Montgomery Co., Box 4, folder 1, pg.1, 3/2/1778
taken by Richard Thompson, in order next to Frederick & Leonard
Kogendorger and John Middaugh.
Prince Georges Co., Md., Charles Tressies
Washington Co., Md., Goodhart Tresal, Geroge Troseel, Abraham
Troxal, Abraham Troxal, Louson Toller

Washington Co., Md., Maryland Militia in Rev. War, F. Edward
Wright, Family Line 1978 pg.237, Washington Co., Md., 1 Corp.
Peter Tresler, Capt. Nichodemus Company 2nd Batt #6
Rsh.30  pg.199, Montgomery Co., Md., Jacob Trisler

pg.207, 8th Co., Montgomery Co., Md., Class #1, Jacob Trisler
pg.247, Washington Co., Md., Capt. Martin Kershners Co., 4th
Corp. Jacob Trisher, 4th Class, George Troxel, 3rd Class,
Abraham Troxell

## PENNSYLVANIA

Pennsylvania Archives, Series 2, Vol.10, LC
pg.448, 2nd Pa., Continental Line, David Trexler, 1/1/1777-
1781; Ludwick Tresler
pg.757, 10th Pa., Colonel's Company, John Troxel, 8/1778
Series 2, Vol.13
pg.228, Rev. Soldiers, 1775-1783, Peter Trexler, Jonathan
Trexler
pg.229, Jacob Troxel, John Troxell
Series 5, Vol.3
pg.789, David Drexler, German Regiment of the Continental
Line under Capt. Peter Boyer, Phila. Co., Pa.
Series 6, Vol.2
pg.637, John Dresler, York Co., Pa., Militia under Capt.
Wm. Heffer, 8/29/1781
pg.528, under Wm. Heffer, George Dressler, Michael
Tressler, York Co., Pa. Militia, Capt. Peter Zollinger

Chester County Archives and Records Services, Chester County,
Pa.
Lawrence Trexler, Revolutionary Soldier, pg.627, Pa., Vol.5,
Series 5

DAR, SEMMES MICROFILM CENTER
Rsh.86      John Peter Trexler, was the child of Jermiah Trexler
            who was born in 1708 in Europe as proved by
            national number 4093634474, and his wife was
            Maria Catherine Schumacher. Their children were:
            John Peter Trexler, b. 12/27/1727, Margaret Trexler,
            John Trexler b 1719 m. Maria Elizabeth Bauer
            Hassler, 2nd wife, Susanna.
Rsh.106, Trexler, Emanuel, b.c. 1760, d. 5/20/1822 m. Catherine,
soldier, Pa., on 3/11/1781 took oath of Allegiance before Peter
Trexler in Northampton Co., Pa. On 4/22/1782 he is found on
Muster Roll of Capt. John Jacoby, Militia Co., 2nd Class, Ist

Battalion, as proved by National number 689587, Mary "Polly" daughter of Jonathan Trexler was b. 5/11/1819, Jackson Ohio, she was the daughter of Jonathan Trexler b. 11/14/1791 and his wife, Rachael Martin. Jonathan Trexler was the son of Emanuel Trexler, proved by National number 590936. Emanuel Trexler was born 1760 in Northampton, Pennsylvania and m. Catherine Cameron of Lancaster, Pennsylvania on 5/7/1785. The children of Emanuel Trexler and Catherine Cameron are:

Susanna Trexler m. John Jacobs  4/25/1809
Mary Trexler m. William Spriggs
Hannah Trexler m. Notingham Mercer, 12/1/1814
Rachael Trexler m. Nathan Stewart, 3/5/1815
Catherine Trexler m. Moses Faught
Elizabeth Trexler m. Collins Bennett
Samuel Trexler b. 6/1/1787, d. 10/24/1850 m. Harriet
    Mercer, 5/4/1828
Jonathan Trexler b. 11/4/1791 d. 1/29/1880 m.
    Rachael Martin 1815
John Trexler m. Nancy Price
David Trexler m. Sarah Crabtree, 4/12/1826

DAR Library Patriots Index
Rsh.27  George Trisler b. 1/25/1754, d. 9/30/1796, m. Elizabeth Robinson; Capt. Pa.
Rsh.30  Jacob Trisler (Trissler) b. 8/25/1744; d. 10/20/1821, m. Mary ____; public service, Md.

DAR Library Revolutionary Pensions
    Tresler, Frederick, service Maryland and Pennsylvania, RI0696, Chambersburg, Franklin Co., Pa., 21st Day, 1842, Frederick Tresler age 83 born 1759, Resided in Frederick Co., Md., Chambersburg, Franklin Co., Pa., volunteer in 1779, at a place called the Trap in north Amton Co., State of Pa., he was born in 1759, and has lived near Pipe Creek, Frederick Co., Md., recently. He served two tours of duty.

NA, Revolutionary War Records
    David Trexler, Pa., recorded as David Trixler, Private 9th Pa. Index 4371
    Ludwick Trexler, Pvt. 5th Pa., filed as Ludwick Tresler Index 4372

Rsh. 5, Anthony Trexler, 4th Company, York, Pa.

# WAR OF 1812 SERVICE

## INDIANA

Rsh.94, James Trasler, <u>NA</u> SO11487, SC15715 Capt. Clements Co., Indiana Militia, James Trasler Connersville Fayette Co., Ind., Capt. Fred Sholts Co., Kent Militia disc. 3/1/1813.  On 4/17/1871 James Trusler was 77 years old and a resident of Fayette Co., Ind.  His wife's maiden name was Anna Martin and he married her in or near Brookville, Ind. on 8/19/1813.

## LOUISIANA

<u>NA War 1812 Index</u>
Andre Troxclair, 5th Reg. (LaBranches) La. Mil. Sgt.
George Troxler, 8th Reg. (Merions) La. Mil. Pvt.
Guan Troxello, 8th Reg. (Merioms) La. Mil. Pvt.
Jasques Troxler, 8th Reg. Merioms) La. Mil. Pvt.
Christopher Troxclair, 5th Reg. LaBranches La Mil. Pvt.
Pierre Troxclair, 5th Reg. LaBranches La. Mil. Pvt
Firmans Troxclair, 5th Reg. LaBranches La. Mil. Pvt
Francaes Troxclair, 5th Reg. LaBranches La. Mil. Pvt
J.B. Troxclair, 5th Reg. LaBranches La. Mil. Pvt
Antoine Troxclair, 5th Reg. (LaBranches) La Mil. Pvt.

## MARYLAND

<u>Maryland Militia War 1812, F. Edward Wright, E359.5.M2W8</u>
Isaac A. Trexler; Peter Trexler; Rsh.76, Ignatius Trexlear

<u>Baltimore City 1st Artillery Regiment Aug. 9-16, 1813, MHS</u>
Rsh.29, John Hitselberger; Rsh.76, Ignatius Trexlear

<u>The Citizen Soldiers at North Point and Fort McHenry on September 12 and 13, 1814, Charles C. Saffell, Baltimore Md. Extracts from Original rolls in 3rd Auditors Office War Department. published on the 75 Anniversary 1889.</u>
Rsh.76        pg.18, "United Maryland Artillery", James Piper Capt., Ignatius Trexlear.

<u>British Invasion of Maryland 1812-1815 by William M. Marine, MHS</u>

pg.265, George Delcher, Private in Capt. Montgomery's Co., Baltimore Artillery; John Delcher, Private in Capt. Hanna's Co., Fells Point Light Dragoons; Thomas Delcher, Private in Capt. Chalmers Co., 51st Rgt.; James Delsher, Private in Capt. Pinkney's Artillery Co.

pg.266, Wlliam Delsher, Private in Capt. Steever's Co., 27th Reg.

## NA, War 1812 Index

George Delcher, Sea Fencildes Vols., Pvt
George Delcher, 51 Reg.(Ameys Md.) Mil.
John Delcher, 5th Regt. Cav.(Biays) Md. Mil.
Thomas Delcher, 51 Reg. (Ameys) Md. Mil., Pvt.
George Delsher, 1st Reg. Art, (Harris) Md. Mil.
James Delsher, Capt. Pinkneys Co., Art, Md. Mil. Pvt.
James Delsher/Delshire, Capt. Wells Co., Arty Md. Mil., Pvt., org. filed under James Duleher
William Delsher, 27th Reg.(Longs) Md. Mil., Pvt.
Rsh.76  Ignatius Trexlear, Pvt., widow, Nancy, Maryland, WO 1942
?Rsh.5  Peter Trexler, Pvt. 2nd Regt.(Heaths) Maryland Mil.
Rsh.69  Jacob Troxal, 2nd Regt.(Heaths) Md. Mil., original filed as Troxell
George Troxel, 2 Reg. Md. Mil., Lieutenant
Jacob Troxel, 2nd Reg. Md. Mil. Pvt.
John Troxel, 1 Reg. (Ragans) Md. Mil., Pvt.
Peter Troxel, 2 Reg. Md. Mil., Pvt.
Jacob Troxell, 32 Reg. (Hoods) Md. Mil., Lieutenant
Philip Troxell, 2nd Reg. (Heaths) Md. Mil., Sgt.
Philip I. Trussell, 4 Reg. Md. Mil., Pvt.
Philip I. Trusil, Capt. Thos Co., Art, Md. Mil., Malroe, Boudardier

## WAR 1812, Maryland Militia, MHS

George Delsher, John Delsher, Thomas Delsher, James Delcher, William Delcher; Henry Tresler, Maryland Militia 3rd Reg.; Isaac A. Trexler, Maryland Militia

## MHS, Newspapers file

8/26/1812, vol. of Conocheague, Philip Tresler, Maryland Militia. (Conocheague area is West of Hagerstown, Md.)

## War of 1812 Files read at NA

John Delcher, widow Sarah J., Pvt. Capt. Hannas Co., Md. Mil., enl. 8/19/1814, disc. 11/18/1814, WO34744/WC20845, residence of widow 1851, 1855, 1879, Baltimore, Md., soldiers first wife Elizabeth Ann Kelly, maiden name of widow Sarah J. Kelley., soldier and widow m. 12/14/1823, Baltimore Md., soldier d. 1/18/1847, Baltimore, Md.

Rsh.63 Henry Tressler, WO33877, WC22082, wife's maiden name Margaret Jordan she was b. 1800. Capt. Galets Co., Md. Mil, drafted in or near Emmitsborough Md., 7/1813 or 14 when he was 22 (b. 1791) a farmer, b. near Abbottstown Pa., 5'll 1/2" tall, dark brown hair, dark eyes, blond completion. Married near Emmitsburgh, Co. of Frederick, Md., on 3/24/1820, he d. Brookfield, Stark Co., Ohio, 8/23/1844. Moved to Ohio from near Emmitsbough in 1834.

Rsh.8 Abraham Troxell, SO 7976, Svs. Capt. Wm. Merediths Co., Pa. Mil., Residence Baltimore, Md. 1871, b. 1788, vol. at Adams Co., Pa., 9/1/1814, disc. at Baltimore, fought in Battle of North Point in defense of Baltimore City. Samuel Jennings and James Elmore test to his loyalty, 7/29/1871. Abraham Troxell made mark.

Rsh.69 Jacob Troxel, SO3115/SC3430, b. 1794, Pvt. Capt. S. Ogles Co., Md. Mil., residence Piney Creek, Carroll Co., Md., 3/20/1871 he is 77 years old, wifes maiden Elizabeth Green, m. in 1838, drafted in Capt. Ogles Co. under Col. Heath, disc. Baltimore 7/1813

Philip J. Trusil, Capt. C. Vickers, Md. Mil., SO3805/SC22531, WO34517, WC22818, 497 W. Lexington St. Baltimore, Md. Capt. E. Vickers, Md. Mil., on 3/8/1871 he is 79 years. Mary Ann Grace was wife's maiden name, m. 12/25/1815, Col. Aulds Md. Mil. disc. Easton, Md. Talbot, at Battle of St. Michales, he enl. at Easton, on 12/5/1878 she was 71, they lived in Gettysburg Pa., for 20 years, then Columbia Pa., then Baltimore, he d. 11/28/1878, at the age of 86, b. Austria, Germany, lived in Baltimore 60 years, bur. at Mt. Olive, children Lezzie V. Gerusil, and Emma P. Mullikiu

Rsh.76 Ignatius Trexlear, WO 1942, His widow, Nancy Ann Murray Trexler, in an attempt to prove service included the following statements by her daughter-in-law, Nancy Ellis Trexler Liggon widow of William Trexler (Rsh.140), in file: Grandson John Ignatius Trexler was named for his grandfather Ignatius and went by the name of Nace until such time as several acquaintances, who to annoy him, would have it Natious. Then he changed his name to John;  Rent Receipt dated 10/12/1870 shows grandson's name to be William Dresler.  "Such errors we know are very common, especially in writing German names."  Ignatius Trexler and Nancy Ann Murray m. 11/8/1812 in St. John's German Catholic Church by Father Nicholas Mertz, Witnesses George Poh, John Robsen, marriage license issued by the Clerk of the Court of Baltimore issued a license to Nathan Truxall and Nancy Murry.  They moved in 1817 to Richmond, Va., where Ignatius d. 8/6/1827. On a 3/14/1855 claim to the Pension Office widow Ann Reseler (Preseler), Pn. No. 901 makes application for bounty land.  Nancy Trexler w/o of Ignatius d. 5/12/1871.  On 4/10/1871 the War of 1812 file states "and I also certify that Mrs. Trexler is ill and seemed to be a great sufferer and I doubt not if she were put in a carriage and carried to the Clerk's Office the result would be quite serious.  Frank T. Sutton, Notary."  Her claim for Pension was approved 9/24/1880 and $22.00 was due her heirs.

## NORTH CAROLINA

NA, Pension Files
Rsh.73  Barney Troxler, SO 27914, SC 19610, Capt. James Grahams Co., N.C. Mil., wife's maiden name Polly Pnletck, he was b. in 1795, his service at Norfolk, Va., living at Summerfield, Guilford Co., N.C.

NA. War of 1812 Index
Rsh.73, Barnabus Troxler, 5 Reg. (Atkinsons) N.C. Mil., Pvt.
Ezekiel Trussell, Major Lillegtons Det. N.C. Mil., Pvt.
Ezekiel Trussell, New Hanover Reg. (Noxons) N.C. Mil., Pvt.
Ezeker Trussel, 4th Reg. (Rowlands) N.C. Mil., Pvt.
Nicholas Troxler, 5yh Reg. (Atkinsons) N.C. Mil., Pvt.
John Troxler, Capt. Sundands Co. N.C. Mil., Pvt.
John Troxler, 5 Reg. (Atkinsons N.C. Mil., Pvt.

## OHIO

Rsh.72  William C. Troxell, WO32957, wife's maiden name Mary Brubaker, he d. Greenfield Ohio, 5/23/1856, when enl. he was 5'8" with light completion, grey eyes, auburn hair and heavy built.  She was b. in 1800. He enl. in Greenfield, Ohio.
Rsh.106  Jonathan Trexler, SO 33437, SC 23665, Capt. John Lindsay Co., Ohio Mil., b. 1792, enl. in Sciota Co., Ohio,

disc. in Chittocothe, Ohio, witness a son William W. Trexler b. 1835, lived in Ohio Jackson Co., 41 years from 1812-1853 and from 1853-1878 in Jasper Co., Ohio. He was 21 years old when enl. in 1812, occp. farmer, b. in Pennsylvania. 5'10" fair hair, eyes blue, completion fair, has brother John I. Trexler. Pension stopped 12/4/1879 because he had died.

NA, War 1812 Index
Isaac Troxell, Renicks Mtd. Reg. Ohio, Vol. and Mil., Pvt.
Joseph Troxell, Adams Reg. Ohio Mil., Pvt.
Jonathan Truxler, 2nd Reg.(Fergusons) Ohio Mil., Pvt.

## PENNSYLVANIA

Catholic Trails West, ibid
pgs.651,652, War of 1812, 33 of parish of St. Michaels followed Capt. Richard McGuire among them was Jacob Troxel, Jacob and John Will. Prince Gattilzin assisted in drilling the troops. 1st Battalion 142 Regt. Pa. Mil. Unit supported attack against Niagria Falls.

NA, War of 1812 Records
Rsh.6  The State of Ohio, Wayne County, Anthony Trexell, (made mark) on 9/28/1850 that he entered the war at Gettysburg, Pa., and was a Private commanded by Captain John McMillan in the 20th Regiment of Pennsylvania Vols., on or about 2/15/1814; served at Buffalo and Ft. Erie received injury to right leg, David Cooper served with Anthony Trexell and confirms what he says, State of Indiana, Allen County 6/10/1852 Anthony Trexell appears and states that he is a native of Adams County, Pa., is 73 years old and entered the service at Gettysburg, Pa., active in the recapture of Fort Erie and while landing crushed his leg causing a bad wound, scouted for the Battle of Chippewa of 7/5/1814, rec. musket or rifle ball wound and was honorably disc. he now resides at Fort Wayne, Allen County, Ind., and his children have since died; State of Wisconsin, County of Marquette, 5/12/1855 resident of Waushara County, State of Wisconsin, signed name.
Rsh.84  Israel Trexler, So8580, Sc6626, age 79, 4/16/1871 (b. 1792), wife's maiden name Hannah Ott, enl. 5/30/1813, disc. Philadelphia, residence Allentown, Lehigh Co., Pa., Hanover Twp.
Rsh.67  Abraham Troxel, WO44,999, WC 35,265, Capt.

John Jenkins Co., Pa. Mil., in 1847 living in Goff, Memaha, Newsha, Kansas, wife's maiden name Margaret Lymann, m. 1/1822 at Canton, Ohio, Peter Troxel has known Margaret for 57 years and Clarasy Troxel has known Margaret for 51 years testify for her. Abraham Troxel d. 8/1847.

Rsh.70 Christian Troxel, WO2701, WC 4761, Capt. Dinkeys Co., Pa. Mil., wifes maiden name Barbara Cru, he d. 1827, she at Allentown, Lehigh Co., Pa., enrolled at Allentown, (disc. Philadelphia,) m. by Rev.Gobrecht, 1/15/1806, she was b. 1787.

Rsh.68 Daniel Troxell, SO 3960, Pa. Mil., wife maiden name Catherine Jacoby, she was b. 1789 and they were married 10/9/1815 at Trexlertown, Leehigh Co., Pa., Solome Wiedes gave test of wedding and Jonathan Schaffer and Philip Beas gave test. of funeral of Daniel.

Rsh.71 Jacob Troxell, WO 32,554, WC 19,305, Capt. Nez Middleworths Co., Pa. Mil., wifes maiden name Sarah Grimm, m. 1819, in Swimeford, Pa., Minister Rev. Freize, vol. Union Co., Pa., d. 8/1852, Pleasant Valley, Illinois. Isaac W. Parkmen age 74 in 1878 and Peter Bishop age 77 in 1878, test to her signature. Jacob Torxell was b. in Union Co., Pa., in 1796 and when enl. he was 5'11" light brown hair, blue eyes, fair complexion. They moved from Pa. to Ill. in 1842, by 1879 pension was stopped because Sarah had died.

Jacob Truxel, SO34555, Sc25493, Pvt. Capt. James McClintock, Pa. Mil., On 7/1/1879 Jacob Trussel was 83 (b. 1796) and living in Ripleyville, Huron Co., Ohio. At time of enlistment he was 5'8" tall had blue eyes, hair was dark and complexion light or brownish. Rubecca Truxel was his guardian in 1879 because he is a "person insane, both deaf and dumb and cannot talk." Jacob Truxel d. 10/19/1882.

NA, 1812 Service Index

Christian Traxal, 1st Regt. Riflemen (Humphreys) original filed as Troxel, Pa. Militia, rank Sgt.

Jacob Traxel, 1st Bat. Riflemen (Uhlers) Pa., Vol. Pvt.

Jacob Traxel, 134th Regt. (Hosacks,) Pa. Mil., Pvt.

Peter Traxell, Capt. Ruch's Troop Light Dragoons, Pa. Mil.

Peter Trraxeller, 2nd Reg. Light Inf. (Bache's) Pa., Orig. filed under Philip Trumheller

John Traxler, 2nd Reg. (Lofas) Pa. Mil., Fifer

John Trexell, 71st Reg. (Hutters) Pa. Mil., Sgt.

Charles Trexler, Pvt., Pa.

Israel Trexler, Pvt., Pa.

Jacob Trexler, Pvt., Pa.

John Trexler, Pvt., Pa.

John Trexler, Pvt., Pa.

Jonas Trexler, Fifer, Pa.

Jonathan Trexler, Pvt.. Pa.

Jacob Trexler, Pa.

John Trexler, Pa.

Daniel Trosall, 71st Regt. (Hullers) Pa. Mil., original filed as Trosell

Abram Troxal, Coheans Batt. Pa., Vol., Pvt. Original filed as Troxel

Abraham Troxel, 5th Batt. (Nelsons) Pa. Mil.

Anthony Troxel, 4th Reg. (Fentons) Pa. Mil.

Jacob Troxel, Mont. Reg. Pa. Mil., Pvt.

Jacob Troxel, 2nd Reg. Riflemons (Pipers) Pa. Mil., Sgt.

William Troxel, 134th Regt. (Hosacks) Pa. Mil., Pvt.

David Troxsell, 2nd Reg. Light Inf. (Baches) Pa. Mil., Pvt.

John Troxsell, 71st Reg. (Hullers) Pa. Mil.

Michael Troxell, 2nd Reg. L. Inf. (Baches) Pa. Mil., Pvt.

Daniel Troxsell, 2nd Reg. L. Inf. (Baches) Pa Mil., Pvt.


### Pennsylvania Archives, 2nd Series, Vol.12, LC

pg.63, Jonathan Bressler, Peter Bressler, 2nd Reg., 2nd Brigade, Pa. Militia, under Lt.Col. John Lotz, at York Pa., from 9/1/1814 to 12/4/1815 from Berks Co.

pg.66, Capt. George F. Coldovey's Co., 10/23/1814, Daniel Draxel

pg.95, Capt. Adam Diller's Co. Infantry, 2nd Reg., 2nd Brig. Pa. Militia under Lt.Col. John Lotz at York, Pa., in service from 9/1/1814 to 3/5/1815, John Trossil

pg.96, Capt. George Dinckeys Co., 18th section of Riflemen, Col. Thomas Humphrey, Sgt. Christian Traxel

pg.142, Capt. George Frysingers, Co., 3rd Regiment, 1st Brigade, Col. LeFever who rendezvoused at Hanover, 10/15 to 22/1814: Jacob Troesler

pg.166, Roll of Capt. Valentine Haas, Co., Inf. 10/31/1814, 77 Regiment: John Trester

pg.182, Capt. Wm. Hamilton Co., Rifle Regiment, 2nd Brigade, Pa., Militia, John Trissler pg.195, Capt. Adam Hawks Co., 1st detachment, 23nd Brigade, Sgt. John Troxel

pg.241, Vol. Rifleman, Capt. John Junkin, 134th Regiment now in 5th Batt. of the 2nd detachment, Comm by Major David Nelson, 10/2/1812 to 4/1813, Abraham Troxel

pg.272, Capt. Richard Maguires Co., Rifle Co., attached to 1st Battalion, 142nd, Regiment, Pa. Militia, Jacob Troxel

pg.351, John Trissler, Roll of Capt. George Musser's Co., Rifle Reg. 2nd Brigade Pa., at York from Lancaster

pg.360, 4th Capt. Nungesser Co., 2nd Reg. Vol. Lighty Inf. under comm. of Col. Louis Bache, 8/27/1814, Michael Troxell

pg.369, Capt. Wm. Painters Co., 2nd Brig. 1st Div. Pa., under Col. John Thompson, Jonathan Trexler

pg.372, Capt. James Perle's Co., 1st Brig. 1st Div. Col. Peter L. Berry, 11/23/1814, to 1/2/1815, Philadelphia, Jacob Trexler

pg.391, Benevolent Blues, under Major Samuel Shacks, Capt. Henry Read from Northern Liberties, John Trexler

pg.506, Lt. Charles Westphals Co., Infantry, 2nd Brigade, 1st division 9/14/1814, Philadelphia: Jonathan Trexler


Pennsylvania Archives, 6th Series, Vol.7, LC
pg.347, Muster Rolls 1812-1814

Rsh.6 Anthony Truxel, return of Capt. John McMillen's Co., 3/9/1814, 26th Regiment, 2nd Brigade and 5th Division of Pennsylvania Militia

pg.59, John Trexler, Pvt., 9/7/1814 for 6 months, Benevolent Blues, Major Samuel Sparks Battalion, Capt. Henry Read, Co. of Philadelphia, Northern Liberties, 12/31/1814

pg.96, Jacob Trexler, Sgt., Philadelphia, Pa., 28th Regiment, Pa. Militia, 1st Co.

pg.144. 1st Brigade, 2nd Div. Pa. Mil., 2/22/1814, John Trexler

Rsh.6   pg.347, Muster Rolls 1812-1814, Adams Co., Pa., Anthony Truxel, return of Capt. John McMillen's Co., 3/9/1814, 26th Regiment, 2nd Brigade and 5th Division of Pennsylvania Militia

pg.438, Pa., Vol. R.S., 87th Reg. 2/1814, John Trexler

pg.555, 94th Regiment, Nicholas Saeger, Brigade 1812, John Droxell, Northampton Co., Pa.

Pennsylvania Archives, 6th Series, Vol.8, pg.16, War of 1812, LC

Lists of NCO's and Privates of Capt. John McMillans Co. of Col. Fenton's Regt. of Pennsylvania Militia who crossed the Niagara into Canada:

Rsh.6 Anthony Troxel, paid $10. 5th Detachment of Pennsylvania Militia, Adams County, Pennsylvania, sworn and subscribed 5/29/1816.

NA, Unindexed Bounty Land Records
Rsh.6 Anthony Troxel, Pvt. Capt. John McMillans Co., 5th Regt. Pa. Mil 5 (Fentons), 6/15 to 8/24/1814, Comm. 2/26/1814, on Command, 2/26 to 6/15/1814, Present: Anthony Truxel, 6/16 to 8/24/1814, travelled 360 Miles, 18 days at .25 per day, 18 rations at .17., Anthony Throxel, 2/26 to 6/15/1814

# VIRGINIA

NA, War of 1812 Index
George Troxall, 5th Regt. Va. Mil., Pvt.
Daniel Troxell, 4 Regt. (Boyds) Va. Mil., Sgt/Pvt
William Trussell, 45 Regt. (Peytons) Va. Mil., Pvt.
Henry Trusler, Flying Camp (McDowells) Va. Mil., Pvt.
John Trussel, 45 Regt. (Peytons) Va. Mil., Pvt.
Charles Trussel, Greens Regt. Mt. Inf. Va. Mil., Pvt.
John Trussel, Robert (Crutchfields) Detach. Va. Mil., Pvt.

VSL, War of 1812 Index
Peter Tresler, 5th Regt. Va. Militia
John Tresslar, 108 Regt. Shanklins, Va. Mil.

NA, Pension Records
John Tresslar, SO 4420, Pvt. Capt. Andrew Beirnes, Va. Mil., enrolled in Montgomery Co., Va. 1/14/1813, served in Ohio Militia 21 days., his wife d. 10/19/1857, does not name her, "witness states Mr. Tressler is quite old and his memory is almost gone., 88 years old (b1782) witnesses Peter A. Trester, John N. Tresler.

Rsh.93 Henry Dressler, WP32565. Capt. Robert Kiles Co., or Capt. Chyles Co., Va. Militia. Henry Dresslar married Elizabeth in Bath Co., State of Virginia on 3/19/1818 and Minister was Elisha Knox. He d. Johnson Co., Indiana. He enl. in Finecastle, Va. was disc. at Norfolk. On 9/30/1878 she was 80 years old. He d. Johnson Co., Ind. 3/17/1858.

Townsend, Trusler, Edmund M. Cobbs, resident of Cooper Co., Missouri, SO1599 SC5691 alleges he served as a substitute for Townsend Trusler in Capt. Wiatts Co., Va. Militia. Cobbs vol. in Lynchburg, Va. as a substitute for Townsend Trisoler in July of 1814 and served 6 months at Ft. Barber near Norfolk. In 1816 he left his brunk remains in Lynchburg, Va. when he went to the western country and during the term of 55 years they were lost. Cobbs d. at Lookout, Mo. 12/1881.

Henry Dresslar, widow, Elizabeth, WO32565, Chyles Co., Va. Mil.

# MILITIA SERVICE

## NEW JERSEY

New Jersey in 1793, Militia Census by James S. Norton, LC
　　pg.191, Peter Traxler, HunterDon County, New Jersey, Kingwood Militia, year 1793
　　pg.176, Henry Traxler, Amwell Militia

## PENNSYLVANIA

Pennsylvania Archives, 6th Series, Vol.3, LC
　　pg.133, Peter Traxler, Haverford Company, Chester Co., Pa., year 1786
　　Rsh.11, pg.688, Lt. Henry Troxel, Montgomery Co., Pa., Militia, 4/1786
　　Rsh.11, pg.720, Henry Troxel, Gwynedd Twp., Montgomery, Pa., 5/2/1786
　　Rsh.11, pg.721, Jacob Troxel, Gwynedd Twp., Montgomery, Pa., 5/2/1786"
　　pg.704, Joseph Traxler, George Ehrman, males between 18 and 53, Whitemarsh Twp., Montgomery, Co., Pa., 5/17/1785
　　pg.710, Lt. Henry Troxel, Jacob Troxel, males of the Lower Dist. of Gwynedd Twp., 1785, Montgomery, Pa.
　　pg.731, Jeremiah Trexler, males 18-53 years, Lower Merrion Twp,, Montgomery Co., Pa.
　　pg.1465 and 66, Michael Ressler/Kessler, Hennery Ressler/Kessler, Muster Roll of Capt. Henery Mathias Co., 1784, York Co., Pa.
　　pg.1476, Michael Ressler/Kessler, Hennery Ressler/Kessler, Muster Roll of Capt. Hennery Mathias Co. 1785, York Co., Pa.
　　pg.769, Jacob Trancklor, 8th Co. Second Batt., Phillip Behm, Northampton Co., Pa., 4/19/1785; Adam Traxel, 5th Co. 34th Bat. 6/1/1784, Northampton Co., Pa.
　　Rsh.85　pg.776, Commanded by Col. Peter Trexler, Capt. Jacob Grims Co., 3rd Batt., Northampton Co. Pa., 6/16/1784
　　pg.777, Rsh.88, Jeremiah Trexler; Rsh.89, Jonathan Trexler; Rsh.87, Peter Trexler
　　pg.781, Adam Traxel, Christian Traxel, 5th Co., 3rd Batt. Northampton, Co., Pa., 4/27/1785
　　pg.814, Traxel, 2nd Co. 6th Batt., Northampton Co., Pa.,

5/8/1784

pg.835, Sgt. Nicholas Traxel, 2nd Co. 6th Batt. Northampton Co., Pa., Capt. Jacob Arndt, Jr.

pg.865, 1st Bat., Capt. Jeremiah Trexler, Capt. Philip Wolfersberger Co., 2nd Batt. of Dauphin Co., Pa., Militia, 5/20/1789

pg.371, Jacob Traxel

pg.372, John Traxel

pg.373,374, Jacob Traxel, John Traxel, 10/27/1789

pg.389, Jacob Troxdel

pg.390, Jacob Troxel, 5th Co. 4th Batt. of Dauphin Co. 1787, Pa. Militia

pg.406, Jacob Troxdale, Capt. Robert McCallens, Co., April and May 1786

pg.447, John Troxtil, Capt. Phillip Wolfelsbarger's, LondonDerry Twp., Dauphin Co., Pa., 10/19/1786, Capt. James Igoe Co., Huntingdon Co., Pa.

pg.33, Christian Troxel, Jr., Bethel Twp., Peter Smith, 2/3/1789, Bedford Co., Pa.

## KENTUCKY

The Kentucky Gazette, 1787-1800, Genealogical and Historical
Abstracts, Karen Mauer Green
  Rsh.147, pg.87, Vol.VIII, number XV, 12/28/1793, John
Troxell, Scott County, Ky., 12/17/1793, living on north Elkhorn
Creek about 2 miles from Georgetown, has land for rent.
  Rsh.147, pg.141, John Troxell, Scott County, Ky.,
12/14/1795, executor of the estate of John Troxwell, deceased
regarding the estate sale to be held at the widow Troxwells.
  Rsh.147, pg.135. Vol.IX number IV, 10/10/1795, John
Troxell, 6/1/1795, found a mare in Scott Co., Ky., about 4 miles
from Georgetown.
  pg.191, Vol.X number 546, 8/5/1797, Wm. Owsley reports
that Jacob Troxel found a mare.
  Rsh.64, pg.211, Dr. Peter Trissler, 6/5/1798, living on the
main fork of Jessamine Creek in Fayette Co., Ky., gives notice to
debtors, please pay your bills.
  Rsh.64, pg.241, Letter at P.O., Lexington, Vol XIII, number
667, 7/4/1799, Doctor Peter Trisler (Trister) in Jessamine Co., Ky.,
  Rsh.64, pg.253, Vol.XIII, number 695, 1/16/1800, Doctor
Peter Trislie (Trislit) of Jessamine Co., Ky., January 14, 1800
regarding a new shipment of medicines at his office.
  pg.261, Vol.XIII number 716, 6/12/1800, Danville Dist. Court
Suit involving Adam Truxall, John Truxall

## MARYLAND

  author's note:  The Baltimore American 1804-1816
  Newspaper is located at Enoch Pratt Free Library, Baltimore,
  Md., and Baltimore Sun Newspaper is located at MHS.

Baltimore, Md., Marriages & Deaths from Baltimore Newspapers
1796-1816, by Robert Barnes, Baltimore Genealogical Publishing
1978 F189.B153 A22
  pg.326, Trisler, Geo., Editor of Winchester Constitutional
Gazette and Rosanna Wetzell of Winchester were married at
Frederickstown by Rev. Strait. (BA, 1/18/1800)
  Rsh.45, pg.326, Troxil, Michael of Gettysburg, Pa., and Miss

Margaret Markle of Baltimore were married Tuesday 21st Instant by Rev. Kurtz (BA, 5/24/1816)

Rsh.9, pg.2, 2/14/1839, Margaret A. Trexler d. 2/8/1839, age 39, born 1800

Rsh.9, pg.2, 1/2/1844, Catharine C. Trexler m. William Braden, Jr., 12/31/1843

Rsh.9, pg.2, 9/26/1844, Mary A. Trexla m. Piercy

Abstracts of Carroll County Newspapers 1831-1846 - Family Line Publications, Westminster, Maryland  Marlene Bates, F187.C26B38

Rsh.25, pg.9, The Carrolltonian, George Trisler, store in Frederick was forcibly entered on Monday night last. Entrance was forced using an iron lever, which was taken from the railing round the Court House Yard, 11/9/1833.

Rsh.13, pg.19, The Carrolltonian, Notice to Bridge Builders, Proposals for bridge across Tom's Creek on road from Frederick to Emmitsburg where old bridge now stands, signed Frederick Troxel,  Felix B. Taney and John Grabill, 3/14/1835.

Frederick Co., Md., The Hornet, years 1802-1814, pub.Frederick Md., MHS

author's note:  from 1803-1806 entire last page printed in German. Obits were very short and told no family history.

Rsh.75, October 29, 1805, Michael Trisler d. 10/22/1805, an old inhabitant of this town.

Hagerstown Newspapers, HSWC

7/5/1798, Peter Tressler has letters remaining at Post Office
2/5/1808, John Troxel, List of Laws Passed (he was a public official)
4/26/1809, Peter Troxell advertises his trade as a Weaver
10/4/1809, David Troxler has letters remaining at Post Office
12/13/1809, Peter Troxel has real estate for sale
1/3/1810, David Troxler has letters remaining at Post Office
1/15/1812, Jacob Troxler has letters remaining at Post Office
8/26/1812, volunteer of Conocheague, Philip Tresler, Md. Mil.

Hagerstown, Maryland Herald and Hagerstown Weekly Advertiser

#39, 8/26/1812   Vol. Corp. 24, Regt. Md. Militia under command of Capt. Thomas Quantrill for the City of Annapolis, Under Capt.

David Cushwa, Philip Troxell volunteered.

Washington Co., Md., Newspaper Abstracts of Allegheny and Washington Counties Maryland 1811-1815, Family Line Publications F 187.A4N48 1990
pg.107, Jacob Tressler, 6/20/1814, The Maryland Herald and Hagerstown Weekly Advertiser, Jacob Tressler, living on Mr. Swope's old place, 1 mile from Mr. Barton's Tavern, on Little Conococheague, offers reward for muley bull, cow and 5 calves

pg.135, Jacob Tressler, The Maryland Herald and Hagerstown Weekly, 3/29/1815, Jacob Tressler, living 4 miles from Williams-Port, on Little Conochogeaague, (Mr. Swopes old Place) offers reward for horse stolen from his wagon at Mr. Neiff's Tavern, 2 miles from Middletown, on Baltimore Turnpike Rd.
pg.81, Jacob Troxell, The Maryland Herald and Hagerstown Weekly Advertiser, 11/17/1813, Journeyman Cooper wanted at John Cushawa's Mill, 2 miles from John T. Mason's. Jacob Troxell
pg.39, Philip Troxell, The Maryland Herald and Hagerstown Weekly Advertiser, David Cushwa Co., Monday, 8/17/1812 volunteers, Philemon Cromwell, Robert Chambers, George Stinemetz, David Stoltz, Stephen Cromwell, James Myers, Philip Troxell and Abraham Watson

## NORTH CAROLINA

Marriages and Deaths from the Western Carolinas, Salisbury, N.C. 1820-1842, compiled by Robert M. Tompkins 1795, The Reprint Co. Pub., Spartansburg, S.C. 1983
Rsh.122, pg.246, Death, Lawrence Trexler, age about 70, 9/13/1827 in Rowan County, N.C. in 9/25/1827 newspaper

Vol II, Abstracts of Vital Records from Raleigh N.C. Newspapers, 1820-1829, compiled by Lois Smathers Neal. The Reprint Co. Pub., Spartansburg, S.C. 1980
pg.707, #5845, George Trexler m. Polly Kelchey (Mary) 7/1/1824
pg.708, #5851, Aggy Trexler daughter of the late George Troxler d. age 19, 9/6/1827

## OHIO

Pioneer Ohio Newspapers 1793-1810 by Karen Mauer Green, The Frontier Press, Galveston 1986

Vol.1, pg.48, Wednesday, 7/2/1800, #52, Lieut. Eli B. Blimson regarding deserters, Peter Trexler, b. York Co., Pa., age 24.

Vol.III, pg.78, Saturday, 7/10/1802, #154, Letters left at Post Office Cincinnati: Joseph Trexell, Gunsmith.

Rsh.106, Vol.IV, pg.209, Saturday, 7/9/1803, #163, Letters at Post Office in Chillicothe: Emanuel Trexler in care of Wm. Lamb.

Vol.VIII, pg.156, #43, Monday, 5/18/1807, Whole # 407, Butler Co., Ohio, Sale of property of Henry Troxell

Vol.VIII, pg.255, Thursday, 1/8/1807, #338, Letters left at P.O. Chillicothe: Emanuel Trexler in care of Adam Hollar

Vol.VIII, Thursday, 9/3/1807 #372, Land Office Sale, E. Traxler

## PENNSYLVANIA

The Lancaster Journal, LHS

pg.460, Helfrich Records, 5/6/1793, Jeremiah Trexslers son Benjamin, Macungie, LeeHigh Co., Pa.

pg.553, 8/15/1801, Ran away from Michael Stoner in Lancaster, Pa., apprentice lad named David Trissler, by Trade a Cabinet Maker, about 19 years of age

Lancaster Co., Pa., Marriages and Deaths, Newspapers of Lancaster Co. Pa., 1821-1830, Family Line 1988, F157.L2M34, Vol.1  Rsh.46, pgs.79 and 214, Trissler, Adam R., wife Juliana age 34 d. 7/19/1822

pg.807, Daniel Trisler d. 3/29/1822

pg.61, 4/5/1822, Margaret Trissler, dau. of Judge Graff, d. in her 51st Year

Rsh.44, date 12/10/1824, Susan Trissler daughter of John m. at Philadelphia, but of Lancaster Pa., to Gerardus Clarkson, son of Rev. Joseph Clarkson.

Rsh.135, pg.60, George Trissler's wife Catherine age 47, d. 8/9/1826

pg.329, 9/21/1827, Catherine Trisler of Lancaster m. Daniel Weidler

pg.348, Mary Ann Trissler daughter of George m. Charles

Gaillard, 2/1/1828

pg.400, 3/27/1829, George Tissler of Lancaster m. Miss Sarah Dietrich

Philadelphia, Pa., Genealogical Data Relating to German Settlers of Pennsylvania and Adjacent Territory, Adv.in German Newspapers, Philadelphia and Germantown, 1743-1800 by Edward Hocker, Geo. Pub. Baltimore, 1989, F160-G3H6 1980

pg.28, 8/16/1751, Sower's Newspapers, Peter Drexler, Macungie, Leehigh Co.

pg.33, 4/16/1752, Sowers, sale of 200 acres in Heidelberg Twp. at Johannes Drechslers, Macungie.

pg.40, 2/1/1754, Martin Schroeder's stepson is in service with Michael Drachel on Great Leehigh.

pg.41, 2/1/1754, Sower's, Martin Schroedius, stepson, Paul Wannebach is in service with Michael Drachsel on the Great Lee High, seeks information about parents.

pg.43, Sower's, 8/1/1754, David Daeschler, Market St., Philadelphia, dealer in Paint and Hardware.

pg.43, Sower's, 8/1/1754, Anthony Taeschler, Market St., Philadelphia, opposite prison, sells Saddler Ware.

pg.49, Sower's, 5/16/1755, between Willowdale and Oley, now Berks Co., Jacob Treibetbliz.

pg.50, 7/16/1755, Jacob Teischer, Miller, Richmond Twp., Berks Co., Pa., advertises his German servant has run away

pg.54, Sower's, 1/16/1756, Johannes Dreschler, Macungie, LeeHigh Co., offers an Inn, Land and Dwelling for sale.

pg.59, Sower's, 12/25/1756, Peter Treszler, New Groshenhoppen, wife Margaretha Weberin.

pg.71, Sower's, 6/24/1758, Michael Drachsel, on the great Leehigh with Paul Ballijet.

pg.90, Sower's, 5/22/1761, Jacob Treibelbitz, Richmond Twp. Berks Co., Pa.

pg.93, Sower's, 9/11/1761, Jacob Traeusch, Heidelberg Twp., Lebanon Co.

pg.95, Sower's, 10/23/1761, Philip Drescher, Longswamp, Berks Co.

pg.137, Staatsbode, Pa., 11/1/1774, Official inquiry from Dfortzheim in Baden-Durlach for Philip Drescher and Fredrich's Drescher's widow, who with several children, left Ellmen Dingen several years ago for Pennsylvania.

York Co., Pa., Abstracts of South Central Pennsylvania
Newspapers, 1785-1790, Carlisle Gazette and York Advertiser,
Familine 1988,
Rsh.128, Carlisle Gazette, 12/14/1785 John Treichler, living
in York Twp., has taken up a stray steer.

York Co., Pa., Abstracts South Central Newspapers, 1791-1795,
Comp. Martha Reamy, Family Line Pub. 1988, Pennsylvania
Herald and York General Adv.
Rsh.128, John Treichler, living in York Twp., has taken up a
stray steer.

York Co., Pa., Abstracts South Central Pa., Newspapers, Family
Line, Comp. F. Edward Wright, Westminister, 1796-1800
pg.374 Adam Desher, Indian King Tavern, informs he has
taken land near his store, near Courthouse in High St., 10/3/1798,
York, Pa.
pg.386, 1/29/1800, York Recorder, Mr. Deshler in York
Borough.
pg.405, 6/25/1800, York Recorder, Appointed by Governor
to Justice of Peace, John Drexler.


## WISCONSIN

Oshkosh, Northwestern 13 Tuesday, 8/23/1960 by Virginia Trexell,
Neshkoro
Rsh.6, "Anthony Trexell was a Veteran of the War of 1812,
He served as a Private in the 26th Regiment Pennsylvania
Volunteers. The United States government has given him a white
marble marker with his name, Regiment and State which gives
him the honor due him as a defender of his Country in time of
War."

O.  ADDADITIONAL DATA

LOUISIANA

New Orleans, La., F380.A2J33 1988 "The German-Arcadian Coast Historical and Genealogical Society, Ancestors Searching List Compiled by Harold A. Jacob
Rsh.33, Troxler, Jacque circa 1742-1809 parents Johann George and Agnes Laile, Jacques and Isabel LeRoux, spouse Isabelle Leroux, 2nd, 3/28/1770, file 04, note: Isabelle, in this record, is interchangeable with Elisabeth
Troxler, Jn George , spouse Agnes Laite file 046
Troxler, Jn (Johannes) George 1698-1759, spouse Hausseran, Magdeline (1), cote des Allemands file 074; spouse Marie
Agnes Lay (2) cote des Allemands file 074, spouse Marie Agens Laile file 043

New Orleans, La., The Settlement of the German Coast of Louisiana and The Creoles of German Descent by J. Hanno Deiler, Balt. Genealogical Publishing, Baltimore, 1969 Author, Professor Emeritus of German at Tulane University of Louisiana, New Orleans, La., published through Americana Germanica Press, Philadelphia 1909 Rsh.33, pgs.80 and 81, right bank of the Mississippi, The German Village of Hoffen, 10 Lieues above New Orleans, 11/12/1724, Census Enumerator proceeds down right side of River number 3, Johann Georg Troxler, of Lichtenberg in Alsace. Catholic; 26 years old. A Mason. His wife "Fort bon  Travailluer". Two and one-half arpents cleared, on which he has been only since the beginning of the year having left the village in the rear. Exposed to inundation. Absent because of bad health. His wife is also sick. Lost his crop and his house. A neighbor, who cooked in a shed attached to Troxler's house, accidentally set fire to it. 1731: Two children. Two negroes; one cow. Johann George Troxler was progenitor of all the "Troxler" and "Trosclair" families in Louisiana.; pg.84, here ends the village of Hoffen, and the census man now leaves the river front and proceeds to the two old villages in the rear, which were mentioned before. Old German Village -three-forths of a mile from the Mississippi. number 24 Balthasar Marx of Wullenberg, Palatinate (one Wollenberg near Wimpfen), Catholic;

27 years old, Nailsmith, 1775 Jean Simon Marx, son of Balthasar and Marianne Agae Marx, married Catharine Troxler, dau. of Nik.T. and Cath. Matern (St.James Parish); pg.118, German girls took German husbands and whole families married into one another, out of the ten children of one Jacob Troxler not fewer than eight married into the Heidel (Haydel) family. In such families the German language survived the longest, and old Creoles of German descent have told me that their grandparents still understood and were able to speak the German language, although they were not able to read and write it, as there were never any German teachers on the German coast.; pg.124, family Troxler changed into, Sroscler, Stroscler, Drozeler, Troesscler, Troxlaire, Drotseler, Trocsler, Trucksler, Trouchsler, Troustre, Troseler, Trocler, Trossclair, Troscler, Trocher, Drotzeler, Droezler, Troxclair, Troslisser

Diocese of Baton Rouge Catholic Church Records, 1770-1803, Vol. 2,3, F368.C37 1978  Vol.2, pub. Diocese of Baton Route, Department of Archives, 1800 South Arcadian Thwy., P.O. Box 2028, Baton Rouge, La. 70821. names in this record:
   Vol.2, pg.707, Trosclair (sometimes Trocsselet, Troxler, Troxeler, Troxlaire, Droezeler, Troscler, Troclister, Troxclaire, Troceler, Troesler, Troclister; Vol.3, pg.837, Trosclair, sometimes, Troxler, Truxcler, Trocsler

The German Coast, Abstracts of the Civil Records of St. Charles and St. John the Baptist Parishes 1804-1812, by Glenn R. Conrad, Center for Louisiana Studies, University of Southwestern Louisiana, Lafayette, Louisiana, Copyright 1081, University of Southwestern Louisiana, Lafayette, La. F377.S124C65Rsh.33, pg.165, No.13, 4/28/1809, Inventory of the Community Property of the Late Jacques Troxler and his wife, Elisabeth Leroux, one son Jacques Troxler, Jr. deceased with three children Firmin 12, Marceline 10 and Emeline 8 represented by their grandfather and tutor Jean Desnoyes. Other heirs born to Jacques Troxler's second marriage to Elisabeth LeRoux were nine children one dead but who had four children. These four children represented by their uncle and tutor, Alphonse Haydel. Other children were Marie, wife of Alphonse Haydel; Christophe; Cleste; wife of Jacques Haydel; Adellaide, wife of Nicholas Haydel; Emelie, wife of George Haydel; Maximillien; Godefroy; and Andre. The four

346

children represented by Alphonse Haydel their uncle and tutor, were Joseph, Carmelite, Nathalie, and Moyse (?) Haydle who were heirs through their mother Felicite Troxler. Deceased left farm 12 arpets wide located about 37.5 miles above New Orleans, 40 arpets deep with 40 arpets of cultivable land fenced.

## MARYLAND

Mdhr, Baltimore, Md., Hawkers and Peddlers License 1817, found in the back of Balt. Co. Agc. Criminal Court Docket date 1817, loc. 2/15/7/29
?Rsh.76, June - September Ordinary Licenses granted, 9/17/1817, Mrs. Murray, residence Baltimore/York Rd.

Baltimore, Md., Notes on History, April 5th, 1826. True return - Charles Howard - Capt. F.M.V., MHS
Rsh.9, Muster Roll of the First Mechanical Volunteer Company, attached to the 5th Regiment Volunteer Infantry, Privates, Jacob Hitscelburger, Nicholas Hitscelburger, Peter Hitschelburger, Samuel Truxler

Carroll Co., Md., Schraf's History of Western Maryland, ibid
Carroll County, Md., District, Taneytown, District No. 1
?Rsh.5, ?Rsh.6, "At the Presbytery meeting at Carlisle, 9/26/1810, charges of a serious nature were made against Mr. Davidson by Mr. Emmitt. Only six were deemed relevant. Of these, # 3, Of falsehood in renting to Anthony Troxel a brick house only, and afterwards giving him possession of orchard, clover, and garden, though said property was claimed by said Emmitt according to contract."

Frederick Co., Md. Poll Books, Mdhr
Rsh.34, 1808 Dist. 5, Emmitsburg, Jacob Troxel, Frederick Troxel; Taneytown, Rsh.24, Adams Troxeler
1810, Emmitsburg, John Troxill of Jacob.

Frederick Co., Md., History of Frederick Co., Md., T.J.C. Williams, Vol.I, Vol.II, pub. L.R. Tilswroth and Co., 1910
Rsh.25        pg.179, George Trisler's store in year 1811
Rsh.75        pg.640, Census 1790, Michael Trisler

**Frederick Co., Md. Vol.2, Scharf, History of Md., ibid, 1995 Carroll Co., ibid.**

Taneytown, The founder of Taneytown was a Catholic and it is reasonable to suppose there were others of the same faith living in the vicinity of the town at an early period. As far back as 1790 there are records of Mass having been said at private dwellings by Fathers Frambaugh, Pellentz, Brosuis and Cefremont. In 1804, Prince Geliven visited the village and built St. Josephs Church. Father Zocchi was the first priest.

**Frederick Co., Md., Monocracy and Catoctin, Vol.II, Some Settlers of Western Maryland and Adjacent Pennsylvania, and their descendants, C.E. Schildknecht, Ed,, Family Line 1989**

Rsh.22, pg.50, Peter Drachsel (Troxell, etc) from Lenk in Simmenthat, Canton, Berne, emig. c. 1680 to Rieschweiler, W. Pfalz and c. 1733 to Lehigh Valley, Pa., (23). Descendant, Peter in Frederick Co., Md.; pg.101, Peter Trachsel (Drachsel,Troxel, etc,) son of Jacob and Margaretha (Brengel) was born at Lenk, Canton Berne, where bapt. 1691; emig. to Wolfersheim in Homburg-Saar area and to Frederick Co., Md., soon after 1754 (Will 1766) see Troxell Trails by Richard M. Troxel, Gateway, 1977, pg.2

**Frederick Co., Md., History of Western Maryland by John Thomas Scharf A.M. Vol.II, Baltimore, Regional Pub. Co. 1968**

Rsh.75, Mary Trisler wife of Michael Trisler d. 4/5/1828, age 87

Rsh.25, Rosanna wife of George Trisler b. 11/19/1799 d. 10/12/1826; Rsh.25, pg.468, George Trisler was b. Frederick Town 1768, d. 9/9/1845 at age 77. His Parents came to Frederick from Lancaster Co., Pa. He was a writer and a poet and ran a print shop, then joined forces with Baltimore mercantile company. He was an importer of German and Irish linens. In 1794 he married Kittie Breidenbough of Baltimore at the German Reformed Church.

Rsh.34, pg.588, The name of the post office was changed from Poplar Fields to Emmitsburg. William Greenmeyer who died in 1802 in the 30th year of his life (born 1772) was the first Postmaster. He was a son in law of John Troxell who built the Brick house adjoining the Eagel Hotel.

pg.611, Jacob Trisler, German Reformed Church Records

348

Washington Co., Md., Maryland Source Records, Colonial, Revolutionary, County and Church, Gaius Marcus Brumbaugh, M.S., M.D., Vols.1 and 2, Genealogical Pub. Co., Inc. 1985

Rsh.15, pg.47, Lease September 15, 1765, Christian Traxall, Conegocheague Manor, Dorchester Co., (note at end of chapter states that this is probably Frederick Co., because this family is later found in Washington Co. It is listed as Washington Co., Md. here, however, Dorchester, Co., Md. records should be checked)

pg.524, January 18, 1794, marriage Joseph Ridenour and Ann Troxall, German Reformed Church, Washington Co., Md

Rsh.106, pg.529, Emanuel Traxler, Catherine Camerer, May 7, 1785, Washington Co., Rev. Jacob Weimer

pg.272, Poll Presidential Election, Frederick Co., Md., November 9 to 12, 1796, George Trisler; Rsh.42, Peter Crise; Rsh.5, Samuel Lilly, Jr; ?Rsh.24, Adam Shisler

pg.290, Poll Presidential Election, Frederick Co., Md., November 9 to 12, 1796, Michael Trisler; Jacob Rohr

## NORTH CAROLINA

History of Rowan County, North Carolina Containing Sketches of Prominent Families and Distinguished Men by Rev. Jethro Rumple, Reprinted with a new Index by Edith M. Clark, Baltimore Regional Publishing Company 1978

pg.286, St. John's Church, Salisbury, oldest Lutheran Church in North Carolina was reorganized in 1822. The document effecting reorganizing was dated September 1822 and was signed by John Beard, Sr., Charles Fisher, Daniel Cress, Peter Crider, John Trexler, John Beard, Jr., Peter H. Swink, Moses Brown, John H. Swink, Bernhardt Kreiter, Lewis Utzman, H. Allemong, M. Bruner, John Albright and Henry Swinkwag.

## OHIO

Clermont Co., Ohio, Vol.7, pgs.163,166, Clermont Co., Genealogy Society

Rsh.82, Michael Trisler b. c. 1750, Wittenberg, Germany m. Catherine. Emigrated to America via Hagerstown, Md. where some children were b., then to Jessamine Co., Kentucky where he d. c. 1800, widow raised four children. One of them John Trisler b. 12/31/1789, Hagerstown Md., Washington Co., moved to

Jessamine Co., Ky., in early childhood, Bible Record of John can
be found in The Living Tree News by Harris Co. Genealogical
Society, Vol.7, #2, 1980 at P.O. Box 391, Pasadena, TX 77501.
Trisler family along with a whole settlement of other German
families were actually Moravian (a province of Czechoslovakia),
via Wittenburg Saxony. Relative of Michael Trisler who came to
America in 1780 was Peter Trisler a medical doctor who led a
group of settlers from Maryland and western Pennsylvania to
Kentucky. Also birthdate on file with Latter Day Saints, source
call number 1260561 for John.

Jackson Co., Ohio, Gateway To The West, Vo. II, Compt. Ruth
Bowers and Anita Short, Geo. Pub. Co., Inc., Balt 1989,
   Rsh.106, pg.664, Jackson Co., Ohio, Index to U.S. Land
Patents 1816 to 1860:
   Emanuel Trexler A-122, Samuel Trexler, A-4,B-198

## PENNSYLVANIA

Berks Co., Pa., The Goshenhoppen Registers, 1741-1819,
reprinted from Records of the American Catholic Historical
Society of Philadelphia Co., Pa., Groshenhoppen (Bally)
Washington Twp., Berks Co., Berks Co., Pa., Pa. Genealogical
Publishing Co. Inc., Bentley, Baltimore,1984 - Registers of
Baptisms, Marriages, and Deaths of the Catholic Mission at
Goshenhoppen (Bally), Washington Township, Berks County,
Pennsylvania (1195 Most Blessed Sacrament Church, 610 Pine
Street, P.O. Box C., Bally, Pa. 19503, (215) 845-2460, The
Museum here has Bell and Vestments from the 1700's. The
following reprinted from the Records of the American Catholic
Historical Society of Philadelphia.; note: The following was
written by Father Thomas C. Middleton, O.S.A., Villanova College,
8/10/1891, "These registers belonged formerly to the old mission
church of St. Paul, known since 1837 as the church of the Most
Blessed Sacrament, at Goshenhoppen, now Bally, in Washington
township, Berks Co., Pa. They contained the records of the
baptisms , conversions, marriages, deaths and burials, as kept by
the Rev. Theodore Schneider and his successor, Rev. John
Baptist Ritter, both Jesuits, who for forty-four years, namely, from
1741 to 1785, were in charge of Goshenhoppen and its outlying
Missions.
   In 1741, the Mission of Goshenhoppen was opened by

Father Schneider, who attended it until his death, 7/10/1764, and was succeeded by Father Ritter, who continued in charge until toward the close of his life, 2/3/1787. These Goshenhoppen Registers are believed to antedate all existing Mission Registers in Pa. The Missions of St. Joseph's Church, in Philadelphia and of Conewago, in Adams Co., are both of earlier foundation than Goshenhoppen, but their early records are, it is believed, no longer in existence. The handwriting in the Goshenhoppen Registers is of three different persons, namely, Father Schneider, Father Ritter and the unknown, the names of three other Jesuit priests, Father Ferdinand Farmer's twice in 1765 and Father Luke Geisler's, twice in 1769, Father James Frambachs in Pa., 1764 and 1768, occasionally place names in eastern Pa., are mentioned where the above named missionaries visited to say Mass or confer the Sacraments. In Father Ritter's Registers the principal ones are: 1. Goshenhoppen, written Gosshenhopen, Gosschenhopen, Cushenhopen, Couissahopen, 2. Falkner's Swamp, in Montgomery Co., now known as Pottsgrove, is variously spelled as Falksner Schwam, Falckner's Swamp, Falkoner Swam, 3. Sharp Mountain, as the English rendering of the name that occurs frequently in the Registers as Asperum Collem, Collem Aculum, or Montem Aculum. Bishop Neumann's visitation book says that prior to 1787 Reading (Pa.) was attended by Father Ritter, who also visited Makunzie, Cedar Creek, and Sharp Mountain. This is presumably the Asperum Collem of Father Ritter, 4. Oley, in Berks Co., which is very frequently met with under the Latin forms of Mt. Olivet, Olivetan mountains, or hills, or even in the vernacular as Oley and Ol, 5. Cedar Creek, which Father Ritter Latinizes as "ad torrentem Cedrou, 6. Easton, in the registers Ostonia, in Northampton Co., 7. Haycock, in Bucks Co., 8. Reading, written once in the Registers as Readingtown, in Berks Co.,,, and, 9. Macungie, in Lehigh Co., which is variously written in the registers as Macunski, Magungi, Magunshi, Macungi, Magunchi, Makunski, Macunhi. From these Registers one discovers that there were some customs of the olden time rather peculiar, that will bear mention here. For instance, it was an almost universal practice for the subjects at baptism to receive the Christian name of one or the other of the sponsors, either the godfather's or the godmother's: at baptisms it was not infrequently the case that one or the other of the sponsors was a non-Catholic; in one instance in 1773 both the sponsors were non-Catholic; marriages were commonly solemnized in church at Mass. Father Ritter had large powers of dispensing in the impediment of consanguinity; In several instances Father Ritter marries parties in church when one of them was a non-Catholic; Father Schneider, from an entry in 1741, marries two non-Catholics, during Mass, on Christmas day, in John Kuhn's house; Sometimes bonds of indemnity were required by the priest before witnessing a marriage contract. This was the case where the parties were slaves, or indentured; From the inversion of the dates, it appears to have been a common practice to make the various entries in the Register weeks, and sometimes months, after the performance of a ceremony. It seems from this that the Registers were not carried around by the missionaries on their journeys, but that on their return home to Goshenhoppen they entered their proceedings, either from memory, or, much more probably, from memoranda they had made at the time. On name observations the name Kraff must be Krast, Hoffmann must be Houstmann, Riffel must be Ristel, Schaffer must be Schaster. The Christian names I have translated are Susanna as Susan, Maria as Mary, Anna as Ann, Helena as Ellen, Jacobus I have, as a rule, translated James, and only in a few cases Jacob." author's note: Cedar Creek was at Allentown, Makunzie. Cedar Creek is listed in these records as home of John George Kuhn, Rsh.5.

Berks Co., Pa., Outline located at York County, Pa., Historical Society, of material assembled by Hilda Bitting Tressler, Blanche Tressler Telfer, Mary A. Tessler and Lillian M. Kell Rsh.21, "Sketch of Family of John Tressler and Elizabeth Loy Tressler" prepared by Dr. George Tressler Scott in 1949; "The Wunderlich Family in America", compiled by Charles Albert Cornman and Daniel Wunderlich Nead, M.D.d; The Biographical Encyclopedia of Juniata Valley; Wills, Deeds, Accounts, Gravestones, etc.; Includes material compiled by Clayton O. Billow prior to 1930 regarding the brothers and sisters of David Tressler note: Hilda B. Tressler is tje wife of General Frank E. Tressler, "Jagsthausen Register, Johann Andreas Dressler b. 11/30/1714, parents John Jacob Dressler and Eva Magdalena nee Rathgeber. The matrimonial Register reads Johann Andreas Dressler, Smith, legimate son of Johann Jacob Dresser, Citizen and Smith m. Anna Barbara, legimate daughter left by deceased Bartholomaus

Bernhardt, former Farmer at Beinberg, Dist. Liebenzell duchy of Wurtemberg, bans pub. 9th, 10th, 11th Sundays after Trinity and m. 9/10/1737. Johann Andreas Dressler b. 11/30/1714, and his w. Anna Barbara Bernhardt Dressler, migrated to Philadelphia in 9/13/1749. One child d. at sea, but arriving with the parents were a dau. and sons George David and Johann Andreas, Jr., aged about 3 years. Soon after landing the family headed north westward and stopped in Goshenhoppen area near the present Pennsburg in Montgomery Co. Graves marked Trexler and Dressler seven miles southeast of Kutztown in a private abandoned cemetery have been located. Later records show that Johann Andreas Dressler, now known as Andrew moved 6 miles father north to Grimsville of Greenwich Township, Berks Co. Andrew Sr. is shown as a Tax Collector in 1765 and Andrew Tressler, Sr., Michael Loy and Frederick Hammon, all of Berks Co. were naturalized. In 1778 Andreas Dressler, Andreas Dressler, Jr. and David Dressler took the Oath of Allegiance. They served in the Pennsylvania Militia. Capt. Smiths Co., 2nd Battalion, Berks Co., Both father and son were Blacksmiths and Farmers. On tombstone in Bethel Zion's church yard at Grimesville says "here rest the remains 1714, the date of Andrew Sr. b. in Jugsthausen, Germany. Hammon, Ship arrivals in Philadelphia, Ship Christian, Peter Hammon, Johann Andreas Dressler. Frederick Hamman enl. 1770/1777? Pa. Militia served until 1780, as Private Capt. Smiths Co., 2nd Battalion, Berks Co., Pa. Frederick and Mary Hamman had eight children. Their second daughter Catherine Hamman became the second wife of Andreas Tressler, Jr., Andrew. John Andreas Dressler, Jr. was b. 5/28/1747 in Germany and d. 10/21/1828. His older brother George David Dressler was b.in 1744. John Andreas Dressler, Jr. married Mary Margaret Ley in 1768. Their son John Jacob Dressler was b. December 25, 1770 (called John). He is the only son who lived to adult hood by first marriage, and he married Susanna Hamman. The only surviving child of Andrew Tressler, Jr.'s m. to Margaret Ley (Loy) was John Jacob and he married the younger sister Susannah Hamman. Catherine Hamman was b. 12/12/1763 and d. 5/12/1850, children of John Andreas Jr. and Catherine Hamman were Joseph b. 8/23/1799, d. 5/28/1890, Sarah Doser d. 9/9/1841, Catherine Sheaer d. 1/14/1888 and Catherine Tressler, Barbara Tressler married Moos of South Carolina. George David Tressler was b.1744. Older brother of

Johann Andreas Tressler, Sr. was John Peter Tressler, who had a son David Dressler, and his youngest brother was George Michael who is said to have landed 9/17/1771. The Bower's Church Records in the Reading Historical Society should be examined for more on this family. It is said that this family came from the Sudenten Mountains, this area was assigned in 1919 to Czechoslovakia.

## Chester Co., Pa., Arrest Records, CCA

Driscoll, Jeremiah, 2/1745/46, petition of those languishing in jail. note: inmates often languished because they could not pay their fines.

Trexler, Peter, Jr., of Charleston, Yeoman, Assault and Battery against Edward Lane, Innkeeper, of Charleston, Commonwealth vs. Peter Trexler, Jr., of Charleston, 1/29/1822. note: Charleston in is the upper part of Chester adjacent to Montgomery Co., the Germans in this area often came out of Philadelphia, Pa.

## Chester Co., Pa., Poor House Index 1800-1858, CCA

Isaac Dresser, 1825, notation aided or assisted out of poor house

John Dresser, 1831, d. Eastown

Joseph Trexler, age 43, 10/14/1843, b.1800, supported in poor house Eastown, 4/21 taken to Delaware Co.

Peter Trexler, age 50, 11/16/1819, b. 1769, Eastown, 1/136, gone without permission

## Leehigh Co., Pa., Genealogies of Pennsylvania Families, from the Pennsylvania Genealogical Magazine, Vol.III, indexed by Robert and Catherine Barnes, Baltimore Genealogical Pub. 1982

Rsh.89, pg.937, Jonathan Trexler, Schmeier and Klein Family Register., Joshus Schmeier, (Schmoyer) Macungie Twp., Leehigh Co., Pa., m. Christina Trexler b. 1/7/1799. They were m. 1/3/1818. She is a dau. of Jonathan Trexler who d. 5/9/1846 at the age of 84 and his wife Elizabeth nee Harlacher d. 4/3/1854 at the age of 82. Elizabeth Harlacher's mother was Eva Harlacher.

Montgomery Co., Pa., MCHS Perkiomen Region, Salford Store Ledger

Rsh.5, pg.40, 6/6/1767, Anthony Trexsel, "Mason at Henry Landis, to sundry goods, Abraham Berky promised to see it paid. L1.9.11"

pg.159, 3/3/1769, George Droxsel, "to sundries his wife had before marriage L.0.6.6."

10/16/1769, George Droxsel, "to 1 pr shears, 1 knife L0.1.8."

12/25/1769, George Droxsel, "to sundry goods L0.10.11 1/2"

6/2/1770, George Droxsel, "to 1 lb sugar, Dd his father-in-law L0.0.8"

pg.6, 10/28/1768 John Drexler in Mochgunsky


York Co., Pa., The Pennsylvania German Society, Vol.XVL, Pub. by the Society, 1907, Records of Indentures,

pg.50, Michael Dressler, Apprentice, taught to read bible, 4 years, Joseph Stainsbury, 1/7/1772

Rsh.126, pg.152, Francis Peter Drexler, apprenticed to Joseph Smith, 3 years, YorkTown, York Co., Pa., 10/26/1772


York Co., Pa., HSYC

Rsh.115, Johann Peter Drechssler b. 12/1727, christened 8/19/1730, Father Jeremias Drechseler, John Casper Stoever Record of Baptisms and Marriages, sponsor Johann George Schuymacher


York Co., Pa., HSYC

Index of Records on Microfilm of Adams Co., Pa.

?Rsh.38, Microfilm # 487, Joseph Trexel, adm. 12/23/1812, exr. Benjamin Whitley, 1/23/1813

# 2153, David Troxell, Will 3/1840

# 2317, John Trostle


York Co., Pa., History and Family Record of John Treichler 1730-1978, John Treichler of York County Pa., and Lineal Descent from his Son Daniel Treichler to the present time. Complied, arranged and published by Gerald E. Treichler 1978, Sanborn, New York. Copies of original history and supplements are Registered in Grosvenor Library, Buffalo, New York

Rsh.139, John Treichler, "Historically, the emigration from Germany of John Treichler's father and two uncles in the year 1730 and his settling near York, Pennsylvania, coincides with the time of arrival of thousands of persecuted Protestant refugees from Palatine for the same reason at an earlier date. Today there are many Treichlers listed in the Berne, Geneva, and Zurich telephone books. In 1710, the Rev. Hans Herr and other leaders of the Mennonite Religion purchased 10,000 acres of land from William Penn in what is now Lancaster County, Pennsylvania, area. A genealogical record published of the Herr family in 1908 lists over 13,000 names, some of whom married Treichlers. These are truly Pennsylvania Dutch, corruption of the German word Duetsch, and the earliest pioneers of this part of the United States. John Treichler was 12 years old when he and his father (first name unknown) were provisioning the British during the French and Indian War in 1755 and his father became ill and died. He returned to the farm which he ran with the aid of his mother and sisters. There is no record of any living brothers. John's marriage in 1760 to Elizabeth Leupsin and his subsequent marriage to the widow Neiswanger resulted in 12 children, 5 sons and 7 daughters, one of the son's died early."

Rsh.128, "In Manchester Twp., York Co., Pa., two known licenses issued to Daniel Treichler for retail of spirits and wines for 1813 and 1814. in 1833 April, Daniel age 58 and his wife Catherine 46 started out with their family, Elizabeth 22, Polly had died young, John 18, Daniel 16, Henry 13, Jacob 10, Samuel 7, Benjamin 4. They made the 414 mile trip to the Niagara Frontier spending 16 days on the road in wagons. A hand-drawn map in the possession of Melvin, grandson of Samuel, shows the trip starting from York, Pa., with its destination "Millers" marked across a river channel (Niagara River). This was shown 212 miles from Boffleoe (Buffalo) and on the river towards Buffalo from the Falls of Niagara. They settled on what is now Ward Road about 1/2 miles south of Sanborn on land that was bought from the Holland Land Co. The City of Buffalo existed as Buffalo Creek in 1805 with a total population of 300 people, later as the Village of Buffalo in 1810 with a population of 500 people.

# Virginia

Blacksmiths listed in 1850, Stephen Trisler
Rsh.76  Coopers listed in 1860, John Trexler

BCH - Bucks County Courthouse, Administration Building, Doylestown, Pa. 18901

BCCH - Berks Co., Pa., Orphans Court and Register of Wills, Berks County Court House, 6th and Court Streets, Reading, Pa. 19601

CAGC - Carroll County Genealogical Society, Care of Carroll County Public Library, 50 East Main Street, Westminster, Md. 21157

CCA - Chester County Archives and Records Services, 601 Westtown Road, Suite 080, West Chester, Pa. 19382-4527

CGS - Clermont County Ohio Genealogical Society, DAR National Society Daughters of The American Revolution, 1776 D. Street, N.W., Washington, D.C. 20006

DGM - Detroit Genealogical Magazine, Care of Detroit Public Library, 5201 Woodward Avenue, Detroit, Michigan 48201

DCPL - Dorchester County Public Library, 303 Gay Street, Cambridge, Md. 21613

FCHS - Historical Society of Frederick County, 24 E. Church St., Frederick, Md. 21701

HCGS - Harford County Genealogical Society, P.O. Box 15, Aberdeen, Md. 21001

HGM - Society for the History of Germans in Maryland, P.O. Box 22585, Baltimore, Md. 21202

HSBC - Historical Society Berks County, Pa., 940 Center Avenue, Reading, Pa. 19601

HSPA - Historical Society of Pennsylvania, 13th and Locust Street, Philadelphia, Pa. 19107

HSWC - Historical Society of Washington Co., Md., 135 West Washington Street, Hagerstown, Md. 21740

HSYC - Historical Society of York County, 250 E. Market St., York, Pa. 17405

JTRHS - John Timon Reily Historical Society, P.O. Box 7, McSherrystown, Pa. 17344-0007

LC - Library of Congress, Washington, D.C. 20540

LCCH - Leehigh County Courthouse, 5th & Hamilton Streets, P.O. Box 1548, Allentown, Pa. 18105

LCCP - Court of Common Pleas of Lancaster Co., Pa., Office of Records and Archives Services, 50 North Duke Street, P.O. Box 3480, Lancaster, Pa. 17603-1881

LHCHC - Leehigh County Historical Society, P.O. Box 1548, Allentown, Pa. 18105

LHS - Lancaster Historical Society, 230 No. President Avenue, Lancaster, Pa. 17603

MCHS - Montgomery County Historical Society, 1654 DeKalb Street, Norristown, Pa. 19401-5415

MCA - Montgomery County Archives, 1800 Markley Street, Norristown, Pa. 19401

Mdhr - Maryland Hall of Records, Rowe Blvd., Annapolis, Md. 21401

ML - Mennonite Historical Library, The Meeting House, Box 82, 565 Yoder Road, Harleysville, Pa. 19438

MGS - Maryland Genealogical Society, Inc., 201 W. Monument Street, Baltimore, Md. 21201

Mdhr - Maryland Hall of Records, Rowe Blvd., Annapolis, Md. 21401

MHS - Maryland Historical Society, 201 W. Monument St.,Baltimore, Md. 21201

NA - National Archives and Records Administration, Washington, D.C. 20408

NCA - Northampton County Archives, 669 Washington Street, Easton, Pa. 18042

NCCH - Northampton County Court House, Easton, Pa. 18042

NGS - National Genealogical Society, 4527 17th Street North, Arlington, Va. 22207-2399

OPL - Oshkosh Public Library, 106 Washington Avenue, Oshkosh, WI 54901

ONN - Oshkosh Northwestern Newspaper, 224 State Street, Oshkosh, WI 54901

PA - Archives of the City and County of Philadelphia, 401 N. Broad Street, Philadelphia, Pa.

SHS - Shippensburg Historical Society, P.O. Box 539, Shippensburg, Pa. 17257

VSL - Virginia State Library and Archives, 11th Street at Capitol, Square, Richmond, Va. 23219-3419

WPA - Works Projects Administration/Library of Congress Washington, D.C. 20540

Berks Co., Pa., Historical and Biographical Annals of Berks Co., Pa., compiled by Morton L. Montgomery, Vol.I, Vol.II, Chicago, J.H. Beers & Co., 1909

Chronicles of Central Pennsylvania, by Frederic A. Godcharles, Litt.D., Vol.IV, Personal and Family History, Lewis Historical Publishing Company,Inc., New York

The Detroit Society for Genealogical Research Magazine, Vol. 33#1,2,3,4, Fall 1969 F574.D4D547, Compiler Jack D. Salmon of Royal Oak, Michigan (Rsh.145 and descendants)

Descendants of George Philip Duddra or Doddderer, Spelling their Names in some 35 Diverse Variations, Throughout the United States, by the Rev. Wm. B. Duttera, PhD,S.T.D., Salisburg, North Carolina 1934, no publisher cited (Rsh.43)

**French Records** - Lower Rhine, Republique Francaise, Departement Du Bas-Rhin, Archives Departementales, 5, rue Fischart, 67000 Strasbourg France, Attention: Le Conservateur en chef, Director des Services d-Archives, du Bas-Rhin, Christian Wolff

> **Area of Upper Rhine named Katzenthal (near Colmar)**
> Parish Registers begin in 1687, Contact for rates: Madam Solange-Agnel-Geissler, 10 rue, Katzenthal,France, or family expert: Dr. Jean Alfred Meyer, President, Historical Society of Katzenthal, 9 rue, Katzenthal, France, note: Upper Rhine translations provided by Professor Femi Ojo-Ade, St. Mary's College of Maryland, St. Mary's City, Maryland 20686

**German Records** - Civil Registration began in 1876, early records available from local church LDS National Archives, Geh. Staatsarchiv Preussischer Kulturbesitz, Archivstr, 1000 Berlin 33, Federal, Republic of Germany, Staatsbibliothek Preussischer Kulturbesitz, Postfach 1407, 1000 Berlin 30, Frederal Republic of Germany, Stadtarchiv und Wissenschaftliche Stadbibliothek, Stadtverwaltung, 5300 Bonn, Federal Republic of Germany, Historic Emigration Office, Museum fur Hamburgische, Geschichte, Holstenwall 24, 2000 Hamburg 36, Federal Republic of Germany

**LDS** - Church of Jesus Christ of the Latter Day Saints, Mormon Records, Salt Lake City, Utah 84199

**Leehigh County, Pa.** - The Family History Center, Van Buren Rd., Whitehall, Allentown, Pa. 18105, Scott Andrew Trexler II Memorial Library, Old Courthouse, Hamilton at 5th, Allentown, Pa. 18101

**Redemptorist Cemeteries, Md.** - Sacred Heart of Jesus, Most Holy Redeemer, Administrative Offices, 4430 Belair Road, Baltimore, Md. 21206

Roberts History of Leehigh County, Pa., Leehigh County Historical Society, Allentown, Pa. 18105

A History of Rowan County, North Carolina, containing Sketches of Prominent Families and Distinguished Men, by Rev. Jetro Rumple, Reprinted with a new Index by Edith M. Clark, Baltimore Regional Publishing 1978 Rsh.122

**Schuylkill County, Pa.**, Office of the Register of Wills, Schuylkill, County, Pa., Pottsville, Pa., 17901, Schuylkill County Court House, 401 N. 2nd Street, Pottsville, Pa. 17901; Historical Society of Schuylkill County, 14 North 3rd Street, Pottsville, Pa. 17901

**Swiss Records** - Civil registration began in 1876, church records much earlier, LDS, National Archives, Schweizerisches Bundesarchiv, Archivstr 4, 3012 Bern, Switzerland, Aargau City Archives, Staatsarchiv des Kantons Aargau, Obere Vorstadt, 5001 Aargau, Switzerland; Basel Arvhives, Staatsarchiv Basel-Stadt, Martinsgasse 2, 4001 Basel, Switzerland, Bern City Archives, Staatsarchiv des Kantons Bern, Falkenpatz 4, 3012 Bern, Switzerland; Graubunden Archives, Staatsarchiv des Kantons, Graubunden, Reichsgasse, Archivegebaude, CH-7001 Chur, Switzerland; Geneva Archives, Archives de L'Etat, 1 rue dei'hotel de Ville, 1211 Geneva 3, Switzerland; Neuchatel Archives, Archives de l'Etat, Le Chateau, CH-2001 Neuchatel, Switzerland; Zurich Achives, Staatsarchiv des Kantons Zurich; Winterhurestr 170, 8057 Zurich, Switzerland; National Library, Schweizerische Landesbibliothek, Hallwylstr.15, 3003 Bern, Switzerland; Zurich Central Library, Zentrabibliothek Zurich; Zahringerplatz 6, 8025 Zurich, Switzerland

History and Family Record of John Treichler 1730-1978, John

Treichler of York County Pa., and Lineal Descent from his Son Daniel Treichler to the present time. Complied, arranged and published by Gerald E. Treichler 1978, Sanborn, New York. Copies of original history and supplements are registered in Grosvenor Library, Buffalo, New York (Rsh.127,128,139)

Tressler: Outline located at York County, Pa., Historical Society of material assembled by Hilda Bitting Tressler, Blanche Tressler Telfer, Mary A. Tessler and Lillian M. Kell

Tressler Families by George T Scott, Loysville, Pa. 1949 (M)

History and Genealogy of the Trexler Family, Compiled and Published by John Trexler Warren, Schlechter's Printers-Publishers, Allentown, Pa. 1972 (Rsh.3 and descendants)

Troxell (Drachsel,etc.) Families by Stanley M. Shartle, Indianapolis, IN 1955

The Troxler Family of North Carolina by Rockie D.Troxler, October 1980, CS71.T8636, no publisher referenced ( Rsh.33)

Troxell Trails by Richard M. Troxel, compiled 1963-1977, Gateway Press, Inc., Baltimore, 1977 (Rsh.145 and descendants)

Dr. George Allen Troxel, "Troxell and Allied Families Notes," manuscripts,Pennsylvania Historical Society Library in Philadelphia, 7 volumes not published or dated (Rsh.143 and descendants)

# FULL NAME INDEX

## Q.

ABERCROMBIE, Capt. James
  264
ABRECHT, Joseph 189
ACKERMAN, Catherine 24 39
  George 241 Jacob 209
  Samuel 74
ADAMS, Charles R. 318 Jacob
  246
AGNEW, John 209
AHUM, Milton 216
ALBRECHT, Christian S. 322
  Conrad 219 Heinrich 262
  Jacob 220 Joseph 189
  Maria 220 Mary 219
  Susannah 189
ALBRIGHT, Caty 314 Christian
  111 George 111 George A.
  223 Gottlieb 111 Jno. 291
  294 John 2 40 216 293 296
  314 349 John P. 43 Jonas
  314 Lauwich 36 Ludwick 36
  315 Maria Catherine 52
  Mary 111 Mary Ann 111
  Peter 230 Rosetta 111
  Virginia 111
ALBRITH, Joseph 236
ALGEYER, Dame Catharine
  143
ALLBRECHT, Christian S. 37
  Christian 37 Eutaw 37
  George Adam 261 Gottlieb
  37 322 Joseph 37 147
  Margaret 37 Mary Louise
  37 Nonnie 37 Virginia 37
ALLEMONG, H. 349
ALLEN, James 44 John L. 53
ALTER, Mary 313

AMAN, Robert L. 47 199
  Samuel 47 199
AMBOUCHER, Sarah 121
ANDERSON, Henry 191
ANGSTADT, Jacob 170 Leah
  170 Mary Ann 170
ANNAN, Robert L.196
APPLEGARTH, S. Hubert 82
ARBRGAST, P.G. 318
ARCHENBRIGHT, Jacob 255
ARCHER, Thomas 203
ARGUST, Thomas B. 46
ARMAT, Thomas 287
ARMENTROUT, Frederick 254
ARMINTROUT, Fredk. 255
ARMONTROUT, Phil. 255
ARNOLD, Arnold's Delight 259
  Catherine 208 Christian 208
  Elizabeth 208 Jacob 29 208
  Mary 208 Sarah 208
ARNOT/ARNOTT, Capt.
  Thomas 261 Thomas 265
ARTZ, Rev. Wm. 314
ASQUITH, Wm. 192
ATEN, John R. 240
AUE, Jacob 152
AUGHENLAUGH, George U.
  197
AULD, Col.Md.Mil.329 Earl
  Kessler 64
AULTHOUSE, W.H. 223
AURAND, Henry 241 244
AUSTRAIN, Fannie 212 Raphel
  212
AXER, Joh.Michael 149
  Michael 28
BABB Jorge 214

# FULL NAME INDEX

BACHMAN, John 226 Lavina
44
BECKEBACH, Casper 123
Sasanna 123
BACTLETON, Samuel 238
BADTITLE, Christopher 189
BAER, Johannes 26 167
Susanna 26 167
BAIRD, John 317
BAKER, Anna Margaretha 6
David C.279 Jacob 146
James 192 John 286
Mathias 245 Valentine 285
Susanna 7 Susannah 10
Treaxler and Baker 181
Wm. G. 230
BALERSTON, D. Jolly 46
BALET, Paul 167
BALL, Mary Ellen 314
BALLIET, Catharina 165
Fannie 72 Magdalena 168
Niclaus 33 Niclaus 168
Nicolaus 166 Paul 165
Stephen 72 168
BALLIJET, Paul 343
BALLY see Goshenhoppen 3
117 137 138 350 351 352
353
BALMAIN, Alex 322
BALTGELL, George 196
BAND, Wm. 205
BARE, Barbara Ann 277
Jacob 277
BARENT, Caterana 269 Daniel
269
BARINGER, Catherine 55 Peter
55
BARNES, John 280
BARNICLE, Mary Ann 140

BARTH, Augustus 229 Lewis
143
BARTHEL, Jacob 175
BARTON, Barton's Tavern 341
Henry 32 Mary Ann 32 126
BASALA John 64
BASCHMAN, Catharine 145
Elisabeth 145, Jacob 145
BASHMAN, Andrew 270
BASSARD, M.T. 283
BAUER, Casper 39 Catharina
150 Elis.145 Joannes 5
150 Joh 145 Marg 145
Maria Elizabeth 324
Susanna 39 52
BAUGHER, Catherine 197
201 202 Joseph 47 199
Isaac 47 199 J.W. 202
James 197 James W. 48
197 200 202 Joseph 47
199
BAUGHMAN, George 185
Joseph 185 Margaret 185
BAUGNER, Conrad 258
BAUMGADEN, Samuel 197
BAUMGARDNER, John B. 209
John H. 211
BAUSCHER, Lydia 43
BAWR, Casper 239
BAYER, Casp. 123 Catherine
48 123 202 James W. 48
BAYIN, Sybilla 8 124 131
BEAM, Elizabeth 54 210 John
54 210 John H. 210
BEAR, Edith Irene 319 George
W. 58 Jacob 277 John 277
BEARD, Fredrick 273 276
George 252 John Sr. 349
Michael 278

BEAS, Philip 332
BEAVER, John K. 287
BECK, Jacob 285
BECKER, Anna Margaretha 6
    Anna Margaretha 25
    Catharine 136 George
    Ernst 25 Henry 136
    Magdalena Helena 25
    Susanna 7 10 156 163
BEERS, James 191
BEILLER, John 239, Nancy
    239
BELLENTZ, Rev. James 250
BELSTERLING, Jacob 242
BEMNETT, Builes 198
BENDEN, Mary Caroline 139
    Mary Elizabeth 139 Robert
    139
BENDER, David 286 George
    223 Hans 285 Johann
    Daniel 1 133
BENNER, Abraham R. 239
    Frederick 239
BENNES, Ludwick 242
BENNETT, Collins 49 325
    Elizabeth 49 Lena Madeline
    63
BENTZ, Anna Maria 53 248
    Barbara 248 Catherina 248
    Christian 248 Elizabeth 248
    Jacob 248 Luzey 248
    Salome 248 Samuel 278
    Susanna 52 248 Ursula 248
    Whylich 53 248
BENZ, Anna Maria 53 Anna
    Mary 148 Christian 148
    Susanna 53 Whylich 53
BERGMANN, A. Elizabeth 119
    Jeffes Joseph 119

BERNHARDT, Anna Barbara
    11 59 352 Bartholomaus 12
    353
    353 Mary 54
BERNHEISEL, Mary Catherine
    29
BERNT, Jesse 69
BERTSCH, Christina 65
    Johannes 166
BERVERMOSTER, James C.
    318
BESCHERER, John 55
BESONE, Henry 284
BETHELL, Dr. J.P. 90
BETTING, Ludwig 189
BETZ, Christian 287 Henry 218
BEYERLIN, Catharina 9 27 160
BIEAM, Hannah A. 319
BIEBER, John 220
BIELER, Elizabeth 21
BIERY, Amanda 69 Catherine
    59 231 John 67 Salome 73
BIGGS, Jacob 33 126 197
    Maria 126 Mary A. 32 201
    Polly 197
BIGLER, Jere G. 319
BIGONE, Joseph W. 287
BILLMEYER, Jacob 251
BINDER, Margaret 175
BINGAMAN, Frederick 241
BIRCHARD, Clara 74
BISCHOFFIN, Elis 24 145
BISCOE, Warren 316
BISHER, Elizabeth 55 316
BISHERER, Miss Elizabeth 316
BISHOP, Catherine 25
    Elizabeth 25 27 J. 240
    Peter 332
BITINGER, Philip 133

(Bitinger Cont.) Susanna
133
BITTNER, Abraham 74
BIXLER, Jacob 57 247 252
Sufania Shophia 246
Susana 247 Susanna 252
Susanna Sophia 57
BLACK, George 196 James
240 John 188 194 Martin
58 Valentine 271 276
BLACKBURN, Robert 112
BLACKLEDGE, Thomas 241
BLAIR, Nettie M. 63
BLANK, Maria Veronica 67
John 67 Elizabeth 231
BLANTON,Dewey W. 63
BLIELER, Elizabeth 72
BLIMSON, Lieu. Eli B. 342
BLOOM, Catherine 41 236
Susannah 41
BLOSSER, Sylva E.319
BLUM, Adam 5 150 153 Anna
Margaretha 5 153
Margaretha 150
BLUMER, William H. 231
BODDER, Jacob 221
BOEHME, Charles Lewis 145
BOHLER, John J. 44
BOILER, Edward 126
BOLICH, Catherine 43
BOLLER, Edward 32 Jeanetta
C. 32
BOLTZHUBER, Melchor 135
Elisabetha 135
BOOKMAN, George 185
Joseph 118 Margaret Ann
5 Mary 118
BOON/BOONE, Boones Berry
Town 279 Boones Mill 111

(Boon/Boone Cont.)
Boonsboro 275 George
279 281, John 206
Susanna 279 William 278
279
BOOSS, Daniel 125, Elizabeth
125 Solomon Susanna 125
BORGER, Charles 56
BORONGLIKER, also
BOROUGHLIKER Molly 322
BOTT, Jacob 178 Peter 178
Ulrich 227
BOUCHER, Sarah Ann 5 121
BOUGHAMAN, George William
185
BOUGHMAN, Barbara 185
Eleanor 185 George 185
George W. 185 George
William 185 Henry 185
Henry E. 185 Joseph 185
Margaret 185
BOUVIER, Emma 77 Michael
77 Louise C. Vernou 77
BOWEN, Mary Ann 117
BOWER, Bowers Church 354
George 187 Helen G. 318
319
BOWES, Peter 278
BOWLES, Ruth S. 63
BOWLEY, David 277
BOWMEN, Samuel 220
BOWSER, Benjamin 277
Catherine 277
BOYER, Marcia 214 Mary 74
Peter 324 Solomon 60 218
BRACKIN, Maria 149
BRADEN, Barbara 6 Catherine
185 Catherine C. 340
Catherine Maria 6 William 6

# FULL NAME INDEX

(Braden Cont.) William 185
340
BRADLEY, Thomas 191
BRADY, Samuel 179
Capt.Thomas 179 262
BRAGONIER, Barbara 187
Daniel 187
BRAMMER, Ignatius 273
BRANAMAN, Anthony 254
BRAND, Daniel 191 192
BRASHEAR, Belt 277
BRAUM, Frederick 147
BRAUNGUL, Jacob 9 132
BREADER, Lawrence 189
BRECHT, Joshia 60 157
BREDER, Lawrence 189
BREIDENBACH, Catherine 313
BREIDENBOUGH, Kittie 348
BREING, Catherine 2 Jacob
215
BREINIG, Angeline C. 43
Catherine 53 Jacob, Jr. 42
James 42
BREISCHER, George 54 210
BREITENBACH, Catherine 14
Susanna 124 Valentin 124
BRENGEL, Anna 66 Christian
66 Elizabeth Bratten 64
Jacob 258 Margaretha 64
65 258 348 Steffen 64
BREMER, John 258
BRENING, Susanna 215
BRENNEMAN, Isaac 253
BRENNER, Abraham R. 239
Adam 161 Anna Maria 161
BRENNING, James 215
BRERING, George 189
BRESSLER, Jonathan 333
Peter 333

BREWER, Elizabeth 313
BREY, Jonas 290
BRIGAMAN, Frederick 244
BRINSTOW, Edward P. 230
BROADRAUF, Charles 197
BROGONIER, Jacob 278
BROOKS, Robert 197
BROSIUS, Rev. Francis X. 208
209
BROSUIS, Father 348
BROUHMEYER, Christiana 313
BROWN, America 55 Miss
America 316 Edward 191
192 Moses 349 Peter 214
Sarah Jane 50
BRUBAKER, Mary 35 330
BRUDER, Elizabeth 319
BRUNER, John 274 M. 349
BRUNNER, John 274
BRUTEL, Catherine 39 122
Hemrich 39 122
BUCK, Jonas 73
BUCKMAN, Barbara 117
Barbara Fisher 117 George
117 Joseph 117 119
Margaret 117 118 Margaret
Ann 3 5 Margareta 120 121
BUECHER, Henry 259
BUEHLER, D.A. 210
BUGER, Matthaeus 162
BULGER, Ann 322
BULLMAN, Thomas P. 240
BUMBARGNER, Nancy 192
BUMBERGER, Christina 192
William 192
BUMGARTNER, Jacob 199
BUMMER, John 321
BUNNER, Henry 226
BURAUS, Zachariah 289

BURCKHALDER, Eva
Catharina 165 167 Peter
165 167
BURGHALDER, Eva Catharina
168 Peter 168
BURICKER, Daniel 322 David
322
BURKHALDER, Catherine 50
Peter 50
BURKHALTER, Magdalene 75
BURNNER, Mrs. Charles 61
BURNS, James H. 64
BURROW, marriage 315
BURNO, Jachariah 289
BUSH, James 40
BUSCHMAM, Catherine 145
Elisabeth 145 Jacob 145
BUSHMAN, Andrew 275 Henry
275 Polly 275
BUSHMILLER, Barbara 5
121 185
BUSHONG, Philip 289
BUTLER, Butler Co. 342 Edith
May 63 James Linwood 63
Percy Linwood 63
BUTNER, Julie Fritz 55
BUTZ, Anthony 137 Elizabeth
Ann 70 Marie 137 Robert
188
BYRD, Wm. C. 193
BYRNE, Agnes Elizabeth 140
Alice 140 Anastasia 140
Barnabas 140 Charles
Thomas 140 Jane Matilda
140 Juliana 140 Margaret
140 Margaret Catherine
140 Mary Ann 140 Mary
Magdalen 140 Mary 140
Michael 140 Sarah Ann 140

(Bryne Cont.) Sarah Jane
140 Silas Augustine 140
Thomas 140
CALLAHAN, Andrew 140
CALLINGER, Mary 18
CALLINGS, Mary 201
CALLOWAY, Mary A. 75
CAMERON, Catherine 40
49 325
CAPLER, Joannes 119 John 4
Maria 4 119 Maria
Magdalena 119
CAREY, J.J. 278 Jane 317
CARLTON, Alice 203 Anne
203 Arthur 188 203 Eleanor
188 204 Jane 203 Mary
203 Penn 203 Thomas 203
Usher 203
CARPENTER, Hannah 24
CARPLER, Joannes 119 120
John 4 Maria 4 119
CARROLL, Rebecca 118
CARTER, B. Frank 47 Mrs. J.A.
62
CASPER, Mary 36 277
CATTINGER, Mary 200
CAUBLE, Katie 55 Margaret
316 William A. 55
CAYLER, Daniel 251
CAYLOR, Catherine 207
CEFREMONT, Father 348
CELLAR, John 204 205
CENTNER, Rosanna 53
CERKMAN, Henry 246
CHALMERS, Capt.328
CHAMBER, Elizabeth 58 J.
Sexton 90 Louise 255
Robert 341
CHANCERY/CIVIL RECORDS

(Chancery/Civil Cont.) 184
CHARLTON, Arthur 203 Jane
203 Penn 203 Usher 203
CHASER, Jeremiah 280
CHEYNEY, Wm.222
CHILDRESS, Clyde H. 64
Horace Beverly 64
CHRISIMER, Anna Maria 58
Mary 136
CHRIST, Henry 213
CHRISTEIN, Catherine
Magdalena 29 Magdalena
Catherine 173
CHRISTMAN, Elizabeth 170
Lillian 71 Michael 170 Peter
40 171
CHUST, John 214
CILLEMENS, Joh Nocol 148
CLAGETT, Alexander 280
CLAP, Nelly 315
CLAPP, Dr. W.R. 90
CLARK, James 192
CLARKSON, Gerardus 342
Rev. 342
CLAYTON, Raymond F. 46
CLEMENTS, Capt. 327
CLEMMER, Henry 239 Sarah
239
CLIPPENGER, Levi H. 283
CLMES, Christian 221
CLYMER, John 239
COATES, James 196
COBBS, Edmund 46 336
COBLE, David 35
COBOLE John 143
COCHRAN, Landon 322
COCKSEL, Christian 9
COLE, Ella 62 John 219
COLES, John 219

COLLIFLOWER, Harriet
Elizabeth 126 Joseph 126
Mary J. 32 Sophia
Elizabeth 32 126
COLLINGEN, Mary 18 196
CONFER, James 74
CONFLANY, Edwart 118
CONNER, Peter 223
COOK, Daniel 284 Emilia 118
Isaac P. 314
COOKSEY, John 54 209
COON, see Kuhn, Adam 323
Catherine 10 137
Modolona 195 200
COOPER, David 331 Elizabeth
313 315
CORSON, Joseph E. 288
COUK, Emilia 118
COUL, Wm. 254
COYER, Jacob 285
CRABBS, Elizabeth 22 Fred
201
CRABS, John 272
CRABTREE, Sarah 50 325
CRADDOCK, Maria Ilsabetha
49 313
CRAMER, Daniel 28 George
76 Jacob 76 Maria 76 Peter
76 284
CRAMPTEN, Thomas 279
CRAPS, Silas Westly 64
CRASSMAN, Anna Marie 170
CRAWFORD, Samuel 191 Ship
265
CREAMER, Daniel 28 Peter
282
CREEGER, John 274
CREMER, George 152
CRESALY, Elizabeth 207

CRESS, Daniel 349
CRESSMAN, Ephram 239
    Maria 239
CRIDER, Peter 349
CRISE, Elizabeth 195 200
    Peter 22 195 198 200 273
    276 349
CRISMAN, John 189
CRISTMAN, Michael 170
CROCKSEL, Christian 9
CROHN, Anna Maria 14 Annen
    Marien Crohnin 156
CROHNIN, Anne Maria 156
CROMWELL, Philemon 341
    Stephen 341
CRON, Anna Maria 86 87
    88 157 158
CRONYN, John 139 Philip 139
CROPER, Johannes 119 Maria
    119
CROUSE, George S. 198 John
    194 Michael 198
CRU, Barbara 26 35 169
    332
CRUMBAUGHER, Catherin
    255 Pet. 255
CURLETT, Thomas 194
CURLINGER, Mary 18
CURRNES, Amos 125 Rachael
    125 Robert 125
CUSHION, Madalena 22
CUSHWA, Capt. David 341
    David Co. 341 John 281
    Mill 341
DABW, Minnie T. 319
DACHERT, Joh. Peter 263
DAESCHLER, David 343
DAESCHNER, Georg 125
    Sophia 126 Sophia

(Daeschner Cont.)
    Margreth 125
DALLAM, Priscilla 203
DALLAS, Richard Boothley 203
DAMER, Abraham 250
DANCE, Annie Phippen 62
    Charles 62 Ella 62 Lawson
    H. 62 Lorettta 62 Powhatan
    J. 62
DANKEL, Catherine 173
    Cinetta 58 Johann Conrad
    173
DANNAY, Jacob 196
DANNER, Abraham 58 219
    David 272 Margaret 219
    Margaretha 58 163
DANSBURY, Raymond 46
DARREN, Charles S. 314
DATZELL, James 193
DAVIDSON, Patrick 272 Mr.
    347
DAVIS, Francis M. 278 Henly
    233 Japheth 317 John 201
    271 272 John A. 48 197
    200 John D. 202 Mary A.
    202 Michael 55 316 Susie
    B. 61
DEBELER, Adam 125 Juliana
    125 Philippina 125
DEBOW, Anna Barbara 5
    Barbara 185 Lemuel 5 185
DEBRULER, Benjamin 194
DECH, Anthony 172 Ejiah 213
    Elizabeth 148 248 Joannes
    267 John Jerg 263
    Joh.Peter 263, Johann
    Georg 263 Johann Peter
    263 Margaret 173, Peter
    148 248

# FULL NAME INDEX

DECHART, Anthony 172 Ejiah 213 Elizabeth 148 249 Joannes 265 Johann Georg 263 Johann Peter 263 John Jerg 263 Joh.Peter 263 Margaret 172 Peter 148 248

DECKHARD, John 235

DEHUFF, Dehuff Family 38 Henry 286 John 285 land 285

DEICHER, Michael 62 249

DEICHLER, Henry 227 Sarah L. 227

DEIGELER, Johannes 155 Mariua Catharina 155

DEIGLER, Jacob 155 Joannes 155, Johannes Eberhart 155 Joh Jacob 155

DEIHL, Jonathan 232

DEILY, Valentine 26

DEISCHER, Christ 174 John Jacob 30 173 174 Julia 173 174

DEISE, Steven 74

DEITZ, Valentine 26 240

DEIXLER, John 80 Mary 80

DELCHER, Mrs. Ann 191 Christian 181 191 296 George 191 192 193 194 296 328 Harriett 192 193 194 James 328 Jemima 192 194 Jeremigh 193 Jerimah 193 Jermima 192 194  Joannes 262 265 John 94 191 193 194 296 328 329 Kitty 191 Mary 191 Sarah 191 Thomas 328 Valentine 181 191 193 194

(Delcher Cont.) 296 William 328

DELONG, Church 170 David 69

DELSHER, also DEILSHIRE, George 328 James 328 John 328 Thomas 328

DELSHER, also DEILSHIRE William 328

DEMERS, Charles 230

DEMUTH, Christopher 156 Elizabeth 159 H.C. 230 Johannes 15 87 89 159 171 John 156 Sophia Elizabeth 157

DENGLER, Jacob 10

DENIG, Lewis 283

DENT, Thomas Hatch 207 Thomas H. 316

DERSHTLER, Michael 225

DERSTLER, Adam 225 226 229 301 306 Catherine 229 Michael 226 229

DESCHIEL, Charles 269

DESCHLER, Adam 26 168 Catharina 165 167 David 165 167 169 John 169 Johan David 265 John Peter 21 Magdalena 165 167 Peter 50 165 Susanna 167

DESCHNER, Georg 125 265 Rosina 178 Sophia 125

DESHER, Adam 344 Maria 43 Philip 43

DESHLER Adam 13 26 39 50 103 167 168 169 270 299 308 310 311 312 313 Catharina 168 170 Charles

(Deshler Cont.) 103 308
309 310 David 103 168 170
189 190 284 285 299 301
308 309 310 312 320
Debora 169 Elizabeth 168
George 168 Jacob 167
John Peter 21 Katy 320
Magdalena 26 Maria 167
168 169 Maria Susanna
169 Mr. 344 Peter 12 26 50
167 168 169 299 308 310
311 312 Peter,Jr. 103 Peter
Sr. 103 Sara 168 Susanna
A. Mueckli 167 widow 103
DESHNER, John 251
DESKIEL, Charles 269
DESLER, Peter 18 129
DESNOYES, Tutor Jean 184
346
DESTLER, Adam 300
DETWEILDER, Samuel 288
DETWEILER, Samuel 287
DEUSCHEL, Johann Andreas
29 Andrew 29
DEUTSEL, Cathaine 178
Johannes 178 John Peter
21 Soloman 178
DEXEL, Barbara 80 Caroline
M. 80 Catherine 80
Cunigunda 80 Elizabeth
147 Michael 80 Philip 80
DEXEMER, Catherine 241
Daniel 241
DICE, George 251
DICKSON, George 203
DIEHL, Abraham 31 Catherine
67
DIEMER, Anna Catherine 28
161 Johan Jacob 161 John

(Diemer Cont.) Jacob 28
DIESCHER, Cath. 173 John
Jacob 30
DIETRICH, Anna 43 Elizabeth
43 George 28 Sarah 60
343
DIFFENIELD, Theodore 287
DIGGS, William 273
DINGER, Peter 49 225 227 229
DINKEY, Capt.Pa.Militia 35
332
DISHER, Conrad 269 David
284
DISLER, Adam 299 Daniel 225
David 241 243 Elizabeth
225 241 243 George 91
213 Goopey 105 Jacob 213
John 103 213 Maria 213
DISSLER, Catherine 225
226 227 228, Daniel 225
Daniel Sr. 226 227 David
103 243 Elizabeth 224 225
227 228 George 213
George David 15 Jacob
103 105 213 225 303 John
105 213 225 227 Maria 213
Sarah 213 Sophia 213
DITTERE, Christian 288
DITZLER, Anthony 213 Betsy
213 Catharine 213 Christina
213 Elizabeth 213 Jacob
213 Magdalen 213
Magdlaena 213 Melchoie
213 Molly 213, Thomas 213
William 213 William V. 213
DIXON, George 188 Mary
Nancy Jane 50 Mason
Dixon Survey Line 117
DLEINFILDER, Hannes 285

# FULL NAME INDEX

DOBBINS, Polly A. 50
DODERO, Elizabeth 126
DOERR, Catherine 9 12 127
    129
DOERSTLER, Adam 227
    Benjamin 228 Carolina 227
    Jacob 228 Jacob B. 227
    Jacob M. 227 Mary 228
    Michael 227 228 Sarah 228
DOESCHLER, Barbara 50 165
    167 Johann Peter 165 167
    Peter 50 165 167
DOIL, Conrad 203 Henry 203
    Mary 203
DOLL, Catherine 15 38 250
    Conrad 15 156 163 203
    245 320 Elizabeth 204
    George 204 Henry 203 245
    Jacob 245 John 38 245
    250 271 306 John D. 245
    Joseph 245 Mariah 38
    Mary 203
DONAGAN, James 220
DONOUGHE, Ann Margare
    140
DORES, Valentine 214
DORSON, Shadrach H. 289
DORVIN, Jeanne 17
DOSCHER, Betze 154
DOSCHIN, Anna Regina 161
DOSELER, Catherine 128
    George 128 Rosina 128
DOSLER, Catherine 128 129
    George 128 129 Margaret
    128
DOTHERO, Conrad 127
DOTTERER, Anna Maria Fisher
    22 Conrad 8 32 247
    Elizabeth 8 248 George

(Dotterer Cont.) 248 History
    of 23 John 248 Judianna
    148 Margaret 233 247
    Margaret Elisabeth 32
    Margaretha 247 Mary 247
    Mary Hefners 233 Mary
    Rilfe 234 Michael 23 233
    247 Sophia 8 12 23 32
    115 165 Suffia 233 247
DOTTERO, Anna Maria 127
DOUGHERTY, Theophilus F.
    194
DOUGLAS, Robert 280
DOUSCHEL, Andreas 178
    Andrew 29
    John Andreas 29
DRACHEL, Michael 343 Peter
    33 166 168 Sibilla 166
    Susanna 166 168
DRACHER, cemetery surname
    89
DRACHSEL, Abraham 51
    Christian 168 Daniel 23 145
    Elias 126 Elizabeth 130 199
    258 Families 368 George
    47 160 162 George Jacob
    19 Jacob 130 148
    Johannes 260 John 199
    John David 45 John
    George 160 162 163 John
    S. Micklaus 33 Johann
    Peter 159 162 Jurg
    Michael 147 Magdalena 45
    146 Margaret 159 160 162
    Margaretha 147 Mary Ellen
    126 Michael 33 343
    Nicklaus 166 168 Peter 12
    33 166 168 170 258 260
    348 Sophia Drachselin 45

# FULL NAME INDEX

(Drachsel Cont.) 145
DRACHSELL, Johannes 260
Jurg Jacob 147 Margaretha
147 Michael 147
DRACHSELLN, Jurg Jacob
147 Magdalena 7 147
DRACHSET, David 130
Elizabeth 130
DRACHZEL, George David 15
Magdalena 15
DRACKSEL, Abraham 244
DRAECHER, George 175
DRANCKEL, Christopher 28
160 161
DRANKLE, Daniel 214
DRASSEL, Elizabeth 133
Margaretha 133 Peter 133
313
DRAUCHER, cemetery
surname
89
DRAUSS, George Peter 127
Juli 127 Peter 127
DRAUTEL, Elizabeth 170 Maria
Elizabeth 170 Michael
170
DRAXEL, Abraham 51 93 224
Adam 103 310 Anna
Elisabetha 130 Anna
Maria 169 Appalonia
131 Catharina 168
Cathrina 131 309
Christian 131 310
Daniel 67 93 103 308
309 310 333 David 28
130 Drederich 131
Elizabeth 93 127
Fridrich 127 131
George 1 131 146

(Draxel Cont.) George
Frederick 7 131 Jacob
13 103 179 297 308
309 310 311 Johannes
127 John 103 168 310
John Nicholas 20 25
Margaretha 132
Marianna 134 Michael
131 Nicholas 308 309
311 Nich's 299 Peter
20 31 33 67 103 168
232 299 308 309 310
312 Polly 134 Sarah
179 Solome 168
Solomon 166 Susanna
179
DRAXELXEL, George 1 Peter
93
DRAXSEL, Peter 50
DRAZEL, Anna Maria 130
Appolonia 130
Frederick 130
Johannes 130
DRCKSLER, Conrad 76 150
DREACHSEL, Abraham 265
DREAR/DREAS, Dewald 214
DRECHLER, Daniel 76 John
David 24 John S.
Daniel 23
DRECHSELER, Appolonia 16
Catherine 148 Catharina 40
Jeremias 176 355 Jeremiah
52 Johann Jurg 147 John
Christopher 50 John Peter
41 355 Maria 148 Peter 147
DRECHSELERN, Catharina 41
147 John Christopher 50
Maria 147 148
DRECHSLER, Anna Barbara

# FULL NAME INDEX

(Drechsler Cont.) 81 Anna
Catharina 152 Catharina
154 Christina 152 154
Christian 154 Conrad 53 76
150 151 152 153 Daniel
151 David 175 321
Elizabeth 149 150 151 153
Franny 151 Froehnry 153
George 153 Helena 152
Johannes 151 343 John
298 John David 24 John
Henry 82 John Peter 1
Joseph 33 176 Maria 150
151 152 153 154 Mary 152
Mary C. 81 Michael 4 77
149 150 151 152 153 154
Nicholas 53 Peter 150 151
152 153 Phronica 151 153
Roehny 152 Rosanna 152
Valentine 53 Wayne
Herman 82
DRECHSSLER, Jeremiah 52
John Peter 41 177 Johann
Pete 176 355
DRECKEL, Anthony 3 246
DRECKLER, Anthony 3 247
John Conrad 28
DRECKSELER, Adam 13
Anmarie 118 Anna Barbara
118 Anthony 137 Appolonia
120 Appolonia Julia 120
Catharina 119 Gerhardt 121
Herbemal 118 Ignatius 37
120 121 Joannes Joseph
120 121 Judith 121
Margaret Buckman 118
Maria 119 121 Marianna
118 Samuel 118 119 121
Samuel Anthony 5 Sarah

(Dreckseler Cont.) 118
Sophia 5 6 119 121
DRECKSLER, Anna Barbara
118 121 Anna Maurry 120
121 Anna Moury 119
Appolonia 120 121
Appolinia Julia 121
Catherine 119 Conrad 150
152 155 Francis Peter 56
Fronica 150 153 Ignatius
119 120 121 Jacob 173
Joannes 119 Joh 150 John
76 153 John Jacob 30
John Joh Jacob 172 174
Judith 120 Maria 119 120
Michael 4 149 150 15 Peter
75 307 Samuel 118 121
Samuels 121 Sophia 121
Theresia 119 William 120
121
DRECKSLERN, Fronica 150
DREHCELL, Theresa 117
DREHER, Anna Marg. 177
Catharine 177 Daniel 177
David 177 Jacob 177 John
177 John Henry 177
Veronica 177 William 177
DREHS, Michael 214
DREIBER, Ludwich 251
Michael 304
DREICHER, Michael 62
Susannah 249
DREICHLER, Barbara 248
251 Elizabeth 230 John 56
61 248 251 Martin 56 250
251
DREICKLER, John 56 305
DREIFOOS, Bernard 213
Catherine 213 Emanuel B.

# FULL NAME INDEX

(Dreifoos Cont.) 213 Henry
F. 213
DREIGELER, Johannes
Eberhart 155 Joh.Jacob
155
DREIGHLER, John 61
DREISBACH, George P. 175
DREISCH, Adam 154 155
Anna Maria 152 Elizabeth
152 Jacob 152 Marlena
155 Magdalena 155 Peggy
155
DREISHLES, John 61
DREISLER, Elizabeth 146
170 Johann George 130
Margaretha 130
DREITTSLER, Conrad 76
150
DREKS, Elizabeth 214
DREKSLER, Conrad 150
Elizabeth 150 Michael 76
150
DRENCKLER, Catharina 174
175 Conrad 172 174 Jacob
172 174 John Conrad 28
John J. 172 174 175 John
Jacob 30 Rosina Catharina
174 Susanna Catharina 172
174
DRENKLE, Caroline 214
Catherine 214 Daniel 214
Elizabeth 214 Henry 214
Maria 214 Sarah 214 Sarah
Ann 214
DRESCHEL, Appolomia 131
Elisabeth 131 Fredrich 131
George Frederick 7
DRESCHER, Cemetery 89
Frederich's widow 343

(Drescher Cont.) Henry 191
John C. 81 John George
175 John Jacob 30 John
Peter 42 Maria 146 Mariga
320 Mary 81 Phillip 343
Samuel 320 Susanna 147
320
DRESCHLER, Carherine F. 79
Casper 258 Frank 79 Fred
79 George 76 George J. 81
Johannes 343 John
Conrad 28 Margaret 138
Peter 12 18 139 Theresa 79
Thomas 79
DRESCLER, Francis Peter 56
Peter 250 Samuel Anthony
5 Samuels 121
DRESEL, Mrs. Clarence 79
Fred 79 George 79 Gotthart
133 Harry 79 Ignatius 319
Johann Georg 124, Marg.
J. 79, Margaretha 124
Maria 133 Mariana 179
Michael 124
DRESELE, Johann Georg 124
Margaretha 124 Michael
124
DRESELL, Elizabeth 179
Jacob 179 Mariana 179
DRESH, Andreas 103 Dewalt
103 Rudolph 304
DRESHER, Abraham 103 238
Catharina 146 320 Conrad
304 307 Eve 238 George
103 238 304 Henry 192 194
Lawrence 304 307 Maria 42
Marianna 118 Phil 304
Philip 42 Samuel 103 218
304 Stofle 304 William 260

(Dresher Cont.) William Henry 192 193 194
DRESHSEL, Herman 260
DRESKLER, Joannes 120
DRESKZELL, Anthony 3 136 Catharine 135 Samuel 135
DRESLER, Andreas 262 Andrew 301 307 Anna M. 81 Anthony 4 176 Daniel 218 David 301 307 Frederick 278 George 103 George D. 38 George David 15 Hannah 154 Ignatius 37 Jacob 34 154 313 324 Johann Andreas 11 29 262 Johann John 326 Max P. 81 Sabra 121 Susanna 154  William 330
DRESS, Conrad 214 260 Dewald 214 304 306 Dewalt 304 George 304 John 215 Michael 215 Mrs.304 Valentine 214
DRESSEL, Anna 125 Anna Maria Chrisimer 57 Anna Maria Weilin 155 Catharine 318 Dressels 220 Fredrich 124 George Frederick 7 Goodhart 2 Gotthart 124 128 157 Jacob 58 Jacobus James 10 John George 6 John Michael 6 Ulrich 220
DRESSER, Daniel 148 David 265 Elizabeth Drautel 172 Eva 128 Goodhart 2 Isaac 354 Jacob 58 James 222 Johan Nicholas 170 John 354 Joseph David 219 222 263 Joseph Johann Jacob

(Dresser Cont.) 352 Jung 173 Margaretha Danner 57 Margretha 148 184 Michael 172 Mary Driskle 179 Peter 219
DRESSLAR, Elizabeth 338 Henry 45 337 338
DRESSLER, Adam 13 Andrew 103 304 305 307 309 Andreas 116 124 129 130 131 148 257 260 298 353 Anna 171 251 353 Barb 134 314 Barbara 124 170 Cathar. 149 Catharina 171 172 173 Catharine 87 157 251 Catherine Hamman 355 Christopher 238 Daniel 148 David 3 38 103 154 170 285 304 353 Eva 148 Frederick 171 251 Goodhart 2 George 8 171 245 250 251 306 324 George Sr.252 George David 14 86 116 158 353 George D. Jacob 38 George Michael 30 124 Henry 97 335 336 Jacob 34 97 134 154 163 170 220 314 354 Jacob Knodel 134 Janathan 155 Joanna 3 Johan Jacob 171 173 353 Johan Peter 265, Johann Andreas 11 29 116 352 353 Johann David 355 Johann Jacob 59 116 Johanna M. 175 Johannes 23 171 173 John 308 211 306 316 John George Michael 6 John Jacob 355 Joseph

# FULL NAME INDEX

(Dressler Cont.) David 9
Jurg 171 172 Margaret 8
132 170 Margaret Danner
164 Maria 86 125 129 130
131 Maria Catharine 86 157
Maria Magdalena 124 129
Michael 36 326 355 Peter
103 234 Phillipina 287
Rebecca 154 Regina 3 175
Rosa Meyer 316 Salome
154 Sophia 3 171 Susanna
154 William 234
DRESTLER, Barb 134
DRESZLER, A. Marg 120
DREXEL, Abraham 224 Adam
K. 1 212 Ancestor 138
Antoni 264 Antonio 246
Anthony 3 137 Appollonia
16 Catherine 80 138 212
Charles 211 212 David 134
Drexel and Company 144
Driskle Drexel 57 Elder 135
Elizabeth 20 76 134 135
320 Francis Anthony 77
144 Francis Martin 77 144
264 Franz George 212
Franz Joseph 77 264
Hannah Langcstroth 77
Henry 1 212 Joseph 266
Jacob 134 211 212 James
137 John 1 177 195 211
212 Katherine 77 266 144
Maria 224 Marianna 118
134 Mary 91 Maud 134
Michael 80 Miss 135 143
name 58 Peter 33 166
Reuben 1 211 212
Rosianna 212 Rosina 177
Samuel 117 212 Susanna

(Drexel Cont.) 177 211 212
Thomas 1 212 Theresa 117
Triskel 144 William 1 212
DREXLER, Anna 80 Anna M.
79 Anthony 4 135
Appolonia 4 16 Carrie May
318 Charles 79 Charles C.
79 Charlotte Wehrly 179
Christian 76 150 Crescentia
80 Daniel 177 David 265
324 Elenore 152 Elizabeth
136 152 242 Emma E. 318
Francis Peter 56 355 Frank
81 Frank P. 80 Frantz Peter
265 Ferdnand 80 Frederick
79 279 George 81 George
A. 319 H.91 Infant 79
Isenberg 321 Jermiah 177
Joannes 49 154 John 80
100 103 344 355 John M.
77 John Peter 40 41
Joseph 4 19 20 33 79 91
135 143 241 242 Juliana
279 Laura May 321
Margaret 80 81 Maria 19
Mark K. 77 Mary 80 81 135
318 Mary K. 79 320
Michael 4 149 152 Mildred
E. 318 Miles Alvina 319
Peter 250 302 303 304 305
306 343 Rachael 170
Regina Kienert 85 Ruth 320
Susanna Shepp 179
William 321 William H. 319
DREXST, David 134
DREYFUS, Catherine 212
Emanuel 212 Harry 212
DREZEL, Anna Maria 131
Appalonia 124 131

# FULL NAME INDEX

(Drezel Cont.) Frederick 124 131 George Frederick 7

DRIEALER, Jacob 124 129 Johann Georg 124 Maria 124 129

DRIEBER, Peter 251

DRIECHLER, Mary 238

DRIEFUSS, Bernard 211 Catherine 211

DRIESCH, Cath. 161 Cath.Eliza 161 Catharina Elizabeth 161 Christian 161 Frederich 161 Frederick Johann Fred. 161 Joseph 161 Fried 161 Maria Barbara 161

DRIESLER, Catharina Barbara 159 160 163 David 159 161 Jacob 130 Johann Jacob 16 Joseph David 9 164 Margaret 130 Margreth 125 Margaretha Barbara 163 Maria 130 Maria Michael 130 Maria Susanna 159 161 164 Susanna 164

DRIESLERN, Margareth 125

DRIESSLER, David 159 307 George David 15 Maria Elizabeth 159 Joseph David 159 160

DRINCKLER, Conrad 172 173 174 Jacob 172 173 174 John Conrad 28 172 174 John Jacob 30

DRINKLE, Caroline 214

DRISCAL, Jacob 136

DRISCOLL, James 136 Jeremiah 354 John 143

(Driscoll Cont.) Margaret 143 Michael 211

DRISEL, Catherine 220 David 220

DRISELER, Margaret Buckman 118 Marianna 118 Samuel 118 Samuel Anthony 5

DRISKELL, Anna 136 Charles 136 Henry 136 Jacob 136 James 136 209 John 136 Margaret 136 William 136

DRISKLE, Anna 136 Charles 103 104 Jacob 58 136 James 103 Mary 136 179 name 58

DRISLER, David 101 102 241 303 George David 14 15

DRISSEL, Abraham 220 221 David 220 Henry 220 John 103 219 241 John Sr.221 Joseph 219 220 221 Leah 221 Olery 103

DRISSLE, Abraham 241 John 241 Margaret 241 Ulrich 241

DRISSLER, Andreas 29 Andrew 29 Anna Maria Cron 158 Barbara 124 Daniel 225 229 David 224 241 Elizabeth 241 242 George 8 132 304 George David 157 242 Henrietta 132 Jacob 49 229 Johannes 124 John George Michael 6 John Jacob 30 Julianna Margaret 132 Margaretha 124 128 131 Michael 124 128 131 Phillip 87 158

(Drissler Cont.) Rosina 132
DRISZLER, George 132 Rosina 132
DRIZLER, George 129 Michael 36
DROCKSEL, Adam 13
Gerhardt
   121 Herbemal 118
   Marianna 118 Sarah 118
DROEF, Valentine 214
DROES, George 214
DROEZLER, surname 257 346
DROPLER, Barney 35
DROSCEL, David 134 Maria 134
DROSLLE, George 304
DROSTEL, Abraham 52 148
   178 Anna Mary 148
   Elizabeth 148 Georg 148
   149 John 148 Maria 148
   Peter 178 Rachael 148
   Sarah 148 Susanna 148
   178
DROTSELER, surname 257 346
DROTZELER, surname 257 346
DROXELL, Catharine, Sr. 279
   Christian 9 278 David 279
   John 334
DROXSEL, George 355
DROZELER, surname 257 346
DRUCKENMILLER, Frederick 244
DRUNCKLER, John Conrad 28
DRUSCHEL, Andres 262
   George Sr.221 Rinehart 221
DRUSHAL, Andrew 262 Peter

(Drushal Cont.) 50 269 270
DRUSHALL, Peter 50 269
DRUSHEL, Elizabeth 178
   Peter 311
DRUSING, Maria 286 Maria
   Susannah 9
DRUSSEL, Andreas 176
   Andrew 29 Anna Catharina
   176 John Andreas 29
   Margaretha 176
DRUXEL, Abraham 51
DUCKER, Jeremiah 277
   Nathan 277
DUENCKEL, Anna Margaret
   177 Gertrude 177 John
   Daniel 177
DUNKEL, Jeanette 44
DUNN, Allen 313
DURSLTER, Adam 161 Johann
   Adam 161 Regina 161
DUSCHL, Caroline 81 John 81
   Mlathias 81
DUSSIEL, John 251 Margaret
   251 William 251
EARLY, Thomas J. 284
EARNHART, Elizabeth 55
EARY, Mottelina 207
EBERHARD, Anna Margaret
   31 James 70
EBERHART, Anna Margaretha
   13 Johannes 155
   Joh.Jacob 155 Joseph 13
   163 164
EBERLY, Martin T. 225 Samuel
   225
EBERMAN, Elizabeth Frank
   156 John 156 Joseph 156
   Peter Gander 60 156
ECH, John 214

# FULL NAME INDEX

ECHELBERGER, George
M.199
ECHELLBERGR, G.M. 196
ECHELLEEGER, George M.
47 199
ECKENROTH, John 138
EDELMAN, Maria Elis 172
Susannah 30 172 173
EDWART, Conflany 5 118
Edwart 121
EGAN, Rt. Rev. Michael 141
EGENDER, Johannes 164
Margaretha 164
EGNER, Lydia 42
EHLER, Catherine 15 59 60 89
156 157 159 Daniel 89 159
160 Margaretha 89 159
EHLSPERGER, Barbara 47
John Urich 47 160
EHRMAN, Andrew 224
Appolona 246 Appolonia
208 209 252 Catherine 23
137 194 252 George 224
337 Joannes 194 John 194
Josans 261 Joseph 121
137 208 209 246 252 261
302 Margaret 224 Peter
224
EICHEBERGER, Margareta 7
EICHELBERGER, G.U. 196
Margaretha 36 Margreta
155
EICHOLTZ, I. 313 Lydia C. 319
EISENHART, Anna 237
ELLENBURGER, Ella L. 230
Ellas L. 230 Frank 230
ELLIOTT, Robert M. 74
ELLIS, Jeremiah 37 Nancy
329 Nancy Ann 37 61 62

Virginia 37
ELLMEN DINGEN, District 343
ELMORE, James 329
EMMITT, Mr. 347 William 272
273
EMROCK, Balser 213
ENGLE, Elenora 152 Johannes
152
ENGLE, Elenora 4 Henry 230
Jacob 230 Jacob S. 228
Joannes 4
EPLER, Adam 189
ERB, Peter 228 230
ERDMANN, Abraham 34
154 Cadarina 34 154
Elizabeth 34 154
EREK, Catherine 186
ERLER, Kitty 320
ERLY, Margaret 313
ERMANN, Catherine 137
Joseph 3
ERNST, Jacos 245
ERUERICK, Simon G. 318
ERWIN, Margaret 316
ESSICK, Catherine 45 211
ESTERLY, Amos 214 Joseph
43
EVANS, Benjamin 236 Daniel
192 Elisha 236 Robert A.
225 227
EVERSOLE, Jacob 187
EYLER, John 275 Peter 275
Margaret 275
FARE, Barbara 313
FARMER, Father/Marriage
144 Father 321 Peter 258
FAUGHT, Moses 49 325
FAW, Mary 294
FEAGLE, Martin 322

# FULL NAME INDEX

FEGELY, Christian 218
FEISER, Juliann 32 126
FELL, Sarah T. 287
FELTON, Matthias 290
FENSTERMACHER, Killy
 Amanda 73 Leah 69
FENWICK Enoch 117
FERREA, Andrew 247
FERRY, Mary 56 143
FICK, Ann Louisa 230
FIESSER, Susanna 125
FIFER, Christopher C. 16
FILBERT, Amelia 43
FILE, Daniel 207
FINCH, Magdalina 196
FINDER, Elizabeth 222
FINES, Helen Gertrude 63
FIROR, Sophia Barbara 32
FISHER, Ann 259 Anna
 Catharina 41 Anna Maria
 23 Barabar 5 Barbara 117
 Catherine 259 Charles 349
 Cordelia 58 David 42 198
 235 Eva King 259 George
 259 Hannah 42 235 Henry
 42 249 Jacob 215 259
 James 286 Joseph 42 235
 Sabina 249 Sarah 42 249
 Thomas 259
FITCH, Henry 314
FITZ, Barbara 56 57 Henry
 283 Laura 283
FITZGERALD, Jane 294 John
 294 Margaret 143 name
 294 William 143
FIXLER, Jos. 11 314
FIZER, Juliann 32
FLANADAY, Mary 314
FLANAGAN, William 223

(Flanagan Cont.) William F.
 284
FLECK, Peter 6
FLEISCHMAN, Martin 176
FLICKWIGER, C.S. 225
FLOCK, George 47 199
FLOHR, Daniel E. 283 John S.
 278
FLOYD, Benjamin 45
FOGEL, Anna 71 Benjamin 45
 232 Carolina A. 71 Maria
 42 Philip 40 189 Rachael
 42 Solomon 231
FOLK, John 42 216 Maria 216
FORD, Arthur T.64
FORNEY, Peter 191
FOSTER, Drusilla 50 Dr. R. 91
 Thomas 50
FRACK, Susanna 57 69
FRACKLIN, Jacob 251
FRAISOR, James 255
FRALEY, David 207
FRAMBAUGH, Father 348
FRANCZ, Henry 232
FRAUDHUEGER, Catharinath
 65 Johannes 65
FRAZER, James 254
FREDERICK, Anna Caroline
 73 Tilghman F. 233
FREIDIG, Anna Juliana 12 115
FRENCH, George 270
FREY, Edward 58 Jacob 153
 Jonathan 286 Mary 71
FREYDIG, Anna Juliana 12
 115
FREYDINGER, Anna Juliana
 12 115
FRICK, Daniel 207 Miss
 Elizabeth 316 John 309

FRICKLER, Thresa 137
FRIDDLE, Catharine 315
FRINK, Wm. 45 229
FROTZ. Henry 215 Julie 55
FRONEFIELD, John 234
FRUCK, Regener 207
FUDGE, Christian 321 Mary
    321
FUGATE, Edward 184
FUNFFROCKC, Child 178
FUNK, Samuel 285
FUNKHAUSER, John Peter 47
    159
GACKLE, Catherine 177
GAGLER, David 278
GAILLARD, Charles 343
GARNER, Jane Eby 74
GARY, Margaret 138 Mary 138
    Michael 138
GATTILZIN, Prince 141 331
GAUMER, Fred 320
GEBHARD, Godfrid 263
    Gottfridt 263, Gottfriedt 263
    Margaretha 149
GEBHARDIN, Margaretha 149
GEBHARTT, Anna 149
    Johannes 149
GEFFENTIO, Francis S. 6 121
    Mary 6 121
GEHRY, John Adam 214 Maria
    25
GEIGER, Eva Barbara 162 Eva
    Catharine 20 26 Leonhardt
    130 Sarah 26
GEIGORN, Anna Maria 130
GEISLER, Father Like 353
GEIST, Barbara 231 Maria 72
GELIVEN, Prince 351
GEORGE, Ella 70 Louisa 242

(George Cont.) William
    Harry 242
GEPHART, Catherine 208
GERANFLO, Jennie 57
GERBER, Hans Christian 263
    Margrit 267 Peter 267
GERHARDT, Pearl Estelle 64
GERHART, Jessee 216
GERI, Jacob 146 170
GERINGER, Catherine 315
GEROCK, Pastor 161
GEROR, Henry 273
GERSH, Mary 36 204
GERUSIL, Lizzie V. 329
GERY, Margaret 138 Mary 138
    Michael 138
GESSENO, Mary 121
GETTS, Daniel 254
GHLING, Mary 227
GILKERSON, Achsah 68
GILMAN, Susannae 120
GLASG, Jacob 283
GLATFELTER, Casper 250
GLEASON, Johanna 47 201
GLIFFENDORFER, Joannes
    118 Maria 118
GLIFFENDORPFLER, Joannes
    119 Maria 119
GLIFFIMORERT, Joannes 119
    Maria 119
GLUDEN, Maria Madgellena
    120
GLUFFEN, Joannes 119 Maria
    119
GOBEL, Adam 190 Christina
    190
GOBRECT, Rev.John 26 John
    166
GODFREY, Raphel 17

# FULL NAME INDEX

GOESLNER, Bernhardt 54 210

GOJLIN, Emanuel 49 229 Mary
49 229

GOLD, Christoph 154

GONIG, Mary 120

GOOD, Mary Elizabeth 43
Peter 57 William 279

GOOK, Peter 223

GORNER, John 285 Paul 285

GOSHENHOPPEN, see Bally,
3 12 137 146 163 170 350
351 352 353

GOSNELL, Mary E. 75

GOSSLAR, George Adam 250

GOST, Johannes 124 129
Rebecca 124 129

GOULD, Henry 57

GRABILL, John 340

GRACE, Mary Ann 329 Zeppa
127

GRAEFF, Henry 245 Johannes
Jacob 15 Johann Jacob 88
158 Susanna Maria 88 158

GRAFF, Andreas 87 156 157
Francis 274 Jacob 87 157
Judge 342 Margaret 226
Maria 87 156 Mattheus 87
157 Rebecca 15 24 156
159

GRAMMER, Benjamin 193

GRAMMES, Peter 231

GRANFORD, Samuel 192

GRANT, Col. James 65 William
74

GRAVES, Betsey 36 315 Henry
229

GRAW, Sebastian 97 228

GRAYSON, George 200 202
Johanna 47

GREACEY, Wm. 289

GREEN, Elizabeth 35 48 329
Green Regt.335 John 284

GREENAMYER, Jacob 187
William 187

GREENAWALT, Henry 282

GREENLEAF, Catherine 285

GREENMEYER, Barbara 201
William 18 348

GREENMYER, William 200

GREENSUEIG, Edwin 239
Emma 239

GREFF, Henry 245 Veronica
245

GREISEMER, Katie 1 212
Solomon 231

GREMED, Warner T. 197

GRIESEMER, Katie 213

GRIESMER, Catherine 44

GRIM, Geittie 242 Gertraut 170
Henrich 170 Henry 68 220
Jacob 219 337 Jonathan
220 Joshua 70 Reuben 68
220 Sarah 332

GRIMAMGER, William 200

GRIMM, Catherine 42 Geittie
242 Sarah 35 332

GRIMSHAW, Dr. A.H. 91

GRIMSVILLE, Town 353

GRINN, John 275

GROEFF, Johannes Jacob 15

GROFF, Elizabeth 7 11
Jeremiah K. 290 291 John
11 Margaret 226 Maris H.
229 Mary 229

GROH, Christian 156 163

GROSCHANG, Abraham 128
Johann 128 Johannes 130
Madelena Cushion 22

(Groschang Cont.) Maria 19 128
GROSH, Mary Carlton 203
GROSS, Barbara 120 121 Frederick 174 175 265 Joannes 5 118 120 121 Johann Jacob 174 John 191 John George 174 Lewis 191 Peter 31 174 275 Phillip 174
GROUL, Henry 57 252
GROVE, Elizabeth 36 204 Henry 57 246 247 John 262 Capt.John 265
GRUBER, Jreamns 121 Susan 121 William 121
GUNBLAT, surname 197
GUNGSEL, Elizabeth 65 Heinrich 65
GUNSET, Heinrich 65
GUNTZ, Appolonia 28 130 Johann Nichol 28 130
GURMNER, John 285
GURNER, John 285 Maria Phillippina 285
GUT, Lorentz 12 164 Peter 56 57 246 247 252 Salome 164
GUTH, Edward 70 Elias 69 71 Rev. Frank 71 Joseph 69 Lucinda 70 Peter 31
HAAK, John 219
HAAS, Mrs. Albert 62 George 245 Hannah 16 Jacob 245 Jonathan 43 146 216 320 Peter 40 Valentine 333
HAELKERUN, Joseph 177
HAFFLINCH, John 243
HAFLEY, John 241

HAGER, John 281 Jonathan 271 280
HAGER, Col. George 318
HAHN, Fred 44
HAINES, Caroline Amelia 71 Elizabeth 44
HALM, Rebecca 29
HAMBRECHT, Elizabeth 27 Elizabeth Barbara 160 John Adam 27 160
HAMBRECHTIN, Eva Catherine 27 160
HAMILSON, Wm. S. 209
HAMILTON, Alex 223 Hamilton 284 James 285 286 Capt. Wm. 333
HAMMAN, Catherine 29 353 Frederick 29 353 Mary 29 353 Peter 353 Susannah 28 353
HAMMOND, Garner 264 Oliver 318
HAMPTON, Obediah 207
HAND, Elizabeth 184
HANNA'S, Capt.328
HANNAN, Jacob 34 154
HANTSCH, George 3 175
HAPSLER, Barnard 258
HARAKAUM, Joseph 144 321
HARBAUGH, George M. 32 Jacob Jr. 274 275 Susannah 201
HARBVAUGH, George M. 198
HARLACKER, Caroline 42 Elizabeth 40 44
HAROLD, Mary 245 Peter 245
HARPSTER, Jacob 243
HARR, Christina 245 Jacob 245

HARRIER, Jacob 196
HARRIS, John 273 Sarah
  A.210
HARROLE, Mary 245 Peter 245
HART, Jacob 48 204 Philip
  286 Thomas 289 290
HARTAFFEL, Elizabeth 156
HARTMAN, Nicholas 147
HASSLER, Maria Catherine
  178 Maria Elizabeth 324
  Susanna 39 52
HATFEILD, Edward 254
  Mansfeild 254
HATHWAY, Livia 313
HATZFIELD, J.A. 58
HAUGH, George 213
HAUN, Mary Ann 67
HAUSE, Naomi 22
HAUSSERAN, Magdeline 256
  345
HAUSSERMAN, Madelaine 17
HAWLEY, Betty Sue 64 Daisy
  Adelaide 64 John Edward
  64 Laura Mae 64
HAWLEYBOWER also
  Hawleybows, Balsor 205
HAWMOND, Charles E. 278
HAYDEL, Adellaide 185
  Alphonse 184 185 Family
  257 George 184 Jacques
  184 Nicholas 184, Rose 18
HCKBOS, Joannes 118
HEAD, John 197
HEADER, David 280
HEANIG, Henry 219
HEATH, Col. 35 329 Marie T.
  61 2nd.Regt. Md. Militia
  328
HEATON, Nancy 68

HECHELMAN, Elizabeth 173
  Johann Conrad 173
  Michael 173
HECKENSMITH, Michael 272
  Sheilds 272
HECKER, Anna Marie 20 166
  Anna Maria Catherine 26
  Jonas 168 Jost Wilhelm
  166 Regina 168 Sibilla
  Veronica 20 33 166 168
HECKEREWITH, Michael 272
  Sheilds 272
HECKLEY, Christianna 278
  279
HEFFER, Capt.Wm.324
HEFFLEBOWER, Balser 280
HEFFNER, Simeon Abraham
  73
HEFNERS, Mary 233
HEIBELE, Christopher 177
  Sophia Catharine 177
HEIDE, John 236
HEIDEL, Family 257 346
HEILBRON, Lillie 212 213
  Louis 212
HEILMAN, Catherine 178 Eliza
  Maria 75 Peter 178
HEIMER, Anna 175
HEISLER, George 215
HEIST, George 219
HEISTANDT, Abraham 246
HEISTER, David 278
HEITZMAN, Hans George 265
HELLER, David 169 G.K. 234
  George K. 235 236 Maria
  26 38 Maria Margaretha 42
  Maire 69
HELLICK, Magdalene 75
HELM, Jacob 153 Rosena 153

# FULL NAME INDEX

(Helm Cont.) Susanna 153
HENDERSON, Frances Ann
203 Philip 203
HENDRICK, Jacob 221 John
255
HENERY, Nicholas 292
HENNINGER, Reuben 44
HENRY, Magdalena 245
Nicholas 245 Thomas Y.
288
HERBS, Samuel 210
HERBST, Jacob 54 177 248
HERDER, Ignatius 192
HERR, Family 356 Rev. Hans
356
HERRMAN, Jacob 131
HERSHBERGER, Daniel 52
HERTZLER, Christian 228
HESLER, Anna Marie 239 Eliza
239 Jacob 239 John 239
William 239
HESSER, Susan Rebecca 32
126
HEYSTECK, Antonie Lodwwyh
193
HICKEL, Dewald 124 Eva 124
HICKMAN, Francis 222
Jefferson K. McKim 240
HICKS, Mary Ida 63
HIDY, Christina 41 John 41
HILDEBRAND, Henrich 131
HILLEGAS, Peter 215
HILLEGASS, Fredereick 291
HILLESON, John 215
HIMEBACH, Emeline V. 46
HIMMEL, May 43
HINCH, Hinch 196 Magdalena
18 201 Magdelina 200
HINDS, Benjamin 240

HINDY, R. 240
HINKLE, Barbara 196 200
Maria Barbara 18 Peter 272
HINTZ, Joseph 245 Magdalena
245
HIRST, Edwin 43 Phoebe 43
HITTEL, Elizabeth 21 69
HITZ, William 121
HITZELBERGER, Anthony 3
117 118 120 121 181 182
269 Antonia 120 Appolonia
117 118 120 Catharina 3
Emilia Catherine 118 Emilia
Couk Cook 118 George
Washington 117 Jacobus
Antonius 120 John 120
John Lewis 117 Joseph
117 Josephius 120
Josephus 120 Lewis
Corban 117 Margaretha
Norbeck 118 Maria Theresa
117 Mary Gonig 120 Mary
Rosanna 117 Nicholas 299
300 303 Nocho. 303 Peter
118 303 305 308 Petri 118
Stephanus Vincent 118
Stephen Franklin 117
widow 299 William
Antonius 120
HITZOLBARGER, Nicholas 300
HIXON, S.T. 283
HOAR, George 245 Susanna
245
HOCK, Samuel 214
HOEGER, Jonathan 133
HOFFMAN, Adam 47 125
Balleis 236 Elias 69 George
41 Hoffman 352
Houstmann 354 Joannes 6

# FULL NAME INDEX

(Hoffman Cont.) 119 121
Joann Georg 125 John 4
117 Jurg 147 Maria
Catherina 125 Maria
Christina 125 Michael 12
164 Teresa 117
Therarlackeresa 117
Theresia 6 121 Wm. 290
291
HOFS, Jacob 269
HOHENSHILT, George 30
HOLLAR, Adam 342
HOLLENBACH, Laura M. 58
HOLLENSTEIN, David H. 216
    William 216
HOLLERSTEIN, Daniel K. 216
    David H. 216 David K. 216
HOLMES, Anna Barbara 172
    Conrad 172 Johann
    George 172
HOLSHOUSER, Margaret 19
HOMER, David 290
HONIG, Johann George 28
    162 Johannes 162 John
    George 28 Maria Agnesa
    28 162
HOOKEY, Anthony 133 242
    Benjamin I. 229 Family 144
    Katherine 77 144
HOOVER, Andrew 273
    Caroline 40 Catherine 16
    89 159 Christian 273
    Daniel/Davie 196 Daniel
    197 Haus 271 Horace 274
    Lizzie 136 Mary A. 283
HORLACHER, Caroline 42
    Elizabeth 40 44
HORN, Andrew 249 Elizabeth
    41 235 236 George 249

(Horn Cont.) John 20 41
    171 184 240 Peter 184
    Susannah 249 widow 35
HORNECKER, John 67 199
HORZE, Frederick 16
HOSELER, Jacob 258
HOTTEL, Elizabeth 21
    Rosannah 322
HOTTENSTEIN, Sarah 43
HOTTENSTINE, David H. 216
HOUCH, Elizabeth 196 200
    George 82 Jacob 36 128
    196 200 315 Mary 82
    Newell Hamilton 64
HOUCHENS, Newell Hamilton
    64
HOUGH, John 272
HOUSEHOLDER, Philip 205
HOUSTMANN, surname 352
HOWERTER, Nathan 57
HUBER, Catharina 88 158
    Catherine 16 88 146
    Christine 146 Jacob 224
    Margaret 224 Peter 224
HICKI, Anthony 138 Catharine
    138 Nicholas 138
HUEST, Henry 156
HUFFMAN, John 36 315 Peter
    35
HUGHES, Clemey 195 James
    61 273 274 322 Joseph
    272 Nancy 61 Nancy Ann
    62
HULIN, William 207
HUMES, William 318
HUMMEL, Wm. 240
HUMMER, John 214
HUMPHREY, Thomas 290
HUNSECKER, Bartel 66 Jacob

(Hunsecker Cont.) 66
HUNSICKER, Lewis D. 69
HUNTER, Cleopatra 68 Edwin
    57 Sarah Ann 42
HURD, Beatrice 71 E.R. 71
    James 71
HURST, E.D. 225
HUSSERMAN, Madeline 17
HUSTON, Thoes 228 Thomas
    228 230
HUTER, Fridrich 130
HYDA, Christanna 236
    Christian 236
HYDE, Christina 41 John 41
IHLING, Mary 227
ISENBERG, Laura May 319
ISLEY, Christian 315
JACKSON, Joseph 214
JACKY, Barbara 12 65
    115
JACOBS, George W. 223 John
    49 325
JACOBY, Catherine 35 332
    John 324
JAGGI, Barbara 65 115
JAMES, Harriet 19
JARRETT, Angeline 71 John
    40 71 239 Joseph 40 41 42
    235 236 238 Maria
    Elizabeth 40
JAYSER, Jacob 160
JENNINGS, Samuel 329
JOBST, Frederick T. 288
JOHNS, Elizabeth F.Roach 64
    Etta May 64 Dr. John
    Alexander 64
JOHNSON, Charles 74 George
    263 265 266 James B. 50
    Mr. 189 Richard 285 Sally

(Johnson Cont.) 56 172
    175 Samuel 47 199 Zada
    46
JOHNSTON, David 315
JONES, Catherine 22 David
    188 Israel 236 Jacob 33
    166 Jonathan 317 Margaret
    188 Peter 188 Thomas 275
JORDAN, Margaret 34 329
    Thomas 245
JORDON, John 247
JUNG, see Young
JURY, Hanna 51
KAFELD, Elizabeth 33 176
KALLEN, Christina 267 Marg.
    267 Verena 267
KALTENBACK, Andrew 245
KAMP, Elizabeth 219
KAPLER, see Carpler, Elizabet
    119 Joannes 119 120 John
    4 Maria 4 119 120
KART, Michael 252
KAST, Eva Barbara 30
KAUFER, Adam 214
KAUTUM, John 215
KAYLOR, Matilda 140
KAZEN, Haroit 120
KECK, Edward 68 John 315
KECKERLY, D. 278
KEEBLER, Johannes 146
KEEFAUVER, Susannah 211
KEEPHAVER, Susannah 45
    211
KEINE, Anthony 143
KEISENDAFFER, Mary 117
KEISER, Eilliam 218 William 68
KELCHEY, Polly 341
KELLER, Christopher 219
    Esther 292 Jacob 292

KELLY, Elizabeth Ann 329
 Sarah J. 329
KELPPINGER, Frederick 76
 153
KELTNER, Catherine 11 31
 Michael 31
KEMMERER, George Adam 21
KEMP, Gertrude 40
KEPFORD, Daniel M. 318
 Gertrude 222
KEPLINGER, Samuel 209
KERCHER, Eliza 43
KERFOOT, R.D. 278
KERNS, Elizabeth 77 221
KERPER, Daniel 218
KERSCHER, Conrad 13
 Susanna 13
KERSHNER, John 188 323
 Capt.Martin 323
KESHER, David 188
KESLER, Jacob 255
KESLINGER, Jacob 255
KETTERING, Jacob 193
KEUTCH, A. 280
KEVELER, Catherine 219
KEY, Charles 213
KICKNLE, Lawrence 189
KIMMELL, F.M. 223 223
KINCAID, Elizabeth 207 James
 Sr. 207
KING, Elizabeth 120 Eve 259
 Henry 248 Jacob 51 224
 Jacobina 51 52 Margaretha
 119 120 James M. 242
KINGBERT, Anna Maria 120
 Jacob 120
KINIMMIELL, F.M. 223
KINTZ, Adam 286 Elizabeth
 118 121

KIRTZER, Peter 216
KISTER, Peter 243
KISTLER, John 29
KITZER, Peter 68
KLADDI, Martin 150
KLEE, Nicholas 259 Susannah
 Maria 259
KLEIN, Adam 219 Catherine
 155 Elisabeth 155
 Frederick 217 Klein Family
 Register 354 Magdalene
 219 Michael 155 Nicholaus
 155
KLEMMIAN, Anna Catherina 2
 Catharina 171
KLEYSS, Catherine 138
 Elizabeth 138
KLINE, Dr. I. 90 George 291
 John D. 281
KLINGENSMITH, Philip 200
KLONK, Elizabeth King 120
 Frau 120 Joseph 120
 Josephus 120 Peter 119
 120
KLUNK, Anne 252 Catherine
 208 246 Catherine Maria
 118 121  Elizabeth 118 121
 252 John 208 246 Joseph
 208 246 Magdelen 252
 Margaret 252 Martin 252
 Mary 208 246 252 Peter 3
 118 121 181 208 246 252
 Teresa 208
KLUTTZ, Eva 55 Moses 55
 Simeon 19
KNAYGE, John 224
KNERR, Elizabeth 46 Emma K.
 44
KNETZ, David 215

KNIGHTS, John M. 284
KNOC, also Knock, Knoc,
    Knoch, Catherine Christina
    26 Hanna Zirckel 163 166
    Henry 163 166 Maria 163
    166 Sarah 33 167
KNODEL, Jacob 314
KNORR, Dr. J.K. 91
KNOWER, Daniel 217
KNOX, Elisha 335
KOCHLER, Matthias 286
KOCKY, Sarah 168
KOEBLER, Johannes 146
KOEHLER, George 7 165 167
    Hans George 161 Vincent
    71
KOGENDORGER, Frederick
    323 Leonard 323
KOHLER, Balthaser 253 Jacob
    147 James 7 Jurg 147
KOHN, Jacob 181 John 181
    J.C. 282
KOMP, Polly Maria 43
KOONS, Henry, Mr.276
KOSER, Ruth 319 Sarah 30
KOYER, George 285 Jacob
    285
KRAMER, Daniel 28 149
    Magdalena 5 150 Maria
    150 153 Peter 5 150 153
KRAST, surname 352
KRATZ, John 290
KRAUS, Elisabeth 4 150
    153
KREISHER, Sarah Elizabeth 75
KREITER, Bernhardt 349
    Sophia Theresa 156
KREMER, Anna Maria 151 153
    George 76 151 Jacob 76

(Kremer Cont.) 151 Maria
    76 150 151 152 Peter 76
    143 150 153
KRESSLER, Jacob 307
KRICHTEN, Joseph 136
KRICKBAUM, Philip 171
KRILE, George 207
KRISE, daughter Krise 276
    Peter 22 Susan 140
KROMER, Francis 57 John 39
    239
KRONER, John 40
KRUMMEE, Elizabeth 237
KRUMOR, Elizabeth 237
KUCKELIN, Susanna 150
KUDER, James 58
KUDIG, Mrs. Leo 61
KUHN, see Coon, Adam 323
    Anna Barbara 138 Anna
    Marie 137 Catherine 3 10
    136 137 138 Catharine
    Riffel 138 Christia 22
    Eleminia 44 George 138
    139 George James 138
    Henry 138 Jacob 137 181
    209 245 246 252 James 3
    137 138 John 138 352
    John George 3 137 138
    352 Jonas 69 Margaret 138
    139 Nonnie 37 Stephen
    Jacob 246 Theresa 3 137
    138 Wm. 37 Willoughby 70
KUHNERT, Betty 4
KUHNLE, Lawrence 189
KUNTZ, also Kuntzel, Jacob
    254 Michael 176 Susanna
    178
KURK, Furgerson 252 Mary
    252 Peter 252

# FULL NAME INDEX

KURR, Thomas 213
KURRIN, Catharina 149
   Catherine 28
KURTZ, John 224 Rev. 340
   Susan 313 Susan D. 14
KUSTER, Peter 243
KUTZ, David 216
LACY, Nicholas 72
LAILE, Agnes 256 345
LAINBACH, Angelina L. 70
LAMAR, Wm. 128
LAMB, Wm. 342
LAMBERT, Bartholomew 18
LANDES, Jessee 201 Henry
   292 Susannah 292
LANDIS, Henry 3 355
LANE, Edward 354
LANG, Anna Barbara 170
   Jacob 170
LANGSTROTH, Eliza Lehman
   77 Hannah 77 144, Piscator
   77
LAY, also Loy, Appolonia 7
   115 Elizabeth 30 352
   George 201 Margaret 353
   Marie Agnes 17 Mary
   Agnes 17 Mary Maria
   Margaret 29 Michael 353
LANTZ, John 207
LAUB, also Laab, Elizabeth
   60 154 Johannes 154 John
   60 215 219
LAUBURGER, J. Michael 87
   157 Margaretha Catherine
   157
LAUX, John Jac 175
   Margaretha 175
LAZARUS, Henry 270 276
LEACH, Elizabeth B.

(Leach Cont.) 280 Nicholas
   280
LEAHER, Anna 42 Dr. 42
   Jacob 42
LEARY, Helen 63
LEATHER, Sam 215
LEBBERL, John 245 Lettia 245
LEBO, Christian 318
LECHLER, George Ernest 138
   M. Magdalen 138 Martin
   138
LEE, Margaretha 6 121
LEEK, Deitrichson 197
LEER, see Lehr, Peter 215
   Sasanna 39 239
LEFFERTS, Alfred 288
LEFTER, George Lewis 250
LEHR, see Leer, Peter 215
LEIBENGOOD, Elizabeth 44
LEININGER, Susanna 43
LEINS, Carrie 46
LEISENRING, Salome 21 72
LEITNER, Hanna 34 154 Jacob
   34 154
LEONHARD, John 148
LEROUX, Elisabeth 184 346
   Esabel 345 Isabel 256
LESHER, see Leaher
LEUPSIN, Elizabeth 56 61
   356
LEVAN, Daniel 220
LEVERING, Anthony 236
LEVITT, Firms 237
LEVY, Abraham 287
LEYTH, John 128
LICHTENBERGER, Casper
   252 253
LICHTENWALNER, Judith 45
LICK, John 142

# FULL NAME INDEX

LIEB, Christian 251
LIEBPE, Catharina 161
    Christian 161
LIES, Henry William 219
LIGGON, Albert 62 112 Alonzo
    Columbus 62 Nancy 112
    329 Reuben H. 112 Ruben
    Henry 62
LILLY, Catherine 140 Henry
    209 Isidore 140 Joseph 140
    209 Samuel 140 209 349
    Thomas 140 245 250 252
    William 140
LINEBACHER, Catherine 259
LISCHY, Jacob 29 179 Private
    Reg. 176 178 179
LITTLE, Mary Ann 126 Mary
    Ellen 126 William 126
LNUMMER, John 45 229
LOCHLER, Eva 143 Martin 138
LOESER, Maria Elizabeth 162
LOHREY, Henry 134
LONG, Barbara 219 Catherine
    219 Harman 251 Jacob 219
    Magdalena 219 Margaret
    219 Maria 219 27th
    Reg.Longs 328
LONGNECKER, John 230
LONGWELE, M. 209
LOOS, also Loose, Harry B.
    71 Jacos 225 Jacob 227
LORISH, Amanda 69
LORTSCHER, Abraham 268
    David 268 Hans Rudolf 268
    Isaac 268 Jakob 268
    Jobam 268 Salome 268
    Susanna 268
LOWE, Patrick 47 199
LUCK, John 142 143 Maria

(Luck Cont.) 142 143
LUCKELL, Wm. 276
LUDEN, Fridrich 148
LUDLOW, Dr. J.L. 91
LUDWIG, Benjamin 230 Daniel
    230 George 216 Peter 72
    Sarah 43
LYERLY, Christopher 55
    Elizabeth L. 19 Margaret 19
    Moses 55
LYMANN, Margaret 34 332
LYNN, Jane 59 John Sr. 59
MABANE, Mary 315
MADERIA, Nicholas 218
    Susanna 218
MAEHEINGER, Dr. G. 91
MAILHOFF, Philip 273
MAISON, Anna Maria 178
MALENY, Joseph 54 210
MALLOW, George 21 254
    George,Jr.254
MANBOCK, John 214
MANN, John 225
MANSFIELDL, Dr. R.G. 90
MAPHEL, William 205
MARCH, John 191
MARCHA, Barbara 248
    Laurence 248
MARKLE, Margaret 340
MARKS, John 18 196 200
    Margaret 196 200
MARQUETANT, Loranz 161
MARR, Margaret 43
MARSHALL, Louisa 53
Marshall
    290 Paul 198
MARSTELLA, Frederick 2 171
MARTIN, Anna 46 327 Antonia
    119 Antonius 229 Barbara

# FULL NAME INDEX

(Martin Cont.) 195 200
Catherine Drecksler 119
Clinton Tilgman 75
Elizabeth 18 22 175 G.E.
318 Herman C.3
Hermangel C. 119
Hermann 119 Jacob 229
Johannes 127 John 18 27
28 233 Mathias 18 22 49
50 127 128 233 Rachel 325
Samuel 185
MARX, Balthasar 257 345
Elizabeth 245 Jean Simon
257 346 Marianne Agae
257 346
MARY, Elizabeth 245 John 245
MASLO, Anna Maria 218
MASON, John T. 341
MATERN, Caherine 17 Cath.
257 Nik.T. 257
MATERNE, Catherine 17
MATHIAS, Capt. Hennery 337
Rosie 319
MAUHERZ, Jesse R. 283
MAUL, Bartholomew 251
MAURRY, Anna 121 Emertinia
120 Nancy 121
MAXEL, Samuel 197
MAY, Tobias 315
MAYER, George Ernst 253
Philip 246 William Frederick
228
McALLISTER, John 275
McBRIDE, James 322
McCAFFER, John 191
McCAMEY, James 36
McCAMIE, James 314
McCAREY, Jane 317
McCARTY, Nicholas H. 221

McCELLAN, David W.B. 270
McCLVEY, Julian 237
McCONALLY, Margaret 143
McCONCHE, also McConachy,
Johannes 151 Robert 151
Susanna 151
McDONALD, Owen 130
McDONOAGH, John 269
McELMEE, Hannah 141
McELROY, John 290 Julian
237
McFARLAND, John 317
McGUIRE, Capt. Richard 138
McKIM, Jefferson K. 240
McLELLAN, William 223 284
McMAHON, John 271
McMANUS, William E. 318
McMECHON, John 276
McMILLAN, Capt. 331 Maris
229
McRITTER, George B. 318
MEIER, Algelina 73
MENCHER, Johannes 9 132
Margaretta 9 132
MERCER, Harriet 49 Louiza
50 Nottingham 49 325
MERKLE, also Markel,
Margaret 24 74
MERTENGEL, Hermangel C.
119 Hermanus 3
MERTZ, Anna Margaret 13
Father Nicholas 330 Rev.
John Nicholas 120 Minister
119
MESIMER, Polly 19 55
METZ, Joseph 287
METZGER, John 45 231 232
MEYERS, Jonathan 280 Ollita
138

**394**

# FULL NAME INDEX

MICHLE, John 269
MICKLE, also Mickley,
Elizabeth 21 69 71 73 75
Esther 69 Marg.167, Martin
50 165 Salome 30
MIDDAUGH, John 323
MIDDLETON, Father Thomas
C. 350 Town 223
MILLER, Abraham 144 Ann
187 Annie 69 Benjamis 242
Casper 252 Catherine 151
Charles 71 Charles J. 235
289 Christian 75 320
Christine 13 23 Elijah 73
Elisabeth 177 316 George
55 144 249 Geraldine 55
Harietta 40 Harry 43 189
James 287 Johannes 151
John 27 57 214 240 246
247 252 319 Joseph 45
231 Louisa 86 Louise L.
316 Madg.144 Maria 151
Mary 246 247 252
McClellen 223 Miss 130
316 Peter 237 287 Susanna
317 Tobias 285 Wilbur 318
William 37 249
MINCE, Catherine 18 196 200
201
MISSIMER, Mary 1 Mary H.
211 212 Samuel 234
Samuel D. 1 211 212
MITCHELL, Mary 194 Mary
Ann 67
MITLER, Lydia 291
MMUIM, Clara J. 319
MOHLER, Elizabeth 23 24 121
MOHN, Catherine 170 Peter
170

MOHR, Peter 70 Samuel 70
MOLOW, Elizabeth 24 175 321
MONRY, Nancy Ann 330
MONTGOMERY'S, Capt.329
MONTPELIER, Daniel 265
MORGAN, Bernard 61
Elizabeth 73 316 Esther 74
MORNINGSTAR, John 253
MORRIS, John 252 Joseph
215 Messrss. 268 Store
266
MORRISON, Hans 269
MOSER, Susan 26
MOSSER, Elizabeth 40
MOSSETER, Christian 199
MOTLEY, Isaac 202 Joshua
202 Lewis M. 202
MOTTER, Jacob 47 200 202
Jermia 197 Jermiam 202
Jeremiah 200 Jocob 202
Joseph 197 Lewis 22
MOURRY, Emertinia 120 121
Joannes 120 Nancy 120
MOYER, Algelina 73 Catherine
68 Clinton 73 John 241 244
Leonary 189 Michael 285
MUECKLE, also Mueckli,
Jacob 50 165 168 Susanna
50 168
MUELLER, Daniel 133 David
133 Juliana 133
MULHOLLAY, Thomas 315
MULLER, Henry 231 Jacob
130 253 Muller 267
MULLIKIU, Emma P. 329
MUMBAUER, George 237 238
George S. 290 291
MUMBOUER, George S. 291
MUMPER, Daniel C. 319

MURDOCK, Eleanor 209
MURPHY, Susan 283
MURRAY, also Murry, Anna
   3 37 Catherine 143 James
   143 181 191 John E. 193
   194 Imavanchaanau 193
   194 Nancy Ann 329 Nancy
   Anna 92
MURTIZ, Joseph 197
MUSSELLMAN, Israel B. 60
   217
MYERS, Edna May 319 James
   341 John W.318
NAILOR, Wm. 192
NEAFF, Henry 292
NEASWITZ, Valentine 209
NEAT, George 271
NEFF, Clyde C. 318
NEIFF, Tavern 341
NEISWANGER, Dorothy 56 61
   widow 356
NENNERMACHEY, William H.
   232
NEUHARDT, also Neuhart,
   Anna Barbara 12 164
   Barbara 7 165 167
   Frederick 164 Maria
   Margaretha 13 164 Michael
   165 166
NEUMANN,Biship 351
NEWCOMB, Elizabeth 44
NEWCOMER, Bishop Christian
   178 John 229 Tobias 127
NEWHARD, Emeline Amelia
   57 Franklin J. 233 Mary A.
   58 69 Mollie 58 70
NEWMAN, Wm. 54 210
NICHODEMUS, Capt.323
NICKUM, Elizabeth 83 201

(Nickum Cont.) John 82 83
   201 John D.48 202
NOEL, Alvin Douglas 63
   Barbara 245 Carlyle 63
   Charles Jefferson 63
   Delores Ann 63 Grace
   Laverne 63 James Leslie
   63 Marian Coleman 63
   Peter 245 William Carlisle
   63
NOLL, Barbara 245 Peter 245
NORBECK, Margaretha 118
NORTH, George 265
NUGENT, Maria B. 72 Thomas
   72
NUSSMAN, Solomon 19
NYCE, Jacob C. 286 John 40
   Phillipinia 40
O'BOLD, Christina 19 135
   Joseph 19 135 O'Bolds
   Family 135 Susan 19 135
O'DEER, Patrick 217
O'NEILL, Bernard 272
OASTER, Adam 130 135 John
   136
OBER, John 72 225
OBERLIN, Daniel 68 John 72
ODENMAN, John G. 38 251
OEHLER, Catherine 15 59 60
   157 Daniel 59 Margaret 59
OEKIN, Alexander 142 Maria
   142
OGLES, Capt.S. Co.35 329
OHLE, Catherine 259
OHLER, Catherine 48 145
   156 George Ad. 48 145
ORLER, Ella 319
ORLINGER, Philip 205
OSBBORNE, Mary Murburger

# FULL NAME INDEX

(Osbborne Cont.) 68
OSMAN, John 265
OSTERTAG, Christian 125
   Juliana 125
OTT, also Otto, Elsie S. 33
   Hanna 40 John Matthew
   175 Matthew 3 171
OTTILIA, Anna 161
OVERMIRE, George 243
OWINGS, Patrick 47 199
   Samuel 269 270 William
   274
OWSLEY, Wm. 339
OYLER, Anna Appolonia 259
PACA, Helen 203
PARKMEN, Isaac W. 332
PAULI, Catherine 73
PEELER, Barbara 35 318
   Daniel 55 David D. 19
   Henry 19 318 Mary 54
   Samuel 55 Sarah
   Clementine 55
PELLENGEN, William B. 197
PELLENTZ, Father 136 348
   James 209
PENCE, Jacob 21 254
PERKINS, Egbert A. 63 Emma
   K. 63 Lottie May 63
PERSINGER, William 21 254
PETERS, Albert 73 Henry 177
   Maria Catherine 177
PETTIS, Mrs. H.D. 62
PFEIFFER, Maria Elizabeth
   175 321
PHEBY, Anne 203
PHIFER, Leonard 280
PHILABNER, Juliana 133
PHILLIPS, Elizabeth 29 John
   223 284

PIERCY, Mary A. 340
PIEREY, Jacob 185
PIERY, Jacob 6 185
PILGRIM, Henrich 76 151
PINKNEY'S, Artillery Co.328
PINKSON, Artamessa 316
PLAEK, Henry 199
PLENSING, Fried 175
PLUFER, Leonard 278
PLUNCK, Samuel 289
PNLETCK, Polly 36 330
POE, see Poh, Eva 61
   Georgeous 119 Henry 221
   Jacob 61 James 286 Mary
   Margaret 61 62 Sebastian
   George 119
POH, George 330
POLHOUSE, Thomas 271
POLK, Conrad 242 John 42
PONESMITH, Clinton E. 318
POOL, Richard 287
POOLE, William 192
POOT, Petter 175
POPPLEIM, Johann George
   193
POPPLIM, Nicholas 191
POPPLIN, Johann Nicholas
   193
POTTS, Geoell 236 Philip 44
   Richard 196
PRATHE, James 280
PRATHER, Perry 313 Thomas
   276
PREIFS, 237
PRESELER, Ann 330 Ignatius
   37 330
PRESLAR, also Prexley,
   Andreas 116 Andrew 116
   Ant Je Ann 116 Christian

# FULL NAME INDEX

(Preslar Cont.) 116 John
Volintine 116 Thomas 116
Wells 116
PREUSS, Thomas 130
PRICE, Augustine Sr. 257
Josua 283 Nancy 49 327
PRIEST, George 243 Louis
Barth 143
PRIOR, Samuel 278
PRITNER, Isaac H. 237
PROSLER, Andrew 116 Ann
116, John Vollintine 116
PUREL, Antonio 18
PUSEY, Sarah 32
QUANTRILL, Capt. Thomas
340
QUICK, John 154
QUICKIE, Adam 21 254
RADELINE, Charles 59
RADER, Charles 237
RADINGER, Catherine 175 321
RAG, Ann Caroline 314
RAGY, Christopher 176
RAMBO, Abel 287
RANDALL, N.A. 196
RAPP, Charles F. 288 289
RATENBUSCHIN, Maria
Drusiana 160
RATHGEBER, Eva Magdalena
59 352
RATZELL, Mary 36 204
RAUGH, Sarah 313
RAULS, Elmer H. 318
RAUTENBUSH, Maria Drusiana
176 Maria Susanna Drusina
9
READIN, Thomas F. 237
REAKIRK, Sarah 42 235
REAM, Mary 37 51 125

REANSER, John 283
REED, also Reedy, Daniel
265 James 143 Juliana 24
25 88 156 158 Margaret
143 Mary 156 Philip 237
238 290 Robert 156
REGAR, David 212 Lillie V. 212
REHMER, also Reimer,
Frederic
54 Frederick 247 252
REICHARD, Christina 30 31
320 Christine 147 Juliana
88 158
REICHART, Anna Marie 15 24
25 88 158 Maria 156 158
REID, Patrick 272
REIDENOUR, John 216
REIGART, Adam 24 Emanuel
226 Mary 89 159
REIGERT, Christophel 285
REILEY, John Timon 135
Nancy 3 4 176
REILLY, Philip 284
REINER, Jacob 215
REINERT, William 58
REISEL, Martin 138
REISS, also Reisser, Elizabeth
40 43 Hans Georg 263
REIST, Christian 228
REITER, Margaret 291
REITNAUER, A. Maria 133
Benjamin 133 Elis 133
REITZELL, George 286
RELITZ, Christian 218
REMP, Jacob 217
RENCHLER, John G. 219
RENO, Judith 42
RENTCH, Andrew 279
REODER, Henry 237

# FULL NAME INDEX

RESELER, Ann 330 Ignatius
37 330
RESH, Augusta E.E. 58
Caroline 58 Ephraim 58
RESSELER, Anna Catharne
123 Christian 123
RETTMANN, Johannes 149
REUTCH, Andrew 279
REYDENOUR, Adam 200
RHOADARMER, J. 223
RHOADES, John 190
RHOADS, Daniel 70 Peter 240
Walter P. 70
RHODE, Peter 189 240
Susanna 313
RHODES, Susanna 313
RHORER, Christian 17 187
David 187 Family 17
Francis 17 187 Maria 188
Maria Barbara 17 188
Samuel 16
187 188
RIAKIRT, Sarah 235
RIBLIN, Agnes Jane Eagle 74
Christina C. 74
RICH, Henry 206
RIDENOUR, Joseph 18 349
RIDNEY, Samuel 143
RIEGART, Emanuel 226 Jacob
285 Jane 285 Mary 159
RIENNER, John 258
RIFE, Mary 233
RIFFEL, also Rifle, Riffle,
Catherine 3 137 138
Christina 245 Elizabeth 3
10 136 George 245 Jacob
138 Matthias 245 name 352
RIGEL, Andrew 213
RISH, David 47 199

RISTEL, surname 352
RITTENHOUSE, James 42
Lucinda 42 290
RITTER, Christina 190 Father
351 352 John Baptist 350
RITZ, Peter 44
ROACH, Elizabeth F. 64
ROBERTS, John J. 288
ROBESON, Johannes 119
Jonathan 236
ROBINSON, Catherine 118 121
Charles 323 Elizabeth 14
15 87 89 157 158 159 327
James 15 87 157 John 323
Samuel 193
ROBSEN, John 330
RODENBITTER, Phillip 276
RODENMAYER, George 192
194
RODGERS, Alen 207 Randel
207 Samuel 207 Zacariah
207
ROEDERBUSH, Amatuina 237
ROELLER, Isaac 43 Rev. 216
ROELOFES, also Roeloles,
Mrs. 192
ROHNEN, Anna 143
ROHR, Jacob 340
ROHRBACH, Christian 258
ROHRER, Family 257 Gottfried
213
ROHRMAN, Conrad 175 John
Henry 175
ROLAND, John 215
ROMMEL, Ana Maria 145
Ludwig 145 Sophia 145
RON, Nathaniel 197
RONIG, John 189
ROOT, B.M. 53 Sebastian 49

RORSE, Jacob 204
ROSE, Hugh 313
ROSEBERRY, Jepe 44
ROSOE, Michael 271
ROSSEL, Jerick 261
ROSSELL, Catherine 261
Maria Crete 66 Mary Crete
261
ROTH, also Rother, Anna
Madalena 21 64 65
Catharina 133 Elisabeth
147 George F. 43 Gottfried
30 Johannes 133 Juliana
13
ROTHENBERGER, Cornelius
K. 1 Cornelias K. 214 Rosa
213 214, Rosianna 213
William 74
ROTHERBERGER, William 74
ROTHROCK, Samuel 208
ROUDENBUSH, Henry 237
239 249
ROUDERBUSH, Henry 237
ROWE, George 209 Jacob 205
Joshua 197 Michael 276
Sarah J. 22
ROYER, Jacob 323 John 284
RRODER, Thomas T. 237
RUBEN, Anna Maria 66
Stephan 66
RUCH, Georg 164 Lizzie 69
Peter 69 Capt.Ruch's
Pa.Mil. 332 Susanna 164
Capt. Thomas 73
RUDOLF, Hans 268 Henry 239
RUDOLPH, Hannah 239
RUDY, Anna Maria 248 George
248
RUHL, Gertrude 177 John

(Ruhl Cont.) William 177
RUMBLE, Amelia A. 58
RUNCKEL, Johann Ludwig
267
RUNNER, Michael 199
RUPP, Daniel 266 Israel 266
John 232
RUSH, Capt. Jno. 255
RUSSEL, also Russell,
Alexander 209 Capt. James
262 James 265
RUTH, George 148 William H.
317
RUTLER, Ann 191 193 Wm.
194
SAEGER, Alfred 71 Anna
Barbara 21 22 66 Margaret
71 Nicholas 334 Thomas E.
71
SALFORD STORE, Ledger 3
355
SALZMANN, Anna 267
SAMM, Peter 271
SAMPLE, Annie M. 283
SAMPSON, Jacob 270
SAMUEL, Louisa C. 75 Ship
12 66
SANDER, John 242
SANDERS, Edmund 135
SANTEE, Charles 235 Chris
235
SASBALTER, Ralph 209
SATTLER, Margaret 44
SAUVRTZ, Catherine 237
SAVANT, Mathieu 17
SAVIGON, Francois 17
SAWYER, Stephen 42
SAXTON, Mary Ellen 46
SAYLOR, Jacob 224

# FULL NAME INDEX

SCHAADT, Esther Hettie 71
Maria Ann Mary 21 Peter
21
SCHAFFER, Jonathan 332
Reuben 72 Schaster 352
SCHALL, Caroline 42 288
George 43 Jacob Henry 44
Mary 43 William 42
SCHARD, Johannes 36 155
SCHBCES, Johannes 5 121
SCHEIBLEY, George 29
SCHELL, and wife 7
SCHENEBRUCH, Casper 190
John 190
SCHENKEL, Maria 126
SCHERMAN, Marg. Elizabeth
34 154 Simon 34 154
SCHILLING, Anna Maria 2 171
Joannes 2 Johanes 171
SCHINDELOF, Elmina 42
SCHIOL, Charles 269
SCHISLER, Catharine 136
SCHLAUCH, Catherine 220
Joseph 220 Judith 220
SCHLEIER, also Schleienson,
Anna 173 Johann Michael
173 Michael 173
SCHLEY, Margaret 19 129
SCHLICHER, Susanna 288
SCHLOUGH, Ursula 69
SCHLUTER, John 64
SCHMECH, Henry 214
SCHMEIER, Family 354
Joshus 45 354
SCHMEYER, John 242
SCHMID, also Schmidt, Anna
Christine 162 Barbara 33
147 Catherine 138 Christina
47 160 Elizabeth 124 128

(Schmid Cont.) 131 Eva
Mary 138 Henrich 124 128
131 173 Magdalane 173
Michael 124 128 131 Phillip
138
SCHMIDITN, Anna Christine
162
SCHMIED, Magd. 268 Rosina
Dorothea 59
SCHMITT, George 7 36 155
John 253
SCHMOYER, Joseph 45
Joshus 354 Mary A. 42
SCHNAUTIGEL, Jacob 125
Margareth 125 Maria
Barbara 125
SCHNEIDER, Catharina 133
Christian 37 Eva 7 147
Father 350 351 352
Frederick 265 Hannah 44
Henrich 7 90 Jacob 133
Johann 7 167 Johann
Henrich 263 Johannes 165
Jonathan 133 Maria
Catharina 149 Michael 149
Rev. Thedore 350
SCHNOBILY, Catharina 8 132
John 8 132
SCHNUYER, Joshua 231
SCHOCK, Jacob 225 John 228
SCHOENBERGER, John 33
SCHOENER, Helena Catharine
20 31 Henry 20
SCHOFF, John 225
SCHOLL, Amelia 42
SCHOOCK, Abraham 57
SCHOPF, John 227
SCHOTT, Anna Catharina 9
SCHRANTZ, Johann Jacob

# FULL NAME INDEX

(Schrantz Cont.) 173
Johannes Phoebe 173
SCHREIBER, Anna Madalena
22 65 66 Catharine Maria
Magdalena 22 66 John
Jacob 22 65 Maria 22 Peter
169 Susanna 169
SCHREIER, Jacob 199
SCHREINER, Elizabeth 36 Eva
Catharina 161 Maria Anna
130 Valentine 36
SCHREYER, Eva 259 John
259 Nichholas 259
SCHRIEDER, Jacob 191
SCHRIENER, Valentine 130
Elizabeth 130
SCHROEDER, also
Schroedius, Martin 343
SCHROLL, Catherine 57
SCHROYER, Jacob 67
SCHRUPP, Matthis 128
SCHULTER, Andres 154
SCHULTZ, Anna 238 Peter
253 Jacob 281
SCHUMACHER, Catherina 41
147 Daniel 147 Maria
Catherine 2 52 172 324
Maurietias 118 Mrurilus
121
SCHURCH, Ulli 267
SCHUYMACHER, Johann
George 176 355
SCHWARTZ, A.A. 319 Eliza 43
Valentine 124
SCHWEICKER, Barbara 60 154
SCHWENCK, Christian 288
SCHWERTZOL, Abraham 133
Catharine Barbara 133
Mathaus 133

SCOTT, George 278 279 280
George T. 362 George
Tressler 352
SEAY, Emma K. 63
SEEGRIST, Hans Urick 252
SEGRIST, John Ulrich 249
SEHNER, Fred. 161
SEIB, Rosina 25
SEIBERLING, Sarah 41
SEIBERT, Benjamin 44
SEICHREST, Barbara 62 Hans
Ulchrist 62 249
SEIDEL, Danie 69 Emma 1
Emma Lousia 212 Mahon
231 Samuel 1 212 Uriah 69
SEIFFERT, Sarah 126
SEIP, Roina 25
SELLL, Mary 259
SEMMEL, Louisa C. 75
SEMONS, James 192
SENTMAN, Samuel S. 282
SEPTER, John 274
SERATTE, Sally 9
SEYBERT, Tobias 285
SHAAFF, Alice 203 Arthur 203
Casper 203
SHAFER, Henry 278 Jacob
177
SHAFFER, Casper 230 Henry
279 John 214 Peter 200
SHAMBACK, George 242
SHARP, Soloman 315
SHATTERBY, Hessey 315
SHATTERLY, marriage 315
SHAW, E. 210 James Emmett
75
SHEADS, Peter 24
SHEARER, Catherine 29 30
Clarence L. 318 Jacob A.

(Shearer Cont.) 318
SHEIB, also Sheip, Michael
240 Rosanna 8 Rosina 8
Rosina Margaret 8
SHEIVE, George 287
SHELDON, Lewis L. 231
SHELL, Thomas 184
SHENEBRUCH, Caspar 190
John 190
SHEPARD, Jesse 289
SHEPHERD, Robert Winfrey 63
SHEPORT, Jesse 289
SHEPP, Susanna 33 177
SHEARER, Catherine 30
Clarence L. 318 Jacob A.
320
SHERER, also Shearer,
Searer, Solomon 232
SHEUMAN, Elizabeth 214
SHEWARDS, John 208
SHICHT, Jesse 238
SHIELDS, Henry 187 James
187 Shields Addition 197
198 200 William 187
SHIFFERT, Andrew 44
SHIFFLET, Andrew 231
SHILLING, Robert 37 William
278
SHIPSLER, Adam 258
SHISLER, Adam 349
SHMIFS, Andrew E. 225
SHOCK, Abraham 246 247
Anna 247 Henry 230 Jacob
227 John 230
SHOLTS, Capt.Fred 327
SHOPP, Henry 230
SHORB, Andrew 194 Faurier
A. 202 Jacob 246 Jannis A.
47 199 John 33 245

SHOVER, Adam 196 Peter 274
SHOWER, Abraham 208 Adam
312 David 48 84 204 208
317 Adam Thomas 18
Deliah 208 Elizabeth 200
201 Polly Ann 208
SHREIBER, Jacob 50 167 168
Peter 26 167
SHREINER, Cemetery 86 Clara
R. 230 Phillip 276
SHROEPE, John 270
SHRYER, John 273
SHRYVER, Jacob 190 Mary
190 320
SHUFF, Harriet Elizabeth 126
SHULTZ, Amous 215
SHUMAN, Adam 229
Catherine 229 John 55
SHUYLER, Jacob 190
SHUYVER, Juliana 190 Mary
320
SIBBEST, John 245 Letia 245
SIDDALL, John Edward 242
SIDLER, Jacob 248 Luzey 248
SIEBERS, Margaret 10
SIEBERT, Isaac 214 John 48
204
SIEGFRIED, Abraham 220
Daniel 220 Elizabeth 21 70
220 Gertraut 220 Henry 70
220 Jacob 220 John 220
Magdalena 68 220
SIGFRIED, also Siegfried,
Abraham 220 Daniel 220
Elizabeth 220 Gertraut 220
Henry 221 Jacob 220, John
220 271 Magdalend 146
220
SIMPSON, James M. 62 Mary

(Simpson Cont.) A.
Elizabeth 62 Sarah 62
SIMS, Elizabeth 241
SINGMASTER, Mary Ann 42
SINN, George Christian 251
SKINNER, William 283
SKRAYORK, H. 280
SLAGLE, Jacob 252
SLEELY, William Henry 47 199
SLEINAUER, also Sleinaur,
Rosa 212 George 212
SMALL, Catharine 177
SMECK, Jacob 219 Susanna
219
SMEE, Blanche M. 321
SMIDT, Jacob 14 144
SMITH, Anna 319 Capt. 353
Charles 265 Christian 272
Christina 214 Daniel 143
Dawn Bieller 314 Mrs. Elis
14 144 Elizabeth 16 Ellen
189 Francis K. 71 Jac. 14
144 John 214 280 Joseph
56 249 250 355 Joseph Jim
275 Mary 143 Mary Ann 47
197 200 201 202 Melchor
189 Robert 281 Rosina
Dorothea 59 Peter 338
Philip 29 Ubbia 43
SMOOT, Jedidah 322 Leonard
322
SMOYER, Kate A. 68 Stephen
42 William 276
SNIDER, Christian 322
Nicholas
198
SNIVLEY, Jacob 278
SNYDER, Cora 74 Edwin 73
John 224 Samuel 44

SOHN, George 251
SOHREINER, Valentine 129
SONTAG, Henry 54 209
SOUTH, Thomas 279
SOUTHWARD, also
Southworth, Zawood 113
Zazhary 114
SPALHOFFER, Reuben 238
SPANGLER, Abraham 210
George 294 Mary 45 211
SPANNSEILER, Jacob 27 160
SPANSAILER, Jacob 286
SPANSEILER, also Spanseller,
Jacob 9 27 160 Joseph
162
SPANSELLER, Julianna 247
Frederick 248
SPATZ, Conrad 220
SPENGLER, Anna Maria
Margaretha 50
SPIECKER, Benjamin 27 160
Margaretha 27 160
SPIERS, Ulrich 28
SPIES, Ulrich 149
SPORRSELLER, Michael 47
199
SPRENCKEL, Peter 251
SPRIGGS, William 49 325
SPRINGEL, George 292
SPRING, Martin 241
SPRINGEL, George 292
SROSCLER, surname 257 346
ST. PAUL'S, Catholic Church
3 138
ST. PETER'S, Catholic Church
121
ST. PETER'S, Lutheran Church
42 180
STAHLER, Anna 71 Reuben

(Stahler Cont.) 231
STAHLNECKER, James 231
STAINSBURY, Joseph 355
STAKE, Martin G.E. 318
STALLSMITT, Daniel 210
STANSLER, Christina 313
STARNES, Michael 207
STARR, Anne E. 314 Catherine
    186 Deborah 4 11 119 314
    Elizabeth 209 210 George
    209 210 Isaac 222 Joseph
    186 Mary J. 314 Moses 222
    Samuel 222 Wm. 222
STATTLEMAYER, Mary E. 32
STAUB, Betsy 136
STAUFFER, Andrew 215 David
    219 Henry 219 Lydia 219
    Vincent 319
STAYER, Christian 250
STAYMAN, Lizzie 223
STECKEL, Anna Maria 68
    Coletta 69 Ephraim 71
    Milton 71
STEDMAN, Charles 263 265
STEELE, Anthony 194
STEEVER'S, Capt.328
STEHLY, John 246
STEIGENWALT, Charles 230
    Charles T. 226 M.T. 226
STEIGEWALT, Charles 226
    Henry 226
STEIN, Catherine 203 Wilhelm
    149
STEINAUER, Rosa 1 213
STEINAUR, Rosa 213
STEINBACH, David 146
    Elizabeth 146 John 146
STEINER, Barbara 156 267
    Elizabeth 15 88 158 Jacob

(Steiner Cont.) 156
    Margartha Thomas 156,
    Michael 15 88 156 158 171
    Rebecca 88 158
STERNER, Sally E. 73
STEWART, Eve 246 252 John
    49 247 Mathias 57 246 247
    252 Nathan 49 325
STIFFLER, John 295
STILLER, Albert 80
STINEMETZ, George 341
STINER, John Conrad 258
STOBER, Barbara 155 George
    155 Jacob 155 John 225
    Michael 155
STOCK, George 54 210
    Melchoir 243 Sarah 210
STOFFEER, Nicholas 213
STOFFIET, Eva 165 John 165
    Maria 33 166 168
STOHR, Dorothea 155
    Frederich 155
STOIFFIET, John 20
STOKE, Abraham 210 Caroline
    229 Catherine C. 210
    George 54 210 Henry 210
    Jacob F. 210 Joseph 210
    229 Robert Young 277
    Samuel 210 Sarah A. 210
    Stoke 210 William 210
STOKES, Robert Young 277
STOLL, Jacob 231
STOLTZ, David 341
STONE, Church 177 John
    Letcher 64
STONEBECK, John 317
STONER, Abraham 283 David
    187 Elizabeth 156 John
    Conrad 258 John Michael

(Stoner Cont.) 342 Michael 156 Rudolph 156
STORA, Hanna 51
STORM, Joseph 19 135
STOUDT, Josephine 74
STOVER, George 223 Jacob 54 177 247 248 252 John Casper 155 John Casper Register 6 Susannah 317
STRICKLER, Henry, Jr. 248 Jacob 247 248 John 57 61 246 247 248 248 292 Joseph 57 246 247 252
STRATOR, Susannah 314
STRAUSE, Angelina L. 70 Clara K. 70 Emanuel S. 70
STREGERWALT, Charles T. 225
STREIT, Christian 322
STRINK, Benjamin 60 217 218
STROBELE, Frederick 285
STROH, Mary Ellen 3 4 Nicholas 244
STROSCLER, surname 257 346
STUCKER, Mary Chloe 207
STUHULL, John 279
STULE, John 279
STULL, John 279
STUMP, Benjamin 217
SUESSEROTT, J.L. 282
SUMMARY, Maria G. 237
SUMMERS, Aaron H. 237
SUNDAY, Elizabeth 38 203 205
SUPER, Philip 291
SUTTON, Frank T. 330
SWAIN, Charles A. 279
SWALB, Anna Maria 175

SWARTZ, Catherine 40 56 237 Jacob 189
SWENK, Martin 243
SWILAR, Catherine 52 204 205
SWINK, John H. 349 Peter H. 349
SWINKWAG, Henry 349
SWINNEY, Joanna 143
SWITZGABLE, Vincent 225
SWOPE, Benedict 269 Luriel 225 Mr.'s old place 341
TAESCHLER, Anthony 343
TAESCLER, Elizabeth 129
TALLEY, Margaret Mary Virginia 63
TANEY, Felix B. 340
TAPPER, Madelean 3 Madelen 137
TAXLER, Hans Atam 261
TAYLOR, Joseph 289
TBALBACH, Peter 287
TCHISL, Charles 269
TEAS, John 186
TECKLER, Valantin 262
TEESLER, David 298
TEICHELER, Johannes 155
TEIGHLER, John 61
TEISCHER, Jacob 343
TEISHER, Jacob 132 204 John 47 204 Mary 204 Michael 62 249 Peter 36 204 Susanna 249
TEITCHER, Barbara 252 Michael 62 252
TELCHER, Johannes 262
TELFER, Blanche Tressler 352
TERECH, Anthony 203 Catherine 203
TESCH, also Tesche, Ada 262

# FULL NAME INDEX

(Tesch Cont.) Adam 262 Catrina 262 Engel 262 Henrich Peter 262

TESCHLER, Adam 26 39 165 167 Apel 167 Maria Barbara 39 165 167 Peter 167

TESIER, Rev. John 185

TESTER, George 109

TESSIER, Anthony 108 Francis Peter 56 Mary Ferry 143 Peter 143

TEUBELBIS, Christian 129 Margaretha 129 Maria Magdalena 129

TEUSCHER, Anna 268 Duchtly 268 Niklaus 267

TEUTSCH, Johan Phillipp 261 Philip 253

TEXTOR, John 286

THAGER, Jonathan 133

THALER, Jim 123 Johannes 123 Margaretha 123 124 Schim 123

THELHOLD, Henry 275

THESER, John 94

THOMAS, Adam 18 196 Anna Magdalena 15 88 89 156 158 159 Catharine 88 158 Charles 139 Elizabeth 18 196 George 15 88 89 156 158 159 George Philip 156 John 38 236 285 Julianen 156 Lambert 193 Margartha 156 Maria 156 158 Percy 74

THOMPSON, John 269 Col.John 334 Richard 323

THRASH, Martin 193 Michael

(Thrash Cont.) 192

THRASHER, Benjamin 94 323

THRELXELD, Henry 270

THRESHER, Polly 313

THRISHER, Martin 199

THROXEL, Anthony 4 335

THUMMA, Clara M. 319

TICE, Joseph 221

TICKLEN, Jeremiah 116

TILGHMAN, John 44 Martin 75

TILZER, Melchior 213

TINKHOUSE, Catherine 242

TIPLER, Margaret 200

TIRISZLER, Valentine 51 129

TISHER, John 47 204 206 Mary 204

TISSALL, Frederick 292

TISSEL, Adam 292 Frederick 292

TISSER, Rev. John 185

TISSLER, George 343

TITSCH, Jacob 262

TITZEL, George 29

TIWXL, Anthoni 269

TIXEL, Anthony 95

TOESCHLER, Apolonia 164 Peter 12

TOLAND, Rachael 50

TOLLER, Louson 323

TOMLINSON, Mrs. Francis 140 Mary Matilda 140

TOOL, Aquila 286

TOOTEL, James 94 323 Richard 94 323

TOPPER, Mary 3 33 135

TORNEY, Joseph 51 225

TORSCLE, Goodhard 313 Goodhart 279

TOSELER, Peter 258

# FULL NAME INDEX

TOSELLER, George 258

TOSLER, Catherine 129
George 2 129 Margaret 129
Rosina 129

TOSSELER, George 258 John
George Michael 6

TOSSELL, Bernard 260

TOSSETT, also Trossett,
Francis 203 Jonathan 203

TOSSLER, Peter 272

TOTELL, Elizabeth 203 Richard
203

TOTTEL, David 237 Elizabeth
237

TOTTY, Estelle 63 Hazel 63
Lena Madeline 63

TOXELLER, George 258

TOXELOR, Peter 258

TOXLE, Abraham 258

TOXLER, Marcia 128 Peter 128
258 Stephan 128

TRACELL, Nicholas 241

TRACHE, Lodowick 282 293

TRACHSEL, also Trachsell,
Abraham 51 123 224 Adam
26 165 167 168 169 170
Anna 165 167 168 267
Bendikt 66 Bernhard 265
Catharina 168 Catherine
167 Christian 9 115 168
David 115 145 178 Elis 145
Eva 165 167 George 160
265 George Frederick 115
George Jacob 19 Hans 65
Hans Jacob 64 Jacob 19
73 128 Jacobina King 51
Johannes 66 115 Johann
Daniel 115 Johann Jacob
115 Johann Peter 164 260

(Trachsel Cont.) John 72
225 John David 24 John
Nicholas 20 165 167 John
S. Daniel 23 Juliana 115
Margaret 160 Maria
Barbara 165 166 167 169
Maria Magdalena 159
Michael 265 Nicholaus 165
Nicolaus 169 Nikel 165
Nickel 167 Peter 12 115
128 164 165 167 258 348
Stephan 168

TRACKLER, Catharina 172
Conrad 172 John Conrad
28

TRACKSEL, also Trackseler,
Tracksell, Abraham 51
Daniel 102 Jacob 13 64
163 164 John 224 260 300
John Peter 21 260 John S.
Daniel 23 Margaretha 164
Peter 164

TRACSLER, Jeremiah 266

TRAEHXEL, Jacob 145

TRAENCKEL, John
Christopher 50

TRAEUSCH, Jacob 343

TRAGESSER, John 211

TRAICHLER, John 56 310

TRAIGHLER, John 55 304

TRAINUM, Georgie 64

TRANCKEL, Catarina 160
Elizabeth Magdalena 160
John 27 John Adam 160
John Stephen 160 Maria
Eva 160 Martin 27 Stephen
27 160

TRANCKLER, Catharina 174
Catherine 173 Conrad 173

408

(Tranckler Cont.) 174 John
Conrad 28
TRANCKLOR, Jacob 337
TRASCEL, Daniel 67 Peter 33
232
TRASEL, Joseph 287
TRASELER, George Michael
10 Michael 104
TRASHER, John 94 323
Thomas 94 323
TRASLER, James 327
TRASSER, George 267
TRAUTHAGER, Anna Julianath
Catherinath 12 115
Johannes Hans 12 115
TRAUTMAN, John 218 Michael
218 Philip 218 Susanna
218 Valentine 218
TRAXAL, also Traxall,
Abraham,Jr.104 Barbara
175 Bernard 263 Christian
9 332 349 Elis 170
Elizabeth Mickly 163
Frederick 7 198 George
199 George Frederick 7
Helena 166 Henrich 170
John 299 John Hans
Nicholas 20 John Nickel 20
Joseph 175 Michael 102
266 Nicholas 240 Peter 146
163 166 Ruben 163 Sally
170 Sara 169 170 Sarah
170 Sophia 170
TRAXEL, also Traxell Traxelin,
Abra 300 Abraham 51 52
102 133 215 219 301 303
Abram 306 Adam 102 125
165 166 168 169 337
Amandus 169 An.Mar 144

(Traxel Cont.) Anna Maria
165 166 168 Anna Susanna
169  Barbara 169 Bernard
261 263 Carl 169 Catharina
133 166 168 169 Catharina
Elisabetha 165 167
Catharine 133 145 Christian
102 127 129 164 169 170
281 293 303 333 337
Christina 169 Daniel 67 165
266 299 Dav. 144 David
133 164 Drusilla 169
Edward 169 Elias 166 169
Elis. 145 146 170 Elizabeth
133 144 145 146 169 170
287 Eva 165 Georg 263
Georg Frederick 164
George 106 170 George
Frederick 7 George Michael
263 Hanna 166 168 169
Hannickle 189 Helena 163
166 Henrich 146 170 Henry
104 287 Isabella 169 Jac.
145  Jacob 51 106 145 332
338 Jacobena 225 Jerge
263 Jeremiah 52 281 292
Joel 166 168 Johannes 8
124 131 133 164 166 169
170 Joh Michael 165 Johan
Peter 266 Johann Andrew
11 Johann George 261 263
265 Johann John 102 104
164 168 170 224 225 227
282 284 287 291 292 293
294 303 338 Johann
Michael 265 Johann Nickel
33 166 John David 24 John
George 264 265 266 John
George Michael 6 John

# FULL NAME INDEX

(Traxel Cont.) Michael 167 John Nickel 20 168 John Nicholas 25 27 165 169 266 John Peter 21 John S. Daniel 23 Jonas 168 Jonanthan 171 Joseph 171 Juliana 169 Juliana Catharina 164 Juliana Margaretha 164 166 Magdalena 145 165 170 Magdlna Seigfried 320 Margaret 134 145 215 313 Margaretha 165 167 169 Maria 169 Maria Margaretha 165 Mary 134 190 Mary Shryver 320 Michael 106 131 263 303 Milton 169 Nickel 167 Nicolaus 106 166 168 169 189 241 282 293 310 338 Owen 169 Paul 170 Peter 20 33 163 164 165 166 168 169 190 239 240 281 292 313 320 332 Robert 169 Sally 170 Salome 169 170 Samuel 169 Sara 146 169 170 Sarah 170 Sibilla Veronica 166 168 169 Solomon 167 Sophia 145 146 170 Stephen 232 Thomas 169 Wilhelm 169

TRAXELER, Jacob 102 Peter 106

TRAXELSIN, Abraham 51 Catharina 133

TRAXERLL, Jacobena 51

TRAXHSEL, Maria Barbara 115

TRAXLER, Anna M. 223 Anthony 3 275 306 Charles

(Traxler Cont.) A. 282 Charles Walker 85 Christena 254 Daniel Errol 282 Doris 85 E. 342 Elizabeth 86 99 152 171 Emanuel 49 297 349 Francis 91 Frank 260 Frederick 113 George 283 George R. 223 282 Henry 337 Jacob 77 152 282 Jacob R. 85 223 282 Jeremiah 52 282 291 293 294 Jeremias 299 John 182 189 254 281 282 291 292 293 294 297 299 332 John E. 282 319 321 John Peter 40 41 42 Jonathan 297 Joseph 337 Mary 206 Mary Jane Wiser 85 Mrs. 189 Peter 45 102 189 281 282 284 292 293 294 299 305 337 Samuel 297 Susanna 171 W.A. 282 285 William A. 85 223 282 283 William D. 319

TRAXSELL, George Jr. 188 Nicholas 189 Peter Jr.190

TRAYXLER, Elizabeth 249 John Peter 41 Mary 249

TREALER, Susannah 236

TREALER, Adam 106 Daniel 106 David 286 Martin Kendrick 285

TREASTER. Catherine 243 Elizabeth 243 George 243 Jacob Joseph 243 John 243 Margaret 243 Martin 243

TREBER, also Trebern,

# FULL NAME INDEX

(Treber Cont.) Catherine 147

TRECHERN, Marsha 128

TRECHSLER, also Trechseler: John Peter 21 42 Michael 152 Soloman 177 178

TRECKLER, Michel 150

TRECKSAL, also Trecksall, Anthony 3 269 270

TRECKSLER, Anna Margaretha 150 Anthony 3 307 Elisabeth 150 Elizabeth Kraus 4 Michael 4 150

TREELER, John 298

TREHSLER, Catherine 123 Christian Jr. 123 Michael 39

TREIBER, Ludwig 253 292

TREIBETBLIZ, Jacob 343

TREICHEL, Chas. 106 Elias Ludwig 175

TREICHLER, Abm. 106 Daniel 57 355 Hans Graft 89 Henry 57 John 56 57 344 355 Martin 56 57 Susanna 317

TREICKLER, John 56

TREIGHLER, Barbara 246 249 Dorothea 246 247 252 John 56 246 248 252 Martin 246

TREIGLER, Johannes 252

TREISCH, Anna 152 David 155 Elizabeth 154 Jacob 155 Catharina 154 Lydia 235 Maria 155 Peter 154 Reichert 151 155 Sarah 235

TREISCHLLER, see Treisch

TREISH, Adam 229 305 Jacob 155 252 Leonart 229 Michael 229

TREISHLER, see Treish

TREISTER, Barbara 161 Frederick 67 216 Margaretta 216 Martin 68 216

TREISTLER, Joseph David 9

TREIXER, John Peter 42 Peter 305

TRENCHSELL, John Peter 21

TRENCKEL, Anna Cath. 162 Anna Maria 162 Anna Maria Agensa 162 Catharina 124 Chris. 162 Christoph 161 162 Eva 162 Eva Catharina 162 John 27 Martin 27 Stephen 27 124 162

TRENCKEN, Christopher 10 Eva Catherine 162 John Christopher 50

TRENCKLER, John Conrad 28 John Jacob 30 173 174

TRENGHLER, Daniel 246 247 John 56 Magdalena 246 247 248 Martin 246 Mary 247

TRENHLER, Dorothea 252 John 56

TRENKEL, also Trenkeln, Anna Catherine 161 162 Christophel 263 Christopher 162 Eva Cath. 162 John 218 Stephan 162 263

TRENSLER, Frederick 285 Philip 285

TRESAL, Goodhart 94 323

TRESCHER, also Treschern, Barbara 147 148 Christina 147 Christopher 147

(Trescher Cont.) Drusilla
128 John Christopher 50
Lydia 234 Margaretha 147
Maria Margarfetha 147 148
Mr. 128
TRESCHNER, Mr. 128
TRESCLER, John Peter 40 41
42 Jonas 216 Peter,Sr.239
Willouby 216
TRESHER, Christopher 300
Conrad 106 John 106
Lorentz 106 Phillip 106
Samuel 106 Sarah 234
TRESHLER, Abraham 234
Lyndia 234 Michael 39
TRESHTER, George 215 Peter
215
TRESITER, Martin 298
TRESKLER, Elizabeth Rifle
136 Jacob 136 Jacobus
James 10
TRESLAR, Andrew 29 298
John Andreas 29 Martin
Kendrick 285
TRESLER, A.C. 278 Adam 203
Andreas 298 Andrew 106
108 109 298 322 Annie E.
113 Anthony 3 10 136 137
Barbara 203 254 Barbara
A. 283, Barby 255
Catherine 122 136 137 256
Charles 254 255 Christian
98 Daniel 104 David 96 104
215 285 286 Elizabeth 137
317 Frederick 203 325 327
Friterich 298 George 38
102 109 203 305 George D.
Jacob 36 38 Hans Joseph
256, Henry 45 254 255 328

(Tresler Cont.) Ignatius 109
Isaac N. 113 Jacob 95 106
108 203 204 205 274 275
322 Jacobus James 10 137
Jesse Wise 113 Johann
Andreas 11 John 36 37 106
146 203 204 205 275 296
312 335 John S. Daniel 23
Jonathan P. 11 Joseph 110
274 275 283 286 Joseph
David 9 Levina 215 Lilian
113 Lucwick 324 325 327
Ludwich 325 Lydia 234
Margaret 322 Maria 177
286 Martin Kendrick 285
Mary 203 322 Michael 39
94 122 275 298 301 303
326 name 186 Nora 278
Oscar B. 114 Oscar T. 113
Peter 36 45 112 189 215
254 255 265 323 335 342
Philip 96 104 106 109 317
328 340 342 Reuben 215
Susan 110 113
TRESLOR, Anderson 106
TRESNER, Bernard 198 203
Jacob 198 203
TRESSE, Hugh 222
TRESSEL, Charles 112
Christian 106 David 109
George 297 Goodhert 323
Jacob 301 John 98 106
307 Joseph 307 Thomas
98 William 93
TRESSELL, Charles 112 Jacob
301 John 307 Joseph 307
TRESSER, Samuel 309
TRESSET, also Tressent, Elis
123 John 123 John Jacob

# FULL NAME INDEX

(Tresset Cont.) Samuel Jack 48 Sam 123
TRESSIES, Charles 94 325
TRESSLAR, John 335 John Frederick 34
TRESSLE, Joseph 243
TRESSLEAR, Ignatius 37
TRESSLER, see Tresler
TRESSLERSH, George 176 Christina 176
TRESSLETT, Nathaniel 110
TRESTER, Daniel 106 John 333 Mary 109 Peter A. 335
TRESTLER, David 285 Goodhart 94 Joseph David 9 Martin Kendrick 285
TRESZLER, Peter 343
TRETCHER, Michael 62 Thomas 253
TRETEHELT, William 270
TREUSDALL, Wm. 297
TREXEE, Joseph 19 209
TREXEL, Abraham 51 224 Anthony 3 4 95 102 105 246 252 Antonio 275 Apollonia 16 Betty 4 Catherine 209 275 Christena 243 Dirskell 209 Elizabeth Martin 175 George 1 Jacob 102 105 John 23 24 27 175 252 John Joseph 106 209 355 Julia Ann 312 Henry 106 Michael 74 name 209 Peter 147 252 Soloman 147 Sybilla 147
TREXELL, Abraham 52 Anthony 102 135 331 344 Appolonia 16 Catherine

(Trexell Cont.) 135 Charles 136 Daniel 102 Elizabeth 136 Emanuel 49 Jacob & others 271 John 136 271 332 John S. Daniel 23 Joseph 342 Samuel 135 Mary 136 Mary Roseanna 16 Miss 136 Mrs. 136
TREXELER, Jaramiah Peter 102 William III 102
TREXELLER, John 99 Lawrence 99 Peter 99
TREXER, Willoby 216
TREXIL, John David 24 Michael 312
TREXLA, Mary 340
TREXLEAR, Ignatius 37 327 328 329
TREXLER, Abial 216 Ada Lee 92 Adam 19 55 99 316 Adelaide 92 Aggy 341 Agness 288 320 Alexander 316 Amanda 153 225 227 Amandus 231 Andrew 234 235 288 Ann 110 234 235 288 316 Ann Margaret 140 Ann Magdalena 140 Anna 216 242 288 Anthony 4 86 92 117 185 270 275 326 Arener 288 Barbara 321 322 Barney 206 Benjamin 55 98 146 231 278 279 283 Bertha A. 304 Bertha J. 318 Bertha McCarthy 64 Caleb 19 Camilla 316 Carlton Urban 64 Caroline 216 Catharina 132 146 206 249 Catharine 90 98 216 236 239 242 249 289 325

(Trexler Cont.) Catharine C.
340 Charles 90 106 183
235 333 Charles Augustus
61 Charles Herndon 64
Charles T. 113 Charles
William 57 Charlotte 80 307
Charlotte Ann 63 Chas. I.
224 Christina 354 Clarissa
231 Cooney 104 Daisy
Adelaide 64 Daniel 215 216
217 David 41 74 90 102
104 106 140 141 216 231
233 235 236 238 266 286
289 324 325 Deborah 186
Doc 64 Donald Lee 63
Donn Gregory 64 181
Edward Coleman 63
Edward Coleman, Jr. 63
Elizabeth 82 123 140 141
149 150 216 222 231 233
235 239 242 289 311 325
338 Elizabeth E. 206 Elmira
289 Emanuel 49 132 208
324 325 342 350 Emma R.
235 Eunice 63 Eva 61 108
Evelyn Edward 64
Ferdinand 55 Ferdinant 228
Francia L. 63 Francis Peter
56 Frank James 63 Frank
James, Jr. 63 Franklin H.
231 Frederica 235 289
Frederick 278 279 313
George 19 51 90 106 108
110 242 316 341 George
Herndon 63 George Nelson
50 George W. 46 113
Gertraut 170 Gladys May
64 Grace Bell 63 Gramier
301 Col. H.C. 71 Hannah

(Trexler Cont.) 235 325
Hannah D. 224 Helen 235
Henry 55 207 316 322
Herbert Julius 63 Herbert
Leslie 64 Hiram 225,
History and Genealogy 348
Horatio 216 289 Ignatius 37
92 111 181 183 193 311
322 330 Isaac 98 186 Isaac
A. 327 328 Isaac S. 11 82
123 183 Isabella 62 92 111
Israel 239 331 J. 182 333
J.F. 86 Jacob 53 55 90 99
106 108 140 142 152 182
207 215 216 217 271 333
334 Jacob Eddie 61  Mrs.
James 140 James 54 58
142 222 231 235 290
James Herman 63 James
M. 235 290 James
Washington 63 Janathan
112 Jeremiah 2 42 52 58
63 104 106 189 231 236
239 242 292 293 304 308
310 321 322 324 337 338
Johann David 73 John 19
37 39 42 52 55 61 73 99
104 106 107 108 111 140
182 183 189 235 239 242
289 291 292 294 308 309
310 313 315 316 324 325
333 334 349 357 John
Andrew 140 John George
Michael 6 John I. 331 John
Ignatius 61 62 329 John
Jacob 18 John Joseph 2
63 John Peter 1 40 42 231
324 John Warren 348
Jonas 11 215 216 217 333

# FULL NAME INDEX

(Trexler Cont.) Jonas P. 11 98 Jonathan 11 44 104 119 231 232 308 324 325 330 333 334 337 Jonathan D. 235 Jonathan P. 782 186 widow of Joseph 173 Joseph 19 33 42 52 55 62 92 102 104 107 108 140 142 182 222 235 236 242 249 289 290 301 305 311 338 354 Joseph, Jr. 133 Joseph Edward 63 Joseph Peter 56 Joshua 282 293 Joyce Ann 63 Judith 216 Juliana 313 Kathrina 237 Katy 92 Laurence 235 Lawrantz 102 Lawrence 40 41 55 235 236 238 301 304 305 316 324 341 Lesher 290 Levi 207 316 Lorentz 55 Lottie May 63 Lucas 231 Lucille Herndon 64 Lucinda 216 Ludwick 325 Lydia 232 Mable Lorraine 63 Madelyn 63 Magdalen 133 Margaret 19 63 142 222 242 250 324 Margaret A. 81 340 Margaret Cecila 318 Maria 216 241 Marian May 64 Mary 63 98 140 182 183 249 311 325 Mary Ann 90 231 322 Mary Caroline 139 Mary Diane 63 Mary Elizabeth 140 Mattias 206 Michael 4 104 149 150 152 153 263 264 265 Minnie 61 Minnie A. 92 Minor Davidson 64 Moses 316 Mrs. Trexler 90 Nancy 63

(Trexler Cont.) 92 98 111 330 Nancy Ann Murray 329 Nancy Ellis Trexler 329 Nancy McCarthy 64 Nathan 216 231 281 294 Nelson 58 Peter 2 11 18 41 63 99 104 107 140 141 142 150 153 186 188 189 192 207 215 216 217 235 236 239 242 249 250 263 266 282 287 288 290 291 293 294 301 304 305 306 308 309 310 312 313 314 316 319 321 324 326 327 328 337 338 342 354 Olive 231 Peter Lynn 63 Philip 39 104 Rachel 91 107 172 235 236 311 325 Rebecca 91 Reuben 215 216 217 232 Robert Earl 63 Rosa Alice 61 Rose Alice 92 Rose Edith 63 Rosetta 62 111 322 Ruth Virginia Pastora 63 Sally 316 Samuel 98 107 132 182 208 296 325 350 Samuel Anthony 5 117 Samuel P. 11 186 Samuel R.B. 195 Sarah 91 216 231 232 235 290 Scott Andrew II 360 Solomon 108 Sophia 6 119 232 316 Susan Krise 140 Susanna 239 325 Trexler Game Reservation 71 Violet 63 Virginia 92 Walter Edward 63 Walter Ignatius 63 Walter H. 114 Walter Warren 63 William 61 62 74 92 114 183 216 217 235 281 287 290 294

# FULL NAME INDEX

(Trexler Cont.) 322 329
William Alexander 58
William H. 92 William III 61
William L. 319 William W.
331 Willoughley 216
TREXLERE, John Peter 41
Lawrence 235
TREXSEL, Anthony 3 355
Catherine 129 Elizabeth
129 Goodhart 2 129
TREXSLER, Benjamin 320
Catharina 320 Jeremiah
342 John Peter 42 Michael
150
TREXTORS, John 242
TREYSCH, Susanna 153
TREZLER, Anna Elizabeth 222
TRICHELL, Elias L. 304
TRICHLER, Catherine 234
Cemetery 90 Eve 221
Jacob 107 Jacob S. 253
John 220 221 Louisa 232
TRICKELL, Fred 97 Sophia 4
312
TRICKLER, John 55 220 305
306 307 John Conrad 28
TRIESCH, Anna Elizabeth 7
160 162 Fred. 160 Fried
162 John Frederick 7
Henrich Wilehlm 7 160
Henry Wilhelm 162
TRIESLER, Anna Margreth
128 131 Anna Maria 161
Barbara Weller 124 David
161 George Michael 6 124
132 Joannes 124 John
George Michael 6 Joseph
David 160 Margaretha
Barbara 160 Maria Susanna

(Triesler Cont.) 160 164
TRIEST, George 242
TRIESTER, Anna Margaret
217 Dorothea 217 Frederic
216 217 George Frederick
217 John 217 John Jacob
217 Margaretha 216 Maria
Dorothea 217 Peter 217
TRILSCHER, John 260
TRIMBUL, Wm. 191
TRIMMER, Mathias 54 209
TRINCKEL, Cath. 161
Christopher 161 Stephen
161
TRINCKER, Conrad 299 John
Conrad 28
TRINCKLER, Catharina 172
Catharine 173 Conrad 172
173 Jacob 172 173 John
Jacob 30
TRINKLE, Charles 243
Elizabeth 243 Mathias 243
TRINKLER, Jacob 308 309
John Jacob 30
TRIPLER, Michael 94 323
TRIPPEL, Casper 143
Catharine Anthony 143
TRISELER, Michael 129
TRISHER, Jacob 324 Joseph
302 Juliana 133 Mr. 128
Peter 270 276 312
TRISKIL, John 142 143
Margaret 142 143 Mary 142
143
TRISLER, also Trislerin,
Amanda 92 Ann Bulger 324
Ann Caroline Rag.316 Anna
Maria Cron 87 Casper 110
Catharina 91 Catherine 93

(Trisler Cont.) 171 322 342
Catherine Breidenbach 315
Daniel 342 David 105 110
225 286 313 Eilliam 197
Elisabeth 128 171 230 313
Fannie 79 George 8 14 37
83 84 98 108 109 110 132
196 200 201 286 313 322
325 339 340 347 348 349
George D. 38 George
David 15 87 George D.
Jacob 38 George Michael
10 Goodhard 270 Henrietta
313 J. 274 Jacob 93 105
110 274 296 304 323 324
325 348 James 110
Jedidah Smoot 324 Joel
110 Johann Jacob 16 John
110 229 322 349 John
George Michael 6 John
Nicholas 25 John Peter 40
Joseph 93 Mrs. Joseph 77
Joseph David 286 Kittie
Breidenbough 350 Kitty
109 Lewis 49 91 111 113
Margaret 37 51 196 200
274 276 277 279 314
Margaretha 129 Maria
Drusina 163 Maria Susanna
161 Marie 38 156 163
Martin Kendrick 285 Mary
83 109 184 277 348 Mary
Margaret 83 Mary Ream 51
126 Michael 36 39 83 94 95
129 188 203 269 270 271
274 276 279 286 312 313
340 347 348 349 350 352
Peter 34 36 91 92 93 111
239 339 350 Philip 96 105

(Trisler Cont.) 107 314
Priscilla 91 92 Rosanna 83
84 322 341 350 Rosina 132
Samuel 111 Stephen 183
357 Susan 111 196 201
322 Susan Kurtz 315
Susanna 87 157 204 Trisler
File 91 Trisler Family 352
Valentine 51 96 125 277
William 37 111 196 William
H. 83
TRISLIE, also Trislit, Peter
34 339
TRISOLER, also Trissoler,
Elizabeth 93 George 93
George Michael 10 Jacob
93 Johann Jacob 16 John
93 Mary 93 Townsend 46
336
TRISSEL, Cemetery 84 David
84 208 Frederick 292 321
Jacob 111 John 105 220
221 310 317 Jos. 310
Joseph 105 107 110 221
290 309 Margaret 317
TRISSELER, Lewis 49
Lodowick 294
TRISSLAR, Barbara 21 254
Catherine 21 254 Elizabeth
21 254 George 21 254
Henry 21 254 Jacob 21 254
Mary 21 254 Michael 21
254 Moses 21 254 Nancy
21 254 Peter 21 254 Sally
21 254 William 21 254
TRISSLER, Adam 59 88 89
157 158 159 Adam R. 342
Ann C. 225 226 Ann
Catharine 226 227 Anna

# FULL NAME INDEX

(Trissler Cont.) Maria 88 157 158 159 Anna Magdalena 88 89 156 158 Annette 227 230 Annette C. 226 Cathaina 87 157 Catharina 159 Catharine 59 60 87 88 89 156 157 159 230 313 342 Christian 89 159 Cristina 280 282 David 86 101 102 146 159 182 227 228 229 230 279 280 281 282 285 286 287 303 304 305 306 313 315 342 344 E.H. 230 Edward H. 230 Eliza 157 Elizabeth 86 87 88 89 156 157 158 Frederick 221 G. 96 George 14 36 59 83 89 101 107 156 157 158 159 182 271 272 273 274 303 305 320 322 342 344 George Conrad 89 159 George David 14 15 87 88 156 157 158 159 285 285 George Thomas 156 226 Jacob 16 87 94 157 323 325 Johann Abraham 25 159 Johann Adam 156 159 Johannes 87 88 156 158 John 16 45 86 88 89 105 107 158 159 226 228 229 230 333 334 John A. 86 89 230 John Adam 25 89 John George Michael 6 John Joseph 6 Joseph 222 Joseph David 9 163 263 265 Joseph R. 86 230 Juliana 89 157 159 342 Juliana Reed 158 Lewis 49 294 Lillie D. 86

(Trissler Cont.) Lodowick 294 Louisa 86 225 226 227 M. 96 Margaret 157 224 226 227 277 342 Margaret R. 157 Margaretha Catherine 87 157 Maria 87 157 225 227 231 Maria Susanna 160 Maria Reichart 156 Martin Frederick 156 Martin Kendrick 285 Mary 89 320 Mary Ann 342 Michael 36 175 230 270 271 321 Mr. Trissler,Sr.128 Peter 34 280 339 Philip 54 321 Rachel W. 86 Richard 25 Richard Dehuff 88 158 Susan 342 Susanna Maria 159 Susannah 226 227 Valentine 51 94 95

TRISSLERIN, Anna Magdalena 156 Elizabeth 156

TRISTELER, Philip 54 146

TRISTER, John George 6 Margaretha 129 Peter 34 339

TRISTLEAR, Martin Kendrick 285

TRISTLER, George 244 George David 15 247 Hannah 145 John 145 Lewis 297 Maria 145 Martin Kendrick 285 Mary 110 Michael 278 Philip 54 145 Polly 146 Sarah 145

TRISZLER, Valentine 129

TRITSCHLER, Chas 232 Henry 232

TRITZLER, Mary Magdalena

(Tritzler Cont.) 213 William V. 213

TRIUSSLER, Susanna 224

TRIXEL, Anthony 3 303 304

TRIXLER, David 105 327 John 322 John George Michael 6 Nancy 110 Peter 105

TRIXSELL, John Nicholas 25 Nicholas 240

TROCHER, surname 257 346

TROCHSALL, also Trochsal, Abraham 52 280 Catherine 280 Goodhard 313

TROCHSEL, Abraham 52 280 Goodhard 313

TROCKSAL, Abraham 276 John 276 Michael 271

TROCKSELL, John 271 272 John Jacob 18 Trocksell's Mill Dam 277 William 277

TROCLEAR, also Trocsler, surname 257 346

TROCSSELET, Family 257 346

TROECKSEL, Georg 155 John George 6 Magdalena Margaretha 155 Michael 36

TROESCHLER, Apolonia 12

TROESHER, Catharina 230 Jacob 228 230 Katharina 230

TROESLER, Jacob 228 333 surname 346

TROESNER, Betzi 154

TROESSCLER, surname 257 346

TROESTER, Abraham 263 Abram 264 John Martin Stephen 27

TROKSELL, Catharina 260

(Troksell Cont.) Catharine 261 Daniel 260 261 John S. Daniel 23 Peter 12 31 260 261

TRONCKLER, Conrad 173 Jacob 173 John Conrad 28 John Jacob 30

TROSALL, Daniel 333 Jacob 221 John 276 Susanna 221

TROSCEL, Barbara 201 George 47 Jacob 221 Jermima 201 John 187 John Jacob 18 William George 201

TROSCELL, Jacob 221

TROSCLAIR, Johann George 17 Family 257 345 346

TROSCLE, Aaron 60 Abraham 60 258 Anna Maria 60 Eli 60 Elizabeth 60 217 George 60 John 60 Julia 217 Leva 60 Margaret 60 Mary 60 Samuel 60 217 William 60 217

TROSCLER, Johann George 17 surname 257 346

TROSEEL, George 94 323

TROSEL, also Trosell, Troselle, Anna 313 Daniel 333 Frederick 93 George 47 Goodhart 279 313 Jacob 201 John Nicholas 38 Joseph Peter 201 Joshua 201 Peter 201 202

TROSELA, Joshua 201

TROSELER, surname 257 346

TROSELL, also Troselle, Daniel 333 Frederick 93 Goodhard 313 Goodhart

# FULL NAME INDEX

(Trosell Cont.) 279 John
Nicholas 38
TROSHELL, George 102 105
TROSHER, Michael 36 276
TROSLER, Jeremiah 52
Joseph 239 Michael 36 276
Myrtle 113
TROSLISSER, surname 257
346
TROSSCLAIR, surname 257
346
TROSSEL, Anna Maria 260
261 Barthart 130 Bendikt
66 Bernard 261 Hans
Bernhardt 260
TROSSELL, Benedik 66
Bernard 261 Hans
Bernhardt 260
TROSSIL, John 333
TROSSLER, Henry 109 Jacob
271 Peter 280
TROSTAL, George 177 John
Peter 21
TROSTEL, Abraham 53 107
154 177 178 210 228 247
248 252 263 264 Barbara
154 Bernard 217 Catherine
178 228 Cathrina 178
Elizabeth 178 Elmer F. 226
Elrnru 227 George 60 217
220 Heinrich 60 156 Henry
60 107 217 228 Jacob 107
178 248 Johannes 60 154
John 107 217 283 John
David 24 Joseph 53 Leir
227 Rosina 217 Sarah 226
283 Susan 177 Susanna
178 217 247 Wilheim 177
William 107 217 Wm. 228

TROSTELL, Daniel 283
TROSTER, Catherine 149 Joh.
Michael 149 Johan Wilhem
149 John Martin 149 John
Martin Stephen 27 Martin
149
TROSTLE, also Trostler,
Trostlerin, Abraham 53 54
85 105 107 108 210 247
248 250 Alda 318 Andrew
210 224 Anna Edua 318
Anna Maria 85 218 Annie
M. 318 Bertha 318 Blanch
M. 318 Boyd 319 Catherine
54 85 177 210 222 Charles
W. 319 Christina 224 Daniel
54 209 210 223 243 283
David 319 Elizabeth 54
Emanuel 54 222 Emma F.
318 Ernest H. 319 Fanny P.
318 Frances C. 318 George
85 108 210 George H. 210
George W. 318 319 Gerhe
318 Gertrude 318 Harry C.
222 Helen S. 223 Henry 54
210 226 227 Henry J. 210
Hiram 210 Isaac B. 210
Isaac R. 211 Jacob 53 54
105 107 136 210 248 249
355 Jacob M. 210, James
S. 319 John 53 54 105 209
210 283 284 355 John C.
223 319 John Christopher
50 Jonas 209 Lester W.
319 Leurena M. 318 Levi
226 Lewis E. 319 M. 223
Maggie 223 Margaret 217
Maria 85 Martha 283 Mary
E. 318 Mary Magdalen

(Trostle Cont.) widow 144
321 McClennan A. 223
Melle 85 Michael 210 Mima
318 Moves 209 Peter 53 54
108 176 209 210 223 Peter
Sr. 211 Polly 54 Rebecca
54 Rev. George 222 Roy
John 319 Sallie M. 318
Samuel 54 209 Sarah 283
Susanna 54 209 210 248
250 W.A. 319 William 54
210 217 248 250 Zora
Elizabeth 319
TROSTLEINN, Anna Maria 217
TROUBLESOM, Thomas 189
TROUCHSLER, surname 257
346
TROUDALL, Samuel 297
TROULST, Jurich Geo. 263
TROUP, David 205
TROUSDALE, Barney 35
TROUSTRE, surname 257 346
TROUTNER, George 243
TROXALL, Abraham 109 110
112 271 278 280 284 293
Adam 195 274 Ann 349
David 94 109 112 Elizabeth
220 245 312 Frederick 94
George 187 335 George J.
108 Isabella 182 Jacob 94
195 272 273 297 313
Jacob,Jr. 272 Jacob of
Peter 94 Jane 112
Jeremiah 107 112 John 67
94 107 187 195 201 245
272 276 300 312 313 315
323 325 Jonathan 107
Margaret 198 312 Peter 20
94 95 110 195 272 300 313

(Troxall Cont.) Sarah 313
William H. 112
TROXCEL, Ann 237 David 280
Peter 280 313
TROXCELE, David 280 Peter
313
TROXCLAIR, Andre 327
Antoine 327 Christopher
327 Firmans 327 Francaes
327 J.B. 327 Johann
George 17 Pierre 327
surname 257 346
TROXCLAIRE, Johann George
17 surname 346
TROXDALE, also Troxdel,
Jacob 338
TROXEL, also Troxell, A.97 Ab.
206 Abby 240 Abr. 123
Abra 299 Abraham 5 17 34
51 52 84 91 94 107 111
121 126 127 133 140 141
186 187 188 197 199 201
204 205 208 218 222 240
253 258 270 278 280 281
297 299 313 324 329 331
332 334 Abram 188 253
323 333 Abrm 297 Ad. 144
Adam 13 26 69 95 109 144
166 199 233 240 Adam S.
232 Adelaide 236 237 A.H.
284 Alexander 241 Amanda
189 197 201 202 Andrew
91 111 253 Ann 237 Anna
204 205 222 Anna Maria
127 166 Anna Susanna 69
Anne 206 Anthony 3 4 305
333 335 347 Appolonia 16
127 Audora 233 Barbara 18
196 Barbara Martin 200

(Troxel Cont.) Barbara S. 223 284 Barbara Welty 197 Barbary 84 Benjamin 57 Catharina Magdalena 127 Catherine 82 83 84 132 139 140 166 195 197 200 202 204 205 209 237 238 240 244 278 290 317 Catherine Ann 83 Catherine Baugher 197 200 201 Catherine Mince 196 Catherine Swilar 204 Cathy 312 Cemetery record 90 Charles 57 253 Charlotte 126 196 200 202 Christian 9 17 35 105 132 199 200 232 281 293 332 338 Christina 144 233 240 Christine Reichard 147 Christopher 93 Clarasy 35 332 Daniel 35 67 70 93 97 102 110 132 145 190 199 200 204 205 232 240 253 259 302 303 304 332 335 Daniel S. 305 Dav. 206 David 28 85 97 107 108 111 126 145 197 198 199 200 201 204 205 210 211 221 233 237 238 240 253 278 279 280 281 290 302 303 304 305 355 Edmund 233 Edward 189 240 Elias 47 97 126 196 199 223 276 Elias S. 284 Eleminia 233 Elis 144 145 Elisabet 155 Elisabeth 126 Eliza 69 Elizabeth 77 82 83 126 141 145 189 195 196 197 200 201 202 204 205 218 220 221 232 237 244 278 290

(Troxel Cont.) 312 313 314 317 Elizabeth Crise 200 Elizabeth Hittel 69 Elizabeth Martin 22 Elizabeth Mickley 69 Elizabeth Nickum 197 201 Elizabeth Wise 197 200 Elizabeth Young 126 Elizabetha 135 155 Ella D. 284 Emanuel 126 198 201 206 208 Emma 237 Erwin 237 E.S. 284 Esculine 79 Family 257 362 Fannie S. 206 Frederick 83 97 127 187 188 195 197 198 199 200 201 259 274 277 312 317 323 339 347 Fredrich 155 Fridrich 127 G.274 George 1 47 60 82 94 95 97 105 107 135 188 195 196 199 200 202 204 205 206 222 240 244 277 305 312 324 328 George Allen 362 George Frederick 7 200 George W. 197 200 George Washington 82 George William 126 H.240 Harriett 202 Harvey B. 221 Henritta 196 200 Henry 31 140 141 184 221 232 233 236 237 238 249 287 290 291 337 342 Henry M.240 Henry S.240 I.Lewis 198 Irvin 237 238 Irvin T.291 Isaac 331 Isabella 126 J.Morris 240 Jac.145 Jacob 13 31 35 72 74 77 83 93 95 98 102 105 107 140 141 142 144 145 146 187 188 195 196 198 199 200 201

# FULL NAME INDEX

(Troxel Cont.) 202 221 222
232 240 273 276 277 297
302 303 305 313 317 324
328 329 331 332 333 334
337 338 339 341 347
Jacob Peter 274 Jacob S.
201 James 70 142 231
James B.221 James M.253
Jane 140 253 Jeremia
Motter 197 Jeremiah 71
111 233 253 Jno.323
Joann Winter 197 Joh 144
Johannes 66 127 132 John
11 27 32 47 58 67 69 73 78
82 83 84 85 93 95 98 105
107 109 125 126 140 145
166 195 196 197 198 199
200 201 202 209 218 221
222 232 238 240 241 243
244 258 271 273 274 276
278 281 284 292 297 299
302 303 305 312 313 324
328 334 339 340 348 John
A.317 John David 24 45
John Frederick 34 John
George Michael 6 John
H.240 John J.39 141 209
John Jacob 18 312 John
Jacob Samuel Jac 48 John
N.232 John Nikel 20 John
Nicholas 25 John Peter 21
John S. Daniel 23 John
T.238 291 Jonas 232
Joseph 19 140 142 198
240 242 297 331 Joseph
P.197 200 201 Joseph
Peter 82 Joseph S.291
Joshua 197 200 201 202
Juliana 90 126 198 199 200

(Troxel Cont.) 201 240
Julianath Catharinath 200
Juliann 240 Katharina 132
Lawrence 240 Levi 205
Lewis 126 208 233 Lidia 79
Lorentz 30 147 232 320
Lucus J.233 Lydia 237 238
M.J.284 Magdalene 82 204
281 293 Magdalina Hinch
196 Magdelena 83 127 166
198 205 210 220 233
Manry 206 Margaret 78 140
141 195 196 197 200 201
205 221 258 280 312 317
332 Margaret Marks 196
Margaret S.198 201
Margaret Savilla 126
Margaretha 127 135 199
Maria 69 237 242 Maria
Barbara 17 126 Maria F.231
Marie Heller 69 Maria
Margaretha 127 Maria
Magdelena 83 Maria Rhorer
187 188 Martha 79 Mary 47
77 98 126 140 195 196 197
198 199 200 201 202 205
208 209 221 233 240 253
276 312 Mary Ann Davis
197 200 201 Mary Ann
Smith 197 Mary Collingen
196 Mary E.201 Mary Jane
222 Mary Margaret 115
Mary Magdalene 98 Martin
D.201 Michael 74 90 105
189 240 242 298 333 334
Michael E.189 Modolna
Coon 200 Modolona 200
N.B.237 Nancy 317
Nicholas 90 105 232 233

(Troxel Cont.) 240 309
Nichs 308 Peter 12 18 20
31 35 47 48 68 71 82 83 93
95 97 115 127 142 166 190
196 198 199 200 201 202
204 220 231 232 240 258
274 276 277 278 280 281
282 287 291 292 293 294
297 298 313 320 328 332
340 348 Peter of J.201 202
Peter Van Buren 83 Phillip
111 205 281 328 341 Phillip
Orlinger 205 Polly 317 Polly
Biggs 197 Rachel 111 125
191 Rebecca 218 237 238
Rosanna 208 Ruth 196
Sally 146 Salome 205 241
Samuel 83 84 139 140 197
200 201 202 208 237 238
239 249 287 290 291
Samuel Anthony 5 Samuel
E.222 Samuel J.126 201
Sara 237 Sarah 69 78 123
126 127 139 140 145 205
221 233 237 238 278 317
Sarah J.111 Sarah Solome
204 Sibylla Veronica
Hecker 166 Solomon 72
166 233 241 Sophia 9 48
132 145 Sophia Elizabeth
82 Stephen 75 232 Suffia
233 247 Susan 9 140 141
Susanna 166 201 204 205
211 222 Susanna Rebecca
Hesser 126 Tax list 179
Thomas 240 319 Thomas
F.185 278 Tighman 232
233 241 Troxel Farm 83
Troxell Mills 18 323 Troxell

(Troxel Cont.) Trails 4 8 10
11 18 23 24 25 26 27 28 31
33 38 67 348 362 Veronica
319 William 112 140 141
197 200 201 202 217 218
222 240 244 278 333
William C.35 329 William
D.201 William Henry 126
William L.79 William W.198
201
TROXELE, Peter 280
TROXELER, Adam 13 296 347
George 201 John S. Daniel
23 Sophia 145 surname
346
TROXELIN, Sophia 14 48 145
TROXELLO, George 329 Guan
327
TROXEY, H. 112
TROXIAL, Christian 286 293
TROXIL, also Troxill, George I.
94 Jacob 347 John 347
John David 24 Michael 339
Peter 95
TROXLAIR, surname 257 346
TROXLAIRE, surname 257
346
TROXLER, Adeline 314 316
Barnabe 314 Barnabus 330
Barnet 315 Barney 35 99
330 Catharina 128 257 314
346 David 36 206 237 315
340 Eli 315 Elizabeth 145
Eva 114 Felicite 185 347 G.
107 G.W. 113 George 47
128 206 256 257 315 316
327 329 341 343 347
George Michael 10
Goodhart 2 J.D. 274 Jacob

# FULL NAME INDEX

(Troxler Cont.) 99 223 257 340 346 Jacques 184 256 327 345 346 Johann Georg 256 345 John 206 315 330 John C. 206 315 317 John David 24, John S. Daniel 23, M. 107 Margaret A. 223 Maria Dorothea 128 Mary 315 Milly 315 Nicholas 330 Nik.T. 348 Powell 315 Powell C. 206 Rebecca O. 223 Rockie D. 362 Rosetta 92 Samuel D. 113 Troxler Family 340 Troxler's house 345 W.A. 223

TROXLLER, Johann George 17

TROXSELL, Christian 107 Daniel 190 333 David 333 Isaac 297 John 122 240 333 George 240 Wm. 240

TROXTIL, John 338

TROXWELL, George W. 112 Greenbury 112 John 66 339 widow 339 William 111

TRRAXELLER, Peter 332

TRSCHER, John Peter 42

TRUAX, Benjamin 300 301 Jacob 300 301 307 John 300 301 307 Joseph 307 Philip 300 301 Samuel 300 301 307

TRUCHAUSER, Johann George 264

TRUCKEL, Matheus 263

TRUCKSAAL, Daniel 306 David 306 John David 24 John S. Daniel 23

TRUCKSALL, Ignatius 37

TRUCKSIL, also Trucksill,

(Trucksil Cont.) Adam 13 306 Daniel 306 David 24 306 Jacob 306 John Jacob Samuel 48 John S. Daniel 23

TRUCKSLER, surname 257 346

TRUCSILL, John S. Daniel 23

TRUEL, Anthony 3 302

TRUEXELL, Samuel 317

TRUMBAUER, Ellen Jane 44

TRUMBOUR, Dr. Lewis T. 221

TRUMBOWER, John 290 L.T. 237

TRUMHELLER, Philip 334

TRUNCKEL, Michael 264

TRUNCKER, John Conrad 28

TRUNCKHLER, Johann Conradt 264 John Conrad 28 John Conradt 262

TRUNCKLER, Catharina 173 Catherine 174 Conrad 173 174 John Conrad 28 265 John Jacob 30

TRUNDEL, John 94 323 Josias 94 323 Thomas 94 323

TRUSAL, Mary 224 Robert 224

TRUSCHEL, Andreas 178 Andrew 29 Johann Andreas 29 Margaretha 178 Mary 270 Peter 50 270

TRUSCLER, Jonathan P. 186

TRUSDALL, James 299

TRUSEL, Charles 244

TRUSELL, William 224 Luther C. 244

TRUSHEL, George 176 Jacob 105 303 John George 176

TRUSIL, Philip I. 328 Philip J.

(Trusil Cont.) 329
TRUSLER, Frederick 98 Henry
254 335 Hezekiah 112
Jacob 309 James 46 113
327 Jessee W. 113 John
112 113 Jonas 11 Jonathan
P. 11 Joseph 112 Julia 112
M. 113 Mary 112 Nancy
113 Niklaus 267 Philipina
176 Richard 112 Samuel
314 Townsend 46 336
William 112
TRUSSEL, Ann 184 Charles
335 Christiana 267 Ezeker
330 F. 110 Henry 107
Jacob 332 Jeff 111 Jilson
93 John 110 111 302 335
Katherine 267 Margaret 244
Nahum 93 Nimrod 110 P.
274 Phinehas 297 Sally 93
Sarah 244 Stini 267
Thomas 110 193 Ull 267
Ulrich 267
TRUSSELL, Archibald 112
David 107 Ezekiel 330 John
E. 221 Manson 244 Moses
B. 112 Philip I. 328 Samuel
112 Sarah A. 244 Thomas
112 William 335
TRUSTER, Frederick 213
Martin 107
TRUXALL, Abraham 108 Adam
339 Daniel 259 Ignatius 37
Isreal 211 John 339 John
S. Daniel 23 Nathan 330
Philip John 39
TRUXCLER, Johann George
17 surname 346
TRUXEL, Adam 292 293

(Truxel Cont.) Anthony 4
334 335 Christian 108
Daniel 108 David 102 105
Elizabetha 110 134 George
2 110 134 Goodhart 2
Jacob 105 332 Johann
Daniel 133 John 102 105
211 224 John B. 223
Rebecca 332 Samuel
Anthony 5
TRUXELL, Abraham 52 280
Daniel 110 Jacob 110 John
110 225
TRUXILL, Joseph 108 Rhodam
195
TRUXLER, Forest 114 Ignatius
181 Jonathan 331 Joseph
92 Samuel 347 Samuel
Anthony 5
TRUXSELL, Thomas 195
TRXTER, Adam 13 307
TSCHAGGELM, Peter 267
TTOTTEL, Elizabeth 237
TUCHTER, Martin 264
TUCKER, Mrs.H.B. 64
TURNER, Joshiua 193
TUSCHER, Anna 267 Nicklaus
267 Tillie 267
TUSSLER, Henry 254
TXLER, Ignatius 112 William
112
TYSON, Elisha 269 270
UETZGER, Maria 220
UHLER, Magdalena 65
Regiment 332
UHLLER, Erasmus 194
ULMAN, Frederick 286
ULRIC, Jacob 289
ULRICH, John 242 Peter 317

# FULL NAME INDEX

UMSTAD, Mary 238
UNBEHIND, Jacob 175
UNGER, Esther 68
UPDEGROVE, Dr. S. 90
URBAN, A.L. 53
UTZMAN, Lewis 349
VALIANT, John 193
VAN READ, Anna 219
VAN WYE, Elisha D. 68
VAN HAVERNESS, Margaret
    78 221
VAN HORN, Isiah M. 46
VANLUVANEE, Benjamin 317
VAUTRIN, Abraham 13
    Johannes Abraham 13
VERHULST, Cornelius 285
VERNOU, Louise C. 77
VOELCKNER, Henrich 29
    124 129 Rosina 29 124 129
VOGEL, Andreas 262
VOGT, Veronicka 150
VOITURIN, Johannes Abraham
    13
VOLLWEILER, Johannes 147
VOLWEILER, John 33
VONDERSMITH, Margaret 59
    89 159
WAGENER, John 190 Melchior
    243
WAGGONER, Samuel 30
WAGNER, Ben James 289
    Henry 213 Susan 212
    Susanna 213
WAGONNER, John 215
WAIRE, Capt. 261 263
WALBERT, John 146 320
WALDER, Catharine 131
    Christian 131 Jacob 131
WALDMAN, Paul B. 212 Mrs.

(Waldman Cont.) Rosa 212
    Rose 212
WALDSCHMIDT, Rev. John
    154
WALLS, James 322
WALP, Sarah C. 40
WALTER, Catherine 131
    Christian 131 Jacob 131
WALTERS, Catherine 120
WALTON, Henry A. 316
WANDEL, Solomon 40
WANNEBACH, Paul 343
WANNER, Maria 219
WANTELLBUSH, Salome 40
    Solomon 40
WARD, Monroe 110 Sarah
    Jane 50
WARDELL, M. 61 Patrick G.
    253
WAREN, Melcher 270
WARFEL, David 229
WARMKESSEL, John 10
WARNER, Melcher 270
WARREN, Briscoe 206 Biscoc
    314 John Trexler 362
    Melcher 50
WATERS, Henry G. 47 199
WATRING, Johannes Abraham
    13
WATSON, Abraham 341
WATTS, George 46
WEAVER, Elizabeth 82
    Henrietta 196 200 Henrita
    37 Henritta 14 James 8 313
    John 82 Levi 25 157 Lewis
    82 Rose Ann 317
WEBB, Addie 61 Joseph 236
WEBER, Leonard 258
WEBERIN, Margaretha 343

# FULL NAME INDEX

WEDEL, Jacob 6 124 128 130
  Maria 6 124 128 130
WEEKLER, David 119
WEHR, Solomon 234
WEHRLY, Charlotte 33 177
WEIDLER, Daniel 60 157 342
WEIFS, Felix 118
WEIGER, Christian 5 153
  Susanna 5 153
WEIGLE, John W. 54 211
WEILIN, Anna Maria 155
WEILL, Anna Maria Margaret 6
  Anna Margaretha 66
WEISER, also Weisser,
  Christian 4 5 149 150 153
  Frederick S. 123 124 125
  129 131 147 148 149 153
  154 155 159 178 Frederick
  Sheely 128 Jacob 76 151
  Maria 75 150 Susanna 5
  151 Susannah 149 150 153
WEISS, John 60 217
WEIST, Samuel 54 209
WELLER, Anna 131 155 Anna
  Christine Kraff 259 Barbara
  37 124 128 131 Elisabeth
  155 Georg Michael 131
  Jacob 155 Joann Georg
  124 Johannes 124 128 131
  John 37 161 Margareth 128
WELTY, Barbara 197 200
  Isabella Agnes 33 John 200
  John J. 33 Joseph 47 197
  201 202
WENDEL, B.F. 91
WENNER, Edgar 69
WERNER, Joannes 119
WERT, Sarah 73
WERTLEY, A.P. 59

WERTMAN, Perma 69
WEST, Henry 73 Sarah 73
WETZEL, also Wetzell,
  Benjamin F. 56 George H.
  73 Jacob 189 Johann
  Henrich 147 John Henry 41
  Rachel 56 Rosanna 339
WHARTON, Jane 140
WHILESIL, Mary 36 315
WHITE, A. White 240 Elmira
  74 James 82 234 Joanna
  47 202 Milly 184
WHITESILL, Mary 36
WHITFIELD, James 118
WHITLEY, Benjamin 209
WHITMAN, John 272
WHITMORE, D.H. 273
WHITSEL, Adam 206
WHITSELL, Nancy 315
WHITSILL, Elizabeth 315
WIBLE, John 45 211 Joseph
  45 211 Polly 45 211
  Stephen 45 210 211
WIEDERENCHT, Peter 177
WIEDES, Solome 35 332
WIGLE, Mary 196
WILEY, William B. 225 228
WILHELM, Magdalin 77 264
WILHIDE, Sophia 18
WILKINS, John 322
WILL, Catherine 136 Elizabeth
  19 135 136 Jacob 141
  John 141 Mary Anna 136
WILLIAMS, Elizabeth M. 114
  William 74
WILLIAMSON, Dr. W. 91
  William 222
WILLIGE, Abraham 133
  Elisabeth 133 Johannes

# FULL NAME INDEX

(Willige Cont.) 133

WILLING, Messr 266

WILSON, Catherine 22 312 David 245 J.H.58 James 22 Susannah 22

WINCHESTER, Stephen 273

WINCK, Casper 40 Catherine 2 40 Gertrude Kemp 40

WINDER, Jacob 197 Henry 202

WINEBARECK, John 255

WINGERT, Anna Catharina 133 Elisabeth 133 Peter 133

WINTER, Joann 197 Joanna 201 Johanna 47

WIRST, Christian 38 251

WISE, also Wiserd, Elizabeth 197 200 Margaret 138 Mary Jane 85 Michael 48 197 200

WISMER, Christian 234

WISSLER, Hans 267

WISTER, Casper 2 285 Catherine 287 Richard 285

WITHERS, George 229

WITMER, Anna Maria 149 152 Henriette 156 Jacob 149 152 Jacob I. 227 228 Jacob S. 227 228 Johannes 149 152

WITMYER, Christian 225

WITT, John Nicholas 219

WIVELL, John 195

WOLF, also Wolff, Christian 360 Elizabeth 45 211 Franz 175 George 68 126 217 Jacob Heinrich 47 160 Valentine 129 William 312

WOLFELSBARGER, Capt. Phillip 338

WOOD, Isaac 41 Jos. 203 Joseph 188

WOOLISON, Samuel 214

WORKING, Harmon 278

WORMAN, Thomas 69

WOTRING, Abraham 115 Johannes Abraham 13 Nicolaus 166

WRIGHT, Mrs. William 62 Willie Ann 62

YAHN, Monroe C. 318

YASTE, Leonard 199

YATES, William 280

YETTES, John 317

YINGST, Rev.69, Ursula 69

YOCUM, Elizabeth 235 John 41 235 242

YOUNG, also Yung, Catherine 34 Catharina 155 Elizabeth 8 34 126 312 Joannes 127 Johann Jacob 127 John Daniel 218 Madelena 127 Magdalena 127 Mathias 285 Matthew 187

YUNDT, Henry 71

ZEIGLER, Catherine 209 210 Christian 209 210 Henry K. 291

ZENSINGER, also Zenziger, Godfried 285

ZEP, Henry 146

ZERBE, Christian 215 Geor 214 Leonard 214 218

ZERGENEW, Josaunowr 279

ZIEBACH, Barthlomaus 149

ZIEGLER, Catherine 210 Lutheran Church 178

Susan 39 74 Warren J. 137
ZIGLER, Bernhard 219 Maria
219
ZIMMER, John 219
ZIMMERMAN, Anna Margareta
119 Elijah F.T. 197
Elizabeth 53 121 316
George 4 6 119 121 197
312 John 196 197 201
John A.J. 197 Nicholas 8
187 195 200 312 314
Sophia Dreckseler 119 121
Sophia Trickell 312
ZINDORFF, Andrew 136
Elizabeth 136 George 136
John 136 Joseph 20 136
Miss Trexell 136 Pius 135
136 Zindorff Family 135
ZINZENDORFFISCH, see
Zinzendorfus
ZINZENDORFUS, Anna
Christine 162 Elizabeth 162
ZIRCKEL, Also Zirckle, Hanna
31 163 Hannah 12 166
HENRY 163
ZNGNER, Zefamer 280
ZOCCHI, Father 348
ZORBE, George 215
ZUJWALT, Baltzer 252

R.

Additional Data 345
Anglican Maryland Church Records 116
Catholic Maryland Church Records 116
Catholic Pennsylvania Church Records 135
Cemetery Records 79
Census Records 93
Church Records 115
City Directory Notes 181
Court and Legal Records 184
Estate Documents 191
Family Units 1
French Church Records 115
Georgia Immigration 256
German Church Records 116
Immigration Records 256
Index 363
Indiana War of 1812 Service 327
Kentucky Cemetery 79
Kentucky Census 93
Kentucky Chancery/Civil Records 184
Kentucky Marriage Records 312
Kentucky Newspaper References 339
Kentucky Probate Records 191
Land Records 269
Louisiana Additional Data 345
Louuisiana Chancery/Civil Records 184
Louisiana Immigration 256
Louisiana War of 1812 Service 327
Lutheran Maryland Church Records 122
Lutheran Pennsylvania Church Records 144
Marriage Records 312
Maryland Additional Data 345
Maryland Cemetery 79
Maryland Chancery/Civil Records 185
Maryland Church Records 116
Maryland City Directory Notes 181
Maryland Immigration 257

Maryland Land Records 269
Maryland Marriage Records 312
Maryland Newspaper References 339
Maryland Probate Records 191
Maryland Revolutionary War Service 323
Maryland Tax and Voting Records 296
Maryland War of 1812 Service 327
Militia Service 337
Moravian Pennsylvania Church Records 156
New Jersey Census 99
New Jersey Militia Service 337
New Jersey Probate Records 206
Newspaper References 339
North Carolina Additional Data 349
North Carolina Census 99
North Carolina Marriage Records 314
North Carolina Newspaper References 341
North Carolina Probate Records 206
North Carolina War of 1812 Service 330
Ohio Additional Data 349
Ohio Cemetery 84
Ohio Immigration 260
Ohio Marriage Records 317
Ohio Newspaper References 342
Ohio Probate Records 208
Ohio Tax and Voting Records 296
Ohio War of 1812 Service 330
Pennsylvania Additional Data 350
Pennsylvania Cemetery 84
Pennsylvania Census 100
Pennsylvania City Directory Notes 182
Pennsylvania Immigration 260
Pennsylvania Land Records 281
Pennsylvania Marriage Records 317
Pennsylvania Militia Service 337
Pennsylvania Newspaper References 342
Pennsylvania Probate Records 208
Pennsylvania Prothonotary Court Records 188
Pennsylvania Revolutionary War Service 324

# GENERAL INDEX

Pennsylvania Tax and Voting Records 297
Pennsylvania War of 1812 Service 331
Probate Records 191
Revolutionary War Service 323
Sources 358
South Carolina Census 100
Tax and Voting Records 296
Virginia Additional Data 356
Virginia Cemetery 91
Virginia Census 108
Virginia City Directory Notes 183
Virginia Land Records 294
Virginia Lutheran Church Records 179
Virginia Marriage Records 321
Virginia Probate Records 253
Virginia Tax and Voting Records 311
Virginia War of 1812 Service 335
War of 1812 Service 327
West Virginia Lutheran Church Records 180
Wills 191
Wisconsin Newspaper References 342

www.ingramcontent.com/pod-product-compliance
Lightning Source LLC
Chambersburg PA
CBHW071827270326
41929CB00013B/1917